P9-DCH-605

CompTIA Network+®
Certification Study Guide,
Fourth Edition

Glen E. Clarke

New York Chicago San Francisco
Lisbon London Madrid Mexico City
Milan New Delhi San Juan
Seoul Singapore Sydney Toronto

The McGraw·Hill Companies

Cataloging-in-Publication Data is on file with the Library of Congress

McGraw-Hill books are available at special quantity discounts to use as premiums and sales promotions, or for use in corporate training programs. To contact a special sales representative, please visit the Contact Us page at www.mhprofessional.com.

CompTIA Network+® Certification Study Guide, Fourth Edition

1234567890 DOC DOC 019

ISBN: Book p/n 978-0-07-161540-2 and CD p/n 978-0-07-161541-9
of set 978-0-07-161538-9

MHID: Book p/n 0-07- 161540-7 and CD p/n 0-07-161541-5
of set 0-07-161538-5

Sponsoring Editor Timothy Green	**Copy Editor** Robert Campbell	**Illustration** ContentWorks, Inc.
Editorial Supervisor Jody McKenzie	**Proofreader** Paul Tyler	**Art Director, Cover** Jeff Weeks
Project Manager Molly Sharp, ContentWorks, Inc.	**Indexer** Jack Lewis	**Cover Series Design** Peter Grame
Acquisitions Coordinator Meghan Riley	**Production Supervisor** Jim Kussow	
Technical Editor Dan Lachance	**Composition** ContentWorks, Inc.	

To my beautiful wife, Tanya, who continues to show amazing patience and support. You are a true inspiration!

Glen E. Clarke, MCSE/MCSD/MCDBA/MCT/CEH/SCNP/Security+/ Network+/A+, is an independent trainer and consultant, focusing on network security and security auditing services. Glen spends most of his time delivering certified courses on Windows Server, SQL Server, Exchange Server, Visual Basic .NET, and ASP.NET. Glen also teaches a number of security-related courses covering topics such as ethical hacking, vulnerability testing, firewall design, and packet analysis topics.

Glen is an experienced author and technical editor whose published work has been nominated for a referenceware excellence award in 2003 and 2004. Glen has worked on a number of certification titles, including topics on A+ certification, Windows 2000/2003 certification, and Network+ and Security+ certification.

When he's not working, Glen loves to spend quality time with his wife, Tanya, and their four children, Sara, Brendon, Ashlyn, and Rebecca. He is an active member of High Technology Crime Investigation Association (HTCIA). You can visit Glen online at www.gleneclarke.com, or contact him at glenclarke@accesswave.ca.

About the Technical Editor

Dan Lachance is a Certified Novell Instructor (CNI), a Certified Novell Engineer (CNE), a Certified Linux Professional (CLP), an IBM Certified Instructor for Lotus Notes, and a Convergent Technology Professional (CTP). Dan also holds the A+, Network+, and Security+ certifications and is a technical trainer for Nexient Learning.

About LearnKey

LearnKey provides self-paced learning content and multimedia delivery solutions to enhance personal skills and business productivity. LearnKey claims the largest library of rich streaming-media training content that engages learners in dynamic media-rich instruction complete with video clips, audio, full-motion graphics, and animated illustrations. LearnKey can be found on the web at www.LearnKey.com.

CONTENTS AT A GLANCE

CONTENTS

2   Network Protocols and Standards 71

ACKNOWLEDGMENTS

I would like to thank the wonderful people at McGraw-Hill Professional, especially Timothy Green and Meghan Riley for their extreme patience and support—you guys are a great team to work with! I thank Timothy Green for giving me the opportunity to work with him once again and for this project—it has been a phenomenal experience! Thank you to a close friend and former coworker, Dan Lachance, for great feedback and encouraging ideas as the technical editor.

A special thank you to my wife, Tanya, who has been extremely supportive and loving through the many hours of writing this book. I would also like to thank my four children, Sara, Brendon, Ashlyn, and Rebecca for helping Daddy enjoy the simple things—playing hockey, skating on the rink, dancing in the living room, and chilling out during movie night! I love the time I spend with all four of you!

Thank you to my Mom and Dad for buying my first computer so that I could learn about computers and excel with my studies—it was a huge help. Thanks!

PREFACE

The objective of this study guide is to prepare you for the Network+ certification exam by familiarizing you with the technology or body of knowledge tested on the exam. Because the primary focus of the book is to help you pass the test, we don't always cover every aspect of the related technology. Some aspects of the technology are only covered to the extent necessary to help you understand what you need to know to pass the exam, but we hope this book will serve you as a valuable professional resource after your exam.

In This Book

This book is organized in such a way as to serve as an in-depth review for the Network+ certification exam for both experienced network professionals and newcomers to the world of network technologies. Each chapter covers a major aspect of the exam, with an emphasis on the "why" as well as the "how to" of working with and supporting networking environments.

On the CD

For more information on the CD-ROM, please see the Appendix, "About the CD," at the back of the book.

Exam Readiness Checklist

At the end of the Introduction you will find an Exam Readiness Checklist. This table has been constructed to allow you to cross-reference the official exam objectives with the objectives as they are presented and covered in this book. The checklist also allows you to gauge your level of expertise on each objective at the outset of your studies. This should allow you to check your progress and make sure you spend the time you need on more difficult or unfamiliar sections. References have been provided for the objective exactly as the vendor presents it, the section of the study guide that covers that objective, and a chapter and page reference.

In Every Chapter

We've created a set of chapter components that call your attention to important items, reinforce important points, and provide helpful exam-taking hints. Take a look at what you'll find in every chapter:

- Every chapter begins with **Certification Objectives**—what you need to know in order to pass the section on the exam dealing with the chapter topic. The Objective headings identify the objectives within the chapter, so you'll always know an objective when you see it!

- **Exam Watch** notes call attention to information about, and potential pitfalls in, the exam. These helpful hints are written by authors who have taken the exams and received their certification—who better to tell you what to worry about? They know what you're about to go through!

- **Step-by-Step Exercises** are interspersed throughout the chapters and included on the CD-ROM in LabBook.pdf. These are designed as hands-on exercises that give you a feel for the real-world experience you need to pass the exam. They help you master skills that are likely to be an area of focus on the exam. Don't just read through the exercises; learning by doing is an effective way to increase your competence.

- **On the Job** notes describe the issues that come up most often in real-world settings. They provide a valuable perspective on certification- and product-related topics. They point out common mistakes, and address questions that have arisen from on-the-job discussions and experience.

- **Inside the Exam** sidebars highlight some of the most common and confusing problems that students encounter when taking a live exam. Designed to anticipate what the exam will emphasize, they help ensure you know what you need to know to pass the exam. You can get a leg up on how to respond to those difficult-to-understand questions by paying extra attention to these sidebars.

- The **Certification Summary** is a succinct review of the chapter and a restatement of salient points regarding the exam.

- The **Two-Minute Drill** at the end of every chapter is a checklist of the main points of the chapter. It can be used for last-minute review.

- The **Self Test** offers questions similar to those found on the certification exams. The answers to these questions, as well as explanations of the answers, can be found at the end of each chapter. By taking the Self Test after completing each chapter, you'll reinforce what you've learned from that chapter, while becoming familiar with the structure of the exam questions.

Some Pointers

Once you've finished reading this book, set aside some time to do a thorough review. You might want to return to the book several times and make use of all the methods it offers for reviewing the material:

1. Re-read all the Two-Minute Drills, or have someone quiz you. You can also use the drills as a way to do a quick cram before the exam. You might want to make some flash cards out of 3 × 5 index cards that have the Two-Minute Drill material on them.

2. Re-read all the Exam Watch notes and Inside the Exam elements. Remember that these notes are written by authors who have taken the exam and passed. They know what you should expect—and what you should be on the lookout for.

3. Re-take the Self Tests. Taking the tests right after you've read the chapter is a good idea, because the questions help reinforce what you've just learned. However, it's an even better idea to go back later and do all the questions in the book in one sitting. Pretend that you're taking the live exam. When you go through the questions the first time, you should mark your answers on a separate piece of paper. That way, you can run through the questions as many times as you need to until you feel comfortable with the material.

4. Complete the Exercises. Did you do the exercises when you read through each chapter? If not, do them! These exercises are designed to cover exam topics, and there's no better way to get to know this material than by practicing. Be sure you understand why you are performing each step in each exercise. If there is something you are not clear on, re-read that section in the chapter.

INTRODUCTION

I f you are new to certifications, we have some good news and some bad news. The good news is that a computer industry certification is one of the most valuable credentials you can earn. It sets you apart from the crowd and marks you as a valuable asset to your employer. You will gain the respect of your peers, and certification can have a wonderful effect on your income.

The bad news is that certification tests are not easy. You may think you will read through some study material, memorize a few facts, and pass the examinations. After all, these certification exams are just computer-based, multiple-choice tests, so they must be easy. If you believe this, you are wrong. Unlike many "multiple-guess" tests you have been exposed to in school, the questions on certification examinations go beyond simple factual knowledge.

The purpose of this introduction is to teach you how to take a computer certification examination. To be successful, you need to know something about the purpose and structure of these tests. We will also look at the latest innovations in computerized testing. Using simulations and adaptive testing, the computer industry is enhancing both the validity and security of the certification process. These factors have some important effects on how you should prepare for an exam, as well as your approach to each question during the test.

We will begin by looking at the purpose, focus, and structure of certification tests, and we will examine the effect these factors have on the kinds of questions you will face on your certification exams. We will define the structure of examination questions and investigate some common formats. Next, we will present a strategy for answering these questions. Finally, we will give some specific guidelines on what you should do on the day of your test.

The Value of Certification

The CompTIA Network+ certification program, like the certification programs from Microsoft, Lotus, Novell, Oracle, and other software vendors, is maintained for the ultimate purpose of increasing the corporation's profits through the creation of skilled workers. A successful certification program accomplishes this goal by helping to create a pool of certification questions that not only test the knowledge of the candidate but also test that candidate's skills.

Vendor certification has become increasingly popular over the years because it helps employers find qualified workers, and it helps software vendors such as Microsoft sell products. Many employers are looking for professionals who hold IT certifications, and a number of individuals without the required certification are overlooked.

A marked characteristic of the computer certification program is an emphasis on performing specific job tasks rather than merely gathering knowledge. It may come as a shock, but most potential employers do not care how much you know about the theory of operating systems, networking, or database design. As one IT manager put it, "I don't really care what my employees know about the theory of our network. We don't need someone to sit at a desk and think about it. We need people who can actually do something to make it work better."

CompTIA's Network+ certification program will test you on current network implementations in wide use today, including network-related hardware and software. The job task orientation of certification is almost as obvious, but testing real-world job skills using a computer-based test is not easy. In Network+, CompTIA have created a great certification exam that ensures a candidate knows the basics of networking.

Test Structure and Specifications

The 2009 version of the Network+ Certification exam is exam number N10-004 and is titled the CompTIA Network+ (2009 Edition) Exam. You can book your exam online at www.2test.com. The Network+ exam cost is approximately $240 U.S., but the price may be different in your country. The exam is approximately 85 questions, and you have 90 minutes to complete the exam.

The topics that you are tested on are divided into domains. The following table lists the different domains and what percentage of the questions are based on each domain.

Domain	% of Examination
1.0 Network Technologies	20%
2.0 Network Media and Topologies	20%
3.0 Network Devices	17%
4.0 Network Management	20%
5.0 Network Tools	12%
6.0 Network Security	11%
Total	100%

The Network+ exam is known as a form test, and this is the type of test that we are most familiar with. A form test is made up of a number of multiple-choice questions, and you can go back to previous questions at any point. For the CompTIA certification, a form consists of 85 questions and allows for 90 minutes to complete.

The CompTIA Network+ exam is a form-based test where each correct answer gives you the same amount of points. The score is on a scale from 100 to 900, and a score of 554 must be obtained in order to pass. An interesting and useful characteristic of a form test is that you can mark a question you have doubts about as you take the test. Assuming you have time left when you finish all the questions, you can return and spend more time on the questions you have marked as doubtful.

CompTIA, like Microsoft, may soon implement *adaptive* testing for the Network+ exam. To develop this interactive technique, a form test is first created and administered to several thousand certification candidates. The statistics generated are used to assign a weight, or difficulty level, for each question. For example, the questions in a form might be divided into levels one through five, with level-one questions being the easiest and level-five the hardest.

When an adaptive test begins, the candidate is first given a level-three question. If he answers it correctly, he is given a question from the next higher level; if he answers it incorrectly, he is given a question from the next lower level. When 15–20 questions have been answered in this manner, the scoring algorithm is able to predict, with a high degree of statistical certainty, whether the candidate would pass or fail if all the questions in the form were answered. When the required degree of certainty is attained, the test ends and the candidate receives a pass/fail grade.

Adaptive testing has some definite advantages for everyone involved in the certification process. Adaptive tests enable the test center to deliver more tests with the same resources, because certification candidates often are in and out in 30 minutes or less. For CompTIA, adaptive testing means that fewer test questions are exposed to each candidate, which enhances the security, and therefore the validity, of certification tests.

One possible problem you may have with adaptive testing is that you are not allowed to mark and revisit questions. Because the adaptive algorithm is interactive, and all questions but the first are selected on the basis of your response to the previous question, it is not possible to skip a particular question or change an answer.

Question Types

Computerized test questions can be presented in a number of ways. Some of the possible formats for questions are listed here, and you may find any of the following types of questions on your Network+ certification exam.

True/False

We are all familiar with True/False questions, but because of the inherent 50 percent chance of choosing the correct answer, you will most likely not see true/false questions on your Network+ certification exam.

Multiple Choice

The majority of Network+ certification questions are in the multiple-choice format, with either a single correct answer or multiple correct answers that need to be selected. One interesting variation on multiple-choice questions with multiple correct answers is whether or not the candidate is told how many answers are correct—you might be told to select all that apply.

Graphical Questions

One or more graphical elements are sometimes used as exhibits to help present or clarify an exam question. These elements may take the form of a network diagram or pictures of networking components on which you are being tested. It is often easier to present the concepts required for a complex performance-based scenario with a graphic than it is with words. Expect to see some graphical questions on your Network+ exam.

Test questions known as hotspots actually incorporate graphics as part of the answer. These questions ask the certification candidate to click a location or graphical element to answer the question. As an example, you might be shown the diagram of a network and asked to click an appropriate location for a router. The answer is correct if the candidate clicks within the hotspot that defines the correct location. The Network+ exam has a few of these graphical hotspot questions, and most are asking you to identify network types, such as a bus or star network. As with the graphical questions, expect only a couple of hotspot questions during your exam.

Free Response Questions

Another kind of question you sometimes see on certification examinations requires a free response or type-in answer. This type of question might present a TCP/IP network scenario and ask the candidate to calculate and enter the correct subnet mask in dotted decimal notation. However, the CompTIA Network+ exam most likely will not contain any free response questions.

Knowledge-Based and Performance-Based Questions

CompTIA Certification develops a blueprint for each certification examination with input from subject matter experts. This blueprint defines the content areas and objectives for each test, and each test question is created to test a specific objective. The basic information from the examination blueprint can be found on CompTIA's Web site at http://certification.comptia.org/network/default.aspx.

Psychometricians (psychologists who specialize in designing and analyzing tests) categorize test questions as knowledge-based or performance-based. As the names imply, knowledge-based questions are designed to test knowledge, and performance-based questions are designed to test performance.

Some objectives demand a knowledge-based question. For example, objectives that use verbs such as list and identify tend to test only what you know, not what you can do. For example:

Objective: Explain the following Transport Layer concepts.

Knowledge-based question: Which two protocols are connectionless-oriented network protocols? (Choose two.)

A. FTP

B. TCP

C. TFTP

D. UDP

C and **D** are correct.

The Network+ exam consists of mostly knowledge-based multiple-choice questions that can be answered fairly quickly if you know your stuff. These questions are very straightforward, lacking a complex situation to confuse you.

Other objectives use action verbs such as install, configure, and troubleshoot to define job tasks. These objectives can often be tested with either a knowledge-based question or a performance-based question. CompTIA are focusing their exam questions to performance-based questions where you will need to know how to perform a task instead of just the theory behind it. For example:

Performance-based question: You want to ensure you have a reliable tape backup scheme that is not susceptible to fire and water hazards. You are backing up three Windows servers and would like to completely back up the entire systems. Which of the following is the most reliable backup method?

A. Configure the backup program to back up the user files and operating system files; complete a test restore of the backup; and store the backup tapes offsite in a fireproof vault.

B. Configure the backup program to back up the entire hard drive of each server and store the backup tapes offsite in a fireproof vault.

C. Copy the user files to another server; configure the backup program to back up the operating system files; and store the backup tapes offsite in a fireproof vault.

D. Configure the backup program to back up the user files and operating system files and store the backup tapes offsite in fireproof vault.

A is correct.

Even in this simple example, the superiority of the performance-based question is obvious. Whereas the knowledge-based question asks for a single fact, the performance-based question presents a real-life situation and requires that you make a decision based on this scenario. Thus, performance-based questions give more bang (validity) for the test author's buck (individual question).

Testing Job Performance

We have said that CompTIA certification focuses on timeliness and the ability to perform job tasks. We have also introduced the concept of performance-based questions, but even performance-based multiple-choice questions do not really measure performance. Another strategy is needed to test job skills.

Given unlimited resources, it is not difficult to test job skills. In an ideal world, CompTIA would fly Network+ candidates to a test facility; place them in a controlled environment with a team of experts; and ask them to plan, install, maintain, and troubleshoot a network. In a few days at most, the experts could reach a valid decision as to whether each candidate should or should not be granted Network+ status. Needless to say, this is not likely to happen.

Closer to reality, another way to test performance is to use the actual software and create a testing program to present tasks and automatically grade a candidate's performance when the tasks are completed. This cooperative approach would be practical in some testing situations, but the same test that is presented to Network+ candidates in Boston must also be available in Bahrain and Botswana. Many testing locations around the world cannot run 32-bit applications, much less provide the complex networked solutions required by cooperative testing applications.

The most workable solution for measuring performance in today's testing environment is a simulation program. When the program is launched during a test, the candidate sees a simulation of the actual software that looks and behaves just like the real thing. When the testing software presents a task, the simulation program is launched and the candidate performs the required task. The testing software then grades the candidate's performance on the required task and moves to the next question.

Simulation questions provide many advantages over other testing methodologies, and simulations are expected to become increasingly important in the computer certification programs. For example, studies have shown that there is a very high correlation between the ability to perform simulated tasks on a computer-based test and the ability to perform the actual job tasks. Thus, simulations enhance the validity of the certification process.

Another truly wonderful benefit of simulations is in the area of test security. It is just not possible to cheat on a simulation question. In fact, you will be told exactly what tasks you are expected to perform on the test. How can a certification candidate cheat? By learning to perform the tasks? What a concept!

Study Strategies

There are a number of different ways to study for the different types of questions you will see on a CompTIA Network+ certification examination. The following section outlines some of the methods you can use to prepare for the different types of questions.

Knowledge-Based Questions

Knowledge-based questions require that you memorize facts. There are hundreds of facts inherent in every content area of every Network+ certification examination. There are several tricks to memorizing facts:

- **Repetition**   The more times your brain is exposed to a fact, the more likely you are to remember it. Flash cards are a wonderful tool for repetition. Either make your own flash cards on paper or download a flash card program and develop your own questions.

- **Association**   Connecting facts within a logical framework makes them easier to remember. Try using mnemonics, such as "All People Seem To Need Data Processing" to remember the seven layers of the OSI model in order.

- **Motor Association**   It is often easier to remember something if you write it down or perform some other physical act, such as clicking a practice test answer. You will find that hands-on experience with the product or concept being tested is a great way to develop motor association.

We have said that the emphasis of CompTIA certification is job performance, and that there are very few knowledge-based questions on CompTIA certification exams. Why should you waste a lot of time learning filenames, IP address formulas, and other minutiae? Read on.

Performance-Based Questions

Most of the questions you will face on a CompTIA certification exam are performance-based scenario questions. We have discussed the superiority of these questions over simple knowledge-based questions, but you should remember that the job task orientation of CompTIA certification extends the knowledge you need to pass the exams; it does not replace this knowledge. Therefore, the first step in preparing for scenario questions is to absorb as many facts relating to the exam content areas as you can. In other words, go back to the previous section and follow the steps to prepare for an exam composed of knowledge-based questions.

The second step is to familiarize yourself with the format of the questions you are likely to see on the exam. You can do this by answering the questions in this study guide, or by using practice tests. The day of your test is not the time to be surprised by the complicated construction of some exam questions.

For example, one of CompTIA Certification's favorite formats of late takes the following form found on Microsoft exams:

Scenario: You have a network with…

Primary Objective: You want to…

Secondary Objective: You also want to…

Proposed Solution: Do this…

What does the proposed solution accomplish?

A. It achieves the primary and the secondary objective.

B. It achieves the primary but not the secondary objective.

C. It achieves the secondary but not the primary objective.

D. It achieves neither the primary nor the secondary objective.

This kind of question, with some variation, is seen on many Microsoft Certification examinations and may be present on your Network+ certification exam.

At best, these performance-based scenario questions really do test certification candidates at a higher cognitive level than knowledge-based questions do. At worst, these questions can test your reading comprehension and test-taking ability rather than your ability to administer networks. Be sure to get in the habit of reading the question carefully to determine what is being asked.

The third step in preparing for CompTIA scenario questions is to adopt the following attitude: Multiple-choice questions aren't really performance-based. It is all a cruel lie. These scenario questions are just knowledge-based questions with a little story wrapped around them.

To answer a scenario question, you have to sift through the story to the underlying facts of the situation and apply your knowledge to determine the correct answer. This may sound silly at first, but the process we go through in solving real-life problems is quite similar. The key concept is that every scenario question (and every real-life problem) has a fact at its center, and if we can identify that fact, we can answer the question.

Exam Readiness Checklist

Official Objective	Study Guide Coverage	Ch #	Pg #	Beginner	Intermediate	Expert
1.0 Network Technologies						
1.1 Explain the function of common networking protocols	TCP Protocol Suite	4	170			
1.2 Identify commonly-used TCP and UDP default ports	TCP/IP Addressing	4	182			
1.3 Identify address formats	TCP/IP Fundamentals	4	180			
1.4 Given a scenario, evaluate the proper use of addressing technologies and addressing schemes	TCP/IP Addressing	4	182			
1.5 Identify common IPv4 and IPv6 routing protocols	Dynamic Routing Protocols	5	256			
1.6 Explain the purpose and properties of routing	Understanding Routing	5	246			
1.7 Compare the characteristics of wireless communication standards	Wireless Basics	7	352			
2.0 Network Media and Topologies						
2.1 Categorize standard cable types and their properties	Network Media and Connectors	1	20			
2.2 Identify common connector types	Network Media and Connectors	1	20			

Exam Readiness Checklist

Official Objective	Study Guide Coverage	Ch #	Pg #	Beginner	Intermediate	Expert
2.3 Identify common physical network topologies	Identifying Network Topologies	1	9			
2.4 Given a scenario, differentiate and implement appropriate wiring standards	Network Media and Connectors	1	20			
2.5 Categorize WAN technology types and properties	Wide Area Network Technologies	9	437			
2.6 Categorize LAN technology types and properties	Network Architectures	1	39			
2.7 Explain common logical network topologies and their characteristics	Identifying Characteristics of a Network Bridges and Switches Virtual Private Networks	1 3 8	2 137 413			
2.8 Install components of wiring distribution	Other Networking Devices	3	149			
3.0 Network Devices						
3.1 Install, configure, and differentiate between common network devices	Hubs, MAUs, and Repeaters Bridges and Switches Routers and Brouters Other Networking Devices	3	131 137 144 149			
3.2 Identify the functions of specialized network devices	Bridges and Switches Routers and Brouters Gateways and Security Devices Network Services Firewalls and Proxy Servers Checking Physical and Logical Indicators	3 4 12 13	137 144 147 206 627 699			
3.3 Explain the advanced features of a switch	Bridges and Switches	3	137			
3.4 Implement a basic wireless network	Implementing a Wireless Network	7	364			
4.0 Network Management						
4.1 Explain the function of each layer of the OSI model	The OSI Model	2	79			
4.2 Identify types of configuration management documentation	Network Documentation	11	578			
4.3 Given a scenario, evaluate the network based on configuration management documentation	Network Documentation	11	578			

Exam Readiness Checklist

Official Objective	Study Guide Coverage	Ch #	Pg #	Beginner	Intermediate	Expert
4.4 Conduct network monitoring to identify performance and connectivity issues	Maintaining Logs Checking Physical and Logical Indicators	11 13	581 699			
4.5 Explain different methods and rationales for network performance optimization	Checking Physical and Logical Indicators	13	699			
4.6 Given a scenario, implement network troubleshooting methodology	Troubleshooting Network Problems	13	690			
4.7 Given a scenario, troubleshoot common connectivity issues and select an appropriate solution	Wireless Basics Checking Physical and Logical Indicators	7 13	352 699			
5.0 Network Tools						
5.1 Given a scenario, select the appropriate command-line interface tool and interpret the output to verify functionality	TCP/IP Utilities	6	267			
5.2 Explain the purpose of network scanners	Gateways and Security Devices Guidelines to Protect the Network Checking Physical and Logical Indicators	3 12 13	147 656 699			
5.3 Given a scenario, utilize the appropriate hardware tools	Network Tools	13	725			
6.0 Network Security						
6.1 Explain the function of hardware and software security devices	Virtual Private Networks (VPNs) Firewalls and Proxy Servers Guidelines to Protect the Network	8 12	413 627 656			
6.2 Explain common features of a firewall	Firewalls and Proxy Servers	12	627			
6.3 Explain the methods of network access security	Remote Connectivity Concepts Firewalls and Proxy Servers	8 12	388 627			
6.4 Explain methods of user authentication	Understanding System Security	12	601			
6.5 Explain issues that affect device security	Guidelines to Protect the Network	12	656			
6.6 Identify common security threats and mitigation techniques	Understanding Attack Types Guidelines to Protect the Network	12	598 656			

1
Basic Network Concepts

Knowing how computers communicate in a network environment is essential to passing the Network+ certification exam and to being a good network professional who can troubleshoot networking issues. This chapter introduces you to the basics of what makes a network tick, and covers basic topics and terminology that will set the foundation for the rest of your studies.

We will look at the various topologies, network operating systems, and common terminology used in day-to-day discussions between IT professionals. In this chapter, you will learn the purpose of a network, the different types of networks, network topologies, cables, and connectors, and you will learn about network architectures. You will finish the chapter by learning about some of the most popular network operating systems.

CERTIFICATION OBJECTIVE 1.01

Identifying Characteristics of a Network

More and more people are building home and small office networks now as a result of the low cost of networking devices such as hubs and home routers. As a Network+ Certified Professional, you will need to ensure that you can support these small, medium, and large networks, so you will start by learning some basic terms.

A network is a group of systems that are connected to allow sharing of resources—such as files or printers—or sharing of services—such as an Internet connection. There are two aspects of setting up a network: the hardware used to connect the systems together and the software installed on the computers to allow them to communicate. This chapter is designed to give you an understanding of the hardware used to build a network, and later chapters discuss the software needed. The network hardware is made up of two basic components: the entities that want to share the information or resources, such as servers and workstations, and the medium that enables the entities to communicate, which is a cable or a wireless medium.

Servers, Workstations, and Hosts

A typical network involves having users sit at workstations, running such applications as word processors or spreadsheet programs. The workstation also is known as a client, which is just a basic computer running a client operating system such as Windows XP or Linux. These users typically store their files on a central server so that they can share the files with other users on the network. The server is a special computer that contains more disk space and memory than are found on client workstations. The server has special software installed that allows it to function as a server. This special software can provide file and print services (to allow sharing of files and printers), provide web pages to clients, or provide e-mail functionality to the company.

The term *host* refers to any computer or device that is connected to a network and sends or receives information on that network. A host can be a server, a workstation, a printer with its own network card, or a device such as a router. We can summarize by saying that any system or device that is connected to the network is known as a host.

WANs, LANs, and MANs

Some other terms that you will hear often are LAN, WAN, and MAN. A *local area network (LAN)* typically is confined to a single building, such as an office building, your home network, or a college campus. A *wide area network (WAN)* spans multiple geographic locations and is typically made up of multiple LANs. For example, I have a company with an office in Halifax, Nova Scotia (that's a city in Canada next door to the penguins) that has 100 computers all connected together. This would be considered a LAN. Now if we expand the company and create an office in Toronto, the network in Toronto also would be considered a LAN. If we want to allow the two offices to share information with one another, we would connect the two LANs together, creating a WAN.

The term *metropolitan area network (MAN)* is not used often anymore; it refers to a network that exists within a single city or metropolitan area. If we had two different buildings within a city that were connected together, it would be considered a MAN.

Types of Networks

Organizations of different sizes, structures, and budgets need different types of networks. A local newspaper company has needs for its network that would be different from the needs of a multinational company. Networks can be divided into one of two categories: peer-to-peer or server-based networks.

Peer-to-Peer Network

A *peer-to-peer* network has no dedicated servers; instead, a number of workstations are connected together for the purpose of sharing information or devices. When there is no dedicated server, all workstations are considered equal; any one of them can participate as the client or the server. Peer-to-peer networks are designed to satisfy the networking needs of home networks or of small companies that do not want to spend a lot of money on a dedicated server but still want to have the capability to share information or devices. For example, a small accounting firm with three employees that needs to access customer data from any of the three systems or print to one printer from any of the three systems may not want to spend a lot of money on a dedicated server. A small peer-to-peer network will allow these three computers to share the printer and the customer information with one another (see Figure 1-1). The extra cost of a server was not incurred because the existing client systems were networked together to create the peer-to-peer network.

The Microsoft term for a peer-to-peer network is a workgroup. Be aware that peer-to-peer networks typically consist of fewer than 10 systems.

Most of the modern operating systems such as Windows XP and Windows Vista already have built-in peer-to-peer networking capabilities, which is why building a peer-to-peer network would be a "cheap" network solution. The disadvantage of a peer-to-peer network is the lack of centralized administration—with peer-to-peer networks, you need to build user accounts and configure security on each system.

A peer-to-peer network

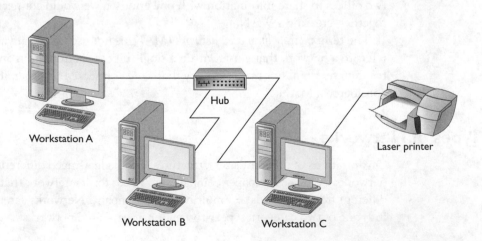

It is important to note that peer-to-peer networks are designed for fewer than 10 systems, and with Microsoft client operating systems such as Windows XP Professional, only 10 concurrent network connections to those clients are allowed. This means that if you have 15 or 20 employees, you eventually will need to implement a server-based network.

Server-Based Networks

A big disadvantage of peer-to-peer networking is that you can't do your day-to-day administration in a single place. With peer-to-peer networking, user accounts typically are created on all the systems, and data files are stored throughout all the systems. This leads to a more complicated environment and makes your job harder as a network administrator. Usually after four or five systems have been networked, the need for a dedicated server to store all of the user accounts and data files becomes apparent—this is a server-based network (see Figure 1-2).

The advantage of a server-based network is that the data files that will be used by all of the users are stored on the one server. This will help you by giving you a central point to set up permissions on the data files, and it will give you a central point from which to back up all of the data in case data loss should occur. With a server-based network, the network server stores a list of users who may use network resources and usually holds the resources as well.

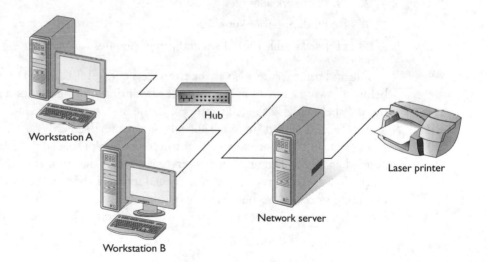

A server-based network

The server in a server-based network may provide a number of different services. The services it will offer to the network usually are decided by the server's role. There are a number of different roles that a server could play on a network:

- File and print servers
- Application servers
- Web servers
- Directory servers

File and print servers control and share printers and files among clients on the network. File and print servers were the original reason to have a network; a large number of users needed access to the same files, so the files were placed on a server, and all clients were connected to the server when they needed to work with the files. File servers often have the following characteristics:

- Large amounts of memory
- Fast hard disks
- Multiple CPUs
- Fast I/O buses
- High-capacity tape drives
- Fast network adapters
- Redundant power supplies
- Hot-swappable hard disks and power supplies

File and print servers also check the access control list (ACL) of each resource before allowing a user to access a file or use a printer. If the user or a group to which the user belongs is not listed in the ACL, the user is not allowed to use the resource, and an "access denied" message appears on the user's screen.

Application servers are servers that run some form of special program on the server. A good example of an application server is a server that runs the company's e-mail server. The e-mail server software is special software that can be run on a server operating system. Another example of software that would run on an application server is a database server product such as Microsoft SQL Server. A database server is a server that holds the company's core business data and typically gives this data to custom applications that run on the workstations. These are some applications that you might find on an application server:

- Microsoft SQL Server
- Oracle
- Microsoft Exchange Server
- IBM Lotus Domino

Web servers are servers that run the Hypertext Transfer Protocol (HTTP) and are designed to publish information on the Internet or the corporate intranet. Web servers are popular in today's businesses because they host web applications (web sites) for the organization. These web applications could be designed for internal use, or they could be used to publish information to the rest of the world on the Internet. Examples of web server software are Microsoft's Internet Information Services that runs on Windows or Apache web server software that runs on UNIX/Linux, Novell NetWare, and Windows.

Directory servers hold a list of the user accounts that are allowed to log on to the network. This list of user accounts is stored in a database (known as the directory database) and can store information about these user accounts such as address, city, phone number, and fax number. A directory service is designed to be a central database that can be used to store everything about such objects as users and printers.

In a server-based network environment, the centralized administration comes from the fact that the directory server stores all user accounts in its directory database. When a user sits at a client machine to log on to the network, the logon request is sent to this directory server. If the username and password exist in the directory database, the client is allowed to access network resources.

It is important to note that a server can have numerous roles at the same time. A server can be a file and print server, as well as an application server, or it can be a file, print, and directory server all at the same time. Because a single server can perform multiple roles, a company will not need to purchase an additional server every time a new product (or feature) is implemented on the network, and this fact reduces the cost of a server-based network.

Internet, Intranet, and Extranet

Internet, intranet, and extranet are three terms that describe "Internet-type" applications that are used by an organization, but how do you know if a web application is part of your intranet or part of the Internet?

- **Internet** If you wish to expose information to everyone in the world, then you would build an Internet-type application. An Internet-type application uses Internet protocols such as HTTP, FTP, or SMTP and is available to persons anywhere on the Internet. We use the Internet and web applications as ways to extend who the application can reach. For example, I no longer need to go to the bank to transfer funds. Because the bank has built a web site on the Internet, I can do that from the comfort of my own home.

- **Intranet** An application is considered to be on the company's intranet if it is using Internet-type protocols such as HTTP or FTP but the application is available only within the company. The information on a company's intranet would not be accessible to persons on the Internet because it is not for public use. For example, a few years ago I was sitting with my banking officer going over my account and noticed that the bank had moved all of its customer account information to a web site and that the banking officer was using a web browser to retrieve my account details. Although the application was being used by a web browser, it was still an "internal" application meant only for banking officers.

- **Extranet** From time to time, an application that has been built for the company's intranet and used by internal employees will need to be extended to select business partners or customers. If you extend your intranet out to select business partners or customers, you have created an extranet. An extranet cannot be used by anyone else external to the company except for those selected individuals. Figure 1-3 displays the basic configurations of Internet, intranet, and extranet.

This section has introduced you to some terms such as peer-to-peer versus server-based networking, Internet, intranet, and extranet; now let's look at how the network is laid out with the different network topologies!

| FIGURE 1-3 | Visualizing the difference between Internet, intranet, and extranet |

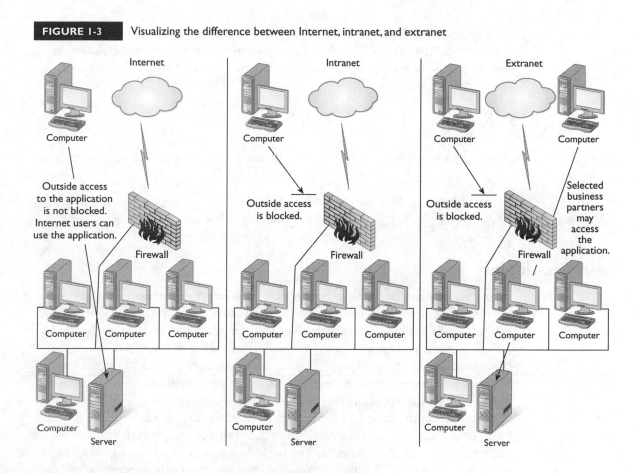

Identifying Network Topologies

This section will introduce you to a number of different network topologies, but this topic is a lead-in to a bigger topic introduced later in the chapter: network architecture. A network architecture is made up of a topology, a cable type, and an access method. Before we can discuss network architectures, we need to specify what the different types of topologies, cables, and access methods are.

A network topology is the physical layout of computers, cables, and other components on a network. There are a number of different network topologies, and a network may be built using multiple topologies. The different types of network layouts are

- Bus topology
- Star topology
- Mesh topology
- Ring topology
- Hybrid topology
- Wireless topology

Bus Topologies

A bus topology uses one cable as a main trunk to connect all of the systems together (shown in Figure 1-4). A bus topology is very easy to set up and requires no additional hardware such as a hub. The cable is also called a trunk, a backbone, or a segment.

With a bus topology, when a computer sends out a signal, the signal travels the cable length in both directions from the sending computer. When the signal reaches the end of the cable length, it bounces back and returns in the direction it came from. This is known as signal bounce. Signal bounce is a problem, because if another signal is sent on the cable length at the same time, the two signals will collide and be destroyed and then must be retransmitted. For this reason, at each end of the cable there is a terminator. The terminator is designed to absorb the signal when the signal reaches the end, preventing signal bounce. If there is no termination, the entire network fails because of signal bounce, which also means that if there is ever a break in the cable, you will have unterminated ends and the entire network will go down, as shown in Figure 1-5.

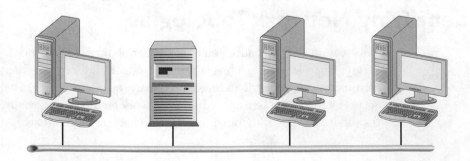

FIGURE 1-4

With a bus topology, all system, are connected to one linear cable.

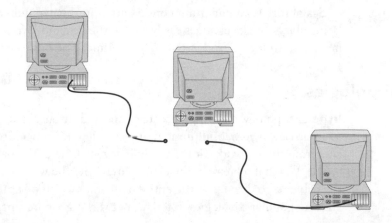

A break in the cable with the bus topology causes the entire network to fail.

With a bus topology, if there is a break in the cable, the entire network will go down.

A bus is a passive topology, which means that the workstations on the bus are not responsible for regenerating the signal as it passes by them. Since the workstations do not play an active role, the workstations are not a requirement of a functioning bus, which means that if a workstation fails, the bus does not fail. But if there is an unterminated end in the bus, the entire network will fail.

Advantages of a Bus Topology

One advantage of a bus topology is cost. A bus topology uses less cable than a star topology or a mesh topology, and you do not need to purchase any additional devices such as hubs. Another advantage of a bus topology is the ease of installation. With a bus topology, you simply connect the workstation to the cable segment or backbone. You need only the amount of cable to connect the workstation to the backbone. The most economical choice for a network topology is a bus topology, because it is easy to work with and a minimal amount of additional devices are required. Most importantly, if a computer fails, the network stays functional.

Disadvantages of a Bus Topology

The main disadvantage of a bus topology is the difficulty of troubleshooting it. When the network goes down, it is usually due to a break in the cable segment. With a large network, this problem can be tough to isolate.

Scalability is an important consideration in the dynamic world of networking. Being able to make changes easily within the size and layout of your network can be important in future productivity or downtime. The bus topology is not very scalable.

Star Topologies

In a star topology, all computers are connected through one central device known as a hub or a switch, as illustrated in Figure 1-6. Each workstation has a cable that goes from the network card to the hub device. One of the major benefits of a star topology is that a break in the cable causes only the workstation that is connected to the cable to go down, not the entire network, as with a bus topology. Star topologies are very popular topologies in today's networking environments.

Advantages of a Star Topology

One advantage of a star topology is scalability and ease of adding another system to the network. If you need to add another workstation to the network with a star topology, you simply connect that system to an unused port on the hub. Another benefit is the fact that if there is a break in the cable it affects only the system that is connected to that cable. Figure 1-7 shows a hub with a few ports available.

Centralizing network components can make an administrator's life much easier in the long run. Centralized management and monitoring of network traffic can be vital to network success. With a star configuration, it is also easy to add or change configurations because all of the connections come to a central point.

With a star topology, if there is a break in the cable, only the system connected to that cable is affected.

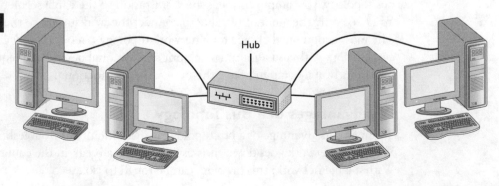

FIGURE 1-6

Computers connected in a star topology are all connected to a central hub or switch.

Hub

FIGURE 1-7

A five-port hub
with four available
ports

Disadvantages of a Star Topology

On the flip side, if the hub fails in a star topology, the entire network comes down, so we still have a central point of failure. But this is a much easier problem to troubleshoot than trying to find a cable break with a bus topology.

Another disadvantage of a star topology is cost. To connect each workstation to the network, you will need to ensure that there is a hub with an available port, and you will need to ensure you have a cable to go from the workstation to the hub. Today, the cost is increasingly less of a disadvantage because of the low prices of devices such as hubs and switches.

Mesh Topologies

A mesh topology is not very common in computer networking today, but you must understand the concept for the exam. In a mesh topology, every workstation has a connection to every other component of the network, as illustrated in Figure 1-8.

FIGURE 1-8

Computers in a
mesh topology
are all connected
to every other
computer on the
network.

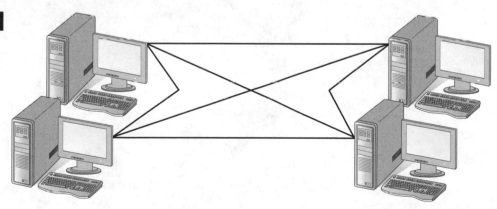

Advantages of a Mesh Topology

The biggest advantage of a mesh topology is fault tolerance, meaning that, if there is a break in a cable segment, traffic can be rerouted through a different pathway because there are multiple pathways to send data from one system to another. This fault tolerance means that it is almost impossible for the network to go down due to a cable fault.

Disadvantages of a Mesh Topology

A disadvantage of a mesh topology is the cost of the additional cabling and network interfaces to create the multiple pathways between each system. A mesh topology is very hard to administer and manage because of the numerous connections.

Ring Topologies

In a ring topology, all computers are connected via a cable that loops in a ring or circle. As shown in Figure 1-9, a ring topology is a circle that has no start and no end. Because there are no ends, terminators are not necessary in a ring topology. Signals travel in one direction on a ring while they are passed from one computer to the next, with each computer regenerating the signal so that it may travel the distance required.

FIGURE 1-9

A ring topology

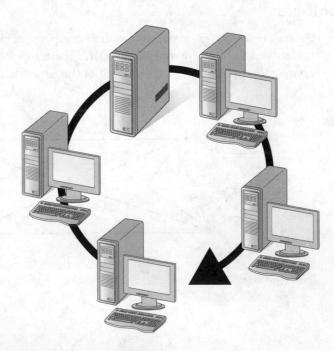

Advantages of a Ring Topology

A major advantage of a ring topology is that signal degeneration is low because each workstation is responsible for regenerating or boosting the signal. With the other topologies, as the signal travels the wire, it gets weaker and weaker as a result of outside interference: eventually, it becomes unreadable if the destination system is too far away. Because each workstation in a ring topology regenerates the signal, the signal is stronger when it reaches its destination and seldom needs to be retransmitted.

Disadvantages of a Ring Topology

The biggest problem with ring topologies is that if one computer fails or the cable link is broken, the entire network could go down. With newer technology, however, this isn't always the case. The concept of a ring topology today is that the ring will not be broken when a system is disconnected; only that system is dropped from the ring.

Isolating a problem can be difficult in some ring configurations. (With newer technologies, a workstation or server will put out a beacon if it notices a break in the ring.) Another disadvantage is that if you make a cabling change to the network or move a workstation, the brief disconnection can interrupt or bring down the entire network.

Hybrid Topologies

It is important to note that it is typical for networks to implement a mixture of topologies to form a hybrid topology. For example, a very popular hybrid topology is a star-bus topology, in which a number of star topologies are connected by a central bus, as shown in Figure 1-10. This is a popular topology because the bus will connect hubs that are spread over distance.

Another very popular hybrid topology is the star-ring topology. The star-ring topology is popular because it looks like a star but acts as a ring. For example, there is a network architecture known as Token Ring (more on this later, in the section "Network Architectures") that uses a central "hub" type device, but the internal wiring makes a ring. Physically it looks like a star, but logically it acts as a ring topology.

Wireless Topologies

A wireless topology is one in which few cables are used to connect systems. The network is made up of transmitters that broadcast the packets using radio

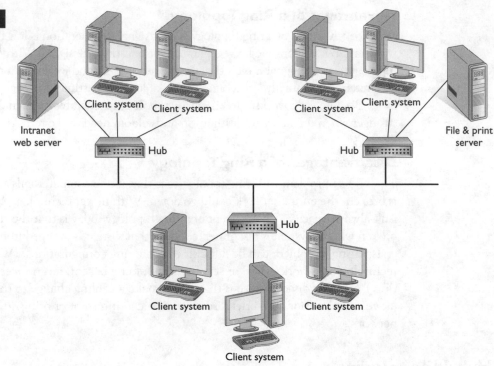

FIGURE 1-10

A star-bus hybrid topology

frequencies. The network contains special transmitters called *cells*, or *wireless access points*, which extend a radio sphere in the shape of a bubble around the transmitter. This bubble can extend to multiple rooms and possibly floors in a building. The PCs and network devices have a special transmitter-receiver, which allows them to receive broadcasts and transmit requested data back to the access point. The access point is connected to the physical network by a cable, which allows it, and any wireless clients, to communicate with systems on the wired network. A wireless network topology is shown in Figure 1-11.

Notice in Figure 1-11 that the wireless cells, or access points, are connected to the network by connecting into the hub or switch that has a connection to the rest of the wired network. Also notice that the clients do not have cables connecting them to the network. These are wireless clients, and they will get access to the network through the wireless cell (or access point).

Another option for wireless networks is the use of a radio antenna on or near the building, which allows one cell to cover the building and the surrounding area. This approach is best in a campus-type arrangement, where many buildings that need to be included in the cell are in a close geographical area. This setup does not easily

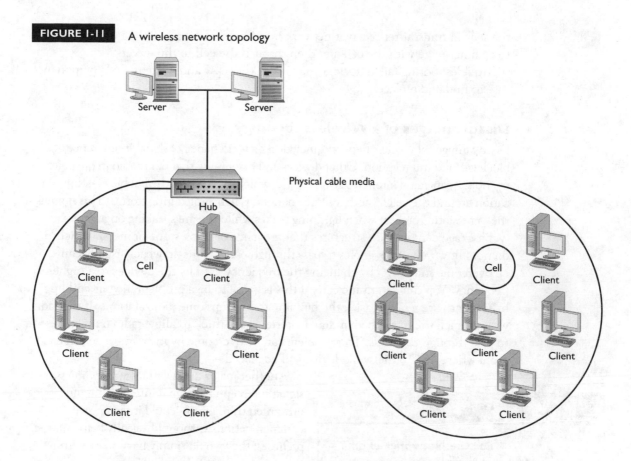

FIGURE 1-11 A wireless network topology

allow you to connect the buildings by a backbone and physical cables and then to each building containing the required cells for all its PCs and devices.

Wireless networks also can consist of infrared communications, similar to a remote-control TV, but this type of communication is slow and requires a direct line of sight—as well as close proximity—for the communication to work. Infrared mainly is used only between two systems. Infrared is not used often as a complete networking solution and should not be considered even as an option for a whole network; it is useful between laptops or a laptop and a printer.

Advantages of a Wireless Topology

The nice thing about wireless networks is the lack of cabling. The wireless network requires only base backbone segments to connect the wireless cells to the wired network if there is one. Once these are set up, the PC and network devices also need the special transmitter-receiver network interface cards to allow the PCs and devices to communicate with the cell and then through the cell to the servers.

Troubleshooting failed devices and cells is very easy and makes failed components easy to find and replace.

Disadvantages of a Wireless Topology

Disadvantages of wireless networks include a greater chance of signal interference, blockage, and interception. Other devices and machinery that emit radio frequencies or "noise" can cause interference and static, which can disrupt the bubble of communication around the cell. Another source of noise is lightning during storms. This noise is the same static you hear when lightning strikes while you are speaking on a phone.

Blockage can occur in structures that are made of thick stone or metal, which do not allow radio frequencies to pass through easily. This drawback usually can be overcome somewhat by changing the frequency used by the devices to a higher frequency. You can determine early if this is going to be a problem in your building by trying to use a radio inside the building to pick up some radio stations. If the radio will not pick them up, the building material is too thick to allow radio frequencies to pass through the walls. This problem can be overcome by installing a cell in each room where a PC or network device will be placed.

For the Network+ exam you need to be able to visually recognize the different network topologies from a network diagram.

Another major disadvantage with wireless is signal interception. Signal interception means unwanted third parties could intercept wireless communications without physically being on the premises; they would simply have to be within the signal range. One of the key steps to securing wireless communication is to limit who can connect to the network and to encrypt the traffic in transit. You will learn about wireless security in Chapter 7.

Point-to-Point and Point-to-Multipoint

There are two popular layouts for topologies: they are either point-to-point or point-to-multipoint. A *point-to-point* topology—also known as host to host—is one system connected directly to another system. In the past these systems would connect directly through the serial ports with a null modem cable, but these days, you could connect them using a crossover cable or a wireless connection.

A *point-to-multipoint* topology uses a central device that connects all the devices together. This topology is popular with wireless. With point-to-multipoint, when the central device sends data, it is received by all devices connected to the central device. But if one of the devices that are connected sends data, then it is received by only the destination system.

Segments and Backbones

With the various topologies you've looked at, you have seen the words segment and backbone mentioned a couple of times. A network segment is a cable length (or multiple cable lengths) that is uninterrupted by network connectivity devices, such as bridges and routers. It is typical that a single network may be broken into multiple network segments through the use of a bridge or router to cut down on network traffic, as shown in Figure 1-12.

In Figure 1-12, notice that there are three network segments named Segment A, Segment B, and Segment C. Also notice that each network segment could have a number of clients and servers all connected through a number of hubs that are then connected to a backbone. This is just one possible solution involving network segments.

FIGURE 1-12   A single network broken into multiple network segments

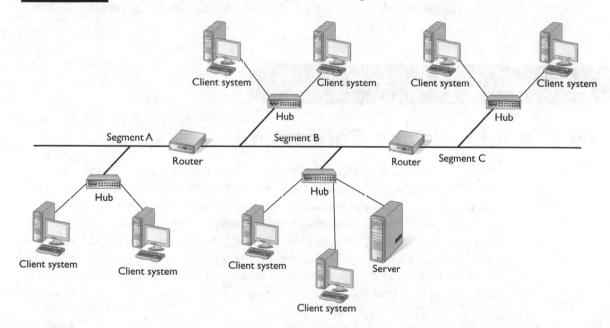

FIGURE 1-13

A network backbone with drop cables connecting the computers

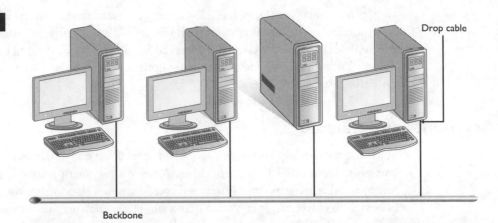

Drop cable

Backbone

You also saw the word backbone mentioned a few times. A backbone is the main cable segment or trunk in the network. In a bus network, you might see a main cable trunk that has smaller cables connecting the workstations. These smaller cables, known as *drop cables*, connect the workstations to the backbone. Figure 1-13 shows a backbone with drop cables.

Another example of a backbone is a satellite linking geographically dispersed local area networks (LANs), making a wide area network (WAN). Such a backbone is an example of a wireless communications network, whereas the previous examples all used cable as the medium.

CERTIFICATION OBJECTIVE 1.03

Network Media and Connectors

Now that you have learned that networks are built using a topology of bus, star, or ring, let's take a look at how the systems will be connected in the topology that you choose. Cabling is the medium for the transmission of data between hosts on the LANs. LANs can be connected together using a variety of cable types, such as unshielded twisted-pair, coax, or fiber. Each cable type has its own advantages and disadvantages, which you will examine in this section.

There are three primary types of cable media that can be used to connect systems to a network—coaxial cable, twisted-pair cable, and fiber-optic cable. Transmission rates that can be supported on each of these physical media are measured in millions of bits per second, or megabits per second (Mbps).

Coaxial Cable

Coaxial, or coax, cable looks like the cable used to bring the cable TV signal to your television. One strand (a solid-core copper wire) runs down the middle of the cable. Around that strand is a layer of insulation, and covering that insulation is braided wire and metal foil, which shields against electromagnetic interference. A final layer of insulation covers the braided wire. Because of the layers of insulation, coaxial cable is more resistant to outside interference than other cabling, such as unshielded twisted-pair (UTP) cable. Figure 1-14 shows a coaxial cable with the copper core and the layers of insulation.

There are two types of coax cabling: thinnet and thicknet. The two differ in thickness and maximum cable distance that the signal can travel. Let's take a look at thinnet and thicknet:

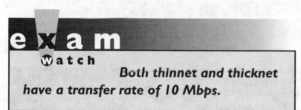

Both thinnet and thicknet have a transfer rate of 10 Mbps.

- **Thinnet**   This refers to RG-58 cabling, which is a flexible coaxial cable about ¼-inch thick. Thinnet is used for short-distance communication and is flexible enough to facilitate routing between workstations. Thinnet connects directly to a workstation's network adapter card using a British naval connector (BNC) and uses the network adapter card's internal transceiver. The maximum length of thinnet is 185 meters. Figure 1-15 displays thinnet coaxial cabling and the BNC connector on the end.

- **Thicknet**   This coaxial cable, also known as RG-8, gets its name by being a thicker cable than thinnet. Thicknet cable is about ½-inch thick and can support data transfer over longer distances than thinnet. Thicknet has a maximum cable length of 500 meters and usually is used as a backbone to connect several smaller thinnet-based networks. Due to the thickness of ½ inch, this cable is harder to work with than thinnet cable. A transceiver often is connected directly to the thicknet cable using a connector known as a vampire tap. Connection from the transceiver to the network adapter card is made using a drop cable to connect to the adapter unit interface (AUI) port connector. Table 1-1 summarizes the characteristics of thicknet and thinnet.

FIGURE 1-14

A coaxial cable

FIGURE 1-15

Thinnet coaxial cable with a BNC connector

TABLE 1-1

Thinnet Versus Thicknet

Coax Type	Cable Grade	Thickness	Maximum Distance	Transfer Rate	Connector Used to Connect NIC to Cable Type
Thinnet	RG-58	0.25 in	185 m	10 Mbps	BNC
Thicknet	RG-8	0.5 in	500 m	10 Mbps	AUI

Twisted-Pair Cable

Coaxial cable is not as popular today as it was a few years ago; today the popularity contest has been dominated by twisted-pair cabling. Twisted-pair cabling gets its name by having four pairs of wires that are twisted to help reduce crosstalk or interference from outside electrical devices. (Crosstalk is interference from adjacent wires.) Figure 1-16 shows a twisted-pair cable. Just as there are two forms of coaxial cable, there are two forms of twisted-pair cabling—unshielded twisted-pair (UTP) and shielded twisted-pair (STP).

e x a m

watch *For the exam know that the RG-59 and RG-6 cable grades are used with home video devices such as TVs and VCRs. RG-59 is used for short distances, while RG-6 is a more expensive coax used for longer distances.*

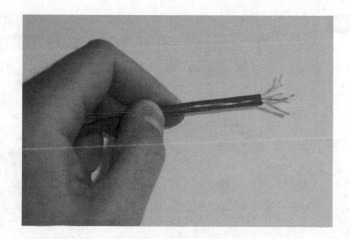

FIGURE 1-16

Unshielded
twisted-pair
(UTP) cable

Unshielded Twisted-Pair (UTP) Cable

Unshielded twisted-pair (UTP) cables are familiar to you if you have worked with
telephone cable. The typical twisted-pair cable for network use contains four pairs of
wires. Each member of the pair of wires contained in the cable is twisted around the
other. The twists in the wires help shield against electromagnetic interference. The
maximum distance of UTP is 100 meters.

UTP cable uses small plastic connectors designated as registered jack 45, or most
often referred to as RJ-45. RJ-45 is similar to the phone connectors, except that
instead of four wires, as found in the home system, the network RJ-45 connector
contains eight contacts, one for each wire in a UTP cable. The bottom cable in
Figure 1-17 is an RJ-45 connector.

It can be easy to confuse the RJ-45 connector with the RJ-11 connector. The
RJ-11 connector is a telephone connector and is shown in Figure 1-17 (the cable
on the top). In an RJ-11 connector, there are four contacts; hence there are four
wires found in the telephone cable. With RJ-45 and RJ-11, you will need a special
crimping tool when creating the cables to make contact between the pins in the
connector and the wires inside the cable.

UTP cable is easier to install than coaxial because you can pull it around corners
more easily due to its flexibility and small size. Twisted-pair cable is more susceptible
to interference than coaxial, however, and should not be used in environments
containing large electrical or electronic devices.

An RJ-11 connector and an RJ-45 connector

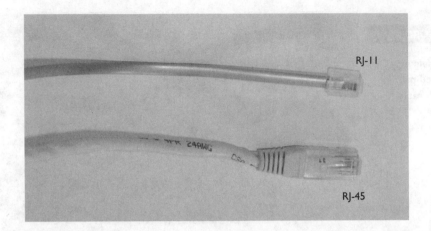

UTP cabling has different flavors, known as grades or categories. Each category of UTP cabling was designed for a specific type of communication or transfer rate. Table 1-2 summarizes the different UTP categories—the most popular today being CAT 5e, which can reach transfer rates of over 1000 Mbps or 1 gigabit per second (Gbps).

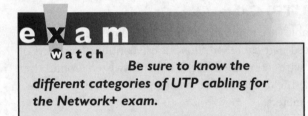

ex**a**m
watch

Be sure to know the different categories of UTP cabling for the Network+ exam.

Wiring Standards

It is important to understand the order of the wires within the RJ-45 connector for both the Network+ exam and in the real world if you intend on creating (also known as crimping) your own cables. Let's start with some basics of comparing a straight-through cable with a crossover cable.

Straight-Through Cables   CAT 5 UTP cabling usually uses only four wires when sending and receiving information on the network. The four wires of the eight that are used are wires 1, 2, 3, and 6. Figure 1-18 shows the meaning of the pins on a computer and the pins on a hub (or switch), which is what you typically will be connecting the computers to. When you configure the wire for the same pin at either end of the cable, this is known as a straight-through cable.

TABLE 1-2	UTP Category	Purpose	Transfer Rate
	Category 1	Voice only	
Different UTP Category Cabling	Category 2	Data	4 Mbps
	Category 3	Data	10 Mbps
	Category 4	Data	16 Mbps
	Category 5	Data	100 Mbps
	Category 5e	Data	1 Gbps (1000 Mbps)
	Category 6	Data	10 Gbps

You will notice in the figure that wires 1 and 2 are used to transmit data (TX) from the computer, while wires 3 and 6 are used to receive information (RX) on the computer. You will also notice that the transmit pin on the computer is connected to the receive pin (RX) on the hub via wires 1 and 2. This is important because we want to make sure that data that is sent from the computer is received at the network hub. We also want to make sure that data sent from the hub is received at the computer, so you will notice that the transmit pins (TX) on the hub are connected to the receive pins (RX) on the computer through wires 3 and 6. This will allow the computer to receive information from the hub.

The last thing to note about Figure 1-18 is that pin 1 on the computer is connected to pin 1 on the hub by the same wire, thus the term *straight-through*. You will notice that all pins are matched straight through to the other side in Figure 1-18.

Crossover Cables   At some point, you may need to connect two computer systems directly together without the use of a hub, from network card to network card. To do this, you would not be able to use a straight-through cable because the transmit pin on one computer would be connected to the transmit pin on another

FIGURE 1-18	

Pinout diagram for a straight-through cable

computer, as shown in Figure 1-19. How could a computer pick up the data if it was not sent to the receive pins? This will not work, so we will need to change the wiring of the cable to what is known as a *crossover cable*.

In order to connect two systems directly together without the use of a hub, you will need to create a crossover cable by switching wires 1 and 2 with wires 3 and 6 at one end of the cable, as shown in Figure 1-20. You will notice that the transmit pins on Computer A are connected to the receive pins on Computer B, thus allowing Computer A to send data to Computer B. The same applies for Computer B to send to Computer A—pins A and B on Computer B are wired to pins 3 and 6 on Computer A so that Computer A can receive data from Computer B.

568A and 568B Standards   Although only four of the wires are used to send and receive data in most environments today, some of the newer standards use all eight wires. Therefore, it is important to know the order of all eight wires in a UTP cable. There are two popular wiring standards today, 568A and 568B, but because 568B is the more popular standard for CAT 5 and CAT 5e, I will discuss the wire order for 568B. Table 1-3 shows the wire order for the 568B standard of a straight-through cable at both ends.

FIGURE 1-19

Using a straight-through cable to connect two computers will not work.

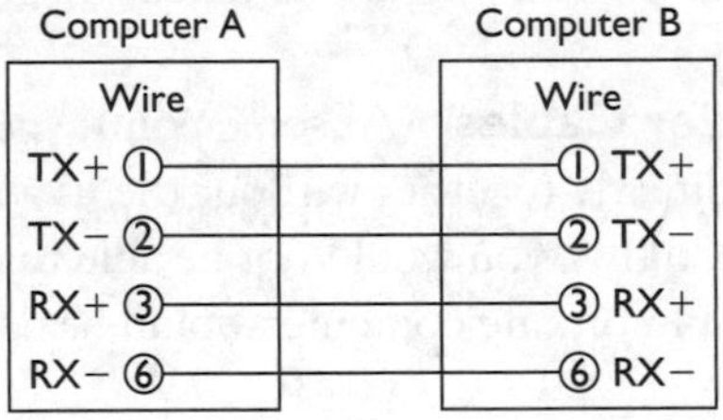

Computer A | Computer B
Wire | Wire
TX+ ① —————— ① TX+
TX– ② —————— ② TX–
RX+ ③ —————— ③ RX+
RX– ⑥ —————— ⑥ RX–

FIGURE 1-20

Pinout diagram of a crossover cable

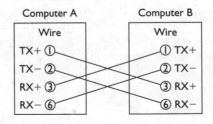

Computer A | Computer B
Wire | Wire
TX+ ① ⟍ ⟋ ① TX+
TX– ② ⟋ ⟍ ② TX–
RX+ ③ ⟍ ⟋ ③ RX+
RX– ⑥ —————— ⑥ RX–

TABLE 1-3	Wire	Connector #1	Connector #2
The 568B Wiring Standard for a Straight-Through Cable	1	White wire/orange stripe (white-orange)	White wire/orange stripe (white-orange)
	2	Orange wire	Orange wire
	3	White wire/green stripe (white-green)	White wire/green stripe (white-green)
	4	Blue wire	Blue wire
	5	White wire/blue stripe (white-blue)	White wire/blue stripe (white-blue)
	6	Green wire	Green wire
	7	White wire/brown stripe (white-brown)	White wire/brown stripe (white-brown)
	8	Brown wire	Brown wire

Following this standard and what you have learned of crossover cables, you would switch wires 1 and 2 with wires 3 and 6 at one end to create a crossover cable. After switching the wires on one end, you would have a cable that has the order of wires shown in Table 1-4.

TABLE 1-4	Wire	Connector #1	Connector #2
The 568B Wiring Standard for a Crossover Cable	1	White wire/orange stripe (white-orange)	White wire/green stripe (white-green)
	2	Orange wire	Green wire
	3	White wire/green stripe (white-green)	White wire/orange stripe (white-orange)
	4	Blue wire	Blue wire
	5	White wire/blue stripe (white-blue)	White wire/blue stripe (white-blue)
	6	Green wire	Orange wire
	7	White wire/brown stripe (white-brown)	White wire/brown stripe (white-brown)
	8	Brown wire	Brown wire

A crimping tool

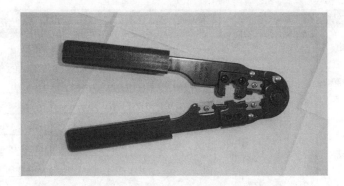

Before moving on to other cable types, apply what you have learned by crimping (creating) your own CAT 5 cable. To create your own network cable, you will need to have a crimper like the one shown in Figure 1-21. You can get a fairly cheap crimping tool at your local electronics store, but you can also buy some fairly expensive crimping tools.

When you select a crimping tool, you want to make sure that you have one that has a built-in crimper as well as a wire stripper and a wire cutter. Exercise 1-1 demonstrates the steps needed to crimp your own CAT 5 cable.

EXERCISE 1-1

Crimping a Category 5 Cable

In this exercise, you will learn how to crimp your own CAT 5 cable. To complete this exercise, you will need to have a crimping tool, a piece of CAT 5 cabling, some RJ-45 connectors, and a little bit of patience! To create a CAT 5 cable, do the following:

1. Ensure that you have a clean-cut end on the cable by using your wire cutters to cut a little off the end of the CAT 5 cable.

2. Once you have cut a clean end on the cable, strip about an inch off the outer jacket from the cable using the wire-stripper portion of your crimping tool, as shown in the next illustration. After stripping the outer jacket off, make sure that you have not cut into any of the individual wires. If you have, cut a clean end off the cable again and start from the beginning.

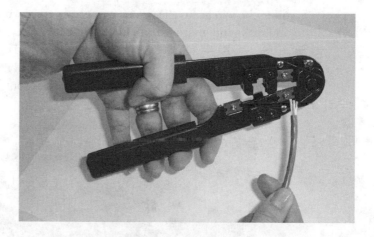

3. Once you have stripped the outer jacket off the cable, order the wires from left to right to follow the 568B standard. This is where your patience will come in, because it will take some time to get the wires in the correct order and placed tightly together so that they will go inside the RJ-45 connector.

4. Once you have the wires aligned in the correct order and you have them all nice and snug together so that they will fit inside the RJ-45 connector, you are ready to insert them into the connector. Before inserting the wires into the connector, make sure that their ends are of equal length; if they are not, just cut the tips a bit with your wire cutters, as shown in the following illustration, to be certain that they will fit nicely into the RJ-45 connector.

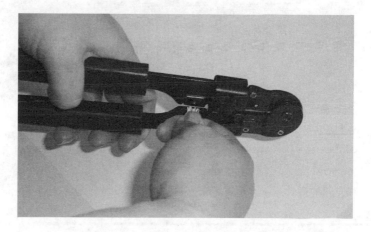

5. Slide the wires into the RJ-45 connector, as shown in the next illustration, and make sure that all wires have made contact with the metal contacts inside the RJ-45 connector by looking at the end of the connector. This is where mistakes happen frequently; there is usually one wire in the middle that is not pushed up to the end of the connector.

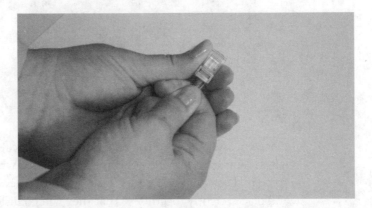

6. Once you are certain that all wires have made contact, you can "crimp" the wire, which will enclose the RJ-45 connector on the wires, creating a permanent fit. Insert the connector into the crimping tool and squeeze the handle tight, as seen in the following illustration.

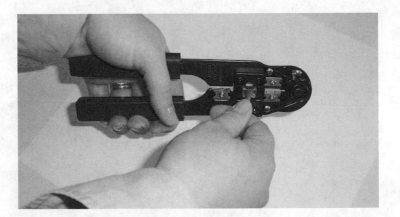

Rollover   A *rollover* cable is a popular cable type in the networking world and is used to connect to a Cisco device such as a router or a switch. Also known as a console cable, this cable connects from the computer's serial port to the console port of the router or switch. Once the network administrator connects to the console port, he or she is then able to configure the router or switch.

Shielded Twisted-Pair (STP) Cable

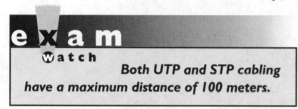

Both UTP and STP cabling have a maximum distance of 100 meters.

Shielded twisted-pair (STP) cable is very similar to UTP cabling, but it differs from UTP in that it uses a layer of insulation within the protective jacket, which helps maintain the quality of the signal. Figure 1-22 shows the size of STP cabling as compared to UTP.

Fiber-Optic Cable

The third type of cabling that we want to discuss is fiber-optic cabling. Fiber-optic cabling is unlike coax and twisted-pair, because both of those types have a copper wire that carries the electrical signal. Fiber-optic cables use optical fibers that carry digital data signals in the form of modulated pulses of light. An optical fiber consists of an extremely thin cylinder of glass, called the core, surrounded by a concentric layer of glass, known as the cladding. There are two fibers per cable—one to

UTP cabling versus STP cabling

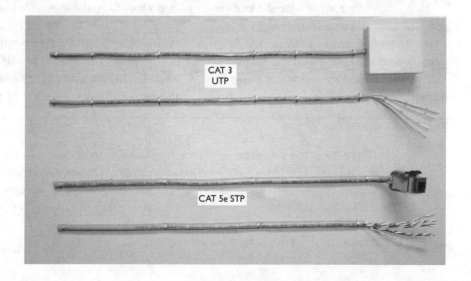

transmit and one to receive. The core also can be an optical-quality clear plastic, and the cladding can be made up of gel that reflects signals back into the fiber to reduce signal loss. Figure 1-23 shows fibers in a fiber-optic cable.

There are two types of fiber-optic cables: single-mode fiber (SMF) and multimode fiber (MMF).

- **Single-mode fiber**   Uses a single ray of light, known as a mode, to carry the transmission over long distances.
- **Multimode fiber**   Uses multiple rays of light (modes) simultaneously, with each ray of light running at a different reflection angle to carry the transmission over short distances.

Fiber-optic cable supports up to 1000 stations and can carry the signal up to and beyond 2 kilometers. Fiber-optic cables are also highly secure from outside interference, such as radio transmitters, arc welders, fluorescent lights, and other sources of electrical noise. On the other hand, fiber-optic cable is by far the most expensive of these cabling methods, and a small network is unlikely to need these features. Depending on local labor rates and building codes, installing fiber-optic cable can cost as much as $500 per network node.

---

exam
watch

You have learned of two electrical phenomena that can disrupt a signal traveling along your network: crosstalk and outside electrical noise. Crosstalk is caused by electrical fields in adjacent wires, which induce false signals in a wire. Outside electrical noise comes from lights, motors, radio systems, and many other sources. Fiber-optic cables are immune to these types of interference because they do not carry electrical signals—they carry pulses of light.

Fiber-optic cables can use many types of connectors, but the Network+ exam is concerned only with the two major connector types: the straight-tip (ST) connector and the subscriber (SC) connector. The ST connector is based on the BNC-style connector but has a fiber-optic cable instead of a copper cable. The SC connector is square and somewhat similar to an RJ-45 connector. Figure 1-24 shows the ST (the connector on the left side) and the SC (the connector on the right side) connector types.

FIGURE 1-23

A fiber-optic
cable

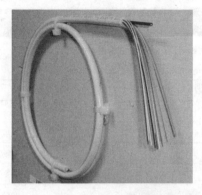

FIGURE 1-24

Fiber-optic ST
and SC connector
types

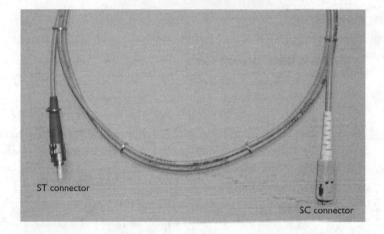

ST connector

SC connector

Regardless of the connector type, the fiber-optic cable still functions at the same speed, which is typically 1000 Mbps and faster. The only thing that you need to worry about is that the connector matches the device to which it is being connected, since the two-connector types are not interchangeable.

To better understand all of the cable types and when to use some specific types, see Exercise 1-2.

ON THE CD

Be sure to take a look at Exercise 1-2 in the LabBook.pdf file that is found on the CD-ROM.

When preparing for the Network+ exam, it is sometimes helpful to have a table listing the differences between the different cable types. Table 1-5 summarizes the different cable types—be sure to review it for the Network+ exam.

Cable	Max Distance	Transfer Rate	Connector Used
Thinnet	185 m	10 Mbps	BNC
Thicknet	500 m	10 Mbps	AUI
CAT 3 (UTP)	100 m	10 Mbps	RJ-45
CAT 5 (UTP)	100 m	100 Mbps	RJ-45
CAT 5e	100 m	1 Gbps	RJ-45
CAT 6	100 m	10 Gbps	RJ-45
Fiber	2 km	1+ Gbps	SC, ST

TABLE 1-5

Summary of Cable Types

Connector Types

Coaxial Connectors

We have discussed coaxial cabling, and you saw the BNC connector that goes on the end of the cable and connects to the network card, but there are a few other BNC connector types you should be familiar with. The BNC-T connector is used to connect to coax cable from either side (so that the cable length can continue on), while a third end of the connector tees out to have a cable length connect to the network card on the client machine. Figure 1-25 displays the BNC-T connector being placed on a network card. Notice the connector on the card that the T-connector connects to, and also notice where the coax cable would continue on through.

FIGURE 1-25

A BNC-T connector connecting to the network card

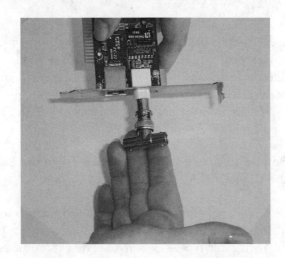

We also discussed the terminator that needs to go at both ends of the coax cable. For example, if we use the BNC-T connector to connect our last system to the network, we would need to terminate one of the ends on the T-connector, as shown in Figure 1-26. Notice that the terminator goes on one end of the T-connector and that the coax cable would connect into the other end.

Twisted-Pair Connectors

We have discussed two major twisted-pair connectors, the RJ-11 for four-wire telephone cable and the RJ-45 for eight-wire network cables. There are also barrel connectors, which are female connectors on both ends that allow you to join two cable lengths together and reach greater distances, not exceeding 100 meters. Figure 1-27 shows an RJ-45 barrel connector connecting two cable lengths together. There are also BNC barrel connectors.

FIGURE 1-26

A 50-ohm BNC terminator

FIGURE 1-27

An RJ-45 barrel connector

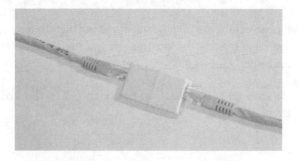

Other Connectors

There are a number of additional connector types that you will come across in networking environments, some of which are listed here:

- **F-type connector**   Another connector style for coax cabling, it is the same connector style that runs to your TV.

- **Fiber local connector (LC) and mechanical-transfer registered jack (MT-RJ)**   Additional fiber-optic connector types that are similar to the registered jack and fiber SC shape. The Fiber LC is the preferred connector of the two for communications exceeding 1 Gbps due to its small form factor.

- **Universal serial bus (USB)**   A high-speed serial bus that supports 127 devices in the chain. USB uses a standard connector type that is used by most devices, including mice, printers, network cards, digital cameras, and flash drives. There are two USB standards: USB 1.1, which has a transfer rate of 12 Mbps, and USB 2.0, which has a transfer rate of 480 Mbps. There are two standard USB connectors, Type A and Type B. Type A connectors connect to the computer, whereas Type B connectors connect to the device. Figure 1-28 displays these two connector styles.

- **IEEE 1394 (FireWire)**   An ultra-high-speed bus that supports 63 devices in the chain and is ideal for real-time applications and devices such as for video. FireWire has two standards: 1394a, which has a transfer rate of 400 Mbps, and 1394b, which has a transfer rate of 800 Mbps.

- **RS-232**   The standard for serial connections using the serial port on a computer. The serial port was a popular way to achieve a point-to-point connection between two hosts or was used for modems. The RS-232 standard defines a transfer rate of 20,000 bits per second, but serial devices support higher transfer rates.

Now that you understand some of the different cable types and connectors, Exercise 1-3 will demonstrate to you the steps to install a bus network using thinnet and BNC connectors.

Be sure to take a look at Exercise 1-3 in the LabBook.pdf file that is found on the CD-ROM.

FIGURE 1-28

USB Type A
and Type B
connectors

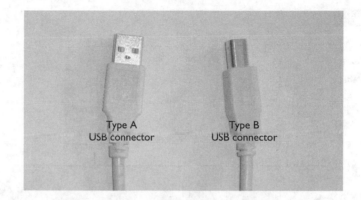

Type A
USB connector

Type B
USB connector

CERTIFICATION OBJECTIVE 1.04

Access Methods

You now know that a network uses a network topology—which is the layout of the network—and you know that some form of media such as cabling connects all hosts on the network. We have discussed the three major types of cabling: coax, twisted-pair, and fiber-optic cabling.

This section will identify what are known as access methods. An access method determines how a host will place data on the wire—does the host have to wait its turn or can it just place the data on the wire whenever it wants? The answer is determined by three major access methods: CSMA/CD, CSMA/CA, and token passing. Let's look at each of these access methods.

CSMA/CD

Carrier sense multiple access with collision detection (CSMA/CD) is one of the most popular access methods in use today. With CSMA/CD, every host has equal access to the wire and can place data on the wire when the wire is free from traffic. If a host wishes to place data on the wire, it will "sense" the wire and determine whether there is a signal already on the wire. If there is, the host will wait to transmit the data; if the wire is free, the host will send the data, as shown in Figure 1-29.

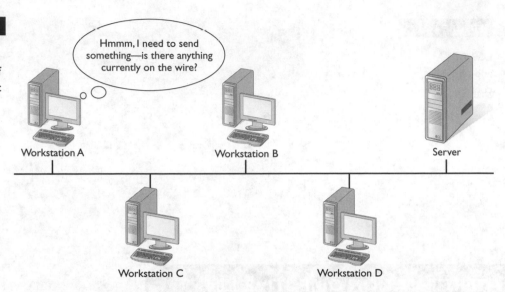

FIGURE 1-29

A host "sensing" the wire to see if it is free of traffic

The problem with the process just described is that, if there are two systems on the wire that "sense" the wire at the same time to see if the wire is free, they will both send data out at the same time if the wire is free. When the two pieces of data are sent out on the wire at the same time, they will collide with one another, and the data will be destroyed. If the data is destroyed in transit, the data will need to be retransmitted. Consequently, after a collision, each host will wait a variable length of time before retransmitting the data (they don't want the data to collide again), thereby preventing a collision the second time. When a system determines that the data has collided and then retransmits the data, that is known as collision detection.

To summarize, CSMA/CD provides that before a host sends data on the network, it will "sense" (CS) the wire to ensure that the wire is free of traffic. Multiple systems have equal access to the wire (MA), and if there is a collision, a host will detect that collision (CD) and retransmit the data.

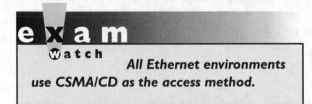

All Ethernet environments use CSMA/CD as the access method.

CSMA/CA

Carrier sense multiple access with collision avoidance (CSMA/CA) is not as popular as CSMA/CD and for good reason. With CSMA/CA, before a host sends data on the wire, it will "sense" the wire as well to see if the wire is free of signals. If the wire is free, it will try to "avoid" a collision by sending a piece of "dummy" data on the wire first to see whether it collides with any other data. If it does not collide, the host in effect assumes "If my dummy data did not collide, then the real data will not collide," and it submits the real data on the wire.

Token Passing

With both CSMA/CD and CSMA/CA, the possibility of collisions is always there, and the more hosts that are placed on the wire, the greater the chances of collisions, because you have more systems "waiting'" for the wire to become free so that they can send their data.

Token passing takes a totally different approach to deciding on how a system can place data on the wire. With token passing, there is an empty packet running around on the wire—the "token." In order to place data on the wire, you need to wait for the token; once you have the token and it is free of data, you can place your data on the wire. Since there is only one token and a host needs to have the token to "talk," it is impossible to have collisions in a token-passing environment.

For example, if Workstation 1 wants to send data on the wire, the workstation would wait for the token, which is circling the network millions of times per second. Once the token has reached Workstation 1, the workstation would take the token off the network, fill it with data, mark the token as being used so that no other systems try to fill the token with data, and then place the token back on the wire heading for the destination host.

All systems will look at the data, but they will not process it, since it is not destined for them. However, the system that is the intended destination will read the data and send the token back to the sender as a confirmation. Once the token has reached the original sender, the token is unflagged as being used and released as an empty token onto the network.

CERTIFICATION OBJECTIVE 1.05

Network Architectures

This section will discuss the different network architectures that are popular in today's networking environments. This section is very important from an exam point of view as well, so be sure to understand how the different architectures are pieced together.

Before we can discuss the different network architectures, we need to start our discussions by defining two terms: broadband and baseband transmissions.

Broadband and Baseband

There are two different techniques that may be used to transmit the signal along the network wire—baseband communication and broadband communication. Let's take a look at each of these techniques.

- **Baseband** Sends digital signals through the media as a single channel that uses the entire bandwidth of the media. The signal is delivered as a pulse of electricity or light, depending on the type of cabling being used. Baseband communication is also bidirectional, which means that the same channel can be used to send and receive signals.

- **Broadband** Sends information in the form of an analog signal, which flows as electromagnetic waves or optical waves. Each transmission is assigned to a portion of the bandwidth, so unlike with baseband communication, it is possible to have multiple transmissions at the same time, with each transmission being assigned its own channel or frequency. Broadband communication is unidirectional, so in order to send and receive, two pathways will need to be used. This can be accomplished either by assigning a frequency for sending and assigning a frequency for receiving along the same cable or by using two cables, one for sending and one for receiving.

Ethernet

To start us out, I first want to point out that network architecture is something that came about one day when someone sat down and said, "We are going to design a network architecture; let's use CAT 3 cabling, a star topology, and CSMA/CD as an access method. Oh, and let's call this architecture 10BaseT!"

In this example, 10BaseT was the name assigned to the architecture because 10 Mbps is the transfer rate of the network, baseband communication is the technique used to transmit the signal, and the T means our cable type—in this case twisted-pair. Now, we have discussed different types of twisted-pair cabling, but CAT 3 is the one that runs at 10 Mbps, so it is the cable used in 10BaseT.

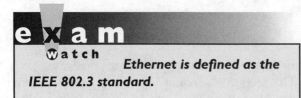

Ethernet is defined as the IEEE 802.3 standard.

The first types of network architecture to look at are the different Ethernet architectures. When designing networks, one of the first decisions we usually make is "Do we want to use Ethernet or the competing network architecture called Token Ring? Oh, we want to use Ethernet. What flavor of Ethernet?" This section will help you understand what the different flavors of Ethernet are.

10Base2

The 10Base2 Ethernet architecture is a network that runs at 10 Mbps and uses baseband transmissions. 10Base2 typically is implemented as a bus topology, but it could be a mix of a bus and a star topology. The cable type that we use is determined by the character at the end of the name of the architecture—in this case a 2. The 2 implies 200 meters. Now, what type of cable is limited to approximately 200 m? You got it; thinnet is limited to approximately 200 m (185 m, to be exact). The only characteristic we have not mentioned is the access method that is used. All Ethernet environments use CSMA/CD as a way to put data on the wire.

The following list summarizes features of 10Base2:

- Baseband communication
- 10 Mbps transfer rate
- Maximum distance of 185 meters per network segment
- 30 hosts per segment
- 0.5 meters minimum distance between hosts

10Base5

The 10Base5 Ethernet architecture runs at 10 Mbps and uses baseband transmission as well. It was also implemented as a bus topology. The cable it uses is limited to approximately 500 meters, which is thicknet, and it uses CSMA/CD as the access method. The thicker copper core in the wire allows the signal to travel farther than is possible with thinnet.

The following list summarizes features of 10Base5:

- Baseband communication
- 10 Mbps transfer rate
- Maximum distance of 500 meters per network segment
- 100 hosts per segment
- 2.5 meter minimum distance between hosts

10BaseT

The 10BaseT Ethernet architecture runs at 10 Mbps and uses baseband transmission. It uses a star topology with a hub or switch at the center, allowing all systems to connect to one another. The cable it uses is CAT 3 UTP, which is the UTP cable type that runs at 10 Mbps. Keep in mind that most cable types are backward compatible, so you could have CAT 5 UTP cabling in a 10BaseT environment. But because the network cards and hubs are running at 10 Mbps, that is the maximum transfer speed you will get, even though the cable supports more. Like all Ethernet environments, 10BaseT uses CSMA/CD as the access method.

10BaseFL

The 10BaseFL Ethernet architecture allows for a 10 Mbps Ethernet environment that runs on fiber-optic cabling. The purpose of the fiber-optic cabling is to use it as a backbone to allow the network to reach greater distances.

Fast Ethernet (100BaseTX and 100BaseFX)

These two standards are part of the 100BaseX family, which is known as fast Ethernet. The different fast Ethernet flavors run at 100 Mbps, use a star topology, use CSMA/CD as an access method, but differ in the type of cabling used. 100BaseTX uses two pairs (four wires) in the CAT 5 cabling, whereas 100BaseFX uses two strands of fiber instead of twisted-pair cabling.

Gigabit Ethernet

Gigabit Ethernet is becoming the de facto standard for network architectures today. With Gigabit Ethernet we can reach transfer rates of 1000 Mbps (1 Gbps), using traditional media such as coaxial, twisted-pair, and fiber-optic cabling. There are two standards (more on the IEEE standards in Chapter 2) for Gigabit Ethernet: IEEE 802.3z and IEEE 802.3ab.

IEEE 802.3z The IEEE 802.3z standard defines Gigabit Ethernet that runs over fiber-optic cabling or coaxial cabling. There are three types of Gigabit Ethernet that fall under this standard:

- **1000BaseSX** The Gigabit Ethernet architecture that runs at 1000 Mbps over multimode fiber (MMF) optic cabling. This architecture is designed for short distances of up to 550 meters.
- **1000BaseLX** The Gigabit Ethernet architecture that runs at 1000 Mbps over single-mode fiber (SMF) optic cabling. This architecture supports distances up to 3 kilometers.
- **1000BaseCX** The Gigabit Ethernet architecture that runs at 1000 Mbps over coaxial cable and supports distances of up to 25 meters.

IEEE 802.3ab The IEEE 802.3ab standard, known as 1000BaseTX, defines Gigabit Ethernet that runs over twisted-pair cabling and uses characteristics of 100BaseTX networking, including the use of RJ-45 connectors and the access method of CSMA/CD. Like 100BaseTX, 1000BaseTX uses CAT 5e or CAT 6 unshielded twisted-pair; the difference is that 100BaseTX runs over two pairs (four wires) while 1000BaseTX runs over four pairs (all eight wires).

10-Gigabit Ethernet

There are standards for 10-Gigabit Ethernet (10,000 Mbps) that have been developed that use fiber-optic cabling:

- **10GBaseSR** Runs at 10 Gbps and uses "short-range" multimode fiber-optic cable, which has a maximum distance of 100 meters.
- **10GBaseLR** Runs at 10 Gbps and uses "long-range" single-mode fiber-optic cable, which has a maximum distance of 10 kilometers.
- **10GBaseER** Runs at 10 Gbps and uses "extra-long-range" single-mode fiber-optic cable, which has a maximum distance of 40 kilometers.
- **10GBaseT** Runs at 10 Gbps using CAT 6 UTP cabling, which has a maximum distance of 100 meters.

There are special WAN versions of 10-Gigabit Ethernet that use fiber-optic cabling to connect to a SONET network (more on SONET in Chapter 9).

- **10GBaseSW** The 10-Gigabit Ethernet standard for short-range, multimode fiber-optic cable, which has a maximum distance of 100 meters
- **10GBaseLW** The 10-Gigabit Ethernet standard for long-range, single-mode fiber-optic cable, which has a maximum distance of 10 kilometers
- **10GBaseEW** The 10-Gigabit Ethernet standard for extended-range, single-mode fiber-optic cable, which has a distance of up to 40 kilometers

Be familiar with the 100 Mbps and 1 Gbps/10 Gbps architectures for the exam. Be familiar with the speeds, cable types, connectors, and maximum distance of each architecture.

Token Ring

A big competitor to Ethernet in the past was Token Ring, which runs at 4 Mbps or 16 Mbps. Token Ring is a network architecture that uses a star ring topology (a hybrid, looking physically like a star but logically wired as a ring) and can use many forms of cables. IBM Token Ring has its own proprietary cable types, while more modern implementations of Token Ring can use CAT 3 or CAT 5 UTP cabling. Token Ring uses the token-passing access method.

Token Ring is defined as the IEEE 802.5 standard.

Looking at Token Ring networks today, you may wonder where the "ring" topology is, because the network appears to have a star topology. The reason this network architecture appears to use a star topology is that all hosts are connected to a central device that looks similar to a hub, but with Token Ring, this device is called a multistation access unit (MAU or MSAU). An example is shown in Figure 1-30. The ring is the internal communication path within the wiring.

Token Ring uses token passing; it is impossible to have collisions in a token-passing environment, because the MAUs do not have collisions lights as an Ethernet hub does (remember that Ethernet uses CSMA/CD and there is potential for collisions).

FIGURE 1-30

A Token
Ring MAU

INSIDE THE EXAM

Unraveling the Ethernet Name Jargon

Most people get very confused by the jargon used to describe the various Ethernet types, but Ethernet is explained easily by breaking down the name of the architecture. Ethernet types follow a ##BaseXX naming convention and are designated as follows:

- ## stands for the speed of the network; examples are 10 (for 10 Mbps), 100 (for 100 Mbps), 1000 (for 1000 Mbps or 1 Gbps), and 10G (for 10 Gbps).
- Base stands for baseband transmission.
- XX stands for the cable type or medium.
  - For example, if there is a 5 at the end of the architecture name, 5 represents the cable medium thicknet. The 5 in the name indicates the maximum length of thicknet, which is 500 meters. A 2 at the end of the name would mean that the medium is thinnet,

which gets its name from the fact that thinnet has a maximum length of 200 meters (actually, 185 meters).

- T stands for twisted-pair cabling and can be further used to show the number of pairs; for example, 10BaseT4 requires four pairs of wires from a twisted-pair cable.
- F is for fiber-optic cable.
- X represents a higher grade of connection, and 100BaseTX is twisted-pair cabling that can use either UTP or STP at 100 Mbps. With fiber-optic cable such as 100BaseFX, the speed is quicker than standard 10BaseF.

If we look at an example such as 100BaseTX, the 100 means 100 Mbps using baseband transmission and twisted-pair cable. Since we know that the speed is 100 Mbps, we also can assume that the type of twisted-pair cable will be at least CAT 5.

FDDI

Fiber distributed data interface (FDDI) is a network architecture that uses fiber-optic cabling, token passing, and a ring topology, but FDDI also uses two counter-rotating rings for fault tolerance on the network. For more information on FDDI, please refer to Chapter 9.

Be sure to take a look at Exercise 1-4 in the LabBook.pdf file that is found on the CD-ROM.

Once again, a table summarizing the core facts is always useful when preparing for an exam. Table 1-6 summarizes the popular network architectures. Be sure to review these before taking the Network+ exam.

TABLE 1-6	Network Architecture	Topology	Cable	Transfer Rate	Access Method
Network Architecture Summary	10Base2	Bus	Thinnet	10 Mbps	CSMA/CD
	10Base5	Bus	Thicknet	10 Mbps	CSMA/CD
	10BaseT	Star	CAT 3	10 Mbps	CSMA/CD
	100BaseT	Star	CAT 5	100 Mbps	CSMA/CD
	1000BaseTX	Star	CAT 5, 5e, 6	1 Gbps	CSMA/CD
	10GBaseLR	Star	Fiber (single mode)	10 Gbps	CSMA/CD
	Token Ring	Star ring	UTP	4 Mbps/16 Mbps	Token passing

CERTIFICATION OBJECTIVE 1.06

Network Operating Systems

Now that you have a general idea of the network topologies, cable types, and network architectures, let's look at the network operating system (NOS). We focus on the three most widely used network operating systems available today:

- Windows 2000 Server and Windows Server 2003/2008
- Novell NetWare
- UNIX

INSIDE THE EXAM

The Role of Network Topology, Cabling, and Connectors

A thorough understanding of how network topology, cabling, and connectors coexist is a very valuable skill set to possess for the Network+ exam. This is especially the case if you are a network engineer who must design and implement a network from the ground up. You must know the characteristics of each network topology and be able to apply them in each unique situation you encounter.

For example, let's say that you are designing a network for a small investment firm with ten users and a minimal budget. Instantly, you may be thinking "star topology," which is relatively inexpensive and easy to implement for smaller networks such as this one.

Your choice of network topology also dictates other characteristics of the network,

such as what your choice of cabling will be and whether additional hardware is required. In our example, we have implemented a star topology, which is conducive to twisted-pair cabling—more importantly of at least CAT 5 UTP. The UTP cables will be connected to a network hub or switch using an RJ-45 connector, which leads us to our final specification: the network connector. Just as the network topology dictates the choice of cabling, it also dictates our choice of connector. The RJ-45 connector is the cornerstone of twisted-pair cabling.

Although this example seems fairly straightforward, the secret lies in understanding the characteristics of each type of network, such as cable types, connectors, and supporting devices. This will come in handy during your Network+ exam, which will definitely test your knowledge of these concepts.

Once you have connected the cables to the hubs and the clients to the cables, it is time to install a network operating system. The network operating system is responsible for providing services to clients on the network. These services could be the sharing of files or printers; the server could be providing name resolution through DNS services or logon services by being a directory server.

Let's take a look at some of the popular network operating systems that provide network services to their clients. For this discussion, any time that we mention Windows 2000 or Windows Server 2003, we can also include Windows NT Server, because Windows 2000 and Windows Server 2003 were built off Windows NT technologies and are the successors to Windows NT.

Windows Servers

Developed from the VMS platform many years ago, Microsoft Windows NT and its successors, Windows Server 2003 and 2008, have grown into very popular network operating systems that provide a number of built-in network services, including

- **File and print services** These allow the administrator to share files and printers among Windows clients.
- **DNS and WINS services** These allow the administrator to configure DNS and NetBIOS name resolution.
- **DHCP services** These allow the administrator to configure the server to assign IP addresses to clients on the network.
- **Directory services** These allow the administrator to build a central list of objects, such as user accounts that may be used by clients to log on to the network. Microsoft's directory service is known as Active Directory.
- **Web services** These allow the administrator to build Internet or corporate intranet sites that are hosted on the server.
- **E-mail services** These allow the administrator to configure the server to send e-mail using the Simple Mail Transfer Protocol (SMTP). This feature was designed to allow application developers to build e-mail functionality into their applications.
- **Group policies** These allow an administrator to deploy settings down to the client operating systems from a central point. Some of the types of settings that can be applied to clients through group policies are folder redirection, file permissions, user rights, and installation of software.

We will look at those network services in a later chapter; the point now is that the network operating systems usually come with these features and all you need to do is install or configure them on the server.

One of the major factors that led to the popularity of the Windows-based server operating systems is that Microsoft developed a user interface on the server that was similar to the client operating systems, such as Windows 98, Windows 2000 Professional, and Windows XP Professional. This dramatically reduces the learning curve that someone new to network operating systems has to go through. Figure 1-31 displays the user interface of a Windows server.

FIGURE 1-31   The Windows server user interface

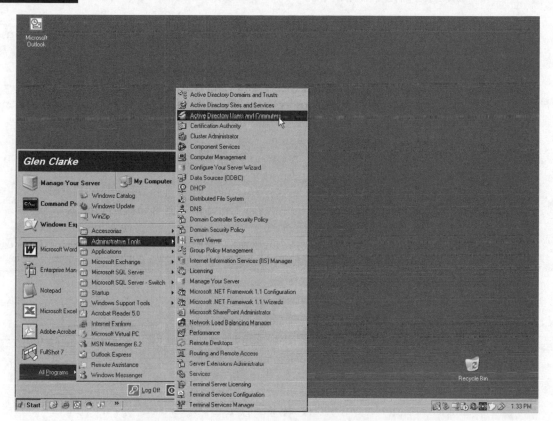

The fact that the user interface on the server operating system is the same as that on the client operating system means that the learning curve for the server operating system is dramatically reduced. The other thing that led to the rapid growth of the installed base for Windows-based servers is the fact that Windows servers made it very easy to configure the services that were mentioned previously. For example, to install a DNS server, WINS server, or DHCP server, you simply go to Add/Remove Programs and install those services as you would install solitaire on a desktop operating system.

Be sure to take a look at Exercise 1-5 in the LabBook.pdf file that is found on the CD-ROM.

Clients and Resources

A major component of successful networking with NOS is the client operating system. The client operating system needs to have client software installed known as the redirector. The term *redirector* comes from the fact that when the client makes the request for a network resource, the redirector redirects the request from the local system to the network server. Whether the workstations are in a workgroup environment (peer-to-peer) or a client/server environment, you need to have client software installed on the client operating systems to connect to the servers. Some examples of client operating systems that can connect to a Windows server are Windows XP Professional, Windows 2000 Professional, Windows NT Workstation 4.0, Windows 95/98, and Windows for Workgroups.

Another reason Windows servers have been so successful is that they support many different client operating systems. Not only can Windows clients such as Windows 98 and Windows XP connect to the Windows servers, but also non-Microsoft clients such as Macintosh clients, NetWare clients, and UNIX clients can connect to Microsoft servers. Microsoft has been very focused on coexisting with other environments.

Directory Services

With Windows servers, the server that holds the central list of user accounts that may log on to the network is called a domain controller. Windows 2000 Server and Windows 2003 Server call the database of user accounts that resides on the domain controllers the Active Directory Database. Active Directory is Microsoft's implementation of a directory service. Typically when users log on to the network, they will sit at a client machine and type a username and password. In the Microsoft world, this username and password combination is sent to the domain controller so that the domain controller can verify that the logon information is correct. If the logon information is correct, the user is allowed to use network resources. A directory service also enables users to locate objects on the network such as printers because the directory stores more than user accounts—it stores additional network objects such as printers and folders so that users can search the directory for these objects.

Novell NetWare

It started as a college project for one individual many years ago; today Novell NetWare is still used in many large organizations. NetWare has evolved into a very powerful network operating system, supporting a number of network services out of the box and an industry-leading directory service. Some of the core services supported by a NetWare server include

- **File and print services** These allow the administrator to share files and printers among NetWare clients.
- **DNS services** These allow the administrator to configure a DNS server for DNS name resolution.
- **DHCP services** These allow the administrator to configure the server to assign IP addresses to clients on the network.
- **Directory services** These allow the administrator to build a central list of objects (such as user accounts) that may be used by clients to log on to the network. Novell's directory service is known as NDS in NetWare 4 and 5, or eDirectory in NetWare 6.
- **Web servers** These allow the administrator to build Internet or corporate intranet sites that are hosted on the server by using Apache web servers provided with the NetWare operating system.

The major difference between Windows servers and NetWare is at the server. Until NetWare 5, the server in NetWare was truly a text-based console with many of the administrative tasks done at a client workstation. As a NetWare administrator, you could manage certain administrative items from the server console, but most of the day-to-day administration such as user account management and file system administration was done from a workstation. This meant that you had to have a workstation with the management tools installed, while with a Windows server you have the management tools already installed on the server and can use them at any time. Figure 1-32 shows a screenshot of a NetWare 6 server console.

FIGURE 1-32

A NetWare 6
server console

```
File server name: DA1
Server Up Time:  54 Minutes 38 Seconds

Novell Ethernet NE1500/2100 and PCnet (ISA, ISA+, PCI, Fast)
     Version 1.39    January 23, 1998
     Hardware setting: Slot 2, I/O ports 1080h to 109Fh, Interrupt Bh
     Node address: 000C295D3FD8
     Frame type: ETHERNET_II
     PACKET EVENIZE_OFF
     Board name: CNEAMD_1_EII
     LAN protocol: ARP
     LAN protocol: IP Addr:192.168.1.10 Mask:255.255.255.0


Tree Name: .DIGITALAIR-TREE.
Bindery Context(s):
     .IS.SLC.DA

DA1:_
```

Clients and Resources

NetWare supports a wide variety of clients. The main ones, of course, are the Windows platform of operating systems, such as Windows 98, Windows 2000 Pro, and Windows XP Pro. It should be noted that NetWare now fully supports Linux client workstations; as a matter of fact, all previously mentioned Novell services can run on Linux server operating systems. Novell client software is required to connect to NetWare 4 and NetWare 5 servers but is no longer required for NetWare 6.*x*, because files, printers, e-mail, and administrative tools are all available using a web browser. The Network+ exam will assume that the Novell client always is required to connect to NetWare servers. The Novell Client software can be downloaded from the Novell web site at download.novell.com.

on the Job

Although Microsoft operating systems come with a "Client for NetWare Networks," it is recommended to install Novell's client to connect to NetWare 4 and 5 networks to ensure that you are getting the full benefit of the networking environment.

Directory Services

One of the driving features of NetWare since version 4 has been Novell's directory services, known as eDirectory (formerly NDS). eDirectory supports a hierarchical grouping of objects that represent resources on the network, as shown in Figure 1-33. The objects in the directory tree can be users, printers, volumes, and servers, along with others.

The directory services built into NetWare make administration easier because everything is organized and centralized within one utility. Some of the features provided by eDirectory include

- **Platform independence**   eDirectory can run on NetWare servers, Windows servers, Linux servers, and UNIX servers.
- **DirXML**   eDirectory uses DirXML software drivers to synchronize directory information with other directories, such as Microsoft Active Directory or Oracle's PeopleSoft.
- **Partitioning and replication**   eDirectory can be split (partitioned) into smaller portions, and these smaller portions (replicas) can be placed on strategically selected servers.

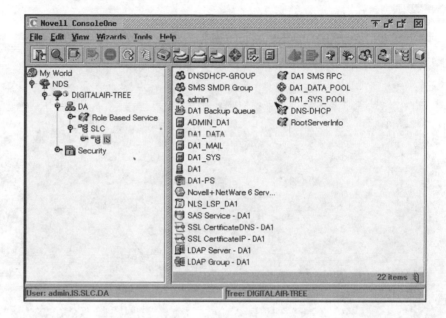

FIGURE 1-33

Objects organized in Novell eDirectory using the ConsoleOne tool

UNIX/Linux

Originally developed by Bell Labs, UNIX is a very popular operating system for powerful networking and database management. UNIX boasts three key features that make it powerful: multitasking, multiusers, and networking capabilities.

UNIX is a very powerful multitasking operating system that can run many processes in the background while enabling users to work in the foreground on an application. The last feature, networking capability, has been standard for some time. UNIX has been the leader in several powerful and diverse utilities that have been ported over to other operating systems. UNIX has a very popular cousin, known as Linux, which is starting to pick up some market share as both servers and clients. Figure 1-34 displays the Linux operating system.

Clients and Resources

Today's versions of UNIX and especially Linux are different than the older versions of UNIX. Today, like Windows, most Linux versions have a graphical shell loaded automatically that allows a user to use the operating system with a mouse. Today's

FIGURE 1-34   The Linux user interface

versions of Linux have programs automatically installed that allow you to configure the operating system and change its settings. Like Windows, most Linux operating systems have popular programs installed for you to use—programs such as a text editor and a calculator. The point is that although most people have traditionally associated Linux or UNIX with the command line only, you can do a lot from the graphical shell as well.

Directory Services

The UNIX and Linux standard directory service is called Network Information Service (NIS), which as been superseded by NIS+ and LDAP. As a matter of fact, Microsoft Services for UNIX and NetWare Services for UNIX both include an NIS service, which allows UNIX and Linux clients to authenticate to Active Directory or eDirectory. These services also allow for the objects from Active Directory and eDirectory to be copied or synchronized with the NIS directory, allowing UNIX clients to authenticate with NIS when the account was built originally in the other directory. Similar to Active Directory and eDirectory, NIS is a central repository of network resources (for example, users, group, printers) that is synchronized to other UNIX and Linux servers on the network.

NIS is the directory service used by UNIX and Linux to store a central list of network objects, such as users, groups, and printers.

CERTIFICATION SUMMARY

This chapter plays a significant role in this book. It serves as an introduction to some very key elements of networking, such as network topologies, cabling, and network architectures. Understanding the basic network structure takes a little knowledge of computing and information sharing. First, remember that for a network to exist, we need to have two things: the entities that want to share information or resources and the medium that enables the entities to communicate (a cable, such as coaxial or unshielded twisted-pair, or a wireless network). In this chapter, you looked at the various topologies that exist in networks: bus, star, ring, mesh, and wireless. You also looked at network terms, such as segments and backbones.

You also looked at the various networking media and connectors. Knowing the various grades of cable can be important for the exam, as well as knowing what connectors go with what type of cabling. Make sure to review this before taking your exam.

You also learned about some of the network operating systems for client/server networks: Windows 2000 Server, Windows Server 2003, Novell NetWare, and UNIX.

✓ TWO-MINUTE DRILL

Identifying Characteristics of a Network

❑ A network is made up of two basic components: the entities that need to share information or resources and the medium that enables the entities to communicate.

❑ A peer-to-peer network is a network that has a number of workstations that connect to one another for the purpose of sharing resources. There is no dedicated server on a peer-to-peer network.

❑ A server-based network is a network that has a central server installed with each client requesting resources from the server.

Identifying Network Topologies

❑ Topology is the physical layout of computers, cables, and other components on a network.

❑ Many networks are a combination of these topologies:

  ❑ Bus

  ❑ Star

  ❑ Mesh

  ❑ Ring

  ❑ Wireless

❑ A bus topology uses a main trunk to connect multiple computers. If there is a break in a cable, it will bring the entire network down.

❑ In a star topology, all computers are connected through one central hub or switch. If there is a break in a cable, only the host that is connected to that cable is affected.

❑ With a mesh topology, every workstation has a connection to every other component of the network. This type of topology is seen more commonly in something like the national telephone network.

❑ In a ring topology, all computers are connected in a ring with no beginning or end. Each system in the ring regenerates the signal. If there is a break in the ring, the entire network goes down.

❑ In a wireless topology, radio frequencies are used instead of physical cables. Wireless clients connect to cells, or access points, through the use of a wireless network card.

❑ A backbone is the main cable segment in the network.

Network Media and Connectors

❑ Cabling is the LAN's transmission medium.

❑ Three primary types of physical media can be used: coaxial cable, twisted-pair cable, and fiber-optic cable.

❑ Coax uses a copper core that carries an electrical signal. There are two types of coax: thinnet and thicknet. Hosts connect to thinnet through BNC connectors, whereas vampire taps and drop cables are used to connect to thicknet.

❑ Twisted-pair cabling is a cable type similar to telephone cable, but there are eight wires instead of four. Telephone cables use an RJ-11 connector, whereas network cabling uses an RJ-45 connector.

❑ Fiber-optic cabling has a glass or clear-plastic core that carries pulses of light. The straight tip (ST) and subscriber connector (SC) are connectors used with fiber-optic cabling.

Access Methods

❑ An access method determines how systems access the network or place data on the wire.

❑ CSMA/CD is the access method used by Ethernet networks and involves a host sensing traffic on the wire. When the wire is free of traffic, the host can send its data.

❑ Token passing is the access method used by Token Ring. When a system on a Token Ring network wants to send data it must wait to receive the token.

Network Architectures

❑ A network architecture is made up of a certain cable type, access method, and topology.

❑ Two popular Ethernet architectures are 10BaseT and 100BaseT. 10BaseT uses twisted-pair cabling at 10 Mbps (CAT 3) and uses CSMA/CD as the access method. 100BaseT runs at 100 Mbps using CAT 5 UTP cabling. Both architectures use a star topology.

❑ Token Ring is a network architecture that uses token passing as the access method and is configured in a star topology.

Network Operating Systems

❑ The three most widely used network operating systems available are

  ❑ Microsoft Windows Server 2003/2008

  ❑ Novell NetWare

  ❑ UNIX

SELF TEST

The following questions will help you measure your understanding of the material presented in this chapter. Read all the choices carefully because there may be more than one correct answer, but you will need to select the most correct answer.

Identifying Characteristics of a Network

1. Which of the following is an example of a network?
   A. A computer attached to a printer and a scanner to input and output information
   B. Computer systems sharing a common communication medium for the purpose of sharing information or devices
   C. Several printers connected to a switch box going to a single terminal
   D. Several diskettes holding information for one workstation

2. In which type of network is there no dedicated server, with each node on the network being an equal resource for sharing and receiving information?
   A. Client/server
   B. Peer-to-peer
   C. Windows Server 2003
   D. Novell NetWare 6.*x*

3. What is the Microsoft term for a peer-to-peer network?
   A. Client/server
   B. Domain
   C. Workgroup
   D. Active Directory

4. A company has offices in Halifax and Toronto. Both networks are connected to allow the two locations to communicate. This is considered what type of network?
   A. LAN
   B. JAN
   C. MAN
   D. WAN

5. Which type of server is responsible for storing files for users on the network?
   A. File and print server
   B. Web server
   C. Directory server
   D. Application server

6. You wish to extend your intranet to certain business partners. What type of network are you building?
   A. Intranet
   B. Internet
   C. Extranet
   D. LAN

Identifying Network Topologies

7. The physical layout of computers, cables, and other components on a network is known as which of the following?
   A. Segment
   B. Backbone
   C. Topology
   D. Protocol

8. Which topology has a centralized location in which all of the cables come together to a central point such that a failure at this point brings down the entire network?
   A. Bus
   B. Star
   C. Mesh
   D. Ring
   E. Wireless

9. Which topology has a layout in which every workstation or peripheral has a direct connection to every other workstation or peripheral on the network?
   A. Bus
   B. Star
   C. Mesh
   D. Ring
   E. Wireless

10. Which network topology requires the use of terminators?

    A. Bus

    B. Star

    C. Mesh

    D. Ring

    E. Wireless

Networking Media and Connectors

11. Which of the following is not a common type of medium used in networking?

    A. Coaxial cable

    B. Twisted-pair cable

    C. Fiber-optic cable

    D. RJ-45

12. What is the distance limitation of 10Base2, or thinnet?

    A. 100 meters

    B. 185 meters

    C. 250 meters

    D. 500 meters

13. Which cable type sends the signal as pulses of light through a glass core?

    A. Thinnet

    B. Thicknet

    C. Fiber optic

    D. CAT 5e

14. What is the maximum distance of CAT 3 UTP cabling?

    A. 100 meters

    B. 185 meters

    C. 250 meters

    D. 500 meters

15. What is the maximum distance of cabling used on a 10Base5 network?

    A. 100 meters

    B. 185 meters

    C. 250 meters

    D. 500 meters

16. You wish to install a 100BaseT network. What type of cabling will you use?
   A. CAT 3 UTP
   B. CAT 5 UTP
   C. Thinnet
   D. Fiber optic

17. Fiber-optic cabling uses which types of connectors? (Select two.)
   A. SC
   B. RJ-45
   C. BNC
   D. ST

18. What is the maximum distance of single-mode fiber (SMF)?
   A. 300 meters
   B. 500 meters
   C. 2 km
   D. 850 meters

19. Which cable type is immune to outside interference and crosstalk?
   A. Thinnet
   B. Thicknet
   C. Twisted-pair
   D. Fiber optic

20. Which type of connector is used on 10Base2 networks?
   A. SC
   B. BNC
   C. RJ-45
   D. RJ-11

21. You want to create a crossover cable to connect two systems directly together. Which wires would you have to switch at one end of the cable?
   A. Wires 1 and 2 with wires 3 and 6
   B. Wires 2 and 3 with wires 6 and 8
   C. Wires 1 and 2 with wires 3 and 4
   D. Wires 2 and 3 with wires 3 and 6

Access Methods

22. Which access method does 100BaseT use?
- **A.** Baseband
- **B.** CSMA/CD
- **C.** CSMA/CA
- **D.** Token passing

23. Which access method does Token Ring use?
- **A.** Baseband
- **B.** CSMA/CD
- **C.** CSMA/CA
- **D.** Token passing

Network Architectures

24. Which network architecture is defined as the IEEE 802.3 standard?
- **A.** Token Ring
- **B.** FDDI
- **C.** Fiber
- **D.** Ethernet

25. Which network architecture uses single-mode fiber-optic cabling?
- **A.** 1000BaseLX
- **B.** 1000BaseSX
- **C.** 1000BaseCX
- **D.** 1000BaseTX

26. How many populated network segments can exist with 10Base2?
- **A.** 1
- **B.** 2
- **C.** 3
- **D.** 5

27. Which type of cabling is used in a 10BaseFL network?
- **A.** STP
- **B.** CAT 3 UTP
- **C.** Thinnet
- **D.** Thicknet
- **E.** Fiber optic

28. Which Gigabit architecture uses multimode fiber cabling?

  A. 1000BaseLX

  B. 1000BaseSX

  C. 1000BaseCX

  D. 1000BaseTX

Network Operating Systems

29. Which network operating system was developed from the VMS platform?

  A. NetWare

  B. UNIX

  C. Windows 95

  D. Windows NT

30. Which operating system was originally developed by Bell Labs and has multitasking, multiuser, and built-in networking capabilities?

  A. UNIX

  B. Windows NT

  C. Windows 95

  D. NetWare

31. Which of the following are network operating systems and not simply desktop operating systems? (Choose all that apply.)

  A. Novell NetWare

  B. Microsoft Windows 98

  C. Microsoft Windows XP

  D. Microsoft Windows Server 2003

32. Novell's directory service is called _____?

  A. Active Directory

  B. NDS / eDirectory

  C. DNS

  D. StreetTalk

33. Microsoft's directory service is called _____?

  A. Active Directory

  B. NDS

  C. DNS

  D. StreetTalk

SELF TEST ANSWERS

Identifying Characteristics of a Network

1. ☑ **B.** Computer systems sharing a common communication medium for the purpose of sharing information or devices is what a network is all about. The entities are usually workstations, and the medium is either a cable segment or a wireless medium such as an infrared signal.
   ☒ **A, C,** and **D** are incorrect because a network, by definition, is two or more computers connected to share information. These three choices do not allow two or more PCs to share information; they are only setups of several connected devices or a PC connected to a peripheral device.

2. ☑ **B.** A peer-to-peer network has no dedicated servers. There are no hierarchical differences between the workstations in the network; each workstation can decide which resources are shared on the network. In a peer-to-peer network, all workstations are clients and servers at the same time.
   ☒ **A** is incorrect because this network type has a dedicated server. **C** and **D** are incorrect because a Windows Server 2003 and Novell NetWare 6.x constitute the server portion of the client/server network.

3. ☑ **C.** The Microsoft term for a peer-to-peer network is a workgroup environment. If you have not installed your Windows clients in a domain (client/server), then they are sitting in a workgroup environment.
   ☒ **A** is incorrect because a client/server network is the opposite of a peer-to-peer network; a client/server network uses a central server. **B** is incorrect because domain is the term for a Microsoft server-based environment. **D** is incorrect because Active Directory is the term for Microsoft's implementation of a directory server.

4. ☑ **D.** Two remote offices that are spread over geographic distances constitute a wide area network (WAN).
   ☒ **A** is incorrect because it is the opposite of a WAN; a LAN is a network in a single geographic location. **B** is incorrect because there is no such thing in networking as a JAN. **C** is a metropolitan area network.

5. ☑ **A** is correct. A file and print server is responsible for providing files and printers to users on the network.
   ☒ **B, C,** and **D** are incorrect because they are each their own type of server. A web server will host web sites; a directory server is a server that contains a central list of objects, such as user accounts on the network; and an application server runs a form of networking application, such as an e-mail or a database server program.

6. ☑ **C.** An extranet allows selected individuals to see your corporate intranet.
☒ **A, B,** and **D** are incorrect. An intranet allows only individuals within your company to access the site; allowing anyone on the Internet to access it would make it an Internet-type application.

Identifying Network Topologies

7. ☑ **C.** The topology is the physical layout of computers, cables, and other components on a network. Many networks are a combination of the various topologies.
☒ **A** is incorrect because a segment is a part of a LAN that is separated by routers or bridges from the rest of the LAN. **B** is incorrect because a backbone is the main part of cabling that joins all of the segments together and handles the bulk of the network traffic. **D** is incorrect because a protocol is a set of rules governing the communication between PCs; a protocol can be thought of as similar to a language.

8. ☑ **B.** In a star topology, all computers are connected through one central hub or switch. A star topology actually comes from the days of the mainframe system. The mainframe system had a centralized point at which the terminals connected.
☒ **A** is incorrect because a bus topology uses one cable to connect multiple computers. **C** is incorrect because the mesh network has every PC connected to every other PC and can resemble a spider's web. **D** is incorrect because a ring topology resembles a circle or ring. **E** is incorrect because there is no physical cabling to represent the topology; it is represented by a bubble or cell.

9. ☑ **C.** A mesh topology is not very common in computer networking, but you have to know it for the exam. The mesh topology is seen more commonly with something like the national telephone network. With a mesh topology, every workstation has a connection to every other component of the network.
☒ **A** is incorrect because a bus topology uses one cable to connect multiple computers. **B** is incorrect because a star topology is made up of a central point or hub with cables coming from the hub and extending to the PCs. **D** is incorrect because this topology resembles a circle or ring. **E** is incorrect because there is no physical cabling to represent the topology; it is represented by a bubble or cell.

10. ☑ **A.** A bus topology uses terminators on any loose end of the bus. The terminator is designed to absorb the signal so that it does not bounce back on the wire and collide with other data.
☒ **B** is incorrect because a star topology does not use terminators; it uses a central hub or switch that connects systems to the network. **C** is incorrect because a mesh topology has each system connecting to each other system. **D** is incorrect because a ring topology has no beginning and no end, so there are no "loose ends" to put a terminator on. **E** is incorrect because a wireless network does not use cables at all.

Networking Media and Connectors

11. ☑ **D.** RJ-45 is not a network medium. Three primary types of physical media can be used: coaxial cable, twisted-pair cable, and fiber-optic cable. Transmission rates that can be supported on each of these physical media are measured in millions of bits per second (Mbps). RJ-45 is a connector type for twisted-pair cabling.
    ☒ **A, B,** and **C** are incorrect because they are all common network media.

12. ☑ **B.** 10Base2 (thinnet) has a distance limitation of 185 meters. 10Base5 (thicknet) has a distance limitation of 500 meters, and 10BaseT (twisted-pair) has a distance limitation of 100 meters.
    ☒ **A, C,** and **D** are incorrect because these are not the distances covered by thinnet.

13. ☑ **C.** Fiber-optic cabling sends pulses of light through a glass core.
    ☒ **A, B,** and **D** are incorrect because each carry an electrical signal.

14. ☑ **A.** All twisted-pair cabling is limited to 100 meters.
    ☒ **B** is incorrect because 185 meters is the maximum distance of thinnet cabling; **D** is incorrect because 500 meters is the maximum distance of thicknet cabling. **C** is incorrect; there is no cable type that has a 250-meter maximum distance.

15. ☑ **D.** 500 meters is the maximum distance of thicknet cabling.
    ☒ **A** is incorrect because all twisted-pair cabling is limited to 100 meters. **B** is incorrect because 185 meters is the maximum distance of thinnet cabling. **C** is incorrect because there is no cable type that has a 250-meter maximum distance.

16. ☑ **B.** 100BaseT uses twisted-pair that runs at 100 Mbps. CAT 5 is twisted-pair cabling type that runs at 100 Mbps.
    ☒ **A** is incorrect because CAT 3 runs at 10 Mbps. **C** is incorrect because thinnet runs at 10 Mbps and is known as 10Base2. **D** is incorrect. Although fiber optic can run at 100 Mbps, it is not used in 100BaseT.

17. ☑ **A** and **D.** Fiber-optic cabling uses a number of connector styles—two of which are the SC and ST connectors.
    ☒ **B** and **C** are incorrect. RJ-45 is used by twisted-pair cabling, and BNC is used by thinnet.

18. ☑ **C.** Single-mode fiber-optic cabling has a maximum distance of approximately 2 km.
    ☒ **A, B,** and **D** are incorrect distances for single-mode fiber, although 300 meters is the maximum distance of multimode fiber.

19. ☑ **D.** Fiber-optic cabling is immune to outside interference and crosstalk.
    ☒ **A, B,** and **C** are incorrect. Thinnet, thicknet, and twisted-pair cabling are susceptible to outside interference.

20. ☑ **B.** The BNC connector is the connector used by 10Base2.
☒ **A, C,** and **D** are incorrect. The SC connector is used by fiber optic, the RJ-45 connector is used by twisted-pair, and the RJ-11 connector is used by the telephone cable.

21. ☑ **A.** To create a crossover cable, you would switch wire 1 and 2 with wire 3 and 6 on one end of the cable.
☒ **B, C,** and **D** are incorrect. These combinations are not used to create crossover cables.

Access Methods

22. ☑ **B.** Carrier-sense multiple access with collision detection (CSMA/CD) is the access method that 100BaseT uses. With CSMA/CD, a host will sense the wire to see if it is free; only if the wire is free of data will the host send data on the wire.
☒ **A, C,** and **D** are incorrect. Baseband is not an access method. CSMA/CA and token passing are access methods but are not used by 100BaseT.

23. ☑ **D.** Token Ring uses the token-passing access method. With token passing, a host must have the token before submitting data on the wire.
☒ **A, B,** and **C** are incorrect. Baseband is not an access method, CSMA/CA is used in AppleTalk networks, and CSMA/CD is used in Ethernet environments.

Network Architectures

24. ☑ **D.** Ethernet (CSMA/CD) is defined by IEEE 802.3
☒ **A, B,** and **C** are incorrect. These architectures are not defined by 802.3, but be aware that Token Ring is defined by IEEE 802.5.

25. ☑ **A.** 1000BaseLX uses single-mode fiber-optic cabling.
☒ **B, C,** and **D** are incorrect. 1000BaseSX uses multimode fiber-optic cabling, 1000BaseCX uses coaxial cabling, and 1000BaseTX uses CAT 5e or above.

26. ☑ **C.** Following the 5-4-3 rule, you are allowed to have five network segments, joined by four repeaters, while three of those segments are populated with nodes.
☒ **A, B,** and **D** are all incorrect because they are not the number of populated segments in a 10Base2 network.

27. ☑ **E.** 10BaseFL uses fiber-optic cabling. Remember to watch the characters at the end of the architecture name to determine what the cable type is—"FL" is for fiber link.
☒ **A, B, C,** and **D** are incorrect. STP, thinnet, thicknet, and CAT 3 UTP are all cable types but are not used in 10BaseFL.

28. ☑ **B.** 1000BaseSX uses multimode fiber cabling. Remember that multimode cannot go as far as single mode, and also the "SX" in the architecture is for "short range"—multimode for short range, single mode for long range.

    ☒ **A, C,** and **D** are all incorrect. 1000BaseLX uses single-mode fiber, 1000BaseCX uses coaxial cable, and 1000BaseTX uses twisted-pair.

Network Operating Systems

29. ☑ **D.** Developed from the VMS platform many years ago, Microsoft Windows NT has grown into a very popular network operating system with a new and different interface.

    ☒ **A, B,** and **C** are incorrect. The graphical interface and look and feel of the other operating systems in the Windows family made Windows NT very popular among users and network administrators. Windows 95 was simply a great enhancement of Windows for Workgroups. NetWare and UNIX were not based on VMS.

30. ☑ **A.** Originally developed at Bell Labs, UNIX is a very popular operating system for powerful networking and database management. UNIX boasts three key features that make it powerful: multitasking, multiuser, and networking capabilities.

    ☒ **B, C,** and **D** are incorrect. Windows 95 and NT were developed by Microsoft; NetWare was developed by Novell.

31. ☑ **A** and **D.** Novell NetWare and Microsoft Windows Server 2003 are NOSs. The major difference between Windows servers and NetWare is at the server.

    ☒ **B** and **C** are incorrect. Windows 98 and Windows XP are client operating systems and not true servers.

32. ☑ **B.** Novell's directory service is known as NDS or eDirectory.

    ☒ **A, C,** and **D** are incorrect. Active Directory is the name of Microsoft's directory service, DNS is the name of a service that performs FQDN–to–IP address name resolution, and StreetTalk is Banyan's directory service.

33. ☑ **A.** Active Directory is the name of Microsoft's directory service.

    ☒ **B, C,** and **D** are incorrect. Novell's directory service is known as NDS, DNS is the name of a service that performs FQDN–to–IP address name resolution, and StreetTalk is Banyan's directory service.

2

Network Protocols and Standards

CERTIFICATION OBJECTIVE 2.01

Network Protocols

Understanding the concepts of networking protocols is critical to being able to troubleshoot communication problems in networking environments. This section will introduce you to four common network protocols found in networking environments and the difference between routable and nonroutable protocols.

A network protocol is a language that is used by systems that wish to communicate with one another. If two systems wish to communicate (or talk) with one another, they need to speak the same language (or protocol). Let's look at an example of a communication problem that could occur when two persons who want to talk are not speaking the same language. Let's say that you were traveling the country on your summer vacation and took a pit stop into a fast food restaurant. When ordering your favorite meal, you would need to ensure that you spoke the same language as the person taking the order. If you speak English and the waiter speaks French, you would be giving your order, but the waiter would not be able to understand you. The same thing will happen on the network when two systems use two totally different protocols—everyone is talking but no one is communicating. The first step to networking is making sure that the two systems that are trying to talk have the same protocol installed.

Four of the major protocols found in networking environments today are

- NetBEUI
- IPX/SPX
- AppleTalk
- TCP/IP

NetBEUI

NetBIOS Extended User Interface (NetBEUI) is a transport protocol developed by IBM but adopted by Microsoft for use in earlier versions of Windows and DOS. NetBEUI commonly was found in smaller networks due to the fact that it is a nonroutable protocol. A nonroutable protocol is a protocol that sends data, but the data is unable to cross a router to reach other networks; communication is limited to the local LAN only. The fact that NetBEUI is a nonroutable protocol has limited the use of NetBEUI on networks today dramatically.

NetBEUI is a nonroutable protocol built by IBM but was popular with earlier versions of Microsoft peer-to-peer networks.

NetBEUI was first implemented with LAN Manager networks and became popular in smaller Microsoft networks back in the Windows 3.11, Windows 95, and Windows 98 days. NetBEUI is an extremely efficient and simple protocol with little overhead because of its inability to route packets. One of the major advantages of NetBEUI is that it is extremely simple to install and configure. There is minimal configuration required to allow the protocol to work—you install it, specify a unique computer name, and it works! Exercise 2-1 demonstrates how to install NetBEUI on a Windows 2000 system.

CertCam 2-1

Be sure to take a look at Exercise 2-1 in the LabBook.pdf that is found on the CD-ROM or watch the CertCam training video found on the CD.

What Is NetBIOS?

NetBEUI has a close friend, NetBIOS (short for Network Basic Input/Output System), with which it works closely when communicating with systems on the network. NetBIOS is an application programming interface (API) that is used to make network calls to remote systems. When you install NetBEUI, it includes the NetBIOS protocol, and NetBEUI relies on NetBIOS for session management functionality. Also, NetBIOS is nonroutable but may be installed with other routable protocols such as IPX/SPX or TCP/IP to allow NetBIOS traffic to travel across networks. NetBIOS has two communication modes:

■ **Session mode** Is used for connection-oriented communication in which NetBIOS would be responsible for establishing a session with the target system, monitoring the session to detect any errors in transmission, and then recovering from those errors by retransmitting any data that went missing or was corrupt.

■ **Datagram mode** Is used for connectionless communication in which a session is not needed. Datagram mode also is used for any broadcast by NetBIOS. Datagram mode does not support error detection and correction services, which are therefore the responsibility of the application using NetBIOS.

Now that you understand a little bit about NetBIOS, here is a list of facts about NetBIOS and NetBEUI:

- NetBIOS is a session protocol, whereas NetBEUI is a transport protocol (more on session and transport later in this chapter, when you learn about the OSI model).

- NetBIOS is used by other protocols as well, such as TCP/IP.

- Since NetBIOS is not a transport protocol, it does not directly support routing but depends on one of three transport protocols—TCP/IP, IPX/SPX, or NetBEUI—to do this.

- NetBIOS uses NetBIOS names as a method of identifying systems on the network. A NetBIOS name, also known as a computer name, can be a maximum of 16 bytes long—15 bytes for the name and 1 byte for the NetBIOS name suffix (a code at the end of the name representing the service running). The NetBIOS computer name must be unique on the LAN.

IPX/SPX

Internetwork Packet Exchange/Sequenced Packet Exchange (IPX/SPX) is a protocol suite (which means there are many protocols in one) that was developed by Novell and was very popular on older NetWare networks. However, newer versions of NetWare (NetWare 5.x and above) have moved away from it and are using TCP/IP as the preferred protocol. Microsoft refers to IPX/SPX as NWLink (NetWare Link).

**IPX/SPX is a routable protocol that was built by Novell and used in older versions of NetWare.**

The IPX protocol of the IPX/SPX protocol suite is responsible for the routing of information across the network. IPX/SPX is a routable protocol, so its addressing scheme must be able to identify each system on the network and the network it exists on. The network administrator assigns each network a network ID. An IPX network ID is an eight-character hexadecimal value—for example, 0BADBEEF.

A complete IPX address is made up of the network ID , a period (.), and then the six-byte MAC address of the network card (a unique address burned into the network card) in the system. For example, the computer I am sitting at right now has a MAC address of 00-90-4B-4C-C1-59. If my system were connected to network ID

0BADBEEF, then my IPX network address would be 0BADBEEF.00904B4CC159. The fact that the MAC address is used in the address means that there is no need to have it resolved when communication occurs—which will make the protocol more efficient than other protocols such as TCP/IP, which does require the IP address to be resolved to a MAC address.

IPX/SPX is not as easy to configure as NetBEUI. When doing an IPX installation, you will need to be familiar with configuration issues such as the network number and frame type (shown in Figure 2-1).

- **Network number**   Is the number assigned to the Novell network segment. It is a hexadecimal value, eight digits maximum.
- **Frame type**   Is the format of the packet that is used by the network. It is important to make sure that all systems on the network are configured for the same frame type. For example, if I wish want to connect to SERVER1, which uses the frame type of 802.2, then I would need to ensure that my frame type was set to 802.2—otherwise, I would not be able to communicate with SERVER1. The four major frame types are 802.2, 802.3, ETHERNET_SNAP, and ETHERNET_II.

FIGURE 2-1

Configuring the IPX/SPX protocol

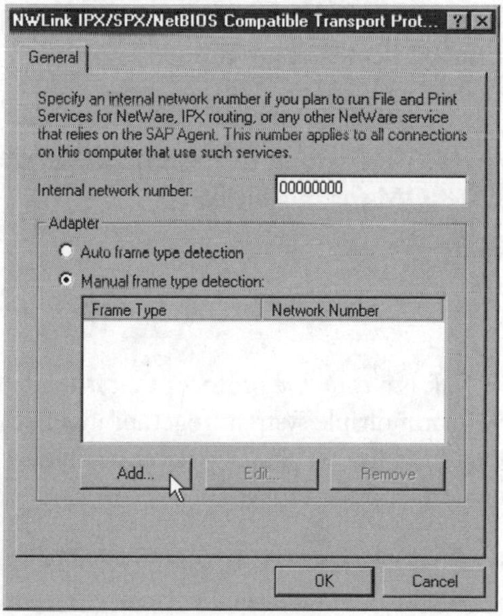

The Microsoft operating systems default to an auto setting on the frame type, which allows the IPX/SPX protocol to "sense" the frame type being used on the network and configure itself for that frame type. This has made the configuration of IPX/SPX much easier during the past few years.

If you are working on a network where there are multiple frame types configured, such as 802.2 and 802.3, the clients that are configured to autodetect the frame type will configure themselves for 802.2, because it is the default frame type.

While IPX is responsible for the routing of packets, it is also a connectionless, unreliable transport. Unreliable means IPX packets are sent to a destination without requiring the destination to acknowledge receiving those packets. Connectionless means that no session is established between sender and receiver before transmitting data. SPX is the protocol in the IPX/SPX protocol suite that is responsible for reliable delivery. SPX is a connection-oriented protocol that will ensure that packets that are not received at the destination are retransmitted on the wire.

To install IPX/SPX in Windows, you will go to your Local Area Connection properties and then choose the Install button. When shown a list of components to install, you then select Protocol and then click Add to add a protocol. When shown the list of protocols, you then select the NWLink IPX/SPX entry and click OK. To configure the network number and frame type, go to the properties of NWLink. Exercise 2-2 demonstrates the steps needed to install and configure IPX/SPX on a Windows 2000 system.

Be sure to take a look at Exercise 2-2 in the LabBook.pdf file that is found on the CD-ROM for this book.

AppleTalk

AppleTalk is a routable protocol that is used primarily in Macintosh environments to connect multiple systems together in a network environment. AppleTalk was implemented in two phases, known as phase 1 and phase 2, with the second phase being more popular today:

- **Phase 1** Was designed for small workgroup environments and therefore supports a much smaller number of nodes on the network. Phase 1 supports nonextended networks; each network segment is allowed to be assigned only a single network number, and only one zone is allowed in a nonextended network. A zone is a logical grouping of nodes—the network administrator will assign nodes to a particular zone.

■ **Phase 2** Was designed for larger networks and supports more than 200 hosts on the network. Phase 2 supports extended networks, thereby allowing one network segment to be assigned multiple network numbers and allowing for multiple zones on that network segment. Each node is part of a single zone on an extended network.

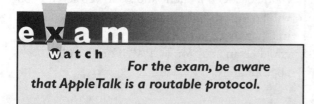

TCP/IP

Transmission Control Protocol/Internet Protocol (TCP/IP) is the most common protocol used today. A routable protocol, TCP/IP is the protocol on which the Internet is built. TCP/IP is very robust and commonly is associated with UNIX and Linux systems.

TCP/IP originally was designed in the 1970s to be used by the Defense Advanced Research Projects Agency (DARPA) and the U.S. Department of Defense (DOD) to connect dissimilar systems across the country. This design required the capability to cope with unstable network conditions. Therefore, the design of TCP/IP included the capability to reroute packets.

One of the major advantages of TCP/IP was the fact that it could be used to connect heterogeneous (dissimilar) environments together, which is why it has become the protocol of the Internet—but what are its drawbacks? TCP/IP has two major drawbacks:

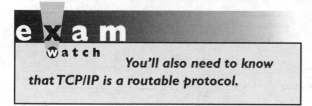

■ **Configuration** TCP/IP is a protocol that requires configuration, and to administer it, you need to be familiar with IP addresses, subnet masks, and default gateways—not complicated topics once you are familiar with them, but there is a bit of a learning curve compared to installing NetBEUI.

■ **Security** Because of the open design of TCP/IP, it has become a very insecure protocol. If security is of concern, you need to make certain that you implement additional technologies to secure the network traffic or systems

The Network+ exam focuses on TCP/IP as the core protocol. Note that Chapters 4, 5, and 6 of this book go into more detail on TCP/IP—please be sure to spend a lot of time with those chapters to prepare for the exam.

running TCP/IP. For example, if you want to ensure that other individuals cannot read the data sent to your web server, you would SSL enable the web site—which would encrypt traffic between a client and your web server. You will be introduced to more on network security in Chapter 12, but be aware that security could be an issue for TCP/IP if not handled appropriately.

Routable vs. Nonroutable Protocols

We have discussed each of the four major protocols, and you have learned that NetBEUI is a nonroutable protocol, whereas IPX/SPX, AppleTalk, and TCP/IP are routable protocols. What exactly is a routable protocol? A routable protocol is a protocol whose packets may leave your network, pass through your router, and be delivered to a remote network, as shown in Figure 2-2.

A nonroutable protocol is a protocol that does not have the capability to cross a router to be sent from one network to another network. This is due to the fact that

---

FIGURE 2-2   A routable protocol sending data through a router

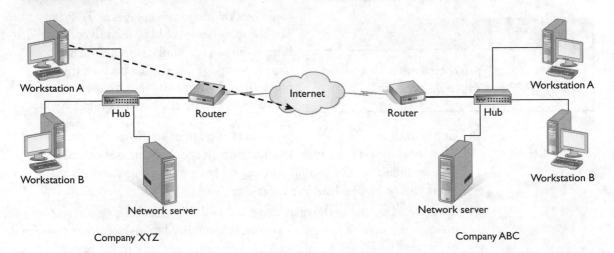

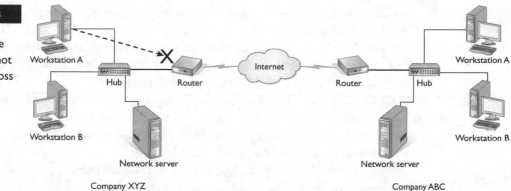

FIGURE 2-3

A nonroutable protocol cannot send data across routers.

the protocol is designed as a simple protocol and does not accommodate addressing patterns in the packets that give knowledge of multiple networks. For example, NetBEUI uses NetBIOS names as a method to send data back and forth, but a NETBIOS name does not identify "what network" the destination system exists on, whereas TCP/IP and IPX/SPX both have a network ID portion to their addressing schemes that identify "what network" the destination system exists on.

When a nonroutable packet reaches the router, the router discards it, as shown in Figure 2-3, because there is no routing information in the packet such as a layer-3 destination address.

TCP/IP, IPX/SPX, and AppleTalk are all examples of routable protocols, while NetBEUI is a nonroutable protocol.

CERTIFICATION OBJECTIVE 2.02

The OSI Model

In 1984, the International Organization for Standardization (ISO) defined a standard, or set of rules, for manufacturers of networking components that would allow these networking components to communicate in dissimilar environments. This standard is known as the Open Systems Interconnect (OSI) model and is a model made up of seven layers. Each layer of the OSI model is responsible for a specific function or task within the stages of network communication. The seven layers of the OSI model, from highest to lowest, are application, presentation, session, transport, network, data link, and physical. Network communication starts at the application layer of the OSI model (on the sending system) and works its way down through the layers to the physical layer. The information then passes along the communication medium to the receiving computer, which works its way back up the layers starting at the physical layer. Figure 2-4 shows an example of packets being transmitted down through the OSI layers of the sending computer, across the medium, and back up the OSI layers on the receiving computer. Be sure to refer to this figure frequently when going through this section.

Each layer of the OSI model is responsible for certain functions within the process of sending data from one system to another. Each layer is responsible for communicating with the layers immediately above it and below it. For example, the presentation layer will receive information from the application layer, format it appropriately, and then pass it to the session layer. As another example, the presentation layer will never deal directly with the network or data link layers.

FIGURE 2-4

Layers of the OSI model

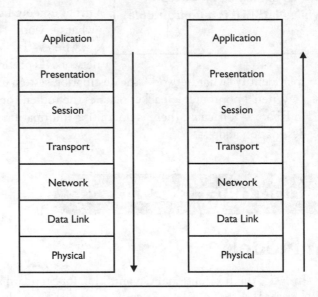

Let's look at the layers from the point of view of two computers that will send data between each other: COMPUTER1 and SERVER1 are going to exchange data on the network. COMPUTER1 will be known as the sending computer, and SERVER1 will be known as the receiving computer, as shown in Figure 2-5.

The data exchange starts with COMPUTER1 sending a request to SERVER1. It is important to notice as you progress through the layers that whatever function is performed at a layer on the sending system must be undone at the exact layer on the receiving system. For example, if the presentation layer compresses the data on the sending system, the presentation layer will decompress the data on the receiving system before passing the data up to the application layer.

Layer 7: The Application Layer

The application layer running on the sending system (COMPUTER1) is responsible for the actual request to be made. This could be any type of networking request—a web request using a web browser (HTTP), an e-mail delivery request using SMTP,

---

FIGURE 2-5   Identifying the function of each layer of the OSI model

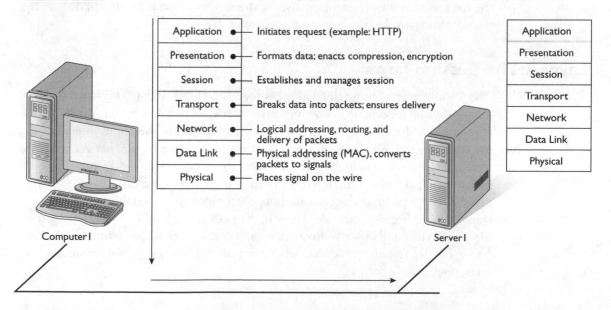

or a file system request using the network client redirector software. On the receiving system, the application layer would be responsible for passing the request to the appropriate application or service on that system. In our example, we will assume that you are sitting at COMPUTER1 and you have typed the address of SERVER1 into your web browser to create an HTTP request.

Layer 6: The Presentation Layer

After the request is made, the application layer passes the data down to the presentation layer, where it is to be formatted so that the data (or request) can be interpreted by the receiving system. When the presentation layer receives data from the application layer to be sent over the network, it makes sure that the data is in the proper format—if it is not, the presentation layer converts the data. On the receiving system, when the presentation layer receives network data from the session layer, it makes sure that the data is in the proper format and once again converts it if it is not.

Formatting functions that could occur at the presentation layer could be compression, encryption, and ensuring that the character code set can be interpreted on the other side. For example, if we choose to compress our data from the application that we are using, the application layer will pass that request to the presentation layer, but it will be the presentation layer that does the compression. Now, at some point, this data must be decompressed so that it can be read. When the data reaches the presentation layer of the receiving computer, it will decompress the data and pass the data up to the application layer.

Layer 5: The Session Layer

The session layer manages the dialog between computers. It does this by establishing, managing, and terminating communications between two computers. When a session is established, three distinct phases are involved. In the establishment phase, the requestor initiates the service and the rules for communication between the two systems. These rules could include such things as who transmits and when, as well as how much data can be sent at a time. Both systems must agree on the rules; the rules are like the etiquette of the conversation. Once the rules are established, the data transfer phase begins. Both sides know how to talk to each other, the most efficient methods to use, and how to detect errors, all because of the rules defined in the first phase. Finally, termination occurs when the session is complete, and communication ends in an orderly fashion.

In our example, COMPUTER1 creates a session with SERVER1 at this point, and they agree on the rules of the conversation.

Layer 4: The Transport Layer

The transport layer handles transport functions such as reliable and unreliable delivery of the data. For reliable transport protocols, the transport layer works hard to ensure reliable delivery of data to its destinations. On the sending system, the transport layer is responsible for breaking the data into smaller packets, so that if retransmission is required, only the packets missing will be sent. Missing packets are determined by the fact that the transport layer receives acknowledgments (ACKs) from the remote system, when the remote system receives the packets. At the receiving system, the transport layer will be responsible for opening all of the packets and reconstructing the original message.

Another function of the transport layer is segment sequencing. Sequencing is a connection-oriented service that takes segments that are received out of order and resequences them in the right order. For example, if I send you five packets and you receive the packets in this order (by their sequence number): 3, 1, 4, 2, 5, the transport layer will read the sequence numbers and assemble them in the correct order.

exam

ⓦatch **TCP is an example of a transport protocol responsible for reliable delivery, whereas UDP is an example of a transport protocol responsible for unreliable delivery.**

The transport layer also enables the option of specifying a "service address" for the services or application on the source and destination computers to specify what application the request came from and what application the request is headed for. All modern operating systems run many programs at once, and each program has a unique service address. Service addresses that are well defined (by networking standards, for example) are called well-known addresses. Service addresses also are called sockets or ports by protocols such as TCP/IP.

At this point in our example, the request is broken into packets in preparation for being delivered across the network, and transport layer information (such as the transport protocol being used and any additional transport information) is appended to the request. In this example, because we are dealing with a TCP/IP application, the source port and destination port are added.

INSIDE THE EXAM

Connection-Oriented Communication

Connection-oriented communication ensures reliable delivery of data from the sender to the receiver. Connection-oriented services must ensure that data is sent reliably across the network. When establishing these services, the protocol must perform some sort of handshaking function. Handshaking takes place at the beginning of a communication session. During handshaking, the two computers determine the rules for communication, such as transmission speed and which ports to use. Handshaking also determines the proper way to terminate the session when finished. This ensures that communication ends in an orderly manner.

A session is a reliable dialog between two computers. Because connection-oriented services can provide reliable communication, they are used when two computers need to communicate in a session. Sessions are maintained until the two computers decide that they are finished communicating. A session is just like a telephone call. You set up a telephone call by dialing (handshaking), speak to the other person (exchange data), say "Goodbye," and hang up when finished.

Connectionless Communication

Connectionless communication is a form of communication in which the sending system does not "introduce" itself—it just fires the data off. Also, the destination computer does not notify the source when the information is received. This type of communication can be unreliable because there is no notification to guarantee delivery. Connectionless communication can be faster than connection-oriented communication because the overhead of managing the session is not there, and after the information is sent, there is no second step to ensure proper receipt of information.

Layer 3: The Network Layer

The network layer is responsible for managing logical addressing information in the packets and the delivery, or routing, of those packets by using information stored in a routing table. The routing table is a list of available destinations that are stored in memory on the routers (more on routing in Chapter 5).

The network layer is responsible for working with logical addresses. The logical addresses are address types that are used to uniquely identify a system on the network, but at the same time identify the network that system resides on. This is unlike a MAC address (the physical address burned into the network card), because a MAC address just gives the system a unique address and does not specify or imply what network the system lives on. The logical address is used by network-layer protocols to deliver the packets to the correct network.

In our example, the request is coming from a web browser and destined for a web server, both of which are applications that run on TCP/IP. At this point, the network layer will add the source address (the IP address of the sending system) and the destination address (the IP address of the destination system) to the packet so that the receiving system will know where the packet came from.

An example of a logical address is an IP address, which might take the form of 192.168.3.24. An IP address is also known as a layer-3 address.

Layer 2: The Data Link Layer

The data link layer is responsible for converting the data from a packet to a pattern of electrical bit signals that will be used to send the data across the communication medium. On the receiving system, the electrical signals will be converted to packets by the data link layer and then passed up to the network layer for further processing. The data link layer is divided into two sublayers:

- **Logical link control (LLC)** Is responsible for error correction and control functions.
- **Media access control (MAC)** Determines the physical addressing of the hosts. It also determines how the host places traffic on the medium, for example CSMA/CD versus Token Passing.

The MAC sublayer maintains physical device addresses (commonly referred to as MAC addresses) for communicating with other devices on the network. These physical addresses are burned into the network cards and constitute the low-level address used to determine the source and destination of network traffic.

In our example, once the sending system's network layer appends the IP address information, the data link layer will append the MAC address information for the sending and receiving systems. This layer will also prepare the data for the wire by converting the

An example of a MAC address is 00-02-3F-6B-25-13, which is also known as a layer-2 address.

packets to binary signals. On the receiving system, the data link layer will convert the signals passed to it by the physical layer to data and then pass the packets to the network layer for further processing.

Layer 1: The Physical Layer

The bottom layer of the OSI hierarchy is concerned only with moving bits of data onto and off the network medium.

This includes the physical topology (or structure) of the network, the electrical and physical aspects of the medium used, and encoding and timing of bit transmission and reception.

In our example, once the network layer has appended the logical addresses and passed the data to the data link layer where the MAC addresses have been appended and the data was converted to electrical signals, the data is then passed to the physical layer so that it can be released on the communication medium. On the receiving system, the physical layer will pick the data up off the wire and pass it to the data link layer, where it will ensure that the signal is destined for that system by reading the destination MAC address.

Now that you have been introduced to the seven-layer OSI model, look at an exercise to put your newfound knowledge to the test.

Be sure to take a look at Exercise 2-3 in the LabBook.pdf file that is found on the CD-ROM for this book.

Protocols and the OSI Layers

Different protocols work at different levels of the OSI model. Here, we look at a few of the main protocols for this exam, apply them to the OSI model, and see how they fit in the OSI model's seven layers. For more information on protocols and services check out Chapter 4.

IPX

IPX is an extremely fast, streamlined protocol that is not connection oriented. IPX was once fairly common because of its widespread use on Novell NetWare. IPX is a routable protocol that is located at the network layer of the OSI model. Because it is also an unreliable connectionless transport, IPX also applies to layer 4—the

transport layer. Remember, unreliable means data is sent without acknowledgment of receipt, and connectionless means that a session is not established before transmitting. IPX is capable of being run over both Ethernet and Token Ring networks using the appropriate network interface card (NIC). For a number of years, IPX over Ethernet was the default use of NICs.

SPX

Sequenced Packet Exchange (SPX) is a transport protocol used by IPX for connection-oriented communication. It is responsible for breaking the message into manageable packets and ensuring the data reaches the destination. SPX is the equivalent to TCP but for the IPX/SPX protocol suite. Because SPX runs at the transport layer, it is considered a layer-4 protocol.

IP

The Internet Protocol (IP) in the TCP/IP protocol suite performs the same routing functions that IPX does for the IPX/SPX protocol suite. IP is responsible for the logical addressing and routing of messages across the network. IP does not ensure the delivery of the packets; that is the responsibility of higher-layer protocols, such as TCP.

The logical address that IP uses is known as an IP address and looks similar to 192.168.3.200—which is different from the physical address (MAC address), which looks like 00-02-3F-6B-25-13. The logical address is responsible for identifying the network the system resides on along with an address of the system, whereas a MAC address is very flat and identifies only the physical system on the LAN—not "where" the system resides.

IP is fully capable of running over either Token Ring or Ethernet networks, as long as an appropriate NIC is used. IP over Ethernet is the most common implementation in networking today, because Ethernet is much less expensive than Token Ring and because TCP/IP is used widely on the Internet.

TCP

The Transmission Control Protocol (TCP) is a transport-layer protocol that is responsible for breaking the data into manageable packets and ensuring that the packets reach their destination. TCP is considered a connection-oriented protocol, which means that it relies on a session being first established. This is different from a connectionless communication, which just sends the data out and if it reaches the destination, great; if not, no big deal. With connection-oriented protocols, a session is established through introductions. ("Hi, I'm Glen Clarke. Nice to meet you, I am going to send you some data.") Connection-oriented protocols will monitor that session to ensure that the packets have reached their destination.

UDP

The User Datagram Protocol (UDP) is part of the TCP/IP protocol suite and is the brother of TCP. When you send data on a TCP/IP network and if you need a connection-oriented conversation, you have learned you would use the TCP protocol. But what protocol do we use if we want to have a connectionless conversation? UDP. Both TCP and UDP are layer-4 protocols. IP is used to deliver both types of data, but TCP and UDP determine whether it is connection oriented or not.

NFS

The Network File System (NFS) is a protocol for file sharing that enables a user to use network disks as though they were connected to the local machine. NFS was created by Sun Microsystems for use on Solaris, Sun's version of UNIX. NFS is still used frequently in the UNIX and Linux worlds and is available for use with nearly all operating systems. NFS is a protocol that is used universally by the UNIX community. Vendor and third-party software products enable other operating systems to use NFS. It has gained acceptance with many companies and can be added to nearly any operating system. In addition to file sharing, NFS enables you to share printers. NFS is located in the application layer of the OSI model and is considered a member of the TCP/IP protocol suite. The primary reason to use the NFS protocol is to access resources located on a UNIX server or to share resources with someone working on a UNIX workstation.

SMB and Novell NCP

Microsoft's Server Message Block (SMB) and Novell's NetWare Core Protocol (NCP) are protocols that are implemented in redirectors. A *redirector* is software that intercepts requests, formats them according to the protocol in use, and passes the message to a lower-level protocol for delivery. Redirectors also intercept incoming messages, process the instructions, and pass them to the correct upper-level application for additional processing.

SMB and NCP are used primarily for file and printer sharing in Microsoft and Novell networks, respectively, and are considered application-layer protocols.

SMTP

The Simple Mail Transport Protocol (SMTP) is the protocol that defines the structure of Internet mail messages. SMTP uses a well-defined syntax for transferring messages. An SMTP session includes initializing the SMTP connection, sending the destination e-mail address, sending the source e-mail address, sending the subject, and sending the body of the e-mail message.

exam
ⓦatch *SMTP is the protocol for sending e-mail on the Internet and is an application-layer protocol.*

FTP and TFTP

The File Transfer Protocol (FTP) is a standardized method of transferring files between two machines. FTP is a connection-oriented protocol, which means that the protocol verifies that packets successfully reach their destinations.

The Trivial File Transfer Protocol (TFTP) has the same purpose and function as FTP, except that it is not a connection-oriented protocol and does not verify that packets reach their destinations. By not verifying that data has been successfully transferred to its destination and therefore requiring less overhead to establish and maintain a connection, TFTP is able to operate faster than FTP. TFTP has no authentication mechanism, whereas FTP can require a username and password.

DECnet

DECnet is a proprietary protocol developed by the Digital Equipment Corporation for use primarily in WANs. You can run DECnet on an Ethernet network, but it is done infrequently. DECnet is a routable protocol.

TCP/IP, IPX/SPX,
AppleTalk, and DECnet are routable
protocols; NetBEUI and DLC are not.

DLC

Data Link Control (DLC) is not a common protocol. DLC, a nonroutable protocol, was sometimes used to connect Windows NT servers to printers.

EXERCISE 2-4

Viewing Protocol Information with Network Monitor

In this exercise, you will install a network-monitoring tool known as Network Monitor that comes with Windows servers, and you will look at network traffic that was captured previously in a file. The example is that a user has filled a credit card number into a web site and you have captured the traffic. Your end goal is to find the credit card number in the packet. Figure 2-6 shows the user filling in the credit card number on a web page.

FIGURE 2-6	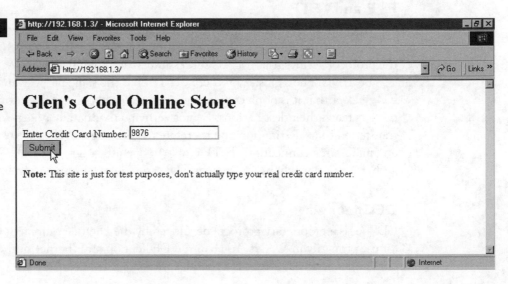
A user typing a credit card number into an insecure web site	

Let's start the exercise by installing the Network Monitor software on your system. These steps were written for Windows 2000 Server but are very similar to those used for Windows Server 2003.

Installing Network Monitor on a Windows Server

1. Go to Start | Control Panel | Add/Remove Programs.
2. In the Add/Remove Programs dialog box, choose the Add/Remove Windows Components on the left side, as shown in the accompanying illustration.

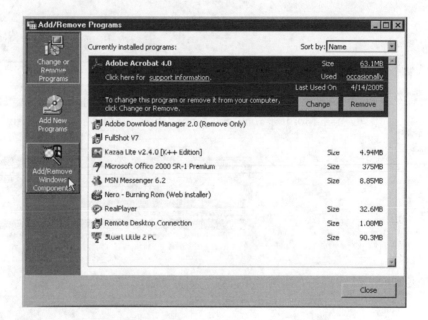

3. In the Windows Components Wizard, scroll down to find Management and Monitoring Tools. As shown in the accompanying illustration, highlight Management and Monitoring Tools and choose Details.

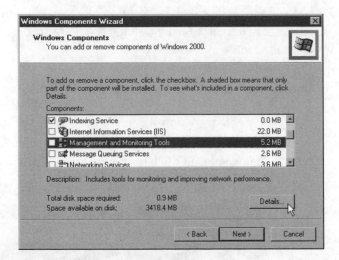

4. In the Management and Monitoring Tools dialog box, check the Network Monitor Tools check box (shown in the accompanying illustration).

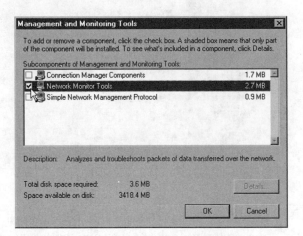

5. Choose OK. You may be asked for the Windows Server CD.
6. When the file copy is complete, choose Finish.
7. Click Close.
8. Close the Control Panel.

Viewing Packet Data with Network Monitor

9. To start Network Monitor, go to Start | Programs | Administrative Tools | Network Monitor.

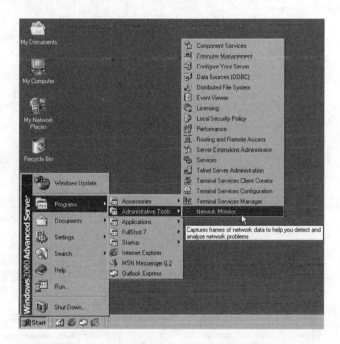

10. When you start Network Monitor, it may ask you to select a network (which means choosing your network card). Select the network card on the left that shows a dial-up adapter on the right as being false (shown next). This will be your network card, as opposed to the modem on the system. We want to capture traffic from this network card eventually.

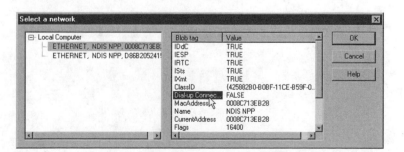

11. Once the network card has been selected, you should have Network Monitor on the screen in front of you. You want to view network traffic that was captured previously, so choose File | Open.

12. In the Open dialog box, open the HTTPTraffic.cap file located in the LabFiles\PacketCaptures folder.

13. The contents of the packet capture are displayed. Notice that there are 24 frames (numbers listed down the left) captured and that frame 16 is the actual HTTP Post Request (seen next), which is the form's information posted to the server. This is the phase where the credit card number was submitted. We will use frame 16 as our learning tool to view network traffic.

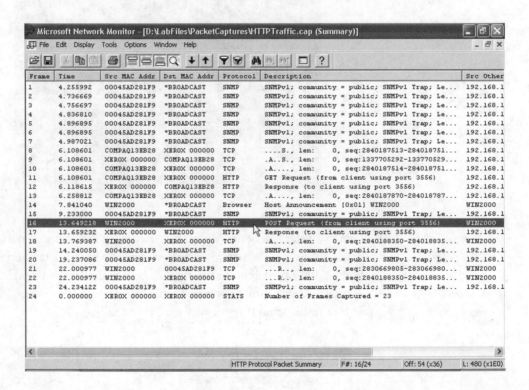

14. Double-click frame 16 to view the details of the traffic (shown in the accompanying illustration).

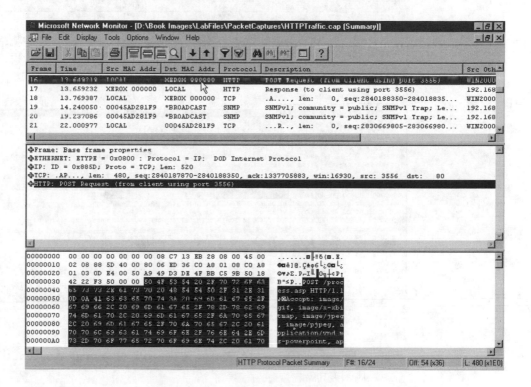

15. The window is divided into three panes; the top pane is the summary pane listing all the frames, the middle pane is the detail pane showing your packet details, and the bottom pane is showing the hex data for that frame. Ensure that frame 16 is still selected in the summary pane so that you can investigate your packet.

16. In the detail pane (middle part of the screen), double-click Ethernet, which will expand the Ethernet section showing you the source and destination (shown in the accompanying illustration) Ethernet addresses or MAC addresses.

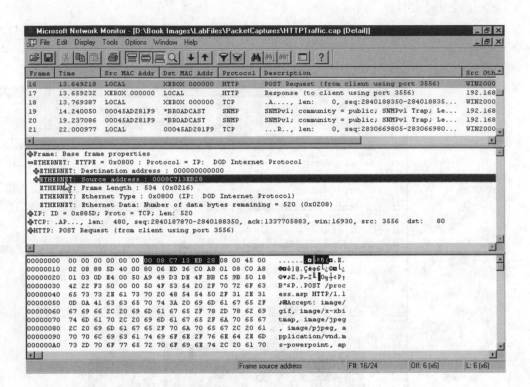

17. Record the source MAC address, which is the system that sent the packet, in the blanks.

    Source MAC Address: _____

    What layer of the OSI model does this information pertain to? _____

18. Below the Ethernet section is the protocol information. What layer-3 protocol is this network traffic using? _____

19. If you answered IP in the preceding question, you are correct! If you double-click the IP section, you will see what layer-3 addresses (IP Address) are the source of the packet and the destination of the packet.

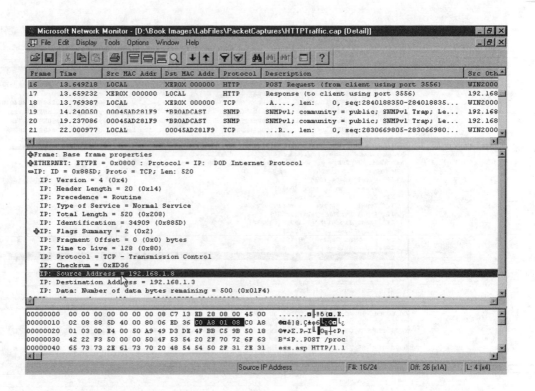

20. Fill in the following information:

    Where is the packet headed? _____

    Where did the packet come from? _____

    Hint: View the source and destination addresses.

21. You also can see what transport protocol was used by IP to deliver this packet. Two lines above the source IP address, you can see that IP is using TCP, a connection-oriented layer-4 protocol, to ensure that the packet reaches the destination (shown in the accompanying illustration).

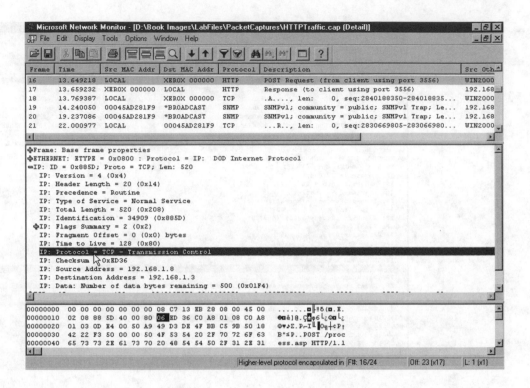

22. If you double-click the IP heading, you will collapse the details of IP. Let's look at the application protocol information for this packet. You want to see the credit card number that was typed into the web page. In the details pane, double-click HTTP to expand the detailed application information.

23. Select the last piece of information for HTTP, which is the HTTP: Data: line. To view the data that was typed into the browser, look in the bottom right of the screen (shown in the next illustration).

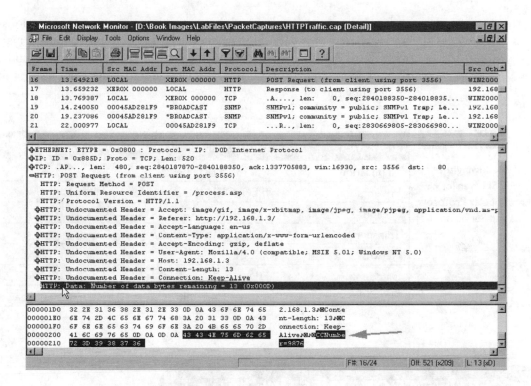

24. What was the credit card number? _____

25. Close Network Monitor.

This exercise has shown you how to view layer-2 information in a packet, such as the source and destination MAC addresses. It has also shown you how to view logical address information, such as the source and destination IP addresses, which were found with layer-3 information. You also saw how the layer-3 protocol (IP) relies on TCP to ensure delivery of the information. Finally, you viewed the application information that was submitted with the request. This will hopefully show you why it is important to ensure that you are using an encryption protocol to encrypt the data typed into an application.

It is important to understand the protocols, services, and applications that we deal with every day and what layer of the OSI model those products may be working with. Table 2-1 summarizes some of the popular protocols, services, and applications that are found in networking environments and specifies what layer of the OSI model they run at.

TABLE 2-1	OSI Layer	Protocols, Services, Methods, and Layers
Identifying the OSI Layer for Popular Protocols and Services	Application	FTP, SMTP, Telnet
	Presentation	JPEG, GIF, MPEG
	Session	NFS, RPC
	Transport	TCP, UDP, SPX, IPX
	Network	IPX, IP
	Data Link	Ethernet, Token Ring
	Physical	Twisted-pair, thinnet coax, AUI, network interface card

CERTIFICATION OBJECTIVE 2.03

802 Project Standards

The Institute of Electrical and Electronics Engineers (IEEE) is a large and respected professional organization that is also active in defining standards. The 802 committee of the IEEE defines one set of standards dear to the hearts of most network professionals. Twelve subcommittees of the 802 committee define low-level LAN and WAN access protocols. Most of the protocols defined by the 802 committee reside in the physical and data link layers of the OSI model.

IEEE 802 Categories

As the use of LANs increased, standards were needed to define consistency and compatibility between vendors. The IEEE began a project in February 1980, known as Project 802 for the year and month it began. IEEE 802 is a set of standards given to the various LAN architectures such as Ethernet, Token Ring, and ArcNet by the LAN standards committee. The goal of the committee was to define more of the OSI's data link layer, which already contained the LLC and MAC sublayers. Several 802 subcommittee protocols are the heart of PC networking. Although there are a number of 802 project categories, a few of them are focused on for the exam and therefore will get a little more focus here in this section.

802.3

Based on the original Ethernet network from DIX (Digital-Intel-Xerox), 802.3 is the standard for Ethernet networks today. The only difference between 802.3 Ethernet and DIX Ethernet V.2 is the frame type. The two Ethernet networks can use the same physical network, but devices on one standard cannot communicate with devices on the other standard.

The MAC sublayer uses carrier sense multiple access with collision detection (CSMA/CD) for access to the physical medium. CSMA/CD keeps devices on the network from interfering with one another when trying to transmit; if they do, a collision occurs. To reduce collisions, CSMA/CD devices listen to the network before transmitting. If the network is "quiet" (no other devices are transmitting), the device can send its data. Because two devices can think the network is clear and start transmitting at the same time (which would result in a collision), all devices listen as they transmit. If a device detects another device transmitting at the same time, a collision occurs. The device stops transmitting and sends a signal to alert other nodes about the collision. Then, all the nodes stop transmitting and wait a random amount of time before they begin the process again.

Remember that Ethernet is defined by the IEEE 802.3 standard.

CSMA/CD doesn't stop collisions from happening, but it helps manage the situations when they do occur. In fact, collisions are a normal part of Ethernet operation. You need to become concerned only when collisions begin to occur frequently.

Ethernet has evolved over the years to include a number of popular specifications. These specifications are due in part to the media variety they employ, such as coaxial, twisted-pair, and fiber-optic cabling.

- The 10Base5 specification, commonly referred to as thicknet, was the original Ethernet specification, and it has a maximum distance of 500 meters (approximately 1640 feet) with a maximum speed of 10 Mbps.
- The 10Base2 specification, commonly referred to as thinnet, uses a thinner coaxial cable than 10Base5 and has a maximum distance of 185 meters (approximately 607 feet) with a maximum speed of 10 Mbps.

- The 10BaseT specification uses twisted-pair cabling with a maximum distance of 100 meters (approximately 328 feet) with a speed of 10 to 100 Mbps.

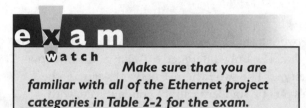

Make sure that you are familiar with all of the Ethernet project categories in Table 2-2 for the exam.

There are a number of Ethernet standards that have been developed in the 802.3 category, and those are shown in Table 2-2.

802.5

Although Token Ring was first designed in the late 1960s, IBM's token-passing implementation did not become a standard until 1985. It became IEEE standard 802.5 under the IEEE Project 802. The 802.5 standard was modeled after the IBM Token Ring network, which had been in use for many years before the standard was even developed.

The 802.5 network introduced a unique access method—token passing. The Token Ring IEEE 802.5 standard passes a special frame known as the token around the network. This token is generated by the first computer that comes online on the Token Ring network. When a workstation wants to transmit data, it grabs the token and then begins transmitting. This computer will send a data frame on the network with the address of the destination computer. The destination computer receives the data frame, modifies it, and sends it on to the network back to the destination computer, indicating successful transmission of data. When the workstation has finished transmitting, the token is released back on to the network. This ensures that workstations will not communicate on the network simultaneously, as in the CSMA/CD access method.

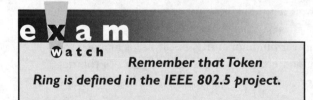

Remember that Token Ring is defined in the IEEE 802.5 project.

TABLE 2-2	IEEE Project Standard	Description
Some Popular Ethernet IEEE 802.3 Project Standards	802.3	Ethernet (CSMA/CD)
	802.3u	Fast Ethernet (100 Mbps)
	802.3z	Gigabit Ethernet over fiber-optic cabling or coaxial cabling
	802.3ab	Gigabit Ethernet over twisted-pair cabling
	802.3ae	10-Gigabit Ethernet

802.11

The IEEE 802.11 standard is the standard that addresses wireless networking (discussed in Chapter 7).

This standard includes the wireless access point (WAP) devices and the wireless network interface cards (NICs) that are used to send and receive broadcasts from the cell or WAP device.

The WAPs and wireless NICs can be set to use different frequencies to allow for cell overlap. This technology does not include the same technology used by cell phones to manage movement of PCs or mobile devices. The wireless NIC is set to a specific frequency and must be changed manually to be able to communicate with another cell. This means that a PC cannot be moved from one cell area to another without changing frequency, unless for some reason the cells operate on the same frequency and have no overlap of coverage area.

There are a few wireless standards that were developed in the IEEE 802.11 category, and those are listed as follows:

There are other wireless standards in the IEEE 802.11 project category, but these four are the most popular and you should be familiar with them for the exam.

- **802.11a** Supports speeds of 54 Mbps at frequencies ranging from 5.725 GHz to 5.850 GHz. 802.11a wireless components are not compatible with 802.11b devices.

- **802.11b** Supports speeds of 11 Mbps at frequency ranges of 2.400 GHz to 2.4835 GHz. 802.11b wireless components are compatible with 802.11g devices, which use an enhancement of the 802.11b standard.

■ **802.11g** Supports speeds of 54 Mbps at the same frequency range as 802.11b, which allows devices from the two standards to coexist. For example, I have an 802.11b wireless access point, but I am connected to it with my 802.11g wireless network card. I am getting only the 11 Mbps transfer rate because it is the lowest common denominator between the two standards.

■ **802.11n** Is a new wireless project that runs at 5 GHz or 2.4 GHz and is backward compatible with 802.11a/b/g standards. The goal of 802.11n is to increase the bandwidth and the range. 802.11n has data transfer rates of over 100 Mbps!

You will need to be familiar with the IEEE 802 projects that have been mentioned, and the exam will focus on those, but you should be familiar with the other 802 standards as well. Table 2-3 lists most of the 802 project standards.

e**x**a**m**
watch

Expect to be asked about the IEEE standards on the exam, especially the ones that map to Ethernet, Token Ring, and wireless.

TABLE 2-3	Project	Description
IEEE 802 Project Standards	802.1	Internetworking
	802.2	Logical link control
	802.3	Ethernet
	802.4	Token bus
	802.5	Token Ring
	802.6	Metropolitan area network (MAN)
	802.7	Broadband technology
	802.8	Fiber-optic technology
	802.9	Voice and data integration
	802.10	Network security
	802.11	Wireless networking
	802.12	Demand priority networking

CERTIFICATION SUMMARY

In this chapter, you have learned about some of the more popular network protocols, such as NetBEUI, IPX/SPX, and TCP/IP. You have learned about the advantages and disadvantages of these protocols, which ones are routable, and which ones are nonroutable.

You also have learned that in order for all of the different manufacturers of networking components to build technologies that will work together, there had to be some standards defined. There are two major standards that manufacturers follow: the 802 project models and the OSI model. In this chapter, you looked at each layer of the OSI model and what functions they perform. An easy way to remember the layers (application, presentation, session, transport, network, data link, and physical) is with the sentence, "All People Seem To Need Data Processing."

TWO-MINUTE DRILL

Network Protocols

❏ Packets and protocols are the fundamental building blocks of data transmission over the network.

❏ Internetwork Packet Exchange/Sequenced Packet Exchange (IPX/SPX) is the protocol most commonly used with older versions of Novell NetWare.

❏ IPX/SPX is the fastest routable network protocol suite available.

❏ The Transmission Control Protocol/Internet Protocol (TCP/IP) is the most common protocol used today. TCP/IP, a routable protocol, is the protocol on which the Internet is built.

❏ The NetBIOS Extended User Interface (NetBEUI) is a transport protocol commonly found in smaller peer-to-peer networks.

❏ NetBEUI is a nonroutable protocol.

❏ AppleTalk is a routable protocol used in Macintosh environments.

The OSI Model

❏ The Open Systems Interconnect (OSI) model is a seven-layer model that defines the function of network protocols and devices.

❏ The seven layers of the OSI model, from highest to lowest, are application, presentation, session, transport, network, data link, and physical.

❏ SMTP, HTTP, Telnet, and FTP are all examples of application-layer (layer 7) protocols.

❏ Compression and encryption are examples of functions that can be performed at the presentation layer (layer 6).

❏ The session layer (layer 5) is responsible for the creation of sessions and the management of those sessions.

❏ The transport layer (layer 4) is responsible for the reliability of the transmission, including breaking the data down into manageable packets and sizes using acknowledgments and packet sequence numbers to ensure that data arrives at the destination and is pieced together in the correct order. Examples of layer-4 protocols are TCP, UDP, and SPX.

❏ Layer 3, known as the network layer, performs logical addressing and delivery functions. Examples of layer-3 protocols are IP and IPX.

❑ The data link layer, layer 2, is responsible for physical addressing and converting the packets to electrical signals. Any device that works with MAC addresses runs at this layer.

❑ The first layer of the OSI model, located at the bottom, is known as the physical layer and is responsible for carrying the signal. Your network media and architectures are defined at this level.

❑ An IP address is known as a layer-3 address and looks similar to 192.168.45.6.

❑ A MAC address is known as a layer-2 address and looks similar to 00-02-3F-6B-25-13.

❑ A port address is known as a layer-4 address and looks similar to 80 (web server port).

802 Project Standards

❑ The Institute of Electrical and Electronics Engineers (IEEE) has created project groups that define networking standards.

❑ 802.3 is the Ethernet (CSMA/CD) standard.

❑ 802.5 defines the Token Ring standard.

❑ 802.11 defines the wireless standard.

SELF TEST

The following questions will help you measure your understanding of the material presented in this chapter. Read all the choices carefully because there may appear to be more than one correct answer and you need to choose the best answer.

Network Protocols

1. What is the name given to languages that are used for network communication?
   A. NIC
   B. Segment
   C. Protocol
   D. Cable

2. Which network protocol did Novell develop for use in its networking environment?
   A. IPX/SPX
   B. TCP/IP
   C. NetBEUI
   D. DLC

3. Which protocol is used on the Internet to give each computer a unique address?
   A. IPX/SPX
   B. TCP/IP
   C. NetBEUI
   D. DLC

4. Which of the following protocols is a nonroutable protocol?
   A. IPX/SPX
   B. TCP/IP
   C. NetBEUI
   D. AppleTalk

5. Which protocol was developed by IBM and used primarily in Microsoft workgroup environments?
   A. NetBEUI
   B. TCP/IP
   C. IPX/SPX
   D. AppleTalk

6. Which protocol configures hosts in zones on the network?

    A. IPX/SPX

    B. TCP/IP

    C. NetBEUI

    D. AppleTalk

7. You are troubleshooting to find out why a client on your NetWare 4.*x* network can communicate only with some of the Novell servers on the network. You have verified that the IPX/SPX protocol is installed; what else would you check?

    A. Ensure that the IP address is configured correctly.

    B. Ensure that all servers and clients are configured for the same frame type.

    C. Ensure that the client has a network card driver loaded.

    D. Ensure that the client software is loaded.

The OSI Model

8. Which of the following is not a layer in the OSI model?

    A. Physical

    B. Transport

    C. Network

    D. Data transmission

9. Which of the following protocols are layer-3 protocols? (Choose two.)

    A. IPX

    B. TCP

    C. IP

    D. SPX

10. Which of the following represents a layer-2 address?

    A. COMPUTER1

    B. 00-02-3F-6B-25-13

    C. 192.168.3.200

    D. www.gleneclarke.com

11. Which of the following functions can be performed at layer 6 of the OSI model? (Select all that apply.)
    A. Routing of the message
    B. Compression
    C. Encryption
    D. Converting the message to a format that is understood by the destination

12. Which of the following protocols are transport-layer protocols? (Choose two.)
    A. IPX
    B. TCP
    C. IP
    D. SPX

13. Which of the following represents a layer-3 address?
    A. COMPUTER1
    B. 00-02-3F-6B-25-13
    C. 192.168.3.200
    D. www.gleneclarke.com

14. Which of the following represents an application-layer protocol?
    A. SMTP
    B. IP
    C. SPX
    D. TCP

15. Which layer of the OSI model is responsible for converting the packet to an electrical signal that will be placed on the wire?
    A. Layer 1
    B. Layer 4
    C. Layer 3
    D. Layer 2

16. Which protocol in the IPX/SPX protocol suite is responsible for logical addressing and delivery?
    A. IP
    B. SPX
    C. ARP
    D. IPX

802 Project Standards

17. Which 802 project standard defines Gigabit Ethernet using fiber-optic cabling?

    A. 802.5

    B. 802.3z

    C. 802.3ab

    D. 802.11g

10. Which 802 project standard defines Token Ring?

    A. 802.5

    B. 802.3z

    C. 802.3ab

    D. 802.11g

19. Which 802 project standard defines 10-Gigabit Ethernet?

    A. 802.3z

    B. 802.3ae

    C. 802.3ab

    D. 802.11g

20. Which 802 project standard defines wireless at speeds of 54 Mbps and a frequency range of 2.4 GHz?

    A. 802.11a

    B. 802.11b

    C. 802.11c

    D. 802.11g

SELF TEST ANSWERS

Network Protocols

1. ☑ **C.** A protocol is the network language used by two systems to communicate across the network.

   ☒ **A, B,** and **D** are incorrect because a NIC is a network card, which is not a language—it is a network device. The segment is the term for a part of network cabling on one side of a router or bridge. The cable is not a language; it is the network medium used to carry the signals.

2. ☑ **A.** IPX/SPX is the protocol developed by Novell for use in NetWare environments.

   ☒ **B, C,** and **D** are incorrect—none of them were developed by Novell. TCP/IP is the protocol of the Internet; NetBEUI was developed by IBM and used in Microsoft workgroup environments. DLC is a protocol used to connect to printers.

3. ☑ **B.** TCP/IP is the protocol of the Internet, and each system is assigned a unique IP address.

   ☒ **A, C,** and **D** are incorrect. IPX/SPX is the protocol developed by Novell for use in NetWare environments, NetBEUI was developed by IBM and used in Microsoft workgroup environments, and DLC is a protocol used to connect to printers.

4. ☑ **C.** NetBEUI is a nonroutable protocol.

   ☒ **A, B,** and **D** are incorrect because IPX/SPX, TCP/IP, and AppleTalk are all routable protocols.

5. ☑ **A.** NetBEUI was developed by IBM and used primarily in Microsoft workgroup environments.

   ☒ **B, C,** and **D** are all incorrect. IPX/SPX was developed by Novell, AppleTalk was developed by Apple, and TCP/IP is the protocol of the Internet.

6. ☑ **D.** The AppleTalk protocol configures hosts into zones.

   ☒ **A, B,** and **C** are incorrect. IPX/SPX, TCP/IP, and NetBEUI do not use zones to organize nodes on the network.

7. ☑ **B.** Using IPX/SPX and having trouble connecting to some of the servers on the network but not others is a classic description of a communication problem, indicating that the client has the frame type set to something different from that used by the servers. You will need to verify the frame type on all systems and ensure that systems that wish to talk to one another are configured with the same frame type.

   ☒ **A, C,** and **D** are incorrect. A is incorrect because IP addresses have nothing to do with the IPX/SPX protocol. C and D are incorrect because both are describing issues that would arise when connecting to "any" server. In our example, the client can connect to some servers, so the client software and the network card driver must already be loaded.

The OSI Model

8. ☑ **D.** Data transmission is not a layer of the OSI model.
☒ **A, B,** and **C** are incorrect because physical, transport, and network are all layers of the OSI mode.

9. ☑ **A and C.** IP is the network-layer protocol in the TCP/IP protocol suite, and IPX is the network-layer protocol in the IPX/SPX protocol suite.
☒ **B and D** are incorrect because TCP and SPX are transport-layer protocols.

10. ☑ **B.** 00-02-3F-6B-25-13 is an example of a MAC address, which is a layer-2 address.
☒ **A, C,** and **D** are incorrect. COMPUTER1 is an example of a NetBIOS name (computer name), 192.168.3.200 is an example of an IP address, which is a layer-3 address, and www. gleneclarke.com is an example of a DNS name.

11. ☑ **B, C,** and **D.** They are all examples of data formatting that is performed at the presentation layer.
☒ **A** is incorrect because the routing of the message is handled by the network layer, which is layer 3.

12. ☑ **B and D.** TCP is the transport protocol that is responsible for reliable delivery in the TCP/IP protocol suite, whereas SPX performs the same function in the IPX/SPX protocol suite.
☒ **A and C** are incorrect. IPX and IP are network-layer protocols that are responsible for the addressing and delivery of data.

13. ☑ **C.** 192.168.3.200 is an example of an IP address that is a layer-3 protocol, and this is a layer-3 address.
☒ **A, B,** and **D** are incorrect. COMPUTER1 is a computer name, 00-02-3F-6B-25-13 is an example of a Mac address (layer-2 address), and www.gleneclarke.com is an example of a DNS-style name.

14. ☑ **A.** An application-layer protocol is a protocol that is responsible for initiating some form of request. SMTP is used to send e-mail from server to server.
☒ **B, C,** and **D** are incorrect. IP is a layer-3 address (network layer), SPX is a transport-layer protocol, and so is TCP.

15. ☑ **D.** Layer 2 (the data link layer) is responsible for converting the packet to an electrical signal.
☒ **A, B,** and **C** are all incorrect. Layer 1 (physical layer) is responsible for placing the signal on the wire, layer 4 (transport layer) is responsible for reliable delivery, and layer 3 (network layer) is responsible for logical addressing, routing, and delivery.

16. ☑ **D.** IPX is responsible for logical addressing and delivery of the message. IPX is similar in function to the IP and UDP protocols found in the TCP/IP protocol suite.

    ☒ **A, B,** and **C** are all incorrect. IP is responsible for logical addressing and delivery but is not found in the IPX/SPX protocol—it is found in the TCP/IP suite. SPX is a transport protocol responsible for reliable delivery, and ARP is an address resolution protocol found in the TCP/IP protocol suite.

802 Project Standards

17. ☑ **B.** Gigabit Ethernet over fiber is defined in the IEEE 802.3z project standard.

    ☒ **A, C,** and **D** are incorrect. The 802.5 standard defines Token Ring, 802.3ab defines Gigabit Ethernet over twisted-pair, and 802.11g defines wireless at 54 Mbps.

18. ☑ **A.** The IEEE 802.5 project standard defines Token Ring.

    ☒ **B, C,** and **D** are incorrect. 802.3z defines Gigabit Ethernet over fiber, 802.3ab defines Gigabit Ethernet over twisted-pair, and 802.11g defines wireless at 54 Mbps.

19. ☑ **B.** The IEEE 802.3ae standard defines 10-Gigabit Ethernet.

    ☒ **A, C,** and **D** are incorrect. 802.3z defines Gigabit Ethernet over fiber, 802.3ab defines Gigabit Ethernet over twisted-pair, and 802.11g defines wireless at 54 Mbps.

20. ☑ **D.** 802.11g defines a wireless standard at 54 Mbps while maintaining compatibility with 802.11b by being on the same frequency.

    ☒ **A, B,** and **C** are incorrect. 802.11a is at 54 Mbps but is not at a frequency of 2.4 GHz, 802.11b is at 11 Mbps but compatible with 802.11g, because it runs at the same frequency, and both are Wi-Fi compatible. 802.11c is not a wireless standard.

3

Networking Components

CERTIFICATION OBJECTIVES

I n this chapter, you will learn about popular networking components found in a LAN environment, such as network cards, hubs, switches, routers, and other network devices. This chapter is a critical chapter not only for the Network+ exam but also for the real world. Be sure to take your time and understand all the concepts presented in this chapter.

Network Interface Cards

The *network interface card (NIC)*, or network card, is a device installed on the system that is responsible for sending and receiving data onto the network. The network card is responsible for preparing data from the system to be transported on the wire by converting the outbound data from a parallel format (due to bus width of the bus architecture that the card is sitting in) to electrical signals that will travel along the network media. On the receiving end, the network card is responsible for receiving the electrical signal and converting it to data that is understood by the system.

The network card also is known as a network adapter; it can be installed in the system after the system has been purchased, or the system comes with a network card built in. A system that comes with a network card built in is said to have an integrated network card—meaning the card is integrated into the system. Figure 3-1 shows an integrated network card port on the side of a laptop; desktop computers typically have the port on the back of the computer.

FIGURE 3-1

An integrated network card on a system

FIGURE 3-2

An ISA network interface card

Network cards that are installed on the computer as an add-on can be installed into the system by inserting the card into the expansion bus of the system (usually PCI, but in the past it was ISA) or by plugging in a USB device. There are a number of different types of expansion slots in the system. When installing a network card, you will need to make sure that you get the correct type of card for the particular type of expansion slot. For example, a PCI card is placed in a PCI slot and will not fit into an ISA or AGP slot. The following is a list of popular expansion bus architectures, and Figure 3-2 shows a picture of an ISA network interface card.

- **ISA**   Industry Standard Architecture (ISA) is an old bus architecture that runs at 8 MHz and supports 8- or 16-bit cards.
- **MCA**   Microchannel Architecture (MCA) was built by IBM and has a 32-bit architecture that runs at 10 MHz.
- **VESA**   Video Electronics Standards Association (VESA, also known as VESA local bus, or VLB) at the time ran at the system speed (which was around 33 MHz); it has a 32-bit architecture.
- **EISA**   Extended Industry Standard Architecture (EISA) is the upgrade to ISA that supports 32-bit cards running at 8 MHz.

- **PCI** Peripheral Component Interconnect (PCI) is the popular bus architecture today for adding cards to the system. PCI runs at 33 MHz and has a 32-bit or 64-bit bus architecture. Most network cards today are PCI.
- **AGP** Advanced Graphics Port (AGP) is the new graphics standard that runs at 66 MHz and is used by video cards.
- **PCMCIA** Personal Computer Memory Card Industry Association (PCMCIA) is the bus architecture used in laptop computers. PCMCIA has a 16-bit architecture that runs at 33 MHz.

Transceivers

A *transceiver* is that portion of the network interface that actually transmits and receives electrical signals across the transmission media. When the signal is traveling along the length of the wire, the transceiver picks the signal up and verifies that the data is destined for the local system. If the data is destined for the local system, the data is passed up to the system for processing; if it is not, it is discarded. There are two types of transceivers: onboard and external.

Onboard Transceivers

Onboard transceivers are built onto the network interface card. With these transceivers, the media connector is built right on the back of the NIC. Common examples of this type include RJ-45 receptacles for twisted-pair cable and BNC connectors for thinnet coaxial cable (shown in Figure 3-3).

FIGURE 3-3

RJ-45 and
BNC onboard
transceivers on a
network card

External Transceivers

With an *external* transceiver, the actual media connection is made external to the network card using a small device that attaches to the NIC via an extension cable. These connections use an attachment unit interface (AUI) connector, also called a Digital-Intel-Xerox (DIX) connector, on the back of the network card. The AUI connector is a female 15-pin D-connector (shown in Figure 3-4) that looks very much like a joystick port and typically is used to connect a workstation to thicknet cabling.

The types of transceivers and media that can be served by a NIC determine the appropriate connector. Each media type has a typical connector type or connection method.

Thicknet Coax

Thicknet, or standard Ethernet coax, uses a connection method that typically involves an external transceiver connected to the adapter's AUI port. This external transceiver has a connection called a vampire tap that attaches to the media by drilling a hole in the cable using a special drilling jig that controls the depth of the hole. This jig prevents the drill from drilling through and severing the center conductor.

The vampire tap consists of a pin that is inserted into the hole drilled in the cable and a clamp that holds the tap onto the cable. One of the challenges of this type of connection is to position the tap so that it contacts the center conductor without shorting to the shield surrounding it. These difficulties, as well as the cost and size of thicknet cable, have rendered it largely obsolete, although it occasionally could be found in existing installations.

FIGURE 3-4

An AUI connector on the back of a network switch

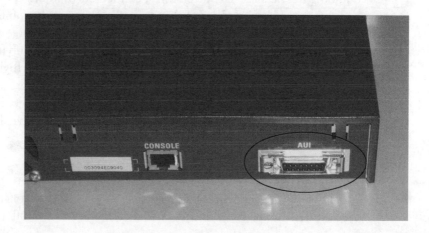

Thinnet Coax

Thinnet coax can be attached directly to a network adapter if an onboard transceiver is used. In this case, a connector called a barrel connector (BNC) on the network card attaches to a T-connector. The T-connector has a female fitting that attaches to the card, as well as two additional male fittings that attach to cable segments or a terminator.

Each end of a thinnet Ethernet segment must be terminated, so the last node on each end could have a terminator attached to the side of the T-connector opposite the inbound cable. All other nodes use T-connectors with cable segments attached to both sides, just like holiday tree lights. A thinnet segment cannot be attached directly to the BNC connector on the network adapter; it must use a T-connector.

Twisted-Pair Wiring

The typical connector for a twisted-pair connection is called an RJ-45 connector. The RJ-45 connector looks like an oversized phone connector. The reason for the difference in size is that a phone connector (RJ-11) has a four-wire connector, whereas an RJ-45 connector is an eight-wire connector.

An RJ-45 patch cable can be plugged directly into the back of the network adapter. The patch cable usually runs to a wall receptacle, which is wired back to a patch panel and ultimately back to a wiring hub.

Fiber-Optic Cabling

Fiber-optic adapters generally have two connectors, one each for incoming and outgoing fiber cables. The mechanical connectors that join the cable, called ST connectors, are designed to pass light seamlessly across the joined fiber segments. For this reason, these connectors must be made with great precision. Fiber-optic runs generally are made back to a concentrator that performs a hub function.

In many situations, fiber-optic cabling is used to connect high-speed computers and provide a high-speed backbone to which slower LANs are attached. The LANs might connect copper media, such as twisted-pair or coaxial cable, to a set of hubs that are then bridged to the fiber-optic backbone for high-speed data transfer between LANs.

Transceiver Configuration

A number of network cards have multiple types of connectors on the back of the card (called combo cards in this case) to allow you to use different types of cabling to connect the system to the network. The transceiver type that is being used by the network card is typically set to the "auto" setting, which means that the card can sense which transceiver you are using and the card will configure itself to use that transceiver. When troubleshooting to find out why the card is not working, the "auto setting" is the first thing you should change. When I have problems connecting to a network, I usually change the transceiver setting to the actual one I am using. For example, if you are using the RJ-45 connector you will want to change the setting to something like TP (for twisted-pair) or TX as shown in Figure 3-5. During configuration, the different transceivers can be referred to in the following ways:

- **DIX or AUI**   The card uses an external thicknet transceiver.
- **Coax, 10Base2, or BNC**   The card has an onboard thinnet Ethernet connector known as a BNC connector.
- **TP, TX, UTP, 10BaseT, or 100BaseT**   The card has an onboard RJ-45 connector.

Another setting that I normally have no problem with but have had trouble with recently is the transfer rate of the network card. A number of today's network cards support 10 Mbps, 100 Mbps, and even 1000 Mbps. Most of the time these

FIGURE 3-5

Changing the transceiver type through the network card properties

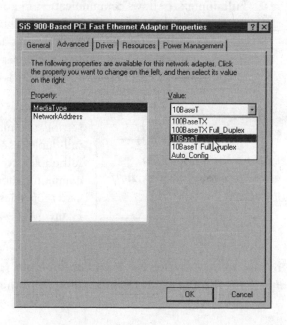

network cards are set to "auto" in order to detect the speed at which the card will run—the card derives its speed from the device it is connected to. For example, if you have a 10/100 Mbps network card but plug it into a 10 Mbps hub, it will run at 10 Mbps—not the full 100 Mbps, because the card detects the speed of the device it is connected to.

Recently, I had a problem when the network card was not able to autoconfigure itself. After troubleshooting for a little bit, I went to the network card properties and forced the speed of the network card to 100 Mbps (shown in Figure 3-6)—and voilà! It worked beautifully.

Another setting you may want to configure on your network card is the transmission method of either simplex, half duplex, or full duplex. The three transmission methods are as follows:

- **Simplex**   Allows communication in one direction only. You will only be able to send or receive with a simplex device—not both directions. It is either one way or the other.
- **Half duplex**   Allows communication in both directions (send and receive), but not at the same time. A network card set to half duplex will not be able to receive data while sending data. Using the half-duplex setting can slow down communication if your device does support full duplex.
- **Full duplex**   Allows communication in both directions at the same time. If a network card supports full duplex, it will be able to receive data when data is being sent because all four pairs of wires are used. If you make sure that a network card that supports full duplex is set to full duplex, you will notice a big difference in throughput if the device is set to half duplex.

w a t c h   **Be sure to be familiar with the differences between simplex, half duplex, and full duplex.**

Most network cards are set to auto. With this setting, you may want to force the setting to the full-duplex mode to be sure that you are getting full-duplex communication. You can change the communication method through the network card properties in Device Manager, as shown in Figure 3-7.

CertCam 3-1

Be sure to do Exercise 3-1 from LabBook.pdf found on the CD-ROM and check out the CertCam training video from the CD-ROM as well.

FIGURE 3-6

Changing the
network card
rate from auto
to 100 Mbps

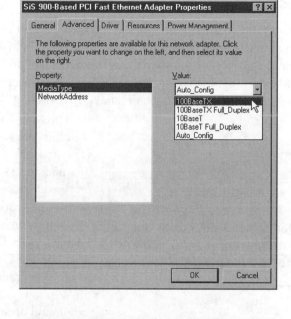

FIGURE 3-7

Changing a
network card's
communication
method from
auto to full
duplex

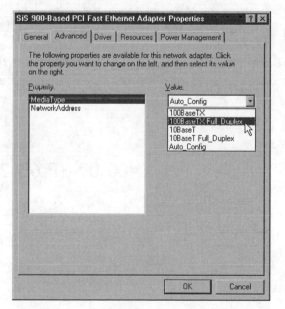

MAC Address

Each network card has a unique address that is burned into the card by its manufacturer. This unique address, known as a MAC address, is used in the header of the packet for the source and destination addresses of the packet. The MAC address is a 48-bit address displayed in a hexadecimal format that looks similar to 00-90-4B-4C-C1-59 or sometimes 00:90:4B:4C:C1:59.

e x a m

ⓦatch *A MAC address is a 48-bit address burned into the network card and is used to send data from one network card to another. A MAC address looks similar to 00-90-4B-4C-C1-59.*

The MAC address is made up of 12 characters and is in hexadecimal format. The first half of the MAC address is the manufacturer's address, while the last half of the address is the unique address assigned to that network card by the manufacturer (shown in Figure 3-8). The combination of the manufacturer ID and the unique address ensure that the MAC address is singular.

To view your MAC address on your system in Windows 2000/XP/2003, you can go to a command prompt and type **ipconfig /all**. You will notice the MAC address of the network card listed within the output as the physical address. To view your MAC address in Linux, go to a terminal prompt and type **ifconfig** to view your MAC address. Exercise 3-2 demonstrates how to view your MAC address and then how to use the Internet to determine the manufacturer of the network card by using the first six characters of the MAC address.

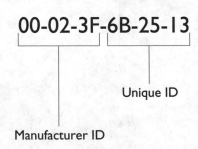

CertCam 3-2

EXERCISE 3-2

Determining Your Local Machine's MAC Address

In this exercise, you will learn how to determine the MAC address of your computer using Windows XP. You will then go to the Internet site of http://www.coffer.com/mac_find/ to determine the manufacturer of your network card.

1. To start a command prompt, select Start | Run, type **cmd**, and then press ENTER.

2. When the command prompt appears, type **ipconfig /all** to view your TCP/IP settings and MAC address (shown next).

```
C:\WINDOWS\System32\cmd.exe                                    _ □ ×

Ethernet adapter Wireless Network Connection:

        Connection-specific DNS Suffix  . :
        Description . . . . . . . . . . . : Broadcom 802.11b/g WLAN
        Physical Address. . . . . . . . . : 00-90-4B-4C-C1-59
        Dhcp Enabled. . . . . . . . . . . : Yes
        Autoconfiguration Enabled . . . . : Yes
        IP Address. . . . . . . . . . . . : 192.168.0.101
        Subnet Mask . . . . . . . . . . . : 255.255.255.0
        Default Gateway . . . . . . . . . : 192.168.0.1
        DHCP Server . . . . . . . . . . . : 192.168.0.1
        DNS Servers . . . . . . . . . . . : 192.168.0.1
        Lease Obtained. . . . . . . . . . : Sunday, June 12, 2005 3:17:14 PM
        Lease Expires . . . . . . . . . . : Saturday, June 18, 2005 6:19:45 PM

C:\>_
```

3. Record your MAC address here:

   Physical Address: _____

4. Once you have recorded the MAC address, start Internet Explorer and navigate to http://www.coffer.com/mac_find/. This site is used to input the first six characters of the MAC address, which represents the address of the manufacturer of the card, and the site will tell you who manufactured the card.

5. Once you access the MAC address find site, fill in the "MAC Address or Vendor to look for" text box with the first six characters of your MAC address and click the String button. For example, the first six characters of my MAC address is 00-90-4B, so I would type 00904B, as shown in the accompanying illustration.

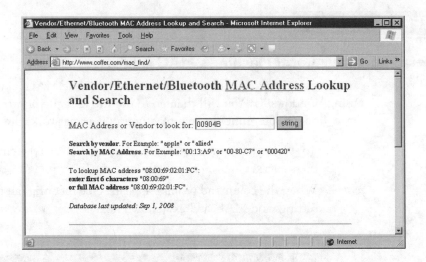

6. In the middle of the page, your network card manufacturer will be displayed. In my example, the manufacturer of all cards starting with 00-90-4B appears to be Gemtek Technology Co., as shown in the next illustration.

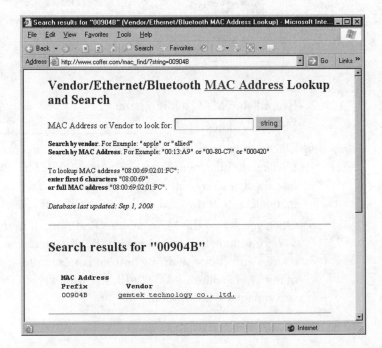

7. Take a few minutes and search for manufacturers of the following MAC addresses. Once you find the manufacturer, fill in the table that follows:

MAC Address	Manufacturer
00-B0-D0-B1-ED-51	
00-0D-60-48-53-9E	
00-A0-C9-C3-D2-E2	

8. Now that you have searched for the vendor of a MAC address by using the manufacturer ID portion of the MAC address, let's search by manufacturer! In the String to search for text box, type **Intel** and choose the String button. Record the first five manufacturer IDs in the spaces provided.

    i. _____

    ii. _____

    iii. _____

    iv. _____

    v. _____

9. Close the browser when you have finished.

The MAC address is also known as the hardware address or physical address of the network card.	*Be sure to remember for the exam that the MAC address is known as a layer-2 address.*

Troubleshooting Network Cards

Along with installing and configuring the network card, you should be familiar with some common steps involved in troubleshooting connectivity issues with a network card. When problems arise in connecting to the network, one of the first things you want to do is check to see that the "link" light is on at the back of the network card. If the link light is on, you may want to make sure that there is activity by looking at the activity light. The activity light should be blinking when there is network activity. If these lights are not on, you will need to reconfigure the cards or replace them if reconfiguration doesn't work. You also may want to try updating the driver for the network card if you are having problems with the device.

Testing

If there is one thing you will do often, it is testing to be sure any updates or changes you made are working properly. Once your network card has been installed, you have to connect the cable to it. Some network cards have multiple transceivers on them. You must connect the appropriate cable for the network into the correct transceiver type.

Once the cable has been connected, you can check a couple of things to see whether the card is operating properly. The first of these is the link light on the back of the card. Some older network cards do not have this feature, but newer ones do. You should see a light next to the transceiver. Some 10 Mbps cards have an activity light and a connection light. Some 10/100 Mbps cards have both a 10 Mbps light and a 100 Mbps light along with the activity light, which tells you the speed at which you are connected.

Once you have verified that the link light is on, which proves to you that there is a physical connection, the next thing you need to do is troubleshoot connectivity issues. Most networks run TCP/IP, so you will likely start pinging addresses on the network. For more troubleshooting tips on TCP/IP, refer to Chapter 6.

Network Card Diagnostics

Another direction to take when troubleshooting the network card is to use a diagnostic program to run a series of tests on the network adapter. You can use generic diagnostic programs or vendor-supplied diagnostics. Many diagnostics must be run without the network drivers loaded, so you may need to boot the operating system to Safe mode first. Figure 3-9 shows a diagnostic and testing program for an Acer card. Diagnostic programs run a variety of tests on the hardware of the card, including the transceiver, and also perform a communication test (such as a loopback test).

Loopback Test The loopback test is one that tests communication in and out of the card. A stream of data is sent out and loops back around into the card. The input is then compared to see whether the data received is the same as that sent.

FIGURE 3-9

Network card
diagnostics
program

Some cards can run an internal loopback test as a method of troubleshooting communication problems. Others must have a loopback adapter that plugs into the card. This way, the data actually is sent out of the card and loops around and comes back into the card as though it were received from another device. Sometimes this is a more accurate and realistic test of the card.

Drivers

When you install a network card on a Windows system, Plug and Play recognizes and configures the hardware by loading the appropriate driver. A driver is a piece of software that enables the operating system to communicate with the device. There are different types of drivers for modems, sound cards, and just about any other component in a computer.

The manufacturer provides the driver, and usually the driver has its own configuration program to set up and install the network adapter. This is usually a SETUP.EXE, INSTALL.EXE, or INSTALL.BAT file. If this isn't the case, and Plug and Play finds the network adapter but no default driver exists, you will have the opportunity to change the driver in Device Manager. If a driver needs updating in Device Manager, it will show with an Unknown Device icon (yellow question mark) in Device Manager, as shown in Figure 3-10.

Unknown
devices in Device
Manager

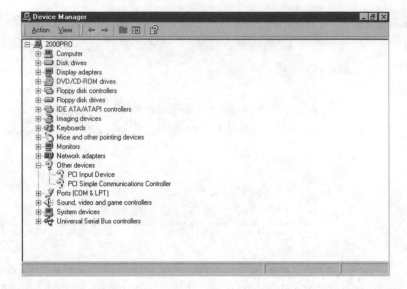

From time to time, you might want to update the drivers for your various devices.
Manufacturers update their drivers if problems are found in current versions. You
can update the driver for your network card through Device Manager with Windows
operating systems. Once in Device Manager, you will need to locate the device and
then right-click and choose Update Driver, as shown in Figure 3-11. Once you choose
the update driver command, you will need to browse to the location of the driver file.

Updating
a network
card driver in
Windows

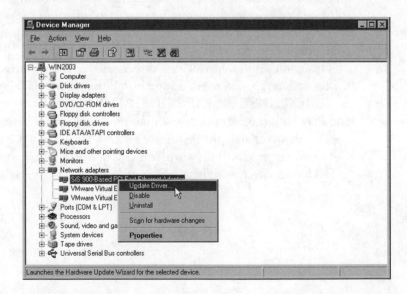

Hubs, MAUs, and Repeaters

Once you have the network card inserted into the computer system or network device, you will next need to connect each of the systems together using devices such as hubs, repeaters, or MAUs. You will need to be familiar with each of these networking devices for the Network+ exam, as well as being familiar with the layers of the OSI model that these devices run at.

Hubs

Hubs are one of the most important components of a network because they act as a central point for all network devices to connect to. You can easily remember the layout of a hub if you think of a wheel and picture how the spokes radiate out from the hub of the wheel. In a network, each spoke is a connection, and the hub of the wheel is the hub of the network where all of the cables come together.

The Role of Hubs in Networking

The hub, also known as a concentrator, is responsible for allowing all systems a central point of connection, so that when a computer sends a piece of data to another computer, the electrical signal leaves the network card of the sending system and reaches the hub, and the hub sends the signal to all ports on the hub so that all systems can check to see whether the data is destined for them. Figure 3-12 shows an example of a five-port hub.

A five-port hub used to connect systems together

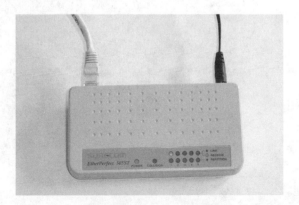

When looking at Figure 3-12, you will notice that the hub displays link lights for each port on the hub that is active. This can be used in troubleshooting, just like the link light on the back of a network card. You also will notice that there is a collision indicator on the hub, which indicates whether or not your network currently is having a lot of collisions. Once again, this could be very useful when troubleshooting network problems—excessive collisions could lead to systems dropping off the network.

Cascading Hubs

Looking at Figure 3-13, you will notice that there is a switch on the hub to indicate that you wish to use the fifth port to cascade, or connect, to another hub. If you were to try to chain two hubs together with the switch set to normal, it would be similar to trying to connect two computers together with a straight-through cable; it can't be done because you need to switch the send and receive wires on one end of the cable. We have discussed using a crossover cable, but manufacturers of hubs have given us a solution that eliminates the need for crossover cables by creating a port on the hub that is already crossed over; you simply need to switch the setting to use the fifth port as the cascade port. Also known as the uplink port, the cascade port connects to a normal port on the next hub.

If you wanted to connect three 24-port hubs together, you would need to uplink from port 24 on the first hub to any port on the second hub (I usually uplink to the first port on the second hub), then use port 24 on the second hub to uplink to the first port on the third hub, as shown in Figure 3-14.

FIGURE 3-13

The uplink switch on a hub

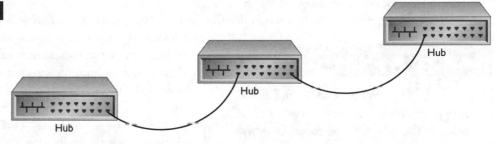

Before we get into the different types of hubs, a point that I want to stress (one that was mentioned earlier) is that a hub sends the signal to all ports on the hub. This means that, if you have a 24-port hub linked to another 24-port hub and a workstation sends data to another workstation, the data will be sent to all 48 ports on the network. This leads to a lot of unneeded traffic and contention across the entire network that will slow network performance. A solution would be to use a switch, which is the subject of an upcoming discussion!

Passive Hubs

The function of a *passive* hub is simply to receive data from one port of the hub and send it out to the other ports. For example, an eight-port hub receives data from port 3 and then resends that data to ports 1, 2, 4, 5, 6, 7, and 8.

A passive hub contains no power source or electrical components, there is no signal processing (such as when the hub receives the electrical signal), and there is no regenerating of the signal to ensure that it is readable at the destination. A passive hub simply attaches the ports internally and enables communication to flow through the network. Regeneration of the signal is a function of an active hub!

Active Hubs

An *active* hub provides the same functionality as a passive hub with an additional feature. Active hubs rebuild (regenerate) the data before sending it to all of the destination ports on the hub. Using active hubs, you can increase the length of your network, because although the signal weakens with distance, when the active hub receives the signal, it rebuilds the data, allowing it once more to go a greater distance. It is important to remember that UTP cabling can be run a maximum of 100 meters. With an active hub, you can run this type of cable 100 meters on each side of the hub. An active hub has a power source and built-in repeaters to boost the signal. Extra electronics built into an active hub allow for signal regeneration.

When exam time comes, remember the difference between an active hub and a passive hub: An active hub can boost the signal, whereas a passive hub cannot.

Hubs are used in Ethernet environments, whereas Token Ring environments use MAUs. Also know that hubs run at layer 1 of the OSI model because they work with the electrical signal.

Hybrid Hubs

A *hybrid* hub is a hub that can use many different types of cables in addition to UTP cabling. A hybrid hub usually is cabled using thinnet or thicknet Ethernet along with popular cable types such as twisted-pair cabling. A few years ago, hybrid hubs were fairly popular. UTP seems to be the popular cable type today, so you may not see the thinnet or thicknet connector on the hub as well. Figure 3-15 displays a hybrid hub.

FIGURE 3-15

A hybrid hub using UTP and thinnet cabling

Multistation Access Units

A *multistation access unit (MAU)* is a device to which multiple workstations are connected in order to communicate on a Token Ring network. A MAU is a hub-type device for Token Ring networks with some features that make it a little bit different from a hub—for example, a MAU regenerates the signal when it reaches the MAU.

Remember that the MAU allows for a physical star topology but is logically a ring topology because it cycles through all ports in order to simulate a ring.

Because Token Ring networks use token passing instead of CSMA/CD, there is no chance for collisions on a Token Ring network. The first difference you will notice with MAUs over hubs is that a MAU does not have collision indicators on it because you can't have collisions on a Token Ring network. Figure 3-16 shows a picture of a MAU; notice that there are no collision indicators on the device.

Another major difference with a MAU is that MAUs don't actually use an uplink port. With Token Ring, there is a logical ring within the MAU, and when you connect to another MAU, you must complete a full ring structure again. Therefore, you will notice on the Token Ring MAU that it has a ring-in port and a ring-out port. When you wish to connect two MAUs together, you must ring out of the first MAU and, with that cable, ring in to the second MAU. Then you must ring out of the second MAU and ring in to the first MAU, as shown in Figure 3-17.

Repeaters

One of the pitfalls of networking environments is that the electrical signal that is traveling the wire is weakened over distance as a result of outside interference. Eventually, if two systems are too far from one another, the signal is so weak that by the time it reaches the other side it is unreadable. This is where repeaters come in.

FIGURE 3-16

A Token
Ring MAU

Connecting two
MAUs using
ring-in and
ring-out ports

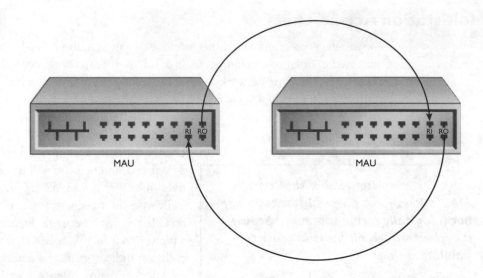

MAU   MAU

e x a m

ᴡ a t c h *Because a repeater works
with the electrical signal, it is considered a
layer-1 device.*

If your network layout exceeds the normal
specifications of the cable, you can use repeaters
to allow the signal to travel the distance by
placing the repeaters at different points in the
network. For example, if you are using thinnet
cabling, you know that thinnet is limited to
185 m. But what if you want to connect two
systems together that are 235 m apart? You would
place a repeater somewhere before the 185 m mark so that the repeater will regenerate
or rebuild the signal, allowing it to travel the extra difference. Figure 3-18 shows a
signal that is weakened over distance but is regenerated through the use of a repeater.

FIGURE 3-18 Using a repeater to regenerate the signal

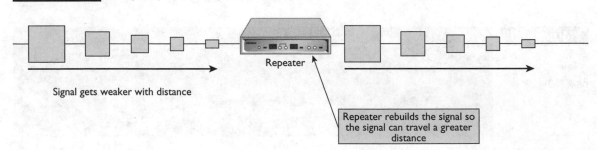

Repeater

Signal gets weaker with distance

Repeater rebuilds the signal so
the signal can travel a greater
distance

Bridges and Switches

Now that we have discussed some of the popular layer-1 devices, let's take a look at some popular layer-2 devices. Layer-2 devices are a little smarter than layer-1 devices in the sense that they actually can make decisions about where the electrical signal needs to go. Remember that a hub, which is a layer-1 device, would forward the signal to all ports on the hub, which will lead to traffic problems as you start adding hubs to the topology.

This section will introduce you to two layer-2 devices that often are used to filter network traffic. By filtering network traffic, we are conserving precious bandwidth on the network, which will have a huge impact on the overall performance of the network.

Bridges

A bridge is a network connectivity device that is used to break the network down into multiple network segments. A bridge runs at layer 2, the data link layer, and is used to filter traffic by only forwarding traffic to the destination network segment. Figure 3-19 shows an example of a bridged network.

FIGURE 3-19

A bridged network with three segments

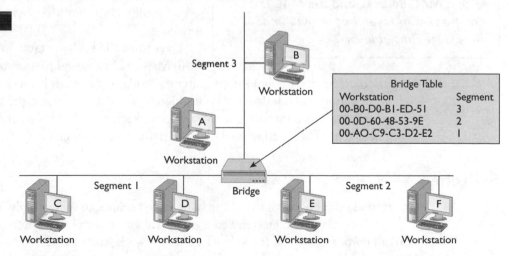

Bridge Table

Workstation	Segment
00-B0-D0-B1-ED-51	3
00-0D-60-48-53-9E	2
00-AO-C9-C3-D2-E2	1

Let's look at an example of how a bridge filters network traffic. Assume that you have just completed connecting the bridge to the network segments shown in Figure 3-19. When Workstation A sends data to Workstation F, the data will go out the network card of Workstation A and will travel the full length of segment 3 in both directions. The signal will reach the bridge, and the bridge will look at the destination MAC address of the packet. Once the bridge looks at the destination MAC address, it will compare that MAC address with the MAC addresses in its bridging table. The bridging table is a table in memory that lists all known MAC addresses and which network segment that MAC address lives on. This table is critical to the bridge's filtering features. Since this is the first piece of data sent on the network, the MAC address for Workstation F is not in the bridging table, so the bridge will need to forward the data to both segment 1 and segment 2. It will not forward the information to network segment 3 because that is where the data came from, and if Workstation F existed on that network, it would already have the data.

When the bridge received the initial data from Workstation A, it recorded the MAC address of Workstation A and the network segment that Workstation A resides on in the bridging table. This way if anyone sends data to Workstation A, the bridge will have an entry for Workstation A in the bridging table, and the bridge will forward the data only to network segment 3 and not to the other segments. Also note that when Workstation F replies to Workstation A, the data will need to pass through the bridge, so the bridge will know what network segment Workstation F resides on and will record that MAC address in the bridging table.

Over time, the bridging table will be filled with MAC addresses and their associated network segments. In our example, after the bridging table has been constructed, if Workstation A sends data to Workstation C, the data will reach the bridge and the bridge will forward the data only to network segment 1. This prevents network segment 2 from being congested with the traffic (shown in Figure 3-20).

Since a bridge works with a MAC address, and the MAC is a component of layer 2 of the OSI model, the bridge runs at layer 2 of the OSI model

Switches

Switches, also known as switching hubs, have become an increasingly important part of our networking today, because when working with hubs, a hub sends the data to all ports on the hub. If you have a large network structure, this means that you

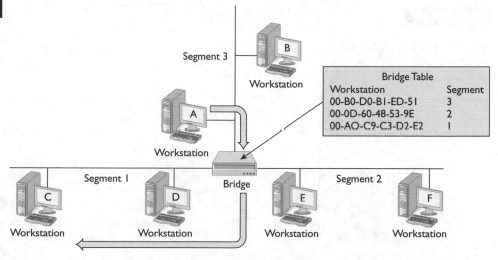

FIGURE 3-20

A bridge forwards the traffic only to the needed network segments.

have probably linked a few hubs together, and when data is sent from one system to another, all computers see the traffic. This leads to a lot of network traffic, which eventually slows network performance. Figure 3-21 shows an example of a 24-port 10/100 Mbps switch.

When you use a switch instead of a hub, the switch acts as a filtering device by associating the MAC address of the system connected to the switch with the port on the switch that the system is connected to. For example, in Figure 3-22, Computer A transmits a packet to Computer C. The packet enters the switch from port 1 and then travels a direct route to port 3, because the switch uses the destination MAC address of the packet and knows that the MAC address is of the device connected

FIGURE 3-21

A 24-port 10/100 Mbps switch

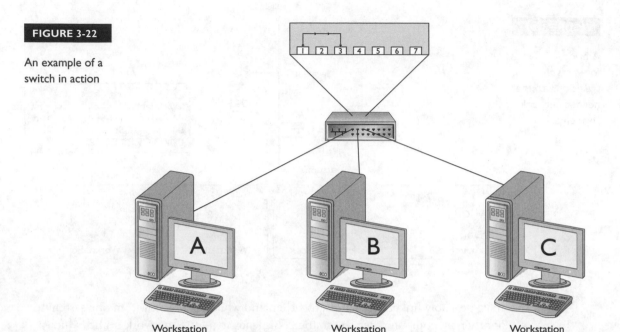

FIGURE 3-22

An example of a
switch in action

Workstation   Workstation   Workstation

into port 3. From port 3, the packet is transmitted to Computer C. During this
process, Computer B is unaware of the traffic between Computers A and C, because
there is a direct path within the switch and no shared bandwidth.

*It is a best practice to use switches whenever possible because of the increase
in performance over a standard hub. The bandwidth with a standard hub is
shared by all users connected to the hub; however, with a switch, all users get
the full network bandwidth. For example, a 100 Mbps network with a 24-port
hub and 24 PCs allows each user to have 100/24 Mbps bandwidth; with a
switch, however, each user would have a full 100 Mbps bandwidth.*

Understanding VLANs

Virtual LANs (VLANs) are a feature of special switches, known as managed switches,
which allow the administrator to group ports on a switch to a "virtual LAN." When
a port is configured for a particular VLAN, it is unable to communicate with systems
that are not on that VLAN without the use of a routing device such as a router. This
is similar to the fact that, if we had two physical networks, a machine cannot send
data from one network to the other without the use of a router.

The purpose of a VLAN is to cut down on broadcast traffic through the use of what are known as broadcast domains. A VLAN acts as a broadcast domain—let's look at how this works. Normally, if we had a 24-port hub or switch and a computer wanted to send data to all systems, it would "broadcast" the data out onto the network. A broadcast will hit every port on that switch or hub. With a VLAN-supported switch, you can create VLANs that act as "broadcast" domains. This means that if Workstation A is on VLAN1, which is made up of ports 1 through 12 on the 24-port switch, when Workstation A sends broadcast traffic (traffic intended for all systems), it will be sent only to ports 1 through 12 because the virtual LAN is acting as a boundary for traffic. The benefit of this is that you are now able to minimize traffic within or across switches, which increases network throughput. Figure 3-23 shows a switch that is divided into two different VLANs.

How you implement your VLAN depends on what type of switch you have. There are a number of different types of switches:

- **Layer-1 switch** A layer-1 switch implements what is known as port switching. Port switching means that the network administrator associates the ports on the switch as being members of a particular VLAN. With port switching, you need to ensure that you are satisfied with the fact that if you move a computer from one port to another, the system may become a member of a different VLAN, because the port is the member of the VLAN, not the network card connected to it. Layer-1 switches do offer benefits; they are great for increasing security and isolation. They also allow an administrator to move a system to a new VLAN by reconfiguring the port for the new VLAN. The benefit is that there is no need to move the system physically.

- **Layer-2 switch** A layer-2 switch doesn't associate the port with the VLAN, but the MAC addresses of systems are associated with the VLAN. The network administrator is responsible for listing all the MAC addresses for each VLAN on the switch. When a packet is sent by a system and reaches the switch, the switch tags the packet as being a member of the VLAN, and it will be sent only to other systems in the VLAN. The benefit of layer-2 switches is that, because the MAC address is associated with the VLAN, it doesn't matter what port the system is plugged into. This is a great feature for laptop users who typically roam around on the network—they will always be a member of the same VLAN unless the switch is reconfigured.

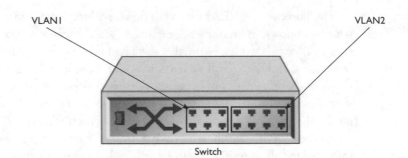

FIGURE 3-23

Ports on a switch associated with VLANs

VLAN1   VLAN2

Switch

For the exam, know that bridges and switches are considered layer-2 devices. You can remember this easily because they both work with MAC addresses (layer-2 addresses).

■ **Layer-3 Switch** A layer-3 switch bases membership to a VLAN on the subnet ID of the layer-3 address of a packet. With layer-3 switches, the workstations do not actually belong to the VLAN, but the packets that are being sent do belong, because they have the source address information which contains the network ID in them.

To create the VLANs, the network administrator will need to run the configuration utility on the VLAN-supported switch. Also note that with a layer-1 switch, if a system needs to be moved from VLAN1 to VLAN2, there is no need to move systems around; you simply need to configure the port that the system is connected to from one VLAN to the other on the switch.

Know that a multilayer switch, such as a layer-2 and layer-3 switch, is a switch that provides the functionality **of a switch (layer-2) and a router (layer-3). These are popular devices today rather than buying both a switch and a router.**

Now that you have an understanding of some of the more popular network components, let's work through an exercise and think about how these devices are used.

Be sure to check out the Cisco switch exercises in LabBook.pdf on the CD-ROM. Exercises 3-3, 3-4, and 3-5 summarize the different types of devices and also walk you through the configuration of a Cisco switch.

Please check out the Exercise 3-3 CertCam training video on the CD-ROM.

Switch Features

Most enterprise-capable switches have a number of features that make the switch attractive for large organizations. The following is a listing of popular features incorporated into big-name switches such as those from Cisco and Juniper Networks.

Spanning Tree Protocol (STP)   The *Spanning Tree Protocol (STP)* runs at layer 2 and is designed to prevent loops on a network that could occur if you connect a number of switches together. For example, a loop is created if you connect Switch1 to Switch2 and then turn around and connect Switch2 back to Switch1 using a different cable and ports on the switches.

Having a loop on the network could cause the network to go down and creates instability in the switches. To prevent this, STP was designed. STP is a protocol that looks at all of the ports used to create a loop and then places one of those ports in a blocking state so that no data traffic can pass through the port. Once the port is in a blocking state, the loop is broken and the network becomes more stable.

The fact that the port is in a blocking state instead of being disabled means that if one of the other links go down, then the port is transitioned into a forwarding state automatically. When a port is in a forwarding state, it is allowed to send and receive data on the port.

Trunking   *Trunking* is a feature on Cisco switches that allows you to connect the switches together and then assign one of the ports as a trunk port. The trunk port is the port that is used to carry VLAN traffic to the other switch. VLANs are allowed to contain ports as members that are from multiple switches. If data is destined for all systems in the VLAN, the VLAN identification information is added to the data packet and then the switch sends the packet out the trunk port. When another switch receives the packet, it checks the VLAN identification information and then sends the data to all of its ports that are a member of that particular VLAN.

ISL and 802.1Q   When a switch assigns the VLAN identification information to a packet, this is known as *tagging*. Two popular protocols for tagging are the *Inter-Switch Link (ISL)* and the IEEE 802.1Q protocol.

ISL is the Cisco proprietary protocol for tagging packets and associating them with a particular VLAN on older switches, while 802.1Q is the IEEE standard for VLAN trunking. Newer Cisco and Juniper Networks switches use 802.1Q as the tagging method.

Port Mirroring *Port mirroring,* also known as port monitoring, is a feature that allows the switch to send a copy of data that reaches certain ports to the mirrored, or monitored, port. Port monitoring allows an administrator to plug his/her workstation into the port that the copy of the data is being sent to, and monitor the network traffic.

Port mirroring is an important feature of a switch because by default the switch filters traffic by only sending the data to the port that the destination system resides on. The switch's filtering feature will prevent the monitoring of traffic, and as a result the administrator will have to enable port mirroring (monitoring) and specify the port that receives the copy of data.

Port Authentication *Port authentication* is another important feature of the switch that allows the administrator to associate the MAC address of the system that will connect to the port. The administrator can also specify that if a system with a different MAC address connects to the port, the port is to be automatically disabled.

Port authentication will help increase the security of the network by allowing only authorized systems to connect to the network—a critical feature of any switch!

Content Switch A *content switch* is a special switch that is designed for optimizing data delivery to clients by incorporating features to improve performance such as data caching or load balancing features on the switch. Here is an example of how the switch can load-balance traffic: if you connect two servers into the switch, the switch creates a virtual server using a virtual IP, and when a request comes in to the virtual IP, the switch then forwards the request to one of the servers connected to the switch. The result is that the load is balanced across both servers and performance is increased.

CERTIFICATION OBJECTIVE 3.04

Routers and Brouters

One of the most popular network devices along with a switch is a network router. A *router* is responsible for sending data from one network to another and is a layer-3 device. This section will introduce you to routers and brouters.

Routers

Routers are layer-3 devices and are responsible for routing, or sending data from one network to another. A router will have multiple network interfaces, as shown in Figure 3-24, with each network connecting to a network or a WAN environment. Routers are typically used to connect the LAN to a WAN environment by having a network interface and a WAN interface connecting to each type of network. The router then passes data from one interface to the other.

In order for data to leave the network, the systems must use routable protocols, such as IPX/SPX, TCP/IP, or AppleTalk.

Routers work with layer-3 addresses, which are logical addresses assigned to the systems that are used to determine how to reach the destination network. Routers use a routing table stored in memory on the router to determine how to reach a system on a destination network. Figure 3-25 shows three networks connected by routers. In the figure, notice that if a system on Network A wants to send data to a system on Network B, it must leave Network A by means of Router 1 and then Router 1 will send the data to Router 2. It is the responsibility of Router 2 to send the data to the destination computer.

Routers are a great way to filter network traffic as well, because they act as a broadcast domain. Traffic will not cross the router unless it is actually destined for a system on the remote network. Most router administrators do not allow broadcasts to pass through the router.

For more information on how routers work and how to manage them, be sure to check out Chapter 5.

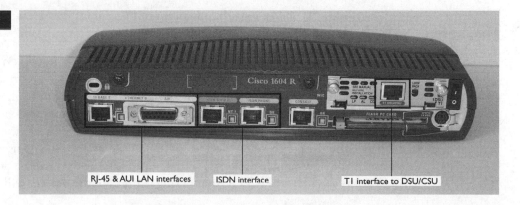

FIGURE 3-24

A Cisco 1604 router with LAN and WAN interfaces

RJ-45 & AUI LAN interfaces   ISDN interface   T1 interface to DSU/CSU

FIGURE 3-25 Routers connecting LANs to a WAN

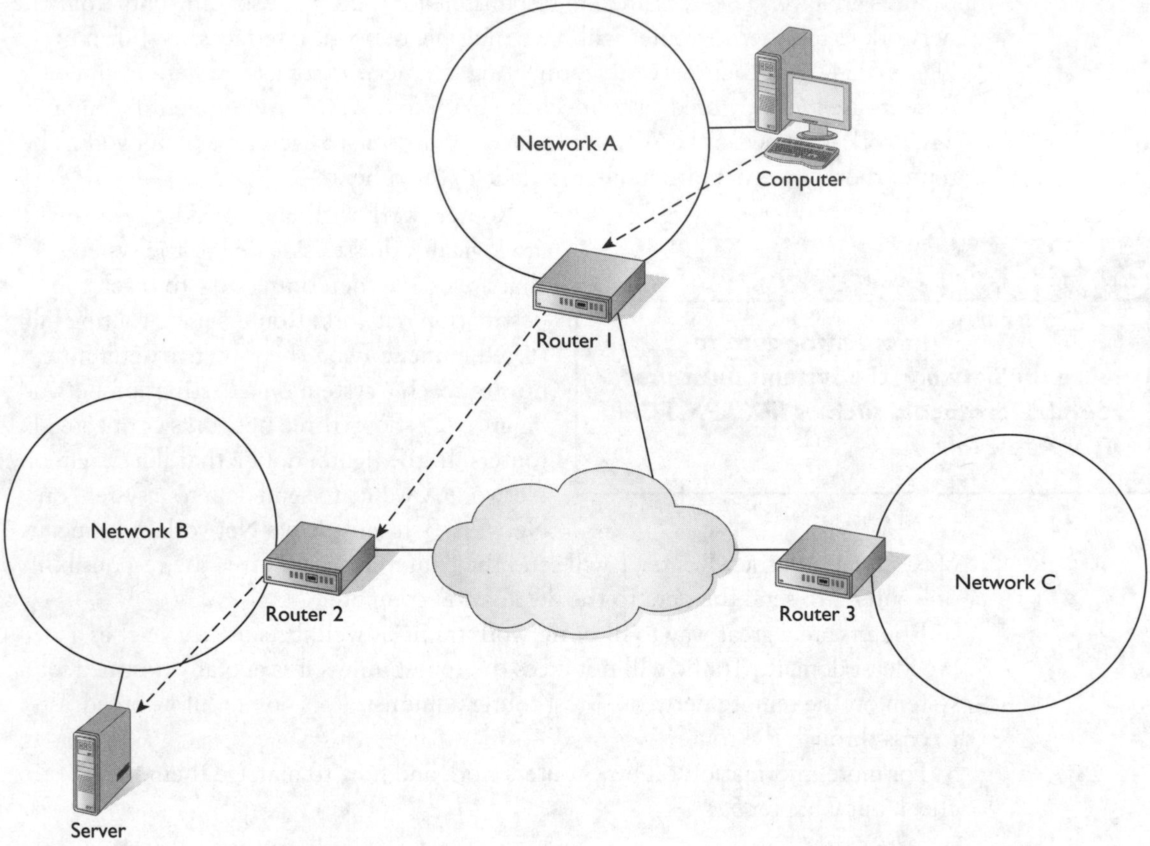

Brouters

A number of network environments use multiple network protocols on the network to support different network applications or services. If you need to route data for one protocol but need the bridging functionality for another protocol, instead of buying both a bridge and a router, you can purchase a brouter. A *brouter* is the combination of a bridge and a router, and it makes the decision whether it needs to bridge the data or route the data according to the protocol being used. If the protocol is a nonroutable protocol such as NetBEUI, the data will be bridged. If the protocol is TCP/IP or IPX/SPX, the routing features of the brouter will be used.

Gateways and Security Devices

Two other types of devices that are found in networking environments are gateways and firewalls. This section discusses gateways and acts as an introduction to security devices such as firewalls and intrusion detection systems. For a more detailed discussion, see Chapter 12.

Gateways

A gateway is responsible for translating information from one format to another and can run at any layer of the OSI model, depending on what information the gateway translates. A typical use of a gateway is to ensure that systems in one environment can access information in another environment. For example, you want to make sure that your PC environment can access information on the company's mainframe. As shown in Figure 3-26, when the packet reaches the gateway, the gateway strips the packet down and repackages it so that it is understood on the other side of the gateway.

In Figure 3-26, notice that the information sent by Workstation 1 has been reformatted after reaching the gateway. Gateways do this by stripping the packet down to just the data and then rebuilding the packet so that it is understood at the destination.

FIGURE 3-26   A gateway translates data from one format to another.

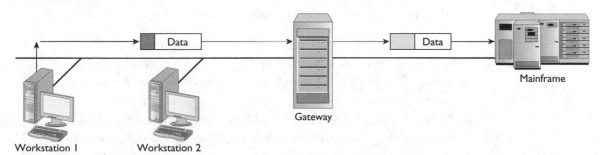

It is also important to note that when you configure TCP/IP and you configure the "default gateway" setting, you are pointing to the address of the router on the network. It really has nothing to do with an actual "gateway" device.

Firewalls

Firewalls are a networking component responsible for protecting the network from outside intruders. The firewall is designed to block specific types of traffic while allowing certain information to pass through. For example, I have a firewall that blocks any data that tries to reach my network from the Internet unless it is HTTP traffic. The reason I have allowed HTTP traffic through the firewall is that I would like my customers to be able to view my web site. The firewall administrator selectively chooses which traffic can and cannot pass through the firewall.

For more information on firewalls, refer to Chapter 12.

on the job

The home router you purchase for home or a small office has firewall features built in. I would highly recommend one to protect your systems from the Internet. To make sure that your computer is not connected directly into the Internet, put one of these devices between you and the outside world!

Intrusion Detection Systems

An *intrusion detection system (IDS)* is a security device that monitors system or network activity and then notifies the administrator of any suspicious activity. Intrusion detection systems are important devices that will complement other security devices such as firewalls. The IDS is an important device because it will notify you not only of suspicious activity against the firewall, but also of suspicious activity inside the network.

There are two types of intrusion detection systems:

- **Host based** Host-based intrusion detection systems monitor the local system for suspicious activity. A host-based IDS is typically a piece of software installed on the system and can only monitor activity on the system the IDS was installed on.

- **Network based** A network-based IDS monitors network traffic for suspicious behavior. A network-based IDS has the capability of monitoring the entire network and comparing that traffic to known malicious traffic patterns. When a match is found an alert can be triggered. Network-based IDSs can be software loaded on a system that monitors network traffic or can be a hardware device.

Intrusion detection systems can be either active or passive. An *active* IDS will monitor activity, log any suspicious activity, and then take some form of corrective action. For example, if a system is doing a port scan on the network, the IDS may log the activity but also disconnect the system creating the suspicious action from the network.

A *passive* intrusion detection system does not take any corrective action when suspicious activity has been identified. The passive IDS will simply identify the activity and then log to file any information needed during an investigation. The passive IDS does not take any corrective action.

For more information on intrusion detection systems, see Chapter 12.

CERTIFICATION OBJECTIVE 3.06

Other Networking Devices

There are a few additional devices that you should be familiar with for the Network+ exam. These are devices that will connect you to a wireless network or a WAN environment. These devices are only quickly mentioned here because they appear again in the chapters on WAN and remote connectivity.

Wireless Access Points

Wireless access points (WAPs) are network devices that can be connected to the wired network to allow a wireless client to pass through to get access to the wired network and its resources. A wireless access point also is known as a cell, which is a device that transmits and receives radio frequencies between the PCs and network devices with wireless transmitters connected to them. The wireless access point is connected to a physical cable, which connects the WAP device to the rest of the network. Figure 3-27 shows an example of a Linksys home router that is a wireless access point as well. Notice the wireless antennas attached to the access point.

FIGURE 3-27

A home router
being used as a
wireless access
point

The typical home router is a multifunctional device; it acts as a wireless access point, firewall, switch, and router, all wrapped up in one device.

Modems

There are other forms of networking devices beyond the typical network card; for instance, modems can be used to communicate with other systems across the public switched telephone network (PSTN). They are used to convert digital data from the PC to analog transmission so that the information can be transmitted over the analog phone lines. The modem on the receiving end is designed to convert the analog signal to a digital format readable by the system. For more information on modems, see Chapter 8.

CSU/DSU

A channel service unit/data service unit (CSU/DSU) is either one device or a pair of devices that allows an organization to get a very-high-speed WAN connection from the telephone company, such as a T1 or T3 link. The CSU is used at the business end to get the connection to the WAN, and the DSU may be used at the provider's end to allow the CSU to connect. For more information on WAN technologies and CSU/DSUs, see Chapter 9.

ISDN

The Integrated Services Digital Network (ISDN) is a communication standard for sending voice and data over normal telephone lines or digital telephone lines. In order to connect to the ISDN lines, a system will need an ISDN modem, which doesn't really act like a modem because, whereas a modem converts digital data to analog, the ISDN modem carries digital data from one digital system to another, and so it really is acting as a terminal adapter connecting you to the ISDN lines.

There are two popular types of ISDN connections:

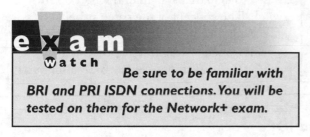

Be sure to be familiar with BRI and PRI ISDN connections. You will be tested on them for the Network+ exam.

- **Basic rate interface (BRI)** This is a 128 Kbps connection that is made up of two 64 Kbps channels (known as B-channels) and one 16 Kbps control channel (known as a D-channel).
- **Primary rate interface (PRI)** This is a 1.55 Mbps connection that is made up of twenty-three 64 Kbps channels (B-channels) and one 64 Kbps D-channel for signaling and control information.

Wiring Distribution

This chapter wouldn't be complete without a discussion of how the cabling for the network is configured. In Chapter 1 you learned about the different types of cables, and this section will identify related terms you need to know for the exam that surround cabling as a topic.

Plenum vs. Nonplenum

For the Network+ exam you need to be familiar with the term plenum. *Plenum* refers to the space between the ceiling tiles and the floor located above them. This space is typically used to route power and network cables. It is important to use plenum-grade cables in this space because if there is a fire and you are not using plenum-grade cables, a toxin is given off that could be carried throughout the building, causing harm to individuals. Plenum-grade cabling uses a low-toxicity material for the jacket of the cable in case of fire.

Patch Panel

Most companies have network jacks located in the walls that allow systems to connect to the network. These jacks have cables connected to them that are then routed a long distance to a patch panel in a server room.

The patch panel then has a *patch cable* that connects to the front of the patch panel and a port on a switch. When a computer connects to the network jack in the wall, the patch cable is used to map that system to the port on the switch. The concept of the patch panel allows ease of administration and flexibility in moving systems from one switch to another without visiting the workstation. Figure 3-28 displays a patch panel.

Cross Connects, MDF, and IDF

When wiring the network you will typically have the outside line coming into the building connect to a panel; this panel is known as the *main distribution frame*, or *MDF*. From the MDF you would typically connect to other panels, known as *intermediate distribution frames (IDFs)*, which is what the workstations connect to. This hierarchy of MDF and IDF panels allows greater flexibility when rearranging the network at a later time.

FIGURE 3-28

A typical patch panel

A typical example of how the MDF and IDFs are used is that the MDF would connect to the cable coming from outside the building. Then there may be a separate IDF panel representing each floor in the building, with the workstations on a particular floor connecting to the panel associated with that floor.

The patch cable that connects to the patch panel is called a horizontal cross-connect (HCC) cable.	*The cable that connects the MDF to the IDFs is called the vertical cross-connect (VCC) cable.*

CERTIFICATION SUMMARY

In this chapter, you learned about some of the popular networking devices that are used on networks to allow systems to communicate on the network. The first of those devices is the network card. The network card is responsible for converting parallel data that is transmitted through the computer's bus to a serial bit stream to be sent on the wire. The network card uses a transceiver. Transceivers constitute that portion of the network interface that actually transmits and receives electrical signals across the transmission media and connects to the media. There are two types of transceivers: built in and external. The NIC usually has a built-in transceiver for twisted-pair and thinnet, but thicknet typically uses an external transceiver.

The network card uses the MAC address burned into the card by the manufacturer as an identifier to determine where the packet is destined and where it came from. The system does this by adding the source MAC address and destination MAC address to the packet, which is read by networking devices to determine where the packet needs to go.

There are a few popular layer-1 devices, such as hubs, repeaters, and MAUs. Remember that these devices are considered layer 1 because they work with the electrical signals. Any data that reaches a layer-1 device will be sent to all ports on the device. A repeater is responsible for regenerating the electrical signal so that the signal may travel a greater distance. A MAU is used in a Token Ring environment and regenerates the signal with each system connected to the MAU. When connecting MAUs, you will need to ring out of one MAU and ring in to the second

MAU; you will then ring out of the second MAU and ring in to the third MAU. Remember to ring out of the last one and ring in to the first MAU.

Bridges and switches are examples of layer-2 devices. A bridge is responsible for filtering network traffic by sending the data only to the network segment where the destination system resides. The bridge builds a bridging table, which has a list of destinations. A switch has replaced the network hub nowadays, and it filters traffic by sending data only to the port on the switch where the destination system is connected. You can increase network performance dramatically by changing your network hubs to switches. A number of switches support VLAN capabilities. A VLAN is used to create virtual networks out of ports on one or more switches. When data is broadcast on the VLAN, it is sent only to members of the VLAN, not the entire switch. Systems can communicate only with other systems on their VLAN and cannot communicate with systems on other VLANs without the use of router.

Some other popular networking components are routers, gateways, and firewalls. Routers are layer-3 devices that are responsible for sending data from one network to another. A gateway is responsible for converting data from one format to another so that the data can be understood on both sides of the gateway. A firewall is a device that stops traffic from passing through it, protecting private network resources.

TWO-MINUTE DRILL

Network Interface Cards

❑ Network interface cards (NICs) function by converting parallel data from the computer to a serial bit stream sent on the network.

❑ The computer must have a software driver installed to enable it to interact with the NIC, just as it must for any other peripheral device.

❑ The media access control (MAC) address, or hardware address, is a 12-digit number that is used to determine where the data is being sent and where it is coming from. The MAC address also is known as a layer-2 address and looks like 00-0D-60-48-53-9E.

❑ A computer bus is the term used for the speed and type of interface the computer uses with various types of interface cards and equipment. Popular bus architectures are ISA, PCI, and PCMCIA for laptops. When you install a network card, you will need to be familiar with what bus slot you will place the card into.

❑ The network card uses a transceiver to pick up the electrical signals and send electrical signals on the wire. There are two types of transceivers: built in and external. The transceivers for twisted-pair and thinnet usually are built into the network card, whereas the transceiver for thicknet is usually an external one.

❑ When you are configuring the network card, you may need to specify the transfer rate so that it supports the device you are connecting to. You also may need to specify the transceiver you intend to use, the transmission type, and whether to use half duplex or full duplex.

❑ Simplex transmissions allow data to be sent in only one direction. Half duplex allows data to be sent and received, but not at the same time. Full duplex allows data to be sent and received at the same time.

Hubs, MAUs, and Repeaters

❑ Hubs are the central location to which all cabling must connect in most topologies.

❑ When exam time comes, remember the difference between an active hub and a passive hub. An active hub contains electronic components to boost the signal. A passive hub does not.

❏ A multistation access unit (MAU) is a device to which multiple workstations are connected in order to communicate on a Token Ring network.

❏ Because the signal gets weaker over distance, repeaters are used to regenerate the signal so that it can continue in its travels.

❏ Hubs, MAUs, and repeaters are layer-1 devices.

Bridges and Switches

❏ A bridge is used to create multiple segments on the network. The bridge will forward network traffic only to the destination segment and not to all segments, thus acting as a filtering device to improve network performance.

❏ A switch filters network traffic by sending data only to the port on the switch where the destination system resides.

❏ Switches are replacing hubs, and network administrators who wish to improve network performance should replace their hubs with switches.

❏ Some switches support virtual LANs (VLANs). A VLAN is a group of ports on the switch that make up their own logical network. Systems on a particular VLAN can communicate only with other systems on the same VLAN unless a router is used. The VLAN also acts as a broadcast domain, because broadcast traffic is sent only to ports in the VLAN where the sender of the broadcast traffic exists.

❏ Bridges and switches are layer-2 devices.

Routers and Brouters

❏ A router is a layer-3 device that sends data from one network to another using a layer-3 address such as an IP address.

❏ Routers are used by routable protocols such as IPX/SPX, TCP/IP, and AppleTalk.

❏ A brouter is a device that combines a bridge and a router. The brouter will act as a router for routable protocols but will act as a bridge for nonroutable protocols such as NetBEUI.

Gateways and Security Devices

❑ A gateway is a device that is used to join dissimilar environments together.

❑ The gateway converts data from one side of the gateway to a format that the other side of the gateway will understand.

❑ A firewall is a device that blocks all network traffic from passing through the firewall in order to protect private network resources. The firewall may be configured to allow selected traffic to pass through. For example, most companies have a web server that publishes their web site, so they will need to allow HTTP traffic to pass through the firewall.

Other Networking Devices

❑ Modems are used as remote connectivity devices to connect systems across telephone wires. The modem converts digital signals to analog on the sending computer and converts analog signals to digital on the receiving computer.

❑ CSU/DSU is a network device that allows an organization to connect to a high-speed link such as a T1 or T3.

❑ ISDN is a digital service that is used to connect systems over a digital phone line and to receive transmission rates faster than conventional modems.

SELF TEST

The following questions will help you measure your understanding of the material presented in this chapter. Read all of the choices carefully, because there might be more than one correct answer. Choose all correct answers for each question.

Network Interface Cards

1. What does a network interface card add to a computer's functionality?
   A. It provides faster communication between the CPU and the hard disk.
   B. It provides the capability to communicate across a phone line to another computer.
   C. It provides the capability to communicate with other computers across a network medium.
   D. It provides the capability to save more information on a diskette than normal.

2. In order for a NIC to interact with the computer, what needs to be installed?
   A. The appropriate documentation for the user to take advantage of the features of the interface card
   B. A driver, which is software that enables the NIC and the computer to communicate with each other
   C. A bus, which enables the interface card to communicate through the various topologies of the Internet
   D. Nothing

3. If a card has the capability to connect to more than one kind of medium, you might have to set which of the following in order to ensure connectivity?
   A. IRQ setting
   B. Link light on/off setting
   C. Transceiver-type setting
   D. PCI setting

4. When troubleshooting to find out why a network card will not connect to the network, which of the following would you check first?
   A. Driver
   B. Link light
   C. Transceiver-type setting
   D. Switch

5. Which of the following is an example of a layer-2 address?

    A. 192.168.2.5

    B. COMPUTER100

    C. Computer100.glensworld.loc

    D. 00-0D-60-48-53-9E

6. What is an AUI connector?

    A. A 9-pin DB male connector

    B. A 15-pin D female connector

    C. A 25-pin D female connector

    D. Same as an RJ-45 connector

Hubs, MAUs, and Repeaters

7. Which of the following types of hubs does not regenerate the signal and therefore is not a repeater?

    A. Active

    B. Hybrid

    C. Passive

    D. Switching hub

8. Which network component is used to extend the distance the signal can travel by regenerating the signal?

    A. Passive hub

    B. Switch

    C. Router

    D. Repeater

9. Which type of hub enables more than one type of cable or medium to connect to it?

    A. Passive

    B. Active

    C. Hybrid

    D. Multistation access unit

10. Which network device is used to connect systems together in a Token Ring environment?

    A. Multisensing action unit

    B. Multistation access unit

    C. Multisplit add transmission unit

    D. Multistation action unit

11. When data is sent to a system on a hub, the data is sent to which port(s) on the hub?
- A. The port of the destination system
- B. All ports on the immediate hub but not any linked hubs
- C. All ports on the immediate hub and any linked hubs
- D. All ports on only the linked hub

Bridges and Switches

12. Which type of network component enables each device to have the full bandwidth of the medium when transmitting?
- A. Hub
- B. Repeater
- C. Switch
- D. Transceiver

13. When data is sent to a system on a switch, the data is sent to what port(s)?
- A. The port of the destination system
- B. All ports on the immediate hub, but not the any uplinked hubs
- C. All ports on the immediate hub and any uplinked hubs
- D. All ports on the uplinked hub

14. Which layer of the OSI model does a bridge run at?
- A. Layer 4
- B. Layer 1
- C. Layer 3
- D. Layer 2

15. Which networking feature allows you to group ports on a switch to create a broadcast domain?
- A. WANs
- B. VLANs
- C. MANs
- D. CANs

Routers and Brouters

16. Which layer of the OSI model does a router run at?

A. Layer 4

B. Layer 1

C. Layer 3

D. Layer 2

17. Which networking device routes data used by a routable protocol but bridges data for nonroutable protocols?

A. Router

B. Bridge

C. Gateway

D. Brouter

18. Which of the following are nonroutable protocols?

A. NetBEUI

B. IPX

C. TCP/IP

D. AppleTalk

Gateways and Security Devices

19. Which of the following layers does a gateway run at (select the best answer)?

A. Layer 4

B. Layer 1

C. Layer 5

D. All layers

20. Which type of device is responsible for connecting dissimilar networking environments together?

A. Router

B. Bridge

C. Gateway

D. Switch

21. Which networking device is used to block unauthorized traffic from entering the network?
A. Bridge
B. Gateway
C. Switch
D. Firewall

Other Networking Devices

22. Which of the following devices is used to connect to digital phone lines?
A. ISDN modem
B. CSU/DSU
C. Modem
D. NIC

23. Which of the following devices is used to prepare the digital data for transmission over the PSTN?
A. ISDN modem
B. CSU/DSU
C. Modem
D. NIC

24. How many B-channels are in a BRI ISDN connection?
A. 1
B. 2
C. 3
D. 4

SELF TEST ANSWERS

Network Interface Cards

1. ☑ **C.** A network card provides the capability to communicate with other computers across a network medium such as a CAT 5 cable. The network card connects to the cable using a transceiver which is responsible for sending and receiving the electrical signals on the wire. Network interface cards (NICs) are known by a variety of names, including network adapters, network cards, network adapter boards, and media access cards. Regardless of the name, they function by enabling computers to communicate across a network. NICs are often defined by the following criteria: 1) The type of data link protocol they support, such as an Ethernet adapter or a Token Ring adapter. 2) The type of medium to which they connect, such as TP or thinnet. 3) The data bus for which they were designed, such as ISA, PCI, or USB.

☒ **A** is incorrect because a NIC does not help increase the bus speed between the CPU and the hard drive; that would require a different, faster system bus that is based on the system clock, which controls the bus speed. **B** is incorrect because a NIC does not provide communications on a phone line—a modem does. **D** is incorrect since the NIC has no bearing or connection to the diskette drive.

2. ☑ **B.** The computer must have a software driver installed to enable the operating system to interact with the NIC, just as it must for any other peripheral device. These drivers enable the operating system and higher-level applications to control the functions of the adapter. The NICs that exist in the various workstations on a network communicate with each other using their own unique addresses. The hardware address, or MAC address as it is commonly called, is unique on each network card on a network.

☒ **A** is incorrect because the documentation for a device or add-in card is for user reference only and has no bearing on the device's functionality. **C** is incorrect because all PCs must already have a bus for all internal components of the PC to communicate with one another. **D** is incorrect because the operating system does need to have instructions to communicate with a device, which requires a driver.

3. ☑ **C.** The transceiver-type setting is required for network adapters that are capable of attaching to more than one media type. Typical cards of this nature include Ethernet cards that have both twisted-pair and coaxial connectors. This is one of the more common oversights in configuring a NIC and renders the card nonfunctional if configured for the wrong media connection. To alleviate this problem, some cards of this type have an auto setting that causes the card to search for the transceiver that has media connected to it. From a troubleshooting point of view, you should be prepared for the auto setting not to be working, and you may need to manually specify the transceiver type.

☒ **A** is incorrect because the IRQ setting allows you to specify that the IRQ is used to get the processor's attention, allowing the device to get some processing time. **B** and **D** are incorrect because the link light on/off setting and the PCI setting do not exist.

4. ☑ **B.** When troubleshooting any kind of problem, you want to check the easy stuff first. When it comes to network cards, the first thing you want to check is the link light on the back of the computer to verify that there is an actual connection to the network.

☒ **A, C,** and **D** are incorrect. Although the driver and switch are definitely things you should verify, they would not be at the top of my list. After verifying that there is a link, I would check the settings on the network card, such as the transceiver type; if that did not work, I would try replacing the driver with a newer version.

5. ☑ **D.** A layer-2 address is a MAC address and looks like 00-0D-60-48-53-9E.

☒ **A, B,** and **C** are incorrect. 192.168.2.5 is an example of an IP address, which is a layer-3 address. COMPUTER100 is an example of a NetBIOS name, and computer100.glensworld.loc is an example of a fully qualified domain name.

6. ☑ **B.** An AUI connector is a 15-pin D female connector. With an external transceiver, the actual media connection is made external to the NIC using a small device that attaches via an extension cable. These types of connections use an adapter unit interface (AUI) connector, also called a Digital-Intel-Xerox (DIX) connector, on the back of the NIC. The AUI connector is a female 15-pin D-connector that looks very much like a joystick port.

☒ **A** is incorrect because a 9-pin male connector is found on the back of PCs and is the serial port. **C** is incorrect because a 25-pin connector is found on the back of a PC as the printer connection. **D** is incorrect because the RJ-45 is used with twisted-pair cable networks.

Hubs, MAUs and Repeaters

7. ☑ **C.** The function of a passive hub is simply to receive data from one port of the hub and send it out to the other ports. For example, an eight-port hub receives data from port 3 and then resends that data to ports 1, 2, 4, 5, 6, 7, and 8. It is as simple as that. A passive hub contains no power source or electrical components. There is no signal processing. It simply attaches the ports internally and enables communication to flow through the network.

☒ **A** is incorrect because the active hub does regenerate the signal, since it is powered. **B** is incorrect because, even though the hybrid hub is powered, the only difference between it and a regular hub is that the hybrid hub has connectors for different media types. **D** is incorrect because a switch is always powered and therefore will regenerate the data signals.

8. ☑ **D.** Repeaters can be used to extend the length of the maximum distance of the different types of cables, because when a signal reaches a repeater, the repeater regenerates the signal.

☒ **A** is incorrect because a passive hub does not regenerate signals, given that it is not powered. **B** is incorrect because a NIC generates a signal but does not regenerate a signal. **C** is incorrect because the IRQ is used to get the CPU's attention by interrupting it to perform processing.

9. ☑ **C.** A hybrid hub is one that can use many types of cables. A popular example of a hybrid hub is a hub that has connectors for thinnet and twisted-pair cabling.

☒ **A** and **B** are incorrect because active and passive hubs deal with the question of whether they will regenerate the signal or not; this has nothing to do with the connector types on the hub. **D** is incorrect because a MAU is for Token Ring networks and does not support multiple connector types.

10. ☑ **B.** A multistation access unit (MAU) is a hub-type device in Token Ring environments. Remember that the MAUs are connected together by a ring-in/ring-out feature.

☒ **A, C,** and **D** are incorrect because they are terms that were made up to trick you!

11. ☑ **C.** Remember that with hubs, when a data signal reaches the hub, the hub sends the signal throughout the entire network bus, which includes ports on that hub and any linked hubs. Hubs perform no filtering of traffic, which is what a switch offers!

☒ **A, B,** and **D** are incorrect because the signal will be sent to all ports on all linked hubs.

Bridges and Switches

12. ☑ **C.** Switching is a fairly involved process that allows the device to have the full bandwidth when transmitting.

☒ **A** is incorrect because the bandwidth is divided among all used ports on a hub. **B** is incorrect because a repeater does not split bandwidth, inasmuch as it is used only to receive signals on one cable and regenerate the signal on another cable. **D** is incorrect because a transceiver is the connection point on a NIC and does not allow for multiple users to send data through the transceiver. The bandwidth on the transceiver is dedicated to the PC in which the NIC is installed.

13. ☑ **A.** A switch is different from a hub in the sense that with a switch the data is sent only to the port that hosts the destination system. This minimizes network traffic and increases throughput on the network.

☒ **B, C,** and **D** are incorrect because a switch will forward the signal only to the port on which the destination system resides.

14. ☑ **D.** Because a bridge works with MAC addresses, it is considered a layer-2 device.

☒ **A, B,** and **C** are incorrect. A hub and a repeater are examples of layer-1 devices; a router is an example of a layer-3 device.

15. ☑ **B.** A VLAN is a way to group ports on a switch so that each grouping is its own virtual network. Systems can communicate only with other systems on their own VLAN, which includes broadcast traffic. If a system sends broadcast traffic on the wire, it will be sent only to other ports on the same VLAN.
☒ **A, C,** and **D** are incorrect. WANs, MANs, and CANs are terms used for types of networks; they have nothing to do with features of a switch.

Routers and Brouters

16. ☑ **C.** A router runs at layer 3 of the OSI model.
☒ **A, B,** and **D** are incorrect. An example of a layer-1 device would be a hub or repeater, and an example of a layer-2 device would be a bridge or a switch. A gateway could be a layer-4 device.

17. ☑ **D.** A brouter will route information using a routable protocol and will bridge information being sent using a nonroutable protocol.
☒ **A, B,** and **C** are incorrect. A router simply routes or sends data from one network to another, whereas a bridge filters data within the network by sending data to the appropriate network segment within a network. A gateway is a device used to translate data from one format to another.

18. ☑ **A.** NetBEUI is an example of a nonroutable protocol.
☒ **B, C,** and **D** are incorrect because they are routable protocols.

Gateways and Security Devices

19. ☑ **D.** A gateway can run at any layer of the OSI model, such as layer 4, 5, 6, or 7, depending on what it is translating. It is very popular in the networking world that layers 4, 5, 6, and 7 are used, but be aware that the gateway could run at any layer.
☒ **A, C,** and **B** are incorrect because a gateway can run at any layer.

20. ☑ **C.** A gateway is responsible for converting data from one format to another to allow dissimilar networking environments to communicate.
☒ **A, B,** and **D** are incorrect. A router sends or routes information from one network to another without reformatting. A bridge and a switch are filtering devices that run at layer 2.

21. ☑ **D.** A firewall is used to block unauthorized traffic from entering the network.
☒ **A, B,** and **C** are incorrect because these devices do not block traffic. A bridge and a switch are filtering devices that run at layer 2, whereas a gateway translates data.

Other Networking Devices

22. ☑ **A.** An ISDN modem is used for digital communication over digital or conventional phone lines.

    ☒ **B, C,** and **D** are incorrect. A CSU/DSU is used to connect to a high-speed WAN link, such as a T1 or T3 link. A modem is used to connect systems over an analog link, and a network card is used to connect a system to the network over network media.

23. ☑ **C.** A modem is responsible for converting digital data to analog and analog data to digital so that digital data can travel over analog lines.

    ☒ **A, B,** and **D** are incorrect. An ISDN modem is used for digital communication over digital or conventional phone lines. A CSU/DSU is used to connect to a high-speed WAN link, such as a T1 or T3 link. A network card is used to connect to another system over network media.

24. ☑ **B.** There are two B-channels in a BRI connection. Each channel is 64 Kbps, so a BRI connection is 128 Kbps.

    ☒ **A, C,** and **D** are incorrect because a BRI connection does not use 1, 3, or 4 B-channels.

4

TCP/IP
Fundamentals

The most popular protocol in use today is Transmission Control Protocol/Internet Protocol (TCP/IP). The Internet and most company intranets currently use TCP/IP because of its popularity, flexibility, compatibility, and capability to perform in both small and large network implementations. TCP/IP can connect a diverse range of hosts, from mainframes to palmtop computers. The popularity of this protocol makes it a likely culprit to appear many times throughout the Network+ exam. Although TCP/IP is the most commonly used protocol, it is not the easiest to configure or even to understand. This chapter gives you an in-depth understanding of TCP/IP, including the architecture, addressing issues, and configuration involved with its use. The Network+ exam will test your knowledge of the protocol, but most importantly, it will test your ability to configure the protocol on workstations. Real-world experience, in addition to this chapter on TCP/IP, will ensure that you can easily answer any TCP/IP-related questions presented to you on the exam.

CERTIFICATION OBJECTIVE 4.01

TCP/IP Protocol Suite

The Transmission Control Protocol/Internet Protocol (TCP/IP) is the protocol suite used by most, if not all, networking environments today. TCP/IP is used on small, medium, and large networks and has been adopted as the protocol of the Internet. TCP/IP is a protocol suite—meaning that there are multiple protocols within the TCP/IP protocol. You will be required to know a number of these protocols for the Network+ exam.

As you learn in this chapter, each protocol in the suite has a specific purpose and function. It is not important for the Network+ exam that you understand the evolution of TCP/IP, so we discuss here the details of the protocol on which you are likely to be tested. Be sure to spend your time on the TCP/IP chapters, because this knowledge will help you throughout your years as a networking professional.

The TCP/IP Model

Contained within the TCP/IP model is a four-layer model similar in concept to the seven-layer OSI model. The four layers of the TCP/IP model map out to the seven layers of the OSI, but you may find that one layer of the TCP/IP model combines multiple layers of the OSI model, as shown in Figure 4-1. There are several protocols that direct how computers connect and communicate using TCP/IP within the TCP/IP protocol suite, and each protocol runs on different layers of the Internet model.

Let's start at the top of this model, which is the application layer. The application layer is responsible for making the network request (sending computer) or servicing the request (receiving computer). For example, when a user submits a request from a web browser, the web browser is responsible for the submission of the request and is running at this layer. When that web request reaches the web server, the web server, running at the application layer, accepts that request. The following are popular application-layer protocols; for more information, see the section "Application-Layer Protocols" in this chapter:

- Hypertext Transfer Protocol (HTTP)
- Simple Mail Transfer Protocol (SMTP)
- Network News Transport Protocol (NNTP)
- File Transfer Protocol (FTP)

FIGURE 4-1	OSI Model	TCP/IP Internet Model

The TCP/IP Internet model versus the OSI model

OSI Model	TCP/IP Internet Model
Application	
Presentation	Application layer (SMTP, HTTP, FTP)
Session	
Transport	Transport layer (TCP, UDP)
Network	Internet layer (IP, ARP, ICMP)
Data Link	Network interface layer (Ethernet, Token Ring)
Physical	

Transport Layer

The next layer under the application layer is the transport layer. The transport layer is responsible for both connection-oriented communication (a session is established) and connectionless communication (a session is not established). When the request comes down from the higher (application) layer, a transport protocol is then chosen. The two transport protocols in TCP/IP are the Transmission Control Protocol (TCP) and the User Datagram Protocol (UDP).

Transmission Control Protocol   The Transmission Control Protocol (TCP) is responsible for providing connection-oriented communication and ensuring delivery of the data. TCP will make sure that the data reaches its destination by retransmitting any data that is lost or corrupt. TCP is used by applications that require a reliable transport, but this transport has more overhead than a connectionless protocol because of the construction of the session and monitoring and retransmission of any data across that session.

Another factor to remember about TCP is that the protocol requires that the recipient acknowledge the successful receipt of data. Of course, all the acknowledgments, known as ACKs, generate additional traffic on the network, which causes a reduction in the amount of data that can be passed within a given time frame. The extra overhead involved in the creation, monitoring, and ending of the TCP session is worth the certainty that TCP will ensure that the data will reach its destination.

User Datagram Protocol   The User Datagram Protocol (UDP) offers a connectionless datagram service that is an unreliable "best-effort" delivery. UDP does not guarantee the arrival of datagrams, nor does it promise that the delivered packets are in the correct sequence. Applications that don't require an acknowledgment of data receipt use UDP. Because of the lack of overhead involved in UDP conversations, it is more efficient than TCP.

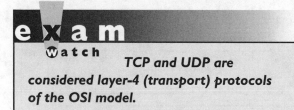

TCP and UDP are considered layer-4 (transport) protocols of the OSI model.

Internet Layer

After a transport protocol has been selected, which boils down to whether the communication should be connection-oriented or connectionless, the information is passed to the Internet layer to determine who is responsible for the delivery of the information. There are a few protocols that run at the Internet layer; IP, ICMP, and ARP are examples.

Internet Protocol The Internet Protocol (IP) provides packet delivery for protocols higher in the model. It is a connectionless delivery system that makes a "best-effort" attempt to deliver the packets to the correct destination. IP does not guarantee delivery of the packets—that is the responsibility of transport protocols; IP simply sends the data.

The IP protocol is also responsible for the logical addressing and routing of TCP/IP and therefore is considered a layer-3 protocol (of the OSI model). The IP protocol on the router is responsible for decrementing (usually by a value of 1) the TTL (time to live) of the packet to prevent it from running around in a "network loop." Windows operating systems have a default TTL of 128.

e x a m

w a t c h   *IP is a layer-3 protocol (of the OSI model) and is responsible for logical addressing and routing.*

Internet Control Message Protocol The Internet Control Message Protocol (ICMP) enables systems on a TCP/IP network to share status and error information. You can use the status information to detect network trouble. ICMP messages are encapsulated within IP datagrams so that they may be routed throughout a network. Two programs that use ICMP messages are Ping and Tracert.

You can use Ping to send ICMP echo requests to an IP address and wait for ICMP echo responses. Ping reports the time interval between sending the request and receiving the response. With Ping, you can determine whether a particular IP system on your network is functioning correctly. You can use many different options with the Ping utility.

e x a m

w a t c h   *ICMP is the protocol in the TCP/IP protocol suite that is responsible for error and status reporting. Programs such as Ping and Tracert use ICMP.*

Tracert traces the path taken to a particular host. This utility can be very useful in troubleshooting internetworks. Tracert sends ICMP echo requests to an IP address while it increments the TTL field in the IP header by a count of 1 after starting at 1 and then analyzing the ICMP errors that are returned. Each succeeding echo request should get one further into the network before the TTL field reaches 0 and an "ICMP time exceeded" error message is returned by the router attempting to forward it.

Also note that Internet Group Management Protocol (IGMP) is another Internet layer protocol and is used for multicast applications.

Address Resolution Protocol The Address Resolution Protocol (ARP) provides IP address–to–physical address resolution on a TCP/IP network. To accomplish this feat, ARP sends out a broadcast message with an ARP request packet that contains the IP address of the system it is trying to find. All systems on the local network see the message, and the system that owns the IP address for which ARP is looking replies by sending its physical address to the originating system in an ARP reply packet. The physical/IP address combo is then stored in the ARP cache of the originating system for future use.

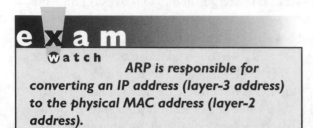

ARP is responsible for converting an IP address (layer-3 address) to the physical MAC address (layer-2 address).

All systems maintain ARP caches that include IP address–to–physical address mappings. The ARP cache is always checked for an IP address–to–physical address mapping before initiating a broadcast. You can learn more about the ARP utility and other related TCP/IP utilities in Chapter 6.

Application-Layer Protocols

Now that you have learned some of the core protocols such as TCP, UDP, and IP in the TCP/IP protocol suite, let's take a look at some of the application-level protocols that run at the application layer of the TCP/IP Internet model.

HTTP and HTTPS

The Hypertext Transfer Protocol (HTTP) is the protocol used on the Internet to allow clients to request web pages from web servers and to allow client interaction with those web servers. HTTP is a stateless protocol, meaning that the web servers are not aware of what a client has or has not requested and cannot track users who have requested specific content. This system does not allow for good interaction with the web server but does allow for retrieving the HTML pages stored on web sites. To aid in tracking client requests, we use cookies—small files stored on the client computer that allow the web server to store data on the client that the client will send back with each request to the server.

The Hypertext Transfer Protocol, Secure (HTTPS) allows you to connect to a web site and receive and send content in an encrypted format using the Secure Sockets Layer (SSL). HTTPS is most commonly used on e-commerce sites to allow you to send personal information without worrying that an Internet hacker is viewing this information, especially credit card numbers and other confidential data. You can determine when HTTPS is being used because the address of the web site starts with https:// and not http://, which marks the regular HTTP protocol. Another sign that HTTPS is in use: In Internet Explorer, a lock appears in the status bar of a page; the lock is either closed or locked (as shown in Figure 4-2).

Normally, HTTPS is not used for an entire e-commerce site, because the encryption and decryption processes slow the connection time, so only the part of the site that requests personal information uses HTTPS.

exam
ⓦatch

For the exam, know that a newer protocol to secure traffic is Transport Layer Security (TLS).

Network Time Protocol (NTP)

The Network Time Protocol (NTP) is used to synchronize the clocks of PCs on a network or the Internet. This is accomplished by configuring a server to be the time server, which then is the server from which all other PCs on the network synchronize their time.

FIGURE 4-2	
Identifying the use of secure traffic by the lock In Internet Explorer	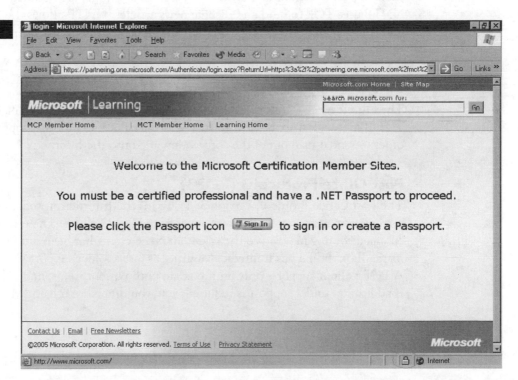

On earlier Windows networks, you can manage time synchronization by placing a command in a logon script to synchronize the time on the client with the time server. Use the following command:

```
NET TIME \\computername /SET
```

Newer Microsoft networks, such as Active Directory networks, have the PDC emulator provide the time to all servers and clients automatically, so there is no need to create a logon script for the clients to synchronize the time with the time server. PDC emulators can also retrieve their time from Internet NTP servers.

Time servers on the Internet allow you to synchronize your PC's clock with the exact time kept by atomic clocks. The time synchronization takes into account time zone settings of your operating system and allows you to synchronize with a time server even if it is not set for your local time zone.

Network News Transfer Protocol (NNTP)

News clients use the Network News Transfer Protocol (NNTP) to send and retrieve news articles to a newsgroup. Newsgroups are typically used as a place for users to post questions and answers on a particular topic area (called a newsgroup). NNTP uses TCP to send and receive news articles. NNTP allows the submission and retrieval of only the news articles that have not previously been sent or retrieved.

Simple Mail Transfer Protocol (SMTP)

The Simple Mail Transfer Protocol (SMTP) is used to send or route mail over a TCP/IP network such as the Internet. Most e-mail server products support SMTP in order to send e-mail out of the corporation and onto the Internet.

Post Office Protocol 3 (POP3)

The Post Office Protocol, version 3 (POP3) is the Internet protocol used to retrieve e-mail from a mail server down to the POP3 client. The e-mail is "popped" or downloaded to the client after the client has been authenticated to its mailbox. POP3 has limited capabilities as far as folder support is concerned. A POP3 client supports only an inbox, an outbox, sent items, and deleted items. If additional folder support is required, you would need to use an IMAP4 client.

Internet Message Access Protocol 4 (IMAP4)

The Internet Message Access Protocol, version 4 (IMAP4) is another protocol similar to POP3 that allows clients to retrieve messages from a mail server. IMAP4 allows additional folders other than the four basic ones provided with POP3. For example, you can use an IMAP4 client to connect to public folders stored on an Exchange Server.

POP3 and IMAP4 are	whereas SMTP is the Internet protocol for
the Internet protocols for reading e-mail,	sending e-mail.

Simple Network Management Protocol (SNMP)

The Simple Network Management Protocol (SNMP) is an Internet standard that provides a simple method for remotely managing virtually any network device that supports SNMP. A network device can be a network card in a server; a program or service running on a server; or a network device such as a hub, switch, or router.

The SNMP standard defines a two-tiered approach to network device management: a central management system and the management information base (MIB) located on the managed device. The management system can monitor one or many MIBs, allowing for centralized management of a network. From a management system, you can see valuable performance and network device operation statistics, enabling you to diagnose network health without leaving your office.

The goal of a management system is to provide centralized network management. Any computer running SNMP management software is referred to as a management system. For a management system to be able to perform centralized network management, it must be able to collect and analyze many things, including the following:

- Network protocol identification and statistics
- Dynamic identification of computers attached to the network (referred to as discovery)
- Hardware and software configuration data

- Computer performance and usage statistics
- Computer event and error messages
- Program and application usage statistics

File Transfer Protocol (FTP)

The File Transfer Protocol (FTP) is a TCP/IP protocol that exists to upload and download files between FTP servers and clients. Like Telnet and Ping, FTP can establish a connection to a remote computer using either the hostname or the IP address and must resolve hostnames to IP addresses to establish communication with the remote computer.

When TCP/IP is installed on the system, there is an FTP utility available, but there are also a number of third-party graphical user interface (GUI) FTP clients available for all operating systems. If you use FTP a great deal, a GUI FTP client could save you a lot of time and frustration in dealing with FTP commands.

Trivial File Transfer Protocol (TFTP)

The Trivial File Transfer Protocol (TFTP) is a simple protocol compared to FTP that supports only reading and writing to files and does not support features such as listing directory contents and authentication. TFTP uses UDP as the transport protocol, as opposed to FTP, which uses TCP. TFTP is typically used to boot diskless workstations.

Secure File Transfer Protocol (SFTP)

The Secure File Transfer Protocol (SFTP) is an interactive file transfer protocol similar to FTP, but it encrypts all traffic between the SFTP client and the SFTP server. SFTP supports additional features such as public key authentication and compression. Unlike TFTP, SFTP does support a number of commands in its interactive shell such as listing directory contents, creating directories, downloading files, and uploading files.

Telnet

Telnet is a terminal emulation protocol that allows a client to run or emulate the program running on the server. A number of devices allow you to telnet into the device and perform remote administration of the network device using the command set available to the Telnet session.

Secure Shell (SSH)

The Secure Shell (SSH) is a program used to create a shell, or session, with a remote system. Once the remote session is established, the client can execute commands within this shell and copy files to the local system. SSH has a major purpose in life, and that is to support remote shells with support for secure authentication and encrypted communication.

Secure Copy Protocol (SCP)

The Secure Copy Protocol (SCP) is responsible for copying files from a remote server to the local system over a secure connection, ensuring that data in transit is kept confidential. A number of SCP products use an SSH connection to ensure the security of the secure copy operation.

Lightweight Directory Access Protocol (LDAP)

The Lightweight Directory Access Protocol (LDAP) is the TCP/IP protocol for directory service access that is supported by all the principal directory services, such as Novell's eDirectory and Microsoft's Active Directory. LDAP is a protocol that allows LDAP clients to connect to the network database, or directory, and query the database for information about its objects, such as user accounts and printers. For example, a user on the network could find out the phone number of another user by using the LDAP protocol.

LDAP is the industry-standard protocol for accessing a directory service and is supported by Active Directory and Novell's eDirectory.

Line Printer Daemon (LPD) and Line Printer Remote (LPR)

The line printer daemon (LPD) is a printer protocol, or service, installed on the print server to allow line printer remote (LPR) clients to send print requests to the print server. When LPD receives the print request, it stores the print request in a queue until the printer becomes available.

Now that you are acquainted with some of the core protocols of TCP/IP and some of the application-layer protocols that run on top of TCP/IP, let's take a look at the possible scenarios involving TCP/IP protocols and services and their appropriate solutions.

TCP/IP Fundamentals

Now that you have learned some of the popular protocols that exist in the TCP/IP protocol suite, this section will introduce you to the configuration of TCP/IP by discussing the addressing scheme and rules for assigning an address to a system.

TCP/IP Settings

TCP/IP is a protocol that requires a little bit of knowledge to configure the systems properly. When you configure TCP/IP, you are required to know the settings for the IP address, subnet mask, and default gateway. Let's start with the IP address!

IP Address

The IP address is a 32-bit value that uniquely identifies the system on the network (or the Internet). An IP address looks similar in appearance to 192.168.1.15. There are four decimal values in an IP address separated by periods (.). Each decimal value is made up of 8 bits (1s and 0s), and there are four decimal values, so 8 bits times 4 equals the 32-bit address.

Since each of the decimal values is made up of 8 bits (for example, the 192), we refer to each of the decimal values as an octet. There are four octets in an IP address. It is very important to understand that the four octets in an IP address are divided into two parts—a network ID and a host ID. The subnet mask determines the number of bits that make up the network ID and the number of bits that make up the host ID. Let's see how this works.

Subnet Mask

When looking at a subnet mask, if there is a 255 in an octet, then the corresponding octet in the IP address is part of the network ID. For example, if I had an IP address of 192.168.1.15 and a subnet mask of 255.255.255.0, the first three octets would make up the network ID and the last octet would be the host ID. The network ID assigns a unique address to the network itself, while the host ID uniquely identifies the system on the network. Table 4-1 summarizes this example.

You can see in Table 4-1 that the network ID (shown with an "N") is 192.168.1, and the host ID is the last octet with a value of 15. This means that this system is on the 192.168.1 network and any other system on the same network will have the same network ID.

To use a different example, if I had a subnet mask of 255.0.0.0, it would mean that the first octet of the IP address is used as the network ID portion, while the last three octets are the host ID portion of the IP address.

So what is the purpose of the subnet masks? Or better yet, why do we have a subnet mask that breaks the IP address into a network ID part and a host ID? The reason is so that when a system such as 192.168.1.15, with a subnet mask of 255.255.255.0, sends a piece of data to 192.198.45.10, the sending system first needs to determine whether the target computer exists on the same network or not. It does this by comparing the network IDs (Table 4-2); if the network IDs are the same, then both systems exist on the same network and one system can send to the other without the use of a router. If the systems exist on different networks, the data will need to be passed to the router so that the router can send the data to the other network.

Let's take a look at an exercise in which you will need to determine whether two systems are on the same network or not.

ON THE CD

Be sure to do Exercise 4-1 found in the LabBook.pdf on the CD-ROM.

TABLE 4-1		Octet 1	Octet 2	Octet 3	Octet 4
Identifying the Network ID and Host ID Portions of an IP Address	IP address	192	168	1	15
	Subnet mask	255	255	255	0
	Address portion	N	N	N	H

TABLE 4-2		Octet 1	Octet 2	Octet 3	Octet 4
Identifying Two Systems on Different Networks Using the Subnet Masks	IP address 1	192	168	1	15
	Subnet mask	255	255	255	0
	IP address 2	192	198	45	10

Default Gateway

When your system wants to send data to another system on the network, it looks at its own network ID and compares that to the destination system's IP address. If it appears that they both have the same network ID, the data is sent directly from your system to the destination system. If the two systems are on different networks, your system must pass the data to the router so that the router can send the data to the destination system's router.

The question is now, how does your system know who the router is? The answer is "that is what the default gateway is." The default gateway is the IP address of the router that can send data from your network.

In order to communicate on the Internet, your system will need to be configured with an IP address, a subnet mask, and a default gateway. If you need to communicate only with other systems on your network, you will need only an IP address and a subnet mask.

To view your TCP/IP settings, you can go to a command prompt and type **ipconfig**—you should see output similar to that shown in Figure 4-3. You will learn more about TCP/IP-related commands later in this chapter and in Chapter 6.

FIGURE 4-3	
Viewing your TCP/IP settings	

```
C:\WINDOWS\System32\cmd.exe

Ethernet adapter Wireless Network Connection:

        Connection-specific DNS Suffix  . :
        IP Address. . . . . . . . . . . . : 192.168.0.100
        Subnet Mask . . . . . . . . . . . : 255.255.255.0
        Default Gateway . . . . . . . . . : 192.168.0.1

C:\>_
```

CERTIFICATION OBJECTIVE 4.03

TCP/IP Addressing

This section will introduce you to the binary representation of an IP address and ensure that before you move onto the next chapter (on subnetting) you feel comfortable with converting binary values to decimal and address classes.

Understanding Binary

You know from the previous discussion that the IP address is a 32-bit address divided into four 8-bit blocks (called octets). The four octets are normally displayed as decimal values but also have a binary representation that looks like

```
11000000 10101000 00000001 00001111
```

Notice that there are four sets of 8 bits (1 or 0), which makes up the 32 bits (8 × 4 sets) of an IP address. Let's take a look at how you can determine the binary representation of an octet. The values of the 8 bits within the octet are shown in Table 4-3.

Looking at Table 4-3, you can see that the first bit in an octet (far right) has a decimal value of 1, the second bit has a decimal value of 2, the third bit has a decimal value of 4, and the values keep doubling with each additional bit. You can also see that the eighth bit has a decimal value of 128. The first bit is known as the least significant bit or low-order bit, while the eighth bit is known as the most significant bit or high-order bit.

To calculate the binary value of an octet with a decimal number such as 192, you need to enable, or turn on, the bits that will add up to the number of 192, as shown in Table 4-4.

Notice that the foregoing table has bit eight and bit seven turned on to give you a value of 128 + 64, which equals 192. The remaining bits will take an "off" state, which means they are not included in the calculation. A bit that has an on state takes a "1," and an off state takes a "0." So the combination of 8 bits to make the number 192 would be 11000000. Now that you know how to convert a decimal value to binary and a binary value to decimal, try out Exercise 4-2 before moving on to the section on address classes.

TABLE 4-3	Bit	8	7	6	5	4	3	2	1
Values Associated with Each Bit in an Octet	Value	128	64	32	16	8	4	2	1

TABLE 4-4	Bit	8	7	6	5	4	3	2	1
Calculating the Decimal Value of 192 in Binary	Value	128	64	32	16	8	4	2	1
	State	On	On						

To practice working with binary, do Exercises 4-2 and 4-3 in LabBook.pdf on the CD-ROM.

Address Classes

Every IP address belongs to a distinct address class. The Internet community defined these classes to accommodate networks of various sizes. The class to which the IP address belongs initially determines the network ID and host ID portions of the address, along with the number of hosts that are supported on that network. The different class addresses are named class A, class B, class C, class D, and class E. This section details each class of addresses.

Class A Addresses

A class A address has a default subnet mask of 255.0.0.0, which means that the first octet is the network ID and the last three octets belong to the host ID portion of the address. Each octet can contain 256 possible values (0–255), so a class A address supports 16,777,216 hosts on the network (256 × 256 × 256). Actually, there are only 16,777,214 valid addresses to use on systems, inasmuch as there are two addresses on each IP network you are not allowed to assign to systems because they are reserved. These are the addresses with all host bits set to 0s (the network ID) and all host bits set to 1s (the broadcast address). So with a class A address, you will not be able to assign *n*.0.0.0 or *n*.255.255.255 (where *n* is your network ID) to any hosts on the network.

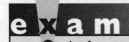

Class A addresses have an IP address in which the first octet is between 1 and 126. Class A addresses also have a default subnet mask of 255.0.0.0.

You can always identify a class A address, because the value of the first octet falls between the numbers 1 and 126. Actually, an address that starts with 127 is a class A address as well, but you are not allowed to use any address that starts with 127, because it is reserved for the loopback address (more on the loopback address later). For example, the IP address 12.56.87.34 is a class A address because the first octet is 12, which falls in the range 1–126.

Class B Addresses

Class B addresses have a default subnet mask of 255.255.0.0, which means that the first two octets are the network ID and the last two octets are the host ID portion of the address. This means that we can have 65,536 hosts (256 × 256) on the network. Oh, but wait! Don't forget to take off the two illegal addresses, so that gives us 65,534 addresses that can be assigned to hosts on the network.

Due to the number of hosts that are supported on a class B address, you usually find that a medium-sized company has a class B address. You can identify a class B address because the first octet starts with a number that falls between 128 and 191.

Class B addresses have an IP address in which the value of the first octet is between 128 and 191. Class B addresses have a default subnet mask of 255.255.0.0.

Class C Addresses

Class C addresses have a subnet mask of 255.255.255.0, which means that the first three octets are the network ID and the last octet is the host ID. Having only one octet as the host ID means that a class C address can support only 254 hosts (256 − 2) on the network.

You can identify a class C address because it has a value for the first octet that ranges between 192 and 223. For example, an IP address of 202.45.8.6 is a class C address because 202 falls between 192 and 223. You also know that this system has a subnet mask of 255.255.255.0 because it is a class C address.

exam

watch *Class C addresses have an IP address in which the value of the first octet is between 192 and 223. In addition, class C addresses have a default subnet mask of 255.255.255.0.*

Class D Addresses

Class D addresses are used for special types of applications on the network known as multicasting applications. Multicasting applications send data to a number of systems at the same time by sending data to the multicast address, and anyone who has registered with that address will receive the data. A multicast address is what class D addresses are used for, so you will not be assigning them specifically to hosts on the network for normal network communication.

Class D addresses have a value on the first octet that ranges from 224 to 239. With that many ranges, class D has the potential for 268,435,456 unique multicast groups that users can subscribe to from a multicast application.

Class E Addresses

The funny thing about class E addresses is that they were designed for experimental purposes only, so you will never see a class E address on a network. Class E addresses have a first octet with a value that falls in the range of 240–247.

Now that you are familiar with the different class addresses, take a look at Table 4-5, which summarizes the address classes. Be sure to know them for the exam.

TABLE 4-5		First Octet Value	Subnet Mask	# of Hosts per Network
Reviewing Address Classes	Class A	1–126	255.0.0.0	16,777,214
	Class B	128–191	255.255.0.0	65,534
	Class C	192–223	255.255.255.0	254

It's guaranteed that you will see questions on identifying class A, B, and C addresses on the exam. Be sure to know their default subnet masks as well.

To practice identifying address classes, check out Exercise 4-4 in LabBook.pdf, which is found on the CD-ROM.

Loopback Address

You have learned that you are not allowed to have a host assigned an IP address that has a value of 127 in the first octet. This is because the class A address range of 127 has been reserved for the loopback address.

The loopback address is used to refer to the local system, also known as the localhost. If you want to verify that the TCP/IP software has initialized on the local system even though you may not have an IP address, you may ping the loopback address, which is typically referred to as 127.0.0.1.

You can test your own local system by typing ping 127.0.0.1, ping localhost, *or* ping loopback, *to verify that the TCP/IP protocol stack is functioning on your system.*

Private Addresses

Another type of address you need to be aware of is what is known as a private address. A *private* address is an address that can be assigned to a system but cannot be used for any kind of Internet connectivity. The private addresses are nonroutable addresses, so any system using them will not be able to function off the network. The following are the three address ranges that are private:

- 10.0.0.0–10.255.255.255
- 172.16.0.0–172.31.255.255
- 192.168.0.0–192.168.255.255

Not being able to route data across the Internet when using these addresses will not pose a problem, because realistically, you will have these private addresses sitting

INSIDE THE EXAM

Illegal Addresses

There are a few IP addresses that are illegal to assign to hosts on the network. You might wonder why a class C address can have only 254 hosts and not 256, as would seem more likely, since an 8-bit number can have 256 possible values. The reason for this seeming discrepancy is that two of the addresses are lost from the available host pool. The first is an address that has all bits set to 0s in the host ID, which signifies the network ID of the network. The second is an address that

has all bits set to 1s in the host ID, which signifies the broadcast address for the network. So, for example, in the class C network 200.158.157.x, the addresses 200.158.157.0 (the network ID) and 200.158.157.255 (the broadcast address) are not available to hosts, reducing the available number of hosts from 256 to 254.

Another illegal address to assign to a host on the network is any system that has the first octet of 127; remember that this is reserved as the loopback address and you will not be able to assign the address to any host.

behind a Network Address Translation (NAT) server that will translate the private address to a public address that can be routed on the Internet. For more information on NAT, refer to the section "Network Services" later in this chapter.

Addressing Schemes

When sending data on the network, there are different ways that the data can be sent to the destination. The data can be sent to a unicast address, a broadcast address, or a multicast address. The following outlines the difference between unicast, broadcast, and multicast:

- **Unicast** Is the sending of information to one system. With the IP protocol this is accomplished by sending data to the IP address of the intended destination system.
- **Broadcast** Is the sending of information to all systems on the network. Data that is destined for all systems is sent by using the broadcast address for the network. An example of a broadcast address for a network is 192.168.2.255. The broadcast address is determined by setting all host bits to 1 and then converting the octet to a decimal number.
- **Multicast** Is the sending of information to a selected group of systems. Typically this is accomplished by having the systems subscribe to a multicast address. Any data that is sent to the multicast address is then received by all systems subscribed to the address. Most multicast addresses start with 224.*x.y.z* and are considered class D addresses.

IPv6

Our entire discussion so far about TCP/IP is based on version 4 of TCP/IP, known as IPv4. The use of TCP/IP over the years has far exceeded expectations, and we are running out of IP addresses. For that reason, TCP/IP has been redesigned and the new version is IP version 6 (IPv6).

There are major changes to IPv6 from what we know of IPv4. For starters, IPv4 uses a 32-bit address scheme, while IPv6 will use a 128-bit address scheme. This will give us an insane number of unique possible addresses—3.4×10^{38} to be exact (2^{128})! This is a huge improvement over 2^{32}=4 billion unique addresses with IPv4.

An IPv6 address will no longer use four octets. The IPv6 address is divided into eight hexadecimal values that are separated by a colon (:) as shown in the following example:

```
65b3:b834:45a3:0000:0000:762e:0270:5224
```

A number of different devices and software now support both IPv4 and IPv6, but it will be a few years yet before we see all systems and devices using only IPv6.

TCP/IP Ports

An application or process uses a TCP/IP port as an identifier for that application running on a system. When you send data from one computer to another, you send data to the port used by that application. For example, when you type the IP address of a web site in your web browser, the web browser connects to the web server (or web application) running at that system by sending data to port 80 (shown in Figure 4-4). Port 80 is the default port of a web server. When the web server answers your request by sending the web page to your browser, the browser is running on a particular port as well and the web server sends the page to the port of the web browser.

Server applications typically use low port numbers that fall under 1024, whereas client applications usually run on ports over 1024. Port numbers that are used by servers are known as *well-known* ports (under 1024), whereas port numbers over 1024 used by client applications are known as *dynamic* ports. They are called dynamic ports because many times the port is selected at runtime by the application

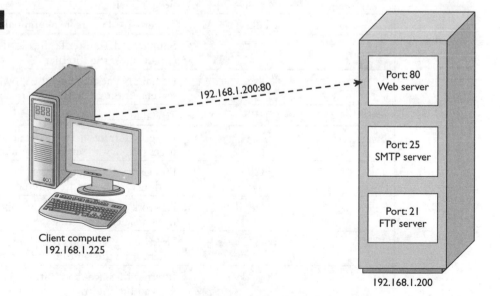

FIGURE 4-4

Sending data to a web server on port 80

192.168.1.200:80

Port: 80
Web server

Port: 25
SMTP server

Port: 21
FTP server

Client computer
192.168.1.225

192.168.1.200

and is different each time the program runs. For example, when you start Internet Explorer, it may use a different port number each time the program is started, but a web server uses the same port each time (port 80).

Table 4-6 is a list of well-known port numbers that are used by different types of applications or protocols. Be sure to know these for the Network+ exam.

exam
watch

For the exam, know the port numbers in Table 4-6, because you will be tested on the well-known port numbers.

Also understand that both TCP and UDP use port numbers.

TABLE 4-6	Port Number	Process	Description
Ports Used by Popular Internet Applications	20	FTP-DATA	File Transfer Protocol—used to transfer data from one machine to another
	21	FTP	File Transfer Protocol—used for control messages of the FTP session
	22	SSH	Secure Shell
	23	TELNET	Telnet—used to create a terminal session
	25	SMTP	Simple Mail Transfer Protocol—used to send e-mail across the Internet
	53	DNS	Domain Name System—used to query DNS servers for the IP address of a remote system
	69	TFTP	Trivial File Transfer Protocol
	80	HTTP	Hypertext Transfer Protocol—used to deliver web pages from a web server to the web client
	110	POP3	Post Office Protocol, version 3—a protocol for reading e-mail over the Internet
	119	NNTP	Network News Transfer Protocol—used to read news articles from a news server
	123	NTP	Used by the Network Time Protocol to synchronize the time on systems
	143	IMAP4	Internet Message Application Protocol, version 4—another Internet protocol for reading e-mail
	443	HTTPS	Secure Hypertext Transfer Protocol—used to encrypt web traffic between a client and server

| EXERCISE 4-5 |

Viewing TCP/IP Port Values

In this exercise, you will look back to the packet capture that you viewed in Chapter 2 for the analysis of web traffic and identify the ports that were used by both the web browser (sending system) and the web server (the receiving system).

1. Start Network Monitor by choosing Start | Programs | Administrative Tools | Network Monitor.

2. Once Network Monitor has started, open the HTTPTraffic capture file from the LabFiles\PacketCaptures folder.

3. Double-click the frame in the packet capture that is posting form data to a web server (frame 16) to expand the details of that packet.

4. In the details panel (middle of screen), select the TCP section by clicking it once (as shown in the accompanying illustration).

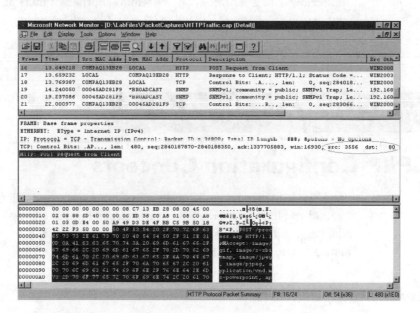

5. Notice that the source port and the destination port are shown on this line on the far right side. Record the following information in the spaces provided:

   Source Port: _____

   Destination Port: _____

6. You should have the following answers recorded in the preceding spaces:

   Source Port: _____3556_____

   Destination Port: _____80_____

7. Keep in mind that the destination port is port 80, which is the default port of a web server. You have found that the source port is 3556, which is a value above 1024. You have learned that a client application usually uses a value above 1024, so this is traffic of a web browser sending data to a web server.

8. Close Network Monitor and don't save any information if asked.

Another term that you will hear a lot is socket. A *socket* is the end point of communication and is made up of three components: the IP address of the system, the port number of the application, and the protocol that is being used—either TCP or UDP. The socket is the end point of communication for a TCP/IP application and is how data is sent from one system to another, or more accurately, from one application to another. The following formula defines what a socket is:

Socket = IP address + Port number + Protocol (TCP or UDP)

CERTIFICATION OBJECTIVE 4.04

TCP/IP Configuration Concepts

You have learned what an IP address, a subnet mask, and a default gateway are used for, and you have learned all about the binary form of addressing, including class addresses. In this section, you will learn to configure TCP/IP on a client system both manually and as a DHCP client.

Manual Configuration

To configure TCP/IP on a Windows XP client, you will click the Start button and then right-click My Network Places and choose Properties.

The network connections window appears, and you should see your LAN connection. If you right-click your LAN connection and choose Properties, you will see your network settings, including the TCP/IP protocol. To configure TCP/IP, select TCP/IP and choose Properties, as the dialog box shows in Figure 4-5.

To configure your system with a specific address, select Use The Following IP Address and then type the IP address, the subnet mask, and the default gateway; then choose OK. Once you have finished configuring TCP/IP, you will be able to communicate with network resources using the newly configured system.

Configuring a system manually is not the best approach to take on a network for a number of reasons:

- **Workload** The amount of work involved in manually configuring each system on the network is too much for any network administrator.

- **Typos** The potential for human error is great when inputting the parameters on multiple systems simply due to the fact that it is such a laborious task. It is also very easy to assign a duplicate address on the network, which would result in an error.

- **Change management** It is very hard to implement major changes to your IP infrastructure when you are manually configuring systems. For example, a change to a router address would require a lot of time to update the default gateway entry on the clients.

FIGURE 4-5

Changing TCP/IP settings

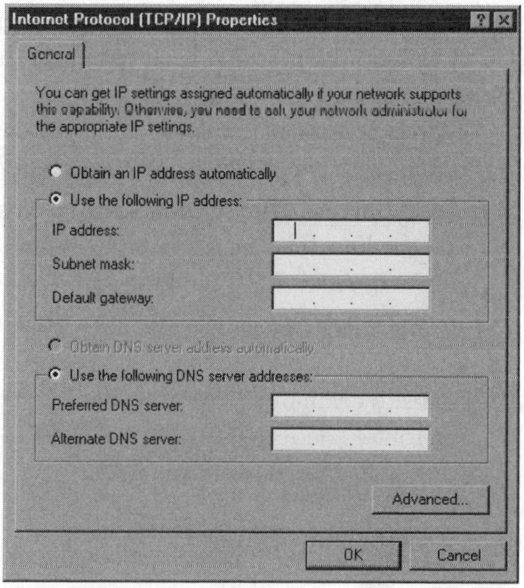

Dynamic Host Configuration Protocol (DHCP)

Configuring IP addressing on a large TCP/IP-based network can be a nightmare, especially if machines are moved from one network to another frequently. The Dynamic Host Configuration Protocol (DHCP) can help with the workload of configuring systems on a network by assigning addresses to systems on boot-up automatically.

The process of dynamically assigning IP addresses is managed via a DHCP server. The DHCP server is configured with a set of usable IP addresses, called a *scope*. The scope can also include the subnet mask, IP addresses of the default gateway, DNS servers, WINS servers, and other necessary addresses. When a PC comes online and is set up to use a DHCP server, it requests an IP address by transmitting a broadcast request packet looking for any DHCP servers on the network (known as DHCP Discovery). The DHCP server responds with an offer containing an IP address that the client can lease (known as the DHCP Offer). The client then accepts the offer by sending a request message for that address from the DHCP server (known as the DHCP Request), and then the server responds with an acknowledgment to the client that it has that address and additional settings for the lease time (known as the DHCP ACK). The DHCP server marks the IP address in its database as being in use so that it is not assigned again. When configuring the DHCP server, you will need to configure a scope with the following settings:

■ **IP addresses**   The DHCP server issues an IP address to each DHCP client system on the network. Each system connected to a TCP/IP-based network is identified by a unique IP address. As you learned in this chapter, the IP address consists of four 8-bit octets separated by periods. The IP address is normally shown in dotted-decimal notation—for example, 192.10.24.62.

■ **Subnet mask**   The IP address actually consists of two parts: the network ID and the host ID. The subnet mask is used to identify the part of the IP address that is the network ID and the part that is the host ID. Subnet masks assign 1s to the network ID bits and 0s to the host ID bits of the IP address.

■ **Default gateway**   A default gateway is required when the client system needs to communicate outside its own subnet. Normally, the default gateway is a router connected to the local subnet, which enables IP packets to be passed to other network segments.

To learn to configure your system for DHCP, be sure to try Exercise 4-6 found in LabBook.pdf on the CD-ROM and check out the CertCam training video to go with this exercise.

Scope Options

A DHCP scope is the range of IP addresses and additional options that the DHCP server will hand out to the DHCP clients on the network. As previously mentioned, the IP address and subnet mask are required items that the DHCP scope must include. Another requirement in the scope is the lease duration. It specifies how long a DHCP client can use an IP address before it must renew it with the DHCP server. This duration can be set for an unlimited time period or for a predetermined time period. You have the option of configuring a scope to reserve a specific IP address for a DHCP client or even for a system on the network that is not DHCP enabled.

Options within the DHCP scope can be configured for settings such as the DNS server, WINS server, router address, and domain name.

Servers

Several versions of Windows server products support having DHCP server capabilities, including Windows Server 2003 and Windows Server 2008. The main factor to consider if you have multiple subnets is that your routers must comply with RFC 1542 so that a DHCP server can receive the broadcast message from a client. It is wise to keep in mind that, if your DHCP server goes down and your DHCP clients cannot renew their lease, the clients will most likely not be able to access network resources.

One of the benefits of using multiple DHCP servers is redundancy. Redundancy can prevent your network from going down. If you decide to use multiple DHCP servers, you should place them on different subnets to achieve a higher degree of fault tolerance in case one of the subnets becomes unavailable. You can manage multiple servers on different subnets with the DHCP Console, the graphical utility used to maintain and configure DHCP servers in Windows.

In most companies, two DHCP servers provide fault tolerance of IP addressing if one server fails or must be taken offline for maintenance. Each DHCP server has at least half of the available addresses in an active scope. The number of addresses on each DHCP server should be more than enough to provide addresses for all clients.

Supported Clients

The following operating systems can perform as DHCP clients on your network:

- Windows clients such as Windows 2000, XP, Vista
- Windows servers such as Windows 2000 Server, Windows Server 2003, and Windows Server 2008
- Older Microsoft clients such as DOS (with network client software loaded), Windows 3.11, and Windows 9x clients.
- Non-Microsoft operating systems such as Linux

Of course, DHCP clients are not limited to Microsoft operating systems. Any system that conforms to RFC 1541 can be a DHCP client. For example, you can have a UNIX, Linux, or Novell NetWare client on the network that obtains an address from your DHCP server as well.

APIPA

Windows clients support a feature known as automatic private IP addressing (APIPA), which is a feature that provides that, when a Windows client boots up and cannot contact a DHCP server, it will configure itself automatically with a 169.254.x.y address. If there is something wrong with the DHCP server and all the systems on the network cannot obtain an address from the DHCP server, the clients will all assign themselves an address within the 169.254 address range and then be able to communicate with one another.

APIPA does not assign a default gateway, so you will be unable to access resources on a remote network and the Internet—but you can still communicate with systems on your network. When troubleshooting to find out why a machine cannot communicate on the network, watch for systems that have the 169.254.x.y address range because it means they could not find a DHCP server.

Boot Protocol

The Boot Protocol, known as BOOTP, is used by diskless workstations. When a diskless workstation boots, it does so using an EEPROM on the network card to allow it to load basic drivers and connect to the network by obtaining an IP address automatically.

A BOOTP server, similar to a DHCP server, assigns the diskless workstation an address for the network to allow it to participate on the network. You will see the term BOOTP a lot when it comes to DHCP and routers; a BOOTP-enabled router will allow the DHCP broadcast to cross the router so that a DHCP server can be found on the other side of the network.

The BOOTP server is usually the same as the DHCP server; the two are considered one and the same. Routers need to be BOOTP compatible to	*allow the DHCP requests to pass through the router to another segment, or else you will require a DHCP server per network segment.*

Domain Name System

One service that is used throughout networks and the Internet is the Domain Name System (DNS). Most users on the network connect to resources by using a friendly name such as www.gleneclarke.com—this style of name, known as a fully qualified domain name (FQDN), must be converted to an IP address before communication can occur. DNS is used as our solution to convert FQDNs to IP addresses.

Let's walk through an example of a name being resolved. You are sitting in your office on your network, and you try to connect to http://www.gleneclarke.com, which means that your client computer will send a query to the DNS server (shown in Figure 4-6) in your office asking, "Do you have an IP address for www.gleneclarke.com?" Your DNS server does not know who www.gleneclarke.com is, so it will then go out and query the DNS root servers and ask them if they have an IP address for www.gleneclarke.com. There are only about 13 DNS root servers on the Internet; they don't actually hold records for individual hosts, but they do forward the request to the name servers at the next level down, which are the .com name servers. DNS will find the IP address of the name requested by reading the name from right to left—in this case, .com is the far-right name part, so the request is forwarded to the .com name servers. The .com name servers look at the request and say, "No, we don't have a clue who www.gleneclarke.com is, but why don't you check out the gleneclarke.com name servers—they might know."

FIGURE 4-6

Finding an IP
address using
DNS

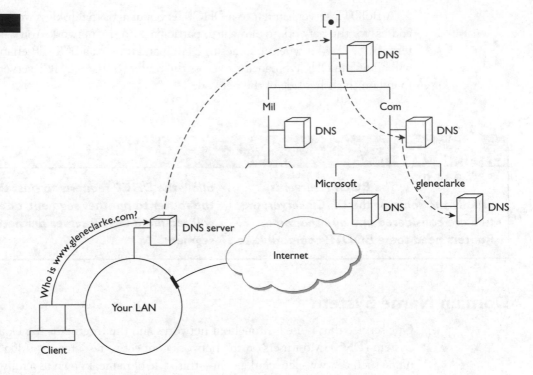

Your DNS server then queries the name servers for gleneclarke.com and asks them, "Do you have an IP address for www.gleneclarke.com?" In this case, the DNS servers for gleneclarke.com do have a record for www and they return the IP address to the DNS on your network. Now, your DNS server is smart—it will cache that data before sending an answer to your client computer that started the whole process, so that if anyone else is interested in the address, your DNS server will have the answer without going out on the web!

Top-Level Domains

The root servers are responsible for ensuring that any requests for an Internet resource are forwarded to the correct top-level domain. To help organize Internet resources in the DNS distributed database, there are specific top-level domain names created, and a company or organization has to register under a top-level domain. For example, if you are trying to connect to microsoft.com, the root DNS server forwards you to the .com top-level domain namespace.

The following is a description of the most popular DNS top-level domains found on the Internet:

- **.com** This is the commercial organizations group and is by far the largest. Almost everyone wants to be found in this domain, because it is where most customers will try to find you.
- **.org** This is for nonprofit organizations.
- **.net** This is for networking organizations such as island.net and nfs.net, as well as for Internet service providers such as netzero.net.
- **.mil** This is for military organizations such as army.mil and navy.mil.
- **.gov** This is for U.S. government offices only.
- **.edu** This is for educational organizations.

Country Domain Names

With only six top-level domain names and the requirement that all organizations register under one of those top levels if they wanted an Internet name, this soon became a problem because there were so many names to be registered and so few choices on the top levels. Eventually, top-level names were created for country domains; therefore, if you resided in a certain country, you could register under that country domain so that your customers could find you easily. Here are a few of the most common country domain names:

- **.ca** Canada
- **.ie** Ireland
- **.uk** United Kingdom
- **.us** United States

DNS Files

Most DNS servers maintain their DNS data in a number of files that exist on the hard disk of the server. In the old days, you managed the records by updating these text files, but today most DNS server environments support a graphic tool like the one shown in Figure 4-7 to create the records for your DNS server. When you create the records graphically, the DNS files are updated. Windows servers store their DNS files in %systemroot%\system32\DNS.

FIGURE 4-7

Managing a
DNS server in
Windows

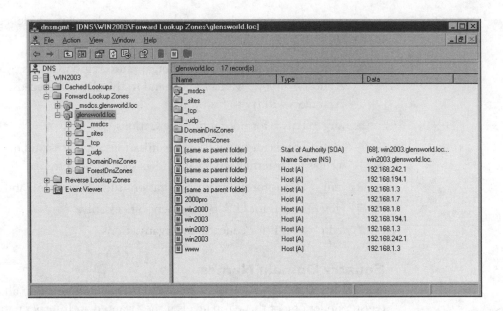

*For Windows servers running Active Directory, the DNS database can be
integrated with Active Directory, which allows you to have the DNS data
replicated with Active Directory and also allows the zone data to be modified
in multiple locations, given that Active Directory is a multimaster environment.
If the DNS database is integrated with Active Directory, it will not be located
in the %systemroot%\system32\DNS directory but be stored within the Active
Directory database.*

Hosts File

Before DNS became a popular solution to hostname resolution, there was a more
manual method of creating and modifying a file on the local hard disk of every
system. This file would need to be updated on every system if a change was made
to a server's IP address and you wanted the client applications to be aware of the
change. This file, known as the hosts file, was located on each client system.

Before DNS servers became a standard, network administrators used to create a
text file known as the hosts file, which was used to resolve the FQDN to matching
IP addresses. This text file was stored locally on each system; in the Windows world,
it is stored in the %systemroot%\system32\drivers\etc folder and contains two
columns—one for the IP address and the other for the FQDN. Figure 4-8 displays
the contents of a hosts file.

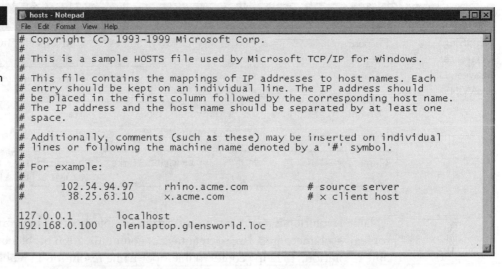

FIGURE 4-8

Looking at the hosts file on a Windows system

```
# Copyright (c) 1993-1999 Microsoft Corp.
#
# This is a sample HOSTS file used by Microsoft TCP/IP for Windows.
#
# This file contains the mappings of IP addresses to host names. Each
# entry should be kept on an individual line. The IP address should
# be placed in the first column followed by the corresponding host name.
# The IP address and the host name should be separated by at least one
# space.
#
# Additionally, comments (such as these) may be inserted on individual
# lines or following the machine name denoted by a '#' symbol.
#
# For example:
#
#      102.54.94.97     rhino.acme.com          # source server
#       38.25.63.10     x.acme.com              # x client host

127.0.0.1       localhost
192.168.0.100   glenlaptop.glensworld.loc
```

Windows Internet Naming Service

The Windows Internet Naming Service (WINS) provides name resolution for NetBIOS names to matching IP addresses and is popular on large Microsoft networks. WINS is very similar to DNS but contains a database of different-style names—NetBIOS names instead of fully qualified domain names.

When a WINS client boots up, it registers its names within the WINS database and then queries that server any time it needs to have a computer name resolved to a matching IP address. When the WINS client shuts down, it also de-registers its names from the WINS database so that another system can register the names while it is offline.

Before WINS, the LMHOSTS file was used to assist with remote NetBIOS name resolution. The LMHOSTS file is a static file that maps NetBIOS names to IP addresses. This file is similar to the hosts file in functionality; the only difference is that the hosts file is used for mapping hostnames to IP addresses. To configure a client for DNS or WINS, follow the steps in Exercise 4-7.

CertCam 4-7

Be sure to try Exercise 4-7 in LabBook.pdf on the CD-ROM and check out the CertCam training video. This exercise demonstrates how to configure your client system for a DNS or WINS server.

Table 4-7 outlines the differences between WINS and DNS.

TABLE 4-7	Feature	DNS	WINS
	Purpose	Converts FQDN to IP address	Converts NetBIOS name to IP address
Identifying Differences Between DNS and WINS	Names	Hierarchical 255-character names	Flat 15-character names
	Dynamic Registration	Yes, with dynamic DNS supported in Windows 2000 and above	Yes
	Name Types	FQDN (ex: www.gleneclarke.com)	NetBIOS name (ex: COMPUTERA)

Name resolution is a very important part of troubleshooting networking problems—chances are a large percentage of communication problems come from name resolution. To help people troubleshoot name resolution in real life and on the Network+ exam, I usually draw for them Figure 4-9, which is a flow chart of the types of names and the technologies used to resolve the type of name. For example, looking at Figure 4-9, you can see that ARP is used to convert IP addresses to MAC addresses, whereas DNS is used to convert the FQDN to the IP address—which is then converted to the MAC address by ARP.

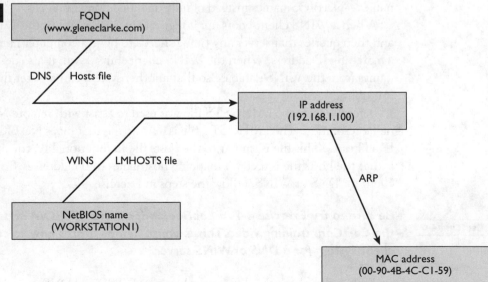

FIGURE 4-9

Name resolution flow chart

Configuring a Linux Machine for TCP/IP

We have spent most of the examples talking about Windows operating systems and how to configure TCP/IP on Windows. Let's take some time now and focus on Linux, one of the biggest competitors to Microsoft Windows. The version of Linux that I have installed for this book is Red Hat Linux 8. If you have Red Hat Linux 9, you should be able to follow the same steps, because there are not a lot of changes regarding this area between the two versions.

on the **job**

To download a free version of the most current version of Linux, visit www.linux.org.

To change your TCP/IP settings in Linux, you will need to log on to the computer with root-level access and then click the Red Hat button in the bottom-left corner of the screen. When the menu appears, select System Settings | Network, as shown in Figure 4-10.

FIGURE 4-10

Selecting the network settings from the Red Hat menu

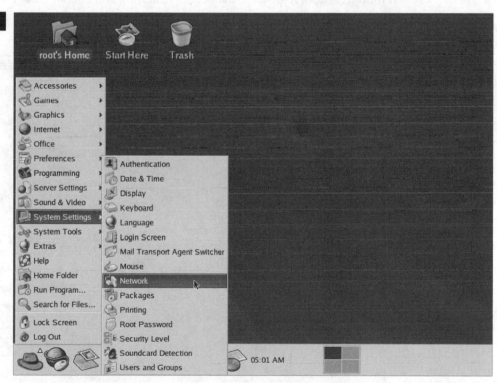

Once the Network Configuration dialog box shows, click the Edit button to change the IP address that is assigned to the Ethernet device in the Linux machine. To statically assign an IP address, select the option Statically Set IP Addresses as shown in Figure 4-11.

If you wish to configure the Linux machine as a DHCP client so that its address information is obtained automatically, you will need to bring the Network Configuration dialog box up again and select the option that says Automatically Obtain IP Address Settings With and ensure that DHCP is selected (as shown in Figure 4-12). You will most likely want to ensure that the setting Automatically Obtain DNS Information From Provider is selected. This setting allows you to configure Linux to obtain the address of the DNS server from DHCP as well.

Once you have configured TCP/IP on the Linux system, you may want to verify the settings by viewing your IP address information. You will look at TCP/IP utilities in Chapter 6, but to make our Linux walkthrough complete, let's take a look at how to view the TCP/IP settings in Linux. To view your IP address information in Linux, you need to bring up a command prompt, known as a terminal session. To start a terminal session, right-click the desktop in Linux and choose New Terminal, as shown in Figure 4-13.

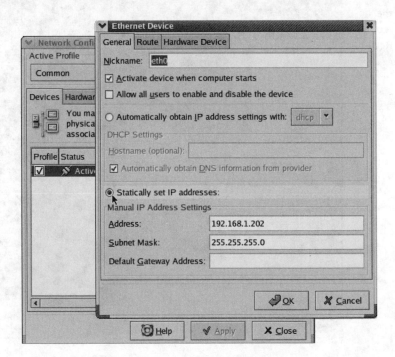

FIGURE 4-11

Configuring a Linux machine with a static IP address

Configuring a
Linux machine as
a DHCP client

Starting a
terminal session
in Linux

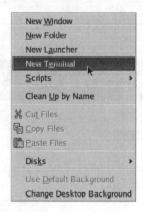

Once the new terminal starts up, you can type **ifconfig** (case sensitive) to
view your TCP/IP settings, or you can use the Ping utility to test connectivity to
another system. Figure 4-14 demonstrates ifconfig being used to view the TCP/IP
settings of the network interface. You may type **exit** at the prompt to exit out of
the terminal.

FIGURE 4-14

Viewing your
TCP/IP settings
with ifconfig in
Linux

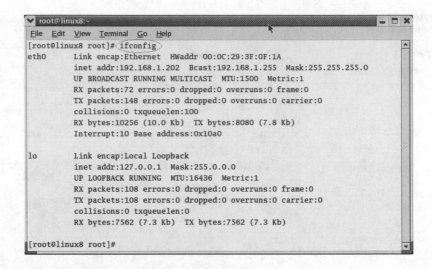

```
[root@linux8 root]# ifconfig
eth0      Link encap:Ethernet  HWaddr 00:0C:29:3F:0F:1A
          inet addr:192.168.1.202  Bcast:192.168.1.255  Mask:255.255.255.0
          UP BROADCAST RUNNING MULTICAST  MTU:1500  Metric:1
          RX packets:72 errors:0 dropped:0 overruns:0 frame:0
          TX packets:148 errors:0 dropped:0 overruns:0 carrier:0
          collisions:0 txqueuelen:100
          RX bytes:10256 (10.0 Kb)  TX bytes:8080 (7.8 Kb)
          Interrupt:10 Base address:0x10a0

lo        Link encap:Local Loopback
          inet addr:127.0.0.1  Mask:255.0.0.0
          UP LOOPBACK RUNNING  MTU:16436  Metric:1
          RX packets:108 errors:0 dropped:0 overruns:0 frame:0
          TX packets:108 errors:0 dropped:0 overruns:0 carrier:0
          collisions:0 txqueuelen:0
          RX bytes:7562 (7.3 Kb)  TX bytes:7562 (7.3 Kb)

[root@linux8 root]#
```

Remember that Linux is case sensitive and that the ifconfig *command is all lowercase characters.*

CERTIFICATION OBJECTIVE 4.05

Network Services

In this chapter, you have already been introduced to a few network services, such as DHCP, DNS, and WINS. This section will review those services briefly and introduce you to some additional services you should be familiar with for the Network+ exam.

A network service is responsible for a specific function on the network. For example, the file and print services are responsible for providing files on the network, and the DHCP service is responsible for assigning IP addresses automatically to systems on the network. Let's identify popular network services found on the Network+ exam.

DHCP

The Dynamic Host Configuration Protocol (DHCP) is responsible for assigning IP address information automatically to systems on the network. The network administrator configures the DHCP server by configuring a scope (a range of addresses) that the server can assign addresses from. The DHCP service may configure a client with all the TCP/IP settings, including the subnet mask, the default gateway, and the addresses of both the DNS server and the WINS server.

CertCam 4-8

To learn the steps to configure a DHCP server in Windows, check out Exercise 4-8 in LabBook.pdf on the CD-ROM. You can also watch the CertCam training video for this exercise, which demonstrates the steps.

DNS

The Domain Name System (DNS) is a network service that is responsible for converting FQDNs to IP addresses so that communication can occur. Most networking applications allow users to type an FQDN (for example, www. gleneclarke.com) as the address of the system they want to communicate with. The FQDN must be converted to an IP address. DNS is responsible for converting this name to the IP address.

Linux, Novell, and Microsoft Windows servers all contain DNS server software that can be installed to create the database of FQDNs and matching IP addresses. The Windows Server DNS Management tool is shown in Figure 4-15. To learn to install a Microsoft DNS server, take a look at the Exercise 4-9 on the CD-ROM.

FIGURE 4-15

Looking at the DNS database in the DNS Management tool for Windows

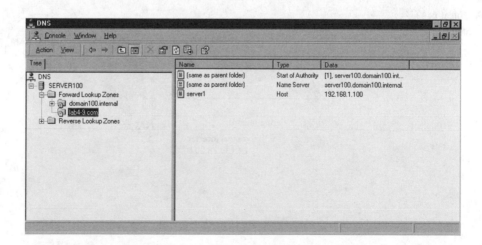

To learn the steps to configure a DNS server in Windows, check out Exercise 4-9 in LabBook.pdf found on the CD-ROM. You can also watch the CertCam training video for this exercise, which demonstrates the steps.

WINS

As you learned earlier in the chapter, the Windows Internet Naming Service (WINS) is used to resolve, or convert, NetBIOS names (computer names) to IP addresses. NetBIOS applications use NetBIOS names as a way to identify the remote system that the application is to communicate with. The NetBIOS name will be converted to the IP address by a WINS server.

NAT/PAT/SNAT

Most networks today are connected to the Internet, and having an Internet connection presents a number of security concerns. For example, if you have your server connected directly to the Internet, it will take no time at all for the system to be hacked. *Network Address Translation (NAT)* is a network service that is responsible for translating internal IP addresses from machines inside the network to a public address used by the NAT service—essentially hiding your internal network addresses. Figure 4-16 displays a typical NAT configuration.

FIGURE 4-16

A typical NAT configuration

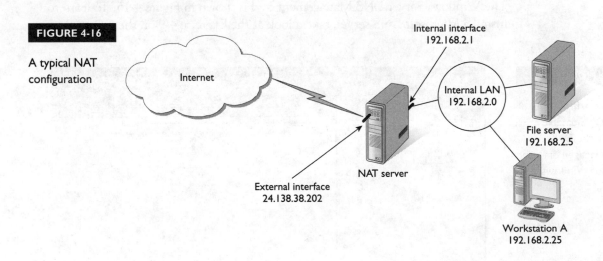

In Figure 4-16, you can see that the NAT server has two network interfaces (cards): the internal interface and the external interface. The internal interface has an IP address within the range of the internal network, whereas the external interface uses an external address. Notice that the NAT server has two IP addresses assigned and that the internal interface uses the IP address of 192.168.2.1. This will be the default gateway address of all other systems on the network because the NAT server is the way off the network.

In Figure 4-16, when Workstation A wants to send information to the Internet, it submits the request to the NAT server. The NAT server then modifies or translates the source address of the packet to 24.138.38.202 so that the packet appears to have come from the external interface of the NAT server. This is beneficial because anyone who intercepts the data on the Internet will believe that the packet came from the NAT server and not the internal computer on the LAN. As a result, anyone who decides to attack the source of the packets will be attacking the NAT server, which will typically be a firewall product as well; if the system is compromised, however, at least it was only the NAT server, not one of the internal systems that holds the company data!

PAT and SNAT

When implementing your NAT solution, you have a few options. You could have each private address inside the network translate to a single public address that is associated with the public interface. This would mean that you need to have multiple public addresses in order to create the one-to-one mapping by which one private IP address translates to one public IP address.

If you only have one public IP address on the NAT device and need to use that for all private addresses on the LAN, then you will need to *overload* the public address with multiple private addresses. NAT overloading is used when each of the private IP addresses is translated to the one public IP address, essentially overloading the poor public address.

The big question is "How does the NAT device know which internal system to send the response to when data is returned from the Internet?" This is an important question because all of the packets will be returned to whatever the public address is on the NAT device. This is where *Port Address Translation (PAT)* comes in. If you look at Figure 4-17, you will see that the NAT device using port addressing is keeping track of not only the IP address of the system sending outbound traffic, but also the port used by the application on the private system. The source address of the outbound packet is converted from the IP address of the private system to the

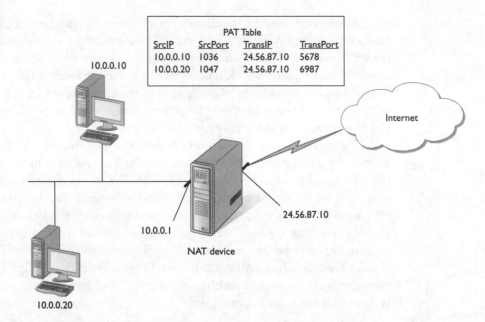

FIGURE 4-17

Port Address
Translation

IP address of the public interface on the NAT device. Also, the port used by the
application on the sending computer is then converted to a unique port address used
by the NAT device. All IP addresses and port addresses are then stored in the NAT
table, known as the port address table, and then the packet is sent to destination
system on the Internet.

When a response comes back from the Internet destined for a port on the NAT
device, the packet is then translated to use the original private IP address and port
number of the original source system. After the header of the packet is replaced with
original IP and port information, the NAT device then sends the data to the internal
system.

Another term you will see that deals with NAT is *Secure Network Address
Translation,* or SNAT. Some NAT devices include proxy features as well. These
features give you the opportunity to configure different types of clients for the NAT
device; for example, you could configure all the clients as proxy clients, or secure
NAT clients.

If you install proxy client software on the client systems, then the clients can use
the NAT device as their method to get out to the Internet and you can leverage
features such as authentication. If you decide you do not want to install the proxy
client software but simply want to use the NAT features of the proxy server, then you

can simply set the default gateway of all the clients to point to the private IP address of the NAT device. All client systems will then send outbound communication to the NAT device, which will then translate the source address as normal. A SNAT solution that does not have client software installed on the stations of the users can leverage features such as application filters but cannot authenticate the users.

ICS

Internet Connection Sharing (ICS) is a service built into Windows operating systems that allows you to share your Internet connection with other users on the network. ICS acts as a NAT server and a DHCP server at the same time. When you enable ICS in Windows, it automatically starts assigning IP addresses out on the network so that the DHCP clients use the ICS computer as their default gateway. When clients send information to the ICS machine to be sent on the Internet, the ICS machine translates the source address (the NAT feature) to use the external interface of the system.

To enable ICS, right-click your Internet LAN connection and choose Properties. On the Advanced page tab, select "Allow other network users to connect through this computer's Internet connection" (shown in Figure 4-18) and then choose OK.

FIGURE 4-18

Enabling ICS in Windows

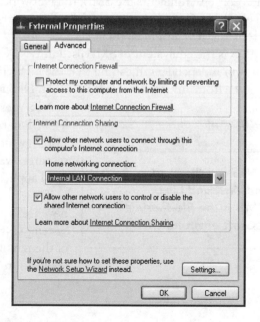

SMB

The Server Message Block (SMB) protocol, used primarily by Microsoft operating systems, is responsible for sharing files and printers on a system and making those resources available to SMB clients on the network. SMB is an application-layer protocol that runs on top of TCP/IP, IPX, and NetBEUI and relies on those protocols for transport functionality.

SMB is a term that is being phased out. Microsoft is now using the term Common Internet File System (CIFS) instead of SMB. Either way, SMB and CIFS *are protocols responsible for allowing access to a remote file system as if it were stored on the local system in a Microsoft environment.*

NFS

Microsoft environments use SMB; the Network File System (NFS) is a protocol developed by Sun Microsystems that allows users to access files stored on a remote system as if it were a local resource.

NFS is the equivalent of SMB used in UNIX and Linux environments and is platform independent, meaning that the NFS client may be accessing a file system resource from any type of server that is an NFS server—not just a Linux server.

NFS is a file-sharing protocol used in UNIX and Linux environments; SMB is the file-sharing protocol in Microsoft environments.

NFS uses an interface that runs on top of TCP/IP networks called the Virtual File System (VFS), which is responsible for making the resource available to a local application. The local application makes the call to the resource as if it were a local resource, and the application never learns that the resource is on a remote system—NFS makes the location and platform of the remote resource transparent to the application and users.

AFP

If SMB is the file-sharing protocol in Microsoft environments and NFS is the file-sharing protocol in UNIX environments, what is responsible for allowing access to files on remote systems in the Macintosh world? You guessed it; the AppleTalk Filing Protocol (AFP) is responsible for allowing Macintosh systems to access remote file systems on an AppleTalk network.

Original implementations of AFP only ran on top of AppleTalk networks, but newer versions of AFP run on top of TCP/IP because of the popularity of the protocol. Like SMB and NFS, AFP provides an environment that allows users to access files on a remote system as if they were on the local system. AFP also provides security as to who accesses the file.

Samba

Samba is an application environment that runs on Linux systems and uses SMB to allow Microsoft clients to access the Samba-enabled UNIX servers as if they were Microsoft servers. A Samba-enabled UNIX server may provide a number of services to Microsoft clients, including

■ Sharing the file system of the UNIX server to Microsoft clients
■ Sharing printer resources from the UNIX environment to Microsoft clients
■ Performing authentication and authorization services to Microsoft clients

Samba is a network service loaded on UNIX/Linux systems that implements SMB services so that Microsoft clients can access files and printers on the UNIX/Linux servers.

This may not sound like a very exciting feature, but it has proven to be a very exciting technology because without it, the Microsoft clients would only be able to access the Microsoft servers in your organization and not the UNIX servers. The reason is that UNIX servers use NFS as a file-sharing protocol, while Microsoft uses SMB—so Samba gives you the best of both worlds because it allows the UNIX server to run its NFS protocol for UNIX clients while Samba provides the SMB service for Microsoft clients. Both types of clients can now share resources with one another! Figure 4-19 shows an example of configuring Samba with Webmin tools in Linux.

FIGURE 4-19

Creating Samba
file shares with
Webmin tools
in Linux

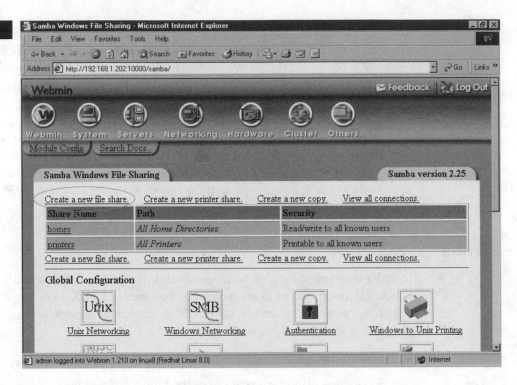

UNIX uses two different services, called *daemons,* to provide Samba services:

- **smbd daemon**   This daemon provides the core services of Samba, offering
  file-and-print services functionality from the UNIX server to Windows
  clients. The smbd daemon also provides authentication and authorization
  services to Windows clients.
- **nmbd daemon**   This daemon is loaded on the UNIX server to provide
  WINS services and network browsing functionality so that the Samba servers
  appear in My Network Places on Windows clients.

*To learn the steps to configure Samba on Linux, check out Exercise 4-10 in the
LabBook.pdf file, found on the CD-ROM.*

ZeroConfig

Zero Configuration Networking (ZeroConfig) is a network service designed to minimize the configuration of the network clients by broadcasting configured services on the network to network clients who automatically discover these network services. After the service has been discovered, the client is automatically configured to use this service with no interaction from the network administrator.

CERTIFICATION SUMMARY

In this chapter you learned the fundamentals of TCP/IP and what makes this protocol so common in today's networking market. The following list summarizes what you learned about TCP/IP:

■ The IP address and subnet mask are the most important configuration settings and must be specified correctly in order to communicate on the TCP/IP-based network. Next in importance is the default gateway, which specifies where to route packets if you are communicating outside the local network.

■ The Dynamic Host Configuration Protocol (DHCP) automatically configures a workstation with the correct TCP/IP settings, relieving you of the burden of manually configuring every workstation.

■ The Domain Name System (DNS) is essential for Internet-based machines and company intranets that use DNS for hostname resolution. You learned about the hostname, domain name, resolution, and Internet domain name server hierarchies.

■ The Windows Internet Naming Service (WINS), which ironically has little to do with the Internet, enables workstations to resolve NetBIOS names to IP addresses rather than using a static LMHOSTS file on each machine.

■ TCP/IP is a suite of protocols, the most popular of which are TCP, UDP, IP, and ARP. (Your Network+ exam will definitely have several questions on some of these TCP/IP protocol suite members.)

■ TCP/IP addressing involves a strong knowledge of the IP address, subnet mask, network classes, and special reserved addresses. (You should memorize each network class for the exam.)

■ The most important portions of TCP/IP as it relates to your Network+ exam are the TCP/IP configuration concepts. You need these to configure workstations with TCP/IP. The concepts include the IP address, the subnet mask, DHCP, DNS, WINS, the default gateway, the hostname, and the NetBIOS name.

With a strong understanding of the material presented in this chapter, you will have no problems with any TCP/IP-related questions on your exam. Not only is the material presented here important for the exam, but it will also be important after you ace the exam and continue on to a career as a networking professional.

✓ TWO-MINUTE DRILL

TCP/IP Protocol Suite

- ❑ TCP/IP is a suite of protocols.
- ❑ TCP is used for connection-oriented communication and ensures delivery.
- ❑ UDP is used for connectionless communication and does not ensure delivery.
- ❑ The Internet Control Message Protocol (ICMP) enables systems on a TCP/IP network to share status and error information.
- ❑ IP provides packet routing and delivery for all other protocols within the suite.
- ❑ The Address Resolution Protocol (ARP) is used to provide IP address–to–physical address resolution.
- ❑ HTTP is used to deliver web pages from the web server to the web browser, while HTTPS is used to deliver the pages securely.
- ❑ The Simple Mail Transfer Protocol (SMTP) is used to send mail over the Internet.
- ❑ The Post Office Protocol (POP) is the Internet protocol for reading e-mail.
- ❑ The Internet Message Access Protocol (IMAP), a protocol similar to POP, is used to retrieve messages from a mail server.
- ❑ The Simple Network Management Protocol (SNMP) is an Internet standard that provides a simple method for remotely managing virtually any network device.
- ❑ The File Transfer Protocol (FTP) is a TCP/IP utility that exists solely to copy files from one computer to another.

TCP/IP Fundamentals

- ❑ The popularity of TCP/IP makes the protocol a likely culprit to appear many times throughout your Network+ exam.
- ❑ TCP/IP addresses are 32-bit addresses.
- ❑ The IP address is a unique value assigned to the system that identifies the system on the network.
- ❑ The subnet mask is used to determine the network ID portion of an IP address.

❑ The network ID is used to determine whether the destination system exists on the same network or not. If the two systems have the same network ID, then they are on the same network.

❑ The host ID identifies the system within the network.

❑ The default gateway refers to the IP address of the router and is used to send data off the network.

TCP/IP Addressing

❑ Class A addresses start with the first octet ranging from 0 to 126 and have a default subnet mask of 255.0.0.0.

❑ Class B addresses have a first octet ranging from 128 to 191 and have a default subnet mask of 255.255.0.0.

❑ Class C addresses have a first octet ranging from 192 to 223 and have a default subnet mask of 255.255.255.0.

❑ Class D addresses are used for multicasting.

❑ An application or process uses a TCP/IP port to communicate between client and server computers.

❑ The most popular, and therefore most likely, exam choices to remember are the FTP ports (20 and 21), SMTP port (25), HTTP port (80), and HTTPS port (443).

TCP/IP Configuration Concepts

❑ You have two options for configuring a workstation: You can configure it manually, or you can use a DHCP server.

❑ DHCP is responsible for assigning IP address to clients automatically and reduces the network administration load.

❑ DNS is used to resolve FQDNs (www.gleneclarke.com) to IP addresses.

❑ WINS is used to convert NetBIOS names (computer names) to IP addresses.

❑ Hosts is a text file on the client that performs the same role as DNS but is configured on each system manually.

❑ LMHOSTS is a text file on the client that performs the same role as WINS but is configured on each system manually.

Network Services

- ❑ DHCP is responsible for assigning IP address information to clients.
- ❑ DNS is a distributed database that is responsible for converting FQDNs to IP addresses.
- ❑ WINS is responsible for converting computer names to IP addresses.
- ❑ NAT is responsible for hiding internal network addresses by configuring all systems to use the NAT system as the default gateway. The NAT server will then change the source address of outgoing packets to its own external address, ensuring that all requests look as though they are coming from the NAT server. The NAT server will receive any responses and then send the response to the internal client—ensuring that no external system can communicate with internal systems.
- ❑ SMB is the e-sharing protocol on Microsoft networks that allows clients to access file systems on remote Microsoft systems.
- ❑ NFS is the file-sharing protocol on UNIX networks that allows UNIX clients to access file systems on NFS servers.
- ❑ AFP is the file-sharing protocol for Macintosh systems, allowing Macs to access remote file systems on Macintosh systems.
- ❑ Samba is a service that implements SMB on UNIX servers, allowing Microsoft clients to access file systems on the UNIX server.

SELF TEST

The following questions will help you measure your understanding of the material presented in this chapter. Read all the choices carefully because there might be more than one correct answer. Choose all correct answers for each question.

TCP/IP Protocols

1. Which layer of the OSI model does the IP protocol run at?
   A. Layer 2
   B. Layer 3
   C. Layer 4
   D. Layer 5

2. Which of the following protocols are layer-4 protocols? (Select all that apply.)
   A. TCP
   B. IP
   C. ARP
   D. UDP

3. Which protocol is responsible for converting the IP address to a MAC address?
   A. IP
   B. TCP
   C. ARP
   D. ICMP

4. Which protocol is responsible for sending e-mail across the Internet?
   A. POP3
   B. IMAP4
   C. HTTP
   D. SMTP

5. Which protocol is responsible for connection-oriented communication?
   A. TCP
   B. IP
   C. UDP
   D. ICMP

6. Which protocol is responsible for error reporting and status information?
   A. ICMP
   B. TCP
   C. UDP
   D. IP

7. Which protocol is responsible for logical addressing and delivery of packets?
   A. ICMP
   B. TCP
   C. IP
   D. UDP

TCP/IP Fundamentals

8. Which TCP/IP setting is not required if you want to communicate on the LAN by IP address only?
   A. IP address
   B. Subnet mask
   C. Default gateway
   D. DNS

9. How many bits in an IP address?
   A. 8 bits
   B. 32 bits
   C. 48 bits
   D. 96 bits

10. How many octets in an IP address?
    A. 1
    B. 2
    C. 3
    D. 4

11. A computer with a subnet mask of 255.255.255.0 has how many octets for the network ID?
    A. 1
    B. 2
    C. 3
    D. 4

12. A computer with the IP address of 134.67.89.12 and a subnet mask of 255.255.0.0 is on the same network with which of the following systems?
    A. 134.76.89.11
    B. 134.67.112.23
    C. 13.4.67.34
    D. 109.67.45.10

TCP/IP Addressing

13. Which network address class supports 65,534 hosts?
    A. Class A
    B. Class B
    C. Class C
    D. Class D

14. What is the default subnet mask for a class C network?
    A. 255.0.0.0
    B. 225.225.0.0
    C. 255.255.255.0
    D. 225.255.255.255

15. Which address is reserved for internal loopback functions?
    A. 0.0.0.0
    B. 1.0.0.1
    C. 121.0.0.1
    D. 127.0.0.1

16. What is the well-known port number for the HTTP service?
    A. 20
    B. 21
    C. 80
    D. 25

17. Which of the following addresses is a private IP address? (Select all that apply.)
    A. 10.0.0.34
    B. 191.167.34.5
    C. 172.16.7.99
    D. 12.108.56.7

18. Which port is used by SMTP?
    A. 23
    B. 25
    C. 443
    D. 110

19. What is the subnet mask for 171.103.2.30?
    A. 255.0.0.0
    B. 255.255.0.0
    C. 255.255.255.0
    D. 255.255.255.255

TCP/IP Configuration Concepts

20. Which network service is responsible for assigning IP addresses out to systems on the network when they boot up?
    A. DNS
    B. WINS
    C. DHCP
    D. Server

21. Which network service is responsible for resolving (or converting) FQDNs to IP addresses?
    A. DNS
    B. WINS
    C. DHCP
    D. Server

22. Bob is having trouble pinging addresses by their FQDN, but he can seem to ping them by their IP address. What should you do to help Bob?
    A. Verify Bob's WINS setting in TCP/IP.
    B. Verify Bob's DNS setting in TCP/IP.
    C. Make sure that the system Bob is trying to connect to is in the LMHOSTS file.
    D. Make sure that the system Bob is trying to connect to is on the network.

Network Services

23. Which network service is responsible for allowing Microsoft clients access to the file system on a UNIX server?

    A. NAT

    B. NFS

    C. SMB

    D. Samba

24. Which network service is responsible for assigning IP addresses out to clients on the network?

    A. NAT

    B. WINS

    C. DHCP

    D. NFS

25. Which network service is responsible for allowing Microsoft clients to access the file system on Microsoft servers?

    A. SMB

    B. NFS

    C. NAT

    D. Samba

26. Which network service is responsible for hiding internal network resources by changing the source address of every outbound packet?

    A. NAT

    B. NFS

    C. SMB

    D. Samba

SELF TEST ANSWERS

TCP/IP Protocols

1. ☑ **B.** The IP protocol is responsible for logical addressing and routing, which is a function of layer 3 of the OSI model.
   ☒ **A, C,** and **D** are incorrect. The IP protocol does not run at those layers or perform the functions of those layers.

2. ☑ **A and D.** TCP and UDP are transport protocols. TCP is responsible for connection-oriented communication and error-free delivery, whereas UDP is responsible for connectionless communication.
   ☒ **B and C** are incorrect. IP is a network-layer protocol, and ARP is a layer-2 protocol.

3. ☑ **C.** The Address Resolution Protocol (ARP) is responsible for converting an IP address to a MAC address so that communication can occur.
   ☒ **A, B,** and **D** are incorrect. IP is used for packet delivery, TCP is used for ensuring packet delivery, and ICMP is used for error reporting and status reporting.

4. ☑ **D.** The Simple Mail Transport Protocol (SMTP) is responsible for sending mail across the Internet.
   ☒ **A, B,** and **C** are incorrect. POP3 and IMAP are e-mail protocols, but they are standards for reading e-mail, not sending e-mail. HTTP is the protocol used by web browsers to receive web pages from the web server.

5. ☑ **A.** TCP is responsible for connection-oriented communication in the TCP/IP protocol suite.
   ☒ **B, C,** and **D** are incorrect. IP is used for packet delivery, UDP is used for connectionless communication, and ICMP is used for error reporting and status display.

6. ☑ **A.** ICMP is responsible for reporting errors and sending back status information when communicating over TCP/IP.
   ☒ **B, C,** and **D** are incorrect. TCP is used for connection-oriented communication, UDP is used for connectionless communication, and the IP protocol is used to deliver the packets.

7. ☑ **C.** IP is responsible for packet delivery and logical addressing.
   ☒ **A, B,** and **D** are incorrect. ICMP is used for error reporting, TCP is used to ensure that the packet reaches the destination, and UDP is used for connectionless communication.

TCP/IP Fundamentals

8. ☑ **C.** If you want to communicate with systems on the local network, you will not need to configure a default gateway.

☒ **A, B,** and **D** are incorrect. An IP address and a subnet mask are always needed when configuring TCP/IP. DNS is needed only if you want to communicate by FQDN, not by IP address.

9. ☑ **B.** An IP address is made up of four 8-bit octets, which gives a total of 32 bits.

☒ **A, C,** and **D** are incorrect, because an IP address is made up of 32 bits.

10. ☑ **D.** An IP address is made up of four 8-bit octets.

☒ **A, B,** and **C** are incorrect, because an IP address is made up of four octets.

11. ☑ **C.** A subnet mask of 255.255.255.0 means that the first three octets are part of the network ID, and the last octet is the host ID portion of the address.

☒ **A, B,** and **D** are incorrect, because a subnet mask of 255.255.255.0 has three octets that map out to the network ID.

12. ☑ **B.** Because the subnet mask is 255.255.0.0, the network ID of the IP address is 134.67.x.y—which means that anyone else with the same first two octets is on the same network.

☒ **A, C,** and **D** are incorrect, because they have different network IDs.

TCP/IP Addressing

13. ☑ **B.** Class B networks support 65,534 hosts because the last two octets are the host ID, and each octet supports 256 possible values. 256 × 256= 65,536—but don't forget there are two addresses that are unusable (the network ID and the broadcast address).

☒ **A, C,** and **D** are incorrect. Class A addresses support 16,777,214 hosts, whereas class C addresses support 254 hosts on the network.

14. ☑ **C.** The default subnet mask of a class C network is 255.255.255.0, which means that the first three octets are the network ID and the last octet is the host ID.

☒ **A, B,** and **D** are incorrect, because they are not the default subnet mask of a class C.

15. ☑ **D.** The loopback address is typically known as the 127.0.0.1 address, but it could be any address starting with 127.x.y.z.

☒ **A, B,** and **C** are incorrect, because they are not reserved for the loopback address.

16. ☑ **C.** The port used by HTTP is port 80.

☒ **A, B,** and **D** are incorrect, because 20 and 21 are used by FTP while 25 is used by SMTP.

17. ☑ **A** and **C.** 10.0.0.34 and 172.16.7.99 are examples of addresses that fall into the private IP address ranges, which are not routable on the Internet.

☒ **B** and **D** are incorrect, because they are not private ranges.

18. ☑ **B.** Port 25 is used by SMTP to send e-mail over a TCP/IP network.
☒ **A, C,** and **D** are incorrect. Port 23 is used by Telnet, port 443 is used by secure HTTP (HTTPS), and port 110 is used by POP3 for reading e-mail on the Internet.

19. ☑ **B.** 171.103.2.30 is a class B address, so it has a subnet mask of 255.255.0.0.
☒ **A, C,** and **D** are incorrect, because they are not the subnet mask of 171.103.2.30.

TCP/IP Configuration Concepts

20. ☑ **C.** DHCP is responsible for assigning IP addresses to systems automatically, so that the network administrator does not have to perform that job manually.
☒ **A, B,** and **D** are incorrect. DNS is used to resolve FQDNs to IP addresses, WINS is used to resolve NetBIOS names to IP addresses, and the Server service is used to connect to files on the server.

21. ☑ **A.** DNS is used to resolve FQDNs to IP addresses.
☒ **B, C,** and **D** are incorrect, because WINS is used to resolve NetBIOS names to IP addresses, DHCP is used to automatically assign IP addresses, and the Server service is used to connect to files on the server.

22. ☑ **B.** If you are having trouble resolving FQDNs to IP addresses, you would make sure that the client is pointing to a valid DNS server in its TCP/IP settings.
☒ **A, C,** and **D** are incorrect, because they do not deal with troubleshooting name resolution for FQDNs.

Network Services

23. ☑ **D.** Samba is responsible for allowing Microsoft clients to access resources on the UNIX system because Samba implements the SMB protocol.
☒ **A, B,** and **C** are incorrect. NAT is used to translate the source address of an outgoing packet to that of the external interface of the NAT server. NFS is the file-sharing protocol on UNIX systems, and SMB is the file-sharing protocol used between Microsoft operating systems.

24. ☑ **C.** DHCP is responsible for assigning IP addresses to clients on the network.
☒ **A, B,** and **D** are incorrect. NAT is used to translate the source address of an outgoing packet to that of the external interface of the NAT server. WINS is used to convert computer names (NetBIOS names) to IP addresses. NFS is the protocol that allows UNIX clients to connect to the remote file system of other UNIX (NFS) systems.

25. ☑ **A.** SMB is the protocol in Microsoft environments that allows Microsoft clients to connect to the file system of other Microsoft systems.

☒ **B, C,** and **D** are incorrect. NFS is the protocol that allows UNIX clients to connect to the remote file system of other UNIX (NFS) systems. NAT is used to translate the source address of an outgoing packet to that of the external interface of the NAT server. Samba is the service loaded on UNIX systems to allow Microsoft clients to access resources of the UNIX server.

26. ☑ **A.** NAT is used to translate the source address of an outgoing packet to that of the external interface of the NAT server.

☒ **B, C,** and **D** are incorrect. NFS is the protocol that allows UNIX clients to connect to the remote file system of other UNIX (NFS) systems. SMB is the protocol in Microsoft environments that allows Microsoft clients to connect to the file system of other Microsoft systems. Samba is the service loaded on UNIX systems to allow Microsoft clients to access resources of the UNIX server.

5

Subnetting and Routing

N ow that you have a handle on binary and TCP/IP addressing, you will learn in this chapter how to take one network address range and break it into multiple network ranges called subnets. Subnetting is one of those topics that most IT professionals tend to avoid because of how tedious it is to sit down and calculate the required information to configure your newly created subnets.

The purpose of subnetting is take one address range that you have and break it down into multiple address ranges so that you can assign each address range to a separate network (subnet) in your internetwork (network made up of multiple networks). You may have multiple networks due to physical locations, or maybe you have one location, but because you want to cut down on traffic, you have decided to segment your one network into multiple network segments by placing a router in between each network segment.

Each segment will need its own network address range so that the router can send data from one network to another. If you were to have two physical networks, but kept the one IP range without subnetting, the router would "logically" think that all systems are on the same network and would never try to route data from one side to the other.

on the job

If you do not subnet a network range that is divided into multiple physical network segments, the IP protocol will "logically" think that all systems are on the same network, and it will not try to route the data across the router separating the network segments. As a result, you will be able to communicate with hosts on your segment but not the other segments.

CERTIFICATION OBJECTIVE 5.01

Understanding Subnetting

In this section you will walk through a subnetting example using a class A address. The example is that you have an address range of 10.0.0.0 and you would like to subnet, or divide, the network into two subnetworks known as subnets. The physical network structure is shown in Figure 5-1. The concept of subnetting is

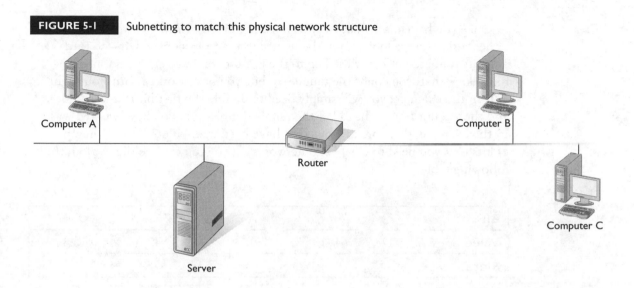

FIGURE 5-1   Subnetting to match this physical network structure

to take some of the host bits from the subnet mask and use them as additional network bits, which will give you more networks. With subnetting, you are taking additional host bits and "masking" them (flagging them as network bits) by setting the bits to a "1" so that they are no longer representing the host ID portion of the subnet mask. This creates additional networks but results in fewer hosts on the network.

To begin, you need to know how many host bits to take to make the desired number of networks. A cheat way that does not involve much math is to look at the eight-bit binary table and then enable the bits that will give you the number of networks you are looking for. For example, you want to divide a class A address of 10.0.0.0 into two networks (be sure to remember that your goal is to have two networks), so you will enable the bits shown in the following table to come up with the decimal value of two.

Bit	8	7	6	5	4	3	2	1
Value	128	64	32	16	8	4	2	1
State							1	

Once you have mathematically enabled the bits that will give you the number of networks you are looking for, the next step is—from right to left—to turn off any bits that are not being used up to the last bit you have enabled. Once you have done that, you count the number of bits you have worked with from right to left. In the example, you will simply need to disable the first bit (far right side), and then count from right to left the number of bits that you have worked with. In the example, there are two bits that have been manipulated, so the number of bits that you need to create two networks is two. You can see the work in the following table:

Bit	8	7	6	5	4	3	2	1
Value	128	64	32	16	8	4	2	1
State							1	0

You can mathematically verify that you have the correct number of bits you want to work with by using this formula: $2^{\text{masked bits}} - 2$ = number of networks. It was decided that two bits were needed to mask the subnet mask to do the subnetting; in checking your work by filling in the formula, you should have $2^2 - 2 = 2$ networks. Having two networks was your goal, so you are on track!

Now that you know that two bits must be masked to create the two subnets, the next step is to look at your IP range of 10.0.0.0 and ask yourself, "What is the default subnet mask of this address?" You should come up with 255.0.0.0, because it is a class A address. Once you know the default subnet mask, the next step is to break the subnet mask down into binary. A default class A subnet mask in binary looks like the following:

Decimal	255	0	0	0
Binary	11111111	00000000	00000000	00000000

Once the subnet mask has been written out in binary, this will be the work area to calculate the new addresses of the two subnets. The first thing you need to do is steal, or "mask," two bits from the host ID portion of the subnet mask and make them network bits by setting them to a "1" state. Remember, the reason for taking two bits is because of your calculation earlier. Because the last three octets of this subnet mask represent the host bits of a class A address, work from left to right and mask two additional bits to get the new binary table that follows:

Decimal	255	0	0	0
Binary	11111111	11000000	00000000	00000000

Notice that the two bits that are now enabled are in the second octet. Also notice that you always work from left to right, except for that little cheat method you saw earlier for calculating the number of bits required to mask. That cheat is just to get the number of bits to work with—but once you actually work with the bits, you always work from left to right.

The next thing you want to do is convert all those octets to decimal values again; then you will have the new subnet mask of the two networks (subnets) we are building. If you convert the new binary value in the preceding table of 11111111.11000000.00000000.00000000, you should get 255.192.0.0 as the new subnet mask of your two new subnets. Write that number down because it will be needed later.

The next step is to calculate the IP ranges for the two different networks, but before that, you should be aware that there are five pieces of information you should know about each network when your calculations are over. These five pieces of information are

- New subnet mask: After subnetting a network you will have a new subnet mask that is used by all subnets you have created.
- Network ID: all host bits set to 0
- First valid address: low-order host bit set to 1; all other host bits are 0
- Broadcast address: all host bits set to 1
- Last valid address: low-order host bit set to 0; all other host bits are 1

You know that the new subnet mask is 255.192.0.0, so you can start by calculating the network ID of each of the two subnets. To determine each piece of information listed previously, you need to determine all of the on/off states of the number of bits that you have stolen. For example, two bits were stolen to create more networks, so there are four possible on/off states with two bits: 00, 01, 10, and 11. As calculated in your binary work area, it would look like the following table:

	First Octet (Decimal)	Second Octet (Binary)	Third Octet (Binary)	Fourth Octet (Binary)
Original IP	10	0	0	0
		00000000	00000000	00000000
		01000000	00000000	00000000
		10000000	00000000	00000000
		11000000	00000000	00000000

The next thing to do after calculating all of the on/off state combinations of two bits is to add in the remaining 0s to the bits that represent the host ID portion. Remember that the original network ID was 10.0.0.0, so the first octet will start with 10, no matter what you change in the binary, because you are starting your work with the second octet.

After you fill in the host bits with all 0s, the next thing you need to do is to cross out the first and last lines; they are illegal, because the subnetted bits are all 0s and all 1s. With the two illegal addresses crossed out, there are only two lines remaining, each representing one of the two networks. This work is shown in the following table:

	First Octet (Decimal)	Second Octet (Binary)	Third Octet (Binary)	Fourth Octet (Binary)
Original IP	10	0	0	0
		~~00000000~~	~~00000000~~	~~00000000~~
		01000000	00000000	00000000
		10000000	00000000	00000000
		~~11000000~~	~~00000000~~	~~00000000~~

The next step is to bring the 10 down to the first octet; each network ID will start with 10 because that is what it was originally. After bringing the 10 down in the first octet, you then calculate the network ID of each of the two networks by leaving all host bits set to 0 (the nonbolded bits) as shown in the following table:

	First Octet (Decimal)	Second Octet (Binary)	Third Octet (Binary)	Fourth Octet (Binary)	Calculation
Original IP	10	0	0	0	
	~~10~~	00000000	00000000	00000000	
	10	01000000	00000000	00000000	10.64.0.0
	10	10000000	00000000	00000000	10.128.0.0
	~~10~~	11000000	00000000	00000000	

In this example, because the two high-order bits are being set, there will be network IDs of 10.64.0.0 and 10.128.0.0. The next number, which can be calculated easily, is the first valid address that can be assigned to a host on each of these networks. To calculate the first valid address, you simply enable the lowest-order bit. The lowest-order bit will be the bit on the far right side. The work area is shown in the following table, and you can see that with the two networks you have a first valid address for each network of 10.64.0.1 and 10.128.0.1:

	First Octet (Decimal)	Second Octet (Binary)	Third Octet (Binary)	Fourth Octet (Binary)	Calculation
Original IP	10	0	0	0	
	~~10~~	00000000	00000000	00000000	
	10	01000000	00000000	00000001	10.64.0.1
	10	10000000	00000000	00000001	10.128.0.1
	~~10~~	11000000	00000000	00000000	

Now that you have calculated the first valid address for each of the two networks, you will need to calculate the broadcast address. The broadcast address is the address that any system will send data to in order to ensure that each system on the network reads the data. To calculate the broadcast address, you will enable all of the host bits and get the outcome in the following table:

	First Octet (Decimal)	Second Octet (Binary)	Third Octet (Binary)	Fourth Octet (Binary)	Calculation
Original IP	10	0	0	0	
	~~10~~	~~00000000~~	~~00000000~~	~~00000000~~	
	10	01111111	11111111	11111111	10.**127**.255.255
	10	10111111	11111111	11111111	10.**191**.255.255
	~~10~~	~~11000000~~	~~00000000~~	~~00000000~~	

As you can see, with all the host bits enabled, if you convert that to decimal, you get 10.127.255.255 and 10.191.255.255 for the broadcast addresses of your two networks. Notice that the first two bits from the left in the second octet have not been changed in this entire process, but they are used in the conversion of that octet from binary to decimal.

on the job

Remember that it is illegal to assign a host an address that has all host bits set to 0 or all host bits set to 1. These are illegal because all host bits set to 0 is reserved for the network ID and all host bits set to 1 is reserved for the broadcast address.

Now that you have calculated the new subnet mask, the network ID, the first valid address, and the broadcast address for your two new subnets, the only additional information you need is the last valid address that may be assigned to hosts on each subnet. To calculate the last valid host address of each subnet, simply subtract one from the broadcast address by disabling the low-order bit (the far right-most host bit). To view what the binary and decimal representation looks like for our last valid address of each network, take a look at the table at the top of the next page.

	First Octet (Decimal)	Second Octet (Binary)	Third Octet (Binary)	Fourth Octet (Binary)	Calculation
Original IP	10	0	0	0	
	~~10~~	~~00000000~~	~~00000000~~	~~00000000~~	
	10	01111111	11111111	11111110	10.127.255.254
	10	10111111	11111111	11111110	10.191.255.254
	~~10~~	~~11000000~~	~~00000000~~	~~00000000~~	

You have now calculated all of the information required to configure the two physical network segments that you have created. The following table summarizes the configuration for each of the two network segments, and Figure 5-2 displays how these two network segments will be configured.

	Network ID	First Valid Address	Last Valid Address	Broadcast Address	Subnet Mask
Subnet 1	10.64.0.0	10.64.0.1	10.127.255.254	10.127.255.255	255.192.0.0
Subnet 2	10.128.0.0	10.128.0.1	10.191.255.254	10.191.255.255	255.192.0.0

FIGURE 5-2 Subnetting a Class A network into two network segments

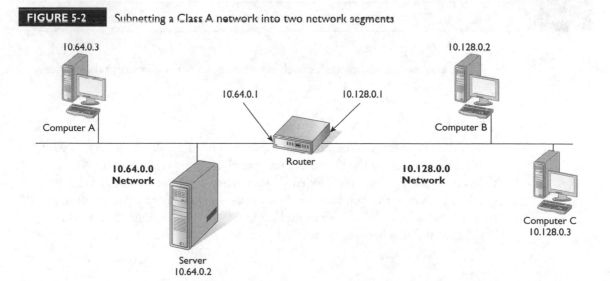

Subnetting a Class A Address

In this exercise you will determine the five pieces of information needed for a class A network that is being divided into four network segments.

Question No. 1

The network ID of the class A address is 120.0.0.0. Take a few pieces of paper and calculate the new subnet mask, the network ID, the first valid address, the last valid address, and the broadcast address of the four subnets. Once you have calculated your answer, fill in the following table. Refer to the subnetting example in this chapter when you need to as a guide to help you calculate the answers for this exercise.

	Network ID	First Valid Address	Last Valid Address	Broadcast Address	Subnet Mask
Subnet 1					
Subnet 2					
Subnet 3					
Subnet 4					

Once you have your answers, check your work against the answer table under "Answer No. 1."

The Work

Given that we want to have four subnets, we will need to take three bits; to verify that answer we enable the bits in our temp work area to get the number 4 and then count the bits from right to left that are used to get to that last enabled bit. 00000100 gives us the number 4, and we have used 4 bits from right to left to get that value. We can also use our formula of $2^{\text{masked bits}} - 2 =$ number of networks to verify that the number is correct, which means we get a formula of $2^3 - 2 = 6$. We get six networks, and we require only four networks. This just means that we have two extra networks that will not be used. If we were to use only two bits, we would have only two networks.

The next thing to calculate is the new subnet mask used by these four new networks. The new subnet mask is determined by masking additional bits in the original subnet mask. The original subnet mask was 11111111.00000000.00000000.00000000, and by masking three additional bits, we get the following:

Binary	11111111	11100000	00000000	00000000
Decimal	255	224	0	0

So your new subnet mask used by all six networks (we actually need only four networks) is 255.224.0.0. Now that we have determined that we have to take three bits, we then figure out all the on/off states of three bits. The following should be the on/off states of three bits. (I have also filled in all the host bits at the same time.)

	First Octet (Decimal)	Second Octet (Binary)	Third Octet (Binary)	Fourth Octet (Binary)
Original IP	120	0	0	0
		00000000	00000000	00000000
		00100000	00000000	00000000
		01000000	00000000	00000000
		01100000	00000000	00000000
		10000000	00000000	00000000
		10100000	00000000	00000000
		11000000	00000000	00000000
		11100000	00000000	00000000

Once you have figured out each of the on/off states of three bits and have filled in the host bits of all 0s, you have the network ID for each of the six networks. If you convert the binary to decimal, you should have the following as the network ID of each subnet:

	First Octet (Decimal)	Second Octet (Binary)	Third Octet (Binary)	Fourth Octet (Binary)	Decimal Value
Original IP	120	0	0	0	
		00000000	00000000	00000000	
	120	00100000	00000000	00000000	120.32.0.0
	120	01000000	00000000	00000000	120.64.0.0
	120	01100000	00000000	00000000	120.96.0.0
	120	10000000	00000000	00000000	120.128.0.0
	120	10100000	00000000	00000000	120.160.0.0
	120	11000000	00000000	00000000	120.192.0.0
		11100000	00000000	00000000	

Once you have calculated the network IDs, continue with figuring out the first valid address by turning on the low-order bit to get the following result:

	First Octet (Decimal)	Second Octet (Binary)	Third Octet (Binary)	Fourth Octet (Binary)	Decimal Value
Original IP	120	0	0	0	
		00000000	00000000	00000000	
	120	00100000	00000000	00000001	120.32.0.1
	120	01000000	00000000	00000001	120.64.0.1
	120	01100000	00000000	00000001	120.96.0.1
	120	10000000	00000000	00000001	120.128.0.1
	120	10100000	00000000	00000001	120.160.0.1
	120	11000000	00000000	00000001	120.192.0.1
		11100000	00000000	00000000	

To calculate the broadcast address, you should have enabled all of the host bits to get the list of addresses shown in the following table:

	First Octet (Decimal)	Second Octet (Binary)	Third Octet (Binary)	Fourth Octet (Binary)	Decimal Value
Original IP	120	0	0	0	
		00000000	00000000	00000000	
	120	00111111	11111111	11111111	120.63.255.255
	120	01011111	11111111	11111111	120.95.255.255
	120	01111111	11111111	11111111	120.127.255.255
	120	10011111	11111111	11111111	120.159.255.255
	120	10111111	11111111	11111111	120.191.255.255
	120	11011111	11111111	11111111	120.223.255.255
		11100000	00000000	00000000	

Finally, calculate the last valid address used by each of these six subnets by turning off the low-order host bit and leaving all other host bits enabled, as shown in the following table:

	First Octet (Decimal)	Second Octet (Binary)	Third Octet (Binary)	Fourth Octet (Binary)	Decimal Value
Original IP	120	0	0	0	
		00000000	00000000	00000000	
	120	00111111	11111111	11111110	120.63.255.254
	120	01011111	11111111	11111110	120.95.255.254
	120	01111111	11111111	11111110	120.127.255.254
	120	10011111	11111111	11111110	120.159.255.254
	120	10111111	11111111	11111110	120.191.255.254
	120	11011111	11111111	11111110	120.223.255.254
		11100000	00000000	00000000	

Now that you have done all the paperwork, you should have come up with the following answer for the first four subnets of the 120.0.0.0 network:

Answer No. 1

	Network ID	First Valid Address	Last Valid Address	Broadcast Address
Subnet 1	120.32.0.0	120.32.0.1	120.63.255.254	120.63.255.255
Subnet 2	120.64.0.0	120.64.0.1	120.95.255.254	120.95.255.255
Subnet 3	120.96.0.0	120.96.0.1	120.127.255.254	120.127.255.255
Subnet 4	120.128.0.0	120.128.0.1	120.159.255.254	120.159.255.255

The subnet mask for each of the four networks is 255.224.0.0.

Question No. 2

You are responsible for subnetting the network ID of 190.34.0.0 into eight subnets. Take some paper and walk through your binary work of subnetting this class B network into eight subnets. Once you have calculated the information on paper, fill in the following table:

	Network ID	First Valid Address	Last Valid Address	Broadcast Address	Subnet Mask
Subnet 1					
Subnet 2					
Subnet 3					
Subnet 4					
Subnet 5					
Subnet 6					
Subnet 7					
Subnet 8					

Answer No. 2

Once you have calculated the information for each of the eight networks and have filled in the preceding table, check your work with the answer that follows. If you made a mistake, double-check your math when converting binary to decimal and also double-check that you have followed the rules given for manipulating the bits to get the desired outcome.

	Network ID	First Valid Address	Last Valid Address	Broadcast Address
Subnet 1	190.34.16.0	190.34.16.1	190.34.31.254	190.34.31.255
Subnet 2	190.34.32.0	190.34.32.1	190.34.47.254	190.34.47.255
Subnet 3	190.34.48.0	190.34.48.1	190.34.63.254	190.34.63.255
Subnet 4	190.34.64.0	190.34.64.1	190.34.79.254	190.34.79.255
Subnet 5	190.34.80.0	190.34.80.1	190.34.95.254	190.34.95.255
Subnet 6	190.34.96.0	190.34.96.1	190.34.111.254	190.34.111.255
Subnet 7	190.34.112.0	190.34.112.1	190.34.127.254	190.34.127.255
Subnet 8	190.34.128.0	190.34.128.1	190.34.141.254	190.34.141.255

The subnet mask used by all segments is 255.255.240.0.

Question No. 3

Your manager has purchased a class C network range and has asked that you subnet this class C network into two subnets for the two network segments that are going to be built. One network segment will host client machines used by customers to do online ordering, and the other segment will host the corporate machines used by your employees.

The class C network ID that you have purchased is 216.83.11.0. Once again, take a piece of paper and start by writing out the default subnet mask of this class C address and then start manipulating the host bits to get the network ID, first valid host ID, last valid host ID, broadcast address, and new subnet mask. Once you have calculated all the required information, fill in the following table:

	Network ID	First Valid Address	Last Valid Address	Broadcast Address
Subnet 1				
Subnet 2				

The new subnet mask for all subnets is _____.

Answer No. 3

Once you have filled in the preceding table, check your answers in the following table to verify that you have calculated everything correctly. This example usually catches people, because they do not see a 255 as the broadcast address, or a 0 as the network ID. Remember to figure things out in binary and you can't go wrong; people usually make mistakes when they try to take shortcuts.

	Network ID	First Valid Address	Last Valid Address	Broadcast Address
Subnet 1	216.83.11.64	216.83.11.65	216.83.11.126	216.83.11.127
Subnet 2	216.83.11.128	216.83.11.129	216.83.11.190	216.83.11.191

The new subnet mask for all subnets is 255.255.255.192.

This section has introduced you to the concept of subnetting, which you will need to know for the Network+ exam. So make sure you are familiar with identifying the class addresses and then have a solid understanding of subnetting!

ON THE CD

Be sure to check out the exercises in LabBook.pdf found on the CD-ROM for more practice on subnetting.

CERTIFICATION OBJECTIVE 5.02

Classful vs. Classless Addressing

Chapter 4 focused on introducing you to the different class IP addresses: class A, class B, and class C. Each IP address that you use on a system falls into one of these three classes—this is known as classful addressing. Table 5-1 summarizes the three major address classes.

TABLE 5-1	Address Class	Value of First Octet	Octet Setup	Number of Host
Reviewing Classful IP Addressing	Class A	1–127	N.H.H.H	16,777,214
	Class B	128–191	N.N.H.H	65,534
	Class C	192–223	N.N.N.H	254

Everything that you have learned about the different address classes, including network IDs, host IDs, and default subnet masks, is based on classful addressing.

Classful IP addressing divides the network ID and host ID portions of an IP address at an octet.	*For example, a class B address uses the first two octets as the network ID and the last two octets as the host ID.*

CIDR

Classless Inter-Domain Routing (CIDR), or classless addressing, is the idea of not following the default concepts of classful addressing. For example, if you wish to break your class A address down into more than one network and subnet the network, then you are creating a variable-length subnet mask. A *variable-length subnet mask (VLSM)* is a subnet mask that does not follow the defaults of address classes but simply specifies which bits in the IP address are part of the network ID by setting the corresponding bit in the subnet mask to a 1.

With the concept of variable-length subnet masks, there needed to be a standard method of indicating how many bits in the IP address were network bits, so the concept of Classless Inter-Domain Routing (CIDR) notation was created. With CIDR notation, you specify the IP address and a / followed by the number of bits that make up the network ID. For example, 10.0.0.0/8 specifies that the network ID is the first eight bits (which would mean the subnet masks is 255.0.0.0).

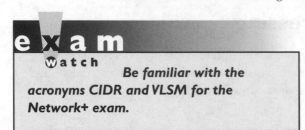

e x a m

ⓦ a t c h *Be familiar with the acronyms CIDR and VLSM for the Network+ exam.*

Supernetting

Supernetting, like subnetting, is part of the CIDR concept where we are altering the default way the IP address scheme works. You learned earlier that the goal of subnetting was to take bits from the host ID portion of an address to create more networks (subnets). Supernetting works the opposite way: you take bits away from the network ID to combine networks. The goal of supernetting is to combine multiple smaller networks into one big network ID.

CERTIFICATION OBJECTIVE 5.03

Understanding Routing

Now that you have an understanding of subnetting, the next topic to discuss is routing. *Routing* is the concept of sending data from one network to another. Once we have the network broken into segments, it is up to the routers to route the data from one network segment to another, as shown in Figure 5-3.

The router is responsible for routing information to the destination network, and it does this by using what is known as a routing table. A routing table is a list of destination networks that resides in memory on the router, and the router uses this to identify where to send data to reach the destination. If the destination is not in the routing table, the router will not be able to send the information to the destination, as shown in Figure 5-3.

FIGURE 5-3   A router depends on its routing table for knowledge of destination networks.

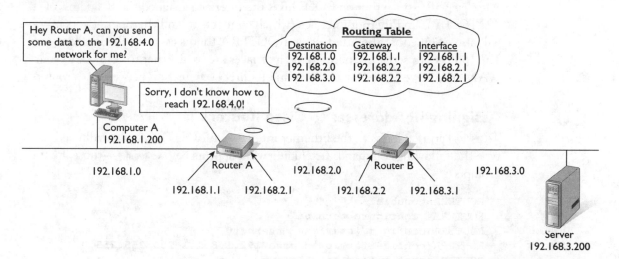

If you take a look at Figure 5-3, you can see that COMPUTERA is trying to send data off the network by sending it to ROUTERA. ROUTERA looks in its routing table to see whether the destination of 192.168.4.0 is listed, and as you can see in the figure, the router does not know how to reach that destination, so it returns an error.

Let's look at the routing table in the figure and learn how to read it. If you take a look at the third entry in the routing table of ROUTERA, you can see that ROUTERA has an entry for the 192.168.3.0 network. If any systems on the 192.168.1.0 network send data to the 192.168.3.0 network, the router will send the information to the "gateway" value of that entry. The gateway is where the router needs to send the data to reach that particular destination. In this case, it will send the data to 192.168.2.2, and it will get to 192.168.2.2 by sending the data out the interface of 192.168.2.1 on ROUTERA. The interface column is important because it lets the router know how that gateway can be reached from ROUTERA.

Cisco Routers

The most popular vendor that supplies routers is Cisco. Cisco routers are used to connect networks together and route data between these networks. A Cisco router connects to different networks by having network cards, known as interfaces, built into the router. Each interface is assigned an IP address and is connected to a network (as shown back in Figure 5-3).

Let's assume that ROUTERA and ROUTERB in Figure 5-3 are Cisco routers. Also, we will assume that on ROUTERA the interface assigned the IP address of 192.168.1.1 is an Ethernet interface (which connects to an Ethernet network). We will also assume that the interface on ROUTERA that is assigned the IP address of 192.168.2.1 is a serial interface. Serial interfaces are used either to connect to your WAN or to serve as a point-to-point link (a direct connection between two routers).

Assigning IP Addresses to Cisco Routers

To assign an IP address to the Ethernet interface on ROUTERA, you will need to type the following commands (excluding what appears before > or #—those are the prompts):

```
ROUTERA> enable
ROUTERA# configure terminal
ROUTERA(config)# interface ethernet0
ROUTERA(config-if)# ip address 192.168.1.1 255.255.255.0
ROUTERA(config-if)# no shutdown
```

Let's take a look at what each of these commands do. The first command, **enable**, is used to move from user exec mode of the router to privilege exec mode. In user exec mode you are unable to make changes, so you had to go to privilege exec mode.

In order to change the settings of the Ethernet interface, you need to go to the interface prompt, which is in global configuration, where most changes are made. To move to global configuration, you typed **configure terminal**, and to move to the interface prompt, you typed **interface ethernet0**. Ethernet0 is the first Ethernet interface on the router; the second Ethernet interface would be Ethernet1 (if you had a second Ethernet interface).

Once at the Ethernet interface prompt, you then assigned the IP address with the **ip address** command. The last command, **no shutdown**, is used to enable the interface. To disable the interface at any time, you could use the **shutdown** command.

To assign the IP address to the Serial 0 port on ROUTERA, you would type the following commands:

```
ROUTERA> enable
ROUTERA# configure terminal
ROUTERA(config)# interface serial0
ROUTERA(config-if)# ip address 192.168.2.1 255.255.255.0
ROUTERA(config-if)# encapsulation hdlc
ROUTERA(config-if)# no shutdown
```

Note that the commands are pretty much the same, except for the fact that we navigate to the Serial0 interface instead of the Ethernet0 interface. After the IP address is assigned with the **ip address** command, you then set the encapsulation protocol for the serial link. Popular encapsulation protocols over a serial link are HDLC or PPP. You need to ensure you are using the same protocol that is on the other end of the serial link.

Viewing the Routing Table on Cisco Routers

Once you have the IP addresses assigned to each interface, you will need to ensure that routing is enabled on the router by typing the following commands:

```
ROUTERA> enable
ROUTERA# configure terminal
ROUTERA(config)# ip routing
```

The **ip routing** command is used to enable routing on the router. Should you wish to disable routing on the router, you would then type the **no ip routing** command.

Once routing has been enabled, the router will automatically add a route for each of the networks it is directly connected to. To view the routing table and verify that the routes are added, type

```
ROUTERA> show ip route
```

If you have a look at Figure 5-4, you will notice that the **show ip route** command was typed and the routing table is displayed. Notice in the figure that the route to the 192.168.1.0 and 192.168.2.0 networks is automatically added because the router is connected to those networks. You will also notice a letter C to the left of each route entry, which means that the route is there because the router is directly connect to the network.

Adding a Route to Cisco Routers

When administering a Cisco router, you will need to add routes for routes that do not exist in the routing table. For example, looking back to Figure 5-4, ROUTERA knows about the 192.168.1.0 and 192.168.2.0 networks but not the 192.168.3.0 network. If you want to configure ROUTERA so that it knows about the 192.168.3.0 network, you will need to add the route manually by typing

```
ROUTERA> enable
ROUTERA# configure terminal
ROUTERA(config)# ip route 192.168.3.0 255.255.255.0 192.168.2.2
```

FIGURE 5-4

Looking at the routing table of a Cisco router

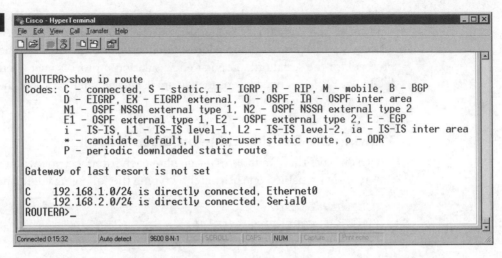

```
ROUTERA>show ip route
Codes: C - connected, S - static, I - IGRP, R - RIP, M - mobile, B - BGP
       D - EIGRP, EX - EIGRP external, O - OSPF, IA - OSPF inter area
       N1 - OSPF NSSA external type 1, N2 - OSPF NSSA external type 2
       E1 - OSPF external type 1, E2 - OSPF external type 2, E - EGP
       i - IS-IS, L1 - IS-IS level-1, L2 - IS-IS level-2, ia - IS-IS inter area
       * - candidate default, U - per-user static route, o - ODR
       P - periodic downloaded static route

Gateway of last resort is not set

C    192.168.1.0/24 is directly connected, Ethernet0
C    192.168.2.0/24 is directly connected, Serial0
ROUTERA>_
```

In this code listing the command is **ip route** (shown in Figure 5-5) to add a route to the routing table. The 192.168.3.0 is the address of the destination network you are adding and its subnet mask, while 192.168.2.2 is the address that ROUTERA is to send information to that is destined for the 192.168.3.0 network. Notice that 192.168.2.2 is the address of an interface on ROUTERB that ROUTERA can communicate directly with. The idea here is that in order for ROUTERA to send data to the 192.168.3.0 network, it will pass the data to ROUTERB via the interface at 192.168.2.2, which will then send the data onto the 192.168.3.0 network.

e x a m
ⓦatch

For the exam know that the *ip route* command is used to add a static route on a Cisco router and the *show ip route* command is used to display your routing table.

If you view the routing table with the **show ip route** command, you will notice that you have routes in the routing table that are there because the router is connected to that network, and you will notice the static routes, which are indicated with a letter *S*. Figure 5-6 displays the new routing table with the static route added.

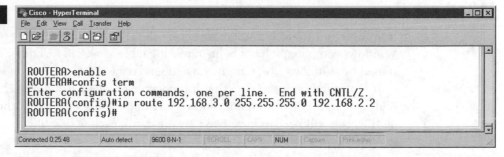

FIGURE 5-5

Adding a static route to a Cisco router

```
ROUTERA>enable
ROUTERA#config term
Enter configuration commands, one per line.  End with CNTL/Z.
ROUTERA(config)#ip route 192.168.3.0 255.255.255.0 192.168.2.2
ROUTERA(config)#
```

FIGURE 5-6

Displaying the routing table after the static route has been added

```
ROUTERA>show ip route
Codes: C - connected, S - static, I - IGRP, R - RIP, M - mobile, B - BGP
       D - EIGRP, EX - EIGRP external, O - OSPF, IA - OSPF inter area
       N1 - OSPF NSSA external type 1, N2 - OSPF NSSA external type 2
       E1 - OSPF external type 1, E2 - OSPF external type 2, E - EGP
       i - IS-IS, L1 - IS-IS level-1, L2 - IS-IS level-2, ia - IS-IS inter area
       * - candidate default, U - per-user static route, o - ODR
       P - periodic downloaded static route

Gateway of last resort is not set

C    192.168.1.0/24 is directly connected, Ethernet0
C    192.168.2.0/24 is directly connected, Serial0
S    192.168.3.0/24 [1/0] via 192.168.2.2
ROUTERA>
```

Deleting a Route on a Cisco Router

It was pretty easy to add a route to the Cisco router with the **ip route** command, and it is just as easy to delete a route with the **no ip route** command. To delete a route from the routing table, use the following syntax:

```
ROUTERA> enable
ROUTERA# configure terminal
ROUTERA(config)# no ip route 192.168.3.0 255.255.255.0
```

Windows Routers

It is important to understand that because the IP protocol is running on your Windows computer, it has a built-in routing table as well. The built-in routing table is used by Windows to determine how to send data.

It is also important to note that it is possible to take a Windows server and install routing features on it so that it routes data from one network to another. In order to do this, you will need to have two network cards, each acting like an interface on a real router.

Once you have both network cards installed and have assigned IP addresses to them, you can then enable the Windows Routing feature by going to Start | Administrative Tools | Routing And Remote Access. Once the *Routing and Remote Access (RRAS)* console is started, you then must enable Routing and Remote Access by right-clicking your server in the left side of the window and then choosing Configure And Enable Routing And Remote Access. This will launch the wizard that will allow you to enable the routing feature of a Windows server. In the RRAS Setup Wizard, you will need to choose Custom Configuration and then choose Next. When you reach the screen asking which services you wish to install, select LAN Routing (shown in Figure 5-7); then press Next and Finish the wizard.

FIGURE 5-7

Enabling LAN
Routing on a
Windows server

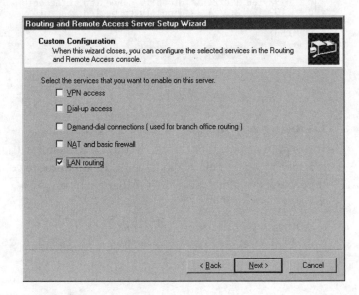

Once you have enabled LAN Routing in Routing and Remote Access, you can then perform tasks such as viewing your routing table, adding routes, or deleting routes by right-clicking Static Routes and choosing the appropriate command shown in Figure 5-8. You can also use a number of commands in Windows to manage your routing table, which is what the next few sections cover.

Viewing Your Routing Table

Because you have TCP/IP installed on your system and the IP protocol uses a routing table to determine the pathway to destination networks, each system running TCP/IP has a routing table. If you wish to view your system's routing table, you can type the following command in a command prompt:

```
route print
```

The **route print** command displays the routing table of your local system, and you should have output similar to that shown in Figure 5-9. Let's look at the contents of the output of the route print shown in Figure 5-9. You can see that there is a route for the 127.0.0.0 network, which is reserved for the loopback test. Notice that any messages sent to the entire network address of 127.0.0.0 are sent to the localhost address of 127.0.0.1 (specified in the gateway column).

You will also notice that there is a route for the 192.168.1.0 network. This is actually the network that this system is plugged into. Therefore, in order for this system to send data to the network, it simply sends data to the 192.168.1.200 address (which is its own network card). You will also notice that there is a route for the 224.0.0.0 network address range, which is the class D range used by multicasting applications.

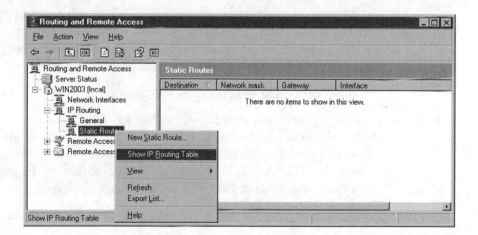

FIGURE 5-8

Displaying the Windows server routing table or adding a new static route

```
C:\WINDOWS\System32\cmd.exe                                    _ □ ×

C:\>route print
============================================================================
Interface List
0x1 ........................... MS TCP Loopback interface
0x10003 ...00 0c 29 4a cd 6c ...... AMD PCNET Family PCI Ethernet Adapter #2 - P
acket Scheduler Miniport
0x10004 ...02 00 4c 4f 4f 50 ...... Microsoft Loopback Adapter
============================================================================
Active Routes:
Network Destination        Netmask          Gateway       Interface  Metric
       127.0.0.0        255.0.0.0        127.0.0.1       127.0.0.1       1
     192.168.1.0    255.255.255.0    192.168.1.200   192.168.1.200      30
   192.168.1.200  255.255.255.255      127.0.0.1       127.0.0.1       30
   192.168.1.255  255.255.255.255    192.168.1.200   192.168.1.200      30
     192.168.2.0    255.255.255.0      192.168.2.1     192.168.2.1      30
     192.168.2.1  255.255.255.255      127.0.0.1       127.0.0.1       30
   192.168.2.255  255.255.255.255      192.168.2.1     192.168.2.1      30
       224.0.0.0        240.0.0.0    192.168.1.200   192.168.1.200      30
       224.0.0.0        240.0.0.0      192.168.2.1     192.168.2.1      30
 255.255.255.255  255.255.255.255    192.168.1.200   192.168.1.200       1
 255.255.255.255  255.255.255.255      192.168.2.1     192.168.2.1       1
============================================================================
Persistent Routes:
  None

C:\>
```

Looking at Figure 5-9, you will also notice that there are two entries for broadcast addresses. The first entry is 192.168.1.255, which is the broadcast address for the 192.168.1.0 network segment; there is also a broadcast address for all network segments, which is known as the 255.255.255.255 address. The 255.255.255.255 address is known as an internetwork broadcast address, and clients can use it to send data to all systems on all subnets, not just their own subnets.

Adding a Route

Let's assume that Figure 5-9 is displaying the routing table of ROUTERA, which was shown in the network diagram of Figure 5-3. In this routing table, we don't have a route for the 192.168.3.0 network, so you will learn how to add a route to the routing table. To add a route to your routing table, you can use the **route add** command. The syntax to use the **route add** command is as follows:

```
route add <destination IP> MASK <subnet mask> <gateway address>
```

In our example, you would like to add a route for the destination address of 192.168.3.0 with a subnet mask of 255.255.255.0. The gateway address is where your system will send the data so that it can reach the destination. If you were adding the route to ROUTERA found in Figure 5-3, you would send to the gateway (how to reach the destination) of 192.168.2.2. Our command is typed as

```
route add 192.168.3.0 MASK 255.255.255.0 192.168.2.2
```

Once you have typed this command into ROUTERA, you can verify that the route has been added by typing the **route print** command again at the command prompt. Figure 5-10 displays both the addition of the route and the routing table after the route has been added.

w a t c h

For the Network+ exam   *use the* route add **command and to view your**
know that in Windows to add a route you   *routing table you use the* route print **command.**

Deleting a Route

You may delete a route from the routing table at any time by using the **route delete** command. The **route delete** command uses one parameter—the destination route that you wish to delete from the routing table. If you wanted to delete the 192.168.3.0 network from your routing table, the syntax for the **route delete** command is as follows:

```
route delete 192.168.3.0
```

FIGURE 5-10

Adding a route on a Windows server and then viewing the routing table

```
C:\WINDOWS\System32\cmd.exe                                              _ □ X

C:\>route add 192.168.3.0 MASK 255.255.255.0 192.168.2.2

C:\>route print
===========================================================================
Interface List
0x1 .......................... MS TCP Loopback interface
0x10003 ...00 0c 29 4a cd 6c ...... AMD PCNET Family PCI Ethernet Adapter #2 - P
acket Scheduler Miniport
0x10001 ...02 00 4c 4f 4f 50 ...... Microsoft Loopback Adapter
===========================================================================
===========================================================================
Active Routes:
Network Destination        Netmask          Gateway       Interface  Metric
        127.0.0.0        255.0.0.0        127.0.0.1       127.0.0.1       1
      192.168.1.0    255.255.255.0    192.168.1.200   192.168.1.200      30
    192.168.1.200  255.255.255.255        127.0.0.1       127.0.0.1      30
    192.168.1.255  255.255.255.255    192.168.1.200   192.168.1.200      30
      192.168.2.0    255.255.255.0    192.168.2.1     192.168.2.1        30
      192.168.2.1  255.255.255.255        127.0.0.1       127.0.0.1      30
    192.168.2.255  255.255.255.255    192.168.2.1     192.168.2.1        30
      192.168.3.0    255.255.255.0    192.168.2.2     192.168.2.1         1
        224.0.0.0        240.0.0.0    192.168.1.200   192.168.1.200      30
        224.0.0.0        240.0.0.0    192.168.2.1     192.168.2.1        30
  255.255.255.255  255.255.255.255    192.168.1.200   192.168.1.200       1
  255.255.255.255  255.255.255.255    192.168.2.1     192.168.2.1         1
===========================================================================
Persistent Routes:
  None

C:\>█
```

CERTIFICATION OBJECTIVE 5.04

Dynamic Routing Protocols

Managing the entries in router routing tables on a large internetwork could be a time-consuming task. To help router administrators manage the routing table of routers throughout the internetwork, the routers could have dynamic routing protocols enabled. *Dynamic* routing protocols are protocols enabled on routers that allow them to share information contained within their routing tables with one another. As a result, routes that are known by one router will be shared with the other routers, thus saving the router administrator from having to add all the routes on all the routers!

The term used for when all the routes on the network are merged into each router's routing table is convergence. *Convergence* occurs when all routing tables have been shared with all other routers and all routers have updated their routing table with that new information.

Convergence is when the routes on each router are shared with all other routers and merged into each router's routing table.

When discussing the different routing protocols, it is important to note that there are two major classes of routing protocols, distance vector and link state. Each routing protocol is either a distance vector protocol or a link state protocol.

Distance Vector

Distance vector routing protocols measure the best route to use based on the lowest hop count. The hop count is increased by one for every router between the source and the destination. With distance vector routing protocols, the route with the lowest hop count is typically selected as the destination path for the data.

exam
watch
Examples of distance vector routing protocols are RIP and IGRP.

RIP/RIPv2

The *Routing Information Protocol (RIP)* is a distance vector protocol and is responsible for sharing its routing table information with neighboring routers by broadcasting the information over UDP every 30 seconds. This broadcasting of the routing table is known as advertising, and advertising the routing table information with neighboring routers exempts the network administrator from having to add the routes manually.

RIP is an industry-standard routing protocol, which means that it is supported by many different vendors, so you could use it as a routing protocol to share routing table information between routers from different manufacturers. RIP will choose the route with the lowest hop count, but if two different routes have the same hop count, RIP will load-balance the traffic over those two routes. Know that RIP is limited to 15 hops, so it is used only on small networks.

RIPv1 has the limitation that it only works with classful addresses because it doesn't send subnet mask information with the routing table. RIPv2 is an update to RIPv1 and does support classless addressing and variable-length subnet masks because it sends the subnet mask information with the routing table.

Let's assume you are the administrator for ROUTERA shown back in Figure 5-3. ROUTERA will have routes to the 192.168.1.0 and 192.168.2.0 networks by default. If you wanted to configure RIP on ROUTERA to advertise knowledge of those two networks, you would type the following commands on ROUTERA (remember not to type what is before the > and # because they are the prompts that would appear on the screen):

```
ROUTERA> enable
ROUTERA# configure terminal
ROUTERA(config)# router rip
ROUTERA(config-router)# network 192.168.1.0
ROUTERA(config-router)# network 192.168.2.0
```

Once RIP, or any other routing protocol, has been enabled on both ROUTERA and ROUTERB, the two routers will then share knowledge of any networks they know about. When ROUTERA receives knowledge of the 192.168.3.0 network and builds the new network into its routing table, this is known as convergence. Figure 5-11 displays the routing table on ROUTERA after RIP has been enabled on both routers. Notice the letter *R* beside the 192.168.3.0 route, meaning that the route was learned through RIP.

The routing table displays the new route learned through RIP.

```
🖥 Cisco - HyperTerminal                                              _ □ ×
File  Edit  View  Call  Transfer  Help
🗋 🖨  🔊 🖇  🗐 🖺  🖆

ROUTERA>show ip route
Codes: C - connected, S - static, I - IGRP, R - RIP, M - mobile, B - BGP
       D - EIGRP, EX - EIGRP external, O - OSPF, IA - OSPF inter area
       N1 - OSPF NSSA external type 1, N2 - OSPF NSSA external type 2
       E1 - OSPF external type 1, E2 - OSPF external type 2, E - EGP
       i - IS-IS, L1 - IS-IS level-1, L2 - IS-IS level-2, ia - IS-IS inter area
       * - candidate default, U - per-user static route, o - ODR
       P - periodic downloaded static route

Gateway of last resort is not set

C    192.168.1.0/24 is directly connected, Ethernet0
C    192.168.2.0/24 is directly connected, Serial0
R    192.168.3.0/24 [120/1] via 192.168.2.2, 00:00:14, Serial0
ROUTERA>_

Connected 0:43:18    Auto detect    9600 8-N-1    SCROLL   CAPS   NUM   Capture   Print echo
```

IGRP

Another example of a distance vector routing protocol is the *Interior Gateway Routing Protocol (IGRP)*. IGRP is a classful routing protocol that was built by Cisco, so you will only use it on networks where you have only Cisco routers.

IGRP was designed to improve on RIP limitations; it has a maximum hop count of 255 and uses the concepts of an *autonomous system (AS)*. An autonomous system is a grouping of routers that share routing table information. Routers using IGRP will only share the routes with other routers in the AS. Another improvement is that the full routing table is advertised every 90 seconds instead of 30 seconds as is the case with RIP.

To enable IGRP on your Cisco router, you type the following commands:

```
ROUTERA> enable
ROUTERA# configure terminal
ROUTERA(config)# router igrp 10
ROUTERA(config-router)# network 192.168.1.0
ROUTERA(config-router)# network 192.168.2.0
```

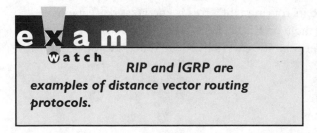

RIP and IGRP are examples of distance vector routing protocols.

In this code listing you will notice that to enable IGRP on a Cisco router is similar to enabling RIP. The difference is that when you enable IGRP, you specify the AS number for the router. In this case I have used 10, so any other router with an AS number of 10 will receive routing information for the 192.168.1.0 and 192.168.2.0 networks.

BGP

The *Border Gateway Protocol (BGP)* is known as an exterior gateway protocol that is responsible for sharing routing table information with routers outside your autonomous system. The protocols discussed before this are known as interior gateway protocols that are responsible for sharing routing tables within your autonomous system (or network).

BGP is designed to send changes made to the routing table when the change occurs versus at a regular interval like RIP. BGP only sends the change, while other routing protocols such as RIP send the entire table. BGP is also a classless routing protocol that supports CIDR.

on the **job**

BGP is a newer version of the Exterior Gateway Protocol (EGP).

Link State

Link state routing protocols are a little more advanced than distance vector routing protocols in the sense that a link state routing protocol knows about the entire network topology. A link state protocol is responsible for monitoring the state of the link between the routers. This link state information is then used to determine the optimal route to a destination network. Although protocols such as RIP have knowledge of neighboring routers, link state protocols have knowledge of the entire network topology and multicast the routing table information to the entire network.

One of the benefits of the link state routing protocols is that if a link is down, that information is stored in the routing table and that pathway will not be used. Because a distance vector routing protocol does not store link state information, it is possible that it will not know of a link that is unavailable for some time and it could still send traffic through that pathway.

OSPF

Open Shortest Path First (OSPF) is an example of a link state protocol. OSPF is an industry-standard protocol, which means that it is available to routers built by different manufacturers and you can use it as a protocol to share routing information between the dissimilar routers.

Like IGRP, OSPF uses autonomous systems, but it also has the capability of dividing the AS into logical groups called areas. OSPF supports VLSM and has an unlimited hop count.

IS-IS

The intermediate system–to–intermediate system (IS-IS) routing protocol competes with OSPF by being a link state routing protocol for inside the network (interior gateway). IS-IS was developed by Digital Equipment Corporation (DEC) and has become an industry-standard protocol, although not as popular as OSPF.

Like OSPF, IS-IS uses a link state algorithm to maintain status information on all the links and routes on the network so that each router running the IS-IS protocol will have knowledge of the entire network topology.

OSPF and IS-IS are examples of link state routing protocols.

Hybrid

There are hybrid routing protocols that combine the features of distance vector and link state. A popular hybrid routing protocol that was built by Cisco is the *Enhanced Interior Gateway Routing Protocol (EIGRP),* which improves upon IGRP by being a classless routing protocol that supports VLSM and supports both IPv4 and IPv6. EIGRP also has a maximum hop count of 255 hops.

EIGRP is an example of a hybrid routing protocol.

CERTIFICATION SUMMARY

In this chapter you have learned more about the TCP/IP protocol and some of its functionality, such as subnetting and routing. You have learned that from time to time you may need to divide a network range into multiple network blocks (subnets) to follow the physical structure of the network. You have also learned that the IP protocol uses a routing table to determine how to deliver data to its destination.

This chapter has also discussed routing protocols, and you have learned the difference between a distance vector routing protocol and a link state routing protocol.

TWO-MINUTE DRILL

Understanding Subnetting

❑ The purpose of subnetting is to break one network ID into multiple subnetworks (subnets) so that you can follow the physical structure of the network.

❑ With subnetting you take host bits from the subnet mask and mask them to be network bits—thus creating more networks but fewer machines per network.

❑ To determine how many bits to take from the host ID portion of the subnet mask, use the formula $2^{masked\ bits} - 2$ = number of networks.

❑ Remember to calculate the network ID, first valid address, last valid address, broadcast address, and new subnet mask of each subnet created.

Classful vs. Classless Addressing

❑ Classful addressing is when the network ID falls into one of the default network IDs of either a class A, class B, or class C address.

❑ Classless addressing is when the network ID is altered from a normal classful address.

Understanding Routing

❑ The IP protocol is responsible for routing data to its destination.

❑ You can view your routing table with **route print**.

❑ You may add a route to a routing table with **route add**.

❑ You may delete a route from the routing table with **route delete**.

❑ You may use a dynamic routing protocol such as RIP or OSPF so that the routers share routing table information with one another, eliminating the need to manually configure the routes individually.

Dynamic Routing Protocols

❑ There are two major types of routing protocols, distance vector and link state.

❑ Distance vector routing protocols share routing information with neighboring routers and measure the best route by how many hops away a destination is.

❑ Link state routing protocols share routing information with all routers on the network and include information on the state of the link.

❑ RIP and IGRP are examples of distance vector routing protocols.

❑ OSPF and IS-IS are examples of link state routing protocols.

SELF TEST

The following questions will help you measure your understanding of the material presented in this chapter. Read all the choices carefully, because there may appear to be more than one correct answer, but you will need to choose the best answer.

Understanding Subnetting

1. You have the network ID of 131.107.0.0 and you would like to subnet your network into six networks. What will be your new subnet mask?
   A. 255.224.0.0
   B. 255.255.224.0
   C. 255.192.0.0
   D. 255.255.192.0

2. You want to divide your network into eight networks. How many bits will you need to take from the host ID portion of the subnet mask?
   A. 2
   B. 3
   C. 4
   D. 6

3. In binary, how do you calculate the broadcast address of a network range?
   A. All host bits set to 0
   B. All host bits set to 0, except for the low-order bit
   C. All host bits set to 1, except for the low-order bit
   D. All host bits set to 1

4. In binary, how do you calculate the network ID of a network range?
   A. All host bits set to 0
   B. All host bits set to 0, except for the low-order bit
   C. All host bits set to 1, except for the low-order bit
   D. All host bits set to 1

5. The last valid address of a subnet is always
  A.   One more than the broadcast address
  B.   One less than the broadcast address
  C.   One more than the network ID
  D.   One less than the network ID

Classful vs. Classless Addressing

6. Which of the following is an example of CIDR notations?
  A.   16/10.34.56.78
  B.   10.34.56.78
  C.   10.34.56.0
  D.   10.34.56.78/16

Understanding Routing

7. You want to add a new route to your Windows router. Which of the following is the correct syntax to add a route to the routing table of the router?
  A.   routetable add 12.0.0.0 255.0.0.0 11.0.0.254
  B.   routetable add 12.0.0.0 MASK 255.0.0.0 11.0.0.254
  C.   route add 12.0.0.0 MASK 255.0.0.0 11.0.0.254
  D.   route add 12.0.0.0 255.0.0.0 11.0.0.254

8. You wish to view the routing table on the router. Which command can you use?
  A.   Routetable view
  B.   Routetable print
  C.   Route view
  D.   Route print

9. You wish to remove a route from the routing table. Which command would you use?
  A.   Router remove
  B.   Route delete
  C.   Remove route
  D.   Delete route

Dynamic Routing Protocols

10. Which dynamic routing protocol is a distance vector protocol?
    A. OSPF
    B. DIP
    C. RIP
    D. NIP

11. Which dynamic routing protocol monitors the state of the links?
    A. OSPF
    B. SIP
    C. RIP
    D. SLIP

SELF TEST ANSWERS

Understanding Subnetting

1. ☑ **B.** Given that we are dealing with a class B address, the default subnet mask is 255.255.0.0. Therefore, if you take three bits (needed for six networks) from the host ID, you will get a new subnet mask of 255.255.224.0.
   ☒ **A, C,** and **D** are incorrect because they don't have the correct subnet mask for the six new subnets.

2. ☑ **C.** The formula to calculate how many bits you wish to take from the host ID portion of the subnet mask is $2^{\text{masked bits}} - 2$ = number of networks. We need to mask four bits to get a minimum of eight networks.
   ☒ **A, B,** and **D** are incorrect, because they will not give us the correct number of networks.

3. ☑ **D.** The broadcast address is calculated by converting all host bits to 1.
   ☒ **A, B,** and **C** are incorrect. All host bits set to 0 is the network ID, all host bits set to 0 except the low-order bit would be used by the first valid address, and all host bits set to 1 except the low-order bit would be used by the last valid address.

4. ☑ **A.** The network ID is determined by setting all host bits to 0.
   ☒ **B, C,** and **D** are incorrect. All host bits set to 1 is the broadcast address, all host bits set to 0 except the low-order bit would be used by the first valid address, and all host bits set to 1 except the low-order bit would be used by the last valid address.

5. ☑ **B.** The last valid address is always one less than the broadcast address.
   ☒ **A, C,** and **D** are incorrect, because they are not used to determine the last valid address.

Classful vs. Classless Addressing

6. ☑ **D.** CIDR notation is used to identify how many bits make up the network ID in the IP address. With CIDR notation, you specify the number of bits that make up the network ID by placing a / after the IP address and then the number of bits that make up the network ID. For example, 10.34.56.78/16.
   ☒ **A, B,** and **C** are incorrect because they do not resemble CIDR notation.

Understanding Routing

7. ☑ **C.** The command to add a route to a router is **route add**, and you must supply the MASK keyword when supplying the subnet mask.
☒ **A, B,** and **D** are incorrect, because they are not the correct commands to add a route to the routing table.

8. ☑ **D.** The command to view a routing table is **route print**.
☒ **A, B,** and **C** are incorrect, because they are not used to view the routing table.

9. ☑ **B.** To delete a route from the routing table, we use **route delete**.
☒ **A, C,** and **D** are incorrect because they are not commands used to delete a route from the routing table.

Dynamic Routing Protocols

10. ☑ **C.** The RIP routing protocol is a distance vector protocol, meaning that it measures how far a destination is in hops.
☒ **A, B,** and **D** are incorrect because they are not routing protocols except for OSPF. OSPF is a routing protocol, but it is not vector based—it is a link state protocol.

11. ☑ **A.** OSPF is a link state protocol, meaning that it monitors the link between the routers and shares that link state information with other OSPF-enabled devices. The preferred route is always selected based on the link state.
☒ **B, C,** and **D** are incorrect, because they are not link state protocols. RIP is a distance vector protocol.

6

TCP/IP Utilities

Many utilities are available to troubleshoot TCP/IP connectivity problems. Most utilities are public domain and are included with the TCP/IP protocol stack provided with the operating system that you are using. This also means that the utilities may vary slightly, depending on the operating system being used. For example, to view your TCP/IP setting on a Windows server, you would use IPCONFIG, whereas on a Linux box you would use ifconfig—each of which may support different command-line switches. Although these utilities generally provide very basic functions, they will prove to be invaluable when troubleshooting network problems.

In the first part of this chapter, we discuss the most commonly used TCP/IP troubleshooting tools, and in the final section, we look at how these tools can be used to help troubleshoot common networking problems. The following list provides a brief description of each utility discussed in this chapter along with its core functions—be sure to know these for the exam:

- **ARP**   Displays and modifies the local ARP cache.
- **Telnet**   Remote terminal emulation, administration, and troubleshooting.
- **NBTSTAT**   Used to troubleshoot NetBIOS over TCP/IP connections.
- **Tracert**   Traces and reports on the route to a remote computer.
- **Netstat**   Displays statistics for current TCP/IP connections.
- **IPCONFIG and ifconfig**   Displays current IP configuration information.
- **FTP**   Enables file transfers between remote computers.
- **Ping**   Verifies hostname, host IP address, and physical connectivity to a remote TCP/IP computer.

CERTIFICATION OBJECTIVE 6.01

ARP

As discussed in Chapter 3, network interface cards (NICs) have a hardware address, or MAC address, burned into the network card itself. When you communicate from one system to another, you normally are familiar with the IP address of the host with which you want to communicate, but underneath the hood, the systems must use the physical MAC address to send and receive data—the problem being, how does one system find out the MAC address of the other system so that it can send the data across the network? The answer—ARP. The Address Resolution Protocol (ARP) was designed to provide a mapping from the logical TCP/IP addresses to the physical MAC addresses.

Address resolution is the process of resolving addresses or converting from one type of address to another. In the case of ARP, the logical address (layer-3 address) is being converted to the MAC address (layer-2 address) by a broadcast out on the network. With ARP, the sending computer yells out on the network, "Whoever has this IP address, I need your MAC address!" This broadcast is sent out on the wire, and every host looks at the broadcast data. The host with that IP address will reply with its MAC address. The address resolution process is complete once the original computer has received the MAC address information of the destination system, and is then able to send data, as shown in Figure 6-1.

ARP maintains the protocol rules for making this translation and providing address conversion in both directions, from a layer-3 address to a layer-2 address (ARP), and from a layer-2 address to a layer-3 address (Reverse ARP) as shown in Figure 6-2. A utility by the same name is available for Windows- and Linux-based

---

FIGURE 6-1　　The ARP process

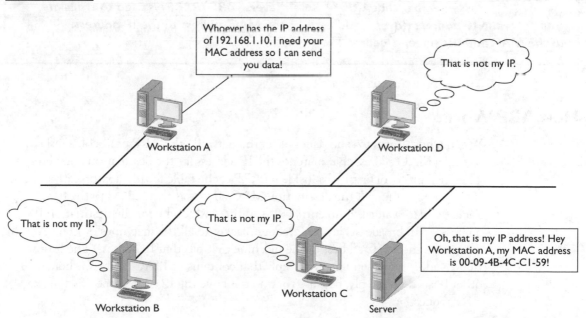

ARP is used
to convert the
logical address to
a physical address.

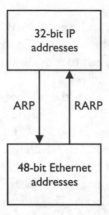

operating systems. This utility is used to display and modify entries within the ARP
cache, which is where the addresses that have been resolved are stored for future
reference. ARP is defined in-depth in RFC 826.

Remember that ARP
translates the IP address (layer-3 address)
to the MAC address (layer-2 address).

Reverse ARP (RARP) is used to translate
the MAC address to the IP address.

How ARP Works

When a host wants to send data out on the network, the ARP protocol is tasked
to find a MAC address that matches the IP address for the destination computer.
The ARP protocol first looks inside its ARP cache table for the appropriate address.
If the address is found, the destination MAC address is then added to the data
packet and forwarded. If no entry exists in the ARP cache for the destination IP
address, ARP broadcasts an ARP request packet to all the machines on the LAN to
determine the MAC address of the machine that has that IP address. The host with
that IP address will send an ARP reply that contains its MAC address, whereas all
other hosts do not reply, because they do not have the IP address specified in the
ARP request.

If the destination is on a remote subnet, the address of the router or gateway used to reach that subnet is ARPed. If the ARP cache does not contain an IP address for the router or gateway, the sending computer will ARP the IP address of the router.

Once the MAC address is determined by the ARP reply, the IP and MAC address of the destination system are stored in the ARP cache (stored in memory) so that next time the address will be resolved from the cache and a broadcast will not be needed.

As protocols go, ARP provides very basic functionality; there are only four types of messages that can be sent out by the ARP protocol, which are as follows:

- ARP request
- ARP reply
- RARP request
- RARP reply

ARP Cache

To reduce the number of address resolution broadcasts, thereby minimizing network utilization, a client caches resolved addresses for a short time in a table in memory. This table, known as the ARP cache, is used to maintain the mappings between each MAC address and its corresponding IP address locally. This is the most important part of this protocol. Since the size of the ARP cache is limited, entries need to be purged periodically. If they are not, the cache could become huge in size and could contain quite a few obsolete entries. Therefore, ARP cache entries are removed at predefined intervals. This process also removes any unsuccessful attempts to contact computers that are not currently running.

Entries in the ARP cache can be viewed, added, or deleted by using the ARP utility. Entries that are added with this utility manually are called *static* entries and will not expire out of cache, whereas the entries that are added automatically through broadcast are known as the *dynamic* entries and will expire from the cache. Being able to view the ARP cache can be helpful in trying to resolve address resolution problems. By displaying the current cache, you can determine whether a host's MAC address is being resolved correctly.

To view the ARP cache, type the following command in a command prompt window and press ENTER:

```
arp -a
```

Figure 6-3 shows an example of an ARP cache.

```
C:\>arp -a
Interface: 207.222.234.73
  Internet Address      Physical Address      Type
  10.37.14.92           00-60-08-72-43-d6     static
  198.70.146.70         20-53-52-43-00-00     dynamic
  199.182.120.2         20-53-52-43-00-00     dynamic
  199.182.120.202       20-53-52-43-00-00     dynamic
  206.246.150.88        20-53-52-43-00-00     dynamic
  207.211.106.40        20-53-52-43-00-00     dynamic
  207.211.106.90        20-53-52-43-00-00     dynamic
  208.223.32.77         20-53-52-43-00-00     dynamic
```

Customizing the ARP Cache

Additional options are available to customize the information found in the ARP
cache. For example, you can filter the entries displayed when you list them with
ARP. When you append the appropriate IP address after the -a switch, the table will
list entries only for that particular IP address, as shown in Figure 6-4. This can be
useful when trying to isolate specific entries in a large table.

Type the following command, and press ENTER to view the ARP cache for a
specific IP address:

```
arp -a <IP address>
```

Computers that contain multiple NICs or multihomed computers have more
than one network interface listed, and the ARP cache maintains addresses for each
interface independently. When you use the ARP -a option, all network interfaces will
be listed. To filter the display by a specific interface, use the -n option. This enables
you to specify which interface to display addresses for, as shown in Figure 6-5.

Type the following command, and press ENTER to view the ARP cache for a
specific interface:

```
arp -a -n <interface>
```

To learn more about ARP, check out Exercise 6-1 and the CertCam training
video for Exercise 6-1 on the CD-ROM.

```
C:\>arp -a 10.37.14.92

Interface: 207.222.234.73
  Internet Address      Physical Address      Type
  10.37.14.92           00-60-08-72-43-d6     static
```

FIGURE 6-5

Displaying the ARP cache by interface

```
C:\>arp -a -n 207.222.234.73

Interface: 207.222.234.73
  Internet Address      Physical Address      Type
  10.37.14.92           00-60-08-72-43-d6      static
  32.97.105.123         20-53-52-43-00-00      dynamic
  198.70.146.70         20-53-52-43-00-00      dynamic
  199.182.120.2         20-53-52-43-00-00      dynamic
  207.211.106.40        20-53-52-43-00-00      dynamic
  207.211.106.90        20-53-52-43-00-00      dynamic
```

EXERCISE 6-1

CertCam 6-1

Using ARP to See Your Local ARP Cache

In this exercise you will view your ARP cache to view the MAC addresses of systems that you have communicated with. You will then ping the IP address of a system that does not appear in your ARP cache and verify that it was added to the cache. After viewing the ARP cache, you will analyze Ping traffic from a capture file and view the ARP request being sent on the network.

1. Go to the command prompt by selecting Start | Run, and then type **cmd**.

2. At the command prompt, type **arp -a** and press ENTER.

3. Make a note of any entries that are in your ARP cache.

4. Ping the IP address of a host on your network that was not in your ARP cache by typing **ping <ip address>**. In the accompanying illustration, notice that the address of 192.168.1.100 is pinged.

```
C:\WINDOWS\System32\cmd.exe

C:\Documents and Settings\Administrator>ping 192.168.1.100

Pinging 192.168.1.100 with 32 bytes of data:

Reply from 192.168.1.100: bytes=32 time=4ms TTL=128
Reply from 192.168.1.100: bytes=32 time=1ms TTL=128
Reply from 192.168.1.100: bytes=32 time=1ms TTL=128
Reply from 192.168.1.100: bytes=32 time=1ms TTL=128

Ping statistics for 192.168.1.100:
    Packets: Sent = 4, Received = 4, Lost = 0 (0% loss),
Approximate round trip times in milli-seconds:
    Minimum = 1ms, Maximum = 4ms, Average = 1ms

C:\Documents and Settings\Administrator>
```

5. At the command prompt, type **arp -a**.

6. Notice that the system that you have pinged is in the cache. This is because in order for any data to be sent to the target system, your system will need to know the MAC address of that system, and an ARP request went out to figure out the address; it was then stored in cache. You can see in the accompanying illustration that the address of 192.168.1.100 and the associated MAC address are stored in the cache.

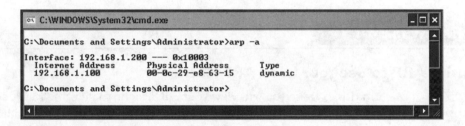

View ARP Traffic with Network Monitor

In this part of the exercise you will open a packet capture made with Network Monitor, and you will analyze the traffic that occurs when you ping another system. Understand that Ping is just one example of communication between two systems and that no matter what type of communication occurs, the MAC address must be determined.

7. Start Network Monitor from Start | Programs | Administrative Tools | Network Monitor. Open the packet capture called ping.cap from the Lab Files\PacketCaptures folder.

8. Once you have the packet capture open, notice that there are 13 frames in the capture, as seen in the accompanying illustration. Further, by looking at the protocol column in the capture you can see that there are two ARP frames (frames 3 and 4). You can also see that frame 3 is the ARP request going out to the network, and frame 4 is the ARP reply coming back to the system.

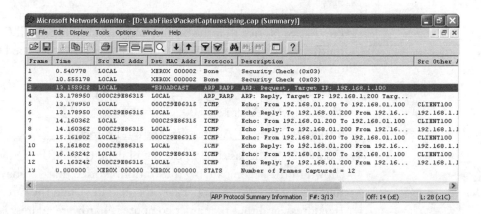

9. Frame 3 is the ARP request; we need to find out whom the request is for. Double-click frame 3 and expand the Ethernet section in the detail pane to determine the destination MAC address of the frame (shown in the accompanying illustration). Record the MAC address information in the space provided:

Destination MAC Address: _____

Source MAC Address: _____

Ethernet Type: _____

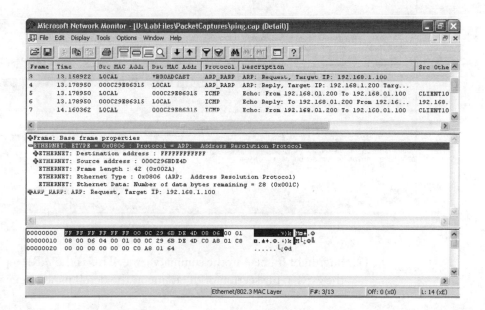

10. You should have the following answers for the information collected previously. Notice that the destination MAC address is all *F*s. This is the hardware address of a network broadcast—which is destined to "All" systems on the network.

 Destination MAC Address: ___FFFFFFFFFFFF___

 Source MAC Address: ___000C296BDE4D___

 Ethernet Type: ___Address Resolution Protocol___

11. Double-click the last line in the detail pane (the ARP: Request line) as shown in the accompanying illustration. Notice that you have the sender's hardware address, the sender's protocol address, and the target computer's IP address, and that the target computer's hardware address is set to all 0s—because it is unknown. That is what ARP is trying to figure out.

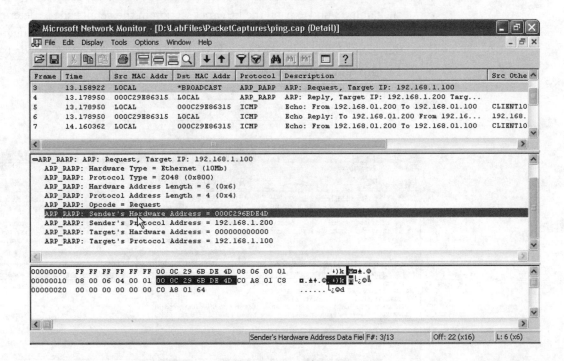

12. Highlight frame 4 in the summary pane. This is the ARP reply. Double-click the ARP reply section of the frame in the detail pane to expand it (as shown

in the accompanying illustration). Notice that in the ARP section of the reply, you have the sender's IP address and MAC address, along with the destination's MAC address and IP address. The sender's MAC address is what the initial system will use to send data to this host.

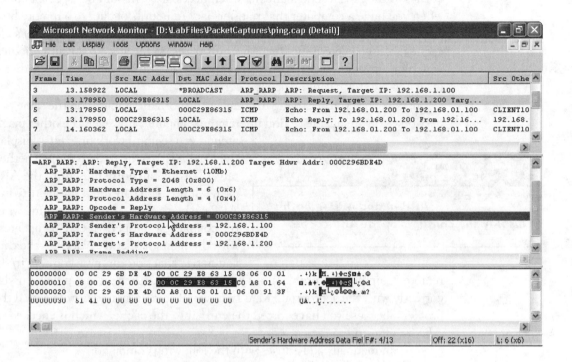

13. Record the following information:

    Source MAC Address: _____

    Source IP Address: _____

    Destination MAC Address: _____

    Destination IP Address: _____

14. What is the MAC address of the system that was pinged (192.168.1.100)?

    _____

15. Close Network Monitor.

Adding Static Entries

When ARP broadcasts out on the network to resolve an address and then adds that entry to the ARP cache, it creates a dynamic entry. A dynamic entry is added and removed from the cache automatically. The systems administrator can add static entries to the ARP cache manually when necessary. This can be especially helpful when you have a computer that transfers large amounts of data to a remote host continually. By adding a static entry for the remote host into the computer's ARP cache table, you determine that ARP broadcasts do not need to occur periodically, which minimizes network traffic. This option can also be used to test whether the local computer is receiving updates correctly.

Suppose that you are trying to connect to another computer on the same network. You are unable to find the remote computer; however, the other machines around you seem to work fine. First, display the local ARP cache to determine whether the target host has an entry present in the ARP cache. If not, you can add a static entry into the ARP cache to allow you to determine whether the computer is properly receiving updates. If, with the new static entry placed in the cache, you notice that you can now connect to the remote computer, the problem was probably that the cache was not being updated correctly with the appropriate MAC address. Adding a static entry bypassed that problem, because you have forced the entry into the cache, which is checked first for ARP resolution.

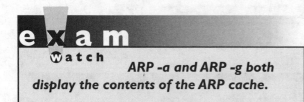

ARP -a and ARP -g both display the contents of the ARP cache.

You can manually add entries with the following command:

```
ARP -s <IP address> <MAC address>
```

Deleting Static Entries

You might need to delete entries that you have manually added or manually remove any entries that have been dynamically added to the ARP cache. Use the following command to delete an entry from the ARP cache:

```
ARP -d <IP Address>
```

ARP Cache Aging

Unlike static addresses, which never age out, dynamic addresses remain for only a predetermined amount of time. The initial cache lifetime of entries is two minutes on Windows systems, but Windows adjusts the size of the ARP cache automatically. If entries are reused within two minutes, they remain for ten minutes. A Registry parameter within Windows is also available to allow for more control over the aging parameters. The Registry parameter is located in the following location:

```
Hkey_Local_Machine\System\CurrentControlSet\Services\Tcpip\Parameters\ArpCacheLife
```

If the ArpCacheLife entry is not found in the Tcpip\Parameters portion of the Registry, the default lifetime of two minutes (120 seconds) will be used. If you want to create the ArpCacheLife Registry entry, create a dword value named ArpCacheLife and set its value to a value in seconds.

RARP

A little-known protocol exists to facilitate the reverse function of ARP. The *Reverse Address Resolution Protocol (RARP)* enables a machine to learn its own IP address by broadcasting to resolve its own MAC address. A RARP server containing these mappings can respond with the IP address for the requesting host. In most cases, a machine knows its own IP address; therefore, RARP is primarily used in situations such as diskless workstations or machines without hard disks. Dumb terminals and NetPCs are good examples of diskless workstations.

To summarize, although ARP is a simple protocol compared to most other protocols, it is just as important as any other to TCP/IP for proper functionality. The utility included with this protocol (ARP) will enable you to display and modify the ARP cache as needed. This enables you to effectively troubleshoot any issues that might arise with ARP. Table 6-1 details the ARP switches and their corresponding definitions.

TABLE 6-1	ARP Switch	Definition
ARP Switches	-a	Displays the entire current ARP cache or a single entry by allowing you to specify the IP address of an adapter.
	-g	Same as -a.
	-N	Shows the ARP entries for a specified IP address and allows for modification.
	-d	Deletes a specified entry or when used by itself it will clear the entire ARP cache.
	-s	Adds an entry to the ARP cache by specifying a MAC address and an IP address.

CERTIFICATION OBJECTIVE 6.02

Telnet

Another utility commonly used is Telnet, a terminal emulation program. This utility was designed to provide a virtual terminal or remote login across the network to a Telnet-based application. This enables the user to execute commands on a remote machine from anywhere on the network as if he or she were sitting in front of the console. The term Telnet refers to both the protocol and the application used to create the remote session.

Telnet was originally designed to allow for a single universal interface in a world that was very diverse. It was an efficient method of simulating a console session when very little else was available. It is still widely used for remotely administering devices such as network equipment and UNIX servers. It can also be a great troubleshooting tool when used correctly.

How Telnet Works

The Telnet service uses TCP port 23 and is defined in depth in RFC 854. It is connection based and handles its own session negotiation, which makes it very efficient and effective. By maintaining its own protocol, it can set up its own sessions and manage them accordingly. This keeps the remote host from spending too much time processing requests and enables it to concentrate on its own processes. A client-based program is used to connect to the remote server, and the remote server must also be running a Telnet service to enable the client to connect.

Telnet uses a concept known as network virtual terminal (NVT) to define both ends of a Telnet connection. Each end of the connection maintains a logical keyboard and printer. The logical keyboard generates characters, and the logical printer displays them. The logical printer is usually a terminal screen, and the logical keyboard is the user's keyboard.

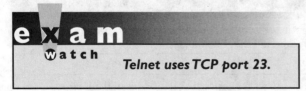

Telnet uses TCP port 23.

Using Telnet

A Telnet client utility is included with most operating systems such as Windows and Linux. You can run the Telnet utility by typing **telnet.exe** at a command prompt in most operating systems. In some operating systems, such as Windows 9*x*, you will use the connect dialog box, as shown in Figure 6-6. You can enter either an IP address or a hostname. To connect via a hostname, the client must be able to resolve the name to an IP address. You must also specify the port to connect to and the terminal emulation type. By default, this Telnet will try to connect to the Telnet port (port 23) on the remote server. VT100 is the default terminal emulation used for Telnet.

Telnet requires a username and password on the server to log on. Different functions and applications are available to assist you in performing remote administration. These depend on what services are being offered by the remote host. Many external devices also offer Telnet capability, such as uninterruptible power supplies (UPSs), remote control server administration cards, and most networking equipment, such as routers and switches.

Customizing Telnet Settings

Because of the different environments in use, Telnet offers multiple types of terminal emulation options. These include setting the terminal emulation, command buffer size, screen fonts, and cursor behavior. Some of these options are required to work on different types of remote hosts, but others are purely cosmetic. Figure 6-7 shows the available options for customizing a Telnet session.

FIGURE 6-6

Connecting to a
Telnet server

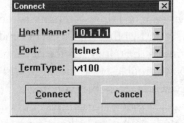

FIGURE 6-7

Telnet session
options

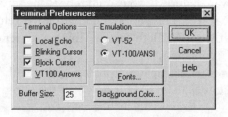

You can change screen fonts and cursor behavior to fit the screen output to your needs. These settings will not affect the server-based process. Some Telnet applications will not function correctly without particular cursor or font settings. The Local Echo option displays all of your keyboard input. The VT100 Arrows option specifies how cursor movement is handled. The Blinking Cursor and Block Cursor options adjust how the cursor is displayed on the screen.

The Buffer Size enables you to customize the amount of history that remains in memory. You can scroll through to see what commands or output have already been processed. The default is 25 lines, but you can set this value as high as 399. The Telnet application will not enable you to specify fewer than 25 lines.

The Emulation option defines what type of remote terminal to use. This controls how commands are interpreted and displayed by the remote server in your terminal session. VT52 is an older standard not commonly used anymore. VT100 is the default standard emulation used today.

Another function of Telnet is logging; it logs the console display to keep a record of all activity. To start or stop logging, select Terminal from the menu bar, and select Start Logging or Stop Logging from the menu. When you select Start Logging, the Open Log File window appears. You need to select the folder that you want Telnet to save the log files to. The log files are saved as telnet.log and are readable by any standard text editor.

Troubleshooting with Telnet

The primary use of Telnet is remote administration. If you are unable to connect to a remote server by other methods, depending upon the problem, Telnet might still work as long as the telnet service or daemon was installed on the server. This will enable you to troubleshoot and work with a remote server without being in front of it. If a server is inaccessible, you might still be able to contact its peripherals.

Suppose a Windows server has crashed and is displaying a blue screen. Some servers include an option to have remote administration cards plugged in. In this case, you could telnet to this card and possibly determine whether there is a hardware failure, or you could reboot the server. Suppose you have a UPS attached to the server. This peripheral might have Telnet capability to enable you to power-cycle the server. Both cases enable you to remotely troubleshoot the server without local interaction.

Another example of troubleshooting with Telnet is to connect to an application's service (e.g., FTP, SMTP, or HTTP) to verify that it is functioning properly. As discussed earlier, every TCP/IP service uses a specific TCP or UDP port. You can specify a particular port to connect to and test the connectivity and functionality of a service by issuing the type of commands for that service. For example, if you have a user that is having trouble sending e-mail, you could connect to your SMTP server from the Telnet utility and issue the SMTP command to try to send an e-mail. The purpose of going to the Telnet utility and not the e-mail client is that you want to verify whether the issue is server based or client based. If you can connect through Telnet and send an e-mail, then the problem is probably with the client.

Exercise 6-2 shows how to enable Telnet services on a Windows server and then use Telnet for remote administration.

CertCam 6-2

Check out Exercise 6-2 in LabBook.pdf on the CD-ROM and watch the CertCam training video from the CD-ROM.

CERTIFICATION OBJECTIVE 6.03

NBTSTAT

The Microsoft TCP/IP stack uses an additional subprotocol for its services, NetBIOS over TCP/IP (NetBT). The purpose of NetBIOS over TCP/IP is to allow you to connect to servers and workstations by their NetBIOS name, also known as the computer name, and behind the scenes that name will be converted to an IP address. Because this is a Microsoft addition to the TCP/IP protocol, Microsoft created the NBTSTAT utility to troubleshoot problems that can arise with NetBIOS over TCP/IP, or NetBIOS name resolution problems.

How NetBIOS over TCP/IP Works

NetBIOS is a software interface and naming convention used in Microsoft networking environments. NetBIOS was built in to NetBEUI and is also a major part of the Microsoft TCP/IP protocol stack. NetBIOS over TCP/IP is the use of the NetBIOS application programming interface over the TCP/IP protocol—using NetBIOS as a method of referencing systems across the network with NetBIOS names. These NetBIOS names need to be resolved to IP addresses for communication to happen on the network.

NetBT Naming

The NetBIOS namespace is a flat structure and is used to give unique NetBIOS names (computer names) to all systems on the network. This means that all computers within a workgroup or domain must have unique names. You will receive a duplicate computername error if two systems are using the same name. Names are composed of 16 bytes; 15 bytes are used by the actual computer name, and the last byte is used by the NetBIOS name suffix. The administrator or user can set the first 15 bytes, representing the computer name, but the 16th byte is created automatically based on a service running on the system. The NetBIOS name suffix is a code that represents a service running on the system. Table 6-2 lists some common NetBIOS name suffix codes.

TABLE 6-2	Suffix	Usage
Popular NetBIOS Name Suffixes	00	Workstation Service
	20	Server Service or File and Print Services
	03	Messenger Service
	1C	Domain Controller
	06	Remote Access Server

Let's look at an example: assume I had a server named SERVER1 and you noticed that there was a name registered on the network (more on this later) that looked like

```
SERVER1      <20>
```

You would know that I have a computer running named SERVER1 and that it is running the server service, which allows clients to connect to it for the purpose of file and print sharing. How do you know that SERVER1 is running the server service? That is what the <20> NetBIOS suffix means. To summarize, the NetBIOS suffix is used to "advertise" which services a system offers.

NetBT Sessions

Because NetBT runs on top of TCP/IP, sessions are set up the same way as though you were connecting through TCP/IP directly. There is additional overhead associated with this due to name resolution, but it is usually very small. When an application attempts to connect to a resource using NetBT, it first resolves the name to an IP address. Next, a TCP connection is established to port 139, designated for the NetBIOS session service. When connected, the computer sends a NetBIOS session request to the server name over the TCP connection. If the server is listening, it will respond with the requested information.

Using NBTSTAT

NBTSTAT is used to troubleshoot connectivity between two computers trying to communicate via NetBT. It displays the protocol statistics and the current connections to each remote host. You can also display the information about a remote host and the names stored in its local name cache.

Displaying the Local Cache

Every NetBIOS name that has been resolved is stored in memory, known as the NetBIOS name cache, so that the name resolution process will not need to go out to the network again. You can display the local cache by using the NBTSTAT -c option. When it comes to name resolution, the goal is to have a computer name that needs to be resolved in cache as quickly as possible so that the name resolves from memory and not through broadcast, or by contacting a WINS server. To have NetBIOS names referenced frequently loaded in cache automatically, you can use the #PRE tag in your LMHOSTS file so that those entries are loaded in cache on boot-up or by using the -R switch.

By using the -n option, you can display the services the local machine is advertising. This lists the registered names for the local machine as well.

Connecting to Remote Machines

When a system boots up, it registers its NetBIOS names in the NetBIOS name table stored in memory on the machine. This NetBIOS name table can be queried by anyone on the network at any point in time by using the -a switch if you are passing in the hostname or the -A switch if you are passing in the remote system's IP address. These options enable you to determine what services the remote machine is offering. Core operating system services such as the Server service or the Computer Browser service are listed here. Applications such as Microsoft Exchange or Microsoft Internet Information Server (IIS) might also list entries here as well. Figure 6-8 shows an example of a remote machine's name table.

Let's analyze the output in Figure 6-8. NetBIOS is exposing some pretty lethal information that can be used against you by a hacker. If I were to view your NetBIOS name table and get the results shown in Figure 6-8, I could probably guess that you are running a Microsoft operating system because of the 00 (workstation service) and the 20 (server service). You will also notice that there is a 03 code (messenger service) registered twice—once for the locally logged-on user and the other for the computer name. In Windows we can send messages to users or computers; therefore, both names need to be registered on the network so that the message being sent can find the user and computer. Because the server service and the workstation service are registered with a name of WORKSTATION1, we know that WORKSTATION1 with the 03 code is the computer, so ADMINISTRATOR with the 03 code must be the locally logged-on user. Pretty scary! As a best practice, you should be renaming the administrator account, but if you don't control who has access to the NetBIOS name table information, someone can find out a username very quickly.

FIGURE 6-8

Viewing the NETBIOS name table of a remote system

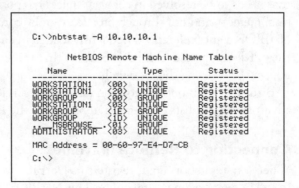

```
C:\>nbtstat -A 10.10.10.1

        NetBIOS Remote Machine Name Table

     Name              Type          Status
---------------------------------------------------
WORKSTATION1    <00>  UNIQUE       Registered
WORKSTATION1    <20>  UNIQUE       Registered
WORKGROUP       <00>  GROUP        Registered
WORKSTATION1    <03>  UNIQUE       Registered
WORKGROUP       <1E>  GROUP        Registered
WORKGROUP       <1D>  UNIQUE       Registered
 .. MSBROWSE _.<01>  GROUP        Registered
ADMINISTRATOR   <03>  UNIQUE       Registered

MAC Address = 00-60-97-E4-D7-CB

C:\>
```

Anytime you have the IP address of a system (maybe by viewing a log file), you can use NBTSTAT -A <ip address> to find out the computer name of that IP address.

Displaying Registration Statistics

Services can register on the network in two ways—via broadcast or with the WINS service. You can display the statistics of how many times you have registered and with what method. You can also display information on how remote NetBIOS names are being resolved. This can help you to determine whether you are using a WINS service correctly or are broadcasting for services. Broadcasting can consume a lot of bandwidth and is generally not recommended except in the smallest networks. To view the registration statistics, use the -r option with NBTSTAT.

The NBTSTAT utility can be crucial in defining problems with Microsoft computers. Since they use the NetBIOS naming standard, this utility is good at finding and isolating connectivity problems. It provides the extra information on NetBIOS statistics that you can't get from regular TCP/IP utilities such as Tracert.

Displaying Session Information

Another option with NBTSTAT is to list the sessions that are currently open. You can see what you are connected to and also list the open sessions that other computers have with your machine. Use the -S (uppercase) option to list names by IP address only. When you use the -s (lowercase) option, NBTSTAT will attempt to resolve the IP addresses to hostnames.

Statistics available with this option include number of bytes in, number of bytes out, current state, and whether the connection is inbound or outbound. Figure 6-9 shows an example of the sessions displayed with this option.

Table 6-3 details the NBTSTAT command-line switches and their definitions.

FIGURE 6-9

Viewing
NetBIOS session
information

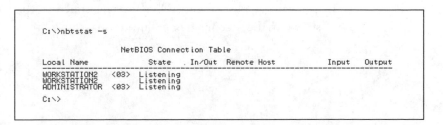

```
C:\>nbtstat -s

                NetBIOS Connection Table
Local Name          State    . In/Out  Remote Host          Input   Output
------------------------------------------------------------------------------
WORKSTATION2  <03>  Listening
WORKSTATION2  <03>  Listening
ADMINISTRATOR <03>  Listening

C:\>
```

TABLE 6-3	NBTSTAT Switch	Definition
NBTSTAT Command Switches	-a	Lists a remote PC's name table by specifying a remote PC's name.
	-A	Lists a remote PC's name table by specifying a remote PC's IP address.
	-c	Displays contents of the name cache, giving the IP address of each name.
	-n	Displays local names.
	-R	Deletes the name cache and reloads entries from the LMHOSTS file that contains the #PRE tag.
	-r	Displays name resolution statistics.
	-S	Lists client and server sessions, listing the remote computers by IP address.
	-s	Displays both client and server sessions, attempting to convert the remote computer IP address to a name using the Hosts file.
	Interval	Specifies the interval to pause display.

EXERCISE 6-3

CertCam 6-3

Using NBTSTAT to View NetBIOS Name Tables

In this exercise, you will view the NetBIOS name table of your local system and of a remote system on the network to determine what names are registered on the network.

1. Go to the command prompt by selecting Start | Run, and then type **cmd**.
2. At the command prompt, type **nbtstat -n**.
3. You will get a list of NetBIOS names registered on the local computer (as shown in the accompanying illustration).

```
C:\WINDOWS\System32\cmd.exe                                    _ □ ×

C:\Documents and Settings\Administrator>nbtstat -n

Local Area Connection 3:
Node IpAddress: [192.168.1.200] Scope Id: []

              NetBIOS Local Name Table

      Name             Type         Status
      ────             ────         ──────
   CLIENT100    <00>  UNIQUE      Registered
   WORKGROUP    <00>  GROUP       Registered
   CLIENT100    <03>  UNIQUE      Registered
   CLIENT100    <20>  UNIQUE      Registered
   WORKGROUP    <1E>  GROUP       Registered
   WORKGROUP    <1D>  UNIQUE      Registered
   ..__MSBROWSE__.<01>  GROUP     Registered
   ADMINISTRATOR <03> UNIQUE      Registered

C:\Documents and Settings\Administrator>
```

4. Record the following information about your system:

   Computername: _____

   Locally logged-on Username: _____

   Is your system running the server service? _____

   How do you know? _____

5. The following answers are coming from the output that was shown in the preceding illustration:

   Computername: _____client100_____

   Locally logged on Username: __Administrator_____

   Is your system running the server service? __Yes____

   How do you know? _<20> code—server service_____

View a Remote Systems Name Table with NBTSTAT

6. At the command prompt, type **nbtstat -A <ip address>** to view the name table of another system on your network. In my example, I am viewing the name table of a system that is using the IP address of 192.168.1.100 (shown in the accompanying illustration).

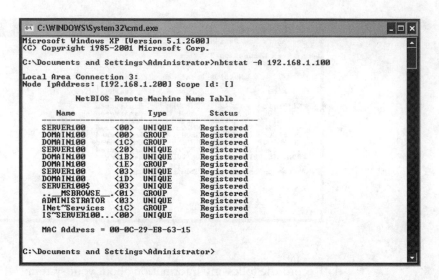

7. Analyzing the preceding output, you can see the <00> and <20> codes, which means that the workstation and server service are running. You can see the <03> code registered twice, once for the computer name of server100 and once for the locally logged-on username of administrator. You can also see that this is a domain controller. You know this because of the <1C> code for the domain named domain100. You also know that the server we hit is running IIS because of the <1C> code for INet Services.

8. Compare my findings with the findings of a computer on your network and record the information in the space provided. You may not have all the answers, depending on the type of system you are analyzing.

   Computername: _____

   Locally logged-on Username: _____

   Is the system running the server service? _____

   Is the system running the workstation service? _____

   Is the system running the messenger service? _____

   Is the system running IIS? _____

9. Type **exit** to close the command prompt.

Watc**h**   *Make sure you know*   *of a command and be expected to know*
the options available with the NBTSTAT   *what command and which switch of the*
command, such as NBTSTAT -R and   *command created the output.*
NBTSTAT -A. You will be given the output

CERTIFICATION OBJECTIVE 6.04

Tracert

Tracert is a command-line utility that was designed to perform a very basic task: to determine the path taken by a data packet to reach its destination. This is different from using the Ping utility. The Ping utility will give you a response if the address you have pinged is up and running. Tracert will send you a response with each router that is hit on the way. This will help you understand the number of networks, or hops, between you and the destination.

This could be useful in a scenario where you know that from the Boston office to the New York office there are 13 hops normally, but one day users start complaining that the network is slow, and when you do a Tracert you notice that there are 19 hops. This means that your packets are taking a different route than usual, and it could be because networks along the usual route are down and your packets are taking a roundabout route to get to the destination.

Watc**h**   *For the exam know that*
the Tracert utility uses ICMP as the
underlying protocol.

When using the utility, you will notice several numbers in the display. Figure 6-10 shows an example of the tracert command used to display the routing path to www.novell.com.

Although a Tracert might look rather confusing at first, it is fairly easy to understand. Each row gathers information about that hop three times. The first column shows the number of hops away that router is. The next three

FIGURE 6-10

Using the Tracert
utility

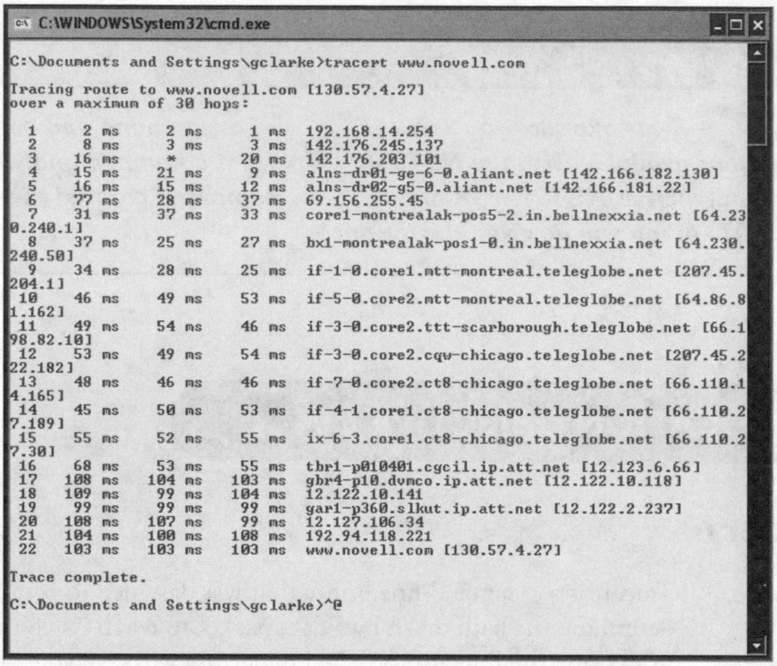

```
C:\WINDOWS\System32\cmd.exe                                          _ □ ×

C:\Documents and Settings\gclarke>tracert www.novell.com

Tracing route to www.novell.com [130.57.4.27]
over a maximum of 30 hops:

  1     2 ms     2 ms     1 ms  192.168.14.254
  2     8 ms     3 ms     3 ms  142.176.245.137
  3    16 ms     *       20 ms  142.176.203.101
  4    15 ms    21 ms     9 ms  alns-dr01-ge-6-0.aliant.net [142.166.182.130]
  5    16 ms    15 ms    12 ms  alns-dr02-g5-0.aliant.net [142.166.181.22]
  6    77 ms    28 ms    37 ms  69.156.255.45
  7    31 ms    37 ms    33 ms  core1-montrealak-pos5-2.in.bellnexxia.net [64.23
0.240.1]
  8    37 ms    25 ms    27 ms  bx1-montrealak-pos1-0.in.bellnexxia.net [64.230.
240.50]
  9    34 ms    28 ms    25 ms  if-1-0.core1.mtt-montreal.teleglobe.net [207.45.
204.1]
 10    46 ms    49 ms    53 ms  if-5-0.core2.mtt-montreal.teleglobe.net [64.86.8
1.162]
 11    49 ms    54 ms    46 ms  if-3-0.core2.ttt-scarborough.teleglobe.net [66.1
98.82.10]
 12    53 ms    49 ms    54 ms  if-3-0.core2.cqw-chicago.teleglobe.net [207.45.2
22.182]
 13    48 ms    46 ms    46 ms  if-7-0.core2.ct8-chicago.teleglobe.net [66.110.1
4.165]
 14    45 ms    50 ms    53 ms  if-4-1.core1.ct8-chicago.teleglobe.net [66.110.2
7.189]
 15    55 ms    52 ms    55 ms  ix-6-3.core1.ct8-chicago.teleglobe.net [66.110.2
7.30]
 16    68 ms    53 ms    55 ms  tbr1-p010401.cgcil.ip.att.net [12.123.6.66]
 17   108 ms   104 ms   103 ms  gbr4-p10.dvmco.ip.att.net [12.122.10.118]
 18   109 ms    99 ms   104 ms  12.122.10.141
 19    99 ms    99 ms    99 ms  gar1-p360.slkut.ip.att.net [12.122.2.237]
 20   108 ms   107 ms    99 ms  12.127.106.34
 21   104 ms   100 ms   108 ms  192.94.118.221
 22   103 ms   103 ms   103 ms  www.novell.com [130.57.4.27]

Trace complete.

C:\Documents and Settings\gclarke>^@
```

columns show the time it took for the router to respond for each attempt. The last column lists the fully qualified domain name of that router, which typically gives you an indication of where the router is. For example, looking at Figure 6-10 again you can see that hop number 12 looks like it is in Chicago!

Using Tracert

Suppose you cannot access a particular web site on the Internet. Your company is directly connected to the Internet via an ISDN line, which is used by approximately 35 people. You are able to hit certain web sites consistently, but others are available only sporadically. Other users begin to notice that they are unable to connect to the same web sites with which you are having a problem.

Tracert fits in well here to begin isolating where the problem is. Although you might have a good idea of what network equipment and options are used within your company, once packets enter the Internet, there is no telling what they might come across. Because routes can be so dynamic, this is a great tool for figuring out where the data is traveling to reach its destination.

You can begin troubleshooting this problem by typing one of the following commands:

```
TRACERT <hostname>
```

or

```
TRACERT <ipaddress>
```

After the utility has run, you might notice the following entry on one of the routers along the way:

```
Destination Net Unreachable
```

The tracert -d form indicates to the utility that you do not want to display hostnames with the tracert output. Specifying -d will speed up the trace because each IP address does not need to be resolved to a name.

Although this utility is unable to determine why the error is occurring, it has effectively found at what point the problem exists. Armed with this information, the owner can then examine that router to resolve the issue.

In the event a name resolution method is not available for remote hosts, you can specify the -d option to prohibit the utility from trying to resolve hostnames as it runs. Without this switch, the program will still work, but it will attempt to translate every hop's IP address to a hostname, thereby slowing the process.

To practice Tracert, check out Exercise 6-4 from the LabBook.pdf on the CD-ROM or watch the CertCam training video on the CD-ROM.

Maximum Number of Hops

One function of the Tracert utility is to provide the number of hops, or networks, that the data is crossing. You may want to limit the number of hops the program will make to search for the remote host; if you don't, Tracert will continue for 30 hops by default. In the unusual case that you must surpass 30 hops, you can also specify a greater interval.

By using the -h option with Tracert, you can specify the maximum number of hops to trace a route to. Figure 6-11 shows an example of limiting the number of hops returned.

FIGURE 6-11

Specifying the
maximum
number of hops
with Tracert

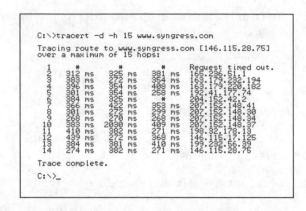

```
C:\>tracert -d -h 15 www.syngress.com

Tracing route to www.syngress.com [146.115.28.75]
over a maximum of 15 hops:

  1    *   ms    *   ms    *   ms  Request timed out.
  2   312 ms   325 ms   381 ms  165.236.51.1
  3   383 ms   272 ms   354 ms  163.179.232.194
  4   396 ms   354 ms   408 ms  163.179.220.182
  5   301 ms   354 ms   258 ms  192.41.177.74
  6   384 ms   325 ms    *   ms  204.152.42.2
  7   366 ms   455 ms   353 ms  207.152.148.41
  8   301 ms   272 ms   299 ms  207.152.148.30
  9   268 ms   270 ms   268 ms  207.152.148.34
 10   583 ms  2030 ms   409 ms  207.152.148.37
 11   410 ms   382 ms   271 ms  198.32.178.13
 12   439 ms   272 ms   368 ms  146.115.17.125
 13   384 ms   381 ms   410 ms  199.232.56.39
 14   274 ms   382 ms   271 ms  146.115.28.75

Trace complete.

C:\>_
```

*Note that some ISPs will not allow an ICMP packet to pass through their gateway, so you may get some lines with * showing there was a hop there but with no information displayed.*

Adjusting Timeout Values

Another option associated with Tracert is to adjust the timeout value using the -w switch. This value determines the amount of time in milliseconds the program will wait for a response before moving on. Using this option will enable you to understand a little more about the problem that is occurring. For example, if you notice that many responses are timing out, you can raise this value. If, after raising this value, remote devices are responding, this could be a good indication that you have a bandwidth problem.

Loose Source Routing Options

An additional option is to use what is known as loose source routing. The -j option can be used to force the outbound datagram to pass through a specific router and back. This enables you to trace the round-trip route for a destination. A normal tracert follows the route until it reaches its destination or times out. When you specify this option, Tracert follows the path to the router specified and returns to your computer. To use loose source routing, enter the following command:

```
TRACERT -j <hop list>
```

Tracert can be a useful tool in determining why a remote host can't be reached. It can also be a good tool to notice other issues, such as bandwidth utilization problems. Its additional options and functionality make it a powerful tool. Table 6-4 lists the Tracert switches and the corresponding definitions.

It is important to note that the Tracert command is used in Windows. The equivalent command in the Linux world is traceroute.

TABLE 6-4	Tracert Switch	Definition
Tracert Command-Line Switches	-d	Does not resolve address to computer names.
	-h	Specifies maximum number of hops.
	-j	Specifies loose source route along host-list.
	-w	Specifies time in milliseconds to wait for reply.
	-target_name	Specifies target computer.

CERTIFICATION OBJECTIVE 6.05

Netstat

Now that you've learned how to trace data packets throughout the network, another utility useful for troubleshooting TCP/IP-specific issues is Netstat. Netstat displays protocol statistics and current TCP/IP network connections. This utility can be used to display in-depth detail about protocol status and statistics for the different network interfaces, as well as viewing the current listening ports and the routing table.

How Netstat Works

TCP-based connections use a three-step handshake method for establishing sessions. This forms the basis for TCP and its reliable data transfer methodology. This enables it to act as a message-validation protocol to provide reliable communication between two hosts. A session is created via this handshake to appropriately handle the transport messages. Netstat displays information about these sessions, the network interfaces, and how they are being used.

By default, Netstat lists the protocol type, local address and port information, remote address and port information, and current state. The information provided explains what connections are open or in progress, through what ports, and what their current states are. Figure 6-12 shows an example of the Netstat utility.

In Figure 6-12 you can see that the local address column references the local system, and the ports on the local system that are being used as connection points to a remote system. Let's use the last entry in the output as the example to be analyzed. You can see in the last entry of the output that I have a connection to the www.syngress.com web site. How do you know this? If you look at the foreign address column, you will notice the FQDN of www.syngress.com (most times you will see an IP address here), and you will notice that the address shows a :80 at the end, which is the default port of a web server. This means that I am connected to port 80 of that FQDN. You will also notice that port 1219 is the port used by my local system—this would be the port used by my web browser, and it is what the web server at www.syngress.com uses to sends its web pages back to my system.

CertCam 6-5

Perform Exercise 6-5 from LabBook.pdf on the CD-ROM or watch the CertCam training video to learn more about Netstat.

The state column displays the current status of TCP connections only. You can determine from the state column whether the connection is currently established or the application running on that port is in listening mode (waiting for a connection). Table 6-5 lists the available states.

FIGURE 6-12

Viewing current connections with Netstat

```
C:\>netstat

Active Connections

  Proto  Local Address        Foreign Address         State
  TCP    workstation2:1192    207.211.106.40:80       TIME_WAIT
  TCP    workstation2:1201    207.211.106.90:80       TIME_WAIT
  TCP    workstation2:1218    www.syngress.com:80     ESTABLISHED
  TCP    workstation2:1219    www.syngress.com:80     ESTABLISHED

C:\>
```

TABLE 6-5	State	Explanation
A Look at the Different Netstat States	SYN_SEND	Indicates an active open.
	SYN_RECEIVED	Server just received a SYN from the remote client.
	ESTABLISHED	Client received SYN, and the connection is complete.
	LISTEN	Server is waiting for a connection.
	FIN_WAIT_1	Indicates an active close.
	TIMED_WAIT	Clients enter this state after an active close.
	CLOSE_WAIT	Indicates a passive close; the server has just received the first FIN from client.
	FIN_WAIT_2	Client just received acknowledgment of its first FIN from the server.
	LAST+ACK	Server enters this state when it sends its own FIN.
	CLOSED	Server received the ACK from the client, and the connection is closed.

Netstat Options

Different types of statistics are available depending on the command-line switches used with Netstat. You can display all connections and listening ports, because server connections are not displayed in the standard output. You can also display Ethernet statistics and per-protocol statistics. The routing table can also be displayed with this command.

You can use the -n option to display addresses and port numbers without resolving the names. Resolving names could take additional overhead if the listing is long, and it might not work properly if you have no form of name resolution set up. Another cool switch is the interval switch—suppose you want the information that is displayed to continually update. By default, the information is displayed once. You can specify an interval in seconds appended to the end of the command to have the utility update itself. The following is an example of the command line:

```
NETSTAT -a 5
```

This command will display the active connections every five seconds. Use CTRL-C to stop this program. This can be helpful when trying to actively monitor connections and their statistics.

Displaying Server Connections and Listening Ports

From the standard output, Netstat does not display your computer's connections and listening ports. This information might be necessary to understand whom the computer is communicating with and whether a port is open and ready to receive data. There are a number of Trojans that hackers plant on systems that open ports so that the hacker can connect to the open port later and send malicious data to that port. A good example is the old Netbus program. When a user ran Netbus, it would do nothing but open port 12345 so that the hacker could connect and do things like eject your CD-ROM, run a program on your system, navigate your system to a URL, and switch your left and right mouse buttons. It is important that you be able to identify whether a system has been hit with such a program, and the best way is to monitor the listening ports with Netstat. To view a list of listening ports, type the following command:

```
Netstat -a
```

Displaying Interface Statistics

Another option available enables you to display the Ethernet interface statistics of your system. The information available with the -e option includes the number of bytes received and sent, the number of discards and errors, and unknown protocols. By understanding what this information means, you can monitor the amount of traffic that is being used in communications. Since this option also displays errors, you can check here to see if communication-related problems are occurring. Figure 6-13 shows an example of the Netstat utility with this option.

Displaying Per-Protocol Statistics

Although the previous option shows Ethernet interface-specific information, protocol-specific information is also available. With the -s option, you can display statistics for all the communications protocols used by TCP/IP. The protocols

FIGURE 6-13

Viewing network interface statistics with Netstat

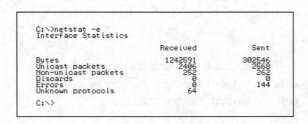

```
C:\>netstat -e
Interface Statistics

                        Received          Sent
Bytes                   1242591         302546
Unicast packets            2406           2568
Non-unicast packets         252            262
Discards                      0              0
Errors                        0            144
Unknown protocols            64

C:\>
```

include TCP, UDP, ICMP, and IP. Detailed information can be obtained with this option that can help you to isolate TCP/IP communications issues.

You can also filter the list of statistics by protocol to focus on a specific area. The -p option can be used alone to display connection information by TCP or UDP, or you can use it with the protocol statistics option (-s) to filter the statistics by TCP, UDP, ICMP, or IP. Figure 6-14 shows an example of this filtering.

One of my favorite switches for Netstat is the -p switch; I can pass it the argument of TCP to view all the TCP-based connections that my system has. If you type the following command, you can view your TCP connection information:

```
Netstat -p TCP
```

Displaying the Current Route Table

Netstat offers another option that enables you to display the current routing table: the -r switch. The output shown by Netstat -r is similar to the output seen with the route print command seen in Chapter 5.

Troubleshooting with Netstat

Using Netstat to monitor TCP protocol activity can enable you to troubleshoot TCP/IP-based connections. Netstat can be used in a variety of ways. You can use the -a option to monitor active connections. I use this a lot to monitor systems connected to my web site. From a security point of view, you can use Netstat -a to view a list of listening ports—useful if you suspect that someone has planted a Trojan on your system. Newer versions of Windows now support the -o switch with Netstat to display the process ID number of the program that is responsible for opening

FIGURE 6-14

Viewing specific protocol information with Netstat

```
C:\>netstat -s -p IP

IP Statistics

    Packets Received                    = 2564
    Received Header Errors              = 0
    Received Address Errors             = 28
    Datagrams Forwarded                 = 0
    Unknown Protocols Received          = 0
    Received Packets Discarded          = 0
    Received Packets Delivered          = 2564
    Output Requests                     = 2801
    Routing Discards                    = 4194332
    Discarded Output Packets            = 0
    Output Packet No Route              = 0
    Reassembly Required                 = 0
    Reassembly Successful               = 0
    Reassembly Failures                 = 0
    Datagrams Successfully Fragmented   = 0
    Datagrams Failing Fragmentation     = 0
    Fragments Created                   = 0

C:\>_
```

the port! Very useful when trying to close down open ports and you need to know what program has opened the port so you know which program to end. Figure 6-15 displays the Netstat command with the -o.

Notice in Figure 6-15 that the -na option was used, which means show all ports in numerical format. The -o is the reason there is a column for the process ID number (PID). Once you know the process ID number, you can then use the Windows **tasklist** command to display which executable is associated with that process ID (shown in Figure 6-16).

Table 6-6 displays popular Netstat command-line switches and the corresponding definitions.

FIGURE 6-15	

The -o switch of Netstat displays the process ID.

```
Command Prompt                                                    _ □ ×
Microsoft Windows [Version 5.2.3790]
(C) Copyright 1985-2003 Microsoft Corp.

H:\>netstat -na -o

Active Connections

  Proto  Local Address          Foreign Address        State           PID
  TCP    0.0.0.0:25             0.0.0.0:0              LISTENING       1668
  TCP    0.0.0.0:53             0.0.0.0:0              LISTENING       1544
  TCP    0.0.0.0:80             0.0.0.0:0              LISTENING       4
  TCP    0.0.0.0:88             0.0.0.0:0              LISTENING       400
  TCP    0.0.0.0:110            0.0.0.0:0              LISTENING       1668
  TCP    0.0.0.0:135            0.0.0.0:0              LISTENING       752
  TCP    0.0.0.0:389            0.0.0.0:0              LISTENING       400
  TCP    0.0.0.0:445            0.0.0.0:0              LISTENING       4
  TCP    0.0.0.0:464            0.0.0.0:0              LISTENING       400
  TCP    0.0.0.0:593            0.0.0.0:0              LISTENING       752
  TCP    0.0.0.0:636            0.0.0.0:0              LISTENING       400
  TCP    0.0.0.0:691            0.0.0.0:0              LISTENING       1668
  TCP    0.0.0.0:995            0.0.0.0:0              LISTENING       1668
  TCP    0.0.0.0:1026           0.0.0.0:0              LISTENING       400
  TCP    0.0.0.0:1027           0.0.0.0:0              LISTENING       400
  TCP    0.0.0.0:1053           0.0.0.0:0              LISTENING       1544
  TCP    0.0.0.0:1168           0.0.0.0:0              LISTENING       1668
```

FIGURE 6-16	

The tasklist command will allow you to match the .exe file with the process ID.

```
Command Prompt                                                    _ □ ×
H:\>tasklist

Image Name                   PID Session Name        Session#    Mem Usage
========================= ======== ================ =========== ============
System Idle Process            0 Console                  0         16 K
System                         4 Console                  0        216 K
smss.exe                     268 Console                  0        460 K
csrss.exe                    316 Console                  0      1,632 K
winlogon.exe                 340 Console                  0     11,808 K
services.exe                 388 Console                  0     48,712 K
lsass.exe                    400 Console                  0     34,592 K
svchost.exe                  592 Console                  0      2,688 K
svchost.exe                  752 Console                  0      3,628 K
svchost.exe                  820 Console                  0      4,588 K
svchost.exe                  840 Console                  0      3,276 K
svchost.exe                  856 Console                  0     22,360 K
spoolsv.exe                 1208 Console                  0     14,452 K
BRSS01A.EXE                 1216 Console                  0      2,036 K
msdtc.exe                   1272 Console                  0      4,200 K
certsrv.exe                 1428 Console                  0      9,120 K
defwatch.exe                1472 Console                  0      2,212 K
dfssvc.exe                  1488 Console                  0      4,288 K
dns.exe                     1544 Console                  0      6,056 K
svchost.exe                 1620 Console                  0      2,148 K
```

TABLE 6-6	Netstat Switch	Definition
Netstat Command-Line Switches	-a	Displays all connections and ports.
	-e	Displays Ethernet statistics.
	-n	Lists addresses and ports in numerical form.
	-s	Lists per-protocol statistics.
	-p	Allows specification of protocol; can be TCP, UDP, ICMP, or IP.
	-r	Lists routing table.
	-o	Displays the process ID number of the process that opened the port.
	-interval	Specifies interval to pause display.

CERTIFICATION OBJECTIVE 6.06

IPCONFIG and WINIPCFG

IPCONFIG and WINIPCFG are utilities used to display the current TCP/IP configurations on the local workstations. IPCONFIG is a command-line utility for Windows NT–based systems, such as Windows 2000/XP/2003/Vista/2008 and later, and WINIPCFG is a graphical interface used in Windows 95, 98, and Windows ME. By default, they both display the IP address, the subnet mask, and the default gateway.

IPCONFIG

IPCONFIG is used in Windows to display TCP/IP information from a command prompt. With this utility, you can also display other related IP settings, such as who your DNS and WINS servers are. You can also view the network interface's physical MAC address with IPCONFIG. If you have more than one network interface, statistics are displayed about each one individually or can be filtered to a particular one.

If you use the IPCONFIG command by itself with no command-line switches, it will display your IP address, subnet mask, and default gateway, but if you use the

/ALL switch with it, it will display all TCP/IP information available. To view all your TCP/IP settings, type the following in a command prompt:

```
ipconfig /all
```

The following output will be displayed. Notice that you can see the hostname, IP address, physical address (MAC address), DNS server, and IP address of the DHCP server that gave your system its IP address.

```
Windows IP Configuration
Host Name . . . . . . . . . . . . : lap-xppro

Primary Dns Suffix . . . . . . . :
Node Type . . . . . . . . . . . . : Unknown
IP Routing Enabled. . . . . . . . : No
WINS Proxy Enabled. . . . . . . . : No
Ethernet adapter Local Area Connection:
Connection-specific DNS Suffix . :
Description . . . . . . . . . . . : Realtek RTL8139/810x Family Fast Ethernet NIC
Physical Address. . . . . . . . . : 00-02-3F-6B-25-13
Dhcp Enabled. . . . . . . . . . . : Yes
Autoconfiguration Enabled . . . . : Yes
IP Address. . . . . . . . . . . . : 192.168.0.108
Subnet Mask . . . . . . . . . . . : 255.255.255.0
Default Gateway . . . . . . . . . : 192.168.0.1
DHCP Server . . . . . . . . . . . : 192.168.0.1
DNS Servers . . . . . . . . . . . : 192.168.0.1
Lease Obtained. . . . . . . . . . : Wednesday, April 20, 2005 4:52:45 PM
Lease Expires . . . . . . . . . . : Wednesday, April 27, 2005 4:52:45 PM
```

IPCONFIG DHCP Parameters

The IPCONFIG command-line utility enables you to control DHCP functions with command-line switches such as /release and /renew.

The /release option removes the assigned IP address from your system. By default, /release removes the assigned IP address from all adapters configured for DHCP use. By specifying the adapter name after the switch, only that adapter will be affected by the command. The /release option can be useful if you are experiencing problems associated with DHCP, such as realizing that you received an address from the wrong DHCP server. It can also be used to release the address if an IP conflict occurs.

The /renew option sends a request to the DHCP server asking for an address. It takes the last address DHCP assigned to your system if it is available. If not, the computer is given the next available address in the pool. As with the /release option, you can specify a particular adapter after the switch to renew the address. This will only work if the adapter has been set up to receive its IP address from a DHCP server.

The IPCONFIG utility also supports switches for troubleshooting DNS name resolution. Since Windows 2000, the operating systems have a DNS resolver cache, which stores responses from the DNS server in memory so that the client will not need to query DNS a second time for an address already stored in the cache—the name is resolved from the cache. If you want to display the DNS resolver cache, you may use the /displaydns switch with IPCONFIG. If you want to clear, or flush, the DNS resolver cache, you may use the /flushdns switch. Flushing the cache will ensure that the client system will query DNS and get up-to-date records.

on the **job**

A number of times I have modified a record in DNS and had troubles communicating with the host that the DNS change was made for. The reason was because the machine I was sitting at had the old DNS data in the resolver cache, and I ended up needing to flush the cache.

To display the DNS resolver cache on your system, type the following at a command prompt:

```
ipconfig /displaydns
```

To clear the entries from the DNS resolver cache, type the following at a command prompt:

```
ipconfig /flushdns
```

WINIPCFG

WINIPCFG is the Windows 95/98/ME–based graphical utility used to display TCP/IP information. The information displayed is the same as that in the IPCONFIG command-line utility used in Windows 2000/XP/2003/Vista/2008. Microsoft has added a graphical interface for ease of use on the Windows 9*x* systems, but it can still be run from the command line with specific switches.

WINIPCFG Options

When you open WINIPCFG, the only information displayed by default is the TCP/IP address, the subnet mask, and the default gateway. There is a button at the bottom for more information. A drop-down box is included in the dialog box to allow you to specify a specific network card and view the TCP/IP configuration of that specific network card. Figure 6-17 shows WINIPCFG—notice the drop-down list in the middle of the screen for you to change network cards in a multicard system.

DHCP Options

The WINIPCFG utility includes buttons for releasing and renewing IP addresses for DHCP. It also contains information pertaining to the time and date the lease was obtained and when it expires. The available options in the winipcfg dialog box are listed as follows:

- **Renew_All**   Renew the IP address on all adapters.
- **Release_All**   Release the IP address on all adapters.
- **Renew**   Renew the IP address for a specified adapter.
- **Release**   Release the IP address for a specified adapter.

FIGURE 6-17

The WINIPCFG
utility in
Windows 9x

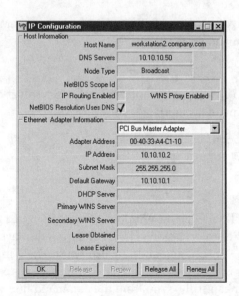

Batch Option

An additional option included with WINIPCFG is the /Batch switch. This enables you to forward the information in this utility to a text file. By default, output is placed in the WINIPCFG.OUT file in the %WINDIR% directory. By appending a path and filename to the end of this switch, you can place this information wherever you prefer. The batch option can be used with any command-line option available for this utility.

CertCam 6-6

Perform Exercise 6-6 from LabBook.pdf on the CD-ROM to experiment with IPCONFIG or watch the CertCam training video.

IFCONFIG

UNIX and Linux operating systems have a command similar to IPCONFIG and it is ifconfig (case sensitive). The ifconfig command stands for Interface Config and is used to control the network interface, which is most commonly referred to as the network card. Let's look at a few ifconfig commands.

The first example is to use ifconfig by itself without any additional switches. When you type **ifconfig** in Linux, you will get a list of network cards and the IP address and MAC addresses associated with each card (shown in Figure 6-18).

FIGURE 6-18

Using ifconfig in Linux to display IP address information

```
root@ linux8:~                                              _ □ ✕
File  Edit  View  Terminal  Go  Help
[root@linux8 root]# ifconfig
eth0      Link encap:Ethernet  HWaddr 00:0C:29:5C:2B:85
          inet addr:192.168.1.8  Bcast:192.168.1.255  Mask:255.255.255.0
          UP BROADCAST RUNNING MULTICAST  MTU:1500  Metric:1
          RX packets:21564 errors:0 dropped:0 overruns:0 frame:0
          TX packets:13 errors:0 dropped:0 overruns:0 carrier:0
          collisions:0 txqueuelen:100
          RX bytes:3174279 (3.0 Mb)  TX bytes:1980 (1.9 Kb)
          Interrupt:10 Base address:0x10a0

lo        Link encap:Local Loopback
          inet addr:127.0.0.1  Mask:255.0.0.0
          UP LOOPBACK RUNNING  MTU:16436  Metric:1
          RX packets:72 errors:0 dropped:0 overruns:0 frame:0
          TX packets:72 errors:0 dropped:0 overruns:0 carrier:0
          collisions:0 txqueuelen:0
          RX bytes:4682 (4.5 Kb)  TX bytes:4682 (4.5 Kb)

[root@linux8 root]# ▮
```

In Windows we can enable and disable a network card by right-clicking the LAN Connection and choosing Enable or Disable. In Linux, if you wish to disable the network card, you will use the **ifconfig** command as follows:

```
ifconfig eth0 up
```

The eth0 part of the command is how you specify the network card you wish to work with. If you had two network cards in the Linux computer, they would be known as eth0 and eth1. This is very similar to how a Cisco router refers to the different network interfaces. The up switch means that you wish to bring the card up, or enable it. If you wished to disable the card, you would use the keyword **down**.

In Linux, if you wish to renew your IP address you use the **dhclient** command (shown in Figure 6-19), which is the equivalent to the Windows **ipconfig /renew** command.

Looking at Figure 6-19, you can see that the **dhclient** command was typed in. You will also notice at the bottom of the output that a DHCPACK came from 192.168.1.3. This means that the Linux machine has received an IP address from the DHCP server running on 192.168.1.3. You will also notice that the Linux network card is bound to address 192.168.1.8.

FIGURE 6-19

Using dhclient to renew the IP address in Linux

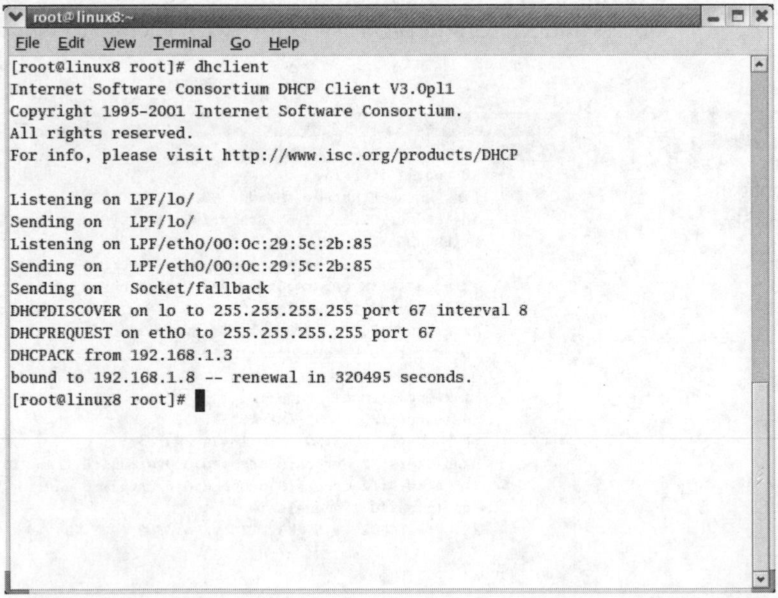

```
[root@linux8 root]# dhclient
Internet Software Consortium DHCP Client V3.0pl1
Copyright 1995-2001 Internet Software Consortium.
All rights reserved.
For info, please visit http://www.isc.org/products/DHCP

Listening on LPF/lo/
Sending on   LPF/lo/
Listening on LPF/eth0/00:0c:29:5c:2b:85
Sending on   LPF/eth0/00:0c:29:5c:2b:85
Sending on   Socket/fallback
DHCPDISCOVER on lo to 255.255.255.255 port 67 interval 8
DHCPREQUEST on eth0 to 255.255.255.255 port 67
DHCPACK from 192.168.1.3
bound to 192.168.1.8 -- renewal in 320495 seconds.
[root@linux8 root]#
```

CERTIFICATION OBJECTIVE 6.07

FTP

The File Transfer Protocol (FTP) is the TCP/IP protocol designed primarily for transferring files from one computer to another. FTP is the name of both a protocol and a utility used for the purpose of connecting to an FTP server and downloading a file. FTP was created to transfer data files from one host to another quickly and efficiently, either by allowing a user to do the download anonymously or by authenticating to the server.

How FTP Works

FTP is unusual in that it uses two TCP channels to operate: TCP port 20 is used as the data transfer channel, and TCP port 21 is used for control commands. The data transfer channel is known as the DTP, or Data Transfer Process, and the command channel is known as the PI, or Protocol Interpreter. The two channels enable you to transfer data and execute commands at the same time, providing a more efficient and faster data transfer.

Like Telnet, FTP requires a server-based program to answer the client requests for file download. An FTP service is available on most network operating systems today, including Windows 2003, Windows 2008, NetWare, UNIX, and Linux.

FTP enables file transfers in several formats based on the type of remote system being used. Most systems have two modes of transfer: text and binary. Text transfers are ASCII based and use characters separated by carriage returns and newline characters, while binary transfer mode is used to download binary files such as executables or non-ASCII data. Most systems default to text mode and require you to switch to binary mode for a binary transfer. Figure 6-20 shows an example of an FTP session.

FIGURE 6-20

An FTP session

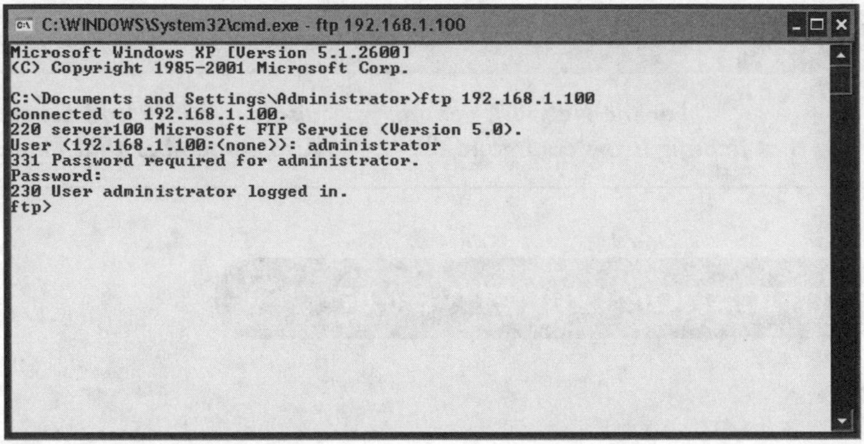

You will notice in Figure 6-20 that to connect to the FTP server you type:

```
ftp 192.168.1.100
```

The server will then ask you for a username and password. Once you type a valid username and password, you will be logged on and placed at the FTP prompt, where you can type FTP commands to potentially view, upload, and download files.

Using FTP

A command-line client utility is included with many versions of Windows and Linux, and many third-party FTP server and client applications are available for connecting to an FTP server and downloading files. Some third-party utilities are Windows-based utilities, adding a graphical interface to the download functionality.

FTP is started by typing **ftp** at a command prompt followed by the fully qualified domain name or IP address of the target machine. As with Telnet, the client computer must be able to resolve the remote computer's name into an IP address for the command to succeed. Once logged on, users can browse through directories, download and upload files, and log out.

There is a wide array of commands available in the FTP utility. These commands are used to control the FTP application and its functions. Table 6-7 lists some of the more common FTP commands that are available in an FTP session.

Command	Description
cd	Changes working directory.
delete	Deletes file.
ls	Lists current directory contents.
bye	Logs out.
get	Downloads a file.
put	Uploads a file.
verbose	Turns verbose mode on and off.

TABLE 6-7

Popular FTP Commands

CertCam 6-7

To use the FTP utility, perform Exercise 6-7 from LabBook.pdf on the CD-ROM or watch the CertCam training video on the CD-ROM.

Configuring FTP

Users require a login ID to access FTP services if anonymous access is disabled. Most systems today enable an anonymous login, but these users should not possess full rights to the system. Common problems with connecting via FTP are an invalid login or insufficient access rights. If you are having problems connecting to an FTP server, contact your FTP server administrator to verify that your login ID is set up correctly.

FTP Options

Several switches are available for the command-line FTP utility. These options enable you to further customize the use of FTP to meet your needs. The -v option suppresses the display of remote server responses. This provides a more user-friendly interface to the utility. By default, when you start FTP, it attempts to log on automatically. You can disable this function by using the -n option.

The -I option turns off the interactive prompting that occurs during multiple transfers, which makes for a more automated approach to FTP. The -d option enables you to turn on the debugging functions. This feature displays all FTP commands that are passed between the client and server.

Another option included with the FTP command-line utility is the capability to run a script of commands after the program is started. The script file is used instead of redirection and can include any standard command. You must append the -s: switch followed by the path and filename of the script.

One of my favorite switches for FTP is -a, which will automatically log on as the anonymous account; this saves you the hassle of having to type the anonymous account name for a logon. Table 6-8 lists the FTP command-line switches.

Troubleshooting with FTP

When it comes to FTP, one of the biggest problems you may hit is with logging on to the FTP server. Make sure that you know the username and password of an account that is allowed to access the FTP server. If you are interested in uploading files to the FTP server, you will need to ensure that you have the appropriate permission to do the upload. Typically, users who log on to the FTP server are granted only read permissions.

The other problem you may have with FTP sessions is understanding the commands that you can type during the session. This is just a matter of practice and getting familiar with the command set.

For the Network+ exam, remember that FTP uses two different TCP ports. Port 21 is used as a control port to send the commands, while port 20 is the data port used to transfer the data between the client and server.

TABLE 6-8	FTP Switch	Definition
FTP Command-Line Switches	-v	Does not list remote server responses.
	-n	Does not autologin on initial connection.
	-I	Disables interactive prompting for multiple file transfers.
	-d	Enables debugging.
	-g	Allows use of wildcard characters.
	-s	Specifies a text file of FTP commands to execute after FTP starts.
	-a	Allows use of any local interface when binding data connection.
	-w	Allows specification of transfer buffer size; the default is 4096.
	-computer	Specifies FQDN or IP address of remote PC with which to connect.

TFTP

The Trivial File Transfer Protocol (TFTP) is a slight variation on FTP. TFTP differs from FTP in two ways: It uses the User Datagram Protocol (UDP) connectionless transport instead of TCP, and you do not log on to the remote machine. Because it uses UDP, TFTP does not provide error-correcting services as TCP does. This has advantages, but it does have to use more complex algorithms to guarantee data integrity. Because users do not log on, user-access and file permission problems are avoided.

TFTP is generally not used for file transfers as FTP is; instead, it is used in situations such as diskless terminals or workstations. Typically, TFTP is used to load applications or for bootstrapping. Because the operating systems are not loaded at this point, the diskless machines cannot execute FTP. TFTP handles access and file permissions by imposing restraints from within the host operating system. For example, by setting the file permissions on the TFTP server, you can limit the security to areas inside the TFTP server.

on the **Ö** o b

TFTP is commonly employed when using Cisco routers. TFTP servers allow you to save the router configuration information to the TFTP server and be able to reload the configuration information from the TFTP server. You can also back up the Cisco IOS to a TFTP server.

CERTIFICATION OBJECTIVE 6.08

Ping and Hping2

The Ping (Packet Internet Groper) command is the most used TCP/IP troubleshooting tool available. This command is used to test a machine's connectivity to another system and to verify that the target system is active.

Usually, using this command is the first step to any troubleshooting if a connectivity problem is occurring between two computers. This can quickly help you to determine whether a remote host is available and responsive.

How Ping Works

Ping uses the ICMP protocol to verify connections to remote hosts by sending *echo request* packets and listening for *echo reply* packets. Ping sends out four different echo messages and prints out feedback of the replies on the screen when the reply is received. Figure 6-21 shows an example of a ping.

To use a Ping command and see the results, perform Exercise 6-8 from LabBook.pdf on the CD-ROM or watch the CertCam training video.

Ping Options

Additional options are available to customize the output that Ping provides. Options include changing packet length, type of service, and TTL settings. You can append the -a option to resolve an IP address to its hostname. The -f option will not enable the packets to be fragmented by a router or gateway. This can be used to further stress connections to determine whether they are failing.

The TTL settings can be specified with the -i option. In addition, the type of service option is available via the -v switch.

Setting the Length Option

By default, packets are sent in 32-byte chunks. You can modify the packet size to further test the response time. When larger packets are involved, you can see what larger loads will do to response time as well as responsiveness. To change the packet size, use the -l option followed by the packet length. The maximum packet length that can be specified is 65,500 bytes.

Setting the Number of Echo Packets

You can specify the number of packets to send to the remote host. By default, only four packets are sent. You can specify any number of packets to send with the -n option. You can also use the -t option to specify a continuous stream of packets, and

---

FIGURE 6-21

The Ping command tests connectivity to another system.

```
C:\>ping 10.10.10.1

Pinging 10.10.10.1 with 32 bytes of data:

Reply from 10.10.10.1: bytes=32 time=1ms TTL=128
Reply from 10.10.10.1: bytes=32 time=1ms TTL=128
Reply from 10.10.10.1: bytes=32 time=1ms TTL=128
Reply from 10.10.10.1: bytes=32 time<10ms TTL=128

C:\>
```

to continuously ping the remote host until you stop the command with a CTRL-BREAK. This functionality is useful in monitoring trends in data transfers.

Timeout Intervals

Timeout intervals are used to interpret the time to travel between hops. A normal LAN usually lists devices as being less than 10 milliseconds away. By default, two seconds is the timeout before a "reply timed out" message is generated. You can use the -w option to raise this value for troubleshooting.

Loose Source Routing

Use Ping to specify intermediate gateways to test against. You can route packets through particular IP addresses or hostnames specified. The -j option enables you to specify the hosts to route through. The -k option enables you to exclude hosts from this route list. The maximum number of hosts you can specify with both options is nine.

Troubleshooting with Ping

Use the Ping utility to verify connectivity by IP address or hostname. You must be able to resolve the hostname to use this functionality. If you are unable to ping by hostname, but you can ping by IP address, you most likely will have a name-resolution problem.

If you are receiving "reply timed out" messages, you might try to bump up the timeout value with the -w option. Maybe the packets are arriving but are timing out before two seconds. After bumping up the value, if the replies are returning, a bandwidth problem might be present. Contact the network administrator where the numbers seem to rise. Table 6-9 details the ping command-line switches.

w a t c h   **The Ping utility uses the**   **ICMP Type 8 is the message type of an**
ICMP protocol instead of TCP as used   **echo request used by Ping, and the echo**
by FTP and Telnet. ICMP has different   **replies come back as ICMP Type 0.**
types of messages that can be sent;

TABLE 6-9	Ping Switch	Definition
Ping Command-Line Switches	-t	Specifies to perform the ping command until interrupted.
	-a	Resolves addresses to computer names.
	-n	Specifies the number of ECHO packets; the default is 4.
	-l	Specifies amount of data to send in ECHO packet. Default is 32 bytes, maximum is 65,500 bytes.
	-f	Specifies to not fragment packets.
	-I	Sets TTL (time to live) value for packets.
	-v	Sets TOS (type of service).
	-r	Records routes of packets.
	-s	Specifies timestamp for number of hops.
	-j	Specifies route for packets (loose source route).
	-k	Specifies route for packets (strict source route).
	-w	Specifies timeout interval in milliseconds.
	-destination-list	Specifies remote PC to ping.

Hping2

The Ping utility that ships with most operating systems uses ICMP as the underlining protocol. There are other Ping-type utilities out there that give you more flexibility, such as Hping or the newer version, Hping2. Hping2 is popular because instead of using ICMP it uses TCP as the underlining protocol and allows you to craft the packets to use whatever port you wish to use. This allows you to ping through firewalls that may be blocking ICMP traffic. The following is a typical Hping2 command:

```
hping2 -c 3 -s 53 -p 80 -S 10.0.0.25
```

In this code example the -c switch is used to specify how many ping messages you wish to send. In this example I have specified to send three messages. The -s switch is used to specify the source port and the -p is used to specify the destination port of the packet. In this example, I have made the traffic look as if it is coming from a DNS server but destined for the web server. The -S specifies that I want to send a TCP SYN message, while the 10.0.0.25 is the target IP address of the system to ping. Figure 6-22 displays the Hping2 utility being used to bypass my firewall, which is blocking ICMP traffic.

FIGURE 6-22

Using Hping2 to craft a TCP ping message

---

e x a m

ⓦatch

       Hping2 is a Ping-style program that allows you to craft your own TCP packet used in the ping operation. This gives you the flexibility of being able *to bypass firewalls because you can create a packet that uses port numbers open on the firewall.*

CERTIFICATION OBJECTIVE 6.09

NSLOOKUP and DIG

The NSLOOKUP command is used to verify DNS name resolution from a DNS server. This is very useful for a Windows network, which depends immensely on the use of DNS. If DNS should fail or return improper information, network communication can slow due to name resolution. If DNS fails, the client systems could have trouble authenticating, and domain controllers could have trouble communicating with one another, because locating a domain controller on the network is a function of DNS. In a Windows network, Active Directory needs DNS, or Active Directory will fail and the domain will fail.

How NSLOOKUP Works

NSLOOKUP will query a DNS server for specific types of records and can be used to troubleshoot why a system cannot connect to another remote system. If there is an incorrect record in DNS, or no record at all, you will be able to determine this with NSLOOKUP.

These items can be verified fairly quickly if you are located at the client PC. You can ping the server by the server IP address. If you can ping the server by IP address and not by the server DNS name, there is a DNS name-resolution issue. You can then pursue the issue further by using NSLOOKUP to verify that the DNS server is operational and that a record exists for the host in the DNS database.

It is possible, but unlikely, that the name to an IP address resolution is incorrect. The DNS name could be matched to an improper IP address. This can cause the data packets to be sent to a PC or network device other than the correct system, or even to a nonexistent IP address.

NSLOOKUP Options

There are two modes in which you can use NSLOOKUP: interactive and noninteractive.

Interactive Mode

In *interactive* mode you simply type the NSLOOKUP command; you are then placed at the NSLOOKUP prompt, where you type one NSLOOKUP command after another. Figure 6-23 displays the interactive prompt. Notice that one command is typed after the other and they all work together to obtain a result.

Interactive mode is used when you have more than one item in the DNS database you will be querying. Interactive mode will allow you enter a command-line state that will keep prompting you for more commands until you type **exit** at the NSLOOKUP command prompt to return to a standard DOS command prompt and exit the NSLOOKUP utility.

Notice in Figure 6-23 that the command **nslookup** was typed to go to interactive mode. In interactive mode, you would then type the different nslookup commands at the prompt that displays with a **>**. Notice that **set type=mx** was typed next—this tells **nslookup** that I want to find MX records for whatever domain I specify next. MX records point to the mail servers for a company, which is what is specified in the next line—glensworld.loc—my fictitious company. Notice in the figure that

FIGURE 6-23

Using nslookup in interactive mode

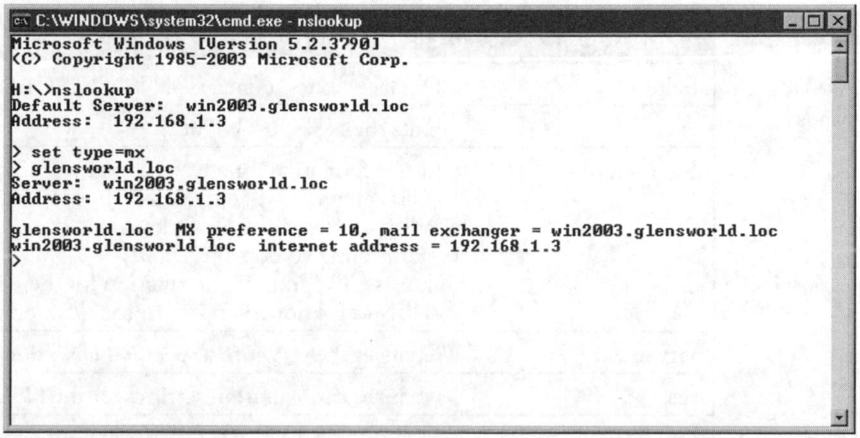

```
C:\WINDOWS\system32\cmd.exe - nslookup                          _ □ X
Microsoft Windows [Version 5.2.3790]
<C> Copyright 1985-2003 Microsoft Corp.

H:\>nslookup
Default Server:  win2003.glensworld.loc
Address:  192.168.1.3

> set type=mx
> glensworld.loc
Server:  win2003.glensworld.loc
Address:  192.168.1.3

glensworld.loc  MX preference = 10, mail exchanger = win2003.glensworld.loc
win2003.glensworld.loc   internet address = 192.168.1.3
>
```

nslookup returns the address of the MX record, which is equal to win2003
.glensworld.loc, which has the Internet address of 192.168.1.3.

Table 6-10 lists the commands available in the NSLOOKUP prompt.

Noninteractive Mode

When using *noninteractive* mode, you will type the NSLOOKUP command followed
by the command options. You are not placed at an interactive prompt where you
type many commands. Figure 6-24 displays the noninteractive use of NSLOOKUP.
In this example, you are simply trying to resolve a single host to an IP address. You
can see from Figure 6-24 that the address www.gleneclarke.com has the IP address of
24.89.233.148.

**To check out NSLOOKUP, perform Exercise 6-9 in LabBook.pdf on the
CD-ROM or watch the CertCam training video from the CD-ROM.**

FIGURE 6-24

Using nslookup
in non-interactive
mode

```
C:\WINDOWS\system32\cmd.exe                                     _ □ X
H:\>nslookup www.gleneclarke.com
Server:  win2003.glensworld.loc
Address:  192.168.1.3

Name:    www.gleneclarke.com
Address:  24.89.233.148

H:\>_
```

TABLE 6-10	Command	Description
NSLOOKUP Commands	help	Displays a brief summary of NSLOOKUP commands.
	exit	Exits the NSLOOKUP utility.
	ls (-t, -a, -d, -h, -s)	Lists information for a DNS domain: -t lists all records of a specified type -a lists aliases in the DNS domain -d lists all DNS domain records -h lists CPU and OS information for the DNS domain -s lists well-known services in the DNS domain
	server	Changes the server to a specified DNS domain.
	set	Changes configuration settings for the NSLOOKUP utility.
	set all	Lists current NSLOOKUP configuration values.
	set cl[ass] = (in, chaos, hesiod, any)	Sets Query class as specified by the option setting: IN Internet class CHAOS Chaos class HESIOD MIT Athena Hesiod class ANY Any of the previously listed wildcards
	set po[rt]	Changes port used by DNS name server.
	set q[uerytype] = (a, any, cname, gid, hinfo, mb, mg, minfo, mr, mx, ns, ptr, soa, txt, uid, uinfo, wks)	Changes type of query: A Computer's IP address ANY All types of data CNAME Canonical name for an alias GID Group name's group identifier HINFO CPU and operating system type of computer MB Mailbox domain name MG Mail group member MINFO Mailbox or mail list information MR Mail rename domain name MX Mail exchanger NS DNS name server for the zone PTR Computer name if the query is an IP address SOA DNS domain's start-of-authority record TXT Text information UID User identifier UINFO User information WKS Well-known service description
	set [no] rec[urse]	Allows you to specify whether to recurse a query to other servers.
	set ret[ry]	Sets the number of retries.
	set ty[pe]	Changes type of information queried.

DIG

DIG is a very popular TCP/IP utility that is available on most Linux systems and is used to query DNS. DIG will give you much the same information as NSLOOKUP but is much more flexible. Let's look at some examples. If you simply want to find out the IP address for a fully qualified domain name (FQDN) you simply type the **dig** command followed by the FQDN as shown in Figure 6-25.

What I love about the dig command is that as you learn the commands, you can place the +short switch on the command to see the "short" version of the results. Looking back to Figure 6-25, you can see that when you typed the command in, it came back and summarized the question and gave us the answer—I don't want all that! Just give me the answer is what the "+short" switch does. Figure 6-26 displays the "+short" switch being used.

There are a wealth of example commands we can use with DIG. I have summarized the commands I use most in Table 6-11.

FIGURE 6-25

Using dig to
query DNS

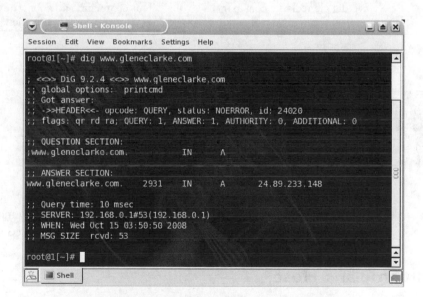

FIGURE 6-26

Using the +short
option with dig

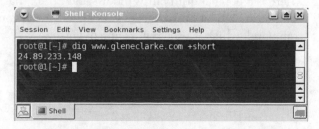

TABLE 6-11	Example Command	Definition
Example dig Commands	dig www.gleneclarke.com	This command will query DNS for the IP address associated with www.gleneclarke.com.
	dig www.gleneclarke.com +short	This command will query DNS for the IP address associated with www.gleneclarke.com but give the short answer version. +short can be used on most dig commands.
	dig gleneclarke.com MX	This command will query DNS for all the MX records for the gleneclarke.com domain. MX records are special records that point to mail servers. This command is used to find out what the IP addresses of a company's mail servers are.
	dig -x 192.168.2.200	This command will perform a reverse query. If you know the IP address and want to know the name of the host, you can use this command.
	dig gleneclarke.com axfr	This command will do a zone transfer of all DNS data for the domain specified.

CERTIFICATION OBJECTIVE 6.10

Other TCP/IP Utilities

This chapter is such a big chapter because there are so many TCP/IP utilities and options with each utility. You need to be familiar with a few more utilities for the Network+ exam—they are the hostname, MTR, and route commands.

Hostname and Host

There is a popular utility in Windows and Linux that you can use to find out the computername, or hostname, of your system—the command is the hostname command, which is shown in Figure 6-27.

FIGURE 6-27

Display your
system name with
the hostname
command.

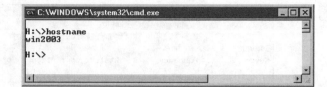

Another useful utility that is available on Linux systems to query DNS is the host utility. There are a number of switches that go along with the host utility, but in its simplest form you could type:

```
host www.gleneclarke.com
```

This will return the IP address of the FQDN www.gleneclarke.com. You can also perform tasks such as finding all the mail servers for the company as you can with DIG or NSLOOKUP. To do this with the host command, you type the following command:

```
host -t MX glensworld.loc
```

In this code example the -t switch allows you to specify which records you wish to query for; in my example I am looking for the MX records from the domain glensworld.loc. Figure 6-28 displays the output of the two host commands discussed.

MTR

MTR is a network diagnostics program available in Linux that combines features of Tracert and Ping. It is a glorified traceroute tool that sends multiple ping messages to each router between the source and the destination. To use MTR, you simply type **mtr** and then specify your destination as shown in Figure 6-29.

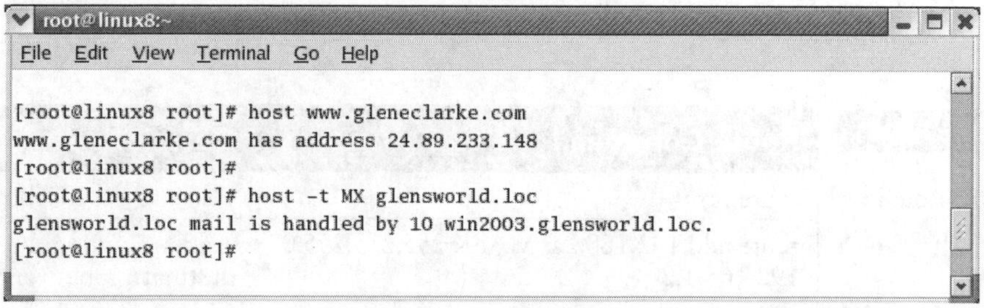

FIGURE 6-28

Using the host
command in
Linux

```
root@linux8:~
File  Edit  View  Terminal  Go  Help

[root@linux8 root]# host www.gleneclarke.com
www.gleneclarke.com has address 24.89.233.148
[root@linux8 root]#
[root@linux8 root]# host -t MX glensworld.loc
glensworld.loc mail is handled by 10 win2003.glensworld.loc.
[root@linux8 root]#
```

FIGURE 6-29

MTR is a Linux utility that combines Tracert with Ping.

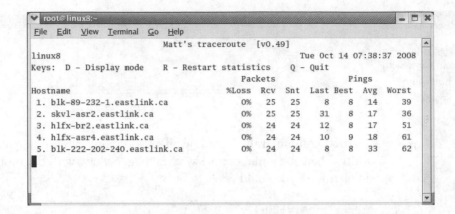

You can see in the figure that there are five hops between my system and the destination. With each destination you can see the packets sent and the packets that have been received as replies along with the percentage of packets lost.

Route

The route command is a very popular TCP/IP utility that is used to manage the routing table of the local system. You learned about the route command in Chapter 5, but just as a refresher Table 6-12 is a listing of popular options to the route command.

Arping

Arping is a popular Linux utility that combines the ping command with the concept of ARP. Remember that ARP is a protocol used to convert the IP address to a MAC address—so when you use arping, you will be sending out ping messages but you will get replies that include the MAC address of the IP address you pinged. Very cool! Figure 6-30 displays the output of the arping utility.

TABLE 6-12

Popular Route Commands

Route Command	Description
route print	Displays the local routing table.
route add 192.168.2.0 MASK 255.255.255.0 192.168.1.2	Adds a route to the local routing table for destination network 192.168.2.0.
route delete 192.168.2.0	Deletes the route from the routing table.

FIGURE 6-30

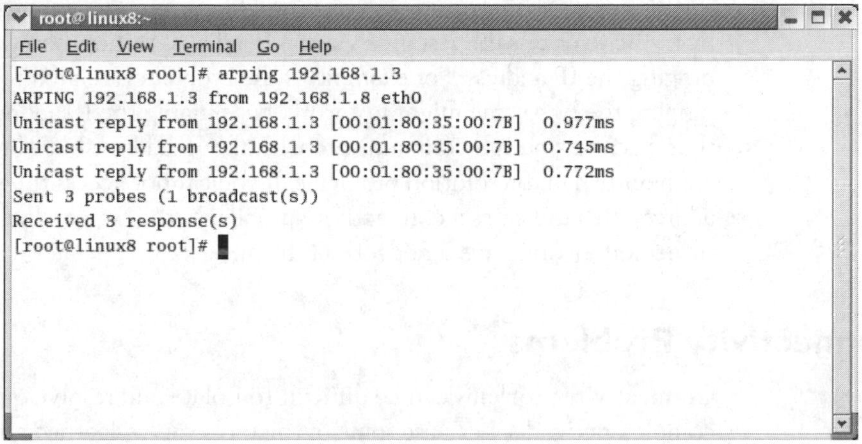

The Linux arping utility returns the MAC address with ping responses.

```
root@linux8:~
File  Edit  View  Terminal  Go  Help
[root@linux8 root]# arping 192.168.1.3
ARPING 192.168.1.3 from 192.168.1.8 eth0
Unicast reply from 192.168.1.3 [00:01:80:35:00:7B]  0.977ms
Unicast reply from 192.168.1.3 [00:01:80:35:00:7B]  0.745ms
Unicast reply from 192.168.1.3 [00:01:80:35:00:7B]  0.772ms
Sent 3 probes (1 broadcast(s))
Received 3 response(s)
[root@linux8 root]#
```

Now that you have an understanding of some of the popular TCP/IP utilities, let's look at some popular troubleshooting situations that can be solved with these utilities.

CERTIFICATION OBJECTIVE 6.11

Troubleshooting with TCP/IP Utilities

The two most common TCP/IP problems are network connectivity and name resolution. In this section, you will learn how to troubleshoot these problems and how to determine where the problems truly reside.

Given the following scenario, how do you troubleshoot the problem?

Scenario   You are trying to use a third-party application to access a remote computer via TCP/IP. You are unable to connect to the remote server.

To properly troubleshoot this problem, you must know where to begin. Most communication problems with TCP/IP can be categorized as one of the following:

■ Basic network connectivity problem
■ Name resolution problem

It is very easy to determine which problem is occurring in a given situation. Start by trying to access the resource via the IP address rather than the hostname by pinging the IP address. For example, if the problem is related to name resolution, pinging the hostname might not work, but pinging the IP address will. This indicates that, because you can communicate with the IP address but not the hostname, you are having name-resolution problems. If you cannot access the resource via the IP address, this indicates a connectivity problem—the system does not exist or it is turned off, or you have a network problem.

Connectivity Problems

Connectivity problems can be difficult to isolate and resolve quickly, especially in complex networks. Let's use some of the tools you've learned about to troubleshoot the earlier problem of using a third-party application to access a remote computer via TCP/IP and being unable to connect to the remote server. You cannot ping the remote host by its IP address.

Check Your TCP/IP Configuration

Start by checking your TCP/IP configuration. TCP/IP requires several settings to be complete and accurate. When you use TCP/IP as your network protocol, an incorrect setting such as a mistyped subnet mask can keep your computer from talking with other hosts on the network. For example, if you have an incorrect default gateway setup, you might not be able to communicate with anyone on a remote network.

Use the IPCONFIG utility or (on Linux or UNIX) the ifconfig utility to determine your computer's basic TCP/IP settings. Verify that the IP address and subnet mask displayed by the IPCONFIG command are the correct values for your computer. Verify that your default gateway is set up with the correct address of the router on the network.

Ping the Loopback Address

Try pinging the loopback address by pinging "localhost," "loopback," or the address 127.0.0.1. You can use the **ping** command to verify that TCP/IP is working properly. By pinging the loopback address, which is 127.0.0.1, you are actually verifying that the protocol stack is functioning properly. You should receive a reply like the one shown in Figure 6-31.

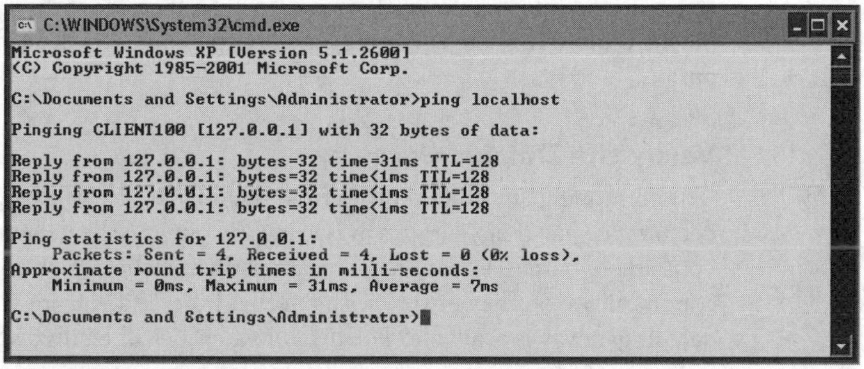

FIGURE 6-31

Pinging the
loopback address

```
C:\WINDOWS\System32\cmd.exe                                          _ □ ×
Microsoft Windows XP [Version 5.1.2600]
(C) Copyright 1985-2001 Microsoft Corp.

C:\Documents and Settings\Administrator>ping localhost

Pinging CLIENT100 [127.0.0.1] with 32 bytes of data:

Reply from 127.0.0.1: bytes=32 time=31ms TTL=128
Reply from 127.0.0.1: bytes=32 time<1ms TTL=128
Reply from 127.0.0.1: bytes=32 time<1ms TTL=128
Reply from 127.0.0.1: bytes=32 time<1ms TTL=128

Ping statistics for 127.0.0.1:
    Packets: Sent = 4, Received = 4, Lost = 0 (0% loss),
Approximate round trip times in milli-seconds:
    Minimum = 0ms, Maximum = 31ms, Average = 7ms

C:\Documents and Settings\Administrator>
```

An error while pinging the loopback address usually indicates a problem with the TCP/IP protocol installed locally. If you do receive an error at this point, you should try uninstalling and reinstalling TCP/IP. You can remove and install TCP/IP from your LAN connection properties.

Ping the Local IP Address

If you can successfully ping the loopback address, try pinging your local computer's IP address. If you do not know what your IP address is, remember that IPCONFIG/ WINIPCFG will display this information for you. By typing the following at a command prompt, you should receive a response similar to the one shown back in Figure 6-31:

```
PING <local IP address>
```

If an error occurs at this point, there might be a problem communicating with the NIC. You can first try reinstalling the adapter driver for the card. If that doesn't work, try removing and reseating the card. This error might only be resolved by completely replacing the NIC.

Clear the ARP Cache Table

If the local IP address responds correctly, try clearing the ARP cache. If an IP address was stored here by mistake, it could cause the client to attempt to contact the wrong computer.

Start by displaying the ARP cache. You can then see if there is an entry located for the remote IP address. If an incorrect entry exists, try deleting it with the -d option.

Verify the Default Gateway

After removing any errant entries from the ARP cache, the next step is to ping the default gateway that your system is using. By pinging the default gateway, you are verifying two items in one step: you are verifying whether or not your system can communicate on the network with another host, and you are verifying that the default gateway is available. The default gateway will be involved in communication only if you are trying to communicate with a host on a remote network. If the gateway does not respond, the packets will not be able to get to the remote host.

on the Job

You can use IPCONFIG or ifconfig (in Linux) to display your default gateway. Once you have that address, try pinging that address to verify that the gateway is up and running.

Trace the Route to the Remote Host

After a packet leaves the default gateway, any route can be taken to reach a remote computer. The next step is to try to trace the route to the remote computer.

A wide array of problems could show up here. You may notice that when the utility gets to a certain point, it responds with "Request timed out." If this occurs, it could indicate a route problem or a device failure. It could also indicate bandwidth issues. Try raising the timeout value. If it responds but with high values, your data transfers could be failing because the application does not wait long enough. Try reconfiguring your application or adding more bandwidth to your network.

Another error message you might receive is "Destination Net Unreachable." This usually indicates a network routing problem. Contact the network administrator responsible for that network segment.

Check TCP/IP Port on the Server

The next thing to try is to verify that you are sending data to the correct port. For example, your web browser automatically tries to connect to port 80 on a server; if the administrator of that server changes the port value, you will need to specify the port when you make the connection. Table 6-13 lists the standard port settings for commonly used protocols.

TABLE 6-13	Port	Protocol
	80	HTTP
Common Ports	443	HTTPS
Used by Network	21	FTP
Services	23	TELNET
	25	SMTP
	110	POP3
	3389	Remote Desktop

You can use the Telnet tool to verify that the other computer is configured to permit connections on the same port you are using. If you do not receive an error message, the other computer is configured to enable connections. If you do receive an error, try looking at the settings on the remote computer to verify that they are set up properly.

Name Resolution Problems

Suppose you are able to connect to a remote host by IP address but are unable to connect via its hostname. This indicates a name resolution problem. In the Microsoft world, there are two types of computer names: fully qualified domain names (FQDNs) used by socket-based applications and NetBIOS names (computer names) used by NetBIOS applications. These names can be resolved in several ways, including using the Domain Name System (DNS), the Windows Internet Naming Service (WINS), a hosts file, or an lmhosts file. Each method has its advantages and disadvantages.

Although there are many techniques used to resolve the two different style names, for the exam, have *it clear that DNS resolves FQDNs to IP addresses whereas WINS resolves NetBIOS names to IP addresses.*

Name-Resolution Order

The two types of Microsoft computer names each work a little differently. They can use the other's services; however, they use their own resolution methods first. When communicating with an FQDN, the name is resolved by the following resolution methods (in order):

1. Checking the local name
2. Checking the local HOSTS file
3. Checking DNS servers
4. Checking the local NetBIOS cache
5. Checking WINS servers
6. Broadcasts

NetBIOS name resolution works in a very similar way. The NetBIOS name is resolved by using the following method:

1. Checking its local NetBIOS cache
2. Checking the WINS server
3. Broadcasting for a computer
4. Checking the LMHOSTS file
5. Checking the local hostname (if Enable DNS For Windows Resolution is checked in TCP/IP properties)
6. Checking the TCP/IP HOSTS file
7. Checking DNS servers

By knowing the order of name resolution, you can better understand how these services work and effectively troubleshoot them.

Check the Hosts File

You can start by checking the hosts file. A hosts file is a text file that can be configured with any standard text editor. It contains static mappings for remote TCP/IP hosts by using an IP address column and a hostname column. Each computer has its own hosts file, HOSTS, located in %windir% for Windows 9x, and HOSTS located in %SystemRoot%\System32\Drivers\Etc for Windows 2000/XP/2003/Vista/2008.

Because every machine maintains its own HOSTS file, they are not generally used in medium or large environments. If a modification or addition has to be made, each machine needs to receive this update by receiving a new version of the hosts file. When you are talking about four or five machines, it's not that bad. When you have to keep 150 machines up to date, it can become very difficult. Figure 6-32 shows an example of a hosts file.

To check your HOSTS file, open it and scan for the entry of the remote host. If your computer resolves addresses using this file, verify that the entry exists and that it contains the correct information. If this is not the resolution method you are using, trying checking your DNS configuration.

Check Your Domain Name System Configuration

DNS provides TCP/IP name-resolution services. DNS is a central server that systems can use to query for name resolution. For example, if any system on your network were to try to contact server1.yourdomain.com, any system can query DNS and have the name resolved. In addition, if an entry is added to the DNS server, all systems know about the change right away, because DNS is a central database that everyone uses (versus the HOSTS file, which all users have their own copy of).

FIGURE 6-32

The hosts file used for FQDN name resolution

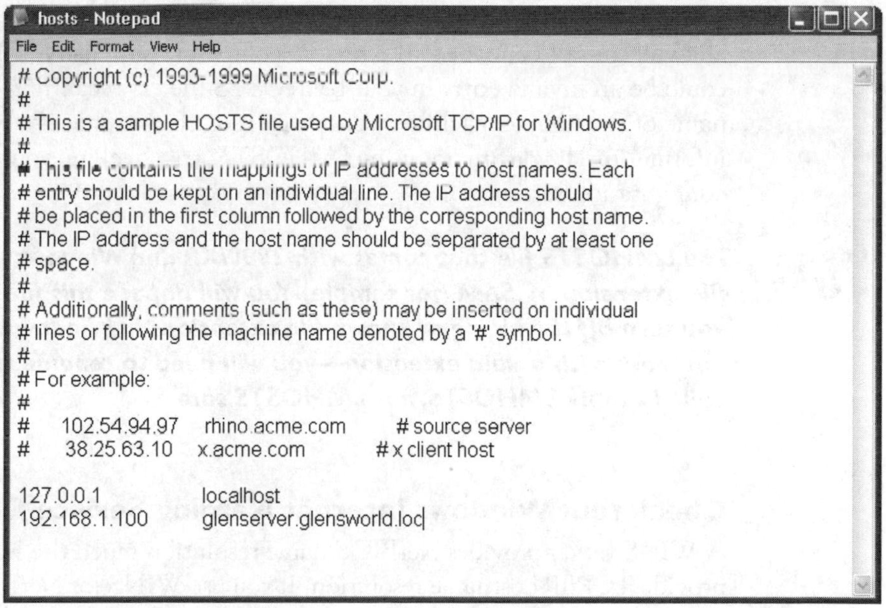

```
# Copyright (c) 1993-1999 Microsoft Corp.
#
# This is a sample HOSTS file used by Microsoft TCP/IP for Windows.
#
# This file contains the mappings of IP addresses to host names. Each
# entry should be kept on an individual line. The IP address should
# be placed in the first column followed by the corresponding host name.
# The IP address and the host name should be separated by at least one
# space.
#
# Additionally, comments (such as these) may be inserted on individual
# lines or following the machine name denoted by a '#' symbol.
#
# For example:
#
#      102.54.94.97     rhino.acme.com        # source server
#       38.25.63.10     x.acme.com            # x client host

127.0.0.1               localhost
192.168.1.100           glenserver.glensworld.loc
```

If you use DNS for name resolution, first verify that you have the DNS client set up correctly on the workstation. From a command prompt, type **ipconfig /all** to list the DNS servers configured on a client. If they exist and are correct, try pinging the DNS server to see if it is online. If it responds, try changing your DNS server to another DNS server, if you have multiple DNS servers. It is possible that one DNS server might have information that is different from what another has. You also might need to contact your DNS administrator to verify that the name exists in DNS and has the correct information.

It is possible that name resolution is a problem because your DNS resolver cache is incorrect. When troubleshooting DNS problems always flush the DNS resolver cache on the client by typing ipconfig /flushdns.

Check the LMHOSTS File

The LMHOSTS file is similar to the hosts file but is used primarily for NetBIOS name resolution, as opposed to FQDN resolution. It can be used to handle TCP/IP hostname resolution, but it is not recommended, because it is low in the name-resolution techniques order.

Like the hosts file, LMHOSTS is a text file that can be edited with any standard text editor. If your network uses LMHOSTS files for NetBIOS name resolution and you cannot connect to the remote computer using its NetBIOS name, there could be an invalid entry in your LMHOSTS file. Try scanning this file for the name of the remote machine. Verify that it exists and that it contains the correct information. If you are not using LMHOSTS, try checking your WINS server configuration settings.

The LMHOSTS file that comes with 2000/XP and Windows 2003 has a hidden file extension of .SAM (for sample). You will not see this file extension unless you turn off the hiding of known file extensions in Windows, and the file will not work with a .sam extension—you will need to rename the file so that it is called simply LMHOSTS, not LMHOSTS.sam.

Check Your Windows Internet Naming Service Configuration

A WINS server provides NetBIOS name resolution much the way DNS servers provide TCP/IP hostname resolution. If you use WINS for NetBIOS name resolution and you cannot connect to the other machine with its NetBIOS name, there might be a problem with your computer's WINS configuration.

Start by verifying that your system is configured to use a WINS server. From a command prompt, type **ipconfig /all**. This will display the current WINS servers configured for your computer. If the correct servers are listed, try pinging the WINS server. If you cannot ping the WINS server address, contact your WINS administrator to correct the problem. You might also need to verify that the remote host you are trying to connect to is registered with WINS correctly.

Check Your Domain Name Server Database

A domain name server (DNS) will provide the DNS domain name–to–IP address resolution when trying to connect to services using domain names, such as on the Internet. If the name and IP address are not matched correctly in the database, you will be unable to access the proper PC for the services you are requesting.

For example, if you were on the Internet and wanted to access an FTP site, but the company had changed the IP address of the FTP server, you would type in the DNS name of the FTP server in the address bar, and this name would be matched to the old FTP IP address. The FTP utility would try to query the old IP address for the FTP service. If no FTP service existed on the old IP address, or a server were not currently using the old IP address, you would receive an error message. Until the company updated the DNS servers on the Internet, the FTP server would be unreachable unless you could find the new IP address of the FTP server.

After querying the DNS server and getting an IP address for the DNS name, you should try to ping the IP address returned to verify that the server at the IP address is functioning.

It is also possible that the DNS server might be unavailable and you will receive no response to your request for the DNS name resolution. If this occurs, you will need to change your DNS server setting on the client to a server that is functioning, or contact someone about the DNS server and report that it is not functioning.

CERTIFICATION SUMMARY

This chapter has introduced you to a number of TCP/IP utilities that are popular for everyday troubleshooting and for the Network+ exam. Be sure that you are familiar with each command-line tool before you book the exam. Also make sure you understand the output shown by the different commands and the command-line switches—you will most definitely be tested in this area.

The ARP utility is used to troubleshoot the ARP process, including the display and modification of the ARP cache. This protocol maintains the mappings between the layer-3 TCP/IP addresses and the layer-2 Ethernet addresses. Each time you access a remote computer, its IP address/MAC address entry is updated in the ARP cache if need be. Entries can also be manually added and deleted. By default, the ARP cache maintains unused entries for two minutes, and it can contain a frequently used entry for up to ten minutes. RARP works in reverse to provide Ethernet addresses to TCP/IP address mappings.

The Telnet utility provides a virtual terminal to execute remote console commands. Telnet uses a TCP protocol connection to port 23. Telnet can also be used to connect to other ports set up to be interactive. The default line buffer size is 25, and it can be configured to a maximum of 399 lines. The default terminal emulation for Telnet is VT100.

NBTSTAT displays NetBIOS over TCP/IP (NetBT) protocol statistics. NetBT is a software standard and naming convention used to connect to remote systems. Each workstation in a domain or workgroup must have a unique NetBIOS name. NetBIOS names are 16 bytes, with the last byte reserved for the NetBIOS name suffix. You can display the name table of a host by using **nbtstat -A <ip address>**.

Tracert is used to determine the route that data travels to reach its destination. It uses the ICMP protocol to display status information such as hop count and timeout values. You can specify the maximum number of hops and timeout values to further customize the utility.

Netstat displays TCP/IP protocol statistics and session information. You can also display the local IP routing table with Netstat. Netstat can display Ethernet-specific statistics, protocol statistics, and session information, including listening ports.

IPCONFIG displays the current TCP/IP configuration for a Windows XP/2003/Vista/2008 computer. WINIPCFG is a graphical interface used on Windows 95/98/ME computers to display TCP/IP configuration information such as IP address, subnet mask, DNS servers, WINS servers, and default gateway. These utilities can be used to release or renew DHCP addresses assigned to a system.

The File Transfer Protocol (FTP) is used for file transfers between two computers. FTP requires two TCP port connections: port 20 for data, and port 21 for control commands. Using the two ports allows for faster transfer speeds than sending both types of data over the one port. A server-based FTP program, called a service or daemon, is used to store files and process commands.

Ping is used to verify a remote computer's connectivity to the network. Additional options for troubleshooting include setting packet lengths, changing the TTL values, and specifying host lists to return routing statistics for.

NSLOOKUP and DIG are used to query a DNS server for information in its database to verify that name resolution is working with DNS names.

✓ TWO-MINUTE DRILL

ARP

❑ The Address Resolution Protocol (ARP) was designed to provide a mapping from the logical 32-bit TCP/IP addresses to the physical 48-bit MAC addresses.

❑ Address resolution is the process of finding the address of a host within a network.

❑ Remember that ARP translates IP addresses (layer 3) into MAC addresses (layer 2). The Reverse Address Resolution Protocol (RARP) is used to find a TCP/IP address from a MAC address.

❑ Only four types of messages can be sent by the ARP protocol on any machine:
  ❑ ARP request
  ❑ ARP reply
  ❑ RARP request
  ❑ RARP reply

❑ The Reverse Address Resolution Protocol (RARP) enables a machine to learn its own IP address by broadcasting to resolve its own MAC address.

Telnet

❑ Telnet was designed to provide a virtual terminal or remote login across the network. It is connection based and handles its own session negotiation.

❑ The primary use of Telnet is for remote administration.

❑ Telnet uses TCP port 23.

NBTSTAT

❑ The Microsoft TCP/IP stack uses an additional protocol for networking services, NetBIOS over TCP/IP (NetBT).

❑ NBTSTAT is used to troubleshoot NetBIOS over TCP/IP.

❑ NBTSTAT -A <ip address> will display the name table of the IP address supplied. This is a useful feature when you know the IP address of a system and want to know the computer name.

❑ NBTSTAT -R purges and reloads the NetBIOS name cache.

❑ NBTSTAT -c will display the NetBIOS name cache, which displays computer names that have been resolved to IP addresses.

Tracert

❑ Tracert is a command-line utility that was designed to perform a very basic task: to determine the path taken by a data packet to reach its destination.

❑ You will use the trace route utility by typing TRACERT <ip address>.

Netstat

❑ Netstat displays protocol statistics and current TCP/IP network connections.

❑ Using Netstat to monitor TCP protocol activity can enable you to troubleshoot TCP/IP-based connections.

❑ Netstat -a will display listening ports—useful if you need to monitor what applications are awaiting a connection.

❑ Netstat -n will display who is connected to your system along with port information.

IPCONFIG and WINIPCFG

❑ IPCONFIG and WINIPCFG are utilities used to display the current TCP/IP configurations on the local workstations and to modify the DHCP addresses assigned to each interface.

❑ IPCONFIG is used in Windows NT/2000/XP/2003 to display TCP/IP information from a command prompt.

❑ WINIPCFG is the Windows 95/98/ME–based graphical utility used to display TCP/IP information.

❑ The ifconfig (lowercase) command is used to display TCP/IP setting on UNIX and Linux.

FTP

❑ The File Transfer Protocol (FTP) is designed primarily for transferring data across a network.

❑ TFTP differs from FTP in two ways: It uses the User Datagram Protocol (UDP) connectionless transport instead of TCP, and it does not log on to the remote machine.

Ping and Hping2

❑ The Ping command is used to test a machine's connectivity to the network and to verify that it is active.

❑ Ping uses the Internet Control Message Protocol (ICMP) to verify connections to remote hosts by sending echo packets and listening for reply packets.

❑ Use the Ping utility to verify connectivity by IP address or hostname.

❑ The two most common problems with TCP/IP are network connectivity and name resolution problems.

❑ Make sure you understand the differences between hostname resolution and NetBIOS (machine) name resolution. The exam will quiz you on both scenarios.

NSLOOKUP and DIG

❑ NSLOOKUP displays information in the DNS server database.

❑ You can use NSLOOKUP to troubleshoot name resolution problems that may arise because of incorrect records on the server.

❑ DIG is a very popular Linux tool used to query and troubleshoot DNS.

Other TCP/IP Utilities

❑ The host and hostname utilities are used to display the local system name.

❑ The route command is used to manage the local routing table.

❑ The MTR command is a Linux command that combines features of Tracert and Ping.

Troubleshooting with TCP/IP Utilities

❑ When troubleshooting connectivity issues first use ipconfig to display and verify your TCP/IP settings.

❑ Use the ping command to test and verify which systems you can communicate with.

❑ Always remember that if you cannot communicate with a system by name, try to use the IP address. Most communication problems are due to name resolution issues.

SELF TEST

The following Self Test questions will help measure your understanding of the material presented in this chapter. Read all the choices carefully, as there may be more than one correct answer. Choose all correct answers for each question.

ARP

1. Which utility can be used to display and modify the table that maintains the TCP/IP address–to–MAC address translation?
   A. NBTSTAT
   B. Telnet
   C. ARP
   D. SNMP

2. Which are not valid message types for ARP? (Choose all that apply.)
   A. ARP reply
   B. ARP decline
   C. ARP response
   D. ARP request

3. How long will a dynamic ARP entry remain in cache if it has not been reused?
   A. 10 minutes
   B. 5 minutes
   C. 2 minutes
   D. None of the above

4. ARP is responsible for converting _____ addresses to _____ addresses.
   A. layer-3, layer-2
   B. layer-4, layer-3
   C. layer-2, layer-3
   D. layer-3, layer-4

5. Which command and command switch were used to generate the following output?

```
Interface: 10.10.10.101
Internet Address Physical Address  Type
12.10.10.10      00-06-6b-8e-4e-e3 dynamic
12.10.10.19      00-c0-ae-d0-bb-f5 dynamic
```

   A. ARP -d
   B. IPCONFIG /DISPLAYMAC
   C. ARP -a
   D. IPCONFIG /ALL

Telnet

6. Which utility enables you to execute console commands remotely through a terminal session?
   A. FTP
   B. Ping
   C. Telnet
   D. NBTSTAT

7. Which protocol is defined to use TCP port 23?
   A. Telnet
   B. FTP
   C. HTTP
   D. SMTP

8. What is the default terminal emulation type for Telnet? (Select two.)
   A. DEC
   B. ANSI
   C. VT52
   D. VT100

NBTSTAT

9. Which protocol uses a 16-byte name, with the last digit reserved as a resource identifier?
   A. TCP/IP
   B. IPX
   C. NetBIOS
   D. NBTSTAT

10. Which utility can be used to troubleshoot NetBIOS over TCP/IP connectivity issues?
- **A.** NetBT
- **B.** NetBEUI
- **C.** NBTSTAT
- **D.** NetBIOS

11. Which NBTSTAT switch enables you to display the computer's NetBIOS name cache?
- **A.** -R
- **B.** -c
- **C.** -a
- **D.** -A

12. In which ways can a computer with a NetBIOS name register its services on the network?
- **A.** Broadcast
- **B.** Hosts file
- **C.** WINS server
- **D.** Both A and C

13. Which command-line utility and command switch were used to generate the following command output?

```
Lan Connection:
Node IpAddress: [192.168.1.100] Scope Id: []
NetBIOS Local Name Table
Name        Type Status
---------------------------
SERVER100 <00> UNIQUE Registered
DOMAIN100 <00> GROUP Registered
SERVER100 <20> UNIQUE Registered
DOMAIN100 <1E> GROUP Registered
```

- **A.** IPCONFIG /ALL
- **B.** NBTSTAT -A
- **C.** NETSTAT -n
- **D.** NBTSTAT -n

Tracert

14. Which utility is used to determine the path that data takes to a remote host?
    A. NBTSTAT
    B. ARP
    C. FTP
    D. Tracert

15. Which command was used to generate the following command output?

```
1 <10 ms <10 ms <10 ms 192.168.0.254
2 <10 ms <10 ms <10 ms 12.127.106.34
3 40 ms 40 ms 50 ms r04.nycmny01.us.bb.verio.net [129.250.10.37]
4 40 ms 40 ms 40 ms r20.nycmny01.us.bb.verio.net [129.250.2.36]
5 40 ms 40 ms 50 ms r00.nwrknj01.us.bb.verio.net [129.250.2.216]
6 110 ms 121 ms 120 ms 192.94.118.221
7 110 ms 130 ms 120 ms www.novell.com [130.57.4.27]
Trace complete.
```

    A. TRACERT www.novell.com
    B. Ping www.novell.com
    C. NSLOOKUP www.novell.com
    D. ROUTE PRINT www.novell.com

Netstat

16. Which utility is used to display TCP/IP-specific protocol and interface statistics?
    A. NBTSTAT
    B. ARP
    C. Netstat
    D. None of the above

17. Which command and command switch were used to generate the following output?

```
Active Connections
Proto Local Address      Foreign Address         Stat
TCP comp1:smtp           2kpc1.domain5.net:0     LISTENING
TCP comp1:http           xppc2.domain5.net:1256  LISTENING
TCP comp1:epmap          2kpc1.domain5.net:0     LISTENING
TCP comp1:https          2kpc1.domain5.net:0     LISTENING
TCP comp1:microsoft-ds   2kpc1.domain5.net:0     LISTENING
TCP comp1:1025           2kpc1.domain5.net:0     LISTENING
```

```
TCP comp1:1245      2kpc1.domain5.net:0     LISTENING
TCP comp1:1277      2kpc1.domain5.net:0     LISTENING
TCP comp1:1312      2kpc1.domain5.net:0     LISTENING
```

   A. NBTSTAT -c

   B. NETSTAT -a

   C. IPCONFIG /ALL

   D. ARP -g

IPCONFIG and WINIPCFG

18. Which items are not available for display in IPCONFIG?

   A. TCP/IP address

   B. MAC address

   C. DHCP lease information

   D. None of the above

19. Which option of IPCONFIG is used to receive a new lease on your IP address?

   A. /all

   B. /release

   C. /obtain

   D. /renew

20. You are troubleshooting to determine why Sue's computer cannot connect to the Internet. What command would you type to view all of Sue's TCP/IP settings in a Windows 2000/XP command prompt?

   A. IPCONFIG

   B. IPCONFIG /ALL

   C. IPCONFIG /SHOWITALL

   D. IPCONFIG /DISPLAYALL

FTP

21. Which utility is used to facilitate file transfers between two remote hosts?

   A. FTP

   B. Telnet

   C. Ping

   D. None of the above

22. What TCP ports are used by FTP services? (Choose two.)
    A. TCP port 20
    B. TCP port 25
    C. TCP port 21
    D. TCP port 80

Ping and Hping2

23. Which utility is used to verify network connectivity of a remote host?
    A. Route
    B. ARP
    C. Ping
    D. None of the above

24. You are having trouble connecting to resources on the Internet, so you use the IPCONFIG utility to verify your TCP/IP configuration. The configuration is shown.

```
Ethernet adapter Lan Connection:
Connection-specific DNS Suffix . : glensworld.loc
IP Address. . . . . . . . . . . : 192.168.1.100
Subnet Mask . . . . . . . . . . : 255.255.255.0
Default Gateway . . . . . . . . : 192.168.1.1
```

    Your configuration seems to be accurate. Which command would you type next to help determine what the problem is?
    A. Ping glensworld.loc
    B. Ping 192.168.1.100
    C. Ping 192.168.1.1
    D. Ping 127.0.0.1

25. The following output was generated from which command?

```
Reply from 10.10.10.1: bytes>32 time<1ms TTL>128
Reply from 10.10.10.1: bytes>32 time<1ms TTL>128
Reply from 10.10.10.1: bytes>32 time<1ms TTL>128
Reply from 10.10.10.1: bytes>32 time<1ms TTL>128
Ping statistics for 10.10.10.1:
Packets: Sent > 4, Received > 4, Lost > 0 (0% loss),
```

```
Approximate round trip times in milli-seconds:
Minimum > 0ms, Maximum > 0ms, Average > 0ms
```

    A. TRACERT 10.10.10.1

    B. ROUTE 10.10.10.1

    C. Ping 127.0.0.1

    D. Ping 10.10.10.1

NSLOOKUP and DIG

26. Which utility is used to verify the DNS database on a DNS server?

    A. Route

    B. ARP

    C. Ping

    D. NSLOOKUP

27. What dig command is used to perform a reverse name query?

    A. Dig www.gleneclarke.com

    B. Dig www.gleneclarke.com +short

    C. Dig -x 192.168.2.200

    D. Dig gleneclarke.com axfr

Other TCP/IP Utilities

28. Which TCP/IP utility is used to manage the routing table on the local system?

    A. Route

    B. ARP

    C. Ping

    D. NSLOOKUP

29. You wish to find out what your system name is. What utility would you use?

    A. Route

    B. hostname

    C. Ping

    D. NSLOOKUP

Troubleshooting with TCP/IP Utilities

30. What command would you use to verify that TCP/IP is running successfully on your system?

A. arp

B. ping 127.0.0.1

C. telnet

D. NSLOOKUP

31. What service is used to convert FQDN to an IP address?

A. WINS

B. Telnet

C. FTP

D. DNS

SELF TEST ANSWERS

ARP

1. ☑ **C.** ARP is responsible for converting a layer-3 address (IP address) to a layer-2 address (MAC address). A utility by the same name is available in most operating systems and is responsible for modifying entries within the ARP cache.

   ☒ **A, B,** and **D** are incorrect. NBTSTAT is used to view the NetBIOS name table of a system, Telnet is used to open a terminal emulation session with a terminal server, and SNMP is used for monitoring of devices.

2. ☑ **B** and **C.** ARP decline and ARP response are not valid ARP messages. There are only four types of messages that can be sent out by the ARP protocol: ARP request, ARP reply, RARP request, and RARP reply.

   ☒ **A** and **D** are incorrect because they are valid ARP messages.

3. ☑ **C.** Two minutes. Unlike static addresses, which never age out, dynamic addresses remain for only a predetermined amount of time. Windows adjusts the size of the ARP cache automatically. Entries not used after two minutes are removed. If entries are used frequently, they remain in the ARP cache for ten minutes.

   ☒ **A, B,** and **D** are incorrect because a dynamic ARP entry remains in cache for two minutes by default.

4. ☑ **A.** ARP is responsible for converting IP addresses (layer-3 addresses) to MAC addresses (layer-2 addresses).

   ☒ **B, C,** and **D** are incorrect because they are not the layered addresses that ARP is responsible for resolving.

5. ☑ **C.** ARP -a will display the ARP cache, which is what the output for this question is showing. Be sure you can identify the output for the exam.

   ☒ **A, B,** and **D** are incorrect because they are the wrong commands or switches to generate this output.

Telnet

6. ☑ **C.** Telnet (telecommunications network) was designed to provide a virtual terminal or remote login across the network. This enables the user to execute commands on a remote machine anywhere on the network as if he or she were sitting in front of the console. The term Telnet refers to both the protocol and the application used for remote management.

   ☒ **A, B,** and **D** are incorrect because FTP allows for file transfers between two PCs; Ping is used to verify that connectivity can be established between two PCs; and NBTSTAT will allow you to view the NetBIOS name table available on a PC.

7. ☑ **A.** Telnet uses TCP port 23 by default.

   ☒ **B, C,** and **D** are incorrect because FTP uses ports 20 and 21, HTTP uses port 80, and SMTP uses port 25.

8. ☑ **B** and **D.** VT100 and ANSI. The terminal emulation option defines what type of remote terminal to use. This controls how commands are interpreted and displayed by the remote server.

   ☒ **A** and **C** are incorrect. VT52 is an older standard not commonly used anymore. VT100/ANSI is the default standard emulation used today. DEC is not an available option.

NBTSTAT

9. ☑ **C.** NetBIOS uses unique 15-character names for each system, known as computer names. Each NetBIOS name is made of 16 bytes; 15 are used for the computer name, and the 16th byte is used as the NetBIOS name suffix, which identifies a service running on the system.

   ☒ **A, B,** and **D** are incorrect because they do not use 16-byte names.

10. ☑ **C.** NBTSTAT is used to troubleshoot connectivity between two computers trying to communicate via NetBIOS over TCP/IP (NetBT). It displays the protocol statistics and the current connections to each remote host. You can also display the information about a remote host and the names stored in its NetBIOS name table.

    ☒ **A, B,** and **D** are incorrect. NetBT stands for NetBIOS over TCP/IP; NetBEUI is a nonroutable protocol; and NetBIOS is a software and naming convention. All of these are protocols, not utilities.

11. ☑ **B.** The -c option is correct. When a system resolves a NetBIOS name to an IP address, that information is stored in the NetBIOS name cache.

    ☒ **A, C,** and **D** are incorrect. The -R option will purge the cache and reload any entries in the cache that have the #PRE tag in the LMHOSTS file. The -a parameter is used to list a name table of a remote PC by specifying the name of the remote PC; -A does the same, but you must specify the remote PC by IP address. You should know all these switches for the exam.

12. ☑ **D.** NetBIOS names are registered in two ways, via broadcast or with a WINS service. You can also display information on how remote NetBIOS names are being resolved using the NBTSTAT utility. This can help you to determine whether you are using a WINS service correctly or are broadcasting for services.

    ☒ **B** is incorrect. The hosts file is used for FQDN–to–IP address resolution for the network.

13. ☑ **D.** The local NetBIOS name table can be viewed with NBTSTAT -n. This output shows the names that this system has registered on the network and indicates what services it runs. In this example you can see that the system runs the server service and workstation service.

☒ **A, B,** and **C** are incorrect. IPCONFIG /ALL is used to view all the TCP/IP settings on the host, NBTSTAT -A is used to view the NetBIOS name table of a remote system, and NETSTAT -n is used to view the active connections.

Tracert

14. ☑ **D.** Tracert is a command-line utility that was designed to determine the path taken by a data packet to reach its destination. This can be very helpful in determining at what point a network connection is no longer active. It can also be helpful in troubleshooting issues with network response times.

☒ **A, B,** and **C** are incorrect. NBTSTAT is used to troubleshoot NetBIOS over TCP/IP. ARP is used to view or modify the ARP cache. FTP is used to transfer files between two PCs.

15. ☑ **A.** Tracert sends back multiple responses, one for each router that it hits on its way to the destination address. In this example we are tracing the pathway to www.novell.com and getting a hop entry with each router on the way.

☒ **B, C,** and **D** are incorrect. Ping is used to send a test message to the destination but does not send a response with each router it hits, NSLOOKUP is used to query DNS and troubleshoot DNS problems, and the route print command is used to view the routing table of a system.

Netstat

16. ☑ **C.** Netstat displays protocol statistics and current TCP/IP network connections. This utility can be used to display in-depth detail about protocol status, statistics for the different network interfaces, and the current routing table.

☒ **A** and **B** are incorrect. NBTSTAT is used to troubleshoot NetBIOS over TCP/IP. ARP is used to troubleshoot the ARP cache.

17. ☑ **B.** The Netstat utility is used to view TCP/IP connection information and listening ports.

☒ **A, C,** and **D** are incorrect. NBTSTAT is used to troubleshoot NetBIOS over TCP/IP, IPCONFIG is used to view your TCP/IP settings, and ARP is used to view or modify your ARP cache.

IPCONFIG and WINIPCFG

18. ☑ **D.** All of the options listed can be displayed in IPCONFIG by using the /ALL option.

☒ **A, B,** and **C** are incorrect because all are available for display in IPCONFIG.

19. ☑ **D.** The /renew switch is used to renew the IP address that you have obtained from the DHCP server.

☒ **A, B,** and **C** are incorrect. /ALL will display all of your TCP/IP settings, and /RELEASE will allow your system to give up its IP address. /OBTAIN is not a switch of IPCONFIG.

20. ☑ **B.** IPCONFIG /ALL is used to view all of the TCP/IP settings on a system.

☒ **A, C,** and **D** are incorrect: /SHOWITALL and /DISPLAYALL are not switches of IPCONFIG, and IPCONFIG by itself shows only basic settings, not all the settings.

FTP

21. ☑ **A.** FTP (the File Transfer Protocol) is designed primarily for transferring data across a network. FTP denotes both a protocol and a utility used for this purpose.

☒ **B, C,** and **D** are incorrect. Ping is used to verify communication between two PCs, and Telnet is used to create a remote session with a Telnet server.

22. ☑ **A** and **C.** FTP uses two TCP channels to operate. It uses TCP port 20 as the data transfer channel and TCP port 21 for control commands. The data transfer channel is known as the DTP, or data transfer process, and the command channel is known as the PI, or Protocol Interpreter. The two channels enable you to transfer data and execute commands at the same time, and they provide a more efficient and faster data transfer. FTP also works in real time. It does not queue up requests as most other utilities do; it transfers data while you watch.

☒ **B** and **D** are incorrect. Port 25 is used by SMTP and port 80 is used by HTTP.

Ping and Hping2

23. ☑ **C.** The Ping (Packet Internet Groper) command is the most-used TCP/IP troubleshooting tool available. This command is used to test a machine's connectivity to the network and to verify that it is active. Usually, using this command is one of the first steps to any troubleshooting if a connectivity problem is occurring between two computers. This can quickly help you to determine whether a remote host is available and responsive.

☒ **A** and **B** are incorrect. Route is a command that we can use to view or modify the routing table in Windows. ARP is used to view or modify the ARP cache.

24. ☑ **C.** When troubleshooting connectivity to the Internet, you first check your TCP/IP settings and then ping the IP address of the default gateway to verify that the router is up and running.

☒ **A, B,** and **D** are incorrect. Although you may start pinging addresses, given that you are having trouble connecting to the Internet, you may want to start by pinging the router.

25. ☑ **D.** In the output you can see that the address of 10.10.10.1 is sending responses back. There are four responses that are the four ping response messages.

 ☒ **A, B,** and **C** are incorrect. The output is coming from a Ping command to the IP address of 10.10.10.1.

NSLOOKUP and DIG

26. ☑ **D.** NSLOOKUP. The NSLOOKUP utility is used to view and test the DNS database on the DNS server.

 ☒ **A, B,** and **C** are incorrect. Route is used to view or modify the routing table in Windows. ARP is used to view or modify the ARP cache. Ping is used to verify communications between two PCs.

27. ☑ **C.** To perform a reverse query with dig, you use the -x switch and then supply the IP address of the system you wish to know the name of.

 ☒ **A, B,** and **D** are incorrect because they are not the switches used to do a reverse query.

Other TCP/IP Utilities

28. ☑ **A.** The route utility is used to manage the local routing table. You can view the routing table with route print and add a route with route add.

 ☒ **B, C,** and **D** are not correct because they do not manage the local routing table of a system.

29. ☑ **B.** The hostname command is used to display the system name.

 ☒ **A, C,** and **D** are incorrect because they are not used to display the local system name.

Troubleshooting with TCP/IP Utilities

30. ☑ **B.** You would ping the loopback address to verify that the TCP/IP software stack is installed and working.

 ☒ **A, C,** and **D** are incorrect because are not used to test the local system. You would use ARP to troubleshoot MAC address resolution problems, telnet to remotely connect to another system, and NSLOOKUP to troubleshoot DNS problems.

31. ☑ **D.** DNS is used to convert the FQDN, for example www.gleneclarke.com, to an IP address.

 ☒ **A, B,** and **C** are incorrect because they are not used to convert the FQDN to an IP address. WINS is used to convert the NetBIOS (computer name) to an IP address, telnet is used to remotely connect to another system, and FTP is a protocol to download files from a remote system.

7
Wireless Networking

Today's networks are no longer limited to using cabled, or wired, devices. Today's networks have a mix of wired systems along with wireless systems that use radio frequencies to send data to a wireless access point (as shown in Figure 7-1). The wireless access point may have a connection to the wired network, allowing the wireless devices to communicate with the entire network.

This chapter introduces you to the world of wireless networks! It is a very popular topic to know for the Network+ certification exam, so be sure to study this well. This chapter will introduce you to wireless basics, show you how to set up the wireless network, and then discuss some security concerns around wireless.

FIGURE 7-1

A wireless access point, also known as a wireless router

CERTIFICATION OBJECTIVE 7.01

Wireless Basics

As mentioned, the wireless network uses radio frequencies to transmit data through the air. This means that if you have a laptop user who wishes to be mobile within the office, you can allow her to access the network through a wireless access point as long as she has a wireless network card in her laptop.

There are two types of wireless networks you can create: an ad hoc mode wireless network or an infrastructure mode wireless network. Each of these is known as a wireless mode, and each has its advantages.

With *ad hoc mode* the wireless device, such as a laptop, is connected to other wireless devices in a peer-to-peer environment without the need for a wireless access point. With *infrastructure mode*, the wireless clients are connected to a central device, known as a wireless access point. The wireless client sends data to the access point, which then sends the data on to the destination (as shown in Figure 7-2). As mentioned previously, the wireless client can access network resources on the wired network once connected to the access point because the access point has a connection to the wired network.

The advantage of ad hoc mode is that you don't need to purchase the access point, but the benefit of infrastructure mode is that when you use the wireless access point you get to control who can connect to the wireless network and filter out types of network traffic. For example, if you use a wireless access point to allow wireless clients to connect to the Internet, you can control which web sites the users can connect to. This type of centralized control makes infrastructure mode extremely popular.

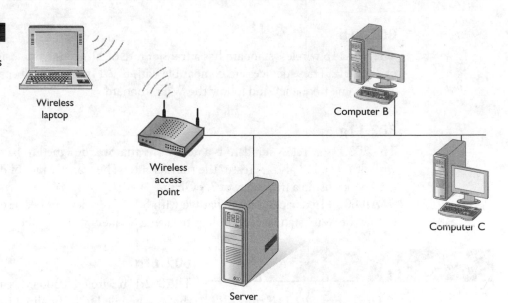

FIGURE 7-2

A typical wireless network running in infrastructure mode

Wireless laptop

Wireless access point

Computer B

Computer C

Server

Standards

The IEEE committee has developed wireless standards in the 802 project models for wireless networking. Wireless is defined by the 802.11 project model and has several standards defined.

802.11a

The 802.11a wireless standard is an older one that runs at the 5 GHz frequency. 802.11a devices can transmit data at 54 Mbps and are incompatible with 802.11b and 802.11g devices.

watch

For the exam remember that 802.11a was an early wireless standard that ran at a different frequency than 80211.b and 802.11g. This makes it incompatible with 802.11b/g. Remember that 802.11a defines wireless environments running at 54 Mbps while using a frequency of 5 GHz.

802.11b

The 802.11b wireless standard has a transfer rate of 11 Mbps while using a frequency of 2.4 GHz. These devices are compatible with 802.11g/n devices because they run at the same frequency and follow the WiFi standard.

802.11g

The 802.11g wireless standard is a newer one that was designed to be compatible with 802.11b but also increases the transfer rate. The transfer rate of 802.11g devices is 54 Mbps using a frequency of 2.4 GHz.

All 802.11g devices are compatible with 802.11b/n devices because they all follow the WiFi standard and run at the same frequency of 2.4 GHz.

watch

Note that 802.11b runs at 11 Mbps, and 802.11g runs at 54 Mbps. The new 802.11n standard is designed to reach up to 600 Mbps!

802.11n

The 802.11n wireless standard is a new one that is scheduled to be finalized in December 2009. The goal of 802.11n is to increase the transfer rate beyond what current standards such as 802.11g support. 802.11n will supposedly support transfer rates up to 600 Mbps! To help accomplish this, 802.11n uses two new features: *multiple input multiple output (MIMO)* and *channel bonding*. MIMO is the use of multiple antennas to achieve more throughput than can be accomplished with only a single antenna. Channel bonding allows 802.11n to transmit data over two channels to achieve more throughput. 802.11n is designed to be backward compatible with 802.11a, 802.11b, and 802.11g and can run at the 2.4 GHz or 5 GHz frequency.

Table 7-1 summarizes key points you need to be familiar with about the different wireless standards for the Network+ certification exam.

e x a m

ⓦatch　　　　**Wireless networks today are called WiFi, which stands for wireless fidelity. 802.11b, 802.11g, and 802.11n are** **all part of the WiFi standard and as a result are compatible with one another.**

It is important to note that 802.11a was an early implementation of wireless networking and is not compatible with the Wi-Fi networks. As an example of the compatibility, my wireless network at my home has an access point that is an 802.11g device, but one of my old laptops has an 802.11b wireless network card. I am still able to have my old laptop communicate on the network because the two standards are 100 percent compatible with one another. In this example, the laptop with the 802.11b card only connects at 11 Mbps, while my new laptop with 802.11g card is connecting at 54 Mbps.

e x a m

ⓦatch　　　**Wireless transmission speeds decrease as your distance increases from the wireless access point.**

TABLE 7-1		802.11a	802.11b	802.11g	802.11n
Comparing the Different Wireless Standards	Frequency	5 GHz	2.4 GHz	2.4 GHz	5/2.4 GHz
	Transfer Rate	54 Mbps	11 Mbps	54 Mbps	Up to 600 Mbps
	Range	150 Feet	300 Feet	300 Feet	300 Feet
	Compatibility	802.11a	802.11b/g/n	802.11b/g/n	802.11a/b/g

Channels

It was stated that 802.11b/g/n all run at the 2.4 GHz frequency, but it is important to understand that 2.4 GHz is a frequency *range*. Each frequency in the range is known as a *channel*.

Most wireless devices allow you to specify which channel you would like to use. The reason this is important is that if you find that you are having trouble with your wireless network failing a lot, then it could be that the wireless devices are conflicting, or interfering with other wireless devices in your area. A good example of this is cordless phones; they run at the 2.4 GHz range as well and could cause issues with your wireless network. As a solution you could change the channel on your wireless access point and clients, which changes the frequency—hopefully preventing any conflicts with other household items!

e x a m

w a t c h

To avoid interference on the wireless network from other household items, try to purchase items like cordless phones that run on a different frequency than 2.4 GHz. If you are experiencing *problems on the wireless network, you could try changing the channel on the wireless equipment and see if a different channel is more reliable.*

Table 7-2 lists the different frequencies used by the different channels.

Remember when troubleshooting wireless networks that you could be getting interference from other wireless devices and household devices running on the same channel. As a fix, experiment by changing the channel used by your wireless network to reduce the amount of interference received. As noted in Table 7-2, adjacent channels have overlapping frequencies and will interfere with one another, so changing from channel 2 to channel 1 will not solve interference problems, but changing from channel 2 to channel 6 might.

Authentication and Encryption

A number of wireless authentication and encryption protocols have been developed over the years. The purpose of these protocols is to help secure your wireless network, and you should consider them for implementation on your wireless network.

TABLE 7-2	Channel	Frequency Range
Different WiFi Channels and Their Operating Frequency Ranges	1	2.3995 GHz – 2.4245 GHz
	2	2.4045 GHz – 2.4295 GHz
	3	2.4095 GHz – 2.4345 GHz
	4	2.4145 GHz – 2.4395 GHz
	5	2.4195 GHz – 2.4445 GHz
	6	2.4245 GHz – 2.4495 GHz
	7	2.4295 GHz – 2.4545 GHz
	8	2.4345 GHz – 2.4595 GHz
	9	2.4395 GHz – 2.4645 GHz
	10	2.4445 GHz – 2.4695 GHz
	11	2.4495 GHz – 2.4745 GHz
	12	2.4545 GHz – 2.4795 GHz
	13	2.4595 GHz – 2.4845 GHz

WEP

Wired Equivalent Privacy (WEP) was designed to give the wireless world a level of security that could equate to what the wired networking world has. In the wired world, someone would have to be in your office to connect a cable to your network, but with wireless networking this is not the case. Someone could sit outside your building in a parked car and connect to your wireless network. WEP was designed to add security to wireless networks.

To configure your wireless network with WEP, you simply specify a shared key, or passphrase, on the wireless access point. The theory is that if anyone wants to connect to your wireless network, he needs to know the shared key and configure his workstation with that key.

When you configure the shared key on the access point and client, any data sent between the client and the access point is encrypted with

WEP can use 64-bit or 128-bit encryption keys that are made up of a 24-bit initialization vector (IV) and then a 40-bit key (for 64-bit encryption) or a 104-bit key (for 128-bit encryption).

WEP. This will prevent unauthorized individuals from capturing data in transit and being able to read the data.

It is important to understand that there were huge flaws in how WEP implemented its encryption and key usage, and as a result both 64-bit and 128-bit WEP have been cracked. For security reasons, you should not use WEP unless you have older access points that do not support WPA or WPA2.

WPA

WiFi Protected Access (WPA) was designed to improve upon security and fix some of the flaws found in WEP. WPA uses a 128-bit key and the *Temporal Key Integrity Protocol (TKIP)*, which is a protocol that is used to change the keys used for encryption for every packet that is sent. This will make it much harder for hackers to crack the key, which is very easy to do with WEP.

WPA had a number of other improvements over WEP; for example, it has improved integrity checking and it supports authentication using the *Extensible Authentication Protocol (EAP)*, a very secure authentication protocol.

WPA operates in two different modes, WPA-Personal and WPA-Enterprise.

- **WPA-Personal**   WPA-Personal is also known as WPA-PSK, which means WPA preshared key. With WPA-Personal you will configure the access point with a starting key value, known as the preshared key, which is then used to encrypt the traffic. This mode is used most by home users and small businesses.
- **WPA-Enterprise**   WPA-Enterprise, also known as WPA-802.1x, is a WPA implementation that uses a central authentication server such as a RADIUS server for authentication and auditing features. WPA-Enterprise is used by larger companies so that they can use their existing authentication server to control who has access to the wireless network and to log network access.

on the
Job   *In order to use WPA, you will need to have devices that support WPA. If you have older wireless cards or access points, they may only support WEP.*

WPA2

WPA2 improves upon the security of WPA and should be used instead of WPA if you have the choice. WPA2 uses the *Advanced Encryption Standard (AES)* protocol instead of TKIP and also supports a number of additional features such as added protection for ad hoc networks and key caching.

Because WPA2 uses AES as its encryption protocol it supports 128-bit, 192-bit, or 256-bit encryption.

e x a m

ⓦ a t c h

Be sure to be familiar with the different wireless authentication and encryption protocols for the Network+ exam.

CERTIFICATION OBJECTIVE 7.02

Securing Wireless

A few years ago when I purchased my first wireless router, I knew nothing about wireless and was concerned that I would not be able to set up the wireless network. Well, my concerns were quickly dismissed when I took the wireless router (access point) out of the box and gave it power. My laptop connected almost immediately! I was amazed at how easy it was to connect to the wireless network—there was no configuration required. Then it dawned on me—if my laptop connected with no configuration, what is stopping the rest of the world from connecting to my wireless network? The answer of course is that nothing is stopping someone from sitting outside my yard and connecting to my wireless network. I needed to figure out how to stop unauthorized access to my wireless access point.

There are a number of different techniques that you can use to prevent unauthorized persons from connecting to your wireless network. You may want to implement some or all of these features. To help secure your wireless infrastructure, you should consider changing settings on the router such as the admin password, the SSID, and MAC filtering, to name a few. The following are some basic best practices that you should follow to secure your wireless router. You can see the steps to configure these features in the later section "Implementing a Wireless Network."

Change Admin Password

The first thing you should do when you take the wireless router out of the box and plug it in is change the admin password. The admin password is needed to connect to the web administration pages and change the settings of the router. All routers have a default admin password, so you want to be sure to change the password from the default.

Figure 7-3 displays how to change the admin password on a D-Link router by going to the Tools link at the top and then choosing the Admin link on the left.

Service Set Identifier (SSID)

The *Service Set Identifier (SSID)* is a name that you give the wireless network, and in order for someone to connect to your wireless network, that person needs to know the SSID. Any client who wishes to connect to your wireless network will need to specify the SSID name in their wireless network card settings. It is important that you change the SSID from the default so that anyone wishing to connect to your wireless network would need to know the name, or SSID.

The problem is that wireless routers are configured to advertise this SSID automatically; so even if you change the SSID to something hard to guess, the router advertises the name out. This means an individual can connect to your network by name without really knowing the name of the network because the router is advertising it. Proof of this is shown when you choose the option in Windows XP or Windows Vista to connect to a network and a dialog box displays (shown in Figure 7-4) showing you all the wireless networks close to you.

FIGURE 7-3

Changing the admin password on a D-Link router

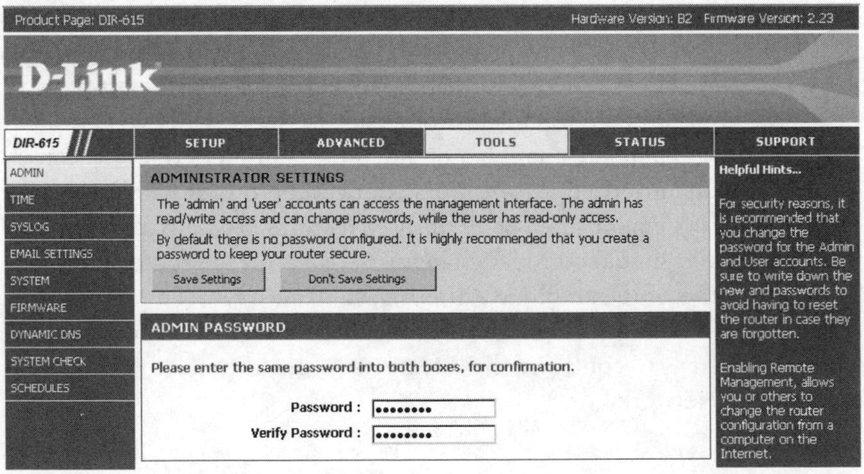

FIGURE 7-4

Displaying wireless networks close to you. Notice the D-Link network.

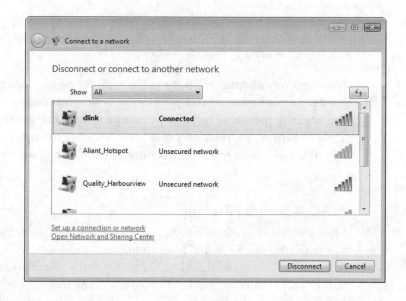

exam

watch   *You can use a tool such as NetStumbler to do a wireless survey to get a list of wireless networks that are close to you.*

To fix this, you should configure your router to not advertise the SSID. This will prevent the Windows users from displaying a list of wireless networks and having your network display in the list. Figure 7-5 displays how to disable SSID broadcasting on a D-Link wireless router (set the Visibility Status to Invisible). Most routers have this as a setting "Disable SSID broadcasting."

FIGURE 7-5

Disabling SSID broadcasting on a D-Link router

WIRELESS NETWORK SETTINGS	
Enable Wireless :	☑ Always ▾ Add New
Wireless Network Name :	dlink (Also called the SSID)
802.11 Mode :	Mixed 802.11n, 802.11g and 802.11b ▾
Enable Auto Channel Scan :	☑
Wireless Channel :	2.437 GHz - CH 6 ▾
Transmission Rate :	Best (automatic) ▾ (Mbit/s)
Channel Width :	20 MHz ▾
Visibility Status :	⦿ Visible ○ Invisible

So to summarize the SSID issue, be sure to change the SSID to something hard to guess (don't use your company name if you are setting up the wireless network for the company) and be sure to disable SSID broadcasting on the router.

Although this chapter is giving you a number of best practices to make it harder for someone to compromise your wireless network, know that most of the security measures have been compromised. For example, when you disable SSID broadcasting, Windows and most wireless scanners such as NetStumbler will not pick up on the wireless network, but tools such as Kismet in Linux can.

MAC Address Filtering

Most wireless networks allow you to limit which wireless network cards can connect to the wireless access point. You can limit systems that can connect to your wireless network by finding out the MAC addresses of the systems you want to allow to connect and then configuring the router to deny traffic from all systems except the MAC addresses you input (see Figure 7-6). This is known as MAC address filtering.

By default, wireless access points are not configured for MAC address filtering, so you want to make sure that you configure it. Be aware that MAC filtering by itself will not keep the determined hacker out. A determined hacker can monitor traffic in the air, see the MAC address of an authorized client, and then spoof that address so that the hacker's traffic is allowed.

FIGURE 7-6

Configuring MAC filtering

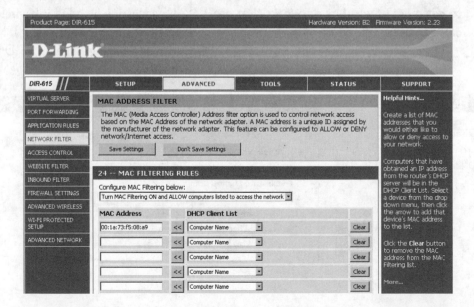

Encrypt Wireless Traffic

You will want to ensure that you are encrypting any traffic from the wireless clients to the access point. You can use WEP, WPA, or WPA2 to encrypt traffic. Remember to use the more secure WPA or WPA2 if you can. To stress the importance of implementing some level of encryption, let's review WEP.

WEP is a feature used to encrypt content between the wireless client and the access point. When configuring WEP, you must configure the wireless access point with an encryption key and then make sure that each wireless client is using the same key. Be aware that WEP encryption has been cracked with products such as AirSnort, so if your devices support WPA or WPA2, then use one of those encryption methods. Always use the largest encryption cipher strength your wireless access point and wireless cards support (for example, 128 bit versus 64 bit).

The other point to make about using WEP or WPA is that not only does it encrypt your traffic but anyone who wishes to connect to your wireless network must know the key and input the key into their wireless card configuration. This helps ensure that people not authorized to use the wireless network cannot connect to the wireless network.

VPN Solutions

Most companies have security concerns with using wireless, and for good reason. Hackers can bypass the MAC filtering, they can crack the WEP key, and they can use Kismet to discover wireless networks even when SSID broadcasting is disabled—so how do you ensure the security of the wireless network?

Most large companies that are using wireless and have security needs of the utmost importance are using VPN solutions with their wireless clients. They are treating the wireless client like any other remote user—"if you want access to the network when not on the premises, you need to connect through VPN"—that is their position. This is due to the high level of security that VPN solutions offer.

In a typical VPN solution for wireless clients, the wireless client would first connect to the wireless network. The wireless network may have some of the security precautions we discussed implemented, such as SSID broadcasting disabled, WEP/WPA, or MAC filtering. The bottom line is if an authorized wireless client connects to the wireless network, that is not where the company network is. After connecting to the wireless network and getting an IP address, the wireless client will then VPN into the network with the VPN software. The VPN software will authenticate the user and also create an encrypted tunnel to secure data transmitting from the client to the corporate network.

on the job *If securing wireless is a concern in your organization, look to using a VPN solution to secure wireless.*

Now that you have an understanding of some of the basic concepts to configure wireless, let's take a look at how to configure a wireless network.

CERTIFICATION OBJECTIVE 7.03

Implementing a Wireless Network

In this section you will learn the steps to configure your wireless access point and the wireless client. Be sure to familiarize yourself with types of settings that exist, but be aware that the screens and steps will be different with different makes and models of wireless routers.

Configuring the Access Point

When you take the wireless access point, or router, out of the box, you will first connect your Internet modem to the WAN port on the wireless router. You can then connect any wired systems on the network to any of the four ports that exist on the switch part of the router as shown in Figure 7-7.

FIGURE 7-7

Looking at the physical ports on a D-Link wireless router

Once you have everything connected, and the router has power, you will need to go through some basic configuration steps to ensure the security of the device. I want to stress that by just plugging everything in the wireless router is working and allowing wireless clients to access the network. You want to control who can connect to the wireless network! The following section outlines some basic settings you can change.

Admin Password

The first thing you will want to do is change the wireless router's administrative password. This password is set by default by the manufacturer, and anyone who has the same router will know the password. In order to change the admin password, you will need to start a web browser and type the IP address of the wireless router. The IP address is normally 192.168.1.1 or 192.168.0.1, depending on the manufacturer.

Once you type in the IP address, you will be asked to log on. In my example I am using a D-Link DIR-615 wireless router, so the password is blank when you take it out of the box. To log on to the router, ensure that admin is chosen as the username and type your password or leave it blank if you don't know the password. Click the Log In button as shown in Figure 7-8 and you will be logged on.

Once logged on, you will change the admin password by going to the Tools link at the top of the page and then selecting the Admin link on the left side of the page (shown in Figure 7-9). In the Admin Password section of the page you will type the password you would like to use for the admin account and then retype it in the verify box. Once you have both password boxes filled in, then you can click the Save Settings button at the top of the page.

FIGURE 7-8	
Logging on to the administration pages of a wireless router	

FIGURE 7-9

Changing the
admin password
on a D-Link
router

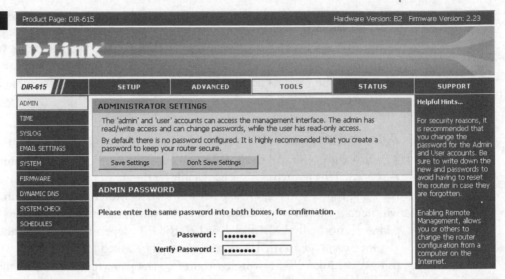

Service Set Identifier

After changing your router admin password, you will want to change the name of
the wireless network, known as the SSID. Remember that in order to connect to
your wireless network, clients have to know the value of the SSID. To change the
SSID on the D-Link router, click the Setup link at the top of the page and then
choose the Wireless Settings link on the left. You can then choose to configure
the wireless network settings manually by scrolling to the bottom of the page and
choosing the Manual Wireless Network Setup button.

You are then placed in the wireless networking setup screen (as shown in
Figure 7-10), where you can change most wireless network settings. To change the
SSID name, type the name you would like to use in the "Wireless Network Name"
box and then click Save Settings.

After changing the value of the SSID, you next want to disable SSID
broadcasting so that your router does not broadcast the name out on the network
to anyone who wants to connect to it. To disable SSID broadcasting on the D-Link
wireless router, set the Visibility Status to invisible and then choose Save Settings
(see Figure 7-10).

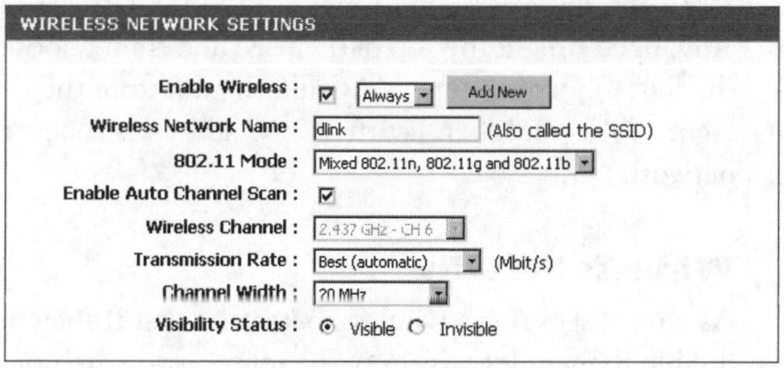

FIGURE 7-10

Changing the
name of the
wireless router
(SSID)

Now that you have SSID broadcasting disabled, users that want to connect to
your network will not see the wireless network through Windows XP/Vista unless
they manually input the SSID name.

While you are looking at the wireless network settings on the router, take a
look at the channel that the wireless network is using. In my example, the router is
autopicking the channel, and you can see in Figure 7-11 that the router has selected
channel 11. If you wish to change the channel used by your wireless network, disable
the Auto Channel Scan check box and then you can pick which channel you wish
to use.

MAC Filtering

The next step to help secure the wireless network is to enable MAC filtering.
Remember that MAC filtering allows you to input the MAC addresses of the
wireless network cards you want to connect to your wireless network. Systems using
any other MAC addresses will not be able to connect to the wireless network.

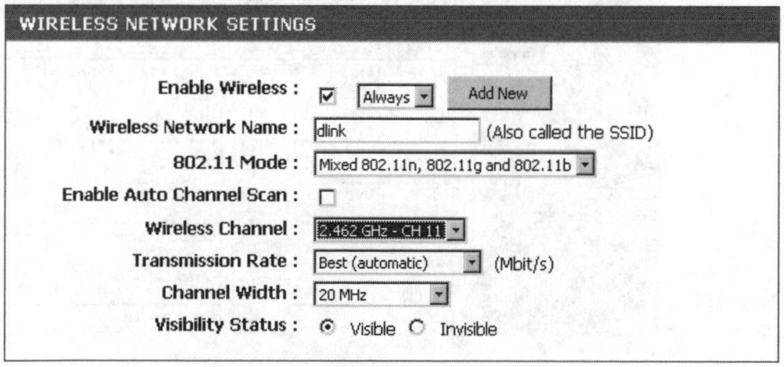

FIGURE 7-11

Choosing a
different channel
to use for the
wireless network

To configure MAC filtering on a D-Link DIR-615 router, you simply click the Advanced link at the top of the page and then choose the Network Filter link on the left. Choose to turn MAC filtering on from the drop-down list (as shown in Figure 7-12) and then list the MAC addresses that are allowed to connect to the network.

Wireless Security

As part of securing a wireless router, the first thing you may decide to do is to disable the wireless aspect of the router if you are not using wireless. A number of people purchase the wireless router and don't actually have any wireless clients at the time—the best thing to do in this case is disable wireless functionality until you need it.

To disable the wireless features on the D-Link router, go to the Setup link at the top of the page and then choose Wireless Settings on the left. At the bottom of the page choose Manual Wireless Network Setup. Once in the wireless settings turn off the Enable Wireless option as shown in Figure 7-13. Also notice that there is an Add New button to the right. This allows you to create a schedule, specifying the times during the day that the wireless is allowed if you want to control the wireless time instead of disabling the feature entirely.

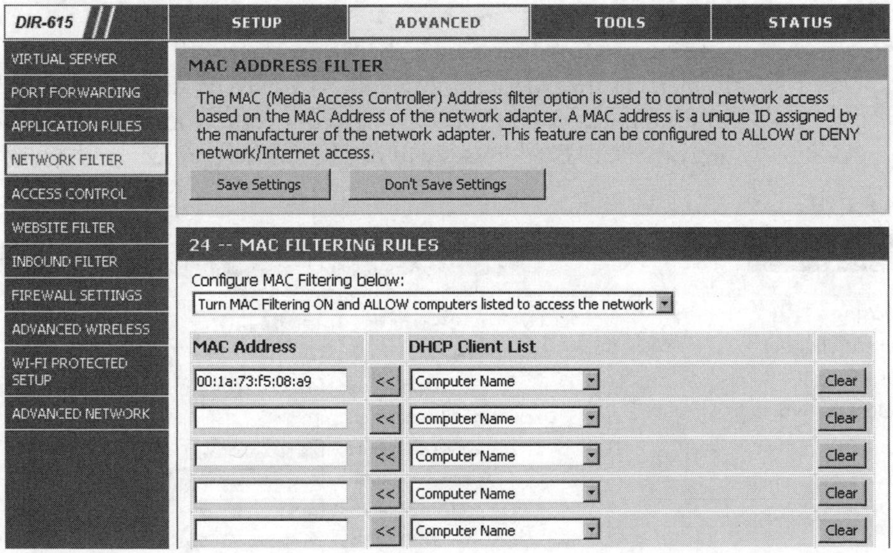

FIGURE 7-12

Filtering which systems can access the network by MAC addresses

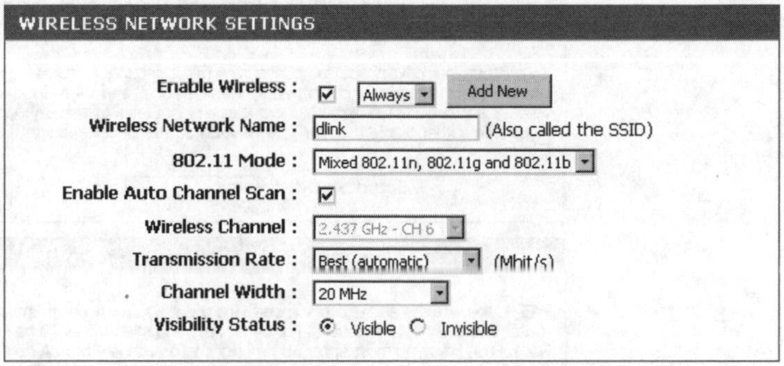

FIGURE 7-13

Disable the
wireless functions
entirely if
you don't use
wireless.

```
WIRELESS NETWORK SETTINGS

        Enable Wireless :  ☑  [Always ▾]  [ Add New ]
   Wireless Network Name :  [dlink          ]  (Also called the SSID)
           802.11 Mode :  [Mixed 802.11n, 802.11g and 802.11b ▾]
  Enable Auto Channel Scan :  ☑
       Wireless Channel :  [2.437 GHz - CH 6 ▾]
      Transmission Rate :  [Best (automatic)  ▾]  (Mbit/s)
         Channel Width :  [20 MHz           ▾]
       Visibility Status :  ⊙ Visible  ○ Invisible
```

As mentioned earlier, you will want to configure some form of encryption on the
wireless router. Most wireless routers will allow you to configure WEP or WPA to
encrypt traffic between the client and wireless access point. Also remember that the
WEP or WPA key must be inputted at the client in order for the client to connect to
the wireless network.

Configure WEP   To configure WEP on the D-Link router, be sure to first log on
to the router. Once you have logged on, click the Setup link at the top of the page
and then the Wireless Settings on the left. Then scroll to the bottom of the page and
choose Manual Wireless Network Setup. Once in the wireless configuration screen,
choose WEP in the Security Mode drop-down list at the bottom of the page. You
will then get options to configure WEP; for instance, you can specify the encryption
strength (such as 128 bit) and then supply four encryption keys of thirteen characters each Figure 7-14 displays WEP being enabled.

Once you have enabled WEP on the wireless access point, you will then need to
configure the wireless clients for WEP (shown later in this chapter).

Configure WPA   To configure WPA on the D-Link wireless router, you will follow very similar steps. Once you have logged on to the router, click the Setup link
at the top of the page and then the Wireless Settings on the left. Then scroll to the
bottom of the page and choose Manual Wireless Network Setup.

Once in the wireless configuration screen, choose WPA-Personal in the Security
Mode drop-down list at the bottom of the page. If you are using a central Radius
server for authentication with WPA, then choose WPA-Enterprise in the Security
Mode drop-down list.

WIRELESS SECURITY MODE

To protect your privacy you can configure wireless security features. This device supports three wireless security modes, including WEP, WPA-Personal, and WPA-Enterprise. WEP is the original wireless encryption standard. WPA provides a higher level of security. WPA-Personal does not require an authentication server. The WPA-Enterprise option requires an external RADIUS server.

Security Mode : [WEP ▼]

WEP

WEP is the wireless encryption standard. To use it you must enter the same key(s) into the router and the wireless stations. For 64 bit keys you must enter 10 hex digits into each key box. For 128 bit keys you must enter 26 hex digits into each key box. A hex digit is either a number from 0 to 9 or a letter from A to F. For the most secure use of WEP set the authentication type to "Shared Key" when WEP is enabled.

You may also enter any text string into a WEP key box, in which case it will be converted into a hexadecimal key using the ASCII values of the characters. A maximum of 5 text characters can be entered for 64 bit keys, and a maximum of 13 characters for 128 bit keys.

If you choose the WEP security option this device will **ONLY** operate in **Legacy Wireless mode (802.11B/G)**. This means you will **NOT** get 11N performance due to the fact that WEP is not supported by Draft 11N specification.

WEP Key Length : [64 bit (10 hex digits) ▼] (length applies to all keys)
WEP Key 1 : [••••••••••]
WEP Key 2 : [••••••••••]
WEP Key 3 : [••••••••••]
WEP Key 4 : [••••••••••]
Default WEP Key : [WEP Key 1 ▼]
Authentication : [Shared Key ▼]

Once you choose WPA-Personal (shown in Figure 7-15), you can then choose below whether you want to support WPA, WPA2, or both. You can also choose which protocol you wish to use, AES being the most secure encryption protocol. With WPA you can also specify how often the key changes with the group key interval.

Controlling Internet Sites

Most wireless routers today allow you to control Internet activity such as what times of the day the Internet is allowed to be used and what Internet sites are allowed to be visited.

There are a number of sites that you may want to block so that your users cannot visit the site. It may be something as simple as a small company using the

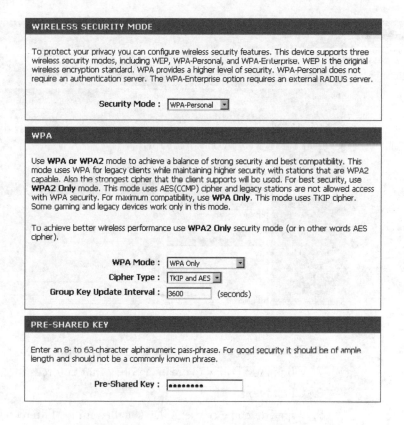

FIGURE 7-15

Enabling WPA-
Personal on a
wireless router

wireless router not wanting its employees wasting company time on a site such as facebook.com, or you may want to block inappropriate sites.

The following steps will guide you through blocking a specific web site on the router so that users cannot visit the site:

1. Log on to the router.

2. Go to the Advanced menu at the top of the page.

3. Click the Website Filter on the left side of the page.

4. Type the URL you would like to block (shown in Figure 7-16). This will prevent users on your network from accessing this site.

5. Now you will have to create a policy that enforces your web site filter at all hours of the day. To do this, click the Advanced link at the top and then choose the Access Control link on the left.

FIGURE 7-16

Blocking access
to specific sites

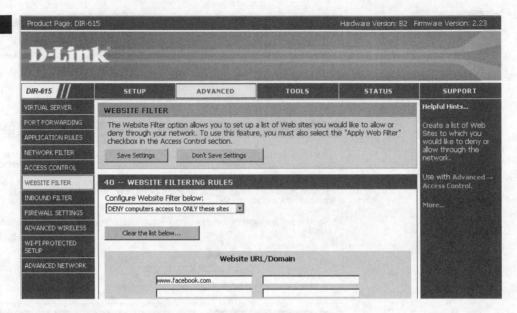

6. Turn on the Enable Access Control option.

7. Click Add Policy to create a policy that enforces the web filter.

8. Click Next.

9. Type the name of the policy (I called mine "FilterSites") and then click Next.

10. Choose Always for when this policy applies and then click Next.

11. Choose Other Machines so that the policy applies to all systems and then click OK.

12. Click Next.

13. Choose Block Some Access and then ensure the Web Filter option is selected so that the web filter is applied (shown in Figure 7-17).

14. Click Next.

15. Ensure that Web Access Logging is enabled. This will allow you to log what sites your users are visiting. After you enable logging, you can view the log at any time to see what sites are being visited.

16. Click Save to save the access policy.

FIGURE 7-17

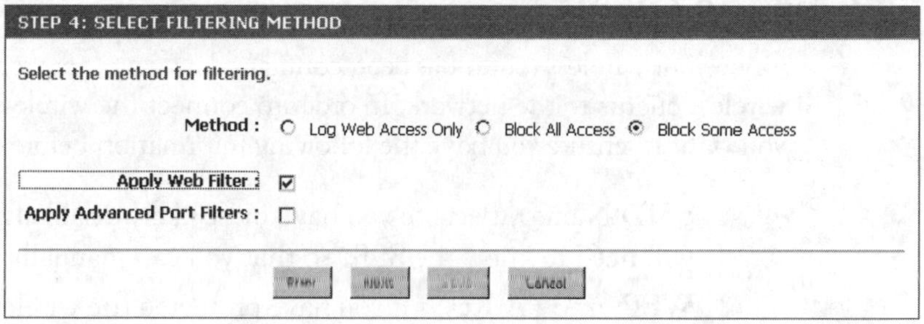

Enabling the Web Filter policy

STEP 4: SELECT FILTERING METHOD

Select the method for filtering.

Method : ○ Log Web Access Only ○ Block All Access ⊙ Block Some Access

Apply Web Filter : ☑

Apply Advanced Port Filters : ☐

View Web Activity

Once you have enabled logging of web activity, you will want to check the logs once in a while. Most routers allow you to view a list of sites that your users have been visiting, or in the case of the D-Link DIR-615 router you can have the log e-mailed to you if you configure the e-mail settings.

To view the log on the router, go to the Status link at the top of the page and then click the Log link on the left. You will see the logged activity for your router in the middle of the screen (shown in Figure 7-18).

CertCam 7-1

To practice configuring a wireless router, check out Exercise 7-1 in LabBook.pdf on the CD-ROM. You can also see the author demonstrate these tasks by checking out the CertCam training video found on the CD-ROM.

FIGURE 7-18

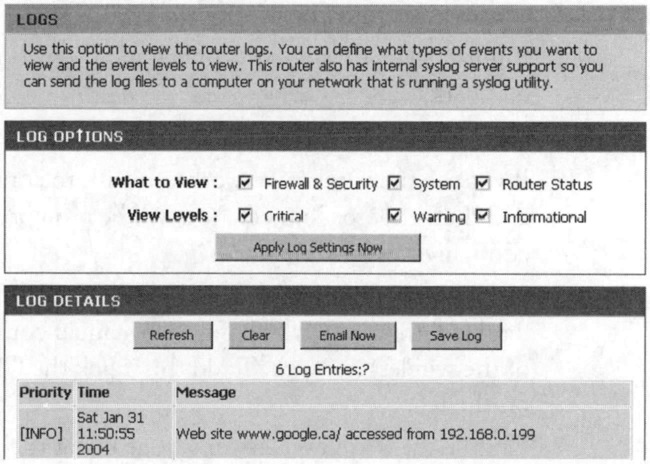

View web sites visited by users with the router's log

LOGS

Use this option to view the router logs. You can define what types of events you want to view and the event levels to view. This router also has internal syslog server support so you can send the log files to a computer on your network that is running a syslog utility.

LOG OPTIONS

What to View : ☑ Firewall & Security ☑ System ☑ Router Status

View Levels : ☑ Critical ☑ Warning ☑ Informational

Apply Log Settings Now

LOG DETAILS

| Refresh | Clear | Email Now | Save Log |

6 Log Entries:?

Priority	Time	Message
[INFO]	Sat Jan 31 11:50:55 2004	Web site www.google.ca/ accessed from 192.168.0.199

Configuring the Client

Once your wireless router has been configured, you are now ready to connect the wireless clients to the network. In order to connect the wireless clients to the network, you want to ensure you have the following information before you get started:

■ **SSID Name** Because you have most likely disabled SSID broadcasting, you will need to know the SSID so that you can manually input it into the client.

■ **WEP or WPA Key** If you have protected the wireless network with WEP or WPA, you will need to know the key.

■ **MAC Address of Client** If you are filtering by MAC addresses, you will need to know the MAC of your client and then input that MAC address into the router.

Once you have all the information in the bulleted list, then you are ready to connect the clients to the wireless network. This section will outline the steps needed to allow your client systems to connect to the wireless network.

Connecting a Windows XP Client

In order to connect your Windows XP client to a wireless network, you will first need to ensure that your wireless network card driver is installed. Once your wireless network card driver is installed, then you can connect to a wireless network by following these steps:

1. Click Start and choose Control Panel.

2. Choose Network Connections.

3. Right-click your wireless connect and then choose View Available Wireless Networks.

4. A list of wireless networks displays (as shown in Figure 7-19).

5. If you see the wireless network you wish to connect to, highlight the network and then choose Connect. You will be prompted for the wireless key if one is configured.

6. If the wireless network you wish to connect to has SSID broadcasting disabled, then you will configure a manual connection and specify the name of the wireless network. To do this, click the Change Advanced Settings link on the left.

7. Choose the Wireless Networks page tab at the top of the dialog box.

FIGURE 7-19

Viewing a list
of wireless
networks from
Windows XP

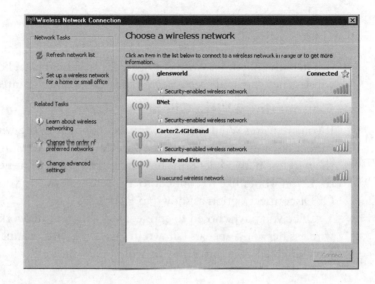

8. Click Add to add a wireless network.
9. Type the SSID and then choose WEP if needed (shown in Figure 7-20).
10. If you are using WEP, turn off the option "The key is provided for me
automatically."

FIGURE 7-20

Adding a wireless
network in
Windows

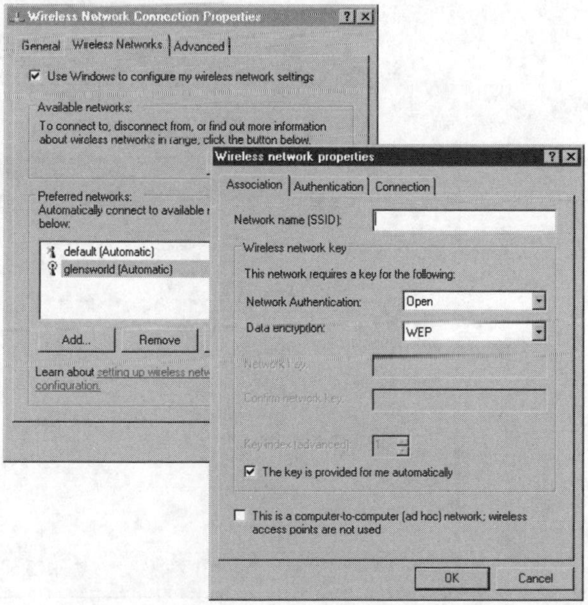

11. Type the WEP key in the field provided.

12. Click OK.

Once the client has been configured, you should then be able to access the wireless network and access network resources and the Internet.

Connecting a Vista Client

If you are using Windows Vista, you can connect to the wireless network in a similar fashion or you can use the wireless network icon in the system tray. Click the wireless network icon in the system tray to see what network you are connected to. If you would like to connect to a different network, you can click the Connect Or Disconnect option as shown in Figure 7-21.

Once you have chosen to connect to a different network, then a list of available wireless networks appears (shown in Figure 7-22). Remember that any networks that have disabled SSID broadcasting will not appear in this list.

FIGURE 7-21

Choosing to connect to a different wireless network in Vista

FIGURE 7-22

Viewing a list of available wireless networks in Vista

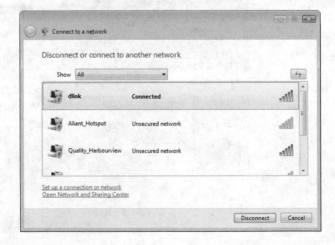

If the wireless network you wish to connect to doesn't appear in the list because SSID broadcasting is disabled, then you will choose the "Set up a connection or network" option and then choose "Manually connect to a wireless network." This will bring you to a dialog box where you can type the SSID name of the wireless network you want to connect to. You can also specify whether the network is using WEP, WPA, or WPA2. You can also specify the key information here as well (shown in Figure 7-23).

When troubleshooting why a client will not connect to wireless networks, there are a number of issues to consider. The following is a list of popular problems when connecting to wireless:

- **Interference**   You could be getting interference from other home equipment, such as a cordless phone. Try changing the channel on the Wireless network.

- **Incorrect encryption**   You could be using the wrong encryption type or even the wrong encryption key. Verify all encryption settings.

- **Incorrect channel or frequency**   You could be using the wrong channel to connect to the wireless network. Verify the channel settings.

- **Extended Service Set ID (ESSID) mismatch**   ESSID is another name for SSID. You must input the correct ESSID name in order to connect to the wireless network.

- **Standard mismatch (802.11a/b/g/n)**   Be sure that the wireless device you are using is compatible with the wireless network.

- **Distance and bounce**   If you are too far from the wireless network, you may not have a strong enough signal to connect. Try moving closer to the access point.

- **Incorrect antenna placement**   Be sure to place the antenna in an open area that will get the best coverage. Try placing it up high, such as on a bookshelf.

FIGURE 7-23

Choosing to connect to a different wireless network in Vista

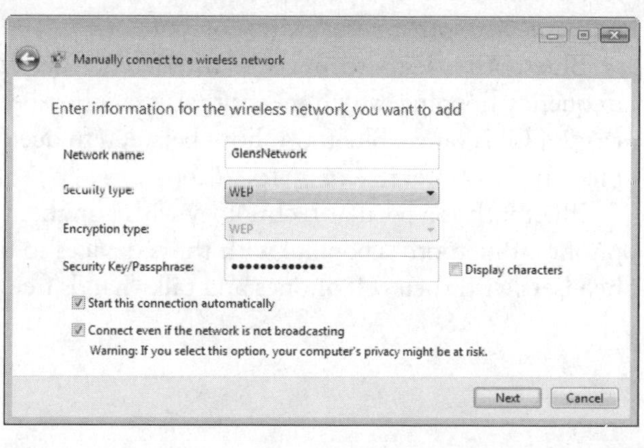

CERTIFICATION OBJECTIVE 7.04

Infrared and Bluetooth

Today's wireless network environments are not limited only to 802.11 wireless LAN equipment. As a Network+ professional, you should be familiar with other popular wireless standards such as infrared and Bluetooth.

Infrared

Infrared wireless is the type of wireless communication that is used by VCR and TV remote controls, along with some computer peripherals. Infrared is typically a line-of-sight technology, which means that the signal is lost if anything blocks the pathway between the two devices. With infrared, the two devices will need to be within one meter of one another.

Infrared devices contain a transceiver that sends and receives light signals as on-off patterns to create the data that travels at transfer rates up to 4 Mbps. Because line of sight is required, you may need to use a radio frequency solution such as Bluetooth if line of sight becomes an issue.

Bluetooth

Bluetooth is a radio frequency wireless technology that allows systems to connect to peripherals over a distance of up to 10 meters away. Bluetooth is more flexible than infrared because it will automatically connect to other Bluetooth devices and does not depend on line of sight. This is a popular technology used by handheld devices to connect to other networking components.

Bluetooth is less susceptible to interference because it uses spread-spectrum frequency hopping, which means that it can hop between any of 79 frequencies in the 2.4 GHz range. Bluetooth hops between frequencies 1600 times per second and provides a transfer rate of up to 1 Mbps.

Bluetooth is a popular technology with handheld devices such as PDAs and cell phones. Bluetooth is popular with these devices so that users can use their wireless headsets with their cell phones and talk "hands free."

There are huge security risks with Bluetooth, as it is possible for a hacker to connect to your cell phone remotely via Bluetooth and steal data off your phone. In order to secure your Bluetooth-enabled device, follow these best practices:

- **Disable Bluetooth**   If you are not using the Bluetooth feature on your phone, then disable Bluetooth through the phone's menu system.
- **Phone Visibility**   If you are using Bluetooth, then set the phone's visibility setting to invisible so that hackers cannot pick up on your phone with a Bluetooth scanner.
- **Pair Security**   Ensure you are using a Bluetooth phone that uses *pair security*, which allows people to connect to your phone only if they know the PIN code you have set on the phone.

CERTIFICATION SUMMARY

In this chapter you have learned about wireless basics and the security issues surrounding wireless. You have learned that wireless networks come in two forms, infrastructure mode or ad hoc mode. Infrastructure mode uses a wireless access point, while ad hoc mode allows clients to connect to one another.

You have also learned about wireless standards such as 802.11b, 802.11g, and 802.11n. 802.11b is an old wireless standard that runs at 11 Mbps, while 802.11g runs at 54 Mbps and 802.11n runs at over 300Mbps.

You have learned that there are many steps to securing a wireless network, such as limiting which systems can connect through MAC filtering, encrypting traffic with WEP or WPA, and making sure to change the SSID and disable SSID broadcasting. You have learned that all these measures have been compromised by hackers, so if security is a concern you should look to using a VPN solution with your wireless network.

✓ TWO-MINUTE DRILL

This chapter has introduced you to a number of concepts related to wireless networking and has shown you how to configure a wireless network. Be sure to remember the following points when preparing for the Network+ exam.

Wireless Basics

❑ Be familiar with the wireless standards such as 802.11a, 802.11b, 802.11g, and 802.11n.

❑ Know that 802.11b, 802.11g, and 802.11n are all compatible because they all run at the 2.4 GHz frequency range.

❑ Know that 802.11a and 802.11n are compatible because they run at the 5 GHz frequency range.

❑ If you are experiencing problems with your wireless clients connecting to the wireless access point, it could be because of interference from other household devices. Try changing the channel on your wireless devices.

Securing Wireless

❑ WEP is a simple form of encryption that uses a passphrase or shared key to secure communications.

❑ You can set up a central authentication server with WPA-Enterprise. This is known as the 802.1x standard.

❑ Be sure to change the SSID and disable SSID broadcasting.

❑ Limit which systems can connect to your wireless network by MAC filtering.

❑ Configure wireless encryption through WEP or WPA.

❑ For the highest level of security, use VPN solutions to secure your wireless infrastructure.

Implementing a Wireless Network

❑ Make sure that you set the admin password on your router.

❑ Configure logging on your router so that you can monitor web sites accessed.

❑ You can implement web site filters to control what sites can be accessed by users on your network.

Infrared and Bluetooth

❑ Bluetooth has a transfer rate of approximately 1Mbps and is used by a number of handheld devices.

❑ Infrared is used by some devices and is a line-of-sight technology.

SELF TEST

Wireless Basics

1. Which wireless mode involves two laptops connecting directly to one another?
   A. Infrastructure mode
   B. Ad hoc mode
   C. Laptop mode
   D. Enterprise mode

2. Which of the following wireless standards does not fall into the WiFi standard?
   A. 802.11n
   B. 802.11g
   C. 802.11b
   D. 802.11a

3. Which wireless standard runs at 54 Mbps per second at the 2.4 GHz frequency?
   A. 802.11n
   B. 802.11a
   C. 802.11g
   D. 802.11b

4. Which wireless standard can reach transfer rates of up to 300 Mbps?
   A. 802.11n
   B. 802.11a
   C. 802.11g
   D. 802.11b

5. Which wireless security protocol changes the key using the TKIP?
   A. WEP
   B. WPA
   C. WEP2
   D. WPA5

Securing Wireless

6. Which of the following is the name you assign to your wireless network?

    A. MAC address

    B. Service Set Identifier (SSID)

    C. WEP key

    D. IP address

7. What should you do with the wireless router to help hide the wireless network from unauthorized users?

    A. Turn it off when it is not being used.

    B. Enable WEP.

    C. Disable SSID broadcasting.

    D. Unplug the network cable from the router.

8. You wish to encrypt traffic between the wireless client and the access point, but you don't have a wireless router that supports WPA or WPA2. What would you do to secure the traffic?

    A. Use a third-party program to encrypt the traffic.

    B. Use WPA on the client but WEP on the router.

    C. Use WPA2 on the client but WEP on the router.

    D. Use WEP on both the client and the router.

Implementing a Wireless Network

9. What is the first thing you should change on the wireless router when it is powered on?

    A. Configure WEP.

    B. Change the admin password.

    C. Change the IP address.

    D. Change the DHCP server scope.

10. You have purchased a wireless router but do not intend on having any wireless clients for the first six months. What should you do to help secure the router?

    A. Enable WEP.

    B. Disable SSID broadcasting.

    C. Enable WPA2.

    D. Disable the wireless feature.

11. What program could be used to do a survey of your area and discover wireless networks?

    A. MBSA

    B. Device Manager

    C. NetStumbler

    D. Routing and Remote Access

Infrared and Bluetooth

12. What is the transfer rate of Bluetooth?

    A. 10 Mbps

    B. 1 Mbps

    C. 4 Mbps

    D. 8 Mbps

SELF TEST ANSWERS

Wireless Basics

1. ☑ **B.** Ad hoc mode is when two laptops connect directly together through a wireless connection.

☒ **A, C, and D** are incorrect. Infrastructure mode is the other wireless topology, which involves having the wireless clients connect to an access point.

2. ☑ **D.** 802.11a was created before the WiFi standard was created and runs at the 5 GHz frequency. 802.11b/g/n all run within the 2.4 GHz frequency range.

☒ **A, B, and C** are incorrect. 802.11b/g/n are all part of the WiFi standard and are compatible with one another.

3. ☑ **C.** 802.11g runs at 54 Mbps and within the 2.4 GHz range.

☒ **A, B, and D** are incorrect. 802.11n supports speeds greater than 54 Mbps, while 802.11b only supports 11 Mbps. 802.11a supports 54 Mbps but runs at the 5 GHz range.

4. ☑ **A.** 802.11n is a new wireless standard that supports transfer rates in the hundreds of Mbps!

☒ **B, C, and D** are incorrect. 802.11a supports a transfer rate of 54 Mbps, 802.11b supports a transfer rate of 11 Mbps, and 802.11g supports a transfer rate of 54 Mbps.

5. ☑ **B.** WPA uses the TKIP protocol to change the key used to secure the wireless network at regular intervals.

☒ **A, C, and D** are incorrect. WEP has static keys configured, while there is no such thing as WEP2 or WPA5.

Securing Wireless

6. ☑ **B.** The SSID is the name of your wireless network. This name should not be easy to guess, and you should also have SSID broadcasting disabled.

☒ **A, C, and D** are incorrect because they are not the name of the wireless network.

7. ☑ **C.** When configuring your wireless router, be sure to disable SSID broadcasting so that the wireless router does not advertise itself.

☒ **A, B, and D** are incorrect. You should enable some form of encryption such as WEP or WPA, but that will not hide the network.

8. ☑ **D.** You will need to use WEP if you have an older router that does not support WPA or WPA2. If you are using WEP on the router, you will need to configure WEP on the client.

☒ **A, B,** and **C** are incorrect because WPA and WPA2 are not supported on the router, so you cannot use them on the client.

Implementing a Wireless Network

9. ☑ **B.** When you first purchase the router, you should set the admin password to prevent others from logging on and changing your router's settings.

☒ **A, C,** and **D** are incorrect. Although you will want to change a number of settings on the router, the admin password should be the first.

10. ☑ **D.** If you do not have a need for the wireless features of the router, then you should disable the wireless features.

☒ **A, B,** and **C** are incorrect because they are all settings you would set if you had wireless clients.

11. ☑ **C.** NetStumbler is a wireless scanner that can detect wireless networks that are close to you.

☒ **A, B,** and **D** are incorrect because they are not wireless scanners.

Infrared and Bluetooth

12. ☑ **B.** Approximately 1 Mbps is the transfer rate of Bluetooth.

☒ **A, C,** and **D** are incorrect because they are not the transfer rate of Bluetooth.

8

Remote Connectivity

Because of the expansion of networks in the world today, user demands for connectivity are increasing dramatically. Users require the ability to connect to network resources from remote locations, at home, and across the Internet. This chapter will introduce you to a number of methods to allow remote users to connect to the network.

As companies expanded and joined an increasingly global market, the need to interconnect offices became crucial to business operations. The Internet is now based on this concept: making information accessible to anyone in the world, from any location. To enable remote installations to communicate with each other and to provide redundancy in case of war, the U.S. government created ARPANET, the first truly remote network. As ARPANET began its transformation into what is now known as the Internet, universities began using it to interconnect and share information and resources. Now, a large portion of the world population uses the Internet for information exchange and research.

Today, companies use networks to interconnect remote sites. They also provide dial-up access to their users to enable them to connect from home or from hotels while on the road. This increased connectivity helps increase productivity and allows the use of additional communication channels. Many technologies we take for granted today implement these concepts. For example, telephone systems use complex networks to enable us to call almost anyone in the world. E-mail is used to send messages and files through the Internet to reach anyone who has access to these services. As with any technology that we come to depend on, remote connectivity has become a part of our everyday lives.

Companies also use features such as Terminal Services or Remote Desktop to connect to systems over a TCP/IP connection and remotely manage those systems or run applications from a particular system. Terminal Services has become a core network service that is required by most organizations and is discussed in this chapter.

CERTIFICATION OBJECTIVE 8.01

Remote Connectivity Concepts

Many technologies and functions are used for remote connectivity. One of the first networks—the telephone system—is still used today by almost everyone in the world. The telephone system concept was based on the idea of enabling two people in different physical locations to speak with each other. The same basic idea is used today for many different applications. Global networks have been created by corporations and institutions alike to enable remote communication and information sharing.

The basic functionality of remote connectivity is available in many different protocols and devices. For example, companies use network links such as Frame Relay and Asynchronous Transfer Mode (ATM), which encompass many different technologies. More common applications include Remote Access Service (RAS), which allows a remote user to use a protocol such as the Point-to-Point Protocol (PPP) to dial in to the RAS server over the public switched telephone network (PSTN).

This chapter will first introduce you to types of connections such as PSTN and ISDN and then talk about RAS services and protocols for dial-up using those connection types. The chapter will then focus on VPN-type connections and protocols as an alternative way to connect to a remote network.

Public Switched Telephone Network (PSTN)

Almost everyone in the world has used a telephone at least once. Today, you can call anywhere in the world and get a direct connection almost instantly using this technology. The PSTN was originally designed as an analog switching system for routing voice calls. Because it has existed for several decades and has been used by so many, it has come to be known as plain old telephone service (POTS). Because PSTN is considered the first wide area network, it was the basis for many of the WAN technologies that exist today and has been instrumental in their evolution.

A History of PSTN

During the initial years of PSTN, digital technologies had not even been considered. The telephone network was based purely on analog signals traveling across copper wire to transport a human voice. The only repetitions of the signal that might have occurred were through one or two repeater devices. The term via net loss (VNL) was coined to calculate the signal degradation that occurred. This degradation was measured in decibels (dB). The only metering equipment needed to test connections consisted of test tones, decibel meters, and volume unit (VU) meters. VU meters were used to measure complex signals such as the human voice. These meters simply measure the loss or gain of a specific circuit.

Prior to the 1960s, PSTN lines could handle nothing more than what they were originally designed for—voice communication. Since then, many great technology leaps have helped the network progress. The beginning of this era was marked by the advent of the Bell T1 transmission system. As T1s became more frequently used in the telephone network, bandwidth and quality increased. This advent also began the true migration from using human operators to route calls to switching these functions electronically.

In the 1970s and 1980s, the phone companies began to invest more resources in improving the quality of the PSTN backbone. This backbone, also known as the digital access cross-connect system (DACCS), was a combination of all the T1 and T3 lines. Although many problems were associated with DACCS at that time, it provided a technology upgrade to help improve services all the way around. Soon companies started looking at PSTN lines as an alternative to the dedicated point-to-point links they were using.

As the industry started to move in the direction of PSTN lines, manufacturers began to market modems for this purpose. As modems became more commonplace, the manufacturers began mass-marketing them for everyday users. Today, although using a modem to dial in to a remote network is not as common as connecting through a broadband connection, it is still an important option for persons not having broadband technologies available. People in rural areas may still need to rely on PSTN and some companies may still rely on using PSTN lines to enable remote users to dial in to private networks as well as to back up data links for computer systems that require remote connectivity.

How PSTN Works

The POTS network originally began with human operators sitting at a switch, manually routing calls. The original concept of the Bell Telephone system was a series of PSTN trunks connecting the major U.S. cities. This was an analog-based system that met its requirements for human voice transmissions at the time. Since the inception of the telephone, the world has changed. PSTN systems still use analog from the end node to the first switch. Once the signal is received, the switch converts the signal to a digital format and then routes the call on. Once the call is received on the other end, the last switch in the loop converts the signal back to analog, and the call is initiated. Because the end node is still analog, modems are used in most homes to facilitate dial-up access. Faster technologies such as ISDN or T1s use a dedicated point-to-point link through a completely digital path, making higher bandwidths attainable. Currently, analog lines can reach only a maximum speed of 56 Kbps. Using digital lines, speeds in excess of 2 Gbps (gigabits per second) can be reached.

The telephone network works much like the TCP transport protocol. It is connection based, and the connection is maintained until the call is terminated. This enables you to hear the other person almost instantaneously. Telephone networks use two copper wires in most homes, but the switching medium is mainly fiber. This allows for the high-speed switching in the back end but slow response in data communications because of the modem device connected to the system.

exam
ⓦ a t c h
Remember that the maximum available speed with an analog modem is 56 Kbps.

Modem Types

Analog modems are used to connect to a remote network via a PSTN line. Although there are many different types and makes of modems, they can be categorized into three classes: single external, single internal, and multiline rack or shelf-mounted.

The *external modem* is the modem most commonly used today. Many ISPs use pools of external modems to enable dial-in access. These modems are also common in server hardware. Many IT workers include modems in production systems to allow for a backup communications link or for remote access.

The *internal modem* belongs to the same device type as the external modem. The only real difference is that it is located inside the computer chassis. Most companies no longer use these modems, because externals are easier to replace and troubleshoot. For example, internal modems do not have the light-emitting diodes (LEDs) that external modems have. This translates into a headache if you have to figure out why the modem won't connect to a remote host via the dial-up connection. Some modem manufacturers provide software interfaces, but they are generally not as full-featured as those in external modems. A common use for internal modems is in laptop computers using PC (PCMCIA) cards. Many laptop vendors still integrate phone jacks into the chassis of their computers. In addition, PC cards can technically be classified as internal modems. These are used widely and do not include the LEDs or lamps an external modem offers. Quite a few businesses use external modems, and home users use internal modems. The cost difference is almost negligible, but home users usually opt for the cheaper of the two.

These solutions are becoming increasingly popular. Many vendors offer solutions that have a single chassis containing a certain number of modem cards that can be connected directly to the network. The modularity and size of these devices makes them much more efficient than trying to maintain a shelf with a stack of external modems sitting on it. These solutions have also been included in some new networking equipment. Manufacturers place analog modems in their equipment to facilitate redundancy features such as a backup network link.

Integrated Services Digital Network (ISDN)

In the past, the phone network consisted of an interconnection of wires that directly connected telephone users via an analog-based system. This system was very inefficient because it did not work well for long-distance connections and was very prone to "noise." In the 1960s, the telephone company began converting this system to a packet-based, digital switching network. Today, nearly all voice switching in the United States is digital; however, the customer connection to the switching office is primarily still analog.

The *Integrated Services Digital Network (ISDN)* is a system of digital telephone connections that enables data to be transmitted simultaneously end to end. This technology has been available for more than a decade and is designed to enable faster, clearer communications for small offices and home users. It came about as the standard telephone system began its migration from an analog format to digital. ISDN is the format portion of the digital telephone system now being used to replace analog systems.

A History of ISDN

The concept of ISDN was introduced in 1972. The concept was based on moving the analog-to-digital conversion equipment onto the customer's premises to enable voice and data services to be sent through a single line. Telephone companies also began using a new kind of digital communications link between each central office. A T1 link could carry twenty-four 64 Kbps voice channels, and it used the same amount of copper wire as only two analog voice calls. Throughout the 1970s, the telephone companies continued to upgrade their switching offices. They began rolling out T1 links directly to customers to provide high-speed access. The need for an efficient solution was greater than ever.

In the early 1990s, an effort was begun to establish a standard implementation for ISDN in the United States. The National ISDN 1 (NI-1) standard was defined by the industry so that users would not have to know the type of switch they were connected to in order to buy equipment and software compatible with it.

Because some major office switches were incompatible with this standard, some major telephone companies had trouble switching to the NI-1 standard. This caused a number of problems in trying to communicate between these nonstandard systems and everyone else. Eventually, all the systems were brought up to standard. A set of core services was defined in all basic rate interfaces (BRIs) of the NI-1 standard. The services include data-call services, voice-call services, call forwarding, and call waiting. Most devices today conform to the NI-1 standard.

A more comprehensive standardization initiative, National ISDN 2 (NI-2), was recently adopted. Now, several major manufacturers of networking equipment have become involved to help set the standard and make ISDN a more economical solution. The NI-2 standard had two goals: to standardize the primary rate interface (PRI) as NI-1 did for BRI, and to simplify the identification process. Until this point, PRIs were mainly vendor-dependent, which made it difficult to interconnect them. Furthermore, a standard was created for NI-2 for identifiers.

ISDN Channels

An ISDN transmission circuit consists of a logical grouping of data channels. With ISDN, voice and data are carried by these channels. Two types of channels, a B channel and a D channel, are used for a single ISDN connection. Each channel has a specific function and bandwidth associated with it. The bearer channels, or B channels, transfer data. They offer a bandwidth of 64 Kbps per channel.

The data channel, or D channel, handles signaling at 16 Kbps or 64 Kbps. This includes the session setup and teardown using a communications language known as DSS1. The purpose of the D channel is to enable the B channels to strictly pass data and not have to worry about signaling information. You remove the administrative overhead from B channels using the D channel. The bandwidth available for the D channel depends on the type of ISDN service; BRIs usually require 16 Kbps and PRIs use 64 Kbps. Typically, ISDN service contains two B channels and a single D channel.

H channels are used to specify a number of B channels. The following list shows the implementations:

- **H0**   384 Kbps (6 B channels)
- **H10** 1472 Kbps (23 B channels)
- **H11** 1536 Kbps (24 B channels)
- **H12** 1920 Kbps (30 B channels, the European standard)

ISDN Interfaces

Although B channels and D channels can be combined in any number of ways, the phone companies created two standard configurations. There are two basic types of ISDN service: BRI and PRI.

- **Basic Rate Interface (BRI)** BRI consists of two 64 Kbps B channels and one 16 Kbps D channel, for a total of 144 Kbps. With BRI, only 128 Kbps is used for data transfers, while the remaining 16 Kbps is used for signaling information. BRIs were designed to enable customers to use their existing wiring. Because this provided a low-cost solution for customers, it is the most basic type of service intended for small business or home use.

- **Primary Rate Interface (PRI)** PRI is intended for users that need greater bandwidth. It requires T1 carriers to facilitate communications. Normally, the channel structure contains twenty-three B channels plus one 64 Kbps D channel for a total of 1536 Kbps. This standard is used only in North America and Japan. European countries support a different kind of ISDN standard for PRI. It consists of 30 B channels and one 64 Kbps D channel, for a total of 1984 Kbps. A technology known as non-facility associated signaling (NFAS) is available to enable support of multiple PRI lines with one 64 Kbps D channel.

<table>
<tr><td>

ⓦatch *For the exam know that BRI uses two 64 Kbps B channels and one 16 Kbps D channel. Also know that PRI uses twenty-three 64 Kbps B channels for data and one 64 Kbps D channel for signaling.*

</td></tr>
</table>

To use BRI services, you must subscribe to ISDN services through a local telephone company or provider. By default, you must be within 18,000 feet (about 3.4 miles) of the telephone company's central office to use BRI services. Repeater devices are available for ISDN service to extend this distance, but these devices can be very expensive. Special types of equipment are required to communicate with the ISDN provider switch and with other ISDN devices. You must have an ISDN terminal adapter and an ISDN router.

ISDN Devices

The phrase *ISDN standard* refers to the devices that are required to connect the end node to the network. Although some vendors provide devices that include several functions, a separate device defines each function within the standard. The protocols that each device uses are also defined and are associated with a specific letter. Also known as reference points, these letters are R, S, T, and U. ISDN standards also define the device types. They are NT1, NT2, TE1, TE2, and TA. The architecture for these devices and the reference points are shown in Figure 8-1 and are explained in the following section.

ISDN Reference Points

Reference points are used to define logical interfaces. They are, in effect, a type of protocol used in communications. The following list contains the reference points:

- **R** Defines the reference point between a TE2 device and a TA device.
- **S** Defines the reference point between TE1 devices and NT1 or NT2 devices.
- **T** Defines the reference point between NT1 and NT2 devices.
- **U** Defines the reference point between NT1 devices and line termination equipment. This is usually the central switch.

Network terminator 1 (NT1) is the device that communicates directly with the central office switch. The NT1 receives a U-interface connection from the telephone company and puts out a T-interface connection for the NT2. NT1 handles the physical layer portions of the connection, such as physical and electrical termination, line monitoring, and multiplexing.

Network terminator 2 (NT2) is placed between an NT1 device and any adapters or terminal equipment. Many devices provide the NT1 and NT2 devices in the same physical hardware. Larger installations generally separate these devices. An

FIGURE 8-1

ISDN device architecture

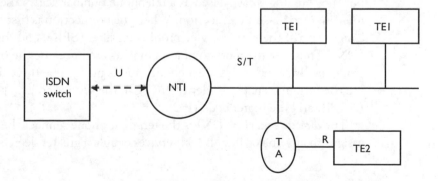

example of an NT2 device is a digital private branch exchange (PBX) or ISDN router. An NT2 device provides an S interface and accepts a T interface from an NT1. NT2 usually handles data link and network layer functions, such as contention monitoring and routing, in networks with multiple devices.

Terminal equipment 1 (TE1) is a local device that speaks via an S interface. It can be directly connected to the NT1 or NT2 devices. An ISDN telephone and an ISDN fax are good examples of TE1 devices.

Terminal equipment 2 (TE2) devices are common, everyday devices that can be used for ISDN connectivity. Any telecommunications device that is not in the TE1 category is classified as a TE2 device. A terminal adapter is used to connect these devices to an ISDN and attaches through an R interface. Examples of TE2 devices include standard fax machines, PCs, and regular telephones.

A *terminal adapter (TA)* connects TE2 devices to an ISDN. A TA connects through the R interface to the TE2 device and through the S interface to the ISDN. The peripheral required for personal computers often includes an NT1 device, better known as ISDN modems.

on the **job**

ISDN modems are used in PCs to connect them to an ISDN network. The term modem is used incorrectly here. ISDN passes data in a digital format, so there is no need to convert the digital data from the computer the way a traditional modem converts the digital data to analog so that it can travel. Conventional modems convert analog to digital and vice versa.

Identifiers

Standard telephone lines use a ten-digit identifier, better known as a telephone number, which is permanently assigned. ISDN uses similar types of identifiers, but they are not as easily used as a telephone number. ISDN uses five separate identifiers to make a connection. When the connection is first set up, the provider assigns two of these: the service profile identifier (SPID) and the directory number (DN). These are the most common numbers used because the other three are dynamically set up each time a connection is made. The three dynamic identifiers are the terminal endpoint identifier (TEI), the service address point identifier (SAPI), and the bearer code (BC).

The *directory number (DN)* is the ten-digit phone number the telephone company assigns to any analog line. ISDN services enable a greater degree of flexibility in using this number than analog services do. Unlike an analog line, where a one-to-one relationship exists, the DN is only a logical mapping. A single DN can be used for multiple channels or devices. In addition, up to eight DNs can be assigned to one device. Because a single BRI can have up to eight devices, it can support up to 64 directory numbers. This is how offices are able to have multiple numbers assigned to them. Most standard BRI installations include only two directory numbers, one for each B channel.

The *service profile identifier (SPID)* is the most important number needed when you are using ISDN. The provider statically assigns the SPID when the ISDN service is set up. It usually includes the DN plus a few extra digits. The SPID usually contains between 10 and 14 characters and varies from region to region. SPIDs can be assigned for every ISDN device, for the entire line or for each B channel.

The SPID is unique throughout the entire switch and must be set up correctly. If it is incorrect, the result is like dialing the wrong phone number—you will not be able to contact the person you are trying to reach. When an ISDN device is connected to the network, it sends the SPID to the switch. If the SPID is correct, the switch uses the stored information about your service profile to set up the data link. The ISDN device will not send the SPID again unless the device is disconnected from the network.

A *terminal endpoint identifier (TEI)* identifies the particular ISDN device to the switch. This identifier changes each time a device is connected to the ISDN. Unlike the SPID or the DN, the TEI is dynamically allocated by the central switch.

The *service address point identifier (SAPI)* identifies the particular interface on the switch to which your devices are connected. This identifier is used by the switch and is also dynamically updated each time a device connects to the network.

The *bearer code (BC)* is an identifier made up of the combination of TEI and SAPI. It is used as the call reference and is dynamic, like the two identifiers included within it. It changes each time a connection is established.

Advantages of ISDN

ISDN offers several major advantages over conventional analog methods. First, it has a speed advantage over normal dial-up lines. Normal dial-up lines use a modem to convert the digital signals from a PC into analog. This enables data to be transferred over public phone lines. This technology does, however, have speed limitations. The fastest standard modem connection that is currently available is 56 Kbps. Given that this is an analog connection, many modems cannot reach this speed, because they are limited by the quality of the connection. This fact accounts for your connecting at different speeds each time you dial in to a remote network. Because phone lines cannot actually transmit at 56 Kbps, a special kind of compression is used to enable these speeds. Two standards are used currently. In order to satisfy all users, ISPs must support both standards, which quickly becomes expensive.

ISDN enables you to use multiple digital channels at the same time to pass data through regular phone lines. The connection made from your computer, however, is completely digital; it is not converted to analog. You can use other protocols that enable you to bind channels together to get a higher bandwidth rate. In addition, ISDN makes a connection in half the time of an analog line.

In addition to speed, ISDN supports multiple devices set up in one link. In an analog system, a single line is required for each device that is attached. For example, a separate phone line is needed for a normal phone, a fax machine, or a computer modem. Since ISDN supports multiple devices, you can use each one of these items on a single line. The connection will also be clearer because the data is being passed in digital format.

Because ISDN uses a separate channel—the D channel for signaling information—it removes the administrative overhead from the B channel so that it can focus on carrying just the data signals. This means that the data is not hindered by the session setups and the signaling information that maintains the session that is required by the devices for communication. The D channel keeps all this information off the data streams (also known as "out of band signaling"). Because of this separation, the setup and takedown of each session is much faster. In addition, ISDN equipment is able to handle calls more efficiently.

CERTIFICATION OBJECTIVE 8.02

Remote Access Service (RAS)

RAS has become a major part of network solutions, using the telephone lines as the physical medium to transfer the data. RAS is a service that allows remote clients to connect to the server over a modem using a RAS-based protocol such as the Serial Line Internet Protocol (SLIP) or the newer Point-to-Point Protocol (PPP).

PPP can run with network protocols such as TCP/IP, IPX/SPX, and NetBEUI; SLIP only supports TCP/IP. This means that you will need to ensure that the client has the network protocol of the destination installed and that the RAS protocol (SLIP or PPP) can run with that network protocol. For example, if the remote network is running IPX/SPX, you will need to ensure that the user who wishes to dial up to that network is running IPX/SPX and that the RAS protocol supports IPX/SPX (PPP in this case).

SLIP and PPP are two communications protocols used by RAS that are used to connect a computer to a remote network through a serial connection using a device such as a modem. When the computer dials up to the remote network, it is treated as an actual node on the network like any other networking device. This setup enables users to run network applications from home as though they were on the network.

SLIP and PPP are fairly similar protocols as far as the overall goal, but they differ in their implementation. They use some of the same underlying technologies, but PPP is newer and better suited for today's expanding networks. The following sections discuss each protocol—how it works, and some of its advantages.

Serial Line Internet Protocol (SLIP)

The *Serial Line Internet Protocol (SLIP)* is a communications protocol used for making a TCP/IP connection over a serial interface to a remote network. SLIP was designed for connecting to remote UNIX servers across a standard phone line. This protocol was one of the first of its kind, enabling a remote network connection to be established over a standard phone line.

SLIP was designed when TCP/IP was the only network protocol commonly used by all UNIX platforms. Although it is still in use today, SLIP has mostly been replaced by PPP. A user can be configured as a SLIP client with Windows 2000/XP/2003, but Windows cannot be a SLIP dial-in server.

Using SLIP to Connect to a Remote Host

To set up a SLIP client in Windows, you must first create the new connection within your Network Connections dialog box. Once you have created the dial-up network connection, you will need to configure its properties and change it from using PPP (the default in Windows) to using the SLIP protocol. Figure 8-2 shows an example of the properties available for configuring a SLIP connection.

FIGURE 8-2

Configuring a
SLIP client in
Windows XP

You might notice that the Settings button is grayed out once you switch from PPP to SLIP; this is because SLIP provides no support for advanced features such as software compression, password encryption, or multilink functionality. Select Internet Protocol (TCP/IP) and click Properties to configure parameters such as the IP address, DNS server addresses, default gateway, and IP header compression.

SLIP is a very simple serial-based protocol. It does not provide the complexity that others, such as PPP, do. Although that can be an advantage, SLIP unfortunately does not include the feature set of other protocols. For example, it does not support option negotiation or error detection during the session setup. It cannot be assigned an address from a DHCP server—it must use static addresses. It also cannot negotiate the authentication method. Issues such as these have helped define the new protocols that are emerging because a given functionality does not exist in SLIP.

The following list summarizes the characteristics of SLIP:

- Runs only with TCP/IP.
- Does not support DHCP functionality.
- Does not support compression or password encryption.
- Used to connect to older UNIX or Linux SLIP servers.

Point-to-Point Protocol (PPP)

The *Point-to-Point Protocol (PPP)* is the default RAS protocol in Windows and is a data link–layer protocol used to encapsulate higher network-layer protocols to pass over synchronous and asynchronous communication lines. PPP was originally designed as an encapsulation protocol for transporting multiple network layer traffic over point-to-point links. PPP also established other standards, including asynchronous and bit-oriented synchronous encapsulation, network protocol multiplexing, session negotiation, and data-compression negotiation. PPP also supports protocols other than TCP/IP, such as IPX/SPX and DECnet.

For PPP to transmit data over a serial point-to-point link, it uses three components. Each component has its own separate function but requires the use of the other two to complete its tasks. The following list explains the three components and their purposes:

- PPP uses the *High-Level Data-Link Control (HDLC)* protocol as the basis to encapsulate its data during transmission.
- PPP uses the *Link Control Protocol (LCP)* to establish, test, and configure the data link connection.
- Various *network control protocols (NCPs)* are used to configure the different communications protocols. This system enables the use of different protocols, such as TCP/IP and IPX, over the same line simultaneously.

Network Control Protocols

Although multiple network protocols are available, Microsoft products use three main protocols for PPP. Each NCP is specific to a particular network-layer protocol such as IP or IPX/SPX. The following is a list of network control protocols.

- The *Internet Protocol Control Protocol (IPCP)* is used to configure, enable, and disable the IP protocol modules at each end of the link.
- The *Internet Packet Exchange Control Protocol (IPXCP)* is used to enable, configure, and disable IPX protocol modules at each end of the link. Although multiple versions of this NCP are available, IPXCP is the most common and is overtaking the other IPX NCPs in popularity.
- The *NetBIOS Frames Control Protocol (NBFCP)* is used to enable, configure, and disable NetBEUI protocol modules at each end of the link.

How PPP Works

PPP uses these three components together to enable it to communicate. It starts by sending LCP frames to test and configure the data link. Next, the authentication protocols are negotiated. Although numerous authentication protocols are available, the most common are the Challenge Handshaking Authentication Protocol (CHAP) and the Password Authentication Protocol (PAP). They determine the type of validation performed for security. The client then sends NCP frames to configure and set up the network-layer protocols to be used during this session. When this step is complete, each network protocol can pass data through this connection. HDLC is used to encapsulate the data stream as it passes through the PPP connection. The link remains active until an LCP or NCP frame closes the link or until an error or external event, such as a user disconnecting the link, occurs.

A control mechanism is included in PPP to enable each protocol to communicate with the others. Finite-state automation (FSA) processes status messages between each layer to coordinate communications. FSA does not actually participate in data flows; it works with the other protocols to keep them in sync and enables them to concentrate on their own jobs.

PPP Framing

PPP framing defines the format in which data is encapsulated before it crosses the network. PPP offers a standard framing solution that enables connections to any standard PPP server because all vendors use the same format. PPP uses HDLC as the basis for its encapsulation framing for serial connections. HDLC is widely used in other implementations and has been slightly modified for use with PPP. The modifications were made to facilitate multiplexing NCP layers.

PPP Devices

PPP is capable of operating across any data terminal equipment or data circuit terminating equipment (DTE/DCE) device. Many examples of these devices are available, including the most common, those following the EIA/TIA-232 standard, better known as modems. PPP is able to use any DTE/DCE devices as long as they support full-duplex circuits. These can be dedicated or switched and can operate in an asynchronous or synchronous bit-serial mode. In addition, the limit on transmission rates is specified by the interfaces and is not controlled by PPP.

You should remember that the DTE is the terminal or PC used to communicate with other systems, and the DCE is the modem that actually does the communicating.

Authentication Protocols

With PPP, each system could be required to authenticate itself. This can be done using an authentication protocol. The most common authentication protocols are PAP, CHAP, and the Microsoft adaptation of CHAP, MS-CHAP. When a connection is being established, either end node can require the other to authenticate itself, whether it is the remote host or the originator of the call. The LCP can be used to send information to the other node to specify the authentication type. Using the authentication protocols, you enable the capability to offer a level of security by requiring authentication to make a remote connection; you also have control over the level of security used.

PAP works much like a regular network login. The client authenticates itself to a server by passing the username and password to it. The server then compares this information to its password store. Because the password is passed in clear text, this system would not work well in an environment in which security concerns are an issue. The system opens the door for anyone "listening" to the line, such as with a network sniffer.

Alternatively, CHAP uses an encryption algorithm to pass the authentication data to protect it from hackers. The server sends the client a randomly generated challenge request with its hostname. The client then uses the hostname to look up the appropriate secret password and returns a response using a one-way hash with the client's hostname. The host now compares the result and acknowledges the client if it matches. CHAP also sends challenges at regular intervals to verify that the correct client is still using this connection. The challenge values change during each interval. Because CHAP is so much more secure than PAP, it is used widely on the Internet. PAP is usually used only in public FTP sites or other public areas.

MS-CHAP is a Microsoft adaptation of CHAP. It uses the same type of encryption methodology but is slightly more secure. The server sends a challenge to the originating host, which must return the username and an MD-4 hash of the challenge string, the session ID, and the MD-4 hashed password. This system enables the authenticator to store the passwords in an encrypted format instead of plain text. Figure 8-3 shows the authentication protocol selections when using PPP as the dial-in protocol for Windows XP. To obtain a list of the supported protocols, go to your dial-in connection properties and select the Security tab. Once on the Security tab, you can select the Advanced security option and then click Settings to view the authentication protocols.

FIGURE 8-3

Authentication
protocols
supported
with PPP in
Windows XP

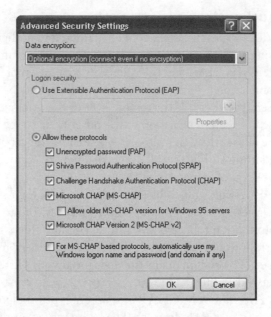

*To learn how to create a PPP dial-up connection in Windows XP, perform the
steps in Exercise 8-1 in LabBook.pdf found on the accompanying CD-ROM
for this book.*

Troubleshooting PPP

When you use PPP to connect to a remote network, you may encounter problems.
These problems can range from no dial tone to a modem misconfiguration or
connectivity problems with the remote PPP server. A log is included with your
communication device to enable you to monitor the steps in opening a PPP
connection and to troubleshoot where the breakdown might have occurred. To
enable modem logging in Windows, go to the properties of the modem device in
Device Manager and click the Diagnostics tab. On the Diagnostics tab choose the
Append To Log option as shown in Figure 8-4.

*To practice enabling modem logging in Windows XP, check out Exercise 8-2 in
LabBook.pdf on the CD-ROM.*

FIGURE 8-4

Enabling modem
logging in
Windows XP

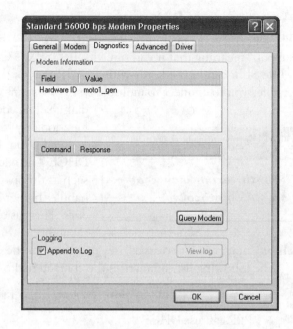

When logging has been enabled, you can see the log file after the next attempt to connect to a PPP server. The log file, modemlog_modemname.txt, is stored in the Windows directory by default. It can be viewed using any standard text editor and is appended each time a new connection is attempted.

Figure 8-5 shows the beginning of a PPP connection to a remote network. It demonstrates the layout of the log file and how detailed it can become. Understanding how to read these log files enables you to troubleshoot almost any PPP problem that could occur.

FIGURE 8-5

Viewing the
modem log

```
05-18-1998 20:10:30.83 - Remote access driver log opened.
05-18-1998 20:10:30.83 - Installable CP VxD SPAP     is loaded
05-18-1998 20:10:30.83 - Server type is  PPP (Point to Point
Protocol).
05-18-1998 20:10:30.83 - FSA : Adding Control Protocol 80fd (CCP) to
control protocol chain.
05-18-1998 20:10:30.83 - FSA : Protocol not bound - skipping control
protocol 803f (NBFCP).
05-18-1998 20:10:30.83 - FSA : Adding Control Protocol 8021 (IPCP) to
control protocol chain.
05-18-1998 20:10:30.83 - FSA : Protocol not bound - skipping control
protocol 802b (IPXCP).
05-18-1998 20:10:30.83 - FSA : Adding Control Protocol c029
(CallbackCP) to control protocol chain.
05-18-1998 20:10:30.83 - FSA : Adding Control Protocol c027 (no
description) to control protocol chain.
05-18-1998 20:10:30.83 - FSA : Adding Control Protocol c023 (PAP) to
control protocol chain.
```

Advantages of PPP over SLIP

PPP offers several advantages over SLIP. First, PPP offers multinetwork protocol support, meaning that it can run with IPX/SPX, TCP/IP, NetBEUI, and AppleTalk while SLIP can be used only with TCP/IP. Any of these protocols can be used, which enables you to connect to multiple types of systems on the remote network through dial-up. The addition of NCPs allows for this functionality in PPP.

In addition, PPP offers the capability to use DHCP. The addition of LCP made options such as this available to PPP. In addition, PPP handles higher-speed links better than SLIP does. This easier use is due to the error-checking capability within the protocol. SLIP does not check datagrams for errors as they pass through the connection.

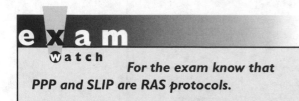

For the exam know that PPP and SLIP are RAS protocols.

The following list summarizes the characteristics of PPP:

- PPP can run with TCP/IP, IPX/SPX, NetBEUI, AppleTalk, or DecNET.
- PPP can use DHCP.
- PPP performs error checking and also supports compression.

CERTIFICATION OBJECTIVE 8.03

Dial-Up Networking

Remote connectivity has had a huge impact on the world market. Many businesses everywhere use remote connectivity to interconnect sites to a single network. It is also used to connect users to the public Internet and to private corporate networks. The New Connection Wizard in Windows allows you to connect to a wealth of different remote servers or to act as a server, depending on how you answer the questions in the wizard. The New Connection Wizard has replaced the dial-up networking feature in previous versions of Windows such as Windows 9x and ME. Figure 8-6 shows the various connections that can be built with the New Connection Wizard in current versions of Windows.

FIGURE 8-6

Creating network
connections
with the New
Connection
Wizard

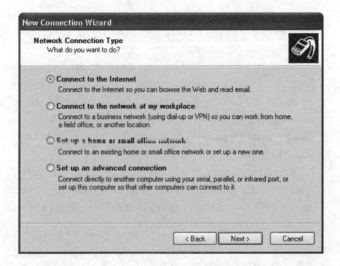

The following list summarizes the options found in the New Connection Wizard
that are used to connect to a remote system in one form or another:

- **Connect to the Internet** This option is used to create a dial-in client that is
set up by the wizard asking you questions about your connection to your ISP.
- **Connect to the network at my workplace** This option is used to create a
dial-in client to a RAS server; it also allows you to create a VPN client that
connects to a VPN server.
- **Set up a home or small office network** This option helps you create a
small home network by running the Network Setup Wizard.
- **Set up an advanced connection** This option is used to create a RAS server
or a VPN server on Windows 2000 Professional or Windows XP Professional.
The RAS and VPN server features that come with these operating systems
allow only one concurrent incoming connection.

Modem Configuration Parameters

Modems are data communication devices that are used to pass data through
the PSTN from node to node. A modem—the word combines modulator with
demodulator —is used to convert a digital signal to an analog format to transmit

across the network. It reverses the conversion process on the other end node to receive the data. Typically, the EIA/TIA-232 serial standard is used to connect the modem to a computer.

Modem communication can be of several types: asynchronous, synchronous, or both. In asynchronous communication, all data is sent separately, relying on the node on the other end to translate the bit order. Synchronous communication sends all data in a steady stream and uses a clock signal to interpret the beginning and end of a packet. Most users today employ synchronous communication in the modems that they buy.

Various system parameters must be set up properly to enable a modem to work. These parameters define the system resources for the modem device to use during its operations. Common parameters include serial ports and baud rates. Let's look at these parameters in more detail.

Serial Port

Serial communications send signals across a point-to-point link. Bits are transmitted one after another in a continuous data stream. Serial ports are the typical means for connecting modems to personal computers. They are based on 9-pin (DB-9) and 25-pin (DB-25) connectors commonly known as COM1, COM2, COM3, and COM4. As we mentioned earlier in the chapter, the computer side of the connection is known as the data terminal equipment (DTE) and the modem is known as the data circuit-terminating equipment (DCE). Various pins are used for different functions inside these connectors. Some are used for transmitting data, others for receiving data, and the remainder for control signals.

You must specify the appropriate serial port settings when you set up a modem. Most modems attempt to use COM1 by default. Each COM port is assigned a specific set of address variables by default when you set up connections. To change the modem COM port after the setup is complete, select Start | Control Panel | Printers And Other Hardware | Phone And Modem Options. Highlight the appropriate modem on the Modem page and click Properties.

Maximum Port Speed

The maximum port speed is defined by the kilobits per second that the modem can support. Maximum rates are defined primarily by the modem hardware; however, the current public telephone network has an upper limit of 56 Kbps through an analog modem. Port speeds are defined by the standards and features available to them.

on the
Job

Note that the terms baud and port speed are not identical. Port speeds define how fast data is traveling; baud measures the signal change per second. With encoding, 2 bits look like 1; therefore, the two terms will not match.

Multiple modem standards exist to define the various features and bandwidths available. Various models provide different standards levels. Before you purchase any modem, you should verify that it fits your current needs and meets the appropriate standard. Table 8-1 illustrates the standards.

To configure the port speed in Windows XP, select Start | Control Panel | Printers And Other Hardware | Phone And Modem Options. Select your modem from the Modems tab and click Properties. When the properties of the modem appear, click the Modem tab. Select the appropriate port speed from the Maximum Port Speed list, as shown in Figure 8-7.

Unimodem

With Windows operating systems, an additional subsystem is available to simplify dial-up networking. Unimodem provides an easy, centralized mechanism for installing and configuring modems, as shown in Figure 8-8. In installing the modem, the wizard enables you to specify configurations included with Windows or to obtain the configuration from disk. Windows ships with over 600 modem configurations included. The information obtained by this process is then accessible to any other application. Many applications written today that run on Windows specifically request information from this process if a modem is required.

TABLE 8-1	Standard	Feature Set
Modem Standards That Define Speeds and Features	V.22	1200 bps, full duplex
	V.22bis	2400 bps, full duplex
	V.32	Asynch/sync, 4800 bps/9600 bps
	V.32bis	Asynch/sync, 14,400 bps
	V.35	Defines high transfer rates over dedicated circuits
	V.42	Defines error-checking standards
	V.42bis	Defines modem compression
	V.34	28,800 bps
	V.34+	33,600 bps

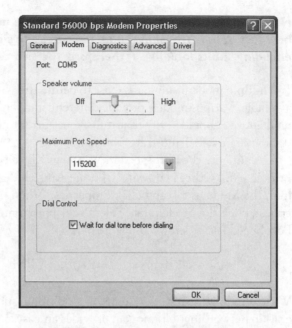

Telephony API

The Microsoft Telephony API (TAPI) is an application interface used for accessing communications features such as connection monitoring. This API is used to provide services such as these without relying on the hardware to set them up. It ties in heavily to the Unimodem mechanism. TAPI functions completely independently from the device hardware. It is now used for modem data transfers; the COMM.API is used for these operations.

When modems were first becoming popular, they could be difficult to configure. You had to understand the settings to use, such as which COM port to set up; the system resources, such as IRQs and DMA channels; and modem baud rates. Each application that was to use this device had to be set up separately. This process could take a great deal of time and become complex quickly when you attempted to use advanced modem initialization strings. TAPI replaced this requirement by providing a standard interface with which the modem would communicate so that the interface could be set up once and all applications could use it.

TAPI also provides other features, such as multiple calling locations. You can set up connection profiles for different dial-up access numbers. You can also customize how the number is dialed. For example, suppose that you set up two separate connection profiles, one with call waiting enabled and the second without it. This setup enables you to manage multiple connections without having to reconfigure your modem setup every time you need a variation.

To access the TAPI options, select Start | Control Panel | Printers And Other Hardware | Phone And Modem Options. Figure 8-9 displays some of the options available for customization.

Requirements for a Remote Connection

Over the course of this chapter, we have addressed several types of remote connectivity technologies. Each has its strengths and weaknesses along with its core functions. Some technologies provide features or functionality that you might not need or want. Understanding how each one works and its benefits and disadvantages enables you to recommend solutions to fit business needs. It is now time to pull all the information together to figure out what is required to make your remote connection work.

FIGURE 8-9

TAPI interface in
Windows XP

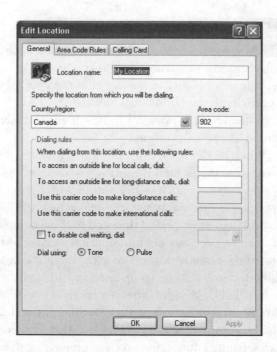

To provide access to a remote server or network, you must properly set up and
configure several items. Each item depends on other items, and this connection will
not work without them all. The following list contains the common components
required to connect to remote resources.

- **Dial-up networking client**   This client must be set up with the appropriate
  parameters defined.
- **Remote server**   You must have a remote server to dial in to reach a remote
  network.
- **User account (PPP, SLIP, RAS)**   You must have a valid ID and password
  on the remote server or network.
- **Modem/ISDN**   You must have a hardware device that enables you to
  communicate with the remote host.
- **Access protocol**   A network-layer protocol must be set up and configured
  properly to access resources on the remote server or network. Examples
  include TCP/IP, IPX, and NetBEUI.

CERTIFICATION OBJECTIVE 8.04

Virtual Private Networks (VPNs)

This chapter has so far discussed how to connect to a remote network using RAS, which typically involves a connection across the PSTN from one system to another. RAS is a great solution to remotely connect to a system, but it does mean that we are incurring long-distance phone calls. The solution to cut down on long-distance calls was to use the Internet as the physical connection. In order to use the public Internet as a physical medium to carry data between a client and the remote network, you first want to create an encrypted tunnel between you and the remote network; then the data is delivered in the encrypted tunnel. This will ensure that no one can intercept the data and read it, because it is transmitted in an encrypted format—the purpose of the VPN.

VPN Overview

Once the Internet became popular, it was an obvious solution to allow users in remote locations to communicate with networks over distance. For example, if we had an office in New York and a user in a hotel room in Boston who wanted to access the network in New York, what better solution than to use the Internet! The problem, of course, is the security issues that surround sending data across the Internet for the entire world to tap into!

Virtual private networks (VPNs) offer a solution. The idea of a VPN is that the user in Boston that is in the hotel will dial up to the Internet using the ISP in Boston provided by the hotel. Once the user in the hotel has the Internet connection, he or she will then dial the IP address of the VPN server in New York to create a "secure tunnel" between the client system and the VPN server in New York. Any data that travels between the two systems will be encrypted and therefore will be considered secure.

Two of the major benefits of VPN are secured communication across an unsecured medium and the lack of long-distance costs incurred to communicate between the two locations. Once all systems have an Internet connection, VPN solutions leverage that Internet connection and add security to it.

w a t c h   *Both PPTP and L2TP are VPN protocols used to create a secure tunnel across an unsecured network such as the Internet.*

Just as there are two primary RAS protocols (SLIP and PPP), there are two primary VPN protocols that provide this tunneling security; they are the Point-to-Point Tunneling Protocol (PPTP) and the Layer 2 Tunneling Protocol (L2TP).

VPN Protocols

The *Point-to-Point Tunneling Protocol (PPTP)* is a network protocol that provides for the secure transfer of data from a remote client to a private server by creating a multiprotocol virtual private network, or VPN. PPTP is used in TCP/IP networks as an alternative to conventional dial-up networking methods. This system enables multiprotocol secure communication over a public TCP/IP network such as the Internet. PPTP takes advantage of an additional level of security that is not currently available in other standard implementations.

PPTP is actually an extension of PPP. It encapsulates PPP packets into IP datagrams for transmission across a network. This system enables the functionality of PPP while taking advantage of the security features offered by the VPN technology. Using both options tied into one protocol, you get the best of both worlds.

A Brief History of PPTP

PPTP became recognized by the IETF (a standards committee) in June 1996. Although many tunneling protocols have been created and implemented, this was the first standard tunneling protocol to become available. Many vendors have adopted it in an attempt to provide a secure method to connect across the public Internet into a corporate internal network.

How PPTP Works

VPNs are used to provide tunneling through a public network with a secure communications channel. Users can employ PPTP to dial into a public network, such as PSTN, to use the Internet to connect to their corporate offices. This system enables users to use the network infrastructure that is already in place; it eliminates the need for dedicated modem banks for users.

PPTP tunneling can be defined as the process of routing packets through an intermediate public network to reach a private network. Only the PPTP-enabled client can access the remote network; other clients on the same segment cannot. The interesting thing about this process is that you can dial into a standard PPP server and use it to establish a PPTP connection to the remote network. No additional setup or option choices are required of your ISP; most offer PPP access already. You could also set up a PPTP server to dial into; this setup would enable you to only require PPP to be set up on the clients.

Once the PPTP server receives the packet from the client connection, it routes the data to the appropriate resource. This occurs by stripping off the PPTP and PPP overhead to obtain the addressing information originally applied to it. The PPTP server must be configured with TCP/IP to communicate with PPTP and whatever other protocols are being passed through this VPN tunnel.

A VPN works by encapsulating the data within IP packets to transport it through PPP. This enables the data to pass through the Internet and use the standards already in place. No configuration changes are required to your existing network stacks; they can be used as-is over the PPTP connection. Other protocols, such as NetBEUI and IPX, can also pass through this secure connection.

VPNs are virtual devices set up as though they were regular devices such as modems. In addition, PPTP must be set up on the client and the server. Host computers in the route between these two computers do not need to be PPTP aware, since the packet's IP header is not encrypted. They need only provide an IP route to the remote server. Figure 8-10 shows the layout of a VPN solution.

FIGURE 8-10   PPTP connections create a secure tunnel over an unsecured network.

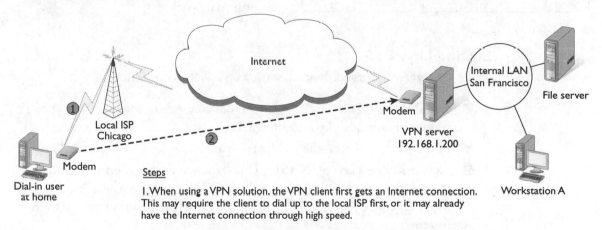

Steps

1. When using a VPN solution, the VPN client first gets an Internet connection. This may require the client to dial up to the local ISP first, or it may already have the Internet connection through high speed.

2. The VPN client dials the IP address or FQDN of the VPN server. When authenticated, a secure tunnel is created by the VPN protocol such as PPTP or L2TP. All traffic between the VPN client and VPN server is encrypted.

PPTP mainly involves three processes to set up a secure communications channel. Each process must be completed before beginning the next process. The following list identifies the processes involved:

■ **PPP connection and communication**   PPTP uses PPP to connect to·a remote network. When connected, PPP is also used to encrypt the data packets being passed between the remote host and the local machine.

■ **PPTP control connection**   When the PPP session is established, PPTP creates a control connection between the client and the remote PPTP server. This process is referred to as tunneling.

■ **PPTP data tunneling**   PPTP creates the IP datagrams for PPP to send. PPP encrypts the data portion of packets, which are sent through the tunnel to the PPTP server. The PPTP server is then used to decrypt the PPP-encrypted packets, disassemble the IP datagram, and route to the appropriate host.

Be sure that you know the three processes involved with PPTP and how PPP applies to each one.

PPTP relies heavily on PPP to perform its job. PPP is used to enable multiple network-layer protocols to be used within the connection. PPP is also used to perform other functions such as establishing and maintaining a connection, authenticating users, and encrypting data packets.

Setting Up PPTP

There are three main components to setting up a PPTP connection:

■ **PPTP client**   This is a client system that connects to the PPTP server by IP address or fully qualified domain name.

■ **PPTP server**   This is the VPN server that allows for PPTP connections.

■ **Network access server (NAS)**   This is the server that connects you to the network that you will use to call the PPTP server. Typically, this is the Internet service provider (ISP) that is responsible for connecting you to the Internet.

These various components are equally important and must be configured properly to enable a user to access resources on a remote network. Each component has its specified functions and requirements. Today, Windows systems can be used as a PPTP client, while Windows 2003 Server also supports PPTP server services through the Routing and Remote Access Service (RRAS).

Also understand that in this day and age the VPN client will typically not need to dial up to the ISP to get an Internet connection before dialing into the VPN server. With the widespread use of high-speed Internet, today's VPN client will most likely already have an Internet connection and therefore simply need to dial the IP address of the VPN server to make a VPN connection.

Exercise 8-3 explains how to set up Windows XP as a PPTP client. The exercise demonstrates using Windows XP as a PPTP client dialing into a PPTP server.

EXERCISE 8-3

Setting Up Windows XP as a PPTP Client

In this exercise you will use the New Connection Wizard to configure your Windows XP client as a PPTP client to dial into a PPTP server.

1. Choose Start and right-click My Network Places and choose Properties.

2. In the New Connection window, click the Create A New Connection link on the left side of the screen in the Network Tasks list.

3. Click Next to pass the welcome screen.

4. Select the type of connection you wish to build. Because you are connecting to a VPN server, choose the Connect To The Network At My Workplace option. You will notice that the description of this option specifies that you are using the dial-up feature or VPN. Also note that the option says that you are connecting to the workplace, but you would use this option anytime you are dialing into a RAS server or a VPN server. Click Next.

5. Now specify whether you want to use the dialup or VPN feature. In this example you are going to connect to a VPN server, so choose Virtual Private Network Connection and click Next (as shown in the accompanying illustration).

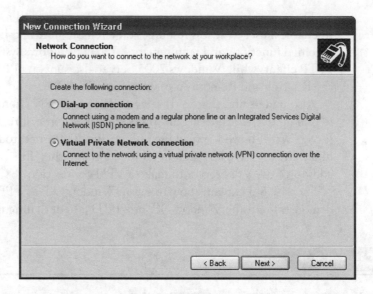

6. You will now give the connection a meaningful name. Type **VPN Server In New York** as the name for the connection (as shown in the accompanying illustration) and choose Next.

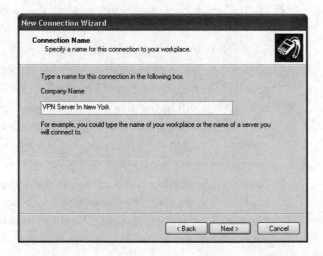

7. You will now specify whether you want to automatically dial up to the Internet when this VPN connection is used. We will assume that you will

already have the Internet connection when you use the VPN connection, so choose the option Do Not Dial The Initial Connection (as shown in the accompanying illustration) and choose Next.

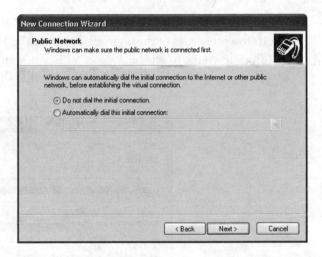

8. You will now provide the IP address or FQDN of the VPN server. This will act as the "phone number" for the VPN server that you will dial once you have a connection to the Internet. Type **192.168.1.200** (as shown in the accompanying illustration) and then choose Next.

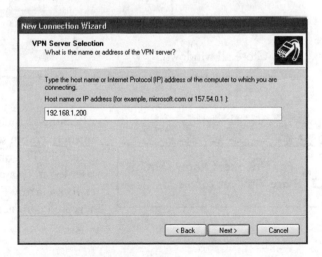

9. Choose Finish to complete the connection wizard.

10. The logon dialog box displays to make a connection to this VPN server. Click Cancel because you will now set that you want to use PPTP instead of L2TP to connect to the VPN server.

11. Right-click the VPN Server In New York connection and choose Properties.

12. In the properties of the connection, go to the Networking tab and click the drop-down list to set the Type of VPN you want to use. Select PPTP VPN from the list (as shown in the accompanying illustration). Then choose OK.

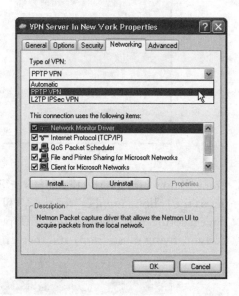

13. Close all windows.

Because of the popularity of PPP and the Internet, a more secure dial-in solution was needed. PPTP grants you the capability to have a user log in to a remote, private, corporate network via any ISP and maintain a secure, encrypted connection. This concept is being implemented by more and more companies every year; its popularity has exploded since its first draft was proposed in 1996.

Most larger companies now have employees traveling for training, seminars, and conventions. Companies require a means for these traveling employees to be able to access the company network securely. Remote access is becoming widely used, whether via direct connections with modems or a VPN connection through the Internet.

CERTIFICATION OBJECTIVE 8.05

Terminal Services

One of the best features that has come from Microsoft servers during the past few years is Windows Terminal Services (WTS). Windows Terminal Services is a feature that allows clients to establish a remote session with the server and have the interface of the server appear on the client. The client can then run the software that is on the server and typically remotely administer the server this way.

Terminal Services uses the Remote Desktop Protocol (RDP) over a TCP/IP network to send screen refreshes from the server to the client. Its primary purpose is to allow fairly old computers to run up-to-date software by allowing the network administrator to install the software on the terminal server and have the clients create a session with the server. Within this session the clients would be able to run whatever software was installed on the server.

Organizations often use this feature for specialized software that needs to be deployed to a selected group of individuals. Instead of the software being installed for that selected group of individuals, those individuals would create a terminal session with the server to run the special software.

Advantages of Terminal Services

There are two major benefits to Terminal Services:

1. The capability to install software on one server.
2. The capability to have that software available to all of the terminal clients instantly. If this software needs to be upgraded, the upgrade needs to be done only on the server; the terminal clients will be aware of the new upgrade immediately.

The other benefit of Terminal Services, which is the reason most people are using it, is that the server supports a remote administration mode that licenses two network administrators to connect to the server at any point in time for remote administration. This feature allows network administrators to lock the servers in the server room and remotely connect to the terminal server over any TCP/IP network (including the Internet) to do their administration. This means that when there are server problems at 9 P.M., you can terminal into the server from your home to solve the problem instead of taking the one-hour drive to the office to fix a small configuration problem.

Another significant advantage to Terminal Services is that you can extend the lifetime of an old computer; older computers with limited RAM and processing power can be used to run new applications, because the software is actually run from the terminal server during a terminal session. You are not using memory or processing power on the client system to run the terminaled applications.

Disadvantages of Terminal Services

The big drawback to Terminal Services is the amount of RAM and processing power the server needs to handle all the remote sessions that are running in its memory. This is one of the key reasons why most terminal servers are probably being used for just the remote administration feature, and are not being used to run the Microsoft Office suite at the desktops through remote sessions.

If you intend to require selected clients to run an application from the terminal server, you will need to ensure that you have installed adequate amounts of memory and processing power on the server. It is recommended that you use multiple processors in the server to handle the processing requirements of a multisession environment.

Remote Desktop

Because most companies were using their Windows 2000 terminal servers for the purpose of remote administration, Microsoft decided to build the "terminal services remote administration" feature into Windows XP and Windows 2003; it was named Remote Desktop.

If you enable the Remote Desktop feature in Windows XP, any Remote Desktop client can connect to your system after being authenticated and then remotely manage the system. Because Windows XP is a desktop operating system, the person sitting at the console will be locked out while you do your remote administration.

In Windows 2003 Server you can have two users connected through Remote Desktop for the purpose of remote administration while the person sitting at the console is left logged in. This is great, because you can use Remote Desktop to access the server and not affect anyone doing administration at the console.

To enable the Remote Desktop feature in Windows Server 2003, click Start and right-click My Computer; then choose Properties. Once the properties have displayed, click the Remote tab and you will see the Remote Desktop feature. If you select the option "Allow users to connect remotely to this computer," you will enable the Remote Desktop feature (shown in Figure 8-11).

Once you have enabled Remote Desktop, you can control who is allowed to use Remote Desktop to access your system by clicking the Select Remote Users button. By default, members of the administrators group are allowed to use Remote Desktop to access the server, but you can select additional user accounts in the dialog box shown in Figure 8-12.

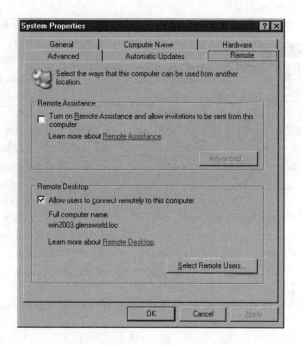

FIGURE 8-12

Selecting
additional users
to use Remote
Desktop to
access a Windows
Server 2003

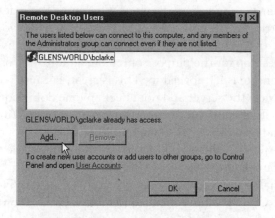

Once you have enabled the Remote Desktop feature on the server, you can connect to it. You can download the Remote Desktop connection client software from Microsoft's web site (it is being shipped with Windows XP and Windows Server 2003).

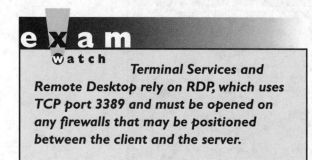

Terminal Services and Remote Desktop rely on RDP, which uses TCP port 3389 and must be opened on any firewalls that may be positioned between the client and the server.

To connect to a remote desktop server or terminal server, choose Start | All Programs | Accessories | Communications | Remote Desktop Connection.

Once you choose to start the Remote Desktop client, you can type the name of the server or its IP address to make the connection (as shown in Figure 8-13). There are a number of options that can be specified before making the connection. Some of the popular ones include specifying that you want to have your local drives and printers available in the Remote Desktop session, along with options to optimize the performance of the session. Most Linux distributions include a Remote Desktop client for connecting to Windows Terminal Services.

In this section you have been introduced to the Terminal Services/Remote Desktop features of the Microsoft Windows operating system. This feature has proven to be quite popular with network administrators to enable remote administration of the servers.

FIGURE 8-13

Logging in to a
terminal server/
remote desktop
system

To learn to enable Remote Desktop on a Windows 2003 server and then remotely connect to that server with the remote desktop client, try Exercise 8-4 in LabBook.pdf on the CD-ROM.

CERTIFICATION SUMMARY

The concept behind remote connectivity is to provide access to a network from a remote location. Originally, the U.S. government used ARPANET to connect remote sites. From there, networks have drastically expanded in size during the past several decades. Many technologies have been spawned from the growing need for remote access.

The Point-to-Point Protocol (PPP) and Serial Line Internet Protocol (SLIP) are communications protocols used to communicate with remote networks through a serial device such as an analog modem. SLIP was originally designed to connect to remote UNIX boxes. SLIP supports only the TCP/IP network-layer protocol. It is rapidly being replaced by PPP.

PPP is a more robust protocol than SLIP. PPP was designed to handle multiple network-layer protocols, such as TCP/IP, IPX, and NetBEUI. It includes additional features such as encapsulation, network protocol multiplexing, session negotiation, and data-compression negotiation. PPP uses three subprotocols: the High-Level Data-Link Control (HDLC), Network Control Protocol (NCP), and Link Control Protocol (LCP). HDLC handles data encapsulation, NCP handles network-layer protocols, and LCP handles connection maintenance and testing. PPP uses three different NCPs: IPCP for TCP/IP, IPXCP for IPX, and NBFCP for NetBEUI. PPP uses authentication protocols such as CHAP, PAP, and MS-CHAP. PPPLOG.TXT is located in the Windows directory, which by default is C:\Windows, and is used to troubleshoot PPP issues.

The Point-to-Point Tunneling Protocol (PPTP) provides a secure communications channel through a public TCP/IP network such as the Internet. PPTP provides multiple network-layer protocol support using PPP as the underlying structure. PPTP uses a technology called virtual private networks (VPNs) to create the encrypted channel through which data is transmitted. You can use a PPTP client to connect to a standard PPP server and create a tunnel to another PPTP server across the network. You can also use a PPP client to connect to a PPTP server and enable it to handle the tunneling. VPN devices are created to facilitate PPTP connectivity following a three-step process: PPP connection and communication, PPTP control connection, and PPTP data tunneling.

The Integrated Services Digital Network (ISDN) is a system of digital telephone connections that enables data to be transmitted simultaneously end to end. ISDN developed as the standard telephone network progressed. ISDN uses channels to make up a logical circuit. Two types of channels are used: a B channel for data transfer and a D channel for circuit-control functions. Each B channel equals 64 Kbps; each D channel represents either 16 Kbps or 64 Kbps. H channels are used to specify a number of B channels. A basic rate interface (BRI) consists of two B channels and one 16 Kbps D channel, totaling 144 Kbps. A primary rate interface (PRI) consists of 23 B channels and one 64 Kbps D channel, totaling 1536 Kbps. ISDN device types define the type of hardware used and include NT1, NT2, TE1, TE2, and TA. Reference points are used to define logical interfaces. Identifiers label the connection and include the service profile identifier (SPID), the directory number (DN), the terminal endpoint identifier (TEI), the service address point identifier (SAPI), and the bearer code (BC).

The public switched telephone network (PSTN) facilitates voice communications globally. Also known as plain old telephone system (POTS), the PSTN was the first telecommunications network of its size in existence. Wide area network technologies are all based to some degree on this network. Various analog device types, including external modems, internal modems, and modem banks, are available to enable data communications.

Dial-up networking functionality is included with all Windows versions since Windows 95. It enables users to connect to their internal networks or the Internet from remote locations. Dial-Up Networking supports four line protocols: NetWare Connect or Netware Remote Networking (NRN), the Remote Access Service (RAS), SLIP, and PPP. Three methods exist to invoke a dial-up session: explicit, implicit, or application invoked. Because modems are used to connect to remote networks, you must know how to configure them. IRQs, I/O addresses, and serial ports all must be configured properly. Modems have a maximum port speed defined by the standards they meet. The Unimodem subsystem provides one interface for all applications to tie into the modem. The Telephony API (TAPI) provides additional features such as connection monitoring and multiple-location support. Specific items are required to use Dial-Up Networking; you must have the appropriate network protocol set up, a line protocol set up, a server to dial into, and a properly set-up modem.

✓ TWO-MINUTE DRILL

Remote Connectivity Concepts

- ❑ The basic functionality that remote connectivity uses is available in many different protocols and devices.
- ❑ Companies use links such as POTS and ISDN to make remote connections.
- ❑ Common applications include PPP dial-up and the public switched telephone network (PSTN).
- ❑ The Integrated Services Digital Network (ISDN) is a system of digital telephone connections that enables data to be transmitted simultaneously end to end.
- ❑ There are two basic types of ISDN service: the basic rate interface (BRI) and the primary rate interface (PRI).
- ❑ Be sure to know the device types and where each type is used. In addition, know the number of channels and speeds associated with the BRI and PRI.
- ❑ The public switched telephone network (PSTN) was originally designed as an analog switching system for routing voice calls.

Remote Access Service (RAS)

- ❑ SLIP and PPP are two communication protocols that are used to connect a computer to a remote network through a serial connection using a device such as a modem.
- ❑ The Serial Line Internet Protocol (SLIP) is a communications protocol used for making a TCP/IP connection over a serial interface to a remote network.
- ❑ The Point-to-Point Protocol (PPP) is a data link–layer protocol used to encapsulate higher network-layer protocols to pass over synchronous and asynchronous communication lines.
- ❑ The most common authentication protocols include the Password Authentication Protocol (PAP), the Challenge Handshake Authentication Protocol (CHAP), and the Microsoft adaptation of CHAP, MS-CHAP.

Dial-Up Networking

- ❑ Remember that the maximum available speed with an analog modem is 56 Kbps.
- ❑ Windows versions 95 to 2003 include a Dial-Up Networking client.

❑ Dial-Up Networking provides support for four types of line protocols.

❑ Modems are asynchronous, synchronous, or both.

Virtual Private Networks (VPNs)

❑ The Point-to-Point Tunneling Protocol (PPTP) is a network protocol that provides for the secure transfer of data from a remote client to a private server by creating a multiprotocol virtual private network (VPN). PPTP is used in TCP/IP networks as an alternative to conventional dial-up networking methods. Be sure to know the three processes involved with PPTP and how PPP applies to each one.

❑ A VPN works by encapsulating the data within IP packets to transport it through PPP. VPNs are virtual devices set up as though they were regular devices such as a modem.

Terminal Services

❑ Terminal Services allow applications to be run completely on the server.

❑ Older PC hardware can still be utilized with Terminal Services.

❑ Connections to a terminal server can be done over a dial-up connection, a LAN connection, and even a direct connection.

❑ A terminal server requires a lot of RAM and processor power.

❑ RDP is the protocol used by Terminal Services and runs over TCP/IP.

❑ Remote Desktop is the feature now used for Terminal Services in remote administration mode.

SELF TEST

The following Self Test questions will help you measure your understanding of the material presented in this chapter. Read all the choices carefully, because there might be more than one correct answer. Choose all correct answers for each question.

Remote Connectivity Concepts

1. What was the first Integrated Services Digital Network standard to be published by the ITU?

- A. ISDN-1
- B. ISDN-NI
- C. NI
- D. NI-1

2. How many B channels are available in a typical ISDN PRI?

- A. 2
- B. 20
- C. 23
- D. 30

Remote Access Service (RAS)

3. Which network-layer protocols can the Serial Line Internet Protocol use during a dial-up session?

- A. TCP/IP
- B. IPX/SPX
- C. PPP
- D. NetBEUI

4. Which remote protocol supports running many different types of network protocols over a serial link?

- A. SLIP
- B. PPP
- C. IPX
- D. NetBEUI

5. Which components are part of the Point-to-Point Protocol?

- A. Network Control Protocol
- B. Link Control Protocol
- C. Internet Protocol
- D. Internet Packet Exchange Protocol

6. Which network control protocol is used in PPP to facilitate the transport of TCP/IP?

    A. IPNP

    B. IPCP

    C. IPXCP

    D. None of the above

7. Which forms of validation can PPP use to authenticate a remote server?

    A. CHAP

    B. Domain account

    C. PAP

    D. KPA

8. How many incoming RAS connections does Windows XP support?

    A. 1

    B. 10

    C. 256

    D. 1024

Dial-Up Networking

9. Where is the logging information for a connection appended when modem logging is enabled?

    A. modemLOG.TXT

    B. PPP.LOG

    C. modemlog_modemname.txt

    D. PPP.TXT

10. Which Windows feature can create a dial-up connection in Windows XP?

    A. Device Manager

    B. Control Panel

    C. Accessories

    D. New Connection Wizard

11. Which application programming interface is used to include features such as call monitoring and multiple localities?

    A. Unimodem

    B. COMM

    C. TAPI

    D. None of the above

Virtual Private Networks (VPNs)

12. What technology do virtual private networks (VPNs) offer to provide a more secure communications channel?

   A. IP header compression

   B. Tunneling

   C. Multiple network protocol support

   D. None of the above

13. Which of the following are protocols used for VPN solutions?

   A. PPTP

   B. PPP

   C. L2TP

   D. SLIP

14. Which of the following is the process for setting up a "tunnel" for PPTP?

   A. PPP connection and communication

   B. PPTP control connection

   C. PPTP data tunneling

   D. PPTP data transfer

Terminal Services

15. What protocol is used by Terminal Services to send screenshots to the client?

   A. RDP

   B. NetBEUI

   C. ICA

   D. TCP/IP

16. What are some advantages of using Terminal Services? (Choose all that apply.)

   A. Use of older workstation PCs is supported.

   B. A higher-performance server is required.

   C. Administrators can watch user sessions.

   D. Less training required for employees.

17. What port number is used by Remote Desktop and Terminal Services?

   A. 443

   B. 3389

   C. 389

   D. 1701

SELF TEST ANSWERS

Remote Connectivity Concepts

1. ☑ **D.** The National ISDN 1 (NI-1) standard was defined by the industry so that users would not have to know the type of switch to which they are connected in order to buy equipment and software compatible with it.

   ☒ **A, B,** and **C** are incorrect because NI-1 is the term used for ISDN.

2. ☑ **C.** PRI is intended for users with greater bandwidth requirements. It requires T1 carriers to facilitate communications. Normally, the channel structure contains 23 B channels plus one 64 Kbps D channel, for a total of 1536 Kbps.

   ☒ **A, B,** and **D** are incorrect numbers of B channels.

Remote Access Service (RAS)

3. ☑ **A.** The Serial Line Internet Protocol, or SLIP, is a communications protocol used for making a TCP/IP connection over a serial interface to a remote network. SLIP was designed for connecting to remote UNIX servers across a standard phone line. This protocol was one of the first of its kind, enabling a remote network connection to be established over a standard phone line.

   ☒ **B, C,** and **D** are incorrect because IPX/SPX and NetBEUI cannot run over SLIP. PPP is incorrect because it is not a network protocol, but a RAS protocol that competes with SLIP.

4. ☑ **B.** PPP established other standards, including asynchronous and bit-orientated synchronous encapsulation, network protocol multiplexing, session negotiation, and data-compression negotiation. PPP also supports protocols other than TCP/IP, such as IPX/SPX and DECnet.

   ☒ **A, C,** and **D** are incorrect because SLIP is limited to running on TCP/IP networks. IPX and NetBEUI are standard network protocols, not protocols for RAS.

5. ☑ **A** and **B.** The following text explains the three components of PPP and their purpose: PPP uses the High-Level Data-Link Control (HDLC) protocol as the basis to encapsulate its data during transmission; PPP uses the Link Control Protocol (LCP) to establish, test, and configure the data link connection; various network control protocols (NCPs) are used to configure the different communications protocols. This enables you to use different protocols such as TCP/IP and IPX over the same line simultaneously.

   ☒ **C** and **D** are incorrect because they are not a part of the Point-to-Point Protocol.

6. ☑ **B.** The Internet Protocol Control Protocol (IPCP) is the NCP used to configure, enable, and disable the IP protocol modules at each end of the link.

   ☒ **A, C,** and **D** are incorrect because **B** is correct and neither of the others exists.

7. ☑ **A and C.** With PPP, each system could be required to authenticate itself. This can be done using an authentication protocol. The most common authentication protocols include the Password Authentication Protocol (PAP), the Challenge Handshake Authentication Protocol (CHAP), and the Microsoft adaptation of CHAP, MS-CHAP.

☒ **B and D** are incorrect because domain authentication is used to validate a user, not the connection, and KPA does not exist.

8. ☑ **A.** Windows XP allows you to create a VPN server or RAS server that allows one connection. You may create these servers through the New Connection Wizard.

☒ **B, C, and D** are incorrect.

Dial-Up Networking

9. ☑ **C.** When logging has been enabled, you can see the log file after the next attempt to connect to a PPP server. The log file, modemlog_modemname.txt, is stored in the Windows directory by default. It can be viewed by any standard text editor and is appended to each time a new connection is attempted.

☒ **A, B, and D** are incorrect because none of them is the name of the log file that modem logging appends logging information to.

10. ☑ **D.** The New Connection Wizard found in your network connections window allows you to create new connections that connect to a RAS or VPN server.

☒ **A, B, and C** are all incorrect because you do not create new connections that way.

11. ☑ **C.** TAPI also provides other features, such as multiple calling locations. You can set up different connection profiles for different dial-up access numbers. You can also customize how the number is dialed. For example, if you set up two separate connection profiles, one with call waiting enabled and the second without it, you can manage multiple connections without having to reconfigure your modem setup every time you need a variation.

☒ **A** is incorrect because Unimodem is a part of Windows that allows for a single installation and configuration of a modem. **B** is incorrect because COMM is not a valid choice, since it is not a common program name with Windows; it is a driver name. **D** is incorrect because there is a correct answer choice.

Virtual Private Networks (VPNs)

12. ☑ **B.** PPTP tunneling is used in TCP/IP networks as an alternative to conventional dial-up networking methods. This enables multiprotocol secure communications over a public TCP/IP network such as the Internet. PPTP takes advantage of an additional level of security that is not currently available in other standard implementations.

☒ **A, C, and D** are incorrect because none of the other choices provides a secure link.

13. ☑ **A and C.** VPNs establish tunnels by using VPN protocols such as PPTP and L2TP.
☒ **B and D** are incorrect because they are RAS protocols, not VPN protocols.

14. ☑ **B.** When the PPP session is established, PPTP creates a control connection between the client and the remote PPTP server. This process is referred to as tunneling.
☒ **A** is incorrect because PPTP uses PPP to connect to a remote network. When connected, PPP is also used to encrypt the data packets being passed between the remote host and the local machine. **C** is incorrect because PPTP creates the IP datagrams for PPP to send. The packets are encrypted by PPP and sent through the tunnel to the PPTP server. The PPTP server is then used to decrypt the PPP-encrypted packets, disassemble the IP datagram, and route to the appropriate host. **D** is incorrect because the transfer of data is not started until the tunnel has been established.

Terminal Services

15. ☑ **A.** Terminal Services use RDP to send screen updates from the server back to the client.
☒ **D and C** are incorrect because they are not complete answers. **B** is incorrect because NetBEUI is a standard network protocol that is not used with Terminal Services.

16. ☑ **A, C, and D.** A Terminal Services environment allows for the use of older equipment and requires less training for users, who can continue to use their existing OS. Administrators are also able to watch user sessions and determine what users are doing as well as to help users who are unable to perform some functions.
☒ **B** is incorrect because a higher-performance server being required is a disadvantage.

17. ☑ **B.** Remote Desktop and Terminal Services use TCP port 3389.
A, C, and D are incorrect because they are not the port numbers used by Remote Desktop and Terminal Services.

9

Wide Area Network Technologies

W ith companies becoming larger and more geographically diverse, wide area networks (WANs) have become increasingly the norm for networks these days. Connecting two different LANs found at different locations within a company is a typical scenario for a WAN environment. For example, Company ABC may have two locations; one is New York and the other in Boston. The company wants the two locations to be able to communicate with one another without using the Internet. You, as the network administrator, will need to choose a WAN technology that connects these two LANs together, basing your decision on the performance and the cost of the technology.

This chapter identifies some of the popular technologies that are used in WAN environments—be sure to be familiar with them for the Network+ exam. Also note that organizations may connect their different offices together using RAS or ISDN technologies as discussed in Chapter 8—be sure to review those for the exam as well.

CERTIFICATION OBJECTIVE 9.01

Packet-Switching vs. Circuit-Switching Networks

This section introduces the concepts of packet-switching networking and circuit-switching networking technologies. Be sure to know these two terms for the Network+ exam.

Packet Switching

Packet switching is used by the Internet and routed networks. The path that is used to send data packets from one point to another through routers is not predetermined, meaning that each packet can take a different pathway to the destination. Packet-switched networks are efficient in that they consume bandwidth only when there is something to send. If you look at the routed network in Figure 9-1, you can see that from point A to point B there exist many paths for packets to travel.

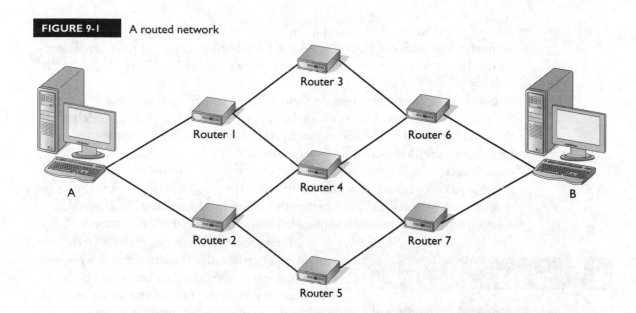

FIGURE 9-1   A routed network

When a user at PC A wants to copy a shared file from PC B, the data path is not a set path between specific routers. Packets are sent from router to router by the quickest or shortest path. If a router is extremely busy, it will not be used, and a different path will be chosen if one exists. Remember that other users are also sending data packets over the same media and routers.

Referring to Figure 9-1, let's now look at an example of how packet switching works. PC B sends its data to the router that is the least busy. For the first data packet, let us assume that it is Router 6. Now that Router 6 has the data packet, it looks at its routing table and determines that Router 3 might be the best way for it to reach PC A. Router 6 sends the data packet to Router 3, which in turn decides that the best path is to forward the packet on to Router 1. Router 1 then sends the packet to PC A. Now, the second packet might be sent to Router 7, because Router 6 has suddenly become very busy. Router 7 receives the data packet and forwards it to Router 4. Router 4 sends the packet to Router 2. Router 2 checks its routing table and sends the packet on to PC A. PC A then starts assembling the entire data file from the packets received. For the third data packet, let's say that it is also sent to Router 7, which sends it to Router 5 again. Now let's say that Router 2 has suddenly gone offline. Router 5 waits to contact Router 2, but eventually it is timed out and sends the data packet back to Router 7, which then tries to send the data packet to Router 4. Router 4 has since determined that Router 2 is offline and sends the data packet to Router 1. Router 1 sends the data packet to PC A. The fourth data packet is sent to Router 6, on to Router 3, then to Router 1, and finally is delivered to PC A.

Let's look more closely at packets 3 and 4: While packet 3 was detained at Router 5 because of the failure of Router 2, packet 4 was able to be delivered to PC A before the arrival of packet 3. This shows that a packet-switched network does not depend on packets being delivered in the order in which they were sent. Actually, if there are enough data paths, it is very common for packets to be received out of order. With routable protocols, data packets are numbered so they can be placed back in the proper order to create the original block of data that existed at the sending PC. It would be counterproductive to receive a jumbled database or an unreadable document.

e x a m
w a t c h
Packet switching is the process of breaking a transmission down into multiple packets, each potentially taking a different route to the destination network. The packets can be received out of order and are assembled at the destination.

Data packets are sent out of order on the Internet constantly. The only time this presents a problem is when the data being sent is streaming voice or video. If you have ever tried to use the Internet as a medium for making telephone calls, you know that the sound quality is not very good on slow network links, such as a 56 Kbps modem.

There are a number of packet-switched network technologies; a few examples of WAN technologies that employ packet-switched networks are Asynchronous Transfer Mode (ATM) and Frame Relay.

Circuit Switching

Circuit switching, on the other hand, is the foundation for the telephone system, but it is also widely used for data communications. When you make a telephone call from your home to someone next door or even 1000 miles away, a circuit is opened between your telephone and the telephone to which you are calling. The circuit is a dedicated pathway used by the communication and is not usable by others, so it is 100 percent dedicated for your use. As you speak, your voice is sent over the media to the other telephone and is not broken up or rerouted. Generally speaking, circuit switching is less efficient than packet switching in that the bandwidth is consumed whether or not there is data to transmit; however, this allows service providers to offer customers a guaranteed bandwidth.

One of the major problems with circuit switching occurs when a circuit fails—the circuit is a permanent path, and there is no redirection of data through another path unless a new circuit is created. For example, if you are speaking with someone on the phone and the line you're using was brought down by a fallen tree, your circuit will be broken and the line will go dead. You will have to hang up and place the call again. When you place the call again, a different circuit will be established and you will use that circuit for the duration of the communication.

e x a m

w a t c h
    Know the differences between packet-switching and circuit-switching networks. In addition, remember that data networks are usually packet-switched, whereas telephone connections are normally circuit-switched.

EXERCISE 9-1

Packet-Switching Network Exercise

In this exercise, you are given a scenario and a network diagram to determine the path of a data packet.

Your company has a headquarters and ten remote offices. All of the offices are connected by a packet-switching network to create a WAN. Look at Figure 9-2, and then answer the following questions.

PC A is at the main headquarters, and PC B is at one of the remote offices. Each router in the diagram designates an office. You are sending data from PC A to PC B, and you want to try to determine the path the data will take on its route. Using a diagnostic utility, you determine that all of the even-numbered routers are extremely busy and are sending slow transmissions from the local LAN and remote LANs.

1. What is the path that data packets could take from PC A to PC B?
2. Is it possible that the data packets could arrive out of order?
3. What are some reasons why Router 1 might be preferred over Router 3?
4. What path would be used if the odd-numbered routers were offline or busy, and the even-numbered routers were online and not busy?
5. What would occur if Routers 1, 2, and 3 were to become extremely busy or go offline?

FIGURE 9-2   A sample network used in the scenario of Exercise 9-1

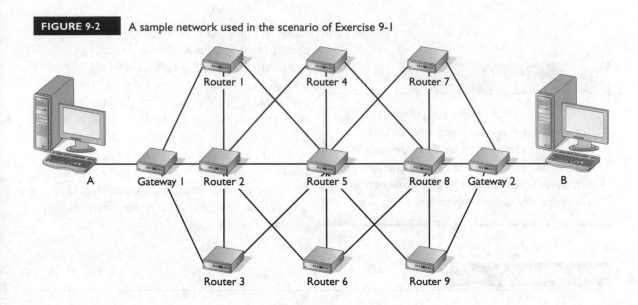

The answers are as follows:

1. The route would be from PC A to the default gateway, then to either Router 1 or Router 3. The packet will then travel from Router 1 or 3 to Router 5, and from Router 5 to Router 7 or Router 9. Then the data packet will go from Router 7 or 9 to the default gateway for PC B, and then to PC B.

2. Yes; since there are still multiple routes, one data path might be less busy than another at any given time. This could allow some data packets to arrive before others. For example, if Router 1 should suddenly become a little busier than Router 3, any packets sent to Router 3 might arrive before those sent to Router 1.

3. Router 3 might be busier than Router 1, which will cause a packet to be delayed a little while. The routers might be configured to have a specific method to determine which route to use as a default or to make one more used than another. This could cause one router to be used until it is too busy, at which point another will be used. The specified method could be determined by hop counts or by some other configured means.

4. From PC A the data packet would be passed to the default gateway, which would then be passed to Router 2. From Router 2, the data packet would be sent to either Router 4 or Router 6. Router 4 or Router 6 would send the

data packet to Router 8. Router 8 would send the data packets to the default gateway for PC B; at that point, the packet would be sent to PC B.

5. No data could be sent from PC A to PC B, because there is no open path from PC A to PC B.

CERTIFICATION OBJECTIVE 9.02

Asynchronous Transfer Mode

Asynchronous Transfer Mode (ATM) is a circuit-switching technology that uses a consistent packet size of 53 bytes, called a *cell*. A 53-byte cell is broken into a 48-byte payload and a 5-byte header. The lack of overhead in the ATM packet (it is always 53 bytes) helps promote the performance of this very fast LAN/WAN technology.

ATM can be used to enhance broadband ISDN to allow for the transmission of voice, data, and multimedia packets over the same media simultaneously. Broadband media use frequencies to be able to manage many "circuits" over one cable. Digital transmissions are electrical or light pulses of on or off, depending on the physical medium over which it is transferred. Broadband is how cable TV works, with multiple channels on one cable using different frequencies for each channel.

ATM will provide for high bandwidth as needed if enough users are requesting the bandwidth. ATM bandwidth ranges from slow speeds (around 12.96–25 Mbps using copper media such as category-3 UTP cable), to high speeds (around 622 Mbps using fiber-optic cable). With advances in technology, ATM speeds can reach 2.488 Gbps.

ATM can be used with physical interfaces such as FDDI and SONET/SDH, which are discussed further on in this chapter. This means that in an FDDI or SONET/SDH network ATM can be used on the network topology for data transmissions. When setting up a switched network similar to that shown in Figure 9-1, ATM can allow for parallel transmissions between nodes. This means that if data is being passed to and from PC A and PC B, the data packets can be

exam
watch

ATM is a WAN technology that allows for speeds of 622 Mbps or more. This fast, reliable WAN technology is great for sending voice or video across great distances.

passed between two routers (nodes) simultaneously. Remember that with ATM, data packets are referred to as cells, and each cell has a fixed length of 53 bytes. There are no variable-length cells as with some transmission standards. This allows all of the devices to be optimized for the specified cell size, thereby providing better performance. Once in place, an ATM network is transparent to users and provides for high data transmission speeds that can grow into a WAN when needed.

ATM can be used in LAN environments, but its use is uncommon due to the high price of ATM networking equipment such as ATM network cards and ATM hubs or switches. ATM also supports Quality of Service (QOS), which allows bandwidth to be allocated to different types of traffic.

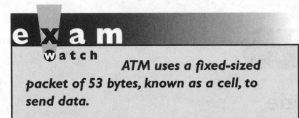

ATM uses a fixed-sized packet of 53 bytes, known as a cell, to send data.

To review the benefits of ATM check out Exercise 9-2 in LabBook.pdf found on the CD-ROM.

CERTIFICATION OBJECTIVE 9.03

Synchronous Optical Network/ Synchronous Digital Hierarchy

The Synchronous Optical Network (SONET) is a North American standard that allows the uniting of unlike transmissions into one single data stream. The Synchronous Digital Hierarchy (SDH) is the European standard designed for the same purpose as SONET. Basically, SONET allows multiple companies to transmit the packets on their networks onto a SONET backbone to be transmitted to a remote location using fiber-optic cabling. Because many companies might be using different network topologies and protocols, the data streams from each company would most likely differ. These companies can transmit their information over SONET without having to conform to a network standard. For example, one company might have a 10 Mbps category-5 Ethernet network using IPX/SPX, while another is using fiber-optic cable with TCP/IP. These can be combined into a single data stream (this is called multiplexing) for transmission over one cable. More companies can be added for transmission over the SONET medium without making any changes to any of the company networks.

This architecture allows for different media types and transmission types to be combined into one stream and sent over a fiber-optic cable. It is measured by optical carrier speed, which is the standard for fiber transmission. SONET runs at the lowest OC rate, which is a minimum speed of 54.04 Mbps, known as SONET-1.

SONET is divided into electrical levels that have varying speeds, termed synchronous transport signals (STSs). The highest level is SONET-192, with a speed of 9953.280 Mbps. SDH has no equivalent for SONET-1 at the speed of 51.84 Mbps, but has a low speed of 155.520 Mbps mapping to SONET-3. The different SDH levels are termed synchronous transfer modes (STMs). Table 9-1 lists the various levels.

The format for SONET is created by multiplexing all data signals into a single data stream called a synchronous transport signal (STS). The multiplexer is managed by the path-terminating equipment (PTE) from various media and transmission types, as shown in Figure 9-3. Now that the STS signal has been created, it must be transmitted on the SONET media. The STS transmission is managed by the line-terminating equipment (LTE), also shown in Figure 9-3. The LTE will send and receive the STS signal on both ends of the SONET media. Remember that the STS signal is in the form of electrical pulses. The SONET link might not be a single connection from one point to another, and entire segments might be composed of sections of SONET media. Therefore, to create the sections and have the entire segment appear as one physical link, section-terminating equipment (STE) is used to begin and end a section, as shown in Figure 9-3.

FIGURE 9-3   A sample network used in the scenario of Exercise 9-1

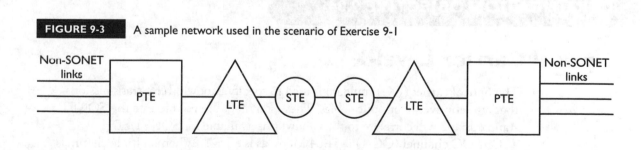

TABLE 9-1	SONET Electrical Level	SDH Level	Bandwidth
SONET and SDH Levels	STS-1	None	51.84 Mbps
	STS-3	STM-1	155.52 Mbps
	STS-9	STM-3	466.56 Mbps
	STS-12	STM-4	622.08 Mbps
	STS-18	STM-6	933.15 Mbps
	STS-24	STM-8	1244.16 Mbps
	STS-36	STM-12	1866.24 Mbps
	STS-48	STM-16	2488.32 Mbps
	STS-96	STM-32	4976.64 Mbps
	STS-192	STM-64	9953.28 Mbps

There is also a scrambling device that allows transmissions to be scrambled. The scrambling device must exist at both ends of the transmission to be able to descramble the stream back into usable data.

ATM (OSI layers 2 and 3) signals can be sent over a SONET/SDH link (OSI layer 1), as was discussed in the preceding section. In addition, PPP (OSI layers 2 and 3) can be transmitted over SONET/SDH.

e x a m

w a t c h

Remember the characteristics and speeds of SONET/SDH.

CERTIFICATION OBJECTIVE 9.04

Optical Carrier Level-X

The optical carrier (OC) standard is used to specify bandwidth for transmissions that are sent over fiber-optic cables. These standards are used to rate the SONET standards and will correlate to the bandwidths available for SONET/SDH.

One OC channel (OC-1) is 51.84 Mbps, as is STS-1. When multiple channels are used, the bandwidth increases by 51.84 Mbps per channel. For example, nine

TABLE 9-2	Optical Carrier Level	SONET Electrical Level	SDH Level	Bandwidth
OC Levels and How They Relate to the SONET/ SDH Transfer Rate	OC-1	STS-1	None	51.84 Mbps
	OC-3	STS-3	STM-1	155.52 Mbps
	OC-9	STS-9	STM-3	466.56 Mbps
	OC-12	STS-12	STM-4	622.08 Mbps
	OC-18	STS-18	STM-6	933.15 Mbps
	OC-24	STS-24	STM-8	1244.16 Mbps
	OC-36	STS-36	STM-12	1866.24 Mbps
	OC-48	STS-48	STM-16	2488.32 Mbps
	OC-96	STS-96	STM-32	4976.64 Mbps
	OC-192	STS-192	STM-64	9953.28 Mbps

OC channels (OC-9) are composed of nine OC-1 channels at 51.84 Mbps each. This results in a total bandwidth of 466.56 Mbps. The OC levels can be matched to the SONET levels, and to the SDH levels as shown in Table 9-2.

CERTIFICATION OBJECTIVE 9.05

X.25 and Frame Relay

This section will introduce you to two popular packet-switched WAN technologies known as X.25 and Frame Relay. The two technologies have been around for many years, and you may be asked a question or two on the exam about them.

X.25

X.25 is a packet-switched network that uses a device called a Packet Assembler/ Dissembler (PAD) to connect a system to the X.25 network. The PAD is a device that connects to serial ports of a device and is therefore considered RS-232 compliant.

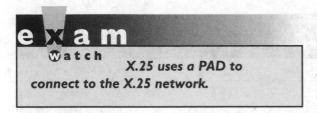

X.25 uses a PAD to connect to the X.25 network.

X.25 runs at layers 1, 2, and 3 of the OSI model and has transfer rates of 2 Mbps. Overall this technology is fairly old and slow compared with some of today's standards. Most X.25 implementations communicate over analog lines.

Frame Relay

Frame Relay is the digital version of X.25 and is much faster than X.25. Frame Relay runs at layers 1 and 2 of the OSI model and supports transfer rates as high as 50 Mbps along with features such as Quality of Service (QoS). It is a choice for WAN networking along with ATM, Broadcast ISDN (BISDN), and Cell Relay.

Frame Relay transmission speeds are not always constant. The data packets, or frames, are sent through a packet-switching network with higher-level protocols managing error checking, such as IPX/SPX or TCP/IP.

Frame Relay is a highly efficient method of transmitting data using bandwidth at an optimal level, allowing for bandwidths well over X.25's 2 Mbps. The nodes, which are used to route the frames in the packet-switching network, each use a routing algorithm that can help determine the efficiency of the Frame Relay network. Frame Relay does send frames as variable-length packets that are not all set at the same size before transmission.

If the bandwidth becomes too congested, Frame Relay will drop any frames that it cannot handle. This can include corrupted frames, as well as those that are unable to be delivered because the destination cannot be reached. Any dropped frames must be requested for retransmission by the protocols being used. When the available bandwidth is at a minimum, the source or destination can be notified to slow the transmissions to avoid overutilization of the bandwidth, which will keep packets from being dropped due to congestion. Although the source or destination is requested to slow the transmissions, the transmissions do not necessarily have to be slow.

To determine which packets are dropped, we must first be aware of who is transmitting over the Frame Relay network. Multiple companies can share a Frame Relay backbone to the Internet or between office buildings. Each company pays for a specific amount of the bandwidth on the Frame Relay medium. If the bandwidth is available, a company can use more bandwidth than that for which they have paid. Once other companies start using their bandwidth, all the companies will be limited to the bandwidth that has been committed to them. The bandwidth that each company pays for is noted by its Committed Information Rate (CIR). The CIR helps determine whether frames can be dropped when the bandwidth becomes congested.

The CIR is included in all frames sent by any company on the Frame Relay network. The Frame Relay nodes will keep statistics on network bandwidth and usage by all companies. If a company is using less bandwidth than what it paid for, its frames will be sent on through the node. If the company is using more bandwidth than the CIR designates, the frames are likely to be dropped.

w a t c h   *X.25 supports transfer rates of 2 Mbps and uses a serial device known as a Packet Assembler/Dissembler*   *(PAD), whereas Frame Relay supports speeds as high as 50 Mbps and is a digital version of X.25.*

To practice what you have learned about Frame Relay, check out Exercise 9-3 in LabBook.pdf on the CD-ROM.

CERTIFICATION OBJECTIVE 9.06

Fiber Distributed Data Interface (FDDI)

The Fiber Distributed Data Interface (FDDI) topology is sometimes referred to as a fast, redundant Token Ring network. FDDI is similar to a Token Ring network in the sense that it uses token passing as the access method, but there are two rings instead of the one found in Token Ring. FDDI uses fiber-optic cable operating at 100 Mbps. If copper cable is used, such as category 5 at 100 Mbps, the topology is termed a Copper Distributed Data Interface (CDDI).

Two rings are used in the FDDI architecture—the primary ring and the secondary ring. The primary ring is used at all times, and the secondary ring is used only if the primary ring fails. The token is passed on each ring in opposite directions.

FDDI is specifically for WAN use, not for LAN use. FDDI is used to connect multiple sites. Even if the individual LANs are using non–Token Ring topologies, they can still be connected by FDDI. Each building or office would have either a dual-attachment concentrator (DAC) that allows both rings to be connected to the

DAC or two single-attachment concentrators (SAC). The SAC connects to a single ring, allowing the SAC to be powered down without affecting the ring.

Now let's examine the FDDI redundancy and find out why the two rings operate in opposite directions. If any ring should break or if an SAC should be shut down, as shown in Figure 9-4 part A, the network will still operate. Operation will continue because the broken section will be bypassed by using the secondary ring to allow the network to go back on itself and function as a continual ring. In Figure 9-4 part B, you can see that part of the ring is broken, so part of the secondary ring will be used to create a complete ring. The reason that the rings must operate in opposite directions is to continue passing the token from one ring to another without causing the direction to change. This allows for continuity if both rings are broken or if a DAC goes offline. If a DAC goes offline, then both rings are "broken."

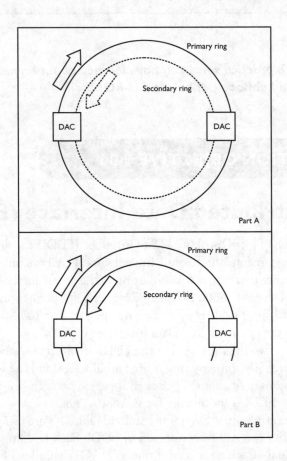

FIGURE 9-4

FDDI redundant rings

Each DAC will have two sets of connectors—one set for both rings coming in and one set for both rings going out. Now consider an example of three office buildings set up with FDDI and how redundancy works to keep them online.

Figure 9-5 shows the three DACs or SACs, depending on which they use. The three companies are all connected with dual rings.

The grayed (inside) areas show the secondary ring, which is not in use. Now, assume that the fiber optic cable is broken between Company B and Company C. Figure 9-6 shows what happens to the secondary ring when part of the primary fails and how the ring is still complete, thereby allowing the WAN to continue operating.

FDDI uses a fault-tolerant ring topology and fiber-optic cabling that reaches speeds of 100 Mbps.

Originally, the token is transferred from Company A to Company B, from Company B to Company C, and then from Company C to Company A. Once the token reaches Company A again, it continues the process. After the break and the redundancy feature starts, the token will go from Company A to Company B, then to Company A again and on to Company C, and back to Company A. Once at Company A, the process will continue until the break is fixed, and the token will be passed as it originally was before the cable break. Multiple cable breaks can take down the entire network or even cause multiple WANs to be created.

FIGURE 9-5

Functional FDDI example

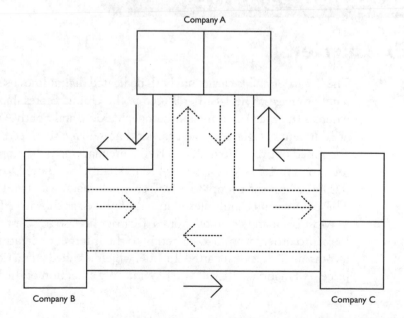

FIGURE 9-6

FDDI redundancy
example

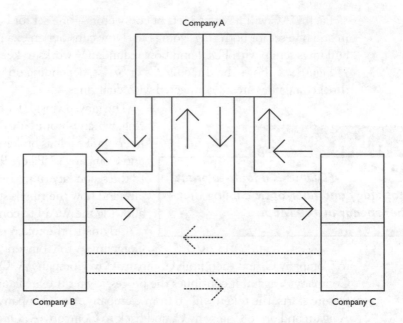

CERTIFICATION OBJECTIVE 9.07

Tx/Ex-Carriers

The T-carrier and E-carrier are both dedicated digital lines used to transmit voice, data, or images. The T-carrier is used in the United States, Japan, and Australia, whereas the E-carrier is used in Europe, Mexico, and South America. There are different categories of each carrier that indicate the speed of the line. T1 is composed of twenty-four channels that are made up of 64 Kbps bandwidth each, for a total of 1.544 Mbps. Each 64 Kbps channel is referred to as digital signal level 0 (DS0), with the twenty-four DS0 channels making a digital signal level 1 (DS1). These lines can be multiplexed into faster links, as shown in Table 9-3.

Most companies cannot afford a T-carrier line, so it is best for some companies to look into other means of connecting to the Internet or creating a WAN. If necessary, a company can lease a partial T1 line, which is called a Fractional T1, at a lower price. A Fractional T1 will also provide only a fraction of the bandwidth.

TABLE 9-3	T-Carrier	Bandwidth
Tx-Carriers and Bandwidth	T1	1.544 Mbps
	T1C	3.152 Mbps
	T2	6.312 Mbps
	T3	44.736 Mbps
	T4	274.176 Mbps

The E1-carrier is similar to the T-carrier, but differs in bandwidth. An E1-carrier is composed of thirty 64 Kbps data channels with two 64 Kbps channels for signaling. The E1-carrier has a total bandwidth of 2.048 Mbps. The E3-carrier is composed of sixteen T1-carrier channels for a total bandwidth of 34.368 Mbps. The Ex-carriers are listed in Table 9-4 with their total bandwidth.

CSU/DSU

The Channel Service Unit/Data Service Unit (CSU/DSU) is a device that allows a business to connect a high-speed data link from the telephone company to the business's router for access to and from the LAN or WAN. The high-speed connections are usually T1 or T3 connections or their European counterparts, E1 and E3. The CSU/DSU used will be specific to the speed of the line being connected to from the telephone company.

TABLE 9-4	E-Carrier	Bandwidth
Ex-Carrier and Bandwidth	E1	2.048 Mbps
	E2	8.448 Mbps
	E3	34.368 Mbps
	E4	139.264 Mbps
	E5	565.148 Mbps

The CSU is the user end of the high-speed connection that will perform encoding and line conditioning as well as protect the LAN or WAN from electrical interference such as lightning. It can also provide statistics for line use. There is also the capability of a loopback test to assure that the high-speed data connection is still intact. The DSU portion is on the side of the telephone company and supports timing functions as well as data conversion.

CERTIFICATION OBJECTIVE 9.08

Internet Access Technologies

There are a number of technologies that are used to connect to the Internet, including some of the high-speed Internet technologies that are used by small businesses or home users. These technologies include ADSL and Cable Modem Internet connections.

ADSL

Asymmetric Digital Subscriber Line (ADSL) is a high-speed Internet service that allows the transfer of data over the phone lines. ADSL is provided by telecom providers and allows the ADSL subscriber to use the phone and the Internet simultaneously with download speeds as high as 9 Mbps and upload speeds around 1 Mbps (hence asymmetric). The transfer rates differ for each service provider.

An ADSL subscriber connects his or her PC to the larger telephone network by connecting to a central office (CO) that must be located within a 5 km distance of the subscriber. A special modem, known as an ADSL modem, is used to connect the ADSL user to a local CO. If there is not a CO close to a user's location, that user would be unable to subscribe to the service.

ADSL Hardware

In order for the ADSL subscriber to connect to the local CO, a splitter will be connected to the phone jack in the wall. The splitter will then connect to the phone and also to the ADSL modem, as shown in Figure 9-7. This splitter is essentially a frequency filter. The human voice falls between 0 and 3.4 KHz, so the splitter sends transmissions below 3.4 KHz to the telephone, and transmissions above

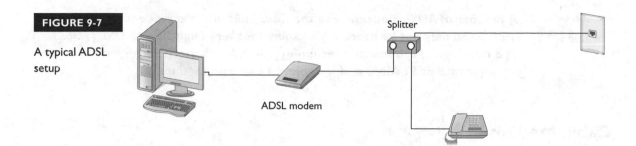

A typical ADSL
setup

3.4 KHz are sent to and from the ADSL modem. The ADSL modem has an RJ-45
jack that is used to connect to the network card in the PC. It is not really a modem
in the sense of a modem that converts digital signals to analog signs; this modem is
really just acting as a terminal adapter.

Asymmetric Digital Subscriber Line (ADSL) uses different download and upload speeds (asymmetric), whereas Symmetric Digital	*Subscriber Line (SDSL) uses an equivalent upload and download bandwidth; home users typically use ADSL, but businesses most often use SDSL.*

Figure 9-8 displays an actual ADSL modem and splitter. The splitter, if needed,
would connect to the phone jack in the wall, and then the computer would connect
to the ADSL modem.

An ADSL
frequency filter
and an ADSL
modem

on the job

A number of ADSL modems have the filter built into the modem, so the filter wall plate may not be needed. Also know that Very High Bitrate DSL (VDSL) is a new high-speed Internet technology that, for short distances, can offer a transfer rate of 52 Mbps and is deployed over copper lines.

Cable Modem

If the phone companies are going to offer high-speed Internet service through the phone lines, you can bet that the cable companies would come up with a broadband, high-speed Internet solution using the coaxial cable TV lines. The cable companies connect you to the Internet over their lines by using a cable modem that connects to the workstation using TP cabling, but then the modem connects to the cable jack in the wall using coaxial cable (as shown in Figure 9-9).

The cable provider supplies each channel on the cable in its own 6 MHz frequency range, and the signal for a particular channel is sent to you in that range. Cable companies supply the Internet data as its own channel, a 6 MHz frequency range being used to send data to your cable modem. Download speeds of cable modems have reached 10 Mbps but may differ with the different suppliers.

One of the drawbacks of the cable modem is that you are sharing this bandwidth with your neighbors if they have subscribed to this Internet service as well. If you have a neighbor that constantly downloads large amounts of data, you may find that times are slow on the occasions when your neighbor uses the precious bandwidth. Keep in mind that the Internet provider can simply provide the data through an additional channel to keep up with neighborhood demands if the provider chooses to do so!

There is an advantage to cable modems and that is that unlike ADSL, you do not need to be within close proximity of a CO. As long as you are receiving cable and your cable provider supplies Internet, you should be able to subscribe to high-speed Internet service. Figure 9-10 displays a cable modem.

FIGURE 9-9

A typical cable modem setup

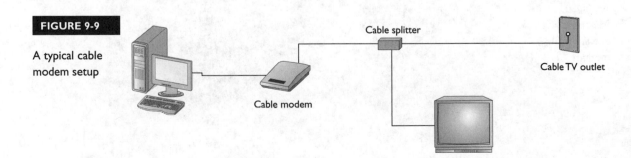

Cable splitter

Cable TV outlet

Cable modem

FIGURE 9-10

A cable modem

High Speed Through Satellite

How can you get high-speed Internet service if you are in a rural area that does not have access to high speed through ADSL or cable modems? There is an option for getting high speed through the use of satellites, which provide download speeds as high as 500 Kbps. Although not as quick as ADSL or cable modems, satellite can provide service to areas that are typically unserviceable and is much faster than the conventional 56 Kbps modem.

Satellite Internet uses a satellite dish that is about two feet high by three feet wide and uses two modems, one for downloads and one for uploads. The modems are typically connected to the satellite dish through coaxial cable.

Other Methods of Internet Access

There are a variety of other methods to connect the Internet if you don't have access to an ADSL or cable modem connection. The following is a list of potential methods to connect to the Internet in addition to those mentioned previously:

- **POTS/PSTN** The plain old telephone service/public switched telephone network provides access through conventional telephone lines using a modem to receive transfer rates as high as 56 Kbps.

- **Wireless** A number of wireless providers now give mobile access to handheld devices.

CERTIFICATION SUMMARY

Networks have become such an important element in the business world that most businesses could not survive the loss of their network. Wide area networks (WANs) have evolved to allow the connection of multiple local area networks (LANs) that are not within close proximity. WANs allow the multiple LANs to operate as a single large network for growing companies.

The different WAN technologies include Asynchronous Transfer Mode (ATM), which can also be used to create a LAN. ATM provides bandwidth on demand for users using an optical network. ATM can provide transfer rates as high as 622 Mbps.

Another WAN technology is SONET/SDH, which uses optical carrier (OC) levels. These use fiber-optic cables to transfer data from different media. Data streams can be taken from different media and combined into one data stream, allowing for transmission speeds from 51.84 Mbps to 9953.28 Mbps. The non-SONET media are connected to a physical terminating equipment (PTE) device, which converts the electrical signals into optical signals. The optical signal is sent to the line-terminating equipment (LTE), which transmits the signal over different sections of fiber-optic cable. The many different sections of fiber-optic cable making up the SONET network are terminated by section-terminating equipment (STE). The OC levels are standards used to specify bandwidth over fiber-optic cable.

Another WAN technology is Frame Relay. Frame Relay is a leased-line solution whereby a company can share the medium and the cost with other companies. The amount of bandwidth available to a company is determined by the amount of bandwidth for which it pays.

FDDI is another WAN technology that is based on the Token Ring topology. It operates at 100 Mbps over fiber-optic or category-5 cables. A setup using category-5 cables is known as a Copper Distributed Data Interface (CDDI). FDDI is composed of two rings operating in different directions. The second ring is used only if the first ring fails.

Popular transmission methods are T-carriers and E-carriers. Each carrier is used in different countries with different bandwidths. The T- and E-carriers are completely digital and operate at speeds as high as 565.148 Mbps.

High-speed Internet services can be provided through ADSL or cable modem. ADSL provides download speeds at approximately 9 Mbps and runs the voice and data services over the copper telephone wires at various frequencies. The cable companies provide high-speed Internet services with download speeds of about 10 Mbps; they supply this data to your home using a different channel on the coaxial cable.

TWO-MINUTE DRILL

Packet-Switching vs. Circuit-Switching Networks

❑ Packet-switching networks use whatever pathway is best at the time to reach the destination network, whereas circuit switching uses a dedicated pathway for the duration of the communication.

❑ Packet switching is a more efficient use of bandwidth than circuit switching.

❑ Packet-switching networks might not deliver packets in the order they were sent.

Asynchronous Transfer Mode

❑ ATM is used by applications that require high amounts of bandwidth.

❑ ATM has a transfer rate of 622 Mbps.

❑ Data packets are referred to as cells and are a consistent 53 bytes in size.

Synchronous Optical Network/Synchronous Digital Hierarchy

❑ SONET is used to unify unlike transmissions into one transmission data stream.

❑ SONET uses fiber-optic cable for transmissions.

❑ SDH is the European standard for SONET.

❑ Bandwidth ranges from 51.84 Mbps to 9953.28 Mbps.

Optical Carrier Level-x

❑ OC is used to specify bandwidth standards over fiber-optic media.

❑ The OC levels are used by SONET and SDH levels.

❑ OC-1 is 51.84 Mbps.

❑ OC-3 is 155.52 Mbps.

❑ OC-48 is 2.488 Gbps.

X.25 and Frame Relay

❑ X.25 uses a PAD to connect the client to the X.25 network.

❑ X.25 supports speeds of 2 Mbps.

❑ Frame Relay is the digital version of X.25 and runs at speeds up to 50 Mbps.

❑ Error correction used by Frame Relay is monitored by higher-layer protocols.

❑ Frame Relay supports QoS.

Fiber Distributed Data Interface (FDDI)

❑ FDDI uses token passing and the ring topology over fiber-optic cabling.

❑ There are two rings operating in opposite directions.

❑ FDDI is for WAN, not LAN, use.

❑ Two rings allow for redundancy.

T*x*/E*x*-Carriers

❑ T*x*/E*x*-Carriers are widely used and very popular.

❑ They are used as a backbone by telephone companies.

❑ They are very expensive.

Internet Access Technologies

❑ Two popular Internet access methods currently in use are ADSL and cable modem.

❑ ADSL provides high-speed Internet service over the phone lines, whereas cable modem uses the television cable.

❑ ADSL provides voice and data over the same wire at the same time while running both at different frequencies.

❑ The cable company supplies the Internet data as another channel. Just as you can receive signals for channel 4, you can receive the "Internet channel."

SELF TEST

The following Self Test questions will help you measure your understanding of the material presented in this chapter. Read all the choices carefully, as there may be more than one correct answer. Choose all correct answers for each question.

Packet-Switching vs. Circuit-Switching Networks

1. Which switching technology is used by the telephone company?

   A. Packet

   B. Circuit

   C. WAN

   D. Hub

2. Which switching method allows for data transmissions even when part of the network fails?

   A. Packet

   B. Circuit

   C. WAN

   D. Hub

Asynchronous Transfer Mode

3. In which area networking environments is ATM usable?

   A. Dial-up

   B. Workgroup

   C. WAN

   D. LAN

4. What is the size of a cell in an ATM network?

   A. 48 bytes

   B. 5 bytes

   C. 53 bytes

   D. 512 bytes

Synchronous Optical Network/Synchronous Digital Hierarchy

5. How many streams does the SONET network transfer?

A. 1

B. 2

C. 3

D. 4 or more

6. Which of the following is in the form of electrical pulses on a SONET network?

A. STM

B. STS

C. PTE

D. LTE

7. What can be used in a SONET network to allow a user's data to remain private?

A. Multiplexer

B. PTE

C. LTE

D. Scrambler

8. What is the speed of one SONET level?

A. 32.24 Mbps

B. 51.84 Mbps

C. 64.08 Mbps

D. 155.52 Mbps

Optical Carrier Level-X

9. What levels are the OC levels matched to?

A. ATM

B. SDH

C. SONET

D. T1

10. What is the highest OC level?

A. 32

B. 64

C. 128

D. 192

X.25 and Frame Relay

11. How is error checking managed on a Frame Relay network?

- **A.** By network devices
- **B.** By the user at the sending PC
- **C.** By the user at the receiving PC
- **D.** By the protocol used

12. If the network is congested and the destination device requests that the source device slow its transmission, what will occur?

- **A.** The source will stop responding for 30 seconds and then continue transmitting.
- **B.** The source will find a different route to send the data.
- **C.** The destination will drop all packets for 30 seconds.
- **D.** Possibly nothing.

13. What happens if a company uses more bandwidth than it has paid for?

- **A.** Its packets will be dropped no matter the state of the network.
- **B.** Its packets will be delivered even if the network is busy.
- **C.** Its packets will be delivered if the bandwidth is available.
- **D.** Its packets will be delivered no matter the state of the network.

Fiber Distributed Data Interface (FDDI)

14. If the primary ring fails, what is used for redundancy?

- **A.** The entire secondary ring
- **B.** A portion of the primary ring that has not failed, and a part of the secondary ring that is equal to the primary ring that failed
- **C.** A portion of the primary ring that has not failed, and a part of the secondary ring that is equal to the primary ring that has not failed
- **D.** A portion of the primary ring that failed, and a part of the secondary ring that is equal to the primary ring that has failed

15. How does the token pass on the rings when functioning normally?

- **A.** From one ring to the other
- **B.** Randomly
- **C.** In opposite directions
- **D.** In the same direction

16. At what speed does FDDI operate?
    A. 10 Mbps
    B. 100 Mbps
    C. 1 Gbps
    D. 2 Gbps

Tx/Ex-Carriers

17. In what countries do E-carriers operate? (Choose all that apply.)
    A. Japan
    B. Europe
    C. Mexico
    D. South America

18. How many channels make up a T1?
    A. 6
    B. 12
    C. 24
    D. 48

Internet Access Technologies

19. Which high-speed Internet service uses the phone lines?
    A. Cable modem
    B. T1
    C. T3
    D. ADSL

20. Which high-speed Internet service supplies the Internet data as its own channel over the television cable?
    A. Cable modem
    B. T1
    C. T3
    D. ADSL

21. At which frequency is the Internet data supplied with ADSL?
    A. 0–3.4 KHz
    B. Above 3.4 KHz
    C. 9–12 KHz
    D. 100–200 KHz

SELF TEST ANSWERS

Packet-Switching vs. Circuit-Switching Networks

1. ☑ **B.** Circuit switching is used by the telephone companies for the network of telephone users.
☒ **A, C,** and **D** are incorrect. Packet switching is used by most data networks. WANs and hubs are not switching types of WAN technology.

2. ☑ **A.** With a packet-switching network, the failed portion will be routed around the point of failure to continue to deliver packets.
☒ **B, C,** and **D** are incorrect. In a circuit-switched network, the connection will be terminated. For example, if you are speaking with someone on the telephone and a telephone line breaks, the call is terminated and must be made again. WANs and hubs are not switching types of WAN technology.

Asynchronous Transfer Mode

3. ☑ **C** and **D** are correct. ATM technology can be used to create LANs and connect them to a WAN.
☒ **A** and **B** are incorrect. Dial-up is a type of connection made from one PC to another, or even possibly a LAN to a LAN. A workgroup is a group of ten or fewer PCs that are connected to share resources with no centralized administration point.

4. ☑ **C.** ATM uses consistent 53-byte cells.
☒ **A, B,** and **D** are incorrect. The payload in the cell is 48 bytes, and the header is 5 bytes, totaling 53 bytes.

Synchronous Optical Network/Synchronous Digital Hierarchy

5. ☑ **A.** The SONET network will multiplex multiple streams into one stream and transmit this single stream over the SONET network. Multiple streams can be combined to form the single SONET data stream.
☒ **B, C,** and **D** are incorrect amounts.

6. ☑ **B.** The synchronous transport signal (STS) is in the form of electrical pulses.
☒ **A, C,** and **D** are incorrect. The electrical pulses are converted by the PTE into one stream and are sent to the LTE as light pulses on fiber-optic cable. STM is a term used to denote the different levels of SDH.

7. ☑ **D.** The scrambler is used to randomize the stream pattern to allow the data to be encrypted. This requires a descrambler on the other end of the connection to convert the data into a usable form.
   ☒ **A, B,** and **C** are incorrect. The multiplexer is used to generate one data stream from many data streams. The electrical pulses are converted by the PTE into one stream and are sent to the LTE as light pulses on fiber-optic cable.

8. ☑ **B.** One SONET level is 51.84 Mbps. If more are added, the value is multiplied by the number of levels.
   ☒ **A, C,** and **D** are incorrect speeds.

Optical Carrier Level-X

9. ☑ **B** and **C** are correct. The OC levels are standards for transmitting over fiber-optic cable. The levels match those of SONET and SDH, which require fiber optics.
   ☒ **A** and **D** are incorrect. ATM and T1 do not have the same standards.

10. ☑ **D.** 192 is the highest level currently set for OC.
    ☒ **A, B,** and **C** are incorrect; they are not the highest OC levels.

X.25 and Frame Relay

11. ☑ **D.** Frame Relay depends on the protocols used to manage error checking.
    ☒ **A, B,** and **C** are incorrect because Frame Relay depends on the protocols used to manage error checking.

12. ☑ **D.** Just because a device is requested to slow transmissions, that does not mean the device will perform the action.
    ☒ **A, B,** and **C** are incorrect; they are not valid choices.

13. ☑ **C.** The packets will be delivered if the bandwidth is available; if it is not, they will be dropped.
    ☒ **A, B,** and **D** are incorrect. The state of the network must be taken into account.

Fiber Distributed Data Interface (FDDI)

14. ☑ **C.** The part that is used for redundancy is the portion of the primary ring that has not failed as well as the same part of the secondary ring that has not failed.
    ☒ **A, B,** and **D** are incorrect. No part of the failed portion of the primary ring can be used, and neither can the same portion of the secondary ring.

15. ☑ **C.** The token is circulated in opposite directions. This helps to keep the flow of the token the same on both rings even after a failure.

☒ **A, B,** and **D** are incorrect. The token passes only from one ring to the other when a failure has occurred. The token is not randomly moved, nor does the token move in the same direction on both rings.

16. ☑ **B.** FDDI operates at 100 Mbps, whether it is fiber or copper cabling.

☒ **A, C,** and **D** are incorrect speeds.

Tx/Ex-Carriers

17. ☑ **B, C,** and **D** are correct. E-carriers are found in Europe, Mexico, and South America.

☒ **A** is incorrect. T-carriers are found in the United States, Japan, and Australia.

18. ☑ **C.** There are 24 channels that are 64 Kbps each to make one T1 for a total of 1.544 Mbps.

☒ **A, B,** and **D** are incorrect channel amounts.

Internet Access Technologies

19. ☑ **D.** ADSL is the high-speed Internet service provided by the phone companies that runs over the phone lines.

☒ **A, B,** and **C** are incorrect because they are not Internet services provided over the phone lines.

20. ☑ **A.** The cable modem receives data over the television cable as its own 6 Mhz channel.

☒ **B, C,** and **D** are incorrect because they are not Internet services provided as their own channel over the television cable. ADSL is an Internet service, but it uses the phone lines.

21. ☑ **B.** ADSL supplies the Internet data over the phone line by using frequencies above 3.4 KHz.

☒ **A, C,** and **D** are incorrect because they are not the frequencies used to send Internet data. Voice travels over the phone lines at frequencies from 0 to 3 KHz.

10

Implementing a Network

Y ou have learned about networking hardware components such as routers, switches, hubs, and network cabling thus far in the book. Being able to identify these components and connect them together is just a small part of implementing the network; you also need to install and configure the network operating system (NOS) on the server to publish resources out to the network.

In this chapter you will learn to implement a network by installing the network operating system, creating user accounts and groups, and subsequently assigning permissions to those user accounts for network resources such as files, folders, and printers.

CERTIFICATION OBJECTIVE 10.01

Installing a Network

Installing the network is one of the first job responsibilities that you may have as a network professional. This duty may include purchasing server hardware, the server NOS, and client desktop systems. You will also need to make choices regarding the type of network you wish to install—will you choose a Novell, Microsoft, or Linux networking environment? Will you go with a peer-to-peer or client/server network? Will you have a mixed environment with a few Microsoft servers and a few Linux or Novell servers? This section will help you answer these questions.

Networking Options

Looking back to Chapter 1, you learned the difference between a peer-to-peer networking environment and a server-based one. You will now need to choose which type of network you intend to build. If you choose to build a peer-to-peer network, you will not be required to purchase server hardware and the network operating system, thereby reducing cost. The disadvantage of a peer-to-peer network is that it is typically limited to ten systems.

If you choose to go with a server-based network, you will need to purchase the server hardware and the server network operating system, so you can expect some additional cost. You will also need to obtain client access licenses. A client access license (CAL) is needed to allow the client to connect to the network operating system. It is important to understand that just because you have purchased the server operating system, that does not mean that you can allow everyone to access data on the server. You will need to purchase a CAL for each client connecting.

Let us say that we have decided to go with a server-based network. When it comes to server-based networking environments, you have three popular types to choose from—Microsoft, Novell, and Linux.

Microsoft Networking

When it comes to networking, Microsoft networking environments have a big market share these days, with Windows Server 2003 being the most popular Windows server version on existing networks. Windows Server 2008 is the newest version of Microsoft's network operating system as of the date of this writing. When you install a Microsoft server, you will have to make a number of choices such as deciding whether to install a standalone server, a member server, or a domain controller.

Standalone System   A *standalone* server is a server that has a local Security Accounts Manager (SAM) database similar to a Windows XP system. The SAM database is a database of accounts that resides on the local system and is used to access resources on the local system only. This is very similar to having a number of Windows XP systems in a workgroup (peer-to-peer) environment—the accounts are not "network" accounts; they are local accounts.

You may install a standalone server if this server is to act as your web server or firewall system. Typically, these systems are not part of the normal "Microsoft network," otherwise called a domain, because they are connected to the Internet.

Domain Controller   A *domain controller (DC)* is a server that has Microsoft's directory service installed, known as Active Directory. The Active Directory database is the term used by Microsoft for the network account database. If you are authenticated by, or you log on to, the Active Directory database, you can access resources across the network. The account is not used just to access resources on the local system, as is the case with the standalone system.

When a user logs on to the network, the logon request is sent to the domain controller on the network where the account information is verified. Once the domain controller has verified the information, the user can access network resources to which they have access anywhere on the network. The term for this Microsoft network is a domain.

When installing a Microsoft domain environment, you need to be familiar with a few more terms—trees and forests. It is possible that a large organization may want to create a network environment that contains multiple domains. The following terms relate to Microsoft network environments:

■ **Domain** A logical grouping of computers and resources. Users log on to the domain and can be authenticated by any domain controller in the domain. A domain is a security boundary and a replication boundary.

■ **Trees** A hierarchy of domains that have a contiguous DNS namespace. For example, if you have a domain named companyabc.loc, you may have a child domain for each region such as eastern, central, or western, or maybe for each country, such as the United States and Canada. Each domain will have a full domain name that includes the domain name joined by the parent domain (companyabc.loc) as shown in Figure 10-1.

■ **Forest** A forest is made up of one or more trees. In the Active Directory world you will always have a domain, a tree, and a forest. It is just a question of how many domains make up this tree-and-forest structure. Each tree in the forest has its own DNS namespace and has a trust relationship to the forest root domain (the first domain installed in the forest).

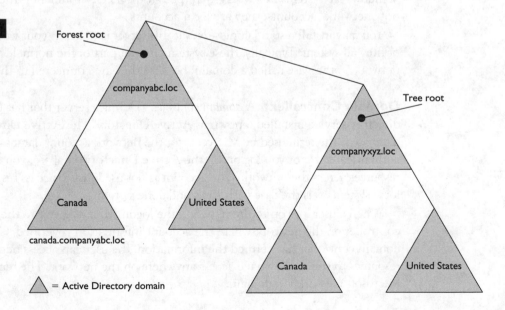

FIGURE 10-1

An Active Directory forest with two trees

Member Server   A *member* server is a machine that is part of a domain, or a member of the domain, and typically is a resource that users would access once they have been authenticated by a domain controller. A member server may be a server that is in the domain that performs any kind of function on the network, such as being a file and print server, a database server, or an e-mail server. The difference between a member server and a standalone server is simply that a standalone server is not part of a domain, so it cannot take advantage of the fact that a domain controller has authenticated the user. This means that the standalone server is responsible for authenticating the user when someone connects to the system. Figure 10-2 displays a typical domain environment in the Microsoft world.

FIGURE 10-2

A typical
Microsoft
network

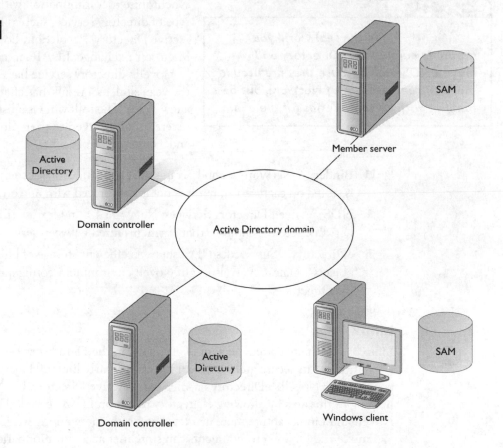

Novell NetWare

Novell's NetWare has been one of the leading networking environments for many years. Novell's directory service is currently called "eDirectory." Like Active Directory, it is a database of network accounts that is automatically synchronized with other servers. One or more NetWare servers sharing the same eDirectory database is called an eDirectory Tree. The administrator decides which servers in which geographic locations will hold a copy of the eDirectory database. One of the major benefits of eDirectory is that you are not limited to installing it on NetWare servers. eDirectory can be installed on NetWare servers, Windows servers, Linux servers, and UNIX servers.

In the real world you probably care about eDirectory and maybe NDS only because they are used in more current versions of NetWare, but be familiar with all three terms for the exam.

With NetWare 6.5, Novell includes a number of dirXML drivers, which allow eDirectory to synchronize user information with any other type of directory service, such as Microsoft Active Directory, PeopleSoft, LotusNotes, Microsoft Exchange, LDAP servers, and so on.

Novell's directory service has evolved over the years and, as a result, has changed names a few times. The following is a listing of the different names given to their directory service and a description of each:

- **Bindery** NetWare 2.*x* and 3.*x* use this; it is a network account database that is stored on each server, but it is not synchronized with any other servers.
- **NDS** Novell Directory Services; NetWare 4.*x* and 5.*x* use this—it is a network account database that is synchronized between servers.
- **eDirectory** Supersedes NDS; supports efficient storage of billions of objects—almost every aspect of Novell environment configurations is stored in eDirectory.

Linux

Linux is starting to command a lot of attention in the IT industry because of its reliability and its secure architecture. Linux has a fairly limited directory service compared to Novell's eDirectory or Microsoft's Active Directory, but Novell is helping in this area by allowing eDirectory to run on Linux servers. This will help Novell and Linux capture more market share in the networking world.

Linux (and UNIX) environments can store user account information in files (/etc/passwd holds user account information, /etc/shadow holds encrypted user passwords, and /etc/group holds group membership information). Without a directory service, this information is specific to each server. Network Information Service (NIS) is commonly used to replicate user account information between servers, but many vendors, such as Sun and IBM, offer modified and enhanced versions of NIS for this purpose.

Network Requirements

This section introduces the hardware and software requirements for building a network. We will review the hardware that is required and then discuss the software requirements needed for a network. This section is in effect a summary of the network components you have already learned about in Chapter 3.

Networking Hardware

The first thing that you will need in each of the systems or hosts that will participate on the network is a network interface card, which is the means the system uses to send and receive data on the network. You will also need to have a hub or a switch to act as a central connection point for all the systems. If your systems are going to send data to another network, you will need a router as well. Figure 10-3 displays the general setup of the networking hardware.

FIGURE 10-3

The networking hardware used to complete the network

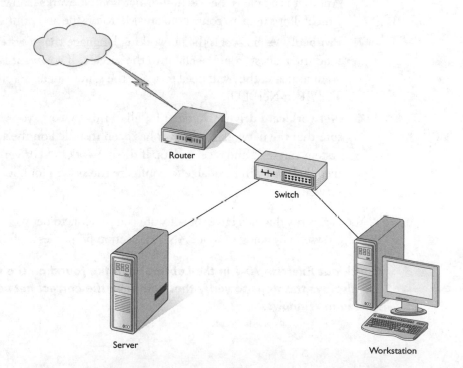

The networking server will also need to have its specs measured out. Today's server will include a RAID controller card that connects and manages the RAID drives. There should be more than 1GB of RAM, depending on the role of the server. If the server is intended to act as a mail server or a database server, you may want a few gigabytes of memory as well as multiple CPUs on the motherboard.

Networking Software

It is extremely important to understand what the network's software requirements are. Certainly, you will need all four of the following software components somewhere on the network.

- **Service** A *service* is what is being provided to clients on the network—it is typically the reason for the network. For example, most networks have a server that offers file and printer sharing services, or maybe web services that offer web pages to web clients on the network. Without a service there is no purpose to the network.

- **Client** A *client* is a piece of software that connects to the service and makes the network request. For example, Internet Explorer is a client that makes requests to a web server (service) for different web pages on the web server. Another example is the Client for Microsoft Networks (shown in Figure 10-4), which allows users to connect to any Microsoft file and print server.

- **Protocol** A *protocol* is the networking language that a system uses to send the request from the client to the service. If you want two systems to communicate, they will need to speak the same language (protocol), such as TCP/IP or NetBEUI.

- **Network card driver** In order for all of this to work, you will need to make sure that the network card driver has been installed on the system so that the system can send and receive data. If the network card driver has not been installed, you will be unable to configure the system for clients, protocols, or services.

You can verify that you have the software components to network the Microsoft operating system by going to your LAN Connection properties as shown in Figure 10-4.

Check out Exercise 10-1 in the LabBook.pdf file found on the CD-ROM. This lab displays the steps to verify that you have the correct network software loaded in Windows.

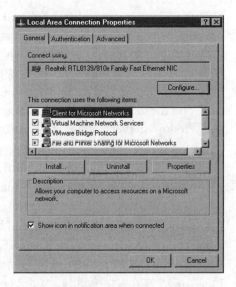

FIGURE 10-4

Client for
Microsoft
Networks in
Windows XP

Just as a side note, in order to connect to older Novell servers (predating NetWare 6), you will need to make sure that you have a Novell client installed on the system. NetWare 6.*x* servers allow users to use a web browser to access all network resources. In order to connect to a Microsoft server, you will need to make sure that you have a Microsoft client installed.

Installing a Network Server

In this section you will learn to install a network server by installing Windows Server 2003 and then configure it as a domain controller for glensworld.loc. After the installation of this server, you will learn to create users and groups on the server.

When installing a Windows server, you want to make sure that you plan for installation by deciding on a number of settings and other issues, such as

- **Server name** You will need to decide what the name of the server will be. Clients will connect to the server by name when accessing folders and printers.
- **Domain name** If your server will be joining a domain, you will need to type in the name of the domain. If you are joining a domain, you will also need to know the username and password of the administrator account that has permission to add servers to the domain. If you will be a domain controller for a domain, you will accomplish that with the dcpromo.exe command, so you should have planned in advance what your domain name will be.

- **Server as domain controller**   You will need to know before you start the installation whether or not the server will be a domain controller, because if the server is to be a domain controller, you will install it as a standalone server and then run dcpromo.exe to promote it to a domain controller.

- **Hardware support**   Make sure that your server hardware (network card, video card, and the like) will work with the server operating system by checking out the Windows Server Catalog at www.windowsservercatalog.com.

- **Partition setup**   During the installation, you will have the opportunity to create and delete the partitions on the hard disk of the server. Plan your partition strategy before the installation so that you are prepared for this step during installation.

- **File system**   After partitioning the disk, you will need to format the partition with a file system such as FAT32 or NTFS. For security reasons you should always go with the NTFS file system on Microsoft servers.

- **Licensing**   When installing a Windows server, you will have to choose either Per Seat or Per Server licensing. With *Per Server* licensing, you obtain a client access license (CAL) for each connection to the server. During the installation of the server you will need to specify how many simultaneous connections you expect. With *Per Seat* licensing, you purchase a license for each individual client that will access the server. The difference between the two is illustrated in this example: If you have ten users accessing two different servers, with Per Server licensing you need 20 licenses, while with Per Seat licensing you only need ten licenses, or one license for each client, no matter how many servers are being accessed.

In order to install the Windows Server operating system, you will first need to place your Windows Server 2003 CD in the CD-ROM drive and then power on the computer. The system boots off the CD and then starts the installation. There are two phases to the installation process:

- **Text-mode phase**   The first is the text-mode portion of the installation, where you partition the disk and format the partition. Then the setup files are copied from the CD-ROM to the hard drive.

- **GUI-mode phase**   The GUI-mode portion of the installation will ask for information such as your product key, computer name, and administrator password.

Let's walk through the steps to install Windows Server 2003, and then you will create a domain controller that runs the Active Directory database. This domain controller will be referred to in all the remaining discussions and exercises in this chapter.

1. Place your Windows Server 2003 CD in the drive and then power on the computer.

2. After some setup files are copied to the system, the Welcome To Setup screen appears (as shown in Figure 10-5). To install Windows Server 2003, press ENTER.

3. Press F8 to agree to the license agreement.

4. You will be shown a list of drives and partitions on which Windows Server 2003 can be installed (as shown in the Figure 10-6); make sure that the first drive is selected. Choose C to create a partition.

5. Type **15000 MB** as the partition size (because of limitations on my system I will choose 4000 as shown in Figure 10-7) and press ENTER.

6. The newly created partition is displayed; select it and press ENTER to install the OS to that partition.

FIGURE 10-5	
Welcome to Setup screen	

```
Windows Server 2003, Enterprise Edition Setup

    Welcome to Setup.

    This portion of the Setup program prepares Microsoft(R)
    Windows(R) to run on your computer.

        •  To set up Windows now, press ENTER.

        •  To repair a Windows installation using
           Recovery Console, press R.

        •  To quit Setup without installing Windows, press F3.




    ENTER=Continue   R=Repair   F3=Quit
```

FIGURE 10-6

Partitioning a
hard disk during
installation

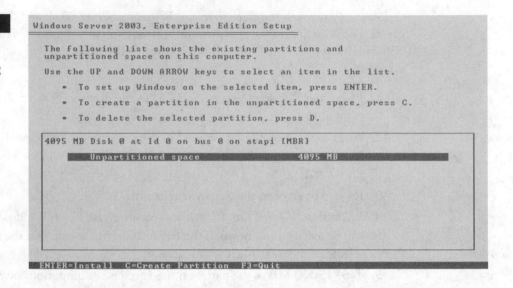

```
Windows Server 2003, Enterprise Edition Setup

    The following list shows the existing partitions and
    unpartitioned space on this computer.

    Use the UP and DOWN ARROW keys to select an item in the list.

      •  To set up Windows on the selected item, press ENTER.

      •  To create a partition in the unpartitioned space, press C.

      •  To delete the selected partition, press D.

    4095 MB Disk 0 at Id 0 on bus 0 on atapi [MBR]
         Unpartitioned space                       4095 MB




  ENTER=Install   C=Create Partition   F3=Quit
```

FIGURE 10-7

Typing a partition
size for the
installation drive

```
Windows Server 2003, Enterprise Edition Setup

    You asked Setup to create a new partition on
    4095 MB Disk 0 at Id 0 on bus 0 on atapi [MBR].

      •  To create the new partition, enter a size below and
         press ENTER.

      •  To go back to the previous screen without creating
         the partition, press ESC.

    The minimum size for the new partition is       8 megabytes (MB).
    The maximum size for the new partition is    4087 megabytes (MB).
    Create partition of size (in MB):   4000






  ENTER=Create   ESC=Cancel
```

7. You will now format (quick) the partition for NTFS by selecting the option shown in the Figure 10-8 and pressing ENTER.

8. The partition is formatted, and setup files are copied to the hard disk. After that, the GUI portion of the installation starts and installs Windows.

9. Select Next to accept the English language.

10. Type your name and organization as shown in Figure 10-9 and then choose Next.

11. Type your product key and then choose Next.

FIGURE 10-8

Quick formatting the partition for NTFS

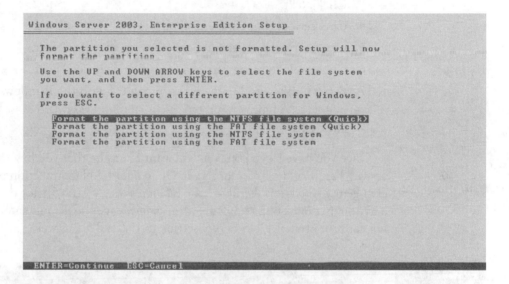

FIGURE 10-9

The GUI-mode portion of the installs prompts for name and organization.

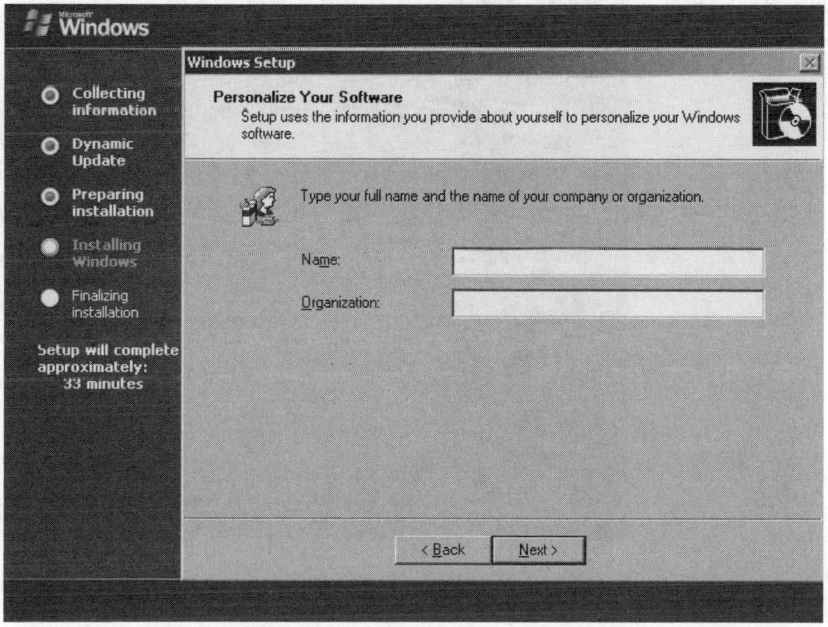

12. Choose to have 100 Per Server licenses (as shown in Figure 10-10) and choose Next. This will allow for 100 clients to connect to the server at one time.

13. Type **win2003-A** as your computer name and **P@ssw0rd** as the password. Click Next.

14. Choose your time zone and click Next.

15. Choose Typical for the network settings and click Next.

16. Choose No to being part of a domain and choose Next.

17. Setup finishes, and then you are presented with the Windows Logon screen. Log on as Administrator, type a password of **P@ssw0rd** (case sensitive), and click OK.

Once you have logged on, you will want to ensure that you have statically assigned an IP address to your server. Go to your LAN Connection properties and change the IP address. I will use the IP address of 192.168.5.1 for this walkthrough and a subnet mask of 255.255.255.0. You may leave the default gateway entry empty, but set your primary DNS Server setting to 192.168.5.1 as well.

FIGURE 10-10

Specifying Per Server licensing

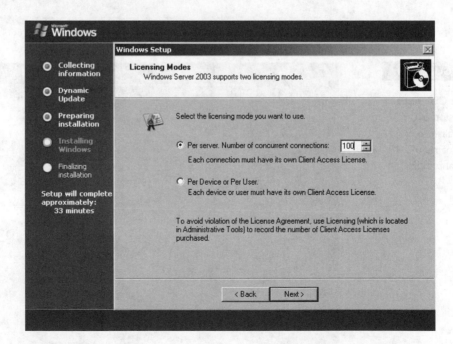

Creating a Domain Controller by Installing Active Directory

18. You will now install Active Directory on this system by running dcpromo. exe. Select Start | Run and then type **dcpromo**. Click OK.

19. The Active Directory Installation Wizard begins; click Next.

20. Click Next on the Operating System Compatibility screen.

21. Choose Domain Controller For A New Domain (as shown in Figure 10-11) and choose Next.

22. Choose Domain In A New Forest and choose Next.

23. Type the DNS name for the new domain—I have used glensworld.loc (as shown in Figure 10-12)—and then choose Next.

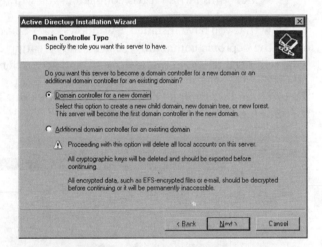

FIGURE 10-11

Installing a domain controller for a new domain

FIGURE 10-12

Setting the DNS name for the new domain

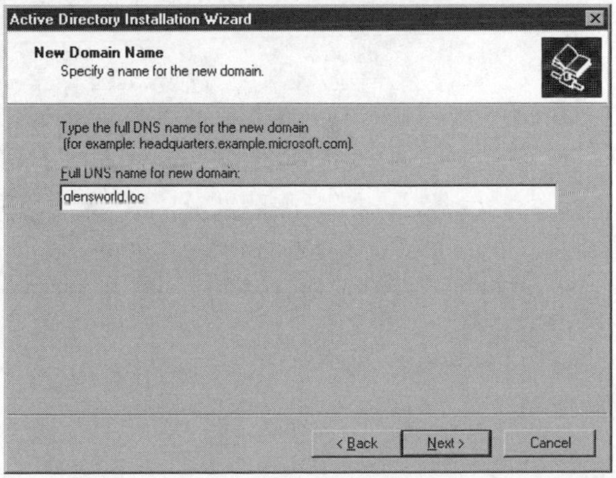

24. Choose Next to accept the NetBIOS name.

25. Choose Next to accept the location of the Active Directory database files.

26. Choose Next to accept the location of the sysvol folder, which is where policies are stored.

27. Accept the default choice to install DNS on this system (as shown in Figure 10-13) and choose Next.

28. Choose Next on the permission compatibility screen.

29. Type a password of **P@ssw0rd** as the directory service restore password, which is used to restore Active Directory.

30. Click Next on the summary screen. Active Directory installs on your system. Click Finish when it has completed; you will then need to reboot.

Now that you have installed a Windows 2003 Server and Active Directory (by using the dcpromo command), you can start creating user accounts for individuals who will need to log on to the network and access network resources.

To practice installing a Windows server, check out Exercise 10-2 in the LabBook.pdf found on the CD-ROM.

FIGURE 10-13

Choosing to install DNS on the system

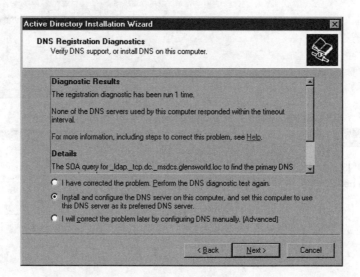

CERTIFICATION OBJECTIVE 10.02

Creating User Accounts

Now that you have the server installed, you will first need to make sure that each user that will access the network has a network user account to log on to the network with. A *user account* is a network object that users on the network use to prove their identity to the network. Once the user logs on with a valid username and password, the user will be able to access resources on the network, such as files, folders, and printers that the user account has permission for.

Built-in Accounts

Before learning how to build a user account for each employee or individual that will access the network, it is important to understand that each operating system has built-in accounts. A built-in account is an account that comes already installed with the operating system and serves a specific purpose.

There are a few built-in accounts that you should be familiar with for the Network+ exam. Each of these accounts is typically used to perform the initial administrative tasks on the server, such as creating user accounts and groups. Table 10-1 displays some popular built-in accounts.

The password for these built-in administrative accounts is normally determined during the installation of the operating system. It is important to be sure that you know that password so that you can log on as that account. Therefore, be sure to make note of the password during the installation and be sure to use a strong password—one that is not easily guessed or cracked. It is also wise to rename the default administrative accounts for security reasons.

Creating User Accounts

Now that you have learned about built-in accounts, let's take a look at how to create and manage user accounts. To create a user account, first make sure that you are comfortable with the naming convention you will use for these accounts. The naming convention is typically made up of the user's first and last name. A popular naming convention is to use the first initial of the first name and then use the entire last name. For example, for my user account you might use a username of gclarke. Once you have decided on the naming convention, you are ready to create your user accounts.

TABLE 10-1	Account Name	Operating System	Description
Built-in Accounts Found with Different Operating Systems	Administrator	Windows	This is an account, built during the installation of the operating system, which is used as the initial administration account. This account is used to build all other accounts and to configure the server.
	Guest	Windows	This built-in account is used to allow individuals to access the network without requiring a user account. Anyone not authenticated with an account that connects to the system can connect as the guest account. This account is disabled by default because of the security concerns involved in allowing individuals to connect to the server without requiring an account.
	Root	Linux/UNIX	This is the main administrative account in the Linux and UNIX world. This account is used to create additional accounts and configure the server.
	Admin	Novell NetWare	This is the main administrative account in NetWare. It is used to create additional accounts and configure the Novell server.

Creating a Local SAM User Account

When creating a user account on a Windows machine in a workgroup environment, you are creating a local user account in the SAM database of that system. This user account will be able to access resources only on the local system; it is typically used where there is no Active Directory environment.

To create a local user account, go to the Computer Management console in the Administrative Tools. Once in the Computer Management console, expand the Local Users And Groups folder on the left. Next, right-click the Users folder and choose New User to create a new user account as shown in Figure 10-14.

Once the New User dialog box appears, type a username and the user's full name. You can also type the description of the user account, such as Accounting Department. Once you have filled in the name information, you can fill in the password for the user account and confirm the password, as shown in Figure 10-15.

FIGURE 10-14

Creating a local user account in the Windows SAM database

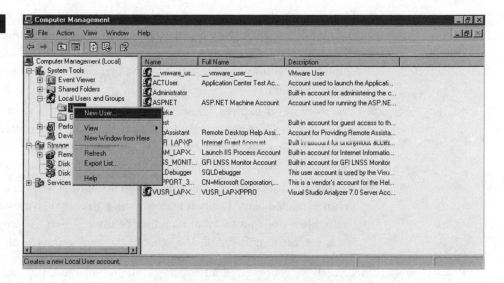

FIGURE 10-15

Filling in the user account properties

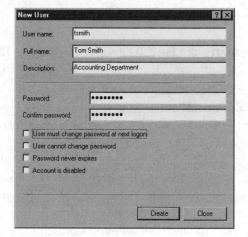

You will notice that there are four additional options at the bottom of the New User dialog box. They are listed with a description, as follows:

■ **User must change password at next logon**   Select this option if you are planning on setting a temporary password for the account and you want to have users change the password once they log on with the account. If you select this option, Windows will force the user to change the password at logon.

- **User cannot change password**   Select this option if you want to control the user account password and you do not want users to change their own passwords. You may set this for a user account that is shared between employees if you want to ensure that one user does not change the password for another user.

- **Password never expires**   Select this option if you don't want this user account to have its password expire based on a policy that forces users to change their password every 30 days. For whatever reason, you have decided that this account is an exception to the password changing policy.

- **Account is disabled**   You may disable an account at any time. If a user goes on an extended leave (such as maternity or paternity leave), you may want to disable the account so that it cannot be used. When the employee comes back, you can simply enable the account by deselecting the check box!

Once you have your desired settings typed in and selected, you can create the account by clicking Create. Once you click Create, you should see the user account in the Users folder.

Creating a User Account in Active Directory

User accounts that are created in the local SAM database cannot be used to access other systems on the network. This becomes a huge problem in most networking environments because you do not want to create the account on each system that the user will access. This is the purpose of creating an Active Directory account. An Active Directory account is a "network" account. When a user is authenticated by Active Directory, that user will have access to every system on the network, assuming that account has been given permission to access those systems.

As a network administrator in a Windows environment, you want to create your accounts in a central directory such as Active Directory so that you do not have to keep building network accounts on each local system.

To create network user accounts in the Active Directory database, go to your server and launch Active Directory Users and Computers from the Administrative Tools (as shown in Figure 10-16).

Once you started the Active Directory Users and Computers console, you can now create a user account by right-clicking and choosing New User. Each user account can be placed in what is called an Organizational Unit (OU). The OU is designed to allow you to group user accounts that require the same policy settings or desktop restrictions. In Figure 10-17 you can see that a new user account is being created in the Halifax OU.

FIGURE 10-16

Launching Active
Directory Users
and Computers

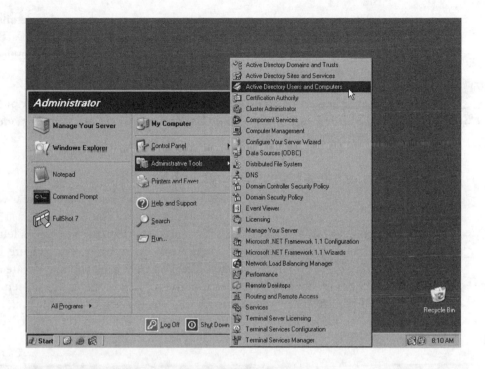

FIGURE 10-17

Creating a new
user account in
Active Directory

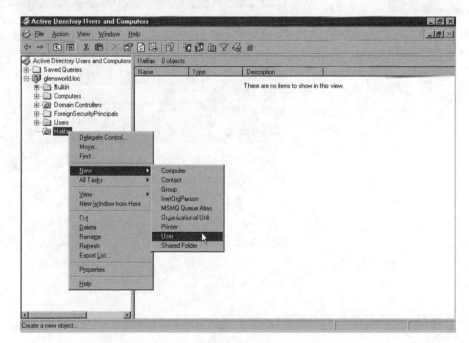

When creating the new user account, you will need to give details such as the first name, last name, and full name of the account (see Figure 10-18). You will also need to specify the user logon name—this is the name that the user will log on to the network with.

To practice creating user accounts in Active Directory check out Exercise 10-3 in LabBook.pdf on the CD-ROM and the CertCam training video.

Creating a User Account in Linux

If you have a Linux or a UNIX operating system, you may create users on your Linux or UNIX server so that users can access resources on those systems. To create a user account in Red Hat Linux, click the Red Hat icon at the bottom left of the screen and select System Settings | Users And Groups as shown in Figure 10-19.

Once you are in the Red Hat User Manager tool, you may create a user account by clicking the Add User button in the top-left corner of the screen. Once you click Add User, you are presented with the Create New User dialog box, in which you will need to fill in the user account information, as shown in Figure 10-20.

FIGURE 10-18

Filling in the user account settings for an Active Directory account

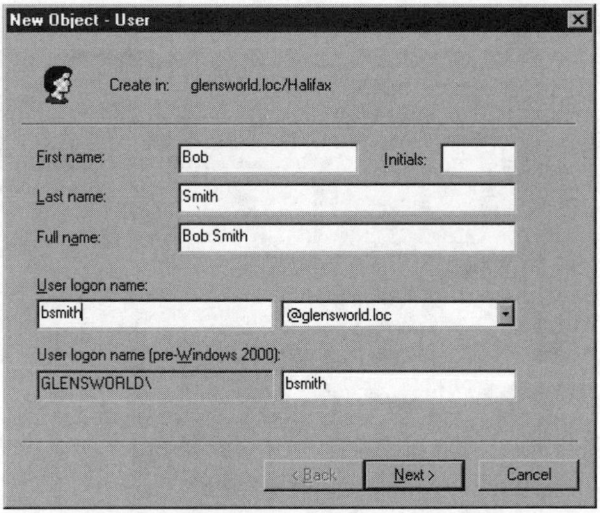

New Object - User

Create in: glensworld.loc/Halifax

First name: Bob   Initials:

Last name: Smith

Full name: Bob Smith

User logon name:

bsmith   @glensworld.loc

User logon name (pre-Windows 2000):

GLENSWORLD\   bsmith

< Back   Next >   Cancel

FIGURE 10-19

Starting the
Red Hat User
Manager tool to
create an account
in Linux

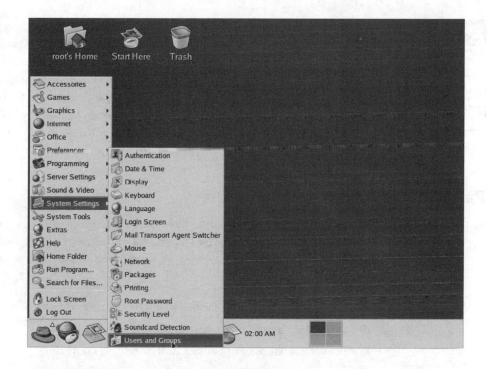

FIGURE 10-20

Supplying account
information for a
new user in Linux

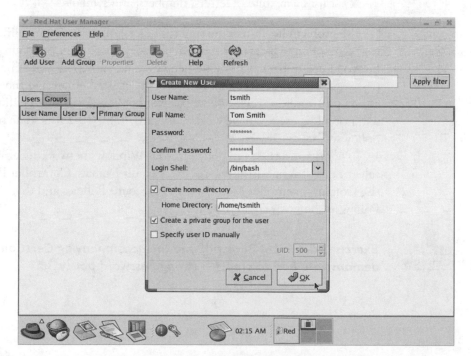

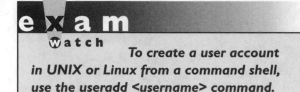

exam

ⓦ**atch** *To create a user account in UNIX or Linux from a command shell, use the useradd <username> command.*

Once you have the user account data filled in, you can click OK and the user account is created. In Linux, the user information is stored in /etc/passwd, and the user's encrypted password is stored in /etc/shadow. Any group the user is a member of is reflected in /etc/group.

Password Policies

When creating your user accounts, make sure that you create strong passwords. Also make sure that when users changes their passwords, they follow guidelines for strong passwords. What is a strong password? A strong, or complex, password is one that meets the following requirements:

- It is not the same as the user's logon name.
- It has a minimum of six (preferably eight) characters.
- It uses a mixture of uppercase and lowercase characters.
- It uses a mixture of letters, numbers, and symbols.

The problem lies in making sure that users follow these guidelines. It is extremely easy to explain to users that they should not choose their pet name as a password, but you need to be certain that when you walk away they don't change their password to a "weak" one that can be easily guessed. To ensure that passwords are strong passwords, you can build a password policy. A password policy, once enabled, will not allow users to have weak passwords. Table 10-2 lists some popular password policy settings.

To configure a password policy in your Windows networking environment, select Start | Administrative Tools | Default Domain Controller Policy. Once in the Domain Controller Policy, expand Account Policies and then select Password Policy, as shown in Figure 10-21.

CertCam 10-4

Exercise 10-4 in LabBook.pdf and the accompanying CertCam training video demonstrate how to create a strong password policy.

TABLE 10-2	Policy Settings	Description
Password Policy Settings	Enforce password history	Enforcing password history means that the server maintains a given number of passwords previously chosen by a user and the user will not be able to choose a password that was already used within the duration of that history. For example, I normally configure my servers to remember at least 12 passwords, so users will not be able to reuse a password that they have chosen 12 times ago.
	Maximum password age	This setting limits the user to having a password for a maximum amount of time. Normally, I set this to 30 days, which means that the user can keep a password for 30 days; after that it will expire, and the user will need to set a new one.
	Minimum password age	Setting the minimum password age means that a user cannot change their password for the amount of time specified after it has been changed. For example, if you force users to change their passwords every 30 days you may not want them to change it for a minimum of 2 days after that, so you can set the minimum password age to 2.
	Minimum password length	The password must have a minimum number of characters. The more characters in a password, the harder it is to crack, because you have increased the number of potential characters. Eight characters or more is the recommendation for a minimum password length.
	Need for password to meet complexity requirements	This is definitely a setting that should be enabled on any server that will hold the network accounts. Enabling complexity requirements means that the passwords must be strong and meet the conditions mentioned previously—a mixture of letters and numbers and employing uppercase and lowercase characters.

FIGURE 10-21

Configuring a password policy on a Windows server

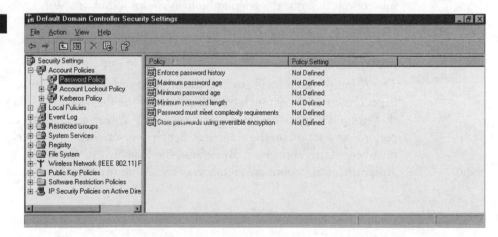

CERTIFICATION OBJECTIVE 10.03

Managing Groups

Once you have created user accounts for your users, you are ready to organize those users into groups. The purpose of creating a group is to allow you to assign permissions or rights on the network to the group. This way, all the users that are members of that group will get the permission or right. For example, if you place all of the accountants in a group called Accountants, when you assign permissions to the accounting team you can assign the permissions once—to the Accountants group; any user who is a member of the group will inherit those permissions.

Groups are also a great way to facilitate role changes within the organization. For example, if you have a new accountant named Bob, you can create the Bob user account and place him in the Accountants group. You will not need to configure the permissions for Bob to access the accounting folder because the group already has the permission. This means that you are working smart as a network administrator and are using features of the network that facilitate change.

Built-in Groups

Before discussing how to create your own groups it is important to understand that there are built-in groups within the network operating system. A built-in group is like a built-in user account in the sense that the group is installed with the operating system and has a predefined purpose within the operating system. The following subsections describe the popular built-in groups found in a Windows operating system.

Administrators

The Administrators local group is the most powerful of all the groups. As you might expect, users in this group have full control of the local system. This means that this group is responsible for managing the local system and has the capabilities to perform any action on the computer. For this reason, only trusted users should be members of this elite group. By default, the Domain Admins global group and the Administrator account are members of the Administrators local group.

Users

The Users local group is a group that all users are members of, and this group has sufficient capabilities to log on to the desktop operating system and run applications that have been installed by the network administrator. The Domain Users global group is a member of the Users local group by default.

Server Operators

The Server Operators group is intended to relieve the burden on the administrator by being able to perform selected server administration tasks. Members of this group can shut down servers, format server hard disks, create and modify shares, lock and unlock the server, back up and restore files, and change the system time.

Print Operators

Users in the Print Operators local group have the capability to create, delete, and modify printers on a Windows system. Printing is one of the most common areas of troubleshooting on the network, and this group is used to alleviate the printing responsibility from the Administrators group.

Backup Operators

Members of the Backup Operators local group can back up and restore files and folders on a Windows system. This group is designed to take over the daily responsibility of doing backups from the Administrators group. Backup Operators can log on to and shut down the server, if needed.

Account Operators

Users in the Account Operators group have permissions to add, modify, and delete user and group accounts in the domain. The Account Operators group is used to create additional user accounts; However, it cannot change characteristics of Administrator accounts or modify members of the Administrators group.

Domain Admins

The Domain Admins global group is a member of the Administrators local group on every computer in the domain by default. To create a network administrator account (as opposed to creating a computer administrator), you should place the user account in the Domain Admins group; then the user can manage any system in the domain.

Domain Users

The Domain Users global group contains all user accounts created in the domain. The Domain Users global group is, by default, a member of the Users local group on every Windows system in the domain. If you need to assign permissions to all users on the network, it is recommended that you give permission to the Users group that contains the Domain Users group (which is all network users).

Placing users into these built-in groups gives them predefined administrative rights within the Windows operating system and Windows Server network operating systems. It is important to always place a user in the group that gives that user the minimum number of rights. For example, although the Administrators group and the Backup Operators group can perform backups, if you want a particular person to do backups, you should place that person in Backup Operators because administrators can perform any administrative tasks.

Creating Groups

You can also create your own groups within most network operating systems, which will allow you to assign permissions to groups of individuals in one action. To create a group within Active Directory, right-click an OU within Active Directory Users and Computers and choose New | Group, as shown in Figure 10-22.

FIGURE 10-22

Creating a new group in Active Directory

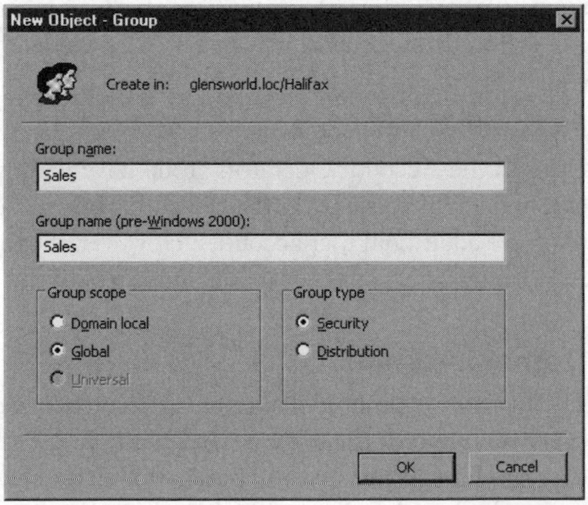

When you create a new group in Active Directory, you will need to choose one of two groups:

- **Distribution**   A distribution group is a group that is used by e-mail applications to send an e-mail to a number of users at once. This is known as a distribution list in a number of e-mail systems.
- **Security**   A security group is a group that is used to assign permissions to groups of people at a time. A security group is also used to e-mail a number of people at once.

When creating a new group, you must also choose the group scope. The purpose of each group scope is given in the following list:

- **Global**   A global group is used to organize users within an Active Directory domain. This group scope can contain any user or global group that exists within the same domain as the global group.
- **Domain local**   A domain local group is used to assign permissions or rights to groups of people within the domain. Domain local groups can contain users or groups from any domain in the enterprise.
- **Universal**   A universal group is used to organize users across domains within the enterprise. For example, if you want to have a group called AllSales that contains the Sales group from two different domains, you will use a universal group to create the AllSales group but use global groups for the two Sales groups.

CertCam 10-5

To practice building groups, try Exercise 10-5 in LabBook.pdf. Also, check out the CertCam training video demonstrating the steps.

Creating a Group in Linux

You can create groups within the Linux environment just as easily as you can within the Windows environment. To create a group within Linux, click the Red Hat icon located in the bottom-left corner and then choose System Settings | Users and Groups. Once the Red Hat User Manager tool appears, click the Groups tab at the top to see a list of existing groups, as shown in Figure 10-23.

FIGURE 10-23

Viewing a list of groups in Linux

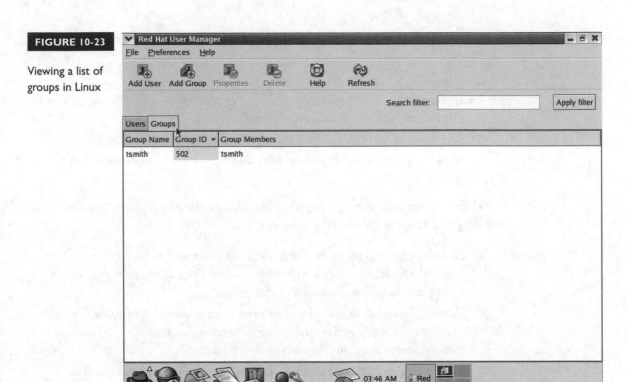

To create a new group, click the Add Group button at the top of the Red Hat User Manager tool and specify a group name, as shown in Figure 10-24.

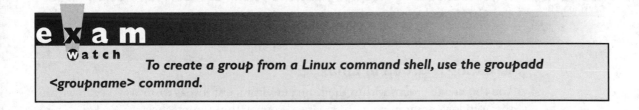

To create a group from a Linux command shell, use the groupadd <groupname> command.

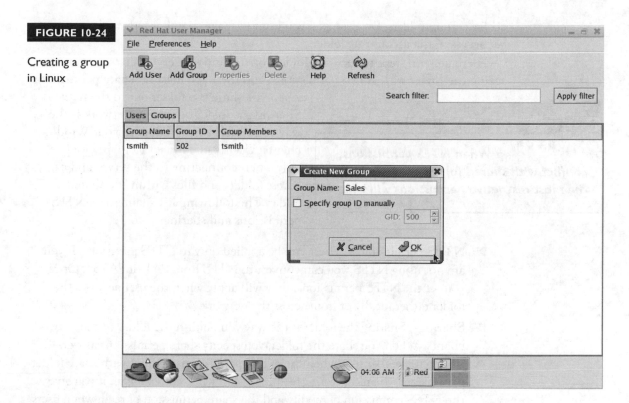

FIGURE 10-24

Creating a group in Linux

CERTIFICATION OBJECTIVE 10.04

Securing Files and Folders

In this section you will learn to secure folders and files by assigning permissions to users and groups within the various network operating systems. You will not be expected to be a security expert for the Network+ exam, but you should be familiar with some of the basic permissions found in the operating systems in current use.

Securing Files in Windows

In the Windows operating systems, once you have your users and groups built, you can then secure the folders and files on these systems so that only certain users can access certain folders. For example, you want to make sure that only accountants can get access to the accounting folder.

There are two steps to securing folders on a Windows server: first you must secure the folder with NTFS permissions, and then you must set share permissions when you share the folder out to the network. Sharing the folder out to the network is the way you "publish" the folder to your Windows clients. Users can connect to shared folders only when connecting to the server and can access folders and files within the shared folder. The following list summarizes NTFS permissions and sharing:

- **NTFS permissions**   These can be applied only to NTFS partitions. If you are not using NTFS, you can convert to NTFS from FAT or FAT32. Once you set the NTFS permissions, they will apply when the user accesses the folder either locally or from across the network.

- **Sharing**   Sharing the folder is the way you publish the folder to the network clients. When you share the folder, you specify share permissions as well. Be sure to remember that when the NTFS permissions conflict with share folder permissions, the most restrictive permission wins. For example, if you give the NTFS permission of modify and the share permission of read, when users come through the share to access that folder, their permission will be read because it is most restrictive.

NTFS Permissions

There are a number of NTFS permissions that you should be familiar with when it comes to securing folders; the popular NTFS permissions are listed in Table 10-3.

Shared Folder Permissions

Once you secure the folders with NTFS permissions, you will need to share the folder to publish it to the network. When sharing the folders, you will need to configure shared folder permissions. There are a few shared folder permissions that you should be familiar with when it comes to securing folders that are shared out on the network. Be aware that when a share permission is applied to a folder, it will be retained for all subfolders as well. For example, if you share the data folder and users have the change permission, when users connect to the data share they will have the change share permission and when they double-click a subfolder they will still have it. You will rely on NTFS to change the permissions at each subfolder level if needed. The share permissions are listed in Table 10-4.

TABLE 10-3	NTFS Permission	Description
Popular NTFS Permissions	List Folder Contents	This is a permission assigned to a folder; it allows a user to view the contents of the folder but not necessarily to "read" the contents of files in the folder.
	Read	This is a folder and file permission that enables a user to open and read the contents of files.
	Read & Execute	This is a folder and file permission that allows users to read the contents of files and to execute an executable.
	Write	This is a file and folder permission that allows a user to modify the contents of a file (write to it) or to create a new file or folder within that folder.
	Modify	This is a folder or file permission that includes all the permissions mentioned previously. Having the Modify permission allows a user to read, execute, delete, list folder contents, and write to the contents of the folder or file.
	Full Control	This is a folder or file permission that gives a user all permissions possible. If you assign the Full Control permission, the user will be able to modify the contents of the file but also change the permissions on the resource as well.

TABLE 10-4	Share Permission	Description
Share Permissions in Windows	Read	This share permission enables a user to open and read the contents of files within the share.
	Change	This share permission enables a user to open and read the contents of files within the share, create new files, and change the contents of files within the share.
	Full Control	This share permission enables a user to open and read the contents of files within the share, create new files, change the contents of files within the share, and change permissions on the share. This permission is typically not assigned to users on the network.

Exercise 10-6 demonstrates how to configure a Windows server for NTFS permissions and publish the resource by sharing it and configuring share permissions.

EXERCISE 10-6

Configuring Permissions in Windows 2003

In this exercise you will learn to set NTFS permissions and shared folder permissions to secure the data folder on your Windows Server 2003 system.

1. Select Start | My Computer.
2. Double-click drive C.
3. Choose File | New | Folder.
4. Type **Data** as the name of the folder.
5. Right-click the data folder and choose Properties, as shown here:

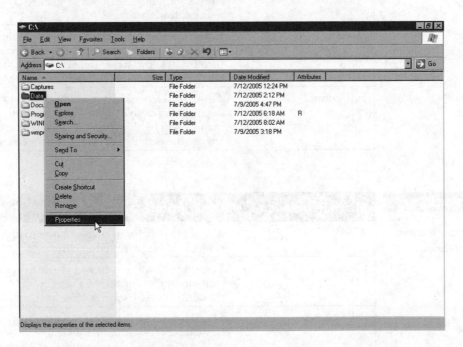

Select the Security tab and then click Advanced.

6. Deselect the Allow Inheritable Permissions check box (as shown in the following illustration) and then choose Remove.

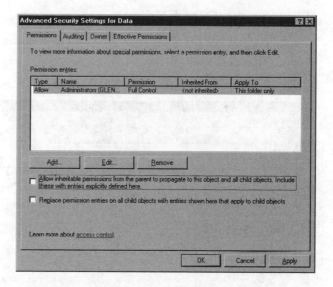

7. Click OK.

8. Click Add to add a user or group to the permission list and then type **Sales** and choose OK.

9. Sales is added to the permission list. Select Sales and then choose the Modify permission as shown here:

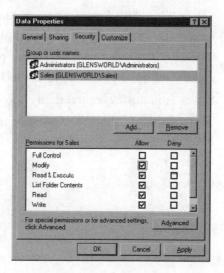

10. Click OK.

Sharing the Data Folder

11. Right-click the Data folder and choose Sharing and Security (as shown in the following illustration).

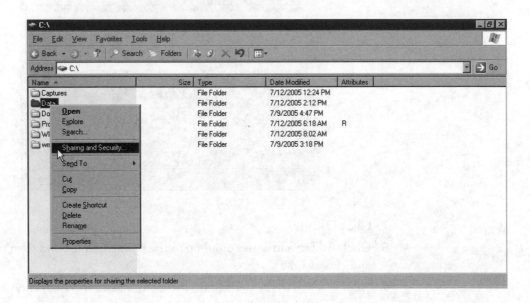

12. Select Share This Folder. Notice that the share name is the same name as the folder—in this case Data. Click Permissions to set the share permissions.

13. Click Remove to remove the default permission of Everyone having Read.

14. Click Add and type **administrators;sales** and then choose OK.

15. Select Administrators and then choose Full Control as the permission.

16. Select Sales and then choose Change as the permission (as shown in the illustration on the next page).

17. Click OK.

18. Click OK again.

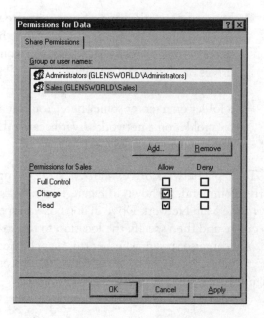

Connecting to a Shared Folder

Once you have configured the permissions on the Windows folder and have shared it out to the network, your clients will need to know how to connect to the shared folder. There are a number of ways to connect to the shared folder; two of my personal favorite methods are to use the run command and then connect to the UNC path of the shared folder, or to map a network drive to the shared folder.

■ **UNC path** The Universal Naming Convention (UNC) path is a standard naming convention to connect to network resources. A UNC path is made up of two \ symbols followed by the name of the computer, another \, and then the name of the share. For example, if you had a shared folder named data on a server called SERVER1, the UNC path would be \\SERVER1\DATA. The beautiful thing about UNC paths is that once you know the name of the server and the share, you can quickly connect by typing the UNC path in the run command!

- **Mapped network drive** Some users are not comfortable with UNC paths and don't know what they are, let alone how to connect to a UNC path. To make your network easier to use, you would normally create mapped network drives on the user's computer. A mapped network drive is a drive in My Computer that does not connect to a drive on the local system but points to a folder on a server somewhere. You can always tell which drives are referring to a folder on a network server because the icon has a cable underneath the drive, as shown in Figure 10-25.

To map a network drive, right-click My Computer and choose the Map Network Drive command, as shown in Figure 10-26.

In the Map Network Drive dialog box you specify the drive letter you would like to create and then specify the location to the shared folder that this drive will point to. You can also specify whether this mapped network drive should be created the next time the user logs on by selecting the Reconnect At Logon option, as shown in Figure 10-27.

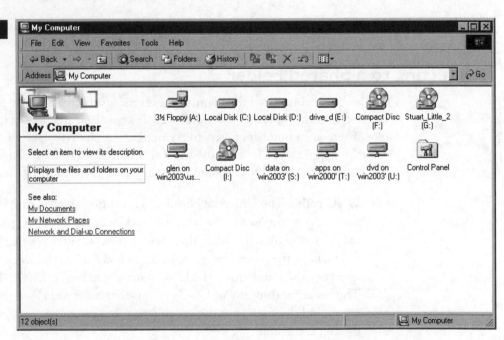

FIGURE 10-25

A cable below the drive icon indicates a mapped drive.

FIGURE 10-26

Choosing the
Map Network
Drive command

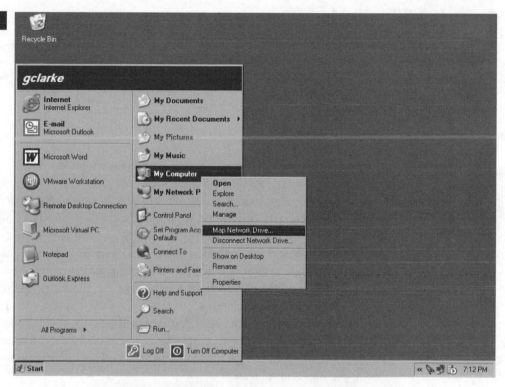

FIGURE 10-27

Mapping a
network drive
in Windows

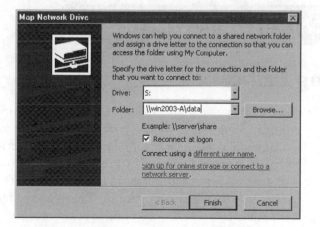

Securing Files in Linux

Securing files in Linux is a little bit different. There are three permissions for files and folders, each having a numeric value:

- Read (R)   4
- Write (W)   2
- Execute (X)   1

There are also three entities that can have these three permissions to a file or folder: the file owner, a group, and everyone else.

The **chmod** (change mode) command is used to set these permissions. For example, **chmod u=rwx /myfile.txt** would set Read, Write, and Execute for the file owner (u) to the file named myfile.txt. The foregoing command could also be expressed using **chmod 700 /myfile.txt**, where 7 assigns read, write, and execute to the file owner while assigning nothing to the group and everyone else.

For another example, **chmod u=rwx,g=rw,o=r /myfile.txt** grants the file owner (u) read, write, and execute, allows a group (g) to read and write, and allows everyone else (o) only read access. Expressed numerically, the command would be **chmod 764 /myfile.txt**. Keep in mind that if you're using **chmod** to set permissions on a folder, you should use the -R switch to recursively change permissions for all subordinate files and folders.

CERTIFICATION OBJECTIVE 10.05

Installing Printers

Another type of resource that appears on the network along with files and folders is printers. Being able to share a printer with other users on the network is one of the fundamental reasons for having a network. This section covers installing a printer and sharing it out to the network.

Before we get into the steps to configure a printer, let's take a look at some terminology that deals with printing. The following terms are used a lot in networking environments to describe the printing environment:

- **Print device**   The print device is the physical printer that takes paper and outputs the printout—in our terms it is the "printer."

- **Printer**   The printer is the software interface to the print device. The printer is the little icon that appears in your printer folder and allows you to configure the settings through the properties of the printer. You can open the printer to see the print jobs that have been submitted. This is also termed the print queue in some environments.

- **Print server**   A print server is the machine that holds the shared printer. Remember that the printer is the icon and not the physical print device. The print server is where clients submit their print jobs. Figure 10-28 displays the relationship between the various printing terms.

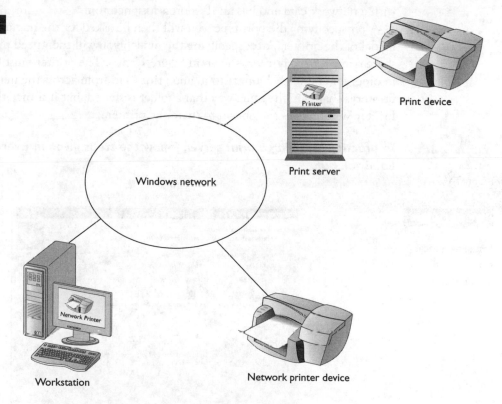

FIGURE 10-28

Identifying printing terminology

Creating a Print Server

To install a print server in the Windows environment, run the Add Printer Wizard on the Windows Server 2003 machine. Clients connect to this shared printer to submit their print jobs.

When installing a printer on the server, run the Add Printer Wizard and select that you are installing a local printer (shown in Figure 10-29). The term local printer means that the printer is a resource of the server and you will manage the printer on that system. Management of the printer could involve things such as adding additional drivers, configuring a schedule, or configuring permissions.

After specifying that you wish to install a local printer in the Add Printer Wizard, you will then need to specify the port the printer is connected to. The port could be a local port such as LPT1 or could be a standard TCP/IP port. A standard TCP/IP port is the port type you use if the print device is connected directly to the network with a network card and has an IP address assigned to it.

After specifying the port type, you will then be asked for the manufacturer and model of the printer. After specifying the model, you will then need to specify a share name for the printer (shown in Figure 10-30). The printer must be shared in order for clients to connect to it, and print to it, from across the network. The printer is shared in the same way that a folder is shared, but it is nice that the Add Printer Wizard gives the option to share the printer.

To practice installing a print server, follow the steps given in Exercise 10-7 in LabBook.pdf.

FIGURE 10-29

Installing a local printer on a Windows server

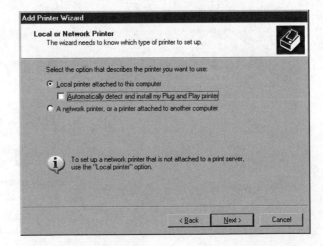

FIGURE 10-30

Giving the printer a share name in the Add Printer Wizard

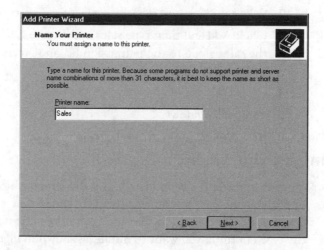

Changing Printer Permissions

Once the printer has been installed, you can then go to the properties of the printer to change its settings. One of the popular settings you may want to change is who has permission to print to the printer. To change the permissions on the printer, follow these steps:

1. Once the printer is installed, right-click the printer and choose Properties (as shown in Figure 10-31).

FIGURE 10-31

Changing the printer properties

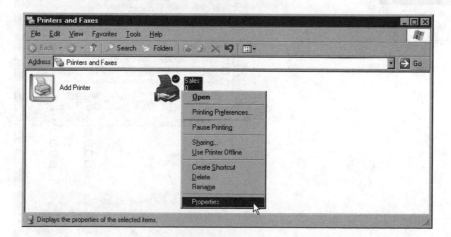

2. Select the Security tab; then select the Everyone group and click Remove.

3. Click Add and then type **sales** and choose OK. In my example I have added the sales group to the permission list and given the print permission as shown in Figure 10-32.

4. Click OK.

5. Close all windows.

Configuring a Print Client

Once the printer has been installed on the server, which now makes the server a print server, you are ready to connect clients to the printer so that they can print. To install a printer on the client, run the Add Printer Wizard and select Network Printer as the type of printer you want to install (as shown in Figure 10-33). The term network printer means that you want to install a printer that references a printer located on a print server and you will reference this printer by its share name. For example, in the preceding section you installed a shared printer on the Windows 2003 Server, and if a client wishes to reference it, the client will specify a UNC path of

```
\\win2003-A\sales
```

Any print jobs destined for the network printer will be redirected to the network print server to handle the print request. The printout will print to whatever print device the print server is pointing to; in our case, LPT1.

FIGURE 10-32

Giving the print permission to Sales

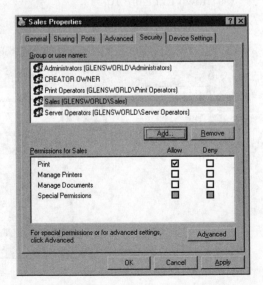

FIGURE 10-33

Installing a
network printer

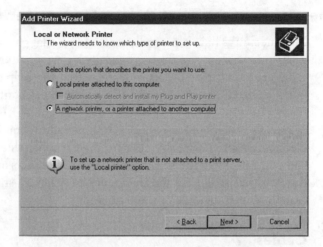

Printing in Linux

CUPS (Common UNIX Printing System) is the standard printing environment used
in Linux. It includes support for the Internet Printing Protocol (IPP), Line Printer
Daemon (LPD), and Line Printer Remote (LPR), among other standards.

LPD is a daemon (or service) that must be running on the Linux server; LPR
refers to the Linux client. There are some basic Linux commands to control printing:

- **lp**   Sends print jobs to a Linux printer—for example, lp myfile.txt.
- **lpstat**   Displays all configured printers and their print job status.

CERTIFICATION OBJECTIVE 10.06

Working with Network Hardware

This section reviews the networking hardware that is required for the network
to function and identifies potential issues surrounding networking hardware and
networking equipment.

Environmental Factors That Affect Computer Networks

Most networks have a centrally located area that can safely house all network appliances and servers. This is typically known as a server room. Within this room are a multitude of special features that can help protect the computers and other environmentally "sensitive" equipment from failing as a result of extreme temperatures.

Because computers are affected by temperature, moisture, vibrations, and electrical interference, you need to create a controlled environment in which you can control each of these elements. If the computers are exposed to these elements, they can act irregularly and sometimes fail. Luckily, standards protect computer components from some of these situations.

Cables

Underneath the protection of most network cables lies a fragile layer of wire (or glass, in the case of fiber optics) that carries the data from one computer to another. Like most other computer components, this wire is not resistant to moisture, heat, or other electrical interference. To protect this cable from harm, a covering is placed over the wire to keep it from breaking or accidentally becoming wet. The main reason for the covering is to prevent cross-talk and electromagnetic interference (EMI).

Cables that bring data to networks come in many different forms, from copper to fiber optic. The type of cable determines its feasible length. When a cable exceeds the recommended distance, the signal begins to fade and becomes unreadable. Be sure to verify that you have not exceeded the maximum distance of your cable types.

e x a m
ⓦ a t c h
Make sure that you know the length limitations for each type of cable. You will be presented with scenario questions for which you are to determine whether the configuration is valid; you must know whether the maximum cable length has been exceeded. Refer to Chapter 1 to review the various cable specifications.

The Network Operations Center

Your Network Operations Center (NOC) is the home base for all of the important servers on your network. The NOC enables you to centrally manage and keep a close eye on all your networked data.

You will be asked to determine which environment of several scenarios is the most appropriate for a server room. Just remember that servers need an environment free of dust, with plenty of ventilation and reasonable temperature and humidity. Placing servers near a window on a sunny day or in a dusty warehouse would not create an ideal operating environment.

A NOC, above all else, needs to be secure and able to house all the data and servers. Normally, the NOC is stored in a secured room that is equipped with various types of fire suppression (halon, foam), raised floors to place the cabling, and temperature control. You can't put a value on your data, so this room should never be compromised in any way.

Your NOC should at all times be cool, dry, and temperature controlled. Computers and other electrical equipment do not like humidity, heat, or extreme cold, so you should be very careful to regulate the temperature of the NOC. When a computer overheats, there is no guarantee that the data on your servers can be saved.

Because computer equipment is very sensitive to moisture, you need to use a form of fire suppression besides water. Putting out a fire in your NOS using a sprinkler system would ruin all your computer equipment. Many types of foams or halon are used to put out fires quickly and safely while minimizing the potential damage to your computer equipment. The laws of your geographical area could require that you not use certain types of fire control methods. Some states require older systems to be upgraded within a certain amount of time and consider older fire control methods dangerous.

For the exam, remember to make sure that you should not expose computers or network equipment to any potential environmental hazards, such as moisture or extreme heat, or to electrical interference, such as that created by generators and television sets. The exam might include questions pertaining to the location of equipment.

Minimizing Electrical Interference

Electromagnetic interference (EMI) can wreak great havoc on any type of computer equipment. You might be aware of certain types of speakers that are magnetically shielded to prevent electrical interference. However, magnets and computers don't mix, so unfortunately this concept doesn't carry over to computer electronics. The alternative is to keep all your computer equipment away from any electrical device that could interrupt the computing power of your equipment.

Computer Chassis

With the rapid advances in today's technology, computers are faster than ever. Today there is more computing power on a single laptop computer than was used by NASA to place the first man on the moon. However, more computing power comes at a price, and the price that we pay is heat. As processors become faster and faster, they become hotter and hotter as they perform billions of calculations. The scenario is the same for disk drives. The larger the drives become, the more work that needs to be done to find the data on the drive. The result is that the temperature within the PC's chassis becomes too hot for the computer to operate. When this happens, the overheating part fails or destroys the PC altogether.

To combat this problem, a cooling fan (or multiple fans) is placed inside the PC to circulate the air and prevent the PC from overheating. Some of the more inventive computer chassis help circulate the air inside the PC to keep the computer cool. The room in which the servers are placed should also be air-conditioned. The air in the PC chassis can only be as cool as the air it is circulating from the room in which it is placed.

One of the things that a number of organizations forget to do as part of their maintenance plan is to clean the inside of the computer. The collection of dust in the system can create problems with the cooling techniques used by the PC manufacturer. I remember trying to fix a client's computer that continued to crash. After trying everything, I opened the case and found that the cooling fan on the processor was jammed with dust. I reached for my can of compressed air and gave the system a good cleaning—problem fixed in five minutes!

Common Peripheral Ports and Network Components

What use is a computer without all the goodies that accompany it? There are literally hundreds of peripherals and network components to choose from in today's fun-filled world of computers. Here, you will learn the basics about the companion pieces you will likely encounter in your day-to-day experience.

All these ports and network components are mainly used to make the experience of using a computer easier and more user-friendly. If you want to be an expert in networking technology, you should know and understand each component in case you have to troubleshoot a problem someday.

Network Interface Cards

Your network interface card (NIC) should be autodetected during setup, but if it is not, you must install the driver for the network card. The driver normally is shipped on a CD that comes with the card or system, and you should also be able to download the driver from the manufacturer's web site. You must make sure that the network driver is installed before attempting any network communication activities.

Binding Protocols

When you install networking protocols on your system, the protocols are bound, or linked, to the network card through a feature called bindings. If you install multiple protocols, each protocol is bound to the network card so that if data leaves the network card, it could use either protocol that is installed. You can optimize network performance by changing the binding order, which specifies which protocol should be used first for communication.

Network Connection

Connecting to the Internet with a networked server requires a large amount of bandwidth to provide connectivity for all users. The amount of bandwidth determines the number of users that can access your site at once. A fast network connection enables easy access to your web site, whereas a slow connection sometimes prohibits users from getting to your web site. If you are on an intranet, you probably do not have to worry about the amount of bandwidth. A normal 100 Mbps Ethernet network card should be sufficient for typical LAN traffic.

You will most likely have a router connected to the Internet using a WAN-type interface. The router will then connect your LAN using an internal network interface that will connect to a hub, or switch, where all other systems are connected. This router acts as the device that allows all users on the network to access the Internet.

Network-Attached Storage

Network-attached storage (NAS) units are standalone devices, usually SCSI, that have a network interface but no PC. A NAS is a containment unit with a power supply, cooling fans, one or two SCSI controller cards, and bays to hold the storage units. The unit usually can be locked to prevent anyone from opening it and removing its contents. The storage units are typically hard disks, although they may be CD-ROM units, and are typically used as mass storage for servers to access.

With CD-ROMs, the unit is usually called a CD tower; it allows you to share the CDs on the network to provide users with easy access to multiple CDs. CD towers can hold as many as 32 CD-ROMs at one time for users to access the contents of. This is typical of CD-ROM libraries used by law firms or in the medical field by doctors.

With hard disks, a NAS allows for a large point of mass storage, and it can possibly include a built-in RAID controller to allow all the hard disks to be fault tolerant and function as a single volume. You manage configuration of a NAS by telnetting to the system or connecting to its web page and setting configuration options to allow sharing and setting up a unit name. The unit name allows you to use the Universal Naming Convention (UNC) to connect to the unit and its devices.

Advantages of NAS   One advantage of using NAS is that the units can be placed anywhere. Most of these units are a little larger than a tower PC and can be placed under a desk with sufficient ventilation. To add storage units, you don't need to purchase a PC and OS into which to place the required devices, such as the hard disks and CD-ROMs. In addition, the units take up less space and can be placed in a server room, even on a desk or table, or in another secure area, so you don't need a large amount of space.

Disadvantages of NAS   A disadvantage of NAS is that the interface requires some knowledge as far as configuration and may require some training to use. Administering these units also requires some monitoring to verify that the unit is still functioning properly with the proper share names. The administration might not be too difficult, but it will cause some overhead. Usually, once it is set up, it won't need further administration unless something goes wrong.

Network-attached storage units are very useful in a large network environment and typically support RAID functions. Typically, clustered environments use NAS for the shared data.

Serial Ports

Serial ports are a slow link that allows data flow with the bits being sent one at a time. This is different from a parallel connection, which sends data eight bits at a time. A serial link typically transmits information at 128 Kbps. You may find a serial link on networking devices such as routers to connect to a WAN interface.

Serial ports are also known as COM ports, or communication ports.

Parallel Ports

Parallel ports yield better performance by sending data eight bits at a time and offer transfer rates as high as 2 Mbps, depending on the parallel port mode. Printers are the most popular type of parallel port devices used on networks.

Universal Serial Bus

Universal Serial Bus (USB) is an innovation in computer peripheral technology that enables you to add devices such as audio players, scanners, printers, network cards, and external hard drives to your computer without having to add an adapter card or even having to turn the computer off. USB comes in two flavors right now:

- **USB 1.0**   USB 1 has a transfer rate of 12 Mbps, which is an amazing speed, considering that serial ports and parallel ports offer only a speed up to 2 Mbps.

- **USB 2.0**   USB 2.0 has a transfer rate of 480 Mbps! This difference in transfer rate dramatically reduces the time it takes to transfer data from one network component to another. For example, last week I was transferring a 3GB file from my USB 2.0 drive to the hard drive on the computer, but because there was not a USB 2.0 driver loaded, the system was treating the device as a USB 1.1 device. As a result, the file copy operation was going to take 67 minutes! I chose Cancel and then updated the driver to USB 2.0 and attempted the file copy a second time; this time it took 3 minutes. Gotta love USB 2.0!

Most systems today have USB ports on both the front and the back of the computer. You can also purchase a USB hub device that will connect to your system and allow additional devices to be connected to it.

Small Computer System Interface

Small Computer System Interface (SCSI) is a standard interface that enables systems to communicate with peripheral hardware, such as disk drives, tape drives, CD-ROM drives, printers, and scanners. What makes SCSI devices so special is the improvement in data transfer over parallel devices. For example, Ultra-Wide SCSI 2 devices can transfer data up to 80 MBps compared to EIDE, which has a transfer rate of 16 MBps. Another benefit of SCSI devices is the capability to daisy-chain as many as 7 or 15 devices (depending on the bus width). SCSI devices are more important for high-performance systems such as servers than they are for the home PC.

Print Servers

Print servers can be either dedicated servers that are responsible for sending documents to various printer pools scattered around a corporation, or they can be used in tandem with file servers. These servers are used to send documents to the print device for printing. This system makes much more sense than having a separate printer for each computer, and it gives you more control over administering the documents that are sent to each network printer.

Bridges

Bridges are intelligent devices used to filter traffic on LANs by forwarding packets to specific network segments based on the source and destination MAC addresses of the packet. Bridges have been popular in the past and seem to have been replaced by switches on today's networks.

Hubs

Hubs enable you to connect systems together at a central point; they have been popular devices on networks for many years. Because hubs send data to all ports on the hub, they have been replaced by switches on networks today. A switch only sends data to the port where data needs to go, not to all the ports like with a hub. The simple filtering features increase overall performance on the network.

Switches

Switches filter traffic by sending the data only to the port where the data should go, essentially not using the bandwidth of the other ports. This is different from a hub, which sends the data to all ports no matter what.

 on the **Job**

Today's computer networks are using switches more than hubs because of both the performance benefits and the security benefits of switches.

Routers

Routers route data packets from one network to another network using the network address of the packet. Remember the OSI model that you learned about in Chapter 2? Routers essentially create broadcast and collision domains and route data destined for a particular network.

Gateways

A gateway can link networks that have different protocols, such as TCP/IP to IPX/SPX. A gateway can change an entire protocol stack into another or provide protocol conversion and routing services between computer networks. Gateways examine the entire packet and then translate the incompatible protocols so that each network can understand the two different protocols. For example, protocol gateways can also be used to convert ATM cells to Frame Relay frames and vice versa.

Peripherals

With today's booming computer industry, you have many options in choosing peripherals for your computer. The standard I/O devices, such as keyboard and mouse, are the mainstays of computer peripherals, but you can choose many other peripherals to make your PC experience even better. Let's look at some now.

The Keyboard A keyboard connects to the computer using a PS/2, DIN, or USB connection, and enables you to input data. Because the keyboard is the primary input device, you rely on the keyboard more than you realize. The keyboard contains certain standard function keys, such as the ESCAPE key, the TAB key, cursor movement keys, SHIFT keys, and CONTROL keys, and sometimes other manufacturer-customized keys, such as the WINDOWS key.

The Mouse A mouse connects to the serial, PS/2, or USB port on your computer and enables you to move a cursor around the GUI of your desktop operating system or server.

Print Device A print device outputs data from your computer to paper or other media, such as labels, transparencies, or envelopes. Sharing print devices is one of the more popular reasons to have a network, which allows multiple users to access a single print device.

Digital Camera A digital camera is a fairly popular peripheral these days, which enables the user to take pictures and store them as files in memory on the camera instead of film used by conventional cameras. The pictures that are saved as digital images on a memory card can be printed at a later time or e-mailed to friends, coworkers, or relatives.

Scanners Scanners are used to convert a photo already in print to a digital image on the computer. This digital image can then be manipulated after the fact. Scanners in the past have connected to a parallel port on the system, but today's scanners are connecting to the USB port.

Modems A modem is a communications device that enables a computer to talk to another computer through a standard telephone line. The modem converts digital data from the computer to analog data for transmission over analog telephone lines. The analog signal is then converted back to digital data by the modem on the receiving computer.

Compatibility and Cabling Issues

All network cables are not created equal. There are four different types of commonly used network cables: thicknet (10Base5), thinnet (10Base2), twisted pair, and fiber optic. For most of your networking needs, twisted pair is the cable of choice because it is relatively inexpensive and available. It is also easy to run in tight places, and many standards are adopted for its RJ-45 interface.

Incompatibilities with Analog Modems and a Digital Jack

An analog modem and a digital jack will not work together, because they use two different technologies. An analog modem works over a standard phone line, and a digital jack for ISDN works with a digital PBX switch, not an analog phone switch.

Uses of RJ-45 Connectors with Different Cabling

An RJ-45 connector is used to connect segments of twisted-pair cabling. To connect two different types of media cable, you need either a hub or bridge that has a specific connection for this type of cabling, or you can use a small transceiver device that has both connection types on it (essentially a converter). For example, you cannot connect a 10BaseT cable that plugs into a bridge that supports connectivity with a BNC connector for 10Base2. You must have the correct network hardware to connect the two different types of cabling media.

Patch Cables and Length of Cabling Segment

A CAT 5 patch cable is normally a couple of feet long or however long you need to connect the client to the network. Commonly, a patch cable is used to "patch" the length it takes to get from your network card to the digital jack on the floor of your office.

CERTIFICATION SUMMARY

In this chapter you have learned the basic elements that make up a network. You have learned that clients connect to servers by using client software. You have also learned that each system will need a network card driver installed and a protocol if they are to communicate on this network.

You have learned that each user who will access the network will need to have a user account. Users identify themselves to the network by user accounts; these are created by the network administrator. You have learned how to create Active Directory accounts in Active Directory Users and Computers and to create Linux accounts in the Red Hat User Manager.

It is important that you create a strong password policy for your user accounts to ensure that the passwords are difficult for someone to guess or crack. A strong password is a password that has a minimum of six characters, has lowercase and uppercase characters, and uses symbols or numbers. You may define your password policy within the Domain Controller Security Policy on a Domain Controller.

You have learned that you can organize your users into groups—this will allow you to assign permissions more easily because you can assign permissions to the groups instead of each user. Windows has two types of groups: a security group for permissions and e-mail and a distribution group for just e-mail. You may use the Active Directory Users and Computers console to create groups with Active Directory, and you may use the Red Hat User Manager to create groups in Linux.

You have learned how to set NTFS permissions to secure a folder and how to share that folder so that users on the network may access the folder. You have learned of a number of permissions in NTFS; be sure to review those before the exam. You have also learned how to create and share a printer on a Windows Server 2003 system.

Finally we have reviewed some of the different types of hardware that you will encounter in your travels as a networking professional, and we have discussed issues surrounding cabling and interference and compatibility.

TWO-MINUTE DRILL

Installing a Network

❑ Microsoft has three types of servers: standalone, member, and domain controller.

❑ A standalone server is not part of a domain and sits on its own. It relies on its own security database known as the SAM database for user and group management and authentication services.

❑ A member server is a member of a domain but does not have the Active Directory database installed. A member server typically runs applications such as Exchange or SQL Server.

❑ A domain controller is a server that holds the Active Directory database.

❑ To have communication on a network, you need to have a network client, protocol, and network card driver installed.

Creating User Accounts

❑ There are two types of accounts: built-in and administrator-created.

❑ Built-in accounts are accounts that are created during the installation of the operating system. There is typically an administrative account built in to the operating system and a guest account that is disabled by default.

❑ The built-in administrative account in Windows is called Administrator, and the one built into Linux/UNIX is called root.

❑ You can create a user account in Active Directory with the Active Directory Users and Computers console.

❑ You may create a user account in Linux with the Red Hat User Manager.

❑ You should create a password policy that enforces strong passwords.

❑ A strong password consists of upper and lowercase characters and has a minimum of six characters and a mix of letters, numbers, and symbols.

Managing Groups

❑ Groups are used to organize users into administrative units.

❑ There are built-in groups in Windows such as Administrators, Backup Operators, Account Operators, and Print Operators.

❑ Backup Operators can perform backups, Printer Operators can install and configure printers, and Account Operators can create and manage user accounts.

❑ Global groups are used to organize users within a domain, domain local groups are used for permissions or rights assignment, and universal groups are used to organize users across domains.

❑ Security groups are used for security or e-mail, and distribution groups are used only for e-mail.

Securing Files and Folders

❑ Use NTFS partitions so that you can configure NTFS permissions on folders.

❑ Use share permissions when creating the shared resource.

❑ When NTFS and share permissions conflict—the most restrictive wins.

❑ In Linux, you can configure permissions with the chmod command.

❑ The Full Control permission allows a user to modify the file contents and modify permissions, while the Modify permission only allows a user to modify the file contents—not permissions.

❑ You can connect to a folder with a UNC path. The UNC path has the following syntax: \\computername\sharename.

Installing Printers

❑ Microsoft terms the print device as the machine that holds the paper and ink and prints the content on paper, whereas the printer is the software interface to the print device.

❑ A print server is a machine that has a shared printer and receives print requests from clients.

❑ A printer (or queue in other network environments) is where the print job is stored while trying to print.

Working with Network Hardware

❑ Because computers are affected by temperature, moisture, vibrations, and electrical interference, you need to create a controlled environment and be in control of each of these elements.

❑ Watch cable distance on the different cable types and be familiar with the components that can create interference in your environment.

❑ Network-attached storage (NAS) is a popular choice for mass storage devices such as RAID drives and CD-ROMs.

SELF TEST

The following questions will help you measure your understanding of the material presented in this chapter. Read all the choices carefully and eliminate the choices you know are wrong; then figure out which one of the remaining choices is the correct answer.

Installing a Network

1. Which networking component is responsible for connecting to the server?

   A. Client

   B. Service

   C. Protocol

   D. Network card driver

2. Which type of Microsoft server holds the network account database known as Active Directory?

   A. Workstation

   B. Standalone

   C. Member server

   D. Domain controller

3. Which networking component is responsible for being the common language used by all systems that are communicating?

   A. Client

   B. Service

   C. Protocol

   D. Network card driver

4. What is the name of Novell NetWare's network account database that can now run on Linux as well?

   A. SAM

   B. Bindery

   C. Active Directory

   D. eDirectory

Creating User Accounts

5. What is the built-in administrative account in Linux?

  A. Admin

  B. Administrator

  C. Root

  D. Guest

6. Which default account in the Microsoft world is disabled by default?

  A. Admin

  B. Administrator

  C. Root

  D. Guest

7. Where are user accounts created on a Windows client system?

  A. SAM

  B. DNS

  C. Active Directory

  D. eDirectory

8. What shell command in Linux is used to create a user account?

  A. Net use

  B. useradd

  C. perm

  D. chmod

Managing Groups

9. Which group scope is used to organize users within a Microsoft domain?

  A. Universal

  B. Global

  C. Domain local

  D. Distribution

10. Which group scope is used to assign permissions within a Microsoft domain?

  A. Universal

  B. Global

  C. Domain local

  D. Distribution

11. Which built-in group would you place Bob in to allow him to manage network user accounts in the domain?

    A. Administrators

    B. Printer Operators

    C. Backup Operators

    D. Account Operators

12. Which group would you place Sue in to allow her to manage your printing environment on the network?

    A. Administrators

    B. Printer Operators

    C. Backup Operators

    D. Account Operators

Securing Files and Folders

13. Which NTFS permission would you use to allow a user to delete a file?

    A. Read

    B. Modify

    C. Read and Execute

    D. Full Control

14. Which command in Linux/UNIX will allow you to change the permissions on a file?

    A. Net use

    B. useradd

    C. perm

    D. chmod

15. When a share permission conflicts with an NTFS permission, which permission will be the effective one?

    A. Both

    B. The share permission

    C. The most restrictive

    D. The NTFS permission

Installing Printers

16. What is the name of the printer component that is the software interface to the print device?

A. Print device

B. Printer

C. Print server

D. Printout

17. Which permission is needed to send a document to the printer in the Windows world?

A. Print

B. Manage documents

C. Full Control

D. Modify

18. You want to install a printer on your Windows server to make it a print server. What would you do?

A. Run the Add Printer Wizard, and then choose network printer.

B. Go to the Registry and create the printer.

C. Go to Active Directory Users and Computers.

D. Run the Add Printer Wizard, and then choose local printer.

Working with Network Hardware

19. Which of the following will most likely create electromagnetic interference with your computer equipment?

A. DVD player

B. Generator

C. TV

D. Dining room table

20. What type of cable is used to connect the workstation to the network jack located in the wall?

A. Crossover

B. Thinnet

C. Patch

D. Thicknet

SELF TEST ANSWERS

Installing a Network

1. ☑ **A.** Client software, also known as the redirector, is responsible for connecting to the server and sending the network request.

   ☒ **B, C,** and **D** are incorrect. A service is what the client connects to on the server such as file and print services, and a protocol is the language the client and server use to communicate. The network card driver is the software that allows the operating system to communicate with the physical network card.

2. ☑ **D.** Domain controllers hold the user account database for the network when it comes to the Microsoft networking environments. You create a domain controller by installing Active Directory with the dcpromo command.

   ☒ **A, B,** and **C** are incorrect. All of these choices are incorrect because they all have a local SAM database.

3. ☑ **C.** A protocol is the language two systems use to communicate on the network.

   ☒ **A, B,** and **D** are incorrect. A service is what the client connects to on the server such as file and print services. The network card driver is the software that allows the operating system to communicate with the physical network card. Client software, also known as the redirector, is responsible for connecting to the server and sending the network request.

4. ☑ **D.** eDirectory is the name given to NetWare's directory service. Older versions of NetWare used the term NDS for the directory service, but that has been changed in recent years.

   ☒ **A, B,** and **C** are incorrect. The SAM database is the name given to the local account database on a Microsoft system that is not a domain controller. The Active Directory database is the network account database in the Microsoft environment that runs on domain controllers, and the bindery is an old name for Novell's directory even before NDS.

Creating User Accounts

5. ☑ **C.** In Linux the administrative account that configures the operating system is known as root.

   ☒ **A, B,** and **D** are incorrect. Admin is the administrative account in NetWare, whereas Administrator is used in Microsoft environments. The guest account is not an administrative account.

6. ☑ **D.** The guest account allows anonymous access to the network, meaning that individuals will not need a user account to authenticate—they will be authenticated as guest. This account is disabled by default.

   ☒ **A, B,** and **C** are incorrect. All of these accounts are administrative accounts, not guest accounts, and are not disabled by default.

7. ☑ **A.** The SAM database is the name of the local account database on a Windows client.
☒ **B, C,** and **D** are incorrect. DNS is a network service used for hostname resolution. Active Directory is Microsoft's network account database, and eDirectory is Novell NetWare's network account database.

8. ☑ **B.** The syntax in a shell command to create a new user account in Linux is useradd <username>.
☒ **A, C,** and **D** are incorrect. Net use is a Microsoft command to map drives and printer ports, perm is not a command, and chmod is a command to change file permissions in Linux.

Managing Groups

9. ☑ **B.** Global groups are used to organize users within a domain.
☒ **A, C,** and **D** are incorrect. Universal groups are used to organize users across domains, but domain local groups are used for permission assignment. Distribution groups are not a group scope, but a group type.

10. ☑ **C.** Domain local groups are used for permission assignment.
☒ **A, B,** and **D** are incorrect. Global groups are used to organize users within a domain and Universal groups are used to organize users across domains. Distribution groups are not a group scope, but a group type.

11. ☑ **D.** Account Operators have permissions to create and manage user accounts throughout the domain.
☒ **A, B,** and **C** are incorrect. Administrators can perform any task, so you do not want to place Bob in this group. Printer Operators can manage the printing environment, and Backup Operators are allowed to perform backup and restore operations.

12. ☑ **B.** You would place Sue in the Printer Operators group so that she can perform any printing functions.
☒ **A, C,** and **D** are incorrect. Administrators can perform any task, so you do not want to place Sue in this group, Account Operators can manage user accounts, and Backup Operators are allowed to perform backup and restore operations.

Securing Files and Folders

13. ☑ **B.** The Modify permission allows users to read, create, delete, and modify the contents of files.
☒ **A, C,** and **D** are incorrect. The read permission allows users only to read the file, whereas read and execute allow users to read the file and execute it if it is an .exe. Full Control allows the delete operation but also gives the permission to change permissions, which is what makes this a wrong choice.

14. ☑ **D.** The chmod command is used to change access permissions to a file in Linux.

☒ **A, B,** and **C** are incorrect. Net use is a Windows command to map network drives and printer ports, useradd is a Linux/UNIX command to create a user account, and perm is not a command.

15. ☑ **C.** When there is a conflict in combining NTFS permissions with shared folder permissions, the most restrictive between them will win.

☒ **A, B,** and **D** are incorrect because the rule is that the most restrictive will win.

Installing Printers

16. ☑ **B.** The software interface to the print device is known as the printer in Microsoft terms.

☒ **A, C,** and **D** are incorrect. The print device is the physical hardware that outputs the printout, the print server is the Windows server on which the printer is installed, and the printout is the piece of paper you have in your hand when the print job completes.

17. ☑ **A.** The print permission is needed to send a print job to a printer.

☒ **B, C,** and **D** are incorrect. The manage documents permission is needed to manage jobs in the printer such as canceling a job. Full Control is needed to change the printer settings, and there is no modify permission on printers.

18. ☑ **D.** You would run the Add Printer Wizard and choose to install a local printer and share it to create a print server.

☒ **A, B,** and **C** are incorrect because they are not the steps to install a printer on a print server.

Working with Network Hardware

19. ☑ **B.** A generator is the most likely to create electromagnetic interference with networking and computer equipment of the choices provided. You need to be aware of potential interference in your environment.

☒ **A, C,** and **D** are incorrect because they are not the most likely to create EMI. A TV may do so, but a generator will typically have greater potential.

20. ☑ **C.** A patch cable is used to connect the workstation to the RJ-45 jack in the wall.

☒ **A, B,** and **D** are incorrect because they are not used to connect the workstation to the wall jack.

11

Maintaining and Supporting a Network

I nstalling and setting up the network is only the beginning of your job as a network professional. You are going to be required to maintain the network by performing some very common day-to-day tasks, such as updating the operating system with any new security patches and installing and maintaining antivirus software to protect your systems against virus attacks.

This chapter looks at these essential tasks along with other common critical tasks, such as backing up data and installing antispyware software. Each task is critical to the day-to-day maintenance of the network!

CERTIFICATION OBJECTIVE 11.01

Network Upgrades

Before we discuss performing operating system upgrades, let's look at software and hardware upgrades and some best practices for dealing with these upgrades. It is important to be sure that before applying any software upgrade and hardware upgrade, you read as much documentation about the upgrade and configure a test environment to test the upgrade. Never perform an upgrade for the first time on production systems.

Software Upgrades

Software manufacturers release upgrades for their products to improve them and make them more powerful. You should always install an upgrade on a standalone machine before distributing it to the network. This enables you to test the application and go through the upgrade process in a nonproduction environment.

Many minor upgrades are free and require a simple download similar to a patch. Upgrading from one version of an application or OS to another usually requires the purchaser to pay a fee for the new product. Sometimes an application can have a minor version change, such as version 5.01 to version 5.02, which may not require a fee, due to the subtle changes contained in the upgrade. Other upgrades, meanwhile, can be ordered for free from the manufacturer, or may come at a minimal cost if you are a registered owner of the older version. Again, be sure to have a good backup before you install the upgrade in order to prevent data loss.

on the
job *Be sure to have a test lab for any software or hardware upgrades so that you can thoroughly test the new changes with all of your existing hardware and software. Be sure that the upgrade has not caused another aspect of the network, including applications on the users' desktops, to stop working.*

Hardware Upgrades

Not only will you be responsible for replacing old devices with new ones, such as an old 10 Mbps hub with a new 10/100 Mbps network switch, you will also be responsible for updating the firmware that is contained in your servers and network devices. The firmware is a special type of ROM chip that controls the functionality of the server or device; it is updated using a special software program called a ROM update, or a flash program. It is recommended that you keep informed about the latest ROM updates for all the components on your network. If there is an update, there is a reason for it, and if you can avoid the problem before it happens, you'll save yourself a lot of headaches. Make sure that you have the correct update and that you have done sufficient research into what the update does.

Manufacturers of hardware devote an area on their web sites to their hardware products and allow you to download the latest firmware so that you can update the components in your servers, routers, switches, and workstations. Figure 11-1 shows how to download the latest BIOS updates from the Dell site for a PowerEdge 1800 server.

FIGURE 11-1

Retrieving BIOS updates for a Dell PowerEdge 1800

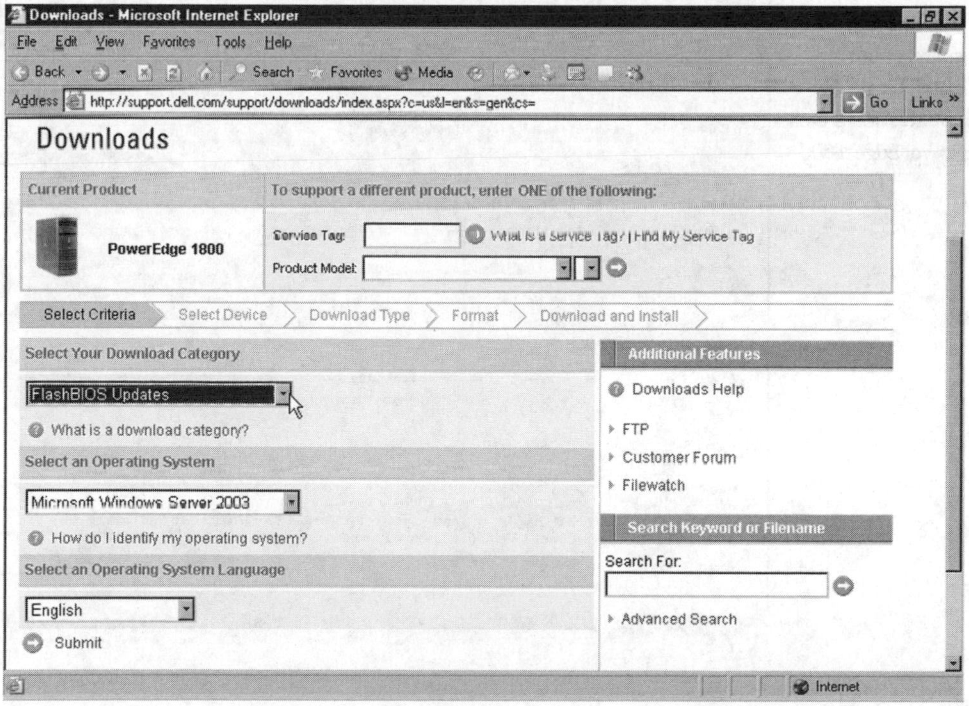

When downloading BIOS updates, be sure that you have the correct and most recent version. On this Dell site, you can see in Figure 11-2 that the site shows the most recent version of the BIOS for this PowerEdge 1800 but also contains a link to view the previous versions. If you click the link for the current version, it will take you to a description of that version and to the file download you will be required to apply to the server.

If you click the link for the current BIOS update for the Dell PowerEdge 1800, you will see the description and download link of the BIOS update as shown in Figure 11-3. Notice in the figure that you can see the release date of the BIOS at the top of the screen, and then at the bottom of the screen you can see the link for the file that needs to be downloaded. Along with the file link, they specify a description on what you will need to do with this file. In most cases, you will download the executable and then either run the update on the system directly or burn to CD and then boot off the CD to perform the update. It is important to make sure that you read the directions first, because each vendor applies the update differently.

FIGURE 11-2	
Viewing the current and previous BIOS updates for a Dell PowerEdge 1800	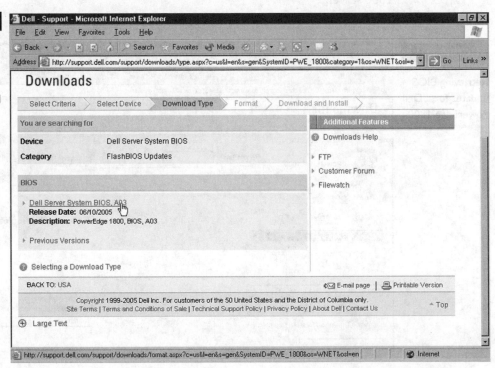

FIGURE 11-3

FIGURE 11-3

Viewing the
BIOS update
description and
download link

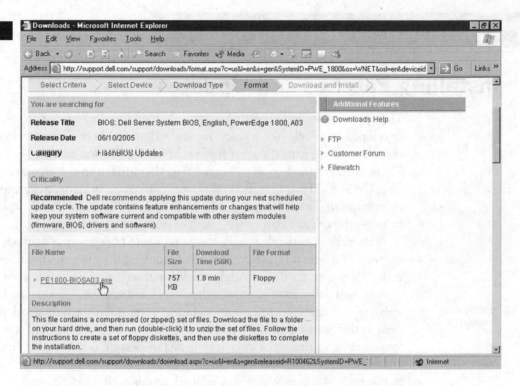

Some hardware items may not allow for ROM updates, and those that do may
require a full hardware upgrade to meet the needs of the company. For example,
if a company upgrades its network from 10 Mbps to 100 Mbps Ethernet and the
company had purchased only 10 Mbps Ethernet cards, there won't be a way to just
update the ROM to allow for 100 Mbps transfer speeds. That would require a full
hardware replacement of the network card.

When new hardware is purchased, you must verify that the hardware will work
with your existing PCs, as well as the OSs and the network environment.

*Be aware of how to perform a ROM BIOS flash upgrade. Remember that the
power cannot be shut off during the upgrade, or else the BIOS will be corrupt
and the system will not function. Also remember that after the upgrade is
complete, the system must be shut off and turned back on for the changes to
take effect.*

CERTIFICATION OBJECTIVE 11.02

Installing Patches and Updates

The applications and operating systems that are installed on our computers are developed by people like you and me and will most likely have mistakes programmed into them along with the great features of the application that we see every day. These mistakes (known as vulnerabilities) that are left in the program code can be found by individuals who then take over your system or network by exploiting that vulnerability! This is known as a network attack, or system attack, depending on whether the entire network was taken over or just a single system.

A number of network attacks can be prevented because the manufacturers of the software and operating systems are always looking for the vulnerabilities in their code. They then fix those mistakes and ship the fixes in what is known as a fix or update. You will normally acquire these fixes and updates through the manufacturer's web site. For example, Microsoft operating systems have a Windows Update program item in the Start menu to go to the company's update web site and scan your system for any updates that need to be installed. This feature is known as Windows Update and may be run from choosing Start | All Programs | Windows Update, as shown in Figure 11-4. After Windows Update determines the updates, or fixes, that are needed on your system, your system will download the updates from the Windows Update site.

There are various types of updates that will be delivered to you through the Windows Update site. They are listed as follows:

- **Security hot-fix**   A security hot-fix is a critical security update that should be applied to your system as quickly as possible because the vulnerability opens the system to serious security risks.

- **Patch**   A patch is a fix to a particular problem in software or operating system code that does not create a security risk but does create problems with the system or the application.

- **Service pack**   A service pack is all updates for a product, including patches and security hot-fixes, from the time the product was released up to the time of the service pack. If you install a service pack, you will not need to install each patch individually, because the service pack includes all updates up to that point in time. You will need to install patches and security fixes that come out after the service pack.

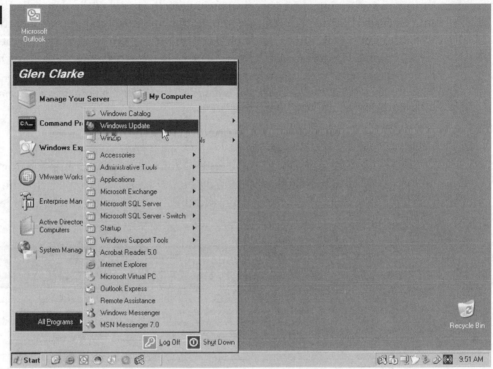

FIGURE 11-4

Starting the
Windows Update
on a Windows
server

Consider now Exercise 11-1, which demonstrates how to patch a system with
Windows Update.

EXERCISE 11-1

Patching a System with Windows Update

In this exercise you will run Windows Update to bring your Windows Server system
up-to-date in order to help protect the system from known vulnerabilities. Windows
2000 Server is used in this example because there are a number of exploits against it.
The point of the exercise is to show you that once the system is patched the exploit
no longer works.

Before patching the system you will first download and leverage an RPC exploit
known as kaht2 that will allow you to connect to the Windows 2000 Server as

the operating system account and take full control of the unpatched system. After verifying that you could connect to the unpatched system, you will then patch the server by running Windows Update and trying the exploit again—the second time you will be unsuccessful because the system has been patched. *Please note that it is illegal to gain unauthorized access to another system, network, or device—this lab is for educational purposes only and is designed to show the importance of patching a system.*

Compromising an Unpatched System

1. On your Windows XP system, download the kaht2.zip file from http://www. securityfocus.com/bid/8205/exploit (as shown in the following illustration). Once you have downloaded the Zip file, extract it to c:\labfiles\tools\kaht2.

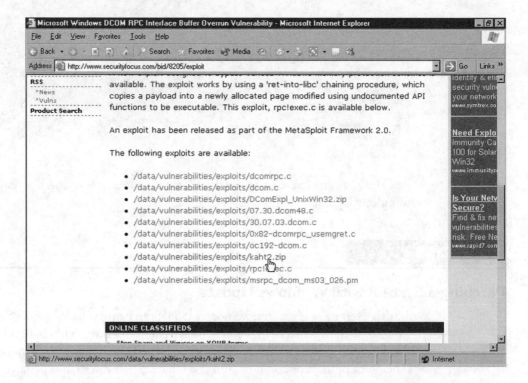

2. Click Start | Run and then type **cmd**.
3. Choose OK.

4. At the command prompt, type **cd c:\labfiles\tools\kaht2**.

5. You will now use two IP addresses with the kaht command-line utility. Address 1 will be the IP address that is one less than the address of your unpatched Windows 2000 Server, whereas address 2 is the IP address of your Windows 2000 Server. Once you know these two addresses, type **kaht2 <address1> <address2>** (as shown in the following illustration) and press ENTER. In my example I intend on hitting the 192.168.1.201 system so I will type **kaht2 192.168.1.200 192.168.1.201**.

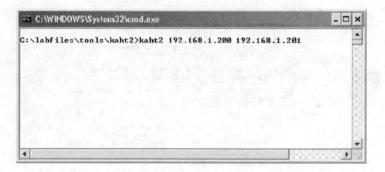

6. If you are connected to the server, you will be sitting at the prompt of c:\winnt\system32—which is the C:\drive of the server you have just compromised! If your screen looks like the screen shown in the illustration that follows, you will need to patch the Windows 2000 Server.

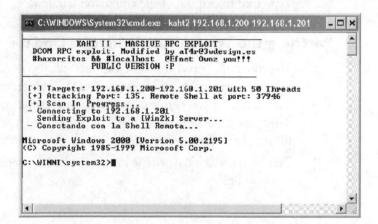

7. To verify that you are connected as the system account and can create your own user account on the server, type **net user bobby password /add**. To place this newly created user account in the administrators group of the server, type **net localgroup administrators bobby /add**. The results are shown in the illustration that follows.

8. You have proven that you can take control of an unpatched system by creating your own administrative account. Type **Exit** to exit out of the kaht2 shell.

9. Type **Exit** to exit out of the command window.

Patching the System with Windows Update

10. To protect the server from the kaht attack, you need to make sure that you patch the server. Microsoft is aware of the vulnerability, and the vulnerability will be fixed if you perform a full Windows update on the system. On the Windows 2000 Server select Start | Windows Update (as shown in the top illustration on the next page).

11. The Windows Update site is loaded in the browser. Click the Scan For Updates link.

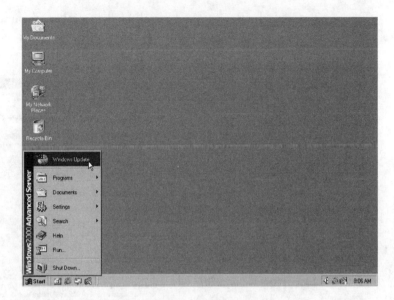

12. Windows scans for updates for your system (as shown in the following illustration).

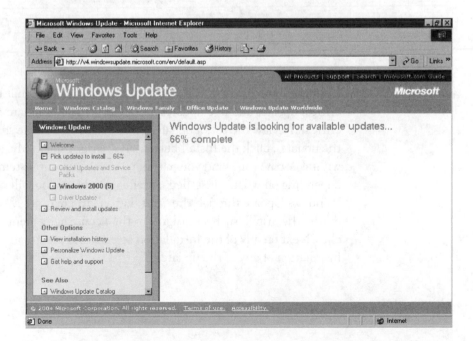

13. Click the Review And Install Updates link and you will be presented with a screen like the one in the illustration that follows.

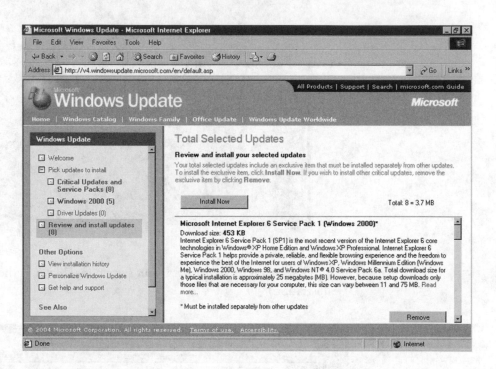

14. In the foregoing screen, you will notice on the left side that there are eight critical updates and five updates for Windows 2000 that are not considered critical. Review the list of updates on the right side of the screen. To install the updates, click the Install button on the right side of the screen. This will take some time, and you may have to reboot your system a few times, depending on what is installed. After each reboot, you will need to restart Windows Update through the Start button. You may get asked questions during the install, such as to agree to the license agreement, and you can click Next on any of the installation screens and accept all defaults for the installation of any of the updates.

Trying to Exploit a Patched System

15. Once the update of the system is complete, let's verify that the patching of the system prevents the RPC exploit from happening again. Go to your Windows XP Professional system and type **kaht2 192.168.1.200 192.168.1.201**—you should be unsuccessful with this attack (as shown in the following illustration).

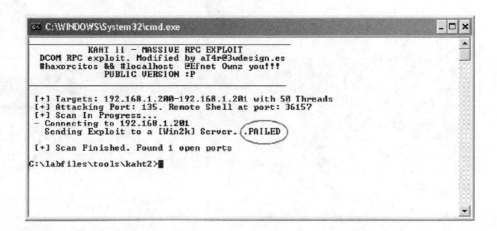

Windows Server Update Services (WSUS)

Running Windows Update on one system is no problem, but what if you have to manage 500 systems and ensure that each system is up-to-date with current patches and hot-fixes? Microsoft has created Windows Server Update Services (WSUS), which allows you to create a WSUS server and download the updates from the Internet to the WSUS server. You can then test the installation of those updates to some test systems to verify that the updates do not conflict with any applications on the systems; then you can send the update out to the 500 systems.

When you send the updates to the 500 systems on the network, you can do it from a central point—the WSUS server. The WSUS server has a web-based management tool that allows you to manually approve updates. Those updates are downloaded to the WSUS server. Within WSUS you can create groups of computers and then send the updates out to the different groups on the network. An update that you have not approved will not be sent to the systems on the network. Figure shows a WSUS structure.

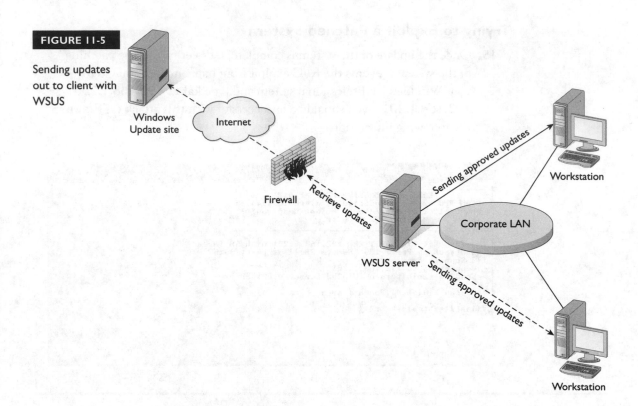

FIGURE 11-5

Sending updates out to client with WSUS

There are many benefits to a product like WSUS; for one thing, you can download the updates to one central machine from the Internet instead of having each system downloading from the Internet. This helps to maintain available bandwidth by not having each person perform the download. Another benefit to WSUS is that clients are receiving only updates that you have approved. This happens because you will configure each client to retrieve the updates from the WSUS server and not the Internet. Once you have approved the update on the WSUS server, the client will get the update automatically through WSUS. Any updates that are not approved will not be downloaded by the clients on the network. It is also important to note that with WSUS the installation is performed by the system itself, not the user who has logged on. This is important because users typically do not have privileges to install software. Figure 11-6 displays the WSUS administration site.

FIGURE 11-6

WSUS is used to distribute updates from a central server.

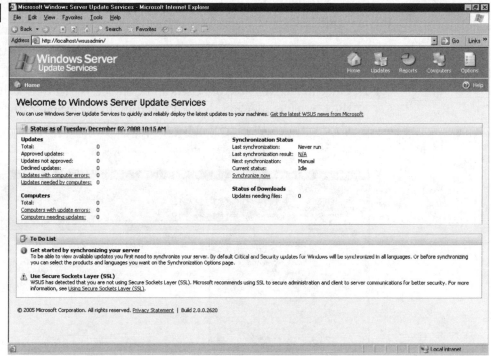

You can download a free copy of WSUS by going to the www.microsoft.com/ download site. Once you download the program, you will need to install it on a Windows server running IIS. After installing WSUS and downloading the updates from the Microsoft site, you then need to approve the updates. After approving the updates, the next step is to configure the clients to point to the WSUS server so that they download the updates from the WSUS server instead of the Windows Update site.

Configuring Clients to Use the WSUS Server for Updates

To configure the Windows clients on your network to use the WSUS server, you will configure a domain policy that configures each client in the domain to point to the WSUS server for the updates. If you are not in a domain environment, you may configure the clients through local policies. To change the default domain policy on the network, follow these steps:

1. Click Start | Administrative Tools | Active Directory Users And Computers.

2. Once in Active Directory Users and Computers, right-click the domain at the top-left corner and choose Properties. In my example, the domain is glensworld.loc (as shown in the following illustration).

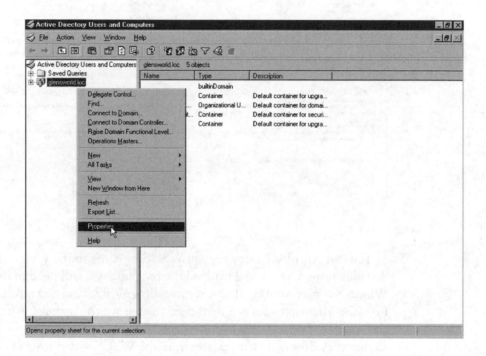

3. Once the properties of the domain are displayed, click the Group Policy tab.

4. Make sure that the Default Domain Policy is selected and click Edit.

5. The Group Policy Object Editor appears. In the Computer Configuration section expand Administrative Templates | Windows Components and then highlight Windows Update (as shown in the top illustration on the next page).

6. To enable automatic updates on the clients in your domain, double-click Configure Automatic Updates.

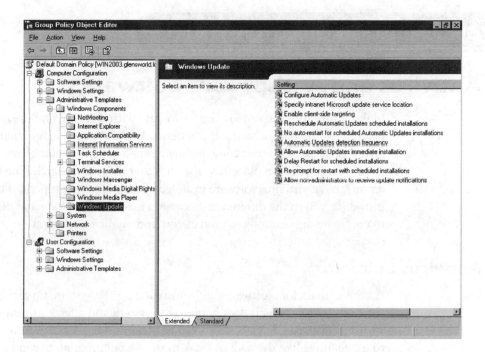

7. In the Configure Automatic Updates Properties, select Enable, choose Auto Download, and schedule the Install option. Specify a schedule of 3:00 A.M. for the automatic installation.

8. Click OK.

9. Double-click the "Specify Intranet Microsoft update service location" policy and enable the policy setting. Set your Intranet server to the name of the server that you installed WSUS on. For example, my server was called win2003, so the Intranet server address is http://win2003.

10. Close the Group Policy Object Editor window.

11. Click OK.

12. Close Active Directory Users and Computers.

Now that the policy is configured in Active Directory, the clients will automatically point to your WSUS server and install any updates that you approve in the WSUS administration site.

CERTIFICATION OBJECTIVE 11.03

Antivirus and Antispyware Software

Making sure that the systems are up-to-date with software and operating system patches is only part of your job as a network professional. It is extremely critical that, given today's threats that come through e-mail systems and the Internet, you have an antivirus policy in place that specifies that all systems, including both clients and servers, have antivirus software installed and configured properly. This section will introduce you to the differences between viruses and spyware and demonstrate how to configure applications to protect you from malicious software.

Antivirus Software

A *virus* is malicious software that is installed on the system, usually by accident or through trickery, which does harm to the system and affects its normal operation. Viruses in the past have been known to prevent the computer from starting up and to use features like the address book in the e-mail program to send e-mail to all recipients in the address book. Bottom line—as a network professional you need to be familiar with installing antivirus software and how to keep it up-to-date.

Antivirus software can be installed on systems automatically through software deployment features such as Group Policies in Active Directory or Zenworks in Novell environments.

There are a number of antivirus software products, the most popular of which appear in the following list:

- Norton AntiVirus
- McAfee Antivirus
- Panda Antivirus
- FProt Antivirus
- AVG Antivirus

Each antivirus product offers pretty much the same type of functionality. Some of the features offered by antivirus products include

- **Scheduled scans**   Each product should offer a scheduling feature that allows you to schedule a virus scan. A virus scan is what the virus protection software does—it scans the system to see whether the system has been infected with a computer virus.

- **Scheduled definition updates**   The virus protection software should allow the scheduling of a virus definition update. A virus definition is a list of all known viruses at the time the definition file was created. After you install the antivirus software, make sure that you are updating the virus definitions on a regular basis; this will ensure that your system is always being protected from the most current viruses. Figure 11-7 shows the option to update your antivirus definitions in Norton AntiVirus.

- **Real-time protection**   Most antivirus products offer real-time protection, which is a feature that scans any file that you access—as you access it. This is an automatic feature—once it is enabled, you will not need to manually invoke the scan on a file before opening the file. Figure 11-8 shows the enabling and disabling of real-time protection. In Figure 11-8 notice that you can enable the real-time protection features but also specify what action the software should take when a virus is found. In this example, Norton will try to clean the virus (remove it); if that is not successful, it will quarantine the virus. You can also specify whether you want to see a message on the system and what file types are being protected.

FIGURE 11-7

Updating virus definitions

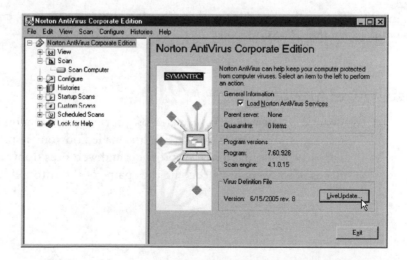

FIGURE 11-8

Enabling real-
time antivirus
protection

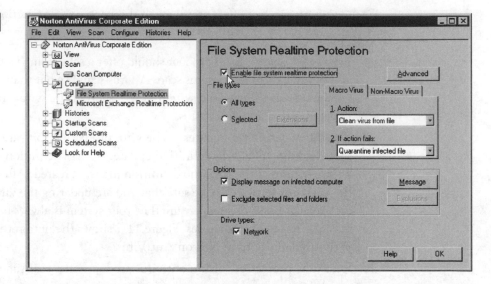

■ **E-mail features** A number of antivirus products integrate with your e-mail
software so that it scans the contents of your e-mail and helps to protect your
system from a virus that is received through e-mail. There are also server-class
antivirus products that you can load on the e-mail server so that the server
scans the e-mail before depositing the e-mail in the user's mailbox. You most
definitely want to load a server-based antivirus product on your e-mail server.
Figure 11-9 shows a version of Norton AntiVirus that will scan e-mails going
to your Exchange Server.

*To practice installing and configuring antivirus software, check out Exercise 11-2
on the CD-ROM.*

Antispyware/Adware

Spyware is software that is loaded on your system that monitors your Internet
activity, and *adware* is software that is loaded on your system that will pop up
with ads promoting different products and web sites from time to time. Both
pieces of software have become the "pain" of the Internet during the past few

FIGURE 11-9

Enabling real-time
protection for
e-mails

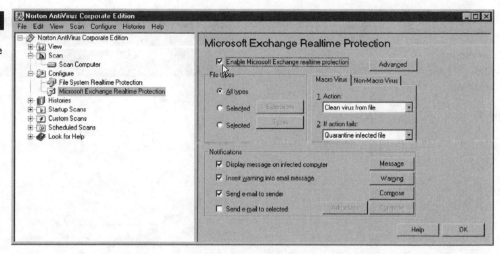

years. They are most often loaded on your system when you surf a malicious or
hacked web site.

Antispyware (and -adware) is software that you can use to remove these
troublesome invaders from your system. There are a number of products that
can be used to remove this malicious software, such as Spybot, Ad-Aware, and
Microsoft's Windows Defender. Antispyware has become as popular as antivirus
software, and a lot of features in newer antispyware products are the same as
those on antivirus software, such as real-time protection and scheduling of scans.
Figure 11-10 shows Microsoft's antispyware software known as Windows Defender,
which includes such features as

- Real-time protection
- Scheduled scans
- Browser hijack protection
- Automatic updates of malicious software definitions

Additionally, you can view software that is running in memory with the Software
Explorer feature!

Check out Exercise 11-3 in LabBook.pdf to see how to install and configure
Windows Defender.

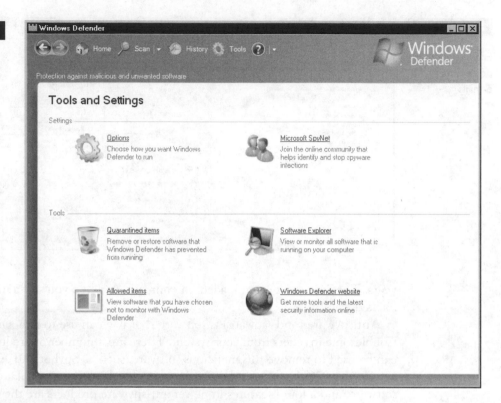

Backing Up Network Data

A critical task to help maintain the network and ensure that users have access to
their data is to regularly back up data on the network to another location. You may
back up the data to tape drives or to a backup file on another server, although tape
drives are the more popular solution.

Tape Drives

The two most common types of tape drives are digital audio tape (DAT) and digital
linear tape (DLT). This section looks at each drive in some detail. The exam will
not delve into as many particulars, but understanding their characteristics will help
you remember the information about the drives and ultimately help you on the test.

Digital Audio Tape (DAT)

Digital audio tape (DAT) was developed in the mid-1980s by Sony and Philips to record music in a digital format, but it has now become very popular as a medium for computer data storage. The DAT drive uses a helical scan, which means that the read/write heads spin diagonally across the tape. DAT uses the digital data storage (DDS) format and a 4 mm tape. Although the speed isn't as good as that of a DLT drive, the capacity can be quite large. Different DDS formats allow for different amounts of storage on a tape. Table 11-1 lists different DDS formats and their storage capacities.

As DDS-1 emerged, so did compression. That is why you'll notice that formats from DDS-1 to DDS-3 have a second number associated with them, which is always double the base storage capacity. Using this equation, standard 4 mm tapes for DAT drives can hold up to 24GB of data. Other technologies have also emerged with the appearance of 8 mm tapes, but you won't need to know these for the exam. Figure 11-11 shows a DAT tape drive.

TABLE 11-1	Type of Format	Storage Capacity
Storage Capacities of DDS Formats	DDS	2GB
	DDS-1	2–4GB
	DDS-2	4–8GB
	DDS-3	12–24GB

FIGURE 11-11

A DAT tape drive

Digital Linear Tape (DLT)

Digital linear tape (DLT) was introduced by Digital Equipment Corporation in the mid-1980s, but Quantum Corporation owns the technology now. The DLT tape is a half-inch reel-to-reel magnetic tape, where the tape cartridge contains one reel and the DLT drive the other. The main advantages are fast data transfer rates, higher storage capacity, and higher reliability over DAT. All this, of course, comes at a price to the customer.

DLT drives store data on the tape differently than DAT drives do. The data path is made up of parallel tracks recorded in a serpentine pattern. What this means is that the first track is written from one end of the tape to the other and then the heads are repositioned and the next track goes the opposite direction (again for the entire length of the tape). The drive continues to go back and forth, writing until the tape is full.

Tape Rotation

When it comes to maintaining the network, you need to schedule a backup job and develop a backup schedule. Many companies do a tape rotation. They have daily, weekly, and monthly tapes, the rotation of which usually consists of 20 to 25 tapes, each with its purpose. Sometimes this is called an autopilot rotation. The backup software keeps a database and expects a certain tape on each day of the year. The most common is a 21-tape rotation consisting of 4 daily tapes for Monday through Thursday, 5 weekly tapes for each Friday (some months have 5 Fridays), and 12 monthly tapes for the last weekday of the month. There are no backups on Saturday or Sunday. It is a good idea to store the weekly or monthly tapes offsite to keep fire or some major catastrophic event from ruining your data and your backups.

Offsite storage of tape backups is a critical part of your backup plan. If you have a fire in the office and it destroys your servers and tape backups, there wouldn't have been much point in having the backup at all. Make sure that copies of backups are stored offsite.

Along with tape rotations come tape libraries and tape arrays. Tape libraries are designed to contain a series of tapes in a holder that is inserted into the tape mechanism to automate the rotation of tapes throughout the week. If the amount of data is very large, the tape library may be used on a daily basis to rotate multiple tapes in and out of the various drives to make sure all data fits onto a tape. Tape arrays, on the other hand, are similar to RAID technology with hard drives, wherein data is spread over a series of drives—for instance, there might be a parity drive to add fault tolerance. Manufacturers claim that tape arrays increase the throughput because multiple drives are writing simultaneously.

It is extremely critical that you store copies of the backup offsite in case there is a disaster, such as fire or flooding in your building. If servers and backups are stored in the same location, the organization will be vulnerable to data loss.

Full, Incremental, and Differential Backups

Backup software enables you to run three types of backups: full, incremental, and differential. These are the three you may see on the exam, so we will focus on them. The key to backing up data is to ensure that you can restore it in the event of a system failure. These three types of backup will function well if you use them together correctly.

Full Backup

A *full* backup backs up every file on the specified volume or volumes (or partitions). Many companies run a full backup every day, no matter what. Under such a system, the restore process requires only the most recent tape. However, a full backup necessitates a large storage capacity and a lot of time. If you have large amounts of data, running a daily full backup may not be practical because it may take too long to perform.

Every file has an archive bit that flags whether or not the file needs to be backed up. When you change a file, this bit is flagged automatically, which means that the file needs to be backed up. In theory, any file that has been changed needs to backed up because we want to be sure we can always bring the file to its most recent state.

To view the archive bit in Windows, right-click the file and go to the properties. Once in the properties, click the Advanced button on the General tab. You will see the option that says File Is Ready For Archiving as shown in Figure 11-12.

exam

watch *Full backups back up every file that is selected and then clear the archive bit.*

FIGURE 11-12

Looking at the
archive bit in
Windows

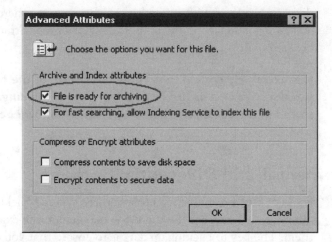

The important thing to understand when a full backup is performed is that the backup backs up all the files that you select (whether the archive bit is set or not), and then clears the archive bit so that the operating system and applications know that the file has been backed up.

Incremental Backup

An *incremental* backup backs up the files that have changed or were added since the last incremental or full backup. It does this by backing only files that have the archive bit set (meaning the file needs to be backed up). This is different from a full backup, in that a full backup will back up any file that is selected because it does not use the archive bit to determine whether to back the file up or not—it simply backs up whatever you tell it to. An incremental backup will back up whatever files you have selected that have the archive bit set.

Using a combination of the full backup and incremental backup is highly effective and less time consuming than running a full daily backup every day. A number of companies will set up a backup schedule that performs a full backup Friday night and then only backs up the changes each night through the week by performing an incremental backup. However, to restore, you will need the last full backup tape as well as every incremental backup tape made since the last full backup.

An incremental backup clears the archive bit to report that the file has been backed up. If you were to perform an additional incremental backup the next day, the same file would not get backed up (unless it was changed) because the archive bit would not be set. Your restore strategy with incremental backups is to restore the full backup and then each incremental backup since the full backup. This will ensure that you get the build-up of changes since the full backup.

e x a m

w a t c h *Differential backups back up any files that have had changes and do not clear the archive bit. Because the archive bit is not cleared, each differential backup will back up all files changed since the last full backup.*

Differential Backup

A *differential* backup backs up the files that have changed or were added since the last full backup by looking for any files that have the archive bit set. The differential backup is different from the incremental in that the differential does not clear the archive bit after the backup is done. This means that if you were to do another differential backup the next time you did a backup, the same files (and any new ones) would get backed up. As a result every differential backup will have all changes since the last full backup. Your restore strategy would be to restore the last full backup and then restore your last differential backup.

e x a m

w a t c h *You will definitely see a question or two on the exam about the different kinds of backups. Be sure to know the differences between full, incremental, and differential backups. You may be given a scenario where you have to choose the backup or restore strategy.*

Differential and incremental backups can make the restoration process a little more complex, because you have to restore from the full backup first, and then restore from the incremental or differential backups to make sure any files that have changed since the last full backup are restored. An important difference between differential and incremental backups is that incremental backups take less time to back up (because you are only getting changes since the last full or incremental backup) but more time to restore (because you restore multiple incremental backups). Differential backups take more time to back up but less time to restore.

If you decide to take a simpler approach by performing full backups each time, you can restore from the most recent full backup and get all the files restored in one session.

Scheduling Backups

Most network administrators would rather be at home late at night while the backup operation is being performed. That's why they schedule the backup operation so that they don't need to be in the office at night to start the backup after everyone else has gone home. Most backup software supports the scheduling of the backup operation, and that is definitely one of the features that you would look for in your backup software.

When scheduling your backup operations, you will need to create a backup plan. A backup plan will contain a listing of the data that will be backed up with each backup operation along with the type of backup that occurs (incremental, differential, or full). You should also make sure that the backup schedule is included in this plan.

For example, you may decide that every Saturday morning at 12 A.M. you will perform a full backup of your data files and your e-mail data. It is really common to have in this backup plan an incremental backup of the same data files and e-mail servers that will be scheduled every morning at 12 A.M. To restore any data that goes corrupt, you would restore the last full backup and then apply on top of that the last differential backup. This will bring your data up-to-date to the point of the last differential.

When developing your backup plan, you should have a detailed plan of what resources on the server (such as folders, databases, or mail stores) will be backed up and what they contain. You should also plot how often these items need to be backed up. This backup plan will serve as great documentation to go in your "Network Documentation" book in which you keep a collection of network diagrams, firewall rules, server configurations, and the like.

Backup Plan Example

The following is an example of a backup plan that you can use as a guideline to build your own plan or maybe adapt in your own backup plan template.

Databases				
Database Name	**File Location**	**Backup Type**	**SQL Job**	**Frequency**
Notes:				

Exchange E-Mail			
Database Name	**File Location**	**Backup Type**	**Frequency**
Notes:			

File System Data Files			
Folder Name	**File Location**	**Backup Type**	**Frequency**
Notes:			

EXERCISE 11-4

Backing Up and Restoring Data on a Windows Server

In this exercise you will learn how to back up files on your Windows server using the Windows backup software, and how to restore a file after it has been accidentally deleted.

1. Select Start | All Programs | Accessories | System Tools | Backup.

2. To do a backup of the labfiles\packetcaptures folder, select the Backup tab. The backup software shows you a list of files on the server you can back up (as shown in the following illustration). Notice that because I have Exchange Server installed, the software allows me to back up my Exchange mailboxes.

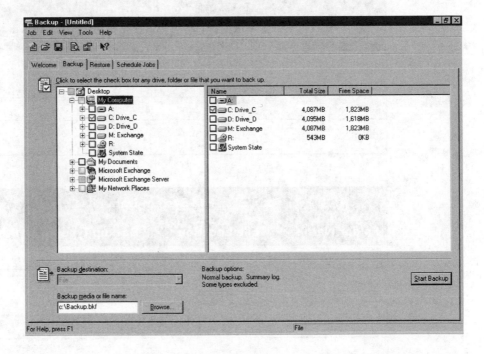

3. Expand out the C drive and then the labfiles folder. Select the check box located beside the PacketCaptures folder to back up the PacketCaptures folder (as shown in the following illustration).

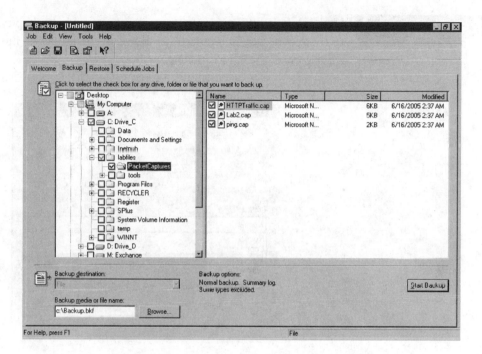

4. At the bottom of the backup screen, change the path of where the files will be backed up to c:\Backup.bkf and then click Start Backup.

5. The backup job information displays (as shown in the following illustration). Click Advanced to verify that the backup type is a full backup.

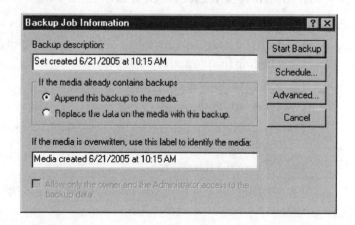

6. In the Advanced Backup Options you can set your backup type from Normal to Incremental or Differential (as shown in the following illustration). Ensure that Normal is selected and then choose OK.

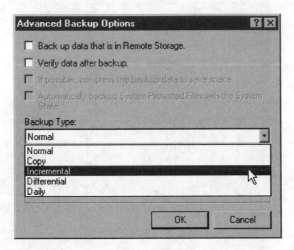

7. You could schedule the backup to occur automatically at certain times by clicking the Schedule button. You will perform the backup manually, so click Start Backup.

8. When the backup completes, it will show a summary. Click Close.

Performing a Restore of a Deleted File

9. Double-click My Computer | Drive C | labfiles | PacketCaptures.

10. In the PacketCaptures folder delete the file named HTTPTraffic.cap by right-clicking the file and choosing Delete.

11. Click Yes to confirm you wish to delete.

12. Close all Windows.

13. To restore the deleted file, choose Start | Programs | Accessories | System Tools | Backup.

14. Choose the Restore tab.

15. Expand the File option on the left by clicking the + sign.

16. Expand the media option and then the folder for drive C by clicking the + sign as well. When a dialog box appears asking the path to the backup file, simply click OK.

17. After the catalog (which is a list of contents that exist in the backup set or tape) is read, the labfiles folder is displayed. Expand the labfiles folder on the left and then highlight the PacketCaptures folder. Choose the check box located beside HTTPTraffic.cap to restore that file (as shown in the following illustration).

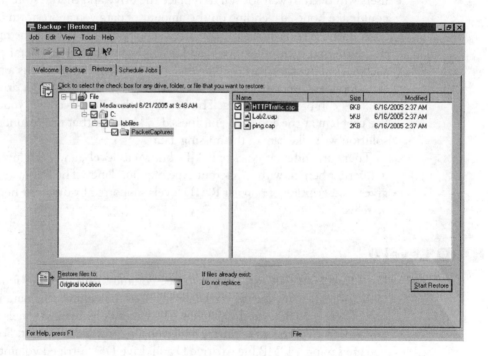

18. Click Start Restore.
19. Click OK.
20. Click OK on the second dialog box.
21. After the restore operation completes, click Close and then close the backup software. Verify that the files now exist in C:\labfiles\PacketCaptures.

Providing Fault Tolerance

Having a data backup is a great idea, and storing a copy of that backup offsite is a better idea to help ensure that you can recover from any type of disaster. One of the problems with relying only on a backup solution is that if a drive fails on the server, users will need to wait for you to replace the drive and then restore all the data—this could take hours, depending on the amount of data you are restoring.

To avoid having to replace the drive and restore the data in the middle of the day during business hours, you could take advantage of fault-tolerant solutions such as Redundant Array of Independent Disks (RAID). RAID is a technology that duplicates data across drives so that if a drive fails, the other drives in the solution can provide the data. The benefit is that if a drive fails, you can wait to fix the problem at the end of the business day, knowing that the redundancy of your solution will take care of the missing data.

There are different types of RAID, known as levels, and each level provides a different benefit with a different type of redundancy. The following subsection gives a description of popular RAID levels supported by different network operating systems.

RAID Level 0

RAID level 0 is called striping or striped volumes. With RAID 0 multiple disks are used to create a volume; when data is saved to the volume, the data is split up and spread across all disks in the volume. The benefit of striped volumes is that all disks are written to at the same time, giving you a performance benefit. For example, if you are saving a 12MB file to drive D and drive D is a striped volume made up of four disks, we can generalize the save operation by saying that each disk will save 3MB of data each and all disks will work at the same time to do the save operation that totals 12MB. If you only had one disk working for that 12MB save operation, it would take four times longer.

The disadvantage of RAID level 0 is that there is actually no duplication of data; therefore, if one of your hard drives fails within the volume, you can't read any of the data. RAID 0 is strictly for the performance benefit in the read and write operations. Figure 11-13 shows an example of a RAID 0 setup.

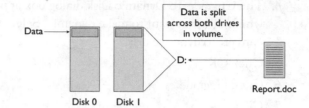

FIGURE 11-13

Looking at
RAID 0

Configuring RAID 0 on a Windows Server

Windows Server offers a software RAID feature, which means that the operating system is responsible for the creation and management of the RAID volume. A hardware RAID solution would offer a better-performing solution, but it would be more expensive.

Before you can start creating fault-tolerant volumes, you must be sure to upgrade your disk to a dynamic disk. Dynamic disk is the disk type used in Windows to create RAID volumes. Take the following steps to convert your disk from a basic disk (which does not support volumes) to a dynamic disk and then create a RAID 0 volume.

1. Right-click My Computer and choose Manage.
2. In the Computer Management console, select Disk Management on the left-hand side.
3. Right-click your disk on the right side and choose Upgrade To Dynamic Disk (see the accompanying illustration).

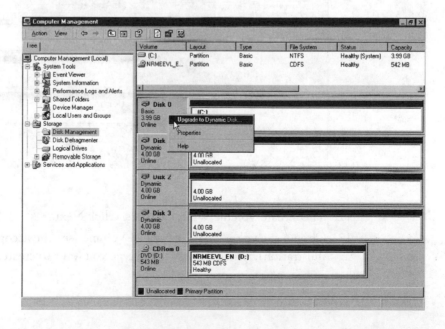

4. The Upgrade To Dynamic Disk dialog box appears, asking you to select which disk you want to make dynamic. Select all disks that you wish to convert to dynamic disk.

5. Click OK.

6. Click Upgrade.

7. Click Yes.

8. Click Yes again.

9. Click OK. You will need to reboot the system.

10. After the system has rebooted, log on as an administrative account, choose No to restarting again, and then start Disk Management.

11. Right-click an area of unallocated space on disk 1 and choose Create Volume (see the accompanying illustration).

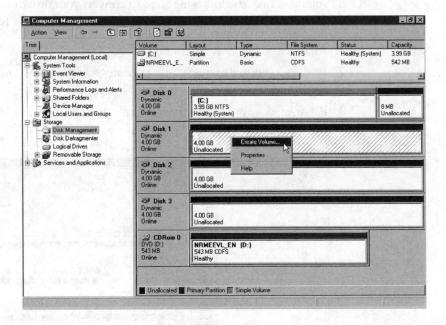

12. The Create Volume Wizard appears. Click Next.

13. Choose the volume type of Striped Volume (see the accompanying illustration), which is the volume type you want to create, and choose Next.

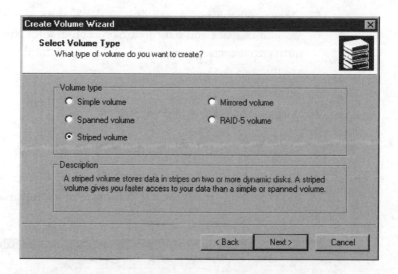

14. You will now need to choose the disks that will participate in the striped volume solution. Select disks 2 and 3 on the left and click Add to add to the striped volume (see the accompanying illustration). Notice that the disk you started the volume on was already selected as a member of the volume. Since I started the volume on disk 1 and added disk 2 and disk 3, I will have three disks in this solution.

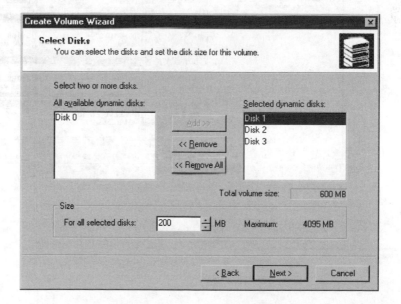

15. Once you have added each disk, at the bottom of the dialog box type the amount of space you want to use on each disk for the volume. Type **200** and notice that each disk will use 200MB—for a total of 600MB for the entire volume.

16. Click Next.

17. Assign a drive letter of S for Striped.

18. Click Next.

19. Click Next to format for NTFS.

20. Click Finish and the new Striped Volume will be created. Notice that drive S shows multiple times because it is made up of multiple disks.

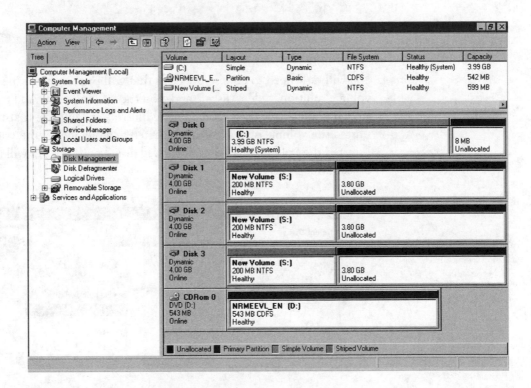

21. Close all windows.

 **a t c h**

RAID 0, known as disk striping, splits the data across all disks in the volume. RAID 0 writes to all disks at the same time, decreasing the time it takes to read or write the data. There is no fault tolerance in RAID 0; it is strictly for performance benefits.

RAID Level 1

RAID level 1 is known as disk mirroring. Disk mirroring uses two hard drives and duplicates the data from one drive to another. The fact that RAID 1 does store a second copy of the data on another member of the volume means that this solution does offer fault tolerance. Fault tolerance is the concept that if one part of the solution fails, the other guy will pick up the workload and the solution will continue to function.

If one of the disks in the mirror fails, you can replace the failed disk by breaking the mirror, adding a new functioning disk, and then rebuilding the mirror from the existing disk that did not fail. Once you have reestablished the mirror, you have your fault tolerance back.

Figure 11-14 displays the concept of a mirror volume. When a user saves data to a mirrored volume, the data is written to both disks that make up the volume.

FIGURE 11-14

A mirrored volume stores a copy of the saved data on both disks.

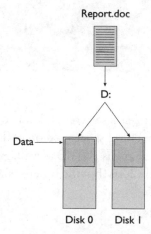

Creating a Mirrored Volume in Windows Server

In this step-by-step you will create a mirrored volume on a Windows server using two of the dynamic disks created in the preceding walkthrough. Remember that a mirrored volume stores all the data on both members (disks) in the volume. To create a mirrored volume, follow these steps:

1. Right-click My Computer and choose Manage.
2. Right-click an area of unallocated space on disk 1 and choose Create Volume.
3. The Create Volume Wizard appears. Click Next.
4. Choose the volume type of Mirrored Volume, which is the volume type you wish to create, and choose Next.

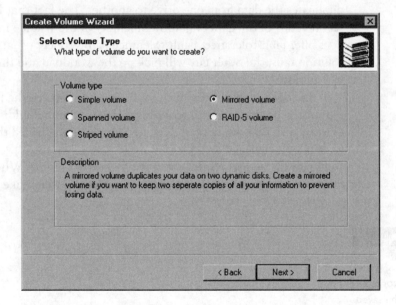

5. Add disk 2 as a selected disk for the mirrored volume and type **200** MB as the total amount of space used on each disk. Also notice that the total space used by the volume is 200MB as well. Although there is 200MB per disk, you can store only 200MB—the other 200MB is to store a copy of the data in case of disaster.
6. Click Next.

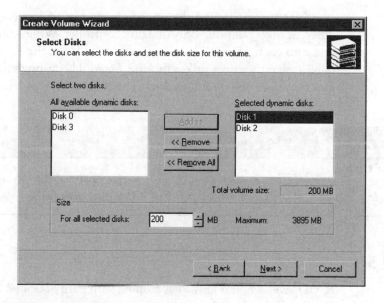

7. Assign drive M as the drive letter and choose Next.

8. Choose Next to format for NTFS.

9. Choose Finish. The mirrored volume is created. Notice that the legend in disk management displays the color codes for each volume type.

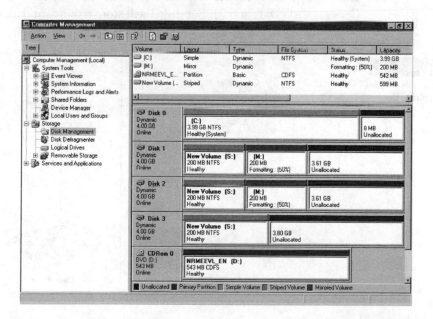

RAID 1 is known as disk mirroring whereby the data is duplicated across two different disks but using only one disk controller. When using two disk controllers, one with each a hard disk connected to it, we term the RAID 1 solution disk duplexing rather than disk mirroring. Figure 11-15 shows the difference between disk mirroring and disk duplexing. They are both considered RAID level 1.

RAID 1 is known as disk mirroring, which "mirrors," or stores a full *copy of the data, on a second disk in case the first disk fails.*

RAID 5

RAID level 5 is also known as striping with parity because a RAID 5 volume acts as a RAID 0 volume but adds the parity information to create redundancy. RAID 5 volumes write data to all disks in the volume but store redundant information on one of the disks per stripe (a stripe is a row made up of 64KB chunks on each disk, as shown in Figure 11-16). For example, when you save data to a RAID 5 volume made up of four disks, the data is split up into 64KB data chunks (that may change, depending on the product or implementation) and written to each disk (let's say disks 0, 1, and 2). But disk 3 will store redundant data (parity data) of the

FIGURE 11-15		
Disk mirroring versus disk duplexing		

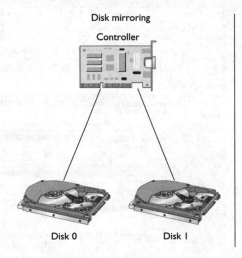
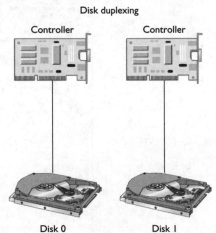

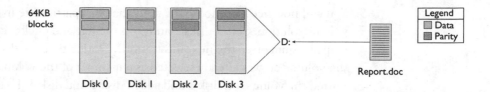

FIGURE 11-16

A RAID 5 volume
stripes the data
and stores parity
information.

three 64KB blocks that have been saved already. If the three 64KB blocks are not
sufficient to complete saving the file, the save operation will continue onto the next
row. There will be parity information for that row as well, but the parity information
is stored on a different disk for each row.

Creating a RAID 5 Volume with Windows Server

In the following walk-through you will see how to create a RAID 5 volume on a
Windows server using three drives. Remember that a RAID 5 volume is similar to a
striped volume but also stores redundant information for each stripe that is written.

1. Right-click My Computer and choose Manage.

2. Right-click an area of unallocated space on disk 1 and choose Create Volume.

3. The Create Volume Wizard appears. Click Next.

4. Choose the volume type of RAID-5 Volume (see the next illustration),
   which is the volume type you wish to create, and choose Next.

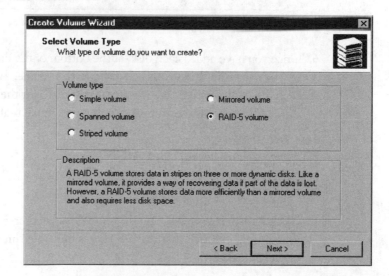

5. You will now need to choose the disks that will participate in the striped volume solution. Select disks 2 and 3 on the left and click Add to add to the striped volume (see the next illustration). Notice that the disk you started the volume on was already selected as a member of the volume. Because I started the volume on disk 1 and added disk 2 and disk 3, I will have three disks in this solution.

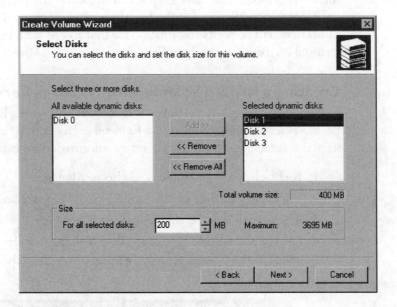

6. Once you have added each disk, at the bottom of the dialog box type the amount of space you want to use on each disk for the volume. Type **200** and notice that each disk will use 200MB—for a total of 400MB for the entire volume, because a third of the space is used for parity and is not actual usable space.

7. Click Next.

8. Assign a drive letter R for RAID-5 Volume.

9. Click Next.

10. Click Next to format for NTFS.

11. Click Finish; the new RAID-5 Volume has been created (see the next illustration). Notice that drive R shows multiple times because it is made up of multiple disks.

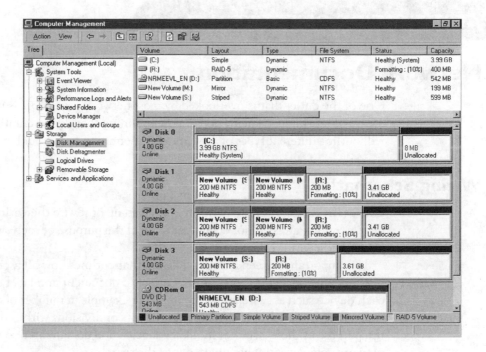

12. Close all windows.

If one of the disks fails, with a RAID 5 volume you can still access the data but you may want to replace the faulty disk. To recover from a disk error with RAID 5, you simply replace the failed disk and regenerate the volume so that the data on the failed disk is created on the newly added disk.

e**x**am
watch

RAID 5 volumes are known as striping with parity because this volume type splits the data across all disks but saves parity data on one of the disks per stripe. The parity information is used to calculate the missing data if a disk in the RAID 5 volume fails.

Network Documentation

One of the duties that is overlooked by most network professionals is the task of creating network documentation and maintaining that documentation. This section will outline different types of network documentation you should maintain.

Wiring Schematics

One of the hardest tasks to perform is to clean up or rewire the wiring closet because most administrators do not document or label the purpose of each switch, router, or cable in the wiring closet.

It is important to keep a wiring diagram that outlines how all aspects of the network are connected. You want to be sure to document and label the purpose of each device such as switches and routers. For example, a number of companies will assign specific switches to specific departments or divisions within the company, so the purpose of those switches should be labeled and documented so that the wrong network cable does not get plugged into the switch.

Be sure to label and document the purpose of each wire or at least group the related wires and then document their purpose.

Physical Network Diagram

The physical network diagram will document the physical network infrastructure including the placement of switches, routers, servers, and workstations. The physical network diagram will display items such as WAN links and the speeds of these links.

A great piece of software to help create the network diagrams is Microsoft Visio. Visio has a number of graphical objects built in that represent routers, switches, and network links. You can create your network diagram with Visio and label each device and network link. Be sure to include information such as the make and model of the device.

Logical Network Diagram

The logical network diagram should be documented. This includes aspects such as IP address ranges used on different network segments and WAN links.

In the logical network diagram you should also document any VLANs that are being used on the network and which computers belong to which VLANs.

The logical network diagram should also include the structure of your directory service, such as the Active Directory Domains and the OU structure.

Baselines

At some point you will end up troubleshooting performance problems with the network and the servers. When troubleshooting performance problems, you will use performance monitoring tools (to monitor the systems) and network monitoring tools (to monitor the network). It is critical after the installation of the network that you use these tools to create a baseline. The baseline is a picture of what your systems and network look like, from a performance point of view, when life is normal.

Once you have saved and documented normal activity in a baseline, you can then refer to the baseline when troubleshooting performance issues later on down the road. What you will end up doing when there is a problem is to use the monitoring tools again to capture activity on the poorly performing system or network and then compare the capture to the information in the baseline to find out what the problem is. It would be really hard to determine what areas of the network are degrading without a baseline to refer to.

Policies and Procedures

When documenting aspects of the network, you want to be sure to document any network policy details. There are a wide range of network policies that you want to be sure to document:

- **Password policy**   The password policy will determine what are valid passwords on the network. It will allow you to set settings such as maximum password length, password complexity, and how frequently passwords should change. Be sure to document all aspects of the password policy.

- **Account lockout**   Be sure to document now many bad logon attempts are allowed before an account is locked. Also document how long the account is locked for.

- **User rights** Document any extra privileges that are given to users on the network. For example, if you allow Bob to back up files from the server, then you want to be sure to document those extra rights.

- **Audit policy** It is important to document your audit policy so that at any point and time you can determine what level of auditing is enabled on the network. Be sure to document what events are being audited and whether you are auditing the success or failure of a given event.

- **Firewall policy** An important network feature to document is the firewall policy. When documenting the firewall policy, document what the default rule is, either accept all traffic or deny all traffic, and then document each rule. You don't want to have to rebuild all those rules without any reference!

- **Software restriction policy** The software restriction policy will determine what applications are allowed to run on the computers. You want to be sure to document the rules in the software restriction policy so that if you have problems with an application running, you can refer to the policy to find out if there is a reason the application does not run.

Along with documenting any policy settings on the network, you will also want to make sure that you document all network procedures. Some examples of network procedures that should be documented are backup procedures, restore procedures, server recovery procedures, device replacement procedures such as for a router or switch, and also hard drive replacement procedures.

Documenting the procedures to perform maintenance on the network will help when the time comes to perform those tasks. You will not need to scramble to figure out how to perform these tasks that were configured so long ago—you simply look at the documentation.

I would like to make two last points about network documentation. The first is to be sure to maintain the documentation by keeping it up-to-date as changes to the network occur. Network documentation that is not kept up-to-date is just as bad as not having any.

The second point is that the network documentation includes critical private information about your network setup that a hacker would love to have! Be sure to store the current copy of your network documentation in a secure location and shred any old copies.

CERTIFICATION OBJECTIVE 11.07

Maintaining Logs

Another form of information that is extremely valuable is log files. Most operating systems and server software maintain a record of activity in a log file. For example, if you are using Microsoft's web server, Internet Information Services (IIS), by default it logs any visits to your web site in a text file. The benefit of having the information in a log is that if you notice suspicious activity with the system, you can look at the log file and view information such as the date and time someone visited the site, their IP address (client IP), what page they requested, and what program they used (User-Agent). Figure 11-17 displays a web log from an IIS Server.

FIGURE 11-17 Looking at a web server log file

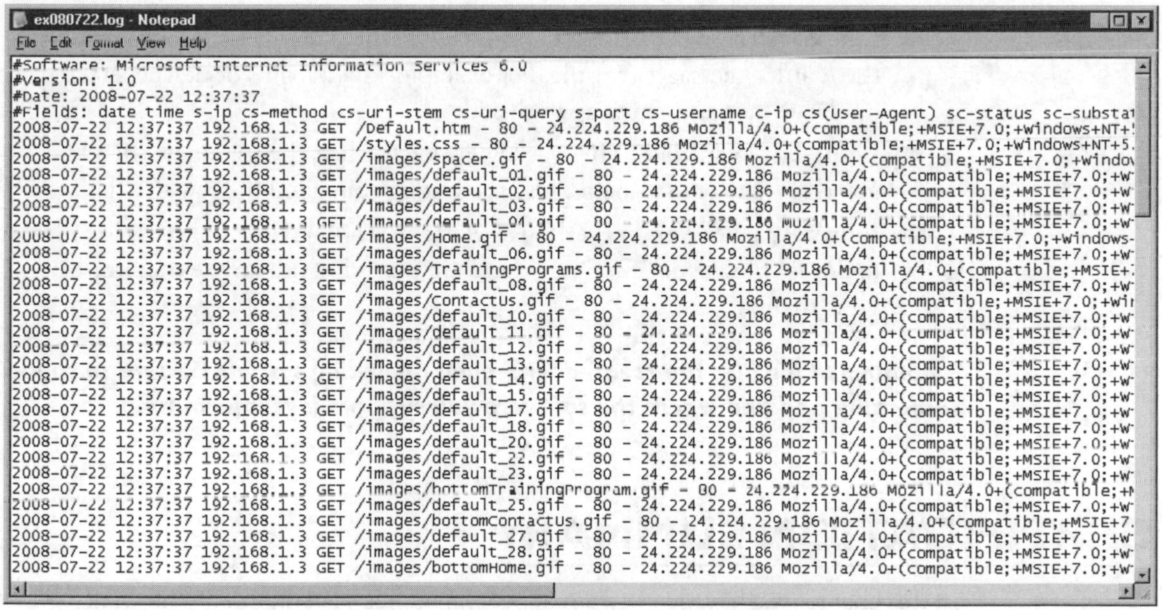

```
ex080722.log - Notepad
File Edit Format View Help
#Software: Microsoft Internet Information Services 6.0
#Version: 1.0
#Date: 2008-07-22 12:37:37
#Fields: date time s-ip cs-method cs-uri-stem cs-uri-query s-port cs-username c-ip cs(User-Agent) sc-status sc-substat
2008-07-22 12:37:37 192.168.1.3 GET /Default.htm - 80 - 24.224.229.186 Mozilla/4.0+(compatible;+MSIE+7.0;+Windows+NT+
2008-07-22 12:37:37 192.168.1.3 GET /styles.css - 80 - 24.224.229.186 Mozilla/4.0+(compatible;+MSIE+7.0;+Windows+NT+5.
2008-07-22 12:37:37 192.168.1.3 GET /images/spacer.gif - 80 - 24.224.229.186 Mozilla/4.0+(compatible;+MSIE+7.0;+Windo
2008-07-22 12:37:37 192.168.1.3 GET /images/default_01.gif - 80 - 24.224.229.186 Mozilla/4.0+(compatible;+MSIE+7.0;+W
2008-07-22 12:37:37 192.168.1.3 GET /images/default_02.gif - 80 - 24.224.229.186 Mozilla/4.0+(compatible;+MSIE+7.0;+W
2008-07-22 12:37:37 192.168.1.3 GET /images/default_03.gif - 80 - 24.224.229.186 Mozilla/4.0+(compatible;+MSIE+7.0;+W
2008-07-22 12:37:37 192.168.1.3 GET /images/default_04.gif - 80 - 24.224.229.186 Mozilla/4.0+(compatible;+MSIE+7.0;+W
2008-07-22 12:37:37 192.168.1.3 GET /images/Home.gif - 80 - 24.224.229.186 Mozilla/4.0+(compatible;+MSIE+7.0;+Windows-
2008-07-22 12:37:37 192.168.1.3 GET /images/default_06.gif - 80 - 24.224.229.186 Mozilla/4.0+(compatible;+MSIE+7.0;+W
2008-07-22 12:37:37 192.168.1.3 GET /images/TrainingPrograms.gif - 80 - 24.224.229.186 Mozilla/4.0+(compatible;+MSIE+
2008-07-22 12:37:37 192.168.1.3 GET /images/default_08.gif - 80 - 24.224.229.186 Mozilla/4.0+(compatible;+MSIE+7.0;+W
2008-07-22 12:37:37 192.168.1.3 GET /images/ContactUs.gif - 80 - 24.224.229.186 Mozilla/4.0+(compatible;+MSIE+7.0;+Wi
2008-07-22 12:37:37 192.168.1.3 GET /images/default_10.gif - 80 - 24.224.229.186 Mozilla/4.0+(compatible;+MSIE+7.0;+W
2008-07-22 12:37:37 192.168.1.3 GET /images/default_11.gif - 80 - 24.224.229.186 Mozilla/4.0+(compatible;+MSIE+7.0;+W
2008-07-22 12:37:37 192.168.1.3 GET /images/default_12.gif - 80 - 24.224.229.186 Mozilla/4.0+(compatible;+MSIE+7.0;+W
2008-07-22 12:37:37 192.168.1.3 GET /images/default_13.gif - 80 - 24.224.229.186 Mozilla/4.0+(compatible;+MSIE+7.0;+W
2008-07-22 12:37:37 192.168.1.3 GET /images/default_14.gif - 80 - 24.224.229.186 Mozilla/4.0+(compatible;+MSIE+7.0;+W
2008-07-22 12:37:37 192.168.1.3 GET /images/default_15.gif - 80 - 24.224.229.186 Mozilla/4.0+(compatible;+MSIE+7.0;+W
2008-07-22 12:37:37 192.168.1.3 GET /images/default_17.gif - 80 - 24.224.229.186 Mozilla/4.0+(compatible;+MSIE+7.0;+W
2008-07-22 12:37:37 192.168.1.3 GET /images/default_18.gif - 80 - 24.224.229.186 Mozilla/4.0+(compatible;+MSIE+7.0;+W
2008-07-22 12:37:37 192.168.1.3 GET /images/default_20.gif - 80 - 24.224.229.186 Mozilla/4.0+(compatible;+MSIE+7.0;+W
2008-07-22 12:37:37 192.168.1.3 GET /images/default_22.gif - 80 - 24.224.229.186 Mozilla/4.0+(compatible;+MSIE+7.0;+W
2008-07-22 12:37:37 192.168.1.3 GET /images/default_23.gif - 80 - 24.224.229.186 Mozilla/4.0+(compatible;+MSIE+7.0;+W
2008-07-22 12:37:37 192.168.1.3 GET /images/bottomTrainingProgram.gif - 80 - 24.224.229.186 Mozilla/4.0+(compatible;+M
2008-07-22 12:37:37 192.168.1.3 GET /images/default_25.gif - 80 - 24.224.229.186 Mozilla/4.0+(compatible;+MSIE+7.0;+W
2008-07-22 12:37:37 192.168.1.3 GET /images/bottomContactUs.gif - 80 - 24.224.229.186 Mozilla/4.0+(compatible;+MSIE+7.
2008-07-22 12:37:37 192.168.1.3 GET /images/default_27.gif - 80 - 24.224.229.186 Mozilla/4.0+(compatible;+MSIE+7.0;+W
2008-07-22 12:37:37 192.168.1.3 GET /images/default_28.gif - 80 - 24.224.229.186 Mozilla/4.0+(compatible;+MSIE+7.0;+W
2008-07-22 12:37:37 192.168.1.3 GET /images/bottomHome.gif - 80 - 24.224.229.186 Mozilla/4.0+(compatible;+MSIE+7.0;+W
```

The following are popular log file locations in Windows that you can use to find log files:

- **Microsoft Web Server**   Stores the log files in the c:\windows\system32\logfiles\w3svc1 directory.

- **Microsoft FTP Server**   Stores the log files in the c:\windows\system32\logfiles\msftpsvc1 directory.

- **Windows Clustering**   Stores the log files in the c:\windows\system32\logfiles\cluster directory.

- **Firewall log**   If you turn on logging in the Windows Firewall in the Advanced Settings of the firewall, you can log dropped packets to the default log file of c:\windows\pfirewall.log.

- **Audit logs**   Stores the log entries in the Security Log of the Windows Event Viewer. The files for the event viewer are stored in the c:\windows\system32\config folder, but you will use the Event Viewer to view the log entries.

Unix and Linux use a number of log files as well to record activity on the system. The following are some popular log files in Linux:

- **Linux system log file**   Most system and kernel messages are logged into the /var/log/messages text file. For example, failed logins or newly detected hardware messages show up in this file.

- **Linux last login file**   The /var/log/lastlog file lists the username, IP address, and date/time of user logins. Use the **lastlog** command to view this data.

- **Linux Apache Web Server logs**   Apache stores error and access log files under /var/log/apache2. Since these are text files, use any text editor to view them.

A number of log files are created with each operating system. Be sure to spend some time and find where the software you support logs information.

CERTIFICATION SUMMARY

In this chapter you have learned a number of methods to maintain the network and ensure that it is in good operational order. This chapter has introduced you to a number of day-to-day tasks that must be performed to help maintain the integrity of the network. When it comes to hardware and software upgrades, make sure that you have tested the upgrade in a lab first so that you do not find out about upgrade problems on production systems. It is critical to back up the system before applying any major upgrade so that if something does go wrong, you have a recent backup to rely on.

Make sure that you have installed antivirus software on all servers and desktop systems. You will also need to schedule a virus scan on the systems regularly and to update the virus definitions often. The virus definitions list is a list of all the known viruses at the time the virus definition file was created.

You will most likely want to load antispyware software on computers on which users spend a lot of time surfing the Internet. Spyware and adware are malicious programs that can be installed on your system without your knowledge. This malicious software is a security risk because it can monitor your activity, and it can dramatically slow system performance.

It is extremely critical that you back up data regularly. You should back up data provided by all services, including file and print services, database servers, and e-mail services. Further, you should make sure that you perform a backup of the operating system so that you can get it up and running quickly when presented with a system failure.

There are three major types of backups: a full backup, an incremental backup, and a differential backup. A full backup backs up any file that you select, whether the archive bit is set or not, and then clears the archive bit. An incremental backup only backs up a file that has the archive bit set, and also clears the archive bit when it is done. A differential backup backs up any files that have the archive bit set and does not clear the archive bit when it is done.

When restoring from an incremental backup, you will need to restore the last full backup and then each incremental since the last full backup. When restoring from a differential backup, you will need to restore the last full backup and then the last differential. If you perform full backups every night, you will need to restore only the last full backup.

Fault tolerance is the concept of trying to keep things running when there is a failure in a device. In this chapter you looked at disk fault tolerance and how to set up your server so that if a disk fails you can still have the server running. To implement disk fault tolerance you implement a level of RAID.

RAID level 0 is known as striping. When a users saves a file to a RAID 0 volume, the file is split across all drives in the RAID 0 volume, which increases performance because you have multiple drives taking care of the save operation at the same time. There is no fault tolerance with RAID level 0. RAID level 1 is known as disk mirroring. Disk mirroring is responsible for duplicating all the data that is saved to the RAID 1 volume to the two drives that are mirrored. RAID level 5 stripes the data as RAID 0 does, but there is data redundancy, or parity information, stored with the data as well. If a drive fails in a RAID 5 volume, the system continues to run, reading the data from the RAID 5 volume.

As a network professional, always remember to set and follow strict policies that control use of software, passwords, account lockout, and auditing. Be sure to get management approval when designing the policies, and then implement the policies on the appropriate systems.

To help prepare for the day when you need them, be sure to be familiar with what level of logging your systems and software can perform. Also, know where the information is logged, so that you can access the logs when you need to.

Always remember that a well-planned network design will always require documentation for the physical and logical aspects of the network. Be sure to store the documentation in a secure location and update it as the network changes.

TWO-MINUTE DRILL

Network Upgrades

❑ Be sure to do an inventory on all your servers and verify that you have the most up-to-date ROMs on the device. Check for updates on the manufacturer's web site for the device.

❑ Be sure to create a test lab to verify that any hardware or software upgrade is tested with all your existing hardware and software. You do not want to do the install on production systems without testing them first.

Installing Patches and Updates

❑ Be sure to keep your systems up-to-date with patches and service packs. Most vulnerabilities are fixed with a software patch.

❑ A hot-fix is something that can't wait for the next service pack release. You should test and then apply any hot-fix as soon as possible.

❑ A service pack includes all updates since the release of the product. If you install a server and service pack 2 is the current service pack, you will not need to install service pack 1 and service pack 2—just service pack 2. You will need to get any updates released since service pack 2 in this example.

❑ You can use the Software Update Service in Microsoft environments to deploy updates across the network. This will simplify the management of the updates.

Antivirus and Antispyware Software

❑ After installing your antivirus software, make sure that you have scheduled regular virus scans.

❑ Make sure that you have the real-time protector enabled on your antivirus software so that any time you access a file, the virus protection software checks the file for viruses.

❑ Make sure that you keep your antivirus software up-to-date by downloading the most current virus definitions.

❑ Install server-based antivirus software on e-mail servers so that incoming mail is scanned before it is deposited into the user's mailbox.

Backing Up Network Data

❏ Make sure that you have a tape rotation schedule, and be sure to store a copy of backups offsite in case of disaster.

❏ Schedule backups to occur regularly.

❏ If the amount of data is too much to perform a full backup each night, create a backup plan that combines your full backup with an incremental or differential backup.

❏ A full backup backs up any selected file whether the archive bit is set or not and then clears the archive bit.

❏ An incremental backup backs up only the selected files that have the archive bit set and then clears the archive bit after the backup.

❏ A differential backup backs up only the selected files that have the archive bit set and does not clear the archive bit.

Providing Fault Tolerance

❏ Fault tolerance is the concept of ensuring that you can still have a solution running if part of the solution fails. For example, if you lose a power supply in a server, there would be a second one waiting to take over.

❏ RAID is a disk fault-tolerance technology that involves multiple drives storing the data. Depending on the RAID level you use, you can still get access to data if a disk fails because a copy of the data is stored on another disk.

❏ RAID level 0, known as disk striping, does not provide any fault tolerance. RAID 0 is used to increase performance with read and write operations because the data is split up and written to all disks in the solution at the same time.

❏ RAID level 1 is known as disk mirroring. RAID 1 stores a full copy of the data on both members of the mirrored volume so that if one disk fails, the other disk still has a copy.

❏ RAID level 5 is also known as disk striping with parity, whereby the data is striped across multiple disks. However, it does store parity information so that if a disk fails, the missing data can be recalculated.

Network Documentation

❑ Be sure to document all aspects of the network, including the physical structure such as placement of routers and switches.

❑ You should document the link speeds between different branches and your routers.

❑ Document the logical structure such as VLAN configuration.

Maintaining Logs

❑ There are a number of log files created with each operating system; be sure to spend some time and find where the software you support logs information.

❑ Most Windows software logs to the c:\windows\system32\logfiles folder.

❑ Review the logs on a regular basis.

SELF TEST

The following questions will help you measure your understanding of the material presented in this chapter. Read all the choices carefully, because there may appear to be more than one correct answer.

Network Upgrades

1. You need to ensure that your server supports a new disk standard—what would you do?
   A. Purchase a new server that supports the new standard.
   B. Go to the server manufacturer's web site and see if there is a BIOS update for that server that will update the BIOS code to make the server aware of the new standard.
   C. Format the hard drives and then restore the data.
   D. All of the above.

2. You are going to upgrade your e-mail server software to a new version. What should you do before the software upgrade?
   A. Perform the upgrade on a test system first.
   B. Delete the e-mails off the server—you need the space for the new software.
   C. Back up the server before attempting the upgrade.
   D. Both A and C.

Installing Patches and Updates

3. What is a hot-fix?
   A. An update that is noncritical
   B. A number of updates that are bundled and will bring your system up-to-date
   C. A critical update that should be applied to your system as soon as possible
   D. All of the above

4. What feature of Microsoft operating systems allows you to update the system fairly easily?
   A. System Restore
   B. Windows Messenger
   C. Backup
   D. Windows Update

5. What Microsoft feature can you use to deliver updates to all clients on the network from a central point?

   A. Windows Update

   B. Backup

   C. WSUS

   D. Active Directory

Antivirus and Antispyware Software

6. What is the name of malicious software that monitors Internet activity?

   A. Virus

   B. Worm

   C. Spyware

   D. Trojan

7. It is critical that you keep what part of your virus protection software up-to-date?

   A. Menu commands

   B. Version

   C. Viruses

   D. Virus definitions

8. What feature of virus protection software is responsible for protecting your system at the time a file with a virus is activated?

   A. Real-time protection

   B. At the time protection

   C. Active protection

   D. None of the above

Backing Up Network Data

9. What type of backup backs up files that have changed and then clears the archive bit?

   A. Full

   B. Incremental

   C. Differential

   D. Copy

10. You have been performing a full backup every Sunday night and have been doing incremental backups on Monday, Tuesday, Wednesday, and Thursday nights. Your server crashes during the day Wednesday. What is your restore strategy?

    A. Restore only Tuesday night's backup.

    B. Restore the last full backup from Sunday and then restore the last incremental, which is Tuesday's.

    C. Restore the last full backup from Sunday and then restore the incremental backups from Monday and Tuesday.

    D. Restore only the full backup from Sunday.

11. Where should you make certain that you have stored a copy of your network backups?

    A. In a central cabinet in the server room

    B. In your manager's office

    C. On a different server for quick restores

    D. Offsite in a safe, trusted location

12. What type of backup backs up files that have changed and does not clear the archive bit?

    A. Full

    B. Incremental

    C. Differential

    D. Copy

13. You have been performing a full backup every Sunday night and have been doing differential backups on Monday, Tuesday, Wednesday, and Thursday nights. Your server crashes during the day Thursday—what is your restore strategy?

    A. Restore only Wednesday night's backup.

    B. Restore the last full backup from Sunday and then restore the last differential backup, which is Wednesday's.

    C. Restore the last full backup from Sunday and then restore all of the differential backups from Monday and Tuesday.

    D. Restore only the full backup from Sunday.

14. How would you make sure that you do not forget to perform a backup each night?

    A. Create a backup plan.

    B. Schedule the backup software to do the backup automatically.

    C. Ask your manager to remind you to do the backup each night.

    D. Set a reminder in Outlook.

15. Before performing a backup operation, what should you have in place to ensure that everyone knows and understands the backup strategy?
    A. An assistant
    B. A backup plan
    C. A security document
    D. A tape

Providing Fault Tolerance

16. Which RAID level stores a full copy of the data on a second disk?
    A. RAID level 0
    B. RAID level 1
    C. RAID level 5
    D. All of the above

17. Which RAID level provides no duplication of data and therefore provides no fault tolerance?
    A. RAID level 0
    B. RAID level 1
    C. RAID level 5
    D. All of the above

18. Which RAID level writes the data across multiple disks and also stores parity information for fault tolerance?
    A. RAID level 0
    B. RAID level 1
    C. RAID level 5
    D. All of the above

19. What tool in Windows is used to create RAID volumes?
    A. Disk Management
    B. Registry
    C. Active Directory Users and Computers
    D. Control Panel

20. A RAID level 1 solution that uses two hard disk controllers is called what?
    A. Mirroring
    B. Striping
    C. Redundancy
    D. Duplexing

Network Documentation

21. Which of the following make up part of the physical structure documentation? (Select all that apply.)

    A. Routers

    B. Active Directory OUs

    C. WAN links

    D. VLAN configuration

22. What should you do with your documentation as changes are made to the network environment? (Select two.)

    A. Throw the outdated documentation out.

    B. Shred the outdated documentation.

    C. Sell the outdated documentation.

    D. Update the documentation.

Maintaining Logs

23. Where does Windows Server store IIS log files?

    A. C:\logs

    B. C:\windows\system32\logfiles

    C. C:\iislogs

    D. C:\windows\iislogs

SELF TEST ANSWERS

Network Upgrades

1. ☑ **B.** It is important to remember that as your hardware gets older you can update the BIOS or ROM code on that server or device to bring it up-to-date with feature or technologies that have come out since the manufacturer built the device.

☒ **A, C,** and **D** are incorrect. Purchasing a new server is a very expensive way to take advantage of new technologies. Simply flashing the BIOS would be a cheaper solution. Formatting the hard drive has nothing to do with the solution.

2. ☑ **D.** Before performing any kind of hardware or software upgrade, you should make sure that you have tested the upgrade first. After you have tested the upgrade, before performing the upgrade on a production server, make sure that you have backed up the production server in case something goes wrong.

☒ **B** is incorrect. You would never delete user data, because you will find yourself very busy restoring that data back from the backup resource.

Installing Patches and Updates

3. ☑ **C.** A hot-fix is a critical update that cannot wait for the next service pack to be supplied. You should apply hot-fixes right away. Make sure that you have tested the hot-fix on a test system first.

☒ **A, B,** and **D** are incorrect because they all imply that the update should not be applied immediately.

4. ☑ **D.** Windows Update is a feature of Microsoft operating systems that allows the user to use Windows Update to connect to the Windows Update site, from which updates are downloaded for that operating system.

☒ **A, B,** and **C** are incorrect. System Restores are a feature of Windows XP to bring the system back to the state of the last restore point. Windows Messenger is an online "chat" type of software, and Backup is the software used to perform a backup of the system.

5. ☑ **C.** Windows Software Update Service is a service that can be installed on a Windows server that allows you to manage deployment of patches and updates from a central point.

☒ **A, B,** and **D** are incorrect. Windows Update is where WSUS gets the updates from, but WSUS helps deploy the update to all your systems. Active Directory is the Microsoft directory service and is not really used to deploy updates.

Antivirus and Antispyware Software

6. ☑ **C.** Spyware is malicious software planted on your system that can monitor your Internet activity.

☒ **A, B,** and **D** are incorrect. A virus, a Trojan, and a worm are all malicious software that damages the system or slows it down.

7. ☑ **D.** It is critical that you keep your virus definitions up-to-date. The virus definitions are the part of the virus protection software that makes the virus protection software aware of what viruses exist. Virus protection software vendors are constantly updating their definitions, and you can download the updates from the Internet through the virus protection software.

☒ **A, B,** and **C** are incorrect because none of those are real features of virus protection software.

8. ☑ **A.** Real-time protection saves you from needing to run a virus scan manually, because as you open files or access files, the virus protection software scans the file being accessed.

☒ **B, C,** and **D** are incorrect because these are not features of virus protection software.

Backing Up Network Data

9. ☑ **B.** Incremental backups clear the archive bit after backing up a file that has changed. Because the archive bit is cleared, the file will not be backed up with the next incremental backup unless it is changed again.

☒ **A, C,** and **D** are incorrect. A full backup backs up any file that is selected whether it has changed or not. A differential backup backs up a file that has changed but does not clear the archive bit. A copy backup does not clear the archive bit; it is like a full backup in that it backs up any file you select.

10. ☑ **C.** You will need to restore the last full backup and each incremental backup up to the crash in this scenario. Each incremental backup applies the changes since the previous incremental, and all incrementals build on the full backup being performed, bringing the server up-to-date.

☒ **A, B,** and **D** are incorrect because they are all incorrect restore strategies when combining full backups with incremental backups.

11. ☑ **D.** You should make sure that you store a copy of your backups offsite in a safe, trusted location. The purpose of having the tapes stored offsite is to be able to recover from a disaster to your premises that would destroy servers and backups.

☒ **A, B,** and **C** are incorrect because they are all locations where a backup could be stored that will still make the backup media vulnerable to disaster along with the server.

12. ☑ **C.** A differential backup backs up any file that has changed but does not clear the archive bit. This is useful because each differential backup includes all changes from the time of the last full backup to the time of the differential backup.

☒ **A, B,** and **D** are incorrect. Full backups back up any file that is selected whether it has changed or not and clears the archive bit. An incremental backup backs up only files that have changed and clears the archive bit, whereas a copy backup backs up any file that is selected and does not clear the archive bit.

13. ☑ **D.** For this scenario you would restore Sunday's full backup to create a starting point and then apply the last differential backup to bring the server up-to-date to the time of the last differential.

☒ **A, C,** and **D** are incorrect because they are not restore strategies used with full backups and differential backups.

14. ☑ **B.** The best thing to do is to schedule your backups so that you are not dependent on memory and the backup is performed automatically.

☒ **A, C,** and **D** are incorrect. Although you should create a backup plan, the plan does not actually ensure that the backups are performed. Make certain that you schedule the backups!

15. ☑ **B.** Make sure that you have a backup plan and that it is up-to-date so that all systems administrators know what is being backed up and what the restore strategy is in case of failure.

☒ **A, C,** and **D** are incorrect because none of these options guarantees that all persons involved in the day-to-day network operations understand the backup strategy.

Providing Fault Tolerance

16. ☑ **B.** RAID level 1 is disk mirroring; it mirrors, or duplicates, the data from one disk to another in case of a disk failure.

☒ **A, C,** and **D** are incorrect. RAID level 0 is known as disk striping and is responsible for saving the data across multiple disks but with no redundancy. RAID level 5 is disk striping but does store parity data as well, which provides fault tolerance.

17. ☑ **A.** RAID level 0 is known as disk striping and is responsible for saving the data across multiple disks but with no redundancy. The benefit is strictly for performance—multiple disks working at saving your data at the same time.

☒ **B, C,** and **D** are incorrect. RAID level 1 is disk mirroring; it mirrors, or duplicates, the data from one disk to another in case of a disk failure. RAID level 5 is disk striping but does store parity data as well, which provides fault tolerance.

18. ☑ **C.** RAID level 5 is also known as striping with parity and stores parity data as well as writing the data across all disks.

☒ **A, B,** and **D** are incorrect. RAID level 0 is known as disk striping and is responsible for saving the data across multiple disks but with no redundancy. RAID level 1 is disk mirroring; it mirrors or duplicates the data from one disk to another in case of a disk failure. RAID level 5 is disk striping but does store parity data as well, which provides fault tolerance.

19. ☑ **A.** Disk Management is the tool used to create volumes on a Windows server.
    ☒ **B, C,** and **D** are incorrect because they are not used to create RAID volumes on a Windows server.

20. ☑ **D.** Disk duplexing is the duplication of data on multiple disks, but the disks are connected to two different disk controllers.
    ☒ **A, B,** and **C** are incorrect. Disk mirroring stores copies of the data on multiple disks but uses only one disk controller. The other choices do not duplicate the data.

Network Documentation

21. ☑ **A and C.** Routers and WAN links make up part of the physical structure of the network and therefore are part of that documentation.
    ☒ **B and D** are incorrect because they are part of documenting the logical structure of the network.

22. ☑ **B and D.** You need to ensure that you update the network documentation as changes are made to the network. For security reasons you want to make sure that you shred any old copies and store the updated documentation in a secure location.
    ☒ **A and C** are incorrect. For security reasons you should shred the documentation, not throw it out.

Maintaining Logs

23. ☑ **B.** The IIS log files are stored in the \windows\system32\logfiles folder. There is then a separate subfolder for each service. If you host multiple web sites on the web server, then there will be a folder per web site with the logs for that web site.
    ☒ **A, C, D** are incorrect because they are not the location of where IIS stores the log files.

12
Network Security

Today's networks are becoming more dispersed and widespread, given the impact the Internet has had on extending the network out to roaming users and business partners. It is extremely important that as you design the network you consider the impact your design will have on the overall security of the organization and its resources. It is important to ensure that resources are protected and that data traveling on the wire or in the air is protected through encryption.

In this chapter you will be introduced to a number of security-related terms and learn what features of the operating system are used to help protect network resources. You will learn what a firewall is and the general steps used to configure a firewall. You will also learn different protocols used to encrypt network traffic for wired networks and wireless networks. This chapter also lists some basic guidelines you could use to help secure your network.

CERTIFICATION OBJECTIVE 12.01

Understanding Attack Types

Due to the complexity of software and networks today, most systems and applications are susceptible to a number of different types of security attacks. Understanding the different types of attacks and methods that hackers are using to compromise systems is essential to understanding how to secure your environment. This section will introduce you to a number of different types of attacks.

There are two major types of attacks:

- Social engineering attacks
- Network attacks

Social Engineering

With a *social engineering* attack, the attacker compromises the network or system through social interaction with an individual, through an e-mail message or phone call, and tricks the individual into divulging information that can be used to compromise security. The information that the victim divulges to the hacker would most likely be used in a subsequent attack to gain unauthorized access to a system or network.

The key to protecting yourself and fellow employees from social engineering attacks is education! Keeping all personnel aware of the popularity of social engineering attacks and the different scenarios that could be examples of social engineering attacks will help raise the security level of the organization.

There are a number of different examples of social engineering attacks. The following are some of the most popular scenarios:

- **Hacker impersonates administrator** In this example, the hacker may call the employee and impersonate the network administrator. The hacker will try to convince the employee to change their password or divulge password information.

- **Hacker impersonates user** In this example, the hacker calls an unsuspecting network administrator and plays the role of a frustrated user who cannot log on to the network. The network administrator naturally helps the "user" by resetting the password and helping them log on—problem being it is actually the hacker!

- **Hacker impersonates vendor** In this example, the hacker may e-mail a customer pretending to be the vendor of a piece of software. In this example, the hacker tries to get the user to install an update, but the user doesn't realize the update is really a Trojan virus that gives the hacker access to the system.

Phishing Attack

A very popular type of attack today is what is known as a phishing attack! A phishing attack is when the hacker creates a fake web site that looks exactly like a popular site such as the bank or eBay. The phishing part of the attack is that the hacker then sends an e-mail message trying to trick the user into clicking a link that leads to the fake site. When the user attempts to log on with their account information, the hacker records the username and password and then tries that information on the real site.

Network-Based Attacks

Most types of attacks are considered network-based attacks where the hacker performs the attack from a remote system. There are a number of different types of network attacks:

■ **Eavesdropping attack** This widely used type of attack typically involves the use of network monitoring tools to analyze and read communications on the network.

■ **Spoof attack** In a spoof attack, the hacker modifies the source address of the packets he or she is sending so that they appear to be coming from someone else. This may be an attempt to bypass your firewall rules.

■ **Hijack attack** In a hijack attack, a hacker takes over a session between you and another individual and disconnects the other individual from the communication. You still believe that you are talking to the original party and may send private information to the hacker unintentionally.

■ **Denial of service** A denial of service (DOS) is a type of attack that causes the system or its services to crash. As a result, the system cannot perform its purpose and provide those services.

■ **Distributed denial of service (DDOS)** The hacker uses multiple systems to attack a single target system. A good example is the SMURF attack, in which the hacker pings a number of computers but modifies the source address of those packets so that they appear to come from another system (the victim in this case). When all of these systems receive the ping request, all systems will reply to the same address, essentially overburdening that system with data.

■ **Buffer overflow** A buffer overflow attack is when the attacker sends more data to an application than is expected. A buffer overflow attack usually results in the attacker gaining administrative access to the system in a command prompt or shell.

■ **Exploit attack** In this type of attack, the attacker knows of a security problem within an operating system or a piece of software and leverages that knowledge by exploiting the vulnerability.

■ **Password attack** An attacker tries to crack the passwords stored in a network account database or a password-protected file. There are three major types of password attacks: a dictionary attack, a brute-force attack, and a hybrid attack. A *dictionary attack* uses a word list file, which is a list of potential passwords. A *brute-force attack* is when the attacker tries every possible combination of characters. With brute force a file is not read. A *hybrid attack* is similar to a dictionary attack in that it uses a word list file, but it also places numbers at the end of the word to catch passwords that are not dictionary words because the user placed a number at the end. For example, a dictionary attack would not find the password "pass1," but a hybrid attack would.

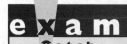

Be sure to know all of the different types of attacks before taking the Network+ exam. Be most familiar **with buffer overflow, denial of service, spoofing, password attacks, and social engineering.**

CERTIFICATION OBJECTIVE 12.02

Understanding System Security

In this section you will be introduced to the differences between authentication and authorization and how those processes are used to allow or deny access to network resources. When securing network resources, you should first have users log on to the network with their own private usernames and passwords; once logged on, they will be able to access network resources to which they have been given permission. The process of logging on to the network is known as authentication, whereas controlling what network resources users may access once they have logged on to the network is known as authorization.

Authentication

Authentication is the process whereby users identify themselves to the network so that they can start accessing network resources. The method used to authenticate a user depends on the network environment and can assume forms such as the following:

- **Username and password**   When the users start the computer or connect to the network, they type a username and password that is associated with their particular network user account.

- **Smartcard**   Using a smartcard for logon is very similar to accessing your bank account at a teller machine. To log on to the network you insert a device similar to a debit card, known as a smartcard, into a smartcard reader and then supply a "PIN." To be authenticated, you must have the smartcard and know its password.

- **Biometrics**   The user would provide a retina scan or fingerprint as a credential. Biometrics is becoming a very popular solution in highly secure environments where special biometric devices would be used.

Whatever method is used to provide the necessary credentials, the outcome is the same in the sense that the credentials are sent to a directory service such as Novell eDirectory or Microsoft Active Directory, where they are verified. For example, if the username and password are correct, the user is authenticated and allowed to access network resources. Network servers also have the ability to authorize users to access different resources depending on how they are authenticated—for example, authentication through biometrics might give a user access to more resources than simple username and password authentication. If the credentials are incorrect, authentication fails and the user is denied access to the network, as shown in Figure 12-1.

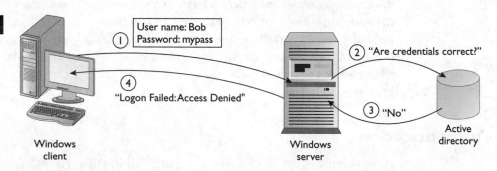

FIGURE 12-1

Logging on to a network

User name: Bob
Password: mypass

① ② "Are credentials correct?"

④ "Logon Failed: Access Denied"

③ "No"

Windows client

Windows server

Active directory

When users provide credentials such as a username and a password, the username and password are passed to the server using an authentication method. A number of authentication methods are used in the Microsoft world as described in the following list:

- **Anonymous Authentication**   You are not required to log on. Windows uses an account for the actual service, and you are passed through as that account. Whatever permissions the anonymous account has are the permissions you will have while you are connected anonymously. This is a popular authentication method for web sites or FTP servers.

- **Basic Authentication**   You are required to log on, and the username and password are sent to the server in clear text. This means that if someone has a packet sniffer between you and the server, that person will be able to capture your password and view it because it is not encrypted.

- **Integrated Windows Authentication**   You are required to log on to the server, but your username and password are sent to the server in an encrypted format. This authentication method is more secure than basic authentication if users are required to log on.

The foregoing authentication methods are very "Microsoftish," but there are standard protocols used to perform authentication as well. The standard authentication protocols used by various network services, such as RAS and VPN, for authentication include the following:

- **Password Authentication Protocol (PAP)**   The Password Authentication Protocol sends the user's credentials in plain text and is very insecure because of how easy it is for someone to analyze and interpret the logon traffic. This is the authentication protocol used by the basic authentication method mentioned previously.

- **Challenge Handshake Authentication Protocol (CHAP)**   With the Challenge Handshake Authentication Protocol, the server sends a client a challenge (a key), which is combined with the user's password. Both the user's password and the challenge are run through the MD5 hashing algorithm (a formula), which generates a hash value, or mathematical answer, and that hash value is sent to the server for authentication. The server uses the same key to create a hash value with the password stored on the server and then compares the resulting value with the hash value sent by the client. If the two hash values are the same, the client has supplied the correct password. The benefit is that the user's credentials have not been passed on the wire at all.

- **Microsoft Challenge Handshake Authentication Protocol (MS-CHAP)** MS-CHAP is a variation of the CHAP authentication protocol and uses MD4 as the hashing algorithm versus MD5 used by CHAP. MS-CHAP also uses the Microsoft Point-to-Point Encryption (MPPE) protocol along with MS-CHAP to encrypt all traffic from the client to the server.

- **MS-CHAPv2** With MS-CHAP version 2 the authentication method has been extended to authenticate both the client and the server. MS-CHAPv2 also uses stronger encryption keys than CHAP and MS-CHAP.

- **Extensible Authentication Protocol (EAP)** The Extensible Authentication Protocol allows for multiple logon methods such as smartcard logon, certificates, Kerberos, and public-key authentication. EAP is also frequently used with RADIUS, which is a central authentication service that can be used by RAS, wireless, or VPN solutions.

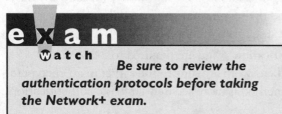

Be sure to review the authentication protocols before taking the Network+ exam.

Authorization

Once you have been authenticated to the network, you will then be authorized to access network resources. There are various types of authorization, depending on what it is that you are trying to be authorized for. For example, if you are trying to access a file on the network, authorization is determined according to the permissions assigned to the file. If you are trying to change the time on the server, authorization is determined by your privileges or rights.

Permissions vs. Rights

In the Microsoft world, there is a difference between a permission and a right, so it is important to make that difference clear.

A *permission* is your level of access to a resource such as a file, folder, or object. The permission is a characteristic of the resource and not a characteristic of the user account. For example, if you would like to give Bob the read permission to a file, you would go to the properties of that file and set the permissions. Notice that you do not go to the user account to assign the permissions.

A *right* is your privilege within the operating system to perform a task. For example, when companies deploy Windows XP Professional to all client systems on the network, users are surprised that they cannot change the time on the computer if they want to. This is because they do not have the Change System Time right. In order to configure an aspect of the operating system, a person must have the appropriate right. This is a significant security feature of the Microsoft operating systems, and it is important to note that administrators can configure the operating system only because the group that they are members of is assigned all the rights.

At times a right can override permissions, because the privilege you have been assigned takes precedence over everything else. For example, when configuring a server I typically configure folders that contain sensitive data with permissions that do not allow administrators access to the folder. It is extremely important to understand that when configuring security, I cannot prevent people from performing their jobs, so the question is, can the administrator still perform backups of the folder if he does not have permissions to read the contents of the folder? The answer is yes, because the administrator has the right to back up files; although he has no permission to the folder, he can read from the folder when running backup software.

Windows Security Subsystem

To help you understand more about authentication and authorization, we will discuss the underlying architecture of Windows and its security subsystem. In this section we overview the logon process and discuss different core services that take part in the authentication and authorization process.

There are a number of components that make up the security subsystem in Windows, each playing an integral part in the security functions provided by the operating system. Table 12-1 lists the security subsystems and gives a brief description of them.

TABLE 12-1	Security Subsystem Component	Description
Components of the Windows Security Model	WinLogon	User interface provided for interactive logon. The WinLogon presents the logon screen when the user presses CTRL-ALT-DEL.
	Local security authority (LSA)	Manages local security policies and user authentication. The LSA is also responsible for generating the access token during the authentication process and writing events to the audit log when an alert is fired by the security reference monitor, based on the audit policy.
	Security reference monitor	Verifies that a user has the appropriate permissions or rights to access an object. It also enforces the audit policy provided by the LSA.
	NetLogon	A service that is used to verify the credentials used during logon against the SAM database.
	Security accounts manager (SAM)	Handles authentication services for LSA on a local Windows system. The SAM is the database of user and group machine accounts on a local Windows system such as Windows XP. The SAM is typically used in a peer-to-peer Windows network.
	Active Directory	Microsoft's Directory Service in Windows 2000/2003/2008 server. Active Directory is the name given to the network account database used to store all user accounts and groups that may access network resources. The Active Directory database resides on domain controllers and is kept synchronized.

The logon process varies depending on whether you are logging on to the local SAM database or to the Active Directory database. The general steps of logging on to a SAM database are as follows:

■ User presses CTRL-ALT-DEL to log on to the local system. The WinLogon process presents the user with the logon dialog box.

■ The user enters a username and password and then presses ENTER.

■ The LSA makes a call to an authentication package and then passes the logon information to the NetLogon service.

■ The NetLogon service then compares the username and password to the local SAM database.

■ Once verified, the NetLogon service returns the user's Security Identifier (SID) and any groups the user is a member of to the LSA.

- The local LSA generate an "access token," which contains the user account, any groups the user is a member of, and any rights the user might have.
- The access token is associated with the user, and the Windows Explorer interface is started. The access token is assigned to any programs that are started by the user. This is important because if the user is not allowed to access a resource, she will be unable to access the resource by starting an application. Each application has the same security context as the user, because the access token is applied to the running program. Figure 12-2 displays this logon process.

The SAM database is the name of the local database of user accounts on a Windows system that is not a domain controller. A domain controller uses the network-wide database, known as Active Directory.

When logging on to the network, the logon process differs dramatically because then users are authenticated by the Active Directory database, not the SAM database. Active Directory uses an authentication service known as Kerberos to log a user on to the network. The following is a general outline of the steps involved when logging on to the network using an Active Directory account and Kerberos authentication:

- The user presses CTRL-ALT-DEL. The WinLogon process displays the username and password dialog.
- The user enters a username, password, and a domain to log on to.
- The logon credentials are passed to the LSA, which then queries DNS for a domain controller that can authenticate the user.

FIGURE 12-2

Logging on to a local SAM database

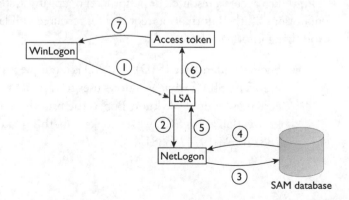

- The LSA then contacts the key distribution center (KDC) on the domain controller and requests a session ticket.
- Kerberos contacts Active Directory to authenticate the user.
- Upon authentication, Kerberos retrieves the user's universal group membership from the global catalog server.
- After the user has been authenticated against Active Directory and every group membership has been determined, Kerberos sends a session ticket to the client that contains the user account's SID and any group memberships.
- The LSA then sends that session ticket to the KDC and requests a session ticket for the local workstation.
- Kerberos sends a session ticket for the local system and the LSA; it then constructs an access token, which is assigned to any processes that the user starts.

You will not be required to know all the steps during the logon process, *but be aware that Kerberos is a ticket-granting service.*

Access Tokens

When a user logs on to a system or network, as part of the logon process an access token is created for the user and is used to determine whether a user should be allowed to access a resource or perform an operating system task. The token maintains all the information required for resource validation and includes the following information:

- **Security Identifier (SID)**   A SID is a unique number assigned to the user. The SID is what Windows uses to identify the user instead of the actual username. We know Bob as the bsmith user account, but Windows knows Bob as his SID, which looks something like S-1-5-21-2752813485-788270693-1974236881-116.

- **Group Security Identifiers**   The access token contains a list of any groups that the user is a member of. This is important because when a user double-clicks a resource, the resource is normally configured with permissions assigned to groups. Windows checks to see which groups the user is a member of through the access token and then checks to see if one of those groups has permission to the resource being accessed. If a group that is contained in the access token is allowed access to the resource, the user will gain access to the resource.

- **Primary Group Security Identifier**   For POSIX compliance you can specify your primary group—this is the group that becomes the owner of files and directories in POSIX environments.

- **Access Rights**   During the logon process, Windows determines the rights you have within the operating system and stores the list of your rights within the access token. For example, if you have the Change the System Time right, that information will be stored in the access token during the logon process. If you try to change the time on the computer, your access token is checked for that right; if the right is in the access token, you would be allowed to change the system time.

It is important to note that the access token is recreated only at logon, so if you add a user to a new group, the user would need to log off and log on again for the access token to contain the new group in the group membership list. After logging on again, the user should be able to access any resources that the newly added group can assess, because the access token has been updated.

To see a list of well-known SIDs used by the Windows operating systems visit http://support.microsoft.com/default.aspx?scid=kb;EN-US;Q243330.

Security Descriptors and Access Control Lists

Most networking environments base their security model on using objects. Everything is an object in the network world. For example, users, groups, computers, folders, and files are all examples of objects that you will work with as a network administrator. Every object has security-related information associated with it, known as a security descriptor, which includes a very important piece of information—the access control list (ACL). In general, the ACL is a list of users and/or groups allowed to access the object as well as the level of permissions those users and groups have. The ACL of an object will have many entries, with each entry representing a security principal (a user or group) that has been given a permission to that resource. Each entry that is contained in the ACL is known as an access control entry (ACE). For example, a folder may be set up to allow the Sales team read-only access, whereas the Marketing group may have the Modify permission. In this example, which is shown in Figure 12-3, the folder (which is the object) has two entries (ACEs) in the ACL, one for the Sales group and one for the Marketing group.

There are two types of ACL within the security descriptor of an object: the system access control list (SACL) and the discretionary access control list (DACL). The security descriptor also contains attributes specifying who the owner of the object is and the primary group for that owner. Table 12-2 gives a summary of the security descriptor attributes that describe the security of an object. Figure 12-4 displays the common attributes contained in the security descriptor of an object.

FIGURE 12-3

Looking at an ACL with ACEs in Windows

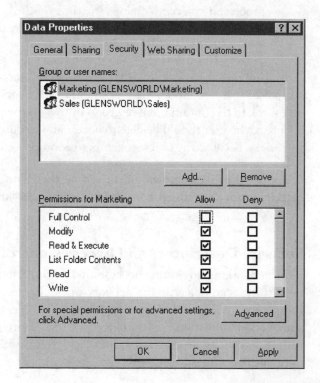

TABLE 12-2	Security Descriptor Attribute	Description
Attributes Contained in the Security Descriptor	System access control list (SACL)	Contains auditing entries for the object if auditing has been enabled for the object. For example, if you decide to audit everyone who fails to read the folder, the folder's SACL will have an entry for the Everyone group with the Failure to Read permission.
	Discretionary access control list (DACL)	Determines which users and groups have access to this object and what their level of access will be. For example, you may want Accountants to be able to modify the contents of a file. The DACL will then have an entry for Accounts Allowed to Modify.
	Owner	Maintains a record of the user who owns the resource. In the Microsoft world, the creator of the object is the person who owns the object. The owner of the object can change permissions of the object at any time. This means that the owner of the object is determined by the security descriptor of the object.
	Primary group	This attribute specifies the primary group ID of the owner of the resource.

In configuring security in a Windows environment, you have two types of security models that you could follow—user-level security and share-level security. With user-level security, when you configure security for the resource, you will use a DACL and pick which users have access to the resource. With share-level security, you simply place a password on the resource when it is shared, and any individual who knows the password can get access to the resource. Let's first take a look at user-level security.

FIGURE 12-4

The security descriptor of an object contains attributes that describe the security of that object.

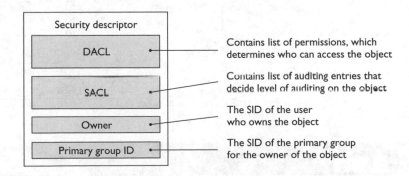

User-Level Security

In Windows operating systems Windows XP, Windows Server 2003/2008, and Vista, you always use user-level security, which gives you no choice but to choose a list of users who can access the resources. Users who are not in the DACL will not be able to access the resource. Figure 12-5 shows a DACL on the security page of a Windows 2003 system.

When configuring the user-level security, you will need to first choose which users or groups (known as security principals) will get access to the resource. In Figure 12-5 you can see that Marketing and Sales have access to the folder. Once you choose which security principals may gain access to a resource, you then assign a set of permissions to each entry in the list. There are a number of permissions in any networking environment; Table 12-3 lists a few of the most common permissions found in the Microsoft world.

FIGURE 12-5

User-level security allows you to select which users have access to the resource.

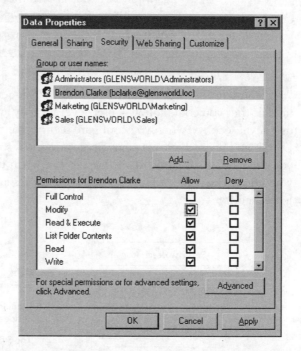

Know the different NTFS permissions for the Network+ exam.

TABLE 12-3	Access Permission	Description
Common NTFS Permissions Assigned to Files and Folders	List Folder Contents	This is a permission assigned to a folder that allows a user to view the contents of the folder but not necessarily to "read" the contents of files in the folder.
	Read	This is a folder and file permission that enables a user to open and read the contents of files.
	Read & Execute	This is a folder and file permission that allows users to read the contents of files and to execute an executable.
	Write	This is file and folder permission that allows a user to modify the contents of a file (write to it) or to create a new file or folder within that folder.
	Modify	A folder or file permission that includes all the permissions mentioned previously. Having the Modify permission allows a user to read, execute, delete, list folder contents, and write to the contents of the folder or file.
	Full Control	A folder or file permission that gives a user all permissions possible. If you assign the Full Control permission, the user will be able not only to modify the contents of the file but also to change the permissions on the resource as well.
	Special permissions	Special permissions are permissions outside of the preceding permission list. You can assign custom permissions such as allowing a user to change permissions but not to modify the file.

Share-Level Security

Share-level security is a security mechanism supported in older Windows operating systems, such as Windows 95 and Windows 98 (as shown in Figure 12-6), that involves configuring the security on a resource, not by selecting which users have access to the resource but by assigning a password to the resource. Anyone who knows the password will have access to the resource.

Share-level security is easy to implement and maintain on small peer-to-peer networks; however, users must remember the password for each resource that is shared. Access is very hard to control because anyone who knows the password can gain access. This is one reason user-level access is much more secure than share-level access and is the most popular method of implementing security.

FIGURE 12-6

Enabling share-
level security in
older versions of
Windows.

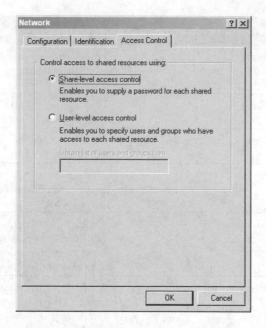

Securing the Registry

Part of securing a Windows system is also securing the Windows Registry. The
Registry is a central database of all the user and computer settings on the system. If
this information were accessible to a malicious user, the results could be disastrous
and could cause the system to be dysfunctional. Because of the risk involved in
accessing the Registry, Microsoft does not even list the utilities provided to modify
the Registry with the rest of the administrative tools. These utilities, REGEDIT.EXE
(for Windows) and REGEDT32.EXE (for Windows NT–based operating systems
such as Windows 2000/XP), are located in the systemroot\system32 directory. In the
past, regedit.exe could not set permissions, while regedt32.exe was the registry editor
you had to use to set permissions. Today's operating systems allow you to use either
regedit.exe or regedt32.exe to set permissions in the registry.

There are two ways to secure the Registry. The first way is to secure the folder
that holds the Registry files; the second way involves securing each section of
the Registry. Let's look at securing the Registry files. The Registry files are stored
in the systemroot\system32\config folder, so you can secure the Registry by
securing this folder—which is done for you by default. Figure 12-7, which shows
the default permissions in Windows Server 2003 for the config folder, reveals that

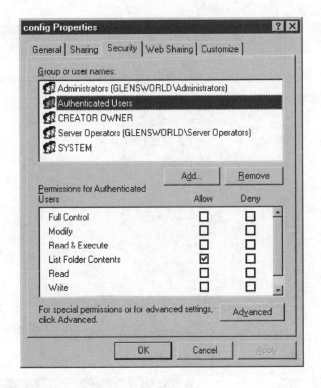

Default permissions on the config folder allow users to see the Registry—not modify it.

authenticated users (users who have logged on) have only the List Folder Contents permission. This means that they can only see that the files are there—they can't modify them.

The second method of securing the Registry is giving users or not giving users specific permissions to a particular area of the Registry. You can control these permissions by using regedt32.exe in Windows operating systems. Once you start regedt32.exe, you can right-click a folder (known as a key) and then choose permissions as shown in Figure 12-8.

Once you choose the permissions command, you can modify the DACL for that section of the Registry. To make sure that users can only read a section of the Registry and not modify it, you can establish that authenticated users have only the Read permission in the permission list but not the Full Control permission. The Full Control permission would allow a user to create and delete items from the Registry. The Permissions dialog box is shown in Figure 12-9, while Exercise 12-1 demonstrates how to secure the Registry with permissions.

FIGURE 12-8

Changing
permissions in
the Windows
Registry with
regedt32.exe

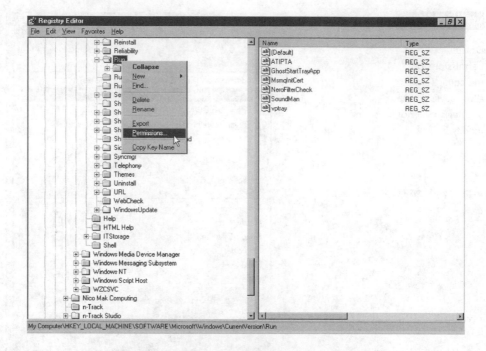

FIGURE 12-9

Ensuring that
authenticated
users have only
Read permission

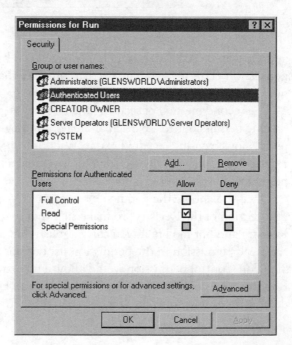

EXERCISE 12-1

Setting Permissions on Registry Keys

In this exercise you will log on to Windows XP as a user named Bob, who does not have access to modify the Registry. You will subsequently log on as a network administrator and configure Registry permissions so that Bob can modify the contents of the Run area of the Registry. Keep in mind that you normally would not allow users to modify the Registry and this part of the exercise is simply for demonstration purposes.

1. Log on to Windows XP as Bob with a password of "password." If you do not have a bob account, you must create one.

2. Select Start | Run and type **regedt32**, and press ENTER.

3. In regedt32, navigate to Hkey_Local_Machine\Software\Microsoft \Windows\CurrentVersion\Run.

4. Right-click the Run folder, and choose New | String Value (as shown in the following illustration).

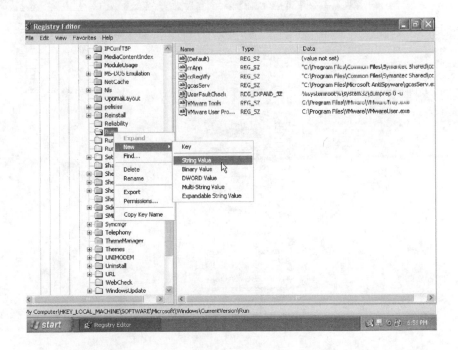

5. An error message should display (as shown in the following illustration), because Bob does not have permission to modify the Registry.

6. Log on to Windows XP as an administrator account.
7. Select Start | Run and type **regedt32**, and press ENTER.
8. In regedt32, navigate to Hkey_Local_Machine\Software\Microsoft\Windows\CurrentVersion\Run.
9. Right-click the Run folder, and choose Permissions (as shown in the following illustration).

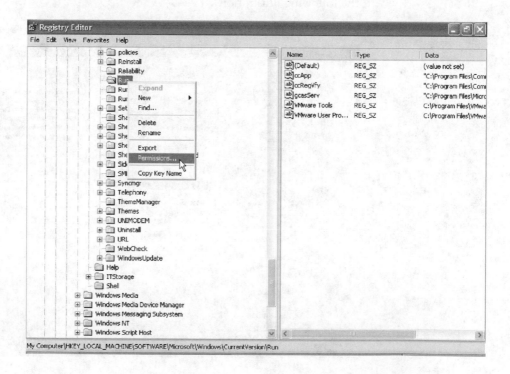

10. In the Permissions dialog box, select the users ACE and assign the Full Control permission (as shown in the following illustration). This allows Bob to create an entry only in the Run portion of the Registry.

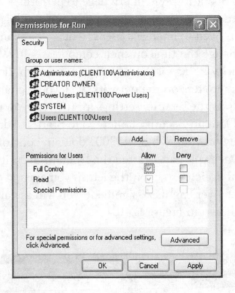

11. Click OK.

12. Log off as administrator.

13. Log on to Windows XP as Bob with a password of "password."

14. Select Start | Run and type **regedt32**, and press ENTER.

15. In regedt32, navigate to Hkey_Local_Machine\Software\Microsoft\Windows\CurrentVersion\Run.

16. Right-click the Run folder and choose New | String Value.

17. Type **test** and press ENTER. You should be able to create the entry this time, because users were assigned full control of the Run portion of the Registry.

Configuring User Rights

In the Windows world, actions users can perform on the network and on their computers are controlled by a feature known as user rights. Remember that a right is an operating system privilege to perform a specific task and that your rights are stored in your access token after you have logged on. As the network administrator, if you need to change a user's rights—for example, you want to allow users to be able to change the time on their computers—in Windows XP you may modify the Local Security Policy of the Windows XP system. If you want users to change the time on all computers on the network, you would change the Domain Security Policy, which controls the security settings for the entire domain. To change the user rights within the Domain Security Policy, go to Start | Administrative Tools | Domain Security Policy on your Windows 2003 domain controller.

Once you have started the Domain Security Policy console, you should see a Local Policies item on the left. If you expand that by pressing the plus sign and then select User Rights Assignment, you will see all the users' rights that can be modified (as shown in Figure 12-10).

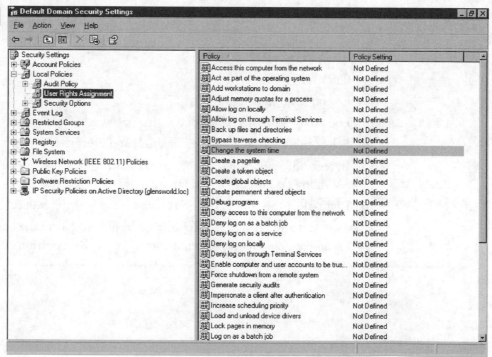

FIGURE 12-10

Looking at user rights assignments

There are a number of user rights displayed on the right side of the screen. If you want to modify a user right, you simply double-click the right and then define the policy and add users or groups to the right to specify that you want those individuals to perform that particular operating system task. Figure 12-11 displays adding the users group to the Change the System Time right.

Table 12-4 is a list of popular user rights assignments and their meaning.

To practice configuring user rights, check out Exercise 12-2 in LabBook.pdf on the CD-ROM.

Configuring Auditing

A major part of configuring network security is making sure that if a user tries to access a protected area of the network, or a hacker tries multiple times to crack a user's password, you are aware of the malicious activity. Configuring auditing on your network server, whether it is Netware, Linux, or Windows, will allow you to identify

FIGURE 12-11

Assigning the
Change the
System Time right
to all users

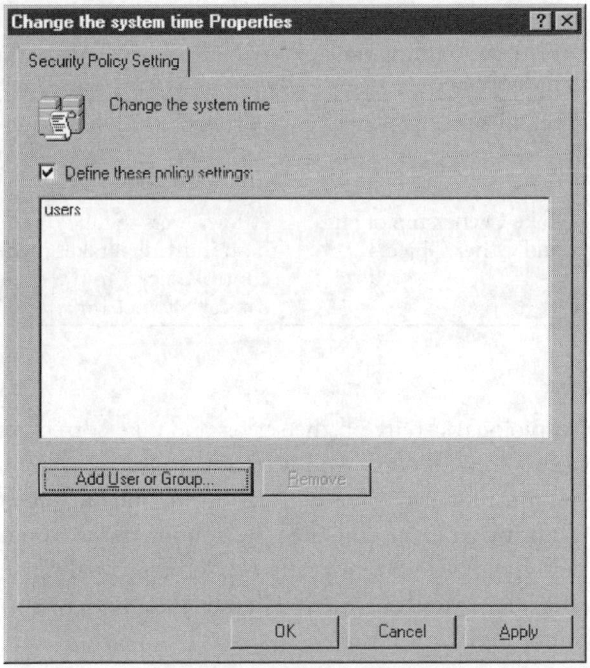

Change the system time Properties   ? ✕

Security Policy Setting

    Change the system time

☑ Define these policy settings:

> users

[Add User or Group...]   [Remove]

    OK   Cancel   Apply

	User Right	Description
TABLE 12-4 Popular User Rights in Windows	Access This Computer from the Network	Allows a user to connect to the system from across the network but not by logging on to the system locally. By default, everyone is allowed to access the system from across the network.
	Allow Log On Locally	Allows users to log on to the system at the keyboard if they have a valid username and password. By default, only administrators have the log on locally right to servers. Everyone has the log on locally right on a Windows client.
	Back Up Files and Directories	Allows users to run backup software and back up any file on the computer or server even if they do not have permissions to the file. By default, only network administrators have this right.
	Restore Files and Directories	Allows a user to perform a restore operation of a backup. By default, only network administrators are given this right.
	Change the System Time	Allows user to change the time on the computer. By default, only network administrators are given this right, even on client systems.
	Allow Logon Through Terminal Services	Allows users to log on to the system through Terminal Services.
	Manage Auditing and Security Logs	Allows users to manage the audit log and security log contained in Windows Event Viewer.
	Shut Down the System	Allows users to shut down a Windows system. If users do not have this right, they will be unable to choose the Windows shutdown command.
	Take Ownership of Files and Other Objects	Allows users to take ownership of files, folders, and printers. If an individual takes ownership of a resource, that individual controls access to the resource. By default, only administrators can take ownership.

suspicious activity on the server and take corrective action. Configuring auditing is a two-step process—you first need to define your audit policy, and then you need to monitor for suspicious activity day in and day out by reviewing the security log. Most auditing software can alert the administrator (usually through e-mail) of suspicious activity. For important network servers, it's always best to have audit logs e-mailed to the administrator (otherwise, a hacker that compromises a machine might clear the audit logs).

Defining the Audit Policy

The first step to configuring auditing is to define your audit policy. When defining your audit policy, you want to enable auditing for specific events within the operating system. An event is something that happens within the system and is usually invoked by a user. For example, logging on or logging off of the network is an event. Accessing a folder is also an event. So you need to determine which events you wish to be notified of, and believe me, you need to be extremely picky as to which events you enable. The important thing to remember is that the more events you audit, the more information that is collected, and you don't want to collect unnecessary information, because it will hide the important audited data.

In the Windows world, there are a number of events you can enable auditing for, and when you enable auditing you have to decide whether you care about the success or the failure of such an event. For example, do you care whether someone successfully logs on to the network or fails to log on to the network? I am going to choose "we care to know if someone fails to log on to the network." Table 12-5 displays a list of the various events in Windows that you can enable the success or failure of.

To enable auditing on Windows 2003 domain controllers, you would configure the Domain Controller Security Policy by going to Start | Administrative Tools | Domain Controller Security Policy. Once in the security policy, expand Local Policies and then select Audit Policy (as shown in Figure 12-12).

FIGURE 12-12

Configuring auditing on a Windows server

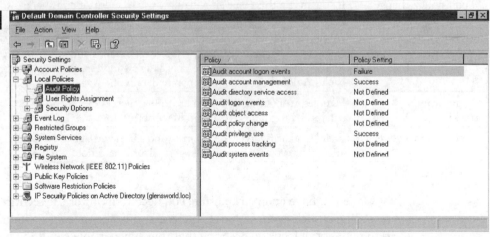

TABLE 12-5   Auditing Events in Windows

Audit Event	Description
Audit account logon events	Logs an entry each time a user logs on to the system, or domain, if auditing is enabled on the domain controller. If you want to monitor when users fail to log on to the network, you would enable this policy on the domain controller and monitor for failures. An entry will be recorded on the domain controller but not the local workstation, because the logon request is sent to the domain controller.
Audit account management	Enable this event if you want to be notified when a user or group is created or modified. This is a great event to enable the success of, because you can monitor when a user account is created. If you enable auditing on account management, you will become aware that a hacker has created a backdoor account, if in fact he got that far. This event also tracks the resetting of user passwords and group membership changes.
Audit directory service access	Audits access to Active Directory objects if auditing is enabled on a particular Active Directory object.
Audit logon events	If you want to audit the event that a user attempted a logon to the domain from the workstation and to record the audit data on the workstation, you would enable this event. If you were to enable audit account logon events instead of this event, there would be no data recorded on the local system when a user logs on to the domain, because the local system did not attempt to answer the logon request.
Audit object access	You can audit folders, files, and printers if you enable this audit policy. Auditing folders, files, and printers is a two-step process—you would need to enable this policy and then enable auditing on any folders or files you want to audit.
Audit policy change	If you enable this event, it will allow you to monitor any changes to the security policy, such as auditing and user rights.
Audit privilege use	Audits anyone who takes advantage of any rights they have been given. For example, if you give Bob the right to back up files and directories, you may want to know when he actually does a backup to prevent him from performing an extra backup and taking private corporate data home with him.
Audit process tracking	Handles events that deal with programs, such as monitoring when a program activates, program exits, and indirect object access.
Audit system events	Enables auditing for system startup and shutdown events; also audits any event that affects the security log or the system security as whole.

Once you have enabled auditing, you need to monitor the security log for the recording of such events. One of the biggest mistakes network administrators make is to put a lot of focus on ensuring that they have enabled auditing but never look at the audit log. As a result, they never know whether their security has been compromised, defeating the purpose of auditing!

Make sure that each day you allow enough time to monitor the security log for suspicious activity. A good idea is to take the first 30 minutes of your morning to review, archive, and then clear the security log while you have your morning coffee.

Monitoring the Security Log

Once you have enabled auditing, you should monitor the security log in Windows Event Viewer, because that is where all audited data appears. Figure 12-13 shows the Windows Event Viewer in Windows 2003. In the event viewer, you can review the various events, save the contents of the log to a file for your own records, and then clear the log to start a clean one for the day. It is important to archive the log in case you need to go back to it at a later time. A lot of security problems are not noticed until long after the event has occurred. Windows also allows you to store the log file to any location, including on another secured host.

To review the security log in Windows Server 2003, select Start | Administrative Tools | Event Viewer. Once in the Event Viewer, select the Security log on the left side, and you will see all the security events. The events with a lock are failure events, and events with a key are success events. Figure 12-13 displays the security log on a Windows Server 2003, and Exercise 12-3 demonstrates how to enable auditing of account management and failures to log on.

Notice in Figure 12-14 that once auditing has been enabled, you can see that a user has failed to log on to the network on June 27, 2005 at 10:41 A.M. When reviewing the security log, if you need more information about the event, double-click the event and the properties appear, as shown in Figure 12-14.

FIGURE 12-13

Reviewing the security log on a Windows server

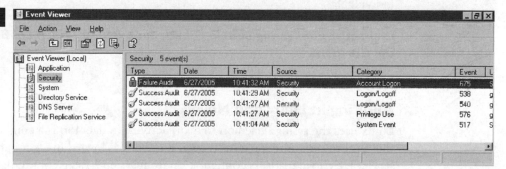

FIGURE 12-14

Viewing details on
a failed logon

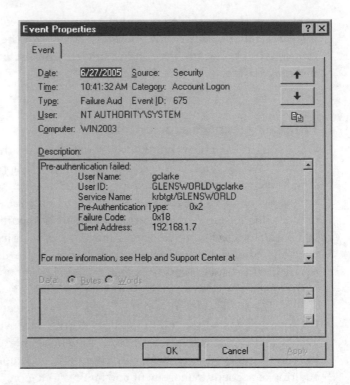

Notice in Figure 12-14 that you can see the date and time someone failed to log on (at the top), but in the description you can see that someone tried to log on with the gclarke user account. Notice that we also have the IP address of the machine at which the person sat to try to log on. This information can help you track down the individual.

To practice configuring auditing, check out Exercise 12-3 in LabBook.pdf on the CD-ROM.

Auditing in Linux and Novell

Linux uses the syslogd daemon to audit activity (a daemon is a computer program that is always running on a host, even if nobody is logged in—similar to a Windows service). Syslogd reads its configuration from sys:etc/syslog.conf to determine what to audit and whether or not to notify the administrator of suspicious activity. Linux administrators also have a wealth of operating system commands, such as last, which lists currently logged-on users, and lastlog, which lists the last logon time for all users.

Novell servers include NSure Audit Services to audit eDirectory and file system activity. As with Windows and Linux, you configure what to audit for whom and decide whether or not to notify someone about suspicious activity.

CERTIFICATION OBJECTIVE 12.03

Firewalls and Proxy Servers

A number of organizations and individuals have an Internet connection allowing them to communicate with the outside world. Although this is a great flexibility allowing access to a wealth of information, there are a number of security risks involved in connecting directly to the Internet. As a general rule, you should always put another device between you and the Internet, and that device is known as a firewall.

Firewall Architecture

Firewalls are designed to protect systems on one side of the firewall from systems on the other side by analyzing packets that reach the firewall and determining whether the packet is allowed to pass through. You will configure rules on the firewall that indicate to the firewall which traffic is to pass through and which is to be blocked.

For example, as a general rule you should configure the firewall to block all traffic, meaning that no traffic can pass through. Once you have configured the "default" rule of blocking all traffic, you can configure exceptions to the rule, allowing selected traffic to pass through. For example, if you have a web server that you want to expose out to the Internet, you would block all traffic except TCP port 80, the port on which web server traffic runs (as shown in Figure 12-15).

Before we consider how to create these firewall rules, let's look at some firewall configurations that are currently used in networking environments.

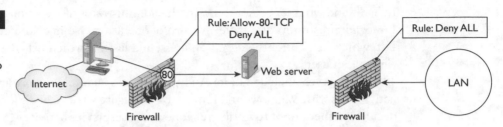

Firewalls allow selected traffic to pass through the firewall.

exam
watch

It is important to note that this chapter is focused on network-based firewalls, which are firewall devices or systems that protect the entire network. For the Network+ exam you need to be familiar with network-based firewalls but also with host-based firewalls. A host-based firewall only protects the one system and is personal firewall software installed on that one system.

Dual-Homed Host Firewalls

A *dual-homed* host firewall consists of a single computer with two physical network interfaces that acts as a gateway between the two networks. The server's routing capability is disabled so that the firewall can handle all traffic management. Either application-level proxy or circuit-level firewall software is run on this system to pass packets from one side of the dual-homed system to the other. You must be careful not to enable routing within the network operating system that will be used as the dual-homed system or you will bypass your firewall software and simply be routing data. Figure 12-16 shows a dual-homed host firewall configuration.

Screened-Host Firewalls

Screened-host firewall configurations are considered by many to be more secure than the dual-homed firewall. In this configuration, you place a screening router between the dual-homed host and the public network. This enables you to provide packet filtering before the packets reach the dual-homed computer, thereby adding an extra layer of network security. The dual-homed computer can then run a proxy to provide additional security to this configuration. Figure 12-17 shows a screened-host configuration.

A dual-homed
system acting
as a firewall has
two network
interfaces.

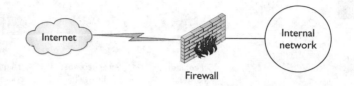

A screened-
host firewall
configuration
adds an extra
layer of network
security by adding
a screening router
to implement
packet filtering.

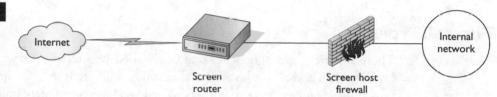

Screened Subnet Firewalls

A *screened subnet* firewall configuration takes security to the next level by further isolating the internal network from the public network. An additional screening router is placed between the internal network and the dual-homed firewall. This provides two additional levels of security. First, by adding a screening router internally, you can protect the dual-homed firewall host from an attack by an internal source. Second, it makes an external attack much more difficult because the number of layers that an attacker must go through is increased. Normally the outside screening router will be configured to pass any data that has passed the filter rule to the dual-homed firewall that will perform more tests on the incoming traffic. Once the incoming traffic has passed the test performed by the dual-homed system, the traffic may then be sent to the internal screening router, where additional tests on the packet are performed. The internal screening router is typically configured to accept only data from the dual-homed firewall, ensuring that hackers can't skip past the outside firewall layers. Figure 12-18 shows the screened subnet firewall configuration.

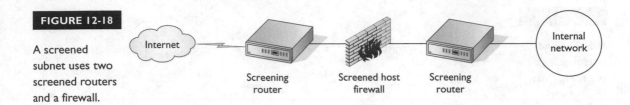

FIGURE 12-18

A screened
subnet uses two
screened routers
and a firewall.

Firewall Types

There are three types of firewalls that can be used: packet-level firewall, application-level firewall, and circuit-level firewall. Each uses different security approaches, thus providing advantages over the others. When you have a complete understanding of the features and the type of security needed from a firewall, you can determine the implementation that bests fits your environment.

Packet-Filtering Firewall

A *packet-level* firewall is usually a form of screening router that examines packets based on filters set up at the network and transport layers. You can block incoming or outgoing traffic according to TCP/IP address or port address rules, so packet-level firewalls map to OSI layers 3 and 4 (network and transport layers, respectively). For example, you may choose to disable all incoming traffic but enable outbound traffic. You can also set up rules that will enable certain types of requests to pass while others are denied. The information that rules can be based on includes source address, destination address, protocol type, and source and destination port address.

For example, if you intend to allow all incoming traffic from any system that is destined for port 80 on your web server's IP address of 24.15.34.89 while disabling all other inbound traffic, you may configure a packet-filtering rule such as the following:

Direction	Protocol	Source Address	Destination Address	Source Port	Destination Port	Rule
Inbound	TCP	Any	24.15.34.89	Any	80	Allow
Inbound	TCP	Any	Any	Any	Any	Deny

Typically, the first rule that applies to the packet is what happens with the data. For example, with the foregoing rule if we have any inbound traffic destined for port 80 on IP address 24.15.34.89, it would be allowed through, but any other traffic would be compared against the following rule, which would deny the traffic at the firewall.

Application-Level Firewall

The *application-level* firewall understands the data at the application level. Application-level firewalls operate at the application, presentation, and session layers of the OSI model. Data at the application level can actually be understood and monitored to verify that no harmful information is included. An example of an application-level firewall is a proxy server. The proxy server can analyze the application data in the packet and decide if it is allowed through the firewall. This is different than a packet-filtering firewall, which can only analyze the header of the packet, including information such as the source and destination IP addresses and port numbers.

In addition, clients often must be configured to pass through the proxy to use it—ideally after they have authenticated themselves properly. Proxy servers are also used to mask the original origin of a packet. For example, an Internet proxy will pass the request on, but the source address listed in the packet will be that of the proxy server address and not of the client that made the request. The overall server doesn't just filter the packets; it actually takes in the original and retransmits a new packet through a different network interface.

Circuit-Level Firewall

A *circuit-level* firewall is similar to an application proxy except that the security mechanisms are applied when the connection is established. From then on, the packets flow between the hosts without any further checking from the firewall. Circuit-level firewalls operate at the transport layer.

Other Firewall Features

As firewalls have evolved, additional feature sets have grown out of—or have been added to—the feature set of a firewall. These features are used to provide faster access to Internet content and better security mechanisms to help protect network resources. A few features that are implemented on firewall products, or are their own standalone products, are discussed in the following subsections.

Caching Servers

Caching servers are used to cache Internet content on a server within your local LAN, so that if additional requests are made for the same content from a client, the content is delivered from the caching server—not retrieved from the Internet a second time. The benefit of such a technology is that you can conserve bandwidth on your Internet connection because the additional request for a resource that has been cached does not create network traffic on the Internet connection, but instead uses bandwidth on the LAN. There is no problem using LAN bandwidth, because LANs are typically a lot faster than a company's Internet connection.

Proxy Servers

By definition, a *proxy* server is a server that performs a function on behalf of another system. The employees who want to access the Internet perform the actions they normally would with their browser, but the browser submits the request to the proxy server. The proxy server then transmits the request on the Internet and receives the results, which are sent to the original requester. The benefit of a proxy is that anyone who captures the traffic sent out on the Internet would have the IP address of the proxy and not that of the internal network systems. Some proxy servers implement caching features as well, allowing the administrator to filter the web sites that are allowed to be viewed by internal clients.

Port Filtering

Port filtering is a major part of building firewall rules. It is extremely important for you to be comfortable with the protocol (either TCP or UDP) and the port number used by an application to establish a socket when administering firewalls. Some of the popular port values and associated protocols for popular network services are listed in Table 12-6.

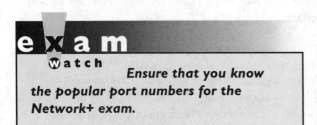

	Port Number	Protocol	Description
TABLE 12-6	20	TCP	FTP server data
	21	TCP	FTP server control
Popular Ports	25	TCP	SMTP server
Used by Network	53	TCP	DNS zone transfers
Services	53	UDP	DNS zone queries
	80	TCP	Web server
	3389	TCP	Terminal Services (RDP)
	110	TCP	POP3
	23	TCP	Telnet

Direction of Transfer

When creating a firewall rule you not only need to supply the layer-3 and layer-4 address information, you also need to specify the direction of the traffic. Most times you will focus on inbound traffic for each of the firewall rules, but you may also control outbound traffic.

Source or Destination Address

On the firewall, we can filter packets based on the source or destination IP address contained in the IP header of the packet. This is a critical tool along with the port number (layer-4 header) because if you want to allow traffic into your network only from one of your other locations, you can specify the source address of your other location in the firewall rule.

A nice feature of layer-3 filtering is that if you detect an intruder accessing the company network from the Internet, you can block any data coming into the network from the IP address of the intruder to help secure your data.

Stateful vs. Stateless Firewalls

A typical packet-filtering firewall is known as a stateless inspection firewall because it simply allows or denies traffic based off the header of the packet (source/destination IP address or source/destination port number). It is possible that the attacker could alter the addresses in the header so that it fits into the rule placed on the firewall and then the firewall allows the packet into the network. In this example, the hacker has simply made up the packet and it really has no context.

A stateful packet inspection firewall will look at the packet and the context of the conversation and if that is the packet that is supposed to be received at that point and time it allows the packet into the network. Stateful packet inspection firewalls use rules to filter traffic as well, but they also are smart enough to know the context of the conversation.

Content Filtering

Another feature available with a number of proxy servers and firewalls is the feature of content filtering. Content filtering allows you to filter what information users are allowed to see when using an application. For example, we may allow web traffic out of the private network onto the Internet but we want to make sure that users on the network are not surfing inappropriate content. At the proxy server or firewall we create content filters that deny any traffic with certain content. For example, we may deny any web pages with the word "sex" in them.

Zones

Firewalls allow the network administrator to divide the network into different network segments known as *zones*. When creating your firewall plan, you will typically create three zones:

- **Private LAN** The firewall placed in front of the private LAN will ensure that no traffic from any other network is sent through the firewall.
- **DMZ** The DMZ is an area between two firewalls that allows selected traffic through from a public network such as the Internet. The DMZ is where we place any servers that need to reached by the general public, such as a web server, FTP server, or DNS server.
- **Public Zone** The public zone is any network not controlled by the network administrator. The best and most popular example of a public zone is the Internet.

EXERCISE 12-4

Enabling a Windows XP/Windows Server 2003 Firewall

In this exercise you will enable the firewall feature on Windows XP or Windows 2003 to block all traffic with the exception of allowing clients to reach the web server that you are hosting and to allow clients to terminal into your server.

Determining Ports to Open

In this part of the exercise you will determine which ports are used by services such as web servers and terminal servers so that you can open those ports on your firewall once it is enabled.

1. First plan which ports will need to be opened on the firewall by filling in the following table.

Service	Port Number	Protocol (TCP/UDP)
HTTP		
SMTP		
RDP (Terminal Services)		

2. Once you have determined the three ports that will be enabled, on your Windows Server 2003 system select Start | Control Panel | Network Connections, and right-click your Local Area Connection, and choose Properties (as shown in the following illustration).

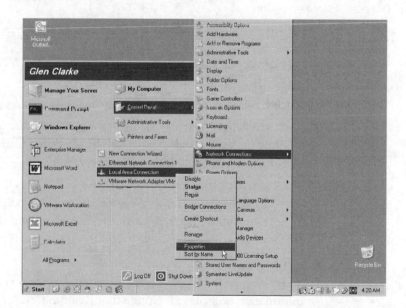

3. Click the Advanced tab.

4. On the Advanced tab, enable the "Protect my computer and network . . ." check box to enable the Windows 2003 or Windows XP firewall (as shown in the following illustration).

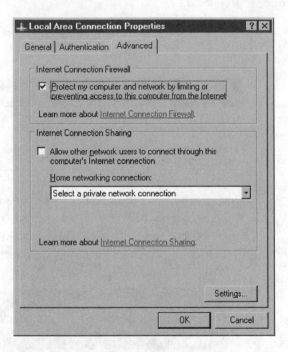

5. Click the Settings button at the bottom of the dialog box.

6. In the Advanced Settings dialog box you can specify which traffic you want to allow to pass through the firewall by selecting the appropriate protocols. Select the check box beside Web Server (HTTP).

7. Once you click the Web Server check box, the Service Settings dialog box appears (as shown in the top illustration on the next page). Notice that port 80 is chosen at the bottom left of the dialog box and that TCP is selected bottom right.

8. Click OK.

9. Select the check box beside the Remote Desktop service. The protocol information is displayed. Notice that Remote Desktop (RDP) uses TCP 3389, and then click OK.

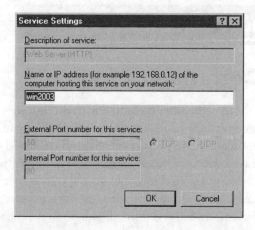

10. Select the check box beside Internet Mail Server (SMTP), and then click OK.

11. You should now have three services selected to allow traffic to pass through the firewall (shown next).

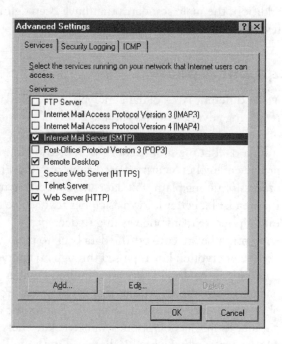

12. Click OK twice.

CERTIFICATION OBJECTIVE 12.04

Securing Communication

As more companies go online with the Internet, the need to protect data becomes more prevalent. The information technology industry has striven to provide a more secure data transfer mechanism because TCP/IP was not designed as a secure network protocol. You can keep up-to-date with worldwide vulnerabilities affecting all vendors by visiting www.cert.org (Computer Emergency Response Team). The idea is to protect the data during a transfer and guarantee that it is sent to its recipient unread and unmodified. From this need, encryption services have grown in popularity. Multiple encryption implementations have been published and are now available to the public. Several standards have also come about that deal with encrypting data in transit, such as SSL and IPsec.

To understand encryption, you must first learn how it works. You will also be introduced to some specific methods and algorithms used for encryption services. In addition, the main standards that have been defined will be explained, as well as a few other data protection methods.

Defining Data Encryption

Many different types of data encryption are available with each methodology, providing advantages and varying levels of security. To date, there are a number of complex encryption standards that have not yet been broken, along with other standards that use simple encryption methods and have been cracked but can still provide a level of security if used appropriately. Encryption can be defined as the process of taking plain text data and converting it to a meaningless format that is unreadable, better known as cipher text. Once the data has been transformed into cipher text, anyone wishing to decrypt the content would need to know the encryption key to convert the data back to plain text, as shown in Figure 12-19.

The encryption key is passed through an encryption algorithm to encrypt the contents of the data. There are a limited number of encryption algorithms, so if a hacker knows the algorithm, that is not considered a security issue, but if a hacker obtains the encryption key, that is a compromise of network security. There are two popular forms of encryption: symmetric key encryption and asymmetric (public-key) encryption, each of which is discussed in the following subsections.

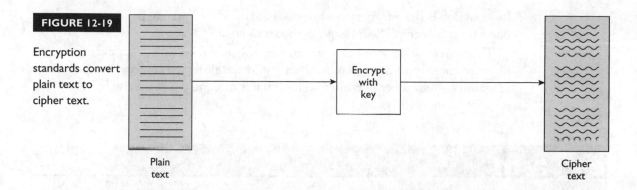

FIGURE 12-19

Encryption standards convert plain text to cipher text.

Plain text

Encrypt with key

Cipher text

Symmetric Key Encryption

The most basic form of encryption is *symmetric key* encryption, so named because both the sender and the receiver of the data use the same key to encrypt and decrypt the data. The problem with symmetric key encryption is that you must have a secure way to transport the encryption key to individuals you wish to exchange data with. If you do not use a secure method to send the key to a recipient, someone may intercept the key. This makes encryption useless, because now the interceptor can decrypt the data knowing the key. In addition, if you are using encryption techniques for multiple recipients, you may not want one person to have access to another's data. Now you must keep multiple single keys per person, which can become extremely cumbersome.

Asymmetric Encryption

A second form of encryption is *asymmetric* encryption, which uses a public-key/private-key pair for the encrypting and decrypting of the data. Asymmetric encryption requires two mathematically related but separate keys in order to perform the encryption/decryption work.

With asymmetric encryption, the public key is freely distributed to anyone you choose. The second key, the private key, is kept in a secure location and is used only by you—hence the term "private." Both keys are required to send data securely over a network structure. For example, say you want to send data to Bob by encrypting the content. You would retrieve his public key and encrypt the data with his public key. Once you have encrypted the data, you can send it over the wire knowing that anyone who intercepts the message would need the related key (Bob's private key) to decrypt the message. Once you send the information on the wire, nothing but the related private key can decrypt the message, not even the public key you have. And because Bob is the only person who possesses the related private key, he is the only one who can decrypt the message, as shown in Figure 12-20.

This system works well because it enables the public key to be sent over an insecure communications channel while still maintaining an appropriate level of security—remember that it would be difficult to share the key securely with symmetric encryption.

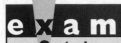

Encryption Methods

When encrypting data, different methods can be used. Each method has its own advantages and drawbacks, and some methods work in cooperation with others to provide an overall solution. The more common methods are discussed and explained here.

FIGURE 12-20

Encrypting data with a public-key/private-key structure

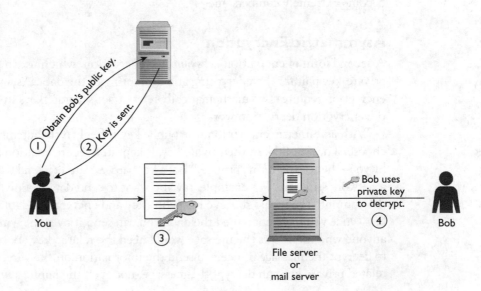

Stream Cipher

Stream cipher algorithms encrypt data one bit at a time. Plain text bits are converted into encrypted cipher text. This method is usually not as secure as block cipher techniques, but it generally executes faster. In addition, the cipher text is always the same size as the original plain text and is less prone to errors. If an error occurs during the encryption process, usually this affects only a single bit instead of the whole string. In contrast, when block ciphers contain errors, the entire block becomes unintelligible.

Block Cipher

Instead of encrypting a bit at a time, *block cipher* algorithms encrypt data in blocks. Block ciphers also have more overhead than stream ciphers, which is provided separately depending on the implementation and the block size that can be modified (the most common size being 64 bits). Because it handles encryption at a higher level, it is generally more secure. The downside is that the execution takes longer. Numerous block cipher options (shown in Table 12-7) are available, such as Electronic Codebook (ECB), Cipher Block Chaining (CBC), Cipher Feedback (CFB), and Output Feedback Mode (OFB).

Padding

When encrypting data, plain text messages usually do not take up an even number of blocks. Many times, padding must be added to the last block to complete the data

TABLE 12-7	Block Cipher Mode	Description
Block Cipher Methods	Electronic Codebook (ECB)	Each block is encrypted individually. If information reappears in the same text, such as a common word, it is encrypted the same way.
	Cipher Block Chaining (CBC)	Feedback is inserted into each cipher block before it is encrypted. It includes information from the block that preceded it. This ensures that repetitive information is encrypted differently.
	Cipher Feedback (CFB)	This enables one to encrypt portions of a block instead of an entire block.
	Output Feedback (OFB)	This works much like CFB. The underlying shift registers are used somewhat differently.

stream. The data added can contain all ones, all zeros, or a combination of ones and zeros. The encryption algorithm used is responsible for determining the padding that will be applied. Various padding techniques are available and used, depending on the algorithm implementation.

Encryption Standards

As encryption has become more popular, the need for industry standards has arisen. Standards for different implementations and algorithms have been defined to move the industry in the same direction. The most popular standards are discussed here with a brief history and explanation.

DES

The Data Encryption Standard (DES) was created and standardized by IBM in 1977. It is a 64-bit block symmetric algorithm and is specified in the ANSI X3.92 and X3.106 standards for both enciphering and deciphering operations, which are based on a binary number. In addition, the National Security Agency (NSA) uses it as the standard for all government organizations. There currently exist 72 quadrillion (72,000,000,000,000,000) encryption keys for DES, in which a key is chosen at random. DES uses a block cipher methodology to apply a 56-bit symmetric key to each 64-bit block. An additional form of DES, known as triple DES, applies three keys in succession to each block.

RSA

Ron Rivest, Adi Shamir, and Leonard Adleman (RSA) were the individuals responsible for creating the RSA standard at MIT, which defines the mathematical properties for using the public-key encryption methodology. The algorithm randomly generates a very large prime number that is used for the public key, which is then consequently used to derive another prime number for the private key via mathematical computations (prime numbers have no pattern). Many forms of RSA encryption are in use today, including the popular PGP. PGP (Pretty Good Privacy) has worked well in the past. Some vendors have included implementations of RSA in their core application code. Versions 4–7 of Novell NetWare have RSA encryption built into the client and server to provide a secure communications channel.

Methods of Securing Traffic

The Network+ exam requires you to be familiar with a number of technologies, along with their related terms, that can be used to secure network traffic. Securing network traffic refers to techniques that can be used to encrypt the network traffic that is sent along the wire (or in the air) between the two systems.

Digital Signatures

Digital signatures are used to verify that a message that was sent is from the appropriate sender and that it has not been tampered with. When using digital signatures, the message is not altered, but a signature string is attached to verify its validity. Digital signatures usually use a public-key algorithm. A public key is used to verify the message, whereas the private key is used to create the signature. A trusted application is usually present on a secure computer somewhere on the network that is used to validate the signature provided. This computer is known as a certificate authority and stores the public key of every user on the system. Certificates are released containing the public key of the user in question. When these are dispensed, the certificate authority signs each package with its own private key. Several vendors offer commercial products that provide certificate authority services. For example, Microsoft Exchange Server can be set up to provide certificates to mail clients by using digital signatures. Lotus Domino also employs this strategy to authenticate client workstations to the server. Employing this methodology doesn't mean you're protecting your data completely, but you will know if it has been tampered with.

It important not only to encrypt data traveling across the network, but also to encrypt it when it gets stored as a file—the lack of file encryption leads to theft of data, which is what we hear about increasingly. On Windows XP/2003/2008, certificates can be used to encrypt files on an NTFS partition through a feature known as the Encrypting File System (EFS). When implementing EFS in Windows 2000, only the user who encrypted the file can decrypt the file and use it, but in the later Windows operating systems you can select additional persons who can decrypt the file. With EFS, the recovery agent always has the capability to decrypt a file as well, and by default the Administrator account is the recovery agent. The benefit of having the recovery agent is that if the person who encrypted the file is no longer available, the recovery agent can decrypt the file so that the organization can access the data. The disadvantage in some Windows versions is if the recovery agent user account is compromised, so is all of the encrypted data. To encrypt a file within the Windows operating systems, perform the steps in Exercise 12-5.

To practice encrypting data on the drive with EFS, check out Exercise 12-5 in LabBook.pdf on the CD-ROM.

Internet Protocol Security

Internet Protocol Security (IPsec) is a fairly new security protocol that can be used to encrypt all IP traffic as well as take part in authentication services and ensure data integrity of information sent across an IP network. One of the things that is so exciting about IPsec is that if you enable IPsec, by means of an IPsec policy, you will not need to configure different encryption methods for each type of application you run on the computer—all IP traffic is encrypted by IPsec once the IPsec policy is implemented. For example, because IPsec encrypts all traffic you do not need to configure a separate encryption technology for your web server, FTP server, and Telnet server. They all run on top of TCP/IP, so IPsec can be used to secure traffic presented by each application. Exercise 12-6 demonstrates how to configure an IPsec policy on your web server and a web client.

When you enable IPsec, you can use one of the default IPsec policies built-in. The IPsec policy is used to determine the type of traffic to be encrypted and the method to be used to encrypt the traffic. The three default IPsec policies are as follows:

- **Client (respond only)**   If asked to communicate securely, this system will respond by using IPsec, but it will never request or initiate secure communication.
- **Server (request security)**   When enabled, this system will request to use IPsec to secure traffic; if the remote system does not support IPsec, the system will communicate insecurely.
- **Secure Server (require security)**   This system will communicate with a remote system only if the remote system supports and uses IPsec.

EXERCISE 12-6

CertCam 12-6

Configuring IPsec to Secure Network Traffic

In this lab you will enable IPsec with a symmetric key between the Windows XP client and Windows Server so that hackers capturing network traffic can't view the data submitted between the XP client and the server.

1. Before enabling IPsec, you may want to verify that you can capture data submitted into the web site of the Windows server from the Windows XP client.

2. On the server, start capturing network traffic with Network Monitor.

3. Go to the Windows XP client and type the address of the server in a web browser to access the web site. In Windows XP, type a credit card number into the site and then click Submit.

4. Go to the 2000 Server and stop capturing the network traffic; view the packet capture to determine whether you can see the credit card number submitted (as shown in the following illustration).

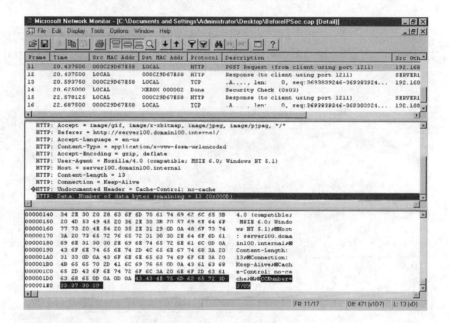

5. The goal of this exercise is that after IPsec has been enabled, you would not be able to view credit card information typed into the site. Also note that the preceding screenshot is from a packet capture called BeforeIPSec.cap stored in the LabFiles\PacketCaptures folder.

Enabling IPsec on the Windows Server

6. To enable IPsec on the Windows server, select Start | Programs | Administrative Tools | Local Security Policy.

7. In the Local Security Policy, select IP Security Policies on Local Machine (as shown in the following illustration).

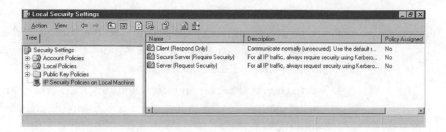

8. Right-click Secure Server and choose Properties.

9. In the properties of the IPsec policy, click the Edit button (as shown in the following illustration) to edit the default policy.

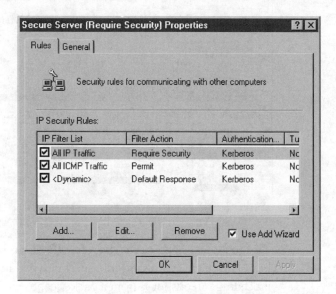

10. Choose the Authentication Methods tab to set the encryption key used by IPsec. You will notice that the default authentication method used by IPsec is Kerberos (as shown in the following illustration). Click Edit to change the authentication method.

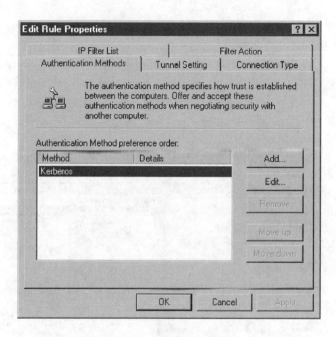

11. Select "Use this string to protect the key exchange," and type the string of mySecret (as shown in the following illustration)—this string is case sensitive.

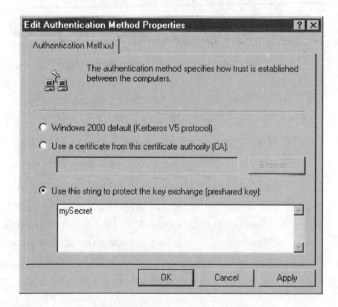

12. Select OK twice.

13. Click Close.

14. Now that you have configured the IPsec policy with the encryption key, you will assign the policy to the system, telling the system to use the policy. Right-click the Secure Server policy and choose Assign (as shown in the following illustration).

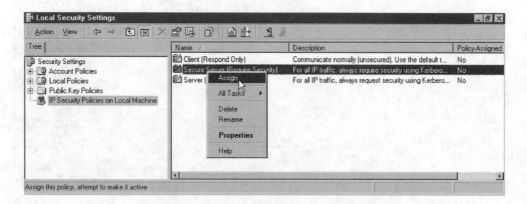

15. When the policy is being used, it will have a little green diamond on it. When you wish to stop using IPsec, you can unassign the policy by right-clicking it and choosing Unassign.

Configuring Windows XP for IPsec

16. Now that the Windows server has been configured for IPsec, we will configure a Windows XP client for IPsec as well. This way any data sent between the Windows XP client and the Windows server will be encrypted. Select Start | All Programs | Administrative Tools | Local Security Policy.

17. In the Local Security Policy, select IP Security Policies on Local Machine.

18. Right-click Secure Server and choose Properties.

19. In the properties of the IPsec policy, click Edit to edit the default policy.

20. Choose the Authentication Methods tab to set the encryption key used by IPsec. You will notice that the default authentication method used by IPsec is Kerberos. Click Edit to change the authentication method.

21. Select "Use this string to protect the key exchange," and type the string of mySecret—again, this string is case sensitive.

22. Select OK twice.

23. Click Close.

24. Now that you have configured the IPsec policy with the encryption key, you will assign the policy to the system, telling the system to use the policy. Right-click the Secure Server policy and choose Assign.

25. Windows XP is now using IPsec. To verify that data is encrypted, capture the network traffic from the Windows XP client to the Windows server by using Network Monitor, submitting the credit card number into the web site again. The following screenshot shows the network traffic captured. Notice that you cannot tell which traffic is the HTTP traffic as opposed to other traffic because it is all Encapsulated Security Payload (ESP) traffic, which is the encryption protocol used by IPsec. The following illustration is from the capture file called AfterIPSec.cap in your LabFiles\PacketCaptures if you want to view the IPsec-enabled traffic.

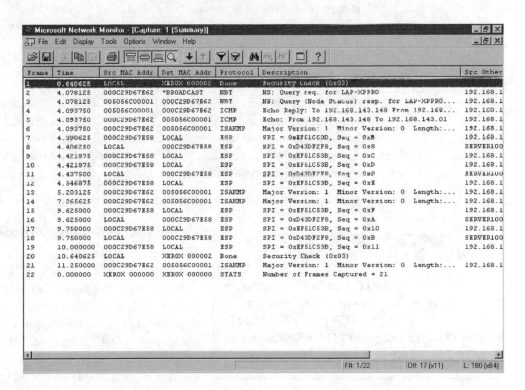

Secure Sockets Layer

Secure Sockets Layer (SSL) is a session-layer protocol that encrypts data sent from any higher-layer program such as FTP, HTTP, SMTP, and so on. SSL has become the standard method of encrypting traffic between a web client and a web server, ensuring that malicious users cannot capture such traffic and read it.

SSL can work only with guaranteed transports—or basically anything using the TCP protocol—and is made up of the two protocols: SSL Handshake and SSL Record.

- SSL Handshake is used to create a secure session between the two systems that are communicating. This includes all methods and parameters used for the encryption.
- SSL Record is used to encrypt all data packets, including the SSL Handshake data packets.

SSL is mainly used on e-commerce web sites during the exchange of personal information such as credit card numbers, because SSL can encrypt the traffic between the client and the server.

Point-to-Point Tunneling Protocol

The Point-to-Point Tunneling Protocol (PPTP) is a VPN protocol used to create an encrypted tunnel over a TCP/IP network such as the Internet. All data that passes through the tunnel is in an encrypted format. The Point-to-Point Tunneling Protocol was dominant in older Microsoft VPN solutions and used Microsoft Point-to-Point Encryption (MPPE) to encrypt the traffic that passed through the tunnel.

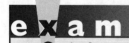

PPTP and L2TP are VPN protocols. PPTP uses MPPE to encrypt VPN traffic and uses TCP port 1723. L2TP uses IPsec to encrypt VPN traffic and uses UDP 500, 4500, and 1701.

Layer Two Tunneling Protocol

The Layer Two Tunneling Protocol (L2TP) is a tunneling protocol similar to PPTP that creates a tunnel over the Internet between two points using PPP data packets encapsulated in TCP/IP protocol packets (for regular networks, you can also use IPX/SPX and NetBEUI). While using IPsec for encryption, the combination will create a VPN. L2TP is supported by Windows

2000 and higher operating systems but does not support implementation over ATM, X.25, or Frame Relay networks.

Kerberos

Kerberos is a distributed authentication security protocol using private keys that verify the validity of a user during logon and will repeatedly do the same every time a request is made. This is useful when a user accesses the network from a workstation that is not secure. A workstation might be in a public kiosk, and anyone may be allowed to log on to the network as a guest, but regular users may visit the kiosk to log on using their individual user accounts.

WEP

The Wired Equivalent Privacy (WEP) protocol is used to encrypt wireless traffic from a wireless client to the wireless access point. Once the data reaches the wireless access point, it is decrypted and then sent along the wired network if needed. WEP uses a symmetric key configured on the access point and then on each client used to encrypt the network traffic. It has been proven that a WEP encryption key is fairly easy to break with products such as Airsnort or WEPCrack.

WPA

WiFi Protected Access (WPA) is the answer from the wireless community to provide more security with wireless communications now that WEP has been proven to be vulnerable to hackers. WPA has improved upon WEP by offering two key features:

- **Improved encryption**   WPA scrambles the encryption keys by passing them through a hashing algorithm and then performing an integrity check to verify that the keys have not been tampered with. The protocol used to scramble the keys is the Temporal Key Integrity Protocol (TKIP), which builds off WEP devices. Typically, only a software upgrade is needed for WEP devices to use WPA.

- **Authentication**   WPA uses EAP as the authentication protocol, which allows for more secure authentication using public-key encryption and authentication. WEP currently does not offer a method of authentication.

on the job *WPA has been superseded by the more secure WPA2. For more information on wireless protocols such as WEP, WPA, and WPA2, read Chapter 7.*

802.1x

Wireless security has generated much interest within the IT industry because it is such a convenient technology. It doesn't need cables all over the place, but still, because of the lack of physical security, some form of authentication is needed to find out who is connecting to the wireless network.

The 802.1x standard provides an authentication technique that leverages EAP and RADIUS to authenticate a user connecting to a network, including a wireless access point. Figure 12-21 displays a typical 802.1x authentication infrastructure.

In the figure you can see that the wireless client is connecting to the wireless access point. The wireless access point sends the request to the *Remote Authentication Dial-In User Service* (RADIUS) server for the user to be authenticated. The RADIUS server challenges the wireless client for a username and password. After the wireless client supplies the username and password to the RADIUS server, the RADIUS server authenticates the client, and the wireless access point allows the wireless client to access the network.

exam watch

Ensure that you are familiar with the protocols used to secure different types of network traffic.

FIGURE 12-21

802.1x using a
RADIUS server
to authenticate a
wireless client

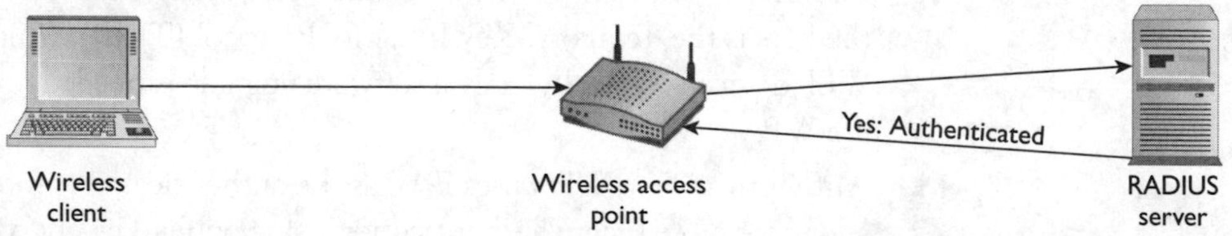

Wireless
client

Wireless access
point

Yes: Authenticated

RADIUS
server

Disaster Recovery and Fault Tolerance

This section introduces two significant topic areas: fault tolerance and disaster recovery. Fault tolerance is the concept of duplicating devices such as drives, power supplies, and network links so that if those components fail, another one becomes operative right away. If for some reason your fault tolerance plan is not effective, a disaster recovery procedure would be in place to help you recover from such failures.

Fault Tolerance

Fault tolerance is the concept of ensuring that systems will continue to function because you have created a solution that involves having backup copies of power supplies, hard drives, and network links. If one of the links goes down, there would be another link ready to kick in at any time, reducing downtime and ensuring an available solution to clients on the network. The following is a list of widely used fault-tolerant components found on the network.

- **RAID solutions**   Redundant Array of Independent Disks (RAID) is the concept of storing redundant data on additional drives in case one drive in the RAID solution should fail. RAID solutions can apply to hardware or software. The hardware solution involves having a RAID controller that controls the RAID array, whereas in a software solution the RAID solution is managed by software such as the network operating system. The software solutions are cheaper, but the hardware solutions offer better performance and are more flexible. For more information on RAID volumes, refer to Chapter 11.

- **Power**   A number of network devices such as servers support a fault-tolerant power source such as a power supply in case the original power supply fails.

- **Network link**   In a number of networking environments a fault-tolerant network link is created to ensure that one network location can communicate with another location at all times or that there is a constant connection to the WAN environment or Internet. A number of business applications require a network link at all times; therefore, when you design the network infrastructure, you should decide whether the organization requires a fault-tolerant network link.

Disaster Recovery

Disaster recovery is a matter of ensuring that you can help the company recover from any kind of disaster. When preparing for disaster, you need to make sure that your disaster recovery plan includes backup and restore plans, contact information for product vendors, and step-by-step instructions on how to recover each part of your information systems.

The disaster recovery plan should contain detailed steps for recovering from any kind of data loss or physical disaster. The step-by-step plan should contain the location of backup tapes, specify which tapes to restore in different scenarios, and list the steps for rebuilding servers, including detailed information on what to do when a disk fails and how to replace and rebuild the data.

A number of disaster recovery documents overlook key elements such as location of software and CD keys needed to rebuild the system. Be sure that contact information for hardware and software vendors is included in the plan so that if you need to replace an item such as a disk you can contact the vendor.

Along with detailed recovery steps, a disaster recovery plan should contain detailed information on backup and restore strategies, offsite storage, hot and cold spares, and hot and cold sites.

Backup and Restore Strategies

Chapter 11 discussed various backup and restore strategies and emphasized the need to guarantee that a strong backup plan is in place to aid disaster recovery. If you have not created a strong backup plan that specifies what to back up and how frequently, you may not be able to recover from disaster. Be sure to review your backup strategy and make certain that you have all the necessary data stored on backup media. You should periodically verify that you can actually restore data using a test environment. Further, make sure that you know and have documented the restore strategy to implement when disaster strikes.

Offsite Storage

It is absolutely critical that you store a copy of the backups offsite in a secure location. You cannot totally rely on the backups stored on your own site, because they will be of no value if the building burns down, destroying all your servers along with the tape backups stored at the location. You must make certain a copy of the backups is stored offsite.

Hot and Cold Spares

When preparing for recovery, organizations typically maintain spares of equipment ready to be used in case of device failures. For example, they may have a spare power supply, hard drive, or network card available in case the original one fails. By having the spare available, you don't need to wait for a part to be delivered to your facility after a device has failed, creating excessive downtime. With a spare available, downtime is minimized. There are two types of directions that you can take with spares, listed as follows:

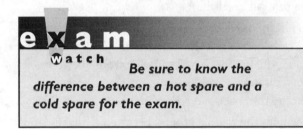

Be sure to know the difference between a hot spare and a cold spare for the exam.

- **Hot spares** A hot spare is a spare component that is typically connected and powered on in case the primary device should fail. When the primary device fails, failover kicks in, allowing the spare device to take over the workload immediately. No time is needed to connect the device or power on the device—hot spares are ready to work.

- **Cold spares** A cold spare is a device that is not powered and is usually sitting on a shelf in a server room. A cold spare involves an increase in downtime, because the device must be connected and powered up before it can take over the function of the original device.

Hot, Warm, and Cold Sites

Disaster involves more than your servers and the data on them; you need to ask yourself, "How can I continue business in the event of a disaster? What if my building burns down? Where can my employees perform their work and continue business operations?" You need to investigate whether your organization will invest in an additional work location, known as a site, in case the original office building becomes unavailable because of fire, flood, or an extended power outage.

When deciding on an alternative location, or site, to continue business operations in the event of a failure, you must choose among a hot site, a warm site, and a cold site. Each site type is explained as follows:

- **Hot site**   A hot site is an alternative location that provides adequate space, networking hardware, and networking software for you to maintain business operations if disaster strikes. This hardware and software should include any data that would be needed by your staff in the event of a disaster, so the provider of the hot site should ensure that the data is up-to-date and the hot site is ready 24/7 if your organization needs it.

- **Cold site**   A cold site is an alternative location where you typically have arranged to have the space available but not the networking hardware or networking software. Providing the hardware and software would be your responsibility in the event of a disaster. A cold site takes time to prepare following a disaster because only the space is made available.

- **Warm site**   A warm site occupies the middle ground between a hot site and a cold site. It is an alternative location with office space and spare networking equipment, such as a server and backup devices, so that you can quickly restore your organization's network in an emergency.

CERTIFICATION OBJECTIVE 12.06

Guidelines to Protect the Network

There are number of concepts that can be applied to your network to help secure the company and its data. This section is intended to provide a best practice guide to guarding your corporate investments. Although it is not designed to be a complete list, this section outlines common practices that should be followed to help create a more secure infrastructure.

One of the most important things to understand about network security is that you should take a layered approach to securing network data. In other words, don't focus too much on just one area of protection but implement all layers of protection.

Physical Security

Physical security plays an important role in any security plan. If someone can get physical access to a system, you can pretty much guarantee they will have access to the system. It is important that you take the necessary steps to ensure physical access to systems is controlled.

The following is a list of physical security measures that should be considered:

- **Physical perimeter security**   In high-secure environments a fence is placed around the perimeter of the location and a guard at a gate are used to control who gets access to the premises.

- **Swipe cards**   Within the facility you can control access to different areas with swipe cards or keypad locks.

- **Locked doors**   It is important that critical systems be locked in a room and access to that room be controlled. Servers should be placed in a locked server room so that physical access to the server can be controlled.

- **CMOS settings**   You can change a number of CMOS settings on the system that deals with physical security. For example, you can ensure that the system cannot boot from CD-ROM. If someone can boot from CD-ROM, that person can load his own operating system and potentially bypass security. You can also disable ports such as USB ports in CMOS, which will ensure someone is not using a thumb drive to take data away.

Firewalls

One of the first things you should do to protect your network from attacks from the Internet is to make sure that you have a firewall between your corporate systems and the Internet. In addition, you should create a demilitarized zone (DMZ), which is an area on the network where you have selected certain data from the Internet to pass through and reach selected services, such as a web server. Figure 12-22 displays a DMZ created by configuring two firewalls; one firewall allows HTTP traffic destined for port 80 to pass through it, and the second firewall connects to the private LAN and allows no traffic to pass through it—essentially protecting internal resources.

FIGURE 12-22

A DMZ is used to publish servers while maintaining security through controlled access to those servers. The DMZ is also used to protect the private LAN.

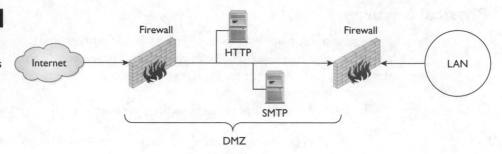

When designing your firewall strategy, do not be afraid to create multiple layers of firewalls by using multiple firewalls and allowing certain traffic to pass through different resources. Also, when using multiple firewalls, be sure to use different vendors for each firewall so that if there is a vulnerability in a firewall and a hacker learns this and bypasses the security of the first firewall, the hacker cannot get past the second firewall using the same technique. For additional security, consider installing personal firewall software on every device on the LAN.

Intrusion Detection Systems

As part of your security best practices you may look to install an intrusion detection system. As you learned in Chapter 3, an *intrusion detection system (IDS)* is a security device that monitors system or network activity and then notifies the administrator of any suspicious activity. The IDS is an important device to complement the firewall because it will notify you not only of suspicious activity against the firewall, but also of suspicious activity inside the network.

There are two types of intrusion detection systems:

- **Host based** Host-based intrusion detection systems monitor the local system for suspicious activity. A host-based IDS is typically a piece of software installed on the system and can only monitor activity on the system the IDS was installed on.

- **Network based** A network-based IDS monitors network traffic for suspicious behavior. A network-based IDS has the capability of monitoring the entire network and comparing that traffic to known malicious traffic patterns. When a match is found, an alert can be triggered. A network-based

IDS can be software loaded on a system that monitors network traffic, or it can be a hardware device.

Intrusion detection systems can be either active or passive. An *active* IDS will monitor activity, log any suspicious activity, and then take some form of corrective action. For example, if a system is doing a port scan on the network, the IDS may log the activity but also disconnect the system creating the suspicious action from the network.

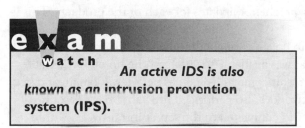

An active IDS is also known as an intrusion prevention system (IPS).

A *passive* intrusion detection system does not take any corrective action when suspicious activity has been identified. The passive IDS will simply identify the activity and then log to file any information needed during an investigation. The passive IDS does not take any corrective action.

Product Updates and Service Packs

A number of people believe that if they have a firewall they are safe from network attacks—a belief that most hackers hope for. The firewall can help protect us against data or services that we have not requested, but what about services that we ask for, such as e-mail? Hackers can attack the system by sending an e-mail that includes an attachment, hoping you open the attachment, which will then attack your system. This is why it is so important that you not open or run any program from an e-mail whose source you are not familiar with.

It is important to note that most vendors, including Microsoft, will never send you an e-mail with an attachment to download. Microsoft has stated that they will send you the URL of a file and downloading it is up to you.

I have received e-mails in the past that appeared to be from Microsoft asking me to run update.exe, which was attached to the e-mail. The hacker doing this was very smart, because the e-mail used the look and feel of the Microsoft site so that it appeared to actually come from Microsoft. The e-mail stated that update.exe would fix a security vulnerability within the operating system, but I knew better and did not run update.exe!

An important part of securing your system is to make sure that you are constantly updating your virus definitions so that your system can protect you from any new known viruses.

Along the lines of updating virus definitions, you will want to make sure that you keep up-to-date on operating system patches and product updates. For example, if you are running a Windows server along with Exchange Server and SQL Server, you must certainly test and apply any patches or updates for each of the products. This is a highly critical step to perform!

About a year ago I was asked to do a security audit on a hotel. During the audit I plugged into a network jack that was available to guests in the hotel. Once I got the IP address, I typed a few Microsoft commands such as net view /domain and saw the domain for the corporate network! I also performed the kaht2 hack described in Chapter 11 on the server and was connected to the server instantly. So within 45 seconds I went from knowing nothing about their network to potentially taking full control of it. Needless to say, the hotel failed the audit!

The lesson here is that the network consultant who configured the network violated every best practice. First, the hotel guest network should never be connected physically to a corporate network. If there is a physical connection, there may always be a way to get access to the data. Second, the server was installed but had never had an update or patch applied to it! If the administrator had run Windows Update on the server, the RPC exploit would not have been successful.

The bottom line here is that you must constantly update your antivirus software and apply any fixes or patches for your server operating systems and network devices. These fixes are provided because of flaws in the products, and hackers are aware of these flaws and use them to gain control of your network. Deny them the opportunity by taking the flaw away! Exercise 12-7 shows how you can delete a file from an unpatched Windows 2000 Server through what is known as the "dot dot" attack typed in the URL of the browser. What is important about this exercise is that a lot of people put their web servers behind a firewall and don't bother doing a Windows update because they figure the system is secure behind the firewall. This attack shows you that the HTTP request will most likely pass through your firewall. You want to publish a web site, but because the system is not patched, anyone in the world can delete files on the server.

EXERCISE 12-7

Understanding the Importance of Patching a Server

In this exercise you will view the contents of drive C on an IIS 5.0 server that has not been patched, using the famous "dot dot" attack. You will then delete a file from drive C of the web server through the URL of a web browser. The goal of this exercise is to demonstrate how dangerous it is not to have up-to-date operating system patches on a server. This vulnerability in IIS 5 would not exist on a patched IIS 5.0 web server.

Create a File on the Windows 2000 Web Server

1. On the Windows 2000 unpatched server double-click My Computer.
2. Double-click drive C to open drive C.
3. Choose File | New | Text Document.
4. Type **secret** as the filename and press ENTER.
5. You will need to know the IP address of your web server. Go to a command prompt, type **ipconfig**, and record the IP address of your web server in the space provided:

Perform the "Dot Dot" Attack from a Windows XP System

6. Start Internet Explorer on the Windows XP system.
7. Type the following URL to connect to your unpatched IIS 5.0 box to view the contents of the web server's hard disk. The IP address of my server is 192.168.1.201—if your IP address is different, you will need to replace the IP address in the URL:

```
http://192.168.1.201/scripts/..%c0%af.../winnt/system32/cmd.exe?/c+dir+c:/
```

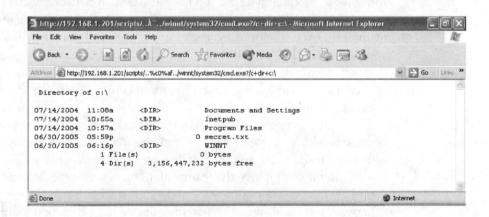

8. In the preceding figure, notice that you can see the file named secret.txt. Now that you have used the **dir** command through the URL, change the command to delete the c:/secret.txt file by changing the **dir** to a **del** command:

```
http://192.168.1.201/scripts/..%c0%af.../winnt/system32/cmd.exe?/c+del+c:/secret.txt
```

9. You get a CGI script error, but the delete operation has been successful. If you change the delete command back to the original command to do a **dir**, you will not see the secret.txt file anymore, because it has been deleted (as shown in the following illustration). You may need to refresh the page.

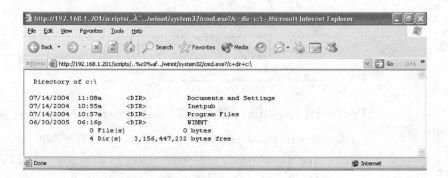

Hardening Devices and Systems

In regard to patching systems, you must also harden network devices and network servers. Hardening a system or a device is the process of removing unnecessary features that you are not using. For example, after installing a Windows 2000 Server you will notice that IIS is installed by default. You learned in the preceding exercise that anyone can delete files on your unpatched IIS 5.0 box. If you are not planning on hosting web sites on the server, you should uninstall the IIS service—this is the concept of hardening.

Hardening an operating system or network device is a time-consuming process because you have to research the operating system or device and find out what software is installed by default. You then must verify whether you actually need that feature, and if not, remove the feature. This process involves a lot of paperwork, and you really must do your homework to determine what is needed and what is not; otherwise, you could cause the system or device to be dysfunctional by removing the wrong operating system component.

Hardening a server and then applying any updates or patches to the server is a very effective method of securing the server. It is not the be-all and end-all of network security, but combined with firewalls and data encryption, it can go a long way to securing your environment.

As part of your hardening practice, you will want to make sure that you have renamed any built-in accounts, such as the Administrator account. Once you have renamed the account, you may even create a new user account named "Administrator" and assign a really strong password to this account. The benefit is that a hacker who obtains the password for that account will only have "user" privileges on the system and also needs to figure out which of your accounts is the real Administrator account.

In connection with passwords, you must also make sure that all accounts are using strong passwords. For more information on creating a password policy, refer to Chapter 10. To audit users' passwords and be certain that their passwords are strong, you could use a password auditor such as LC4.

Data Encryption

In this chapter you have learned about various technologies used to secure network traffic, such as SSL for web traffic or IPsec for all IP traffic. If you want to make sure that a hacker cannot read the traffic on the network, you need to encrypt your traffic to protect its confidentiality.

If you have a wireless network, you need to enable some form of encryption, such as WEP. Remember that WEP encryption has proved to be crackable; use it only if you don't have another method of encrypting wireless traffic, but try to implement another form of encryption if possible.

Another really important point to make about a hacker's capturing network traffic is that on a wired network, the hacker must be connected to the network. If you enforce rules of physical security, you can protect network traffic. For example, many companies will not allow anyone with a laptop to connect to the physical network, because they know that a laptop connected to the network can run a number of security hacks and potentially yield access to corporate data.

Make sure that you have a policy in place that limits who can connect to the network with devices such as laptops. You can enforce this by deactivating network ports until someone wants to use any of them. Even then, the user must be granted permission by management, and the port will be activated for only that MAC address.

Vulnerability Testing

The last point I want to make about network security is that there are a number of vulnerability scanners available that can scan your network, making you aware of common security mistakes and unpatched systems. These vulnerability scanners can inform you of such things as

- The number of network administrator accounts
- Group memberships
- Updates that have not been applied
- Weak passwords used by user accounts
- Common security practices not followed

The foregoing list is a small example of the features available from vulnerability scanners, such as the Microsoft Baseline Security Analyzer (MBSA) or GFI's Languard. You can download both of these tools from the following URLs:

- **MBSA** www.microsoft.com/downloads
- **Languard** www.gfi.com/pages/files.htm

Languard is my favorite of the two and does a better security assessment of your network infrastructure. Languard reports a long list of items to you such as a list of user accounts, groups, permissions, open ports, services that are running, and missing patches. The benefit of a security scanner is that it can scan the entire network and report all of these issues to you in one screen—for all the systems on the network! Figure 12-23 displays Languard.

ON THE CD

To practice performing a vulnerability assessment with Languard, check out Exercise 12-8 in LabBook.pdf on the CD-ROM.

This section has introduced a few best practices relating to securing network resources. Network security is a huge topic and can't be covered in just a few pages, so I hope that I have given you worthwhile information on just a few quick points. If you are interested in learning more on network security, one of the best books on the topic is McGraw-Hill's *Hacking Exposed, Sixth Edition* (2009). I highly recommend it!

FIGURE 12-23

Languard is a security scanner that reports on a number of security issues.

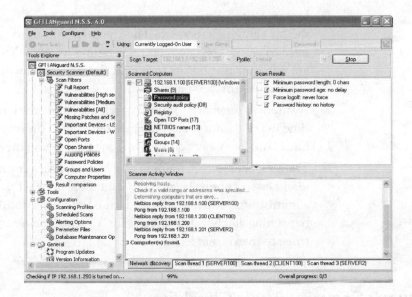

Training and Awareness

One of the most overlooked security measures that can be taken within any organization is training and awareness. It is vital to the success of any security protection program that all employees within the organization are given seminars that make employees aware that their actions could cause security incidents.

One of the best examples I can give is an employee password. Passwords should be changed frequently, and when they are changed, they should be strong passwords (mix of letters, number, symbols, and case). If I were the security manager for a company, I would ensure that all employees saw a demonstration on how easy a program such as LC4 can crack simple passwords, but at the same time have difficulty cracking strong passwords. This style of training and awareness will show the value of policies such as frequent password changes and the need for strong passwords. If we don't make the employees aware, they won't really care.

There are a number of methods that you can use to train employees. The following are a few popular delivery methods:

■ **Lunch and learn** A popular method of raising awareness is to have small one-hour sessions during lunch hour. These sessions, termed lunch and learn, are typical short sessions focused on one topic. For example, today there may be a session on protecting passwords, while tomorrow the topic may be physical security.

- **Intranet site** You could create training videos and post them on a intranet site for employees to watch. These are typically not as effective because you need to ensure you have control measures in place that ensure employees are watching the videos. You could also post documents on the intranet that explain security best practices.

- **Awareness seminars** Instead of relying on lunch time, you could allocate time in the day for short awareness seminars. This is the same idea as the lunch and learn, but you are not using up the employees' lunch time.

- **Training courses** A training course is a longer version of awareness seminars and normally goes into a lot more detail. Typically the network administrators will need to be educated on how security compromises are happening and how to protect against them. These courses could range from three to five days in length.

Network Security Audit Checklist

As a network professional responsible for ensuring that network resources are protected, you may find it hard to keep up with securing all resources and implementing best practices. I have created a general network security checklist that you can use to audit the network and its servers. It is not designed to be complete, but it serves as a guide that you can build from. The checklist is also contained in the LabFiles\Checklist folder on the CD that accompanies this book.

General Security Questions	
How many network segments are present?	
Does the corporate network have a separate network segment from the guests/students/customers network?	☐ Yes ☐ No
Is there a physical connection between the corporate network and the guests/students/customers network?	☐ Yes ☐ No
How many administrator accounts exist?	

Wireless Security	
Is there a wireless network?	☐ Yes ☐ No
Is wireless using WEP? (Use only if WPA encryption is not supported between wireless access point and connecting clients.)	☐ Yes ☐ No
Is wireless limited by MAC addresses?	☐ Yes ☐ No
Is wireless using an SSID different from the company name?	☐ Yes ☐ No
Is SSID broadcasting disabled?	☐ Yes ☐ No
Is authentication (user, smart card) enabled for the wireless access point?	☐ Yes ☐ No
Is DHCP disabled on the wireless access point?	☐ Yes ☐ No
Does the wireless access point admin page support SSL?	☐ Yes ☐ No
Have the wireless access point admin name and password been changed?	☐ Yes ☐ No
Server Security	
Have built-in accounts been renamed?	☐ Yes ☐ No
Is password complexity enabled?	☐ Yes ☐ No
Is auditing enabled?	☐ Yes ☐ No
Are servers up-to-date with service packs and security fixes?	☐ Yes ☐ No
Have web services been removed?	☐ Yes ☐ No
Is NTFS being used?	☐ Yes ☐ No
Is the server in a locked server room?	☐ Yes ☐ No
Have unnecessary services been removed?	☐ Yes ☐ No
Are backups being performed?	☐ Yes ☐ No
Is RAID implemented?	☐ Yes ☐ No
Is antivirus software installed and up-to-date?	☐ Yes ☐ No
Is local file system encryption enabled?	☐ Yes ☐ No
DNS Security	
Are secure dynamic updates enabled?	☐ Yes ☐ No
Are zone transfers being limited?	☐ Yes ☐ No
Is TCP 53 blocked on the firewall?	☐ Yes ☐ No
Is UDP 53 blocked on the firewall?	☐ Yes ☐ No
Are there separate zones for internal use and external use?	☐ Yes ☐ No

Web Server Security	
Authentication type?	☐ Anonymous ☐ Basic ☐ Windows
Are non-public files secured with NTFS?	☐ Yes ☐ No
Is the server up-to-date with patches?	☐ Yes ☐ No
Is the web server behind a firewall?	☐ Yes ☐ No
Has the IIS lockdown tool been run?	☐ Yes ☐ No
Is antivirus software installed and up-to-date?	☐ Yes ☐ No
Is the web server in its own domain or workgroup (Microsoft) or in its own tree (Novell)?	☐ Yes ☐ No
Exchange Server Security	
Are message size limits placed on incoming and outgoing mail?	☐ Yes ☐ No
Are there limits placed on Mailbox size?	☐ Yes ☐ No
Is the e-mail server behind a firewall?	☐ Yes ☐ No
Is the e-mail server up-to-date with patches?	☐ Yes ☐ No
Has message filtering been enabled?	☐ Yes ☐ No
Has antivirus software been installed and kept up-to-date?	☐ Yes ☐ No
Client Desktop Security	
Are virus definitions up-to-date?	☐ Yes ☐ No
Are clients logging in to a domain?	☐ Yes ☐ No
Have the local built-in accounts been renamed and password protected?	☐ Yes ☐ No
Are laptop users and publicly accessible desktop PCs using a lockdown cable?	☐ Yes ☐ No
Do users have admin access to local systems?	☐ Yes ☐ No
Are client systems patched?	☐ Yes ☐ No
Is spyware removal software installed and up-to-date?	☐ Yes ☐ No
Is there personal firewall software installed?	☐ Yes ☐ No
Is local file encryption enabled?	☐ Yes ☐ No
Has the CMOS been hardened?	☐ Yes ☐ No
Has USB port usage been restricted?	☐ Yes ☐ No

Network Vulnerability Testing	
Attack type	System has passed?
Discovery information (net view /domain, nbtstat)	☐ Yes ☐ No
Ping sweep/port scan	☐ Yes ☐ No
Exploits—Example: RPC Exploit (KAHT2)	☐ Yes ☐ No
Password attack	☐ Yes ☐ No
DNS zone transfer	☐ Yes ☐ No
Languard Vulnerability Scanner	☐ Yes ☐ No
Microsoft Baseline Security Analyzer	☐ Yes ☐ No
Firewall test	☐ Yes ☐ No

CERTIFICATION SUMMARY

In this chapter you learned some best practices for securing your network. It is important to remember to implement security in layers and not to rely on just one method of securing your systems. In this chapter you have seen the "dot dot" attack, which is launched by a hacker typing a URL into the web browser that navigates the folder structure on the server and can be used to delete files. This shows that if you were not patching the server but relying only on a firewall, you would be vulnerable to the attack.

You have learned a number of operating system features that are used to secure systems, such as authentication and authorization. Authentication is the process by which a user presents logon credentials that are then verified by the network server against a database; if the credentials are correct, the user is allowed to access the network. After a user has been authenticated, an access token is generated that is used to authorize the user to access various network resources. A network resource uses an access control list to determine who is allowed access.

A firewall is a device used for protecting one network from a second interconnected network, such as the Internet. Firewalls compare the data passing through them with rules set up to allow or deny access. There are several architectures for firewalls; three of them are dual-homed host, screened host, and screened subnet. A dual-homed host firewall has two network interfaces and acts as a gateway between the two networks. A screened-host firewall has a screening router placed between the public network and the dual-homed host firewall. This provides an additional level of security against outside intrusion. A screened subnet firewall, meanwhile, puts a screening router on either side of the firewall host. This provides protection on both sides of the host.

Three firewall types are in use: packet-level firewall, application-level firewall, and circuit-level firewall. The packet-level firewall controls data at the network and transport layers. The type that works at the application level acts as a proxy and controls the top three layers of the OSI model. A circuit-level firewall works like an application-level firewall but operates at the transport layer. Additional security features have been added to firewalls to provide better service, such as support for VPNs and caching and better management tools. Proxy servers can also function as firewalls and can be used to enhance Internet access as well as function as firewalls by filtering ports.

Data security has become increasingly important as networks are becoming interconnected. Data encryption provides a way to ensure that the data is kept secure. Encryption is the process of taking plain text data and converting it into a format that is unreadable. A key is used to encrypt the data and then to return the data to a readable format. Two types of encryption are in use: symmetric and asymmetric (public-key/private-key). Two common encryption methods include stream cipher and block cipher. Two standards for encryption have been accepted: the Digital Encryption Standard (DES) and RSA. Both use different methodologies and are in wide use today. Digital signatures can be used to verify that a message arrived without being tampered with. Digital signatures do not encrypt a message. Instead, they attach a signature that can be verified against a certificate authority. Windows 2000/XP/2003/2008 use certificates to encrypt files on an NTFS volume.

You have learned a number of different disaster recovery concepts, including backing up data and storing a copy of the data offsite. You also learned that there are two types of spares for equipment such as hard drives or other network components—hot spares and cold spares. A hot spare is connected to the system and has power already supplied to the device so that if there is a failure in the original device, the hot spare can take over right away. The cold spare is typically close by but not connected to the system at the time of the failure. Because the spare is not readily available without any kind of changeover time, it will take longer to recover from the failure. You have also learned that companies serious about disaster recovery are likely to have an alternative location set up in case of a disaster affecting the original location. There are hot, cold, and warm disaster recovery sites. A hot site is a fully furnished site that has servers and a copy of the corporate data ready to go in case of disaster. A cold site is a company just paying to have the facility available; a warm site includes the facility with a server and backup devices ready for the restore operation.

You have also learned a number of guidelines used to protect the network, such as patching systems and keeping them up-to-date and using firewalls to protect the network and its data. It is extremely critical that you keep your knowledge up-to-date about known vulnerabilities within the operating systems you are supporting. Be sure to perform a vulnerability scan on your network frequently with products such as Languard.

✓ TWO-MINUTE DRILL

Understanding Attack Types

❑ Social engineering attacks are when the hacker tries to trick a person into compromising security through social contact such as an e-mail address or phone call.

❑ Denial of service attacks result in the system crashing or being so busy servicing requests from the hacker that the system cannot answer requests from valid clients.

❑ There are three main types of password attacks—dictionary, hybrid, and brute-force attacks.

❑ Spoof attacks are when the hacker alters the source address to make the data look like it came from a different source. There are different types of spoof attacks—IP spoofing, MAC spoofing, and e-mail spoofing.

❑ A buffer overflow attack typically results in the hacker getting shell access to the system with administrative permissions.

Understanding System Security

❑ When a user logs on to the network, an access token is created that contains the user account and any groups the user is a member of; the token is then used to authorize the user to access resources.

❑ Security descriptors are broken down into several components: the system access control list (SACL), the discretionary access control list (DACL), an owner, and a primary group.

❑ The DACL is a list that shows the users and/or groups allowed to access the object as well as the level of permissions applied.

❑ User-level security used in all new Windows operating systems allows administrators to select which users can access a resource and specify the permission they have.

❑ Share-level security is available on client operating systems such as Windows 95 and Windows 98, which place a password on the share. Anyone who knows the password can access the resource.

❑ Share-level security is easy to implement and maintain on small peer-to-peer networks. However, users must remember the password for each shared resource.

❑ You can secure the Registry for Windows systems by using regedt32.exe and setting permissions on different areas in the Registry.

❑ Auditing allows you to monitor the security of the system and any administration activity performed.

❑ A permission is a level of access to a resource, whereas a right is a privilege within the operating system to perform an operating system task.

Firewalls and Proxy Servers

❑ A firewall protects the network by analyzing packets trying to pass through it and either allowing or denying the packet.

❑ Traffic can be controlled through the firewall by building a firewall rule that specifies the traffic that can pass through by source, destination IP address, or port address.

❑ A screened-host firewall places a router between the firewall and the Internet that filters and analyzes the traffic before it reaches the firewall.

❑ A dual-homed firewall is made up of a computer with two network interfaces that filters traffic from one interface to the other.

❑ A DMZ is a network segment that allows selected traffic through the firewall to the DMZ. The DMZ can host the web servers and the e-mail server for a company, but it does not host any private corporate servers—they are located behind an additional firewall.

Securing Communication

❑ Symmetric encryption uses the same encryption key for encrypting and decrypting traffic.

❑ Asymmetric encryption uses a different key to encrypt from the one it uses to decrypt the traffic.

❑ There are multiple methods of securing communication; you need to choose the best method for your situation.

❑ Encryption can be defined as the process of taking plain text data and converting it to cipher text.

❑ Internet Protocol Security (IPsec) allows for encryption of all data on an IP network by configuring an IPsec policy.

❑ The Secure Sockets Layer (SSL) is used to encrypt web site information transferred between a user and the web server (online credit card information is encrypted this way).

❑ The Layer Two Tunneling Protocol (L2TP) and PPTP are VPN protocols that are used to encrypt traffic between a VPN client and the VPN server.

❑ Kerberos is a distributed authentication security mechanism used by Windows 2000/2003/2008 Active Directory for user validation.

Disaster Recovery and Fault Tolerance

❑ Fault tolerance is a matter of ensuring that your systems will still function when a component fails, because you have another component ready to take over the work. RAID is an example of a fault-tolerant solution for your data.

❑ Disaster recovery is the concept of ensuring that you can recover from any type of disaster by preparing for the disaster. You can prepare for disaster by building a disaster recovery plan, which contains step-by-step procedures for recovering a system from different failures.

❑ You can create a disaster recovery alternative site for your organization. There are three types of alternative sites: hot, cold, and warm sites.

❑ There are two types of spares when it comes to having standby components: hot spares and cold spares. A hot spare is a component that is connected and powered on, ready for failover; a cold spare must be powered up to be made available.

Guidelines to Protect the Network

❑ Place your web servers, FTP servers, and mail servers in a DMZ to protect them from the outside world.

❑ Make sure that you patch all systems and devices. Patching a system or device helps remove known vulnerabilities from the system or device, which in turn helps secure it.

❑ Review your firewall rules to be certain that you are allowing only needed traffic through the firewall.

❑ Physically secure servers behind a locked door in a controlled-access server room. If a hacker can get physical access to the system, the system can be compromised.

❑ Encrypt the traffic of sensitive data so that it cannot be captured and analyzed by network intruders. You can use such technologies as SSL or IPsec to secure network traffic.

❑ Be sure to spend time hardening your servers. Hardening a server involves removing unnecessary services from the system. The less software running on the server, the fewer security holes.

❑ Make sure that you perform a vulnerability scan of the network with tools such as Languard on a regular basis.

SELF TEST

The following questions will help you measure your understanding of the material presented in this chapter. Read all the choices carefully, because there may appear to be more than one correct answer.

Understanding Attack Types

1. What type of attack involves the hacker altering the source address of a packet?
   A. Buffer overflow
   B. Dictionary attack
   C. Social engineering attack
   D. Spoof attack

2. What type of password attack involves using dictionary words and appending numbers to the end of those words?
   A. Brute-force
   B. Dictionary
   C. Hybrid
   D. Buffer

Understanding System Security

3. What portion of the Windows security subsystem handles both local security policies and user authentication, and generates audit log messages?
   A. Local Security Authority (LSA)
   B. Security Accounts Manager (SAM)
   C. Security Reference Monitor
   D. None of the above

4. What portion of the Windows security architectures maintains the database used for storing user and group account information on a local Windows XP system?
   A. Local Security Authority (LSA)
   B. Logon Process
   C. Security Reference Monitor
   D. Security Accounts Manager (SAM)

5. What access control list object determines which users and groups have permissions to an object?

    A. System access control list (SACL)

    B. Discretionary access control list (DACL)

    C. Owner

    D. User

6. Which of the following allows a user to modify the contents of a file?

    A. Read and Execute

    B. Read

    C. List Folder Contents

    D. Modify

7. A user's credentials are checked against a database of accounts that are allowed to access the network. This process is known as _____?

    A. Authorization

    B. Authentication

    C. Rights

    D. Permissions

Firewalls and Proxy Servers

8. What type of device analyzes packets that attempt to enter the network and then either allows or denies the traffic, based on rules?

    A. Encryption

    B. Firewall

    C. Router

    D. None of the above

9. What kind of firewall provides a single computer with two physical network interfaces?

    A. A dual-homed host firewall

    B. A screened-host firewall

    C. A screening router

    D. A screened subnet firewall

10. Which component(s) is/are included in a screened subnet firewall configuration?

    A. Single screening router

    B. Host firewall server

    C. Circuit application

    D. Two screening routers

11. Which type of firewall is used to provide security based on rules governing the network or transport layers?
    A. Packet level
    B. Application level
    C. Circuit level
    D. None of the above

Securing Communication

12. Which encryption scheme uses the same encryption key to decrypt the data as the one that encrypted the data?
    A. Asymmetric
    B. RSA standard
    C. Symmetric
    D. Public-key algorithm

13. Which of the following is classified as an encryption method? (Choose all that apply.)
    A. Stream cipher
    B. Data cipher
    C. Byte cipher
    D. Block cipher

14. Which block cipher mode encrypts each block individually during the encryption process?
    A. Electronic Codebook (ECB)
    B. Cipher Block Chaining (CBC)
    C. Cipher Feedback Mode (CFB)
    D. None of the above

15. What encryption standard is based on a fixed 56-bit symmetric key encryption algorithm?
    A. RSA
    B. DES
    C. CPA
    D. DSE

16. What technology uses certificate authorities to verify that a message has not been tampered with?
    A. RSA encryption
    B. Local Security Authority

C. Digital signatures

D. None of the above

Disaster Recovery and Fault Tolerance

17. Which disaster recovery site provides only the facility, but no equipment or copy of the original data?

A. Hot site

B. Warm site

C. Blue site

D. Cold site

18. Which disaster recovery site provides the facility and ensures that the site has an up-to-date copy of the data needed to have a fully functional site?

A. Hot site

B. Warm site

C. Blue site

D. Cold site

19. What type of spare component has power supplied to it and is ready to take over if the original component fails?

A. Cold spare

B. Network spare

C. Warm spare

D. Hot spare

Guidelines to Protect the Network

20. Which of the following pieces of software provide a vulnerability scan of the network? (Select all that apply.)

A. Languard

B. Norton AntiVirus

C. Microsoft Baseline Security Analyzer

D. Microsoft AntiSpyware

E. Spybot

21. After installing a network operating system, what should you do before placing the machine on the network to help secure it?

    A. Harden the operating system

    B. Install a firewall

    C. Configure e-mail

    D. Build user accounts

22. After hardening the operating system, what should you do to ensure that your server has all security fixes applied to it?

    A. Install antivirus software

    B. Install antispyware software

    C. Patch the server

    D. None of the above

SELF TEST ANSWERS

Understanding Attack Types

1. ☑ **D.** Spoof attack is the term used for when the hacker alters the source address of the packet. There are different types of spoofing depending on what source address is being altered—IP spoofing, MAC spoofing, and e-mail spoofing.

   ☒ **A, B,** and **C** are incorrect. A buffer overflow attack is when too much information is sent to an application and as a result the hacker can run arbitrary code. A dictionary attack is a form of password attack using a word list file, and a social engineering attack is when the hacker calls or e-mails an individual and tries to trick them into compromising security.

2. ☑ **C.** A hybrid attack, like a dictionary attack, uses a word list file but also tries popular modification on the words such as adding a number to the end of the dictionary word.

   ☒ **A, B,** and **D** are incorrect. A brute-force attack is when all the possible character combinations are calculated to try to figure out a password. A dictionary attack uses a word list file but doesn't try variations of the word. There is no such thing as a buffer password attack.

Understanding System Security

3. ☑ **A.** The Local Security Authority (LSA) handles these functions above the Security Accounts Manager and Security Reference Monitor. Those services are used to provide specific functions for the LSA.

   ☒ **B, C,** and **D** are incorrect. SAM is a local database of users and groups. The Security Reference Monitor is used to validate a user right to perform a task and permission to access resources.

4. ☑ **D.** The Security Accounts Manager (SAM) is the database of users and groups contained on a local Windows 2000 Professional or Windows XP Professional system.

   ☒ **A, B,** and **C** are incorrect. The LSA initiates the authentication process in Windows and validates against the SAM database. The Logon Process is applied to allow a user to log on and be verified. The Security Reference Monitor is used to validate a user right or permission to access resources.

5. ☑ **B.** The discretionary access control list (DACL) determines which users and groups have permissions to an object.

   ☒ **A, C,** and **D** are incorrect. The SACL controls security auditing. The owner maintains ownership of the object, and a user is not a valid ACL object type.

6. ☑ **D.** The Modify permission is the permission that allows a user to modify a file.

   ☒ **A, B,** and **C** are incorrect. Read and Execute allow a user to read the contents of a file and execute a program from that location. Read allows the user only to read the file contents, and List Folder Contents allows a user to see the files that exist in a folder but not read the contents of a file.

7. ☑ **B.** Authentication is the process of logging on to the network.

   ☒ **A, C,** and **D** are incorrect. Authorization comes after authentication and involves determining whether a user can access a resource after being authenticated. Permissions and rights are methods of authorization.

Firewalls and Proxy Servers

8. ☑ **B.** A firewall is used to secure the internal network from the outside world by rules configured on the firewall that specify which packets to drop and which packets to allow through.

   ☒ **A, C,** and **D** are incorrect. Encryption converts plain text to cipher text. A router is used to provide routing functions to the network, but it may have firewalling features.

9. ☑ **A.** A dual-homed host firewall contains two physical network interfaces.

   ☒ **B, C,** and **D** are incorrect because a screened-host firewall passes data through a screening router first and then onto the firewall. A screened-subnet firewall provides two screening routers with a firewall in between, providing an extra layer of security.

10. ☑ **B and D.** A firewall and two screening routers are required in a screened subnet configuration.

    ☒ **A and C** are not included in a screened subnet firewall configuration.

11. ☑ **A.** The packet level controls the network or transport layer within packets, creating rules that allow or deny traffic based on IP address (layer 3) or port number (layer 4).

    ☒ **B, C,** and **D** are incorrect because the application-level type controls the layers above the transport level and the circuit-level type works at the transport layer.

Securing Communication

12. ☑ **C.** In symmetric encryption both parties use the same key to encrypt and decrypt the encrypted data.

    ☒ **A, B,** and **D** are incorrect. Asymmetric encryption has two related keys—one is used to encrypt and the other decrypts.

13. ☑ **A and D.** Stream cipher and block cipher are valid encryption methods.

☒ **B and C** are incorrect because data cipher and byte cipher do not exist.

14. ☑ **A.** The Electronic Codebook (ECB) mode encrypts each block individually, but the Cipher Block Chaining and Cipher Feedback modes do not.

☒ **B, C,** and **D** are incorrect because the Cipher Block Chaining and Cipher Feedback modes do not encrypt each block individually.

15. ☑ **B.** The Data Encryption Standard (DES) uses this algorithm.

☒ **A, C,** and **D** are incorrect because the RSA uses a different type of algorithm, and CPA and DSE are not valid encryption standards.

16. ☑ **C.** Digital signatures technology does not encrypt the message—it only verifies that it arrived without being tampered with.

☒ **A, B,** and **D** are incorrect because RSA is an encryption standard and the Local Security Authority is a Windows NT subsystem.

Disaster Recovery and Fault Tolerance

17. ☑ **D.** A cold site provides only the disaster recovery facility. The equipment and data are the responsibility of the company using the facility.

☒ **A, B,** and **C** are incorrect. A hot site provides the facility and the equipment, and it will ensure that an up-to-date copy of an organization's data is available in case of disaster. A warm site provides the facility and the backup equipment to perform a restore when needed. There's no such thing as a blue site.

18. ☑ **A.** A hot site provides the facility and the equipment, and it will ensure that an up-to-date copy of an organization's data is available in case of disaster.

☒ **B, C,** and **D** are incorrect. A cold site provides only the disaster recovery facility. The equipment and data are the responsibility of the company using the facility. A warm site provides the facility and the backup equipment to perform a restore when needed. There's no such thing as a blue site.

19. ☑ **D.** A hot spare is connected and already has power supplied to it so that there is minimal delay for failover.

☒ **A, B,** and **C** are incorrect. A cold spare is not connected and immediately available. When needed, it must be connected and powered up to become available. The other choices are not types of spares.

Guidelines to Protect the Network

20. ☑ **A and C.** Languard and the Microsoft Baseline Security Analyzer are examples of vulnerability scanners that allow you to audit the network for security-related problems.
    ☒ **B, D,** and **E** are incorrect because they are not vulnerability scanners.

21. ☑ **A.** After installing the network operating system, you should harden the operating system, which involves removing unnecessary services. Removing unnecessary services helps secure the system, because each additional piece of software running provides more security holes for a hacker to find.
    ☒ **B, C,** and **D** are incorrect. You would not enable a firewall on the server because your users would then not be able to connect to it.

22. ☑ **C.** After hardening the operating system, you should patch the server to apply security fixes to any software running on the server.
    ☒ **A, B,** and **D** are incorrect because they are not ways to apply security fixes to the system.

13

Troubleshooting the Network

K nowing how to deal with network problems when they arise is one of the most important parts of operating a network. In this chapter you will learn a methodology to find and diagnose problems in a systematic and logical manner. Teaching that methodology is the goal of this chapter.

Managing Network Problems

Data communication is still not bulletproof. Many things can go wrong when you are networking several different types of computers, mainframes, printers, and network devices using different operating systems, protocols, and data transfer methods. When problems occur, you need not only an understanding of each of the devices on your network—but an understanding of the network as a whole. Learning how each device coexists with and contributes to the network provides you with a strong foundation for understanding how and why network-related problems occur and how to resolve them. For example, if you don't understand how a router works, you will be quite overwhelmed when one segment of your network cannot communicate with another segment. If you have a very good understanding of routers and routing and one segment of your network cannot communicate with another segment, you will immediately know that there is a problem with routing—that, possibly, a router is malfunctioning. It is helpful to classify the types of problems you are having and to ask yourself questions concerning the problem in order to stimulate your network problem-solving abilities.

Does the Problem Exist Across the Network?

When you first encounter a problem, it is important to determine its scope. Does this problem occur with a specific machine, or does the problem exist across the network? You need to narrow the problem as soon as possible. If more than one computer is having the same problem at one time, it is obvious that you have a network problem, not a computer-specific one. This phase of the problem-solving process often requires you to check the status of other computers on the network to determine whether they are having the same problem.

If you are having a network-related problem, the problem's symptoms are helpful in determining its cause. In the example of one segment of the network not being able to communicate with another segment, you could quickly determine that you had a routing problem. Another symptom is that everyone on the coaxial-based bus network is unable to communicate. The cause of this situation is most likely a problem with the network bus backbone, which requires terminators on each end. If the network backbone becomes severed, the end points will not be terminated and the data will echo throughout the network, rendering the entire network unusable. Another symptom is that one department of the company on a twisted-pair Ethernet network can no longer communicate with the rest of the network. The cause is most likely a problem with the hub used to connect this group. As you know, a hub connects groups of computers. The hub itself is then connected to the network backbone, and in this case, the connection to the network backbone from the hub might have been severed.

As you can see, quickly determining the scope of a problem is the first step in gathering information about the nature of the problem.

Workstation, Workgroup, LAN, or WAN Problem?

To continue the discussion on determining the scope of a problem, larger networks present even more possibilities for error. Not only are you faced with computer-specific problems, but you can have problems within your workgroup, your local area network, or even the wide area network.

For example, say that accounting department users employ a terminal-based order-entry system to transfer orders to corporate headquarters. This system operates through terminal sessions on user computers across the WAN to the corporate mainframe. One day the connection on a user's computer is not working. How can you diagnose such a complicated issue? First, you need to determine whether the problem is occurring with a workstation, a workgroup, the LAN, or the WAN. You continue by going over to another computer and trying the connection. You find that this computer is having the same problem. Therefore, the problem is not computer specific. Luckily, the same order-entry program can be used to acquire the monthly sales orders from another terminal session, this time at the regional headquarters. You find that the user is able to connect to the regional headquarters mainframe with no problems. Therefore, you have proved that you can at least get out to another remote location, but you still haven't determined the cause of the problem.

As it stands now, you could be having a routing problem with the corporate headquarters, a name resolution problem, or a mainframe connectivity problem. You can test the routing problem theory by trying to communicate with another computer on the corporate headquarters' network. For example, you could ping another computer on this network by using the Ping utility and pass it the IP address of a system on the remote network. You receive a response from this computer. This response determines that you don't have a routing problem to this remote network. Next, you get the IP address of the mainframe and attempt to ping it:

```
Pinging 207.149.40.41 with 32 bytes of data:
Request timed out.
Request timed out.
Request timed out.
Request timed out.
```

You have found your problem. The mainframe system at corporate headquarters is down. You're sure that corporate headquarters is aware of the problem, so you decide not to pester them. You can check back every so often to determine whether the problem has been fixed. Luckily, it's their problem, not yours!

on the **J o b**

It is beneficial to know the IP addresses of some of the core servers on your network so that when you do connectivity testing with Ping, you will not need to dig up those addresses.

See how quickly you can determine the scope of the problem? It took only a few minutes to determine whether you had a workstation, workgroup, LAN, or WAN problem. Unfortunately, all problems won't be this easy to fix, but armed with the troubleshooting methodology presented here, you are on your way to solving any network problem that occurs.

Is the Problem Consistent and Replicable?

Sometimes you are faced with weird problems that are not so easy to solve and require you to gain more information beyond the scope of the problem. You might already know you are having a LAN or WAN problem, for example, but you need more information to get you down the road to solving the problem. Next, you need to ask yourself, "Is the problem consistent and replicable?" To answer this question, you need to determine a way to replicate the problem.

For example, let's say that when someone in the purchasing department sends a job to the printer, it takes over five minutes for the job to print. As in the preceding section, we need to find out if more than one computer is having this problem. We send a print job from another computer only to discover that the print job once again takes five minutes to print. We now have a consistent problem that is replicable. The problem is not computer specific because we were able to replicate the problem on another computer.

When we take a look at the print server's health we notice that its processing power and memory utilization are high—we need to know why, but at least we have found the source of our problem. Chances are, if we can free up system resources we will have a better performing print server.

Once again, notice how quickly we narrowed the problem to a possible source. Furthermore, notice how we used logic to determine the cause of the problem. We went to the next logical source in our printing problem—the print server. We didn't immediately go to the router and check to see whether it was routing correctly, and we didn't go to the domain controller to check whether the user had rights to print to this printer. We used logical troubleshooting methodology to arrive at the solution to the problem.

Standard Troubleshooting Methods

As you learned in the preceding section, it is important to isolate the subsystem involved with a problematic process. When you work with a problem internal to one computer, you learn to isolate the subsystem involved. For example, say that your system is not detecting your primary hard drive. What subsystem do you check? You check the disk subsystem, which includes the hard disk drive, the drive controller, and the drive cable. You wouldn't begin your troubleshooting by removing the video card and the CD-ROM drive.

You must apply this methodology to solving network-related problems as well. In the preceding section, you knew you had a printing problem, so your troubleshooting remained focused on the printing subsystem; you tracked the problem by following the flow of information. You would have been led to a problem outside the printing subsystem if you researched the problem and found out that everything you did on the network, not just printing, took five minutes.

CertCam 13-1

To verify that your network card is working properly, check out Exercise 13-1 in LabBook.pdf on the CD-ROM and watch the CertCam training video.

CERTIFICATION OBJECTIVE 13.02

Troubleshooting Network Problems

When you are troubleshooting network problems, it is important to follow a logical troubleshooting methodology. Always assume that the problem is a simple one. It might sound counterintuitive, but the simple solutions are most likely to elude you. As your experience grows, you can easily find yourself caught in a web of always assuming that the problem is more complicated than it actually is. When that happens, it can result in an excessive waste of troubleshooting time. Don't forget to ask yourself three basic troubleshooting questions:

1. Did the device ever work?
2. When was it last known to be working?
3. What has changed since then?

Remember this: As an administrator, you are a "doctor." Your patients are computers and networking equipment. As with any doctor, your first step to finding a cure is making a proper diagnosis. Use logic and the scientific method, and do not forget to use one variable at a time. To put it in plain English: fix one thing at a time!

Always remember to start with the simplest things before checking the more complicated items. Most of the time, the problem is caused by something simple. It's easier to check simple items than complicated ones, and doing so can save a great deal of time. Complicated items can take hours to check, whereas simple items can take only seconds or minutes. A process you can follow to help you troubleshoot a problem is presented in the eight steps to troubleshooting that follow:

1. Identify the symptoms.
2. Identify the affected area.
3. Establish what has changed.
4. Select the most probable cause.
5. Implement a solution.
6. Test the result.
7. Recognize the potential effects of the solution.
8. Document the solution.

Before we continue, let's look more closely at the steps to determine the symptoms and causes of a problem and the process of solving the problem in more detail. First, identify the symptoms. Doing so allows us to know the exact effects the problem is causing. You'll use this information later to determine that the problem has been resolved, because these symptoms will disappear. For example, we need to know what the network users are experiencing—whether this is a matter of not being able to connect to a specific server or to all servers.

Second, determine which areas of the network are affected. For example, you need to determine whether the problem affects all systems on the network or just a selected group of systems. No matter what, the affected areas will always have something in common. This "something" could, of course, be the entire network, but that is something that the affected components have in common.

Third, identify any differences between the affected areas and the unaffected areas by determining what has changed since the last time there were no problems. For example, if you are unable to get a network connection with all your workstations that are connected to a thinnet coax cable, but all other workstations are functioning, it's more than likely that your problem resides in that thinnet coax cable.

Fourth, after narrowing down the list of effects caused by the problem, pinpointing the scope of the problem, and determining what has changed, we can then most likely come up with a few things to check. We choose the most probable problem and determine a solution. For example, if we have a whole segment of the network unable to connect to the server even though all other users can connect to the server, we know we have an issue with a specific segment. We can then say that the segment has been disconnected from the rest of the network.

Fifth, once a specific problem has been determined, we need to find a solution to that problem and implement that solution. For example, in the previous step we had a segment that was unable to connect to the rest of the network. If we think the problem is that the segment is disconnected from the rest of the network, our solution is to reconnect the segment.

Sixth, once we have implemented a solution, we need to verify that the problems we found in Step 1 have all disappeared. For example, we could go back to the PCs that could not contact the server and make sure they can do so now.

Seventh, we need to make sure that our solution will not cause other problems. One thing that a technician or administrator needs to realize is that at times there could be multiple solutions to a single problem. Some solutions could cause other problems. For example, when installing service packs on a NOS, you need to determine which items the service packs will fix. You might have previously circumvented a problem on the server with a fix that the service pack will undo and cause a problem again.

Finally, you need to document the solution you implemented. This information will assist others working with you and those who might take your place someday so that they can fix the problem, benefiting from your experience rather than having to perform all the same troubleshooting routines and waste a lot of time trying to arrive at the same solution.

Subsequently in this chapter you will learn about the various tools available for diagnosing and correcting network problems.

Identify the Symptoms

Identifying the symptoms is always the first step to resolving a problem. Whether you are an administrator or a technician, this part is usually the easiest. This portion of the problem-solving process is usually brought to your attention by network users. They will contact you and tell you what they are experiencing, but you need to be careful about taking at face value what they say about the effects they are seeing.

Sometimes people who have little or no technical knowledge about computers and networks give explanations for the problems they are experiencing that are completely opposite to what is really occurring. Always remember that user error is always a possible cause of the problem.

Working at a help desk can be difficult because most situations require a person to actually see the problems to be able to determine and the scope of the issue and possible solutions. Some help desks are set up to assign problems to a specific technician. For example, I once received a call from a user who could not access the server. The user's explanations were that the PC was disconnected from the network or the server was down. I was able to determine that the server was online and running fine, but after looking at the user's PC, I found out that the user had not logged on to the network. The user had been using Windows 98, which allows you to press the ESCAPE key at logon and have access to the local computer only. This was no real network issue, just an issue of the user's failing to properly log on to the network.

Once someone is present to see the problem, the user needs to make sure that the problem still exists and that the problem is a network issue and not a user error. A technician or administrator should try to see the problem first-hand to make sure the information she was given about the problem is correct.

Identify the Affected Areas

Once you have found the exact issues that are occurring as a result of the problem, you need to find out how many and which users are being affected. This step not only helps you determine the scope of the problem so that you can narrow it down to specific segments or devices—it also enables you to determine the priority to place on the issue.

Sometimes this portion of the troubleshooting process allows you to find the problem's source, especially if it is something like a failing router or a broken hub. The scope of the issue can point to the exact cause of the problem, because the affected area will be controlled by a single network device or cable.

Knowing the scope of the problem will let you determine its priority and how long it can wait to be fixed. This is important when there are other problems that need to be considered—you need to fix the crucial problems first.

Same Line, Different Computer

One method to isolate the network problem is to replace the problem workstation with a workstation that is known to be working. You could even use a laptop in place of the workstation to verify the connections, since a laptop would be easier to carry around. If the workstation or laptop that is known to be good has difficulties, the problem cannot be isolated to the original workstation. You should then begin troubleshooting network components such as the cable, hub, repeater, or network backbone, because the problem is not computer specific.

Same Computer, Different Line

In a similar method, the workstation having difficulties is moved to another line. If the workstation is able to function correctly in the new line, the problem is on the original line, not with the workstation itself. This method can also be tested using a network cable from a workstation that is close by without having to move any PCs. Technicians should always try to carry an extra patch cable that can be used to swap with the existing cable to make sure that that cable is not bad and that the wall jacks are all working. This can be done easily if you carry a laptop in a case and place the extra patch cable in a pocket of the case.

Swapping Components

Swap the components that are between the failing workstations. These components include hubs, cables, and terminators—anything that could possibly go bad. This is a quick way to return the network to a functioning state. After the network is functioning, you can test the components that were replaced to determine which component failed. A lightning strike or some other type of electrical problem can sometimes cause a NIC to behave unpredictably. By swapping components, you can solve this problem quickly and efficiently.

Isolating Segments of the Network

You will want to review the network to find out what areas are affected by the problem. With today's networks it is fairly straightforward to isolate the network in the sense that you normally just have to unplug one cable to disconnect an entire segment. If you are using a thinnet coax network, isolating your network is easy. Simply choose a workstation to act as the dividing line for the isolation. Next, unplug the network cable from the T-connector and replace it with a terminator. You have now quickly isolated the network trouble.

Steps for Problem Isolation

Table 13-1 shows you the steps you should take to diagnose and isolate network problems.

TABLE 13-1 Techniques for Problem Isolation	Step	Action
	Determine which workstations are and are not experiencing symptoms.	Separate the working and nonworking workstations from each other using a hub or terminator.
	Rule out simple problems.	Reset all major components that are affected by unplugging the devices and plugging them back in.
	Further determine which workstations are and are not experiencing symptoms.	Separate the nonworking network segment in half and determine which half is not working properly.
	Eliminate simple cable problems.	Examine the cable for any physical damage.
	Eliminate complicated cable problems.	Examine cables with a TDR to find any problems.
	Get more help.	Consult resources such as TechNet, resource kits, or vendor web sites for further information.

Establish What Has Changed

Establishing what has changed since the last time all components worked correctly can be an important step, depending on the problem. In some situations, this step may not have any bearing on the issue. On the other hand, if something has changed recently and everything worked before the change, you know the change has possibly had an adverse effect.

This is the step that will help determine the problem that has occurred when a network device has been reconfigured and the settings are not the same as before. For example, let's say that a network printer has its network interface card replaced and the new card is not given the same IP address as in the previous configuration. This mistake will prevent anyone who could previously print from printing.

This step can also point to server upgrades not only of hardware but of software—drivers, software patches, and even application installation. Settings can be overwritten on the server, .DLL files can be replaced or removed, and many other things can happen to cause adverse effects for users.

This step can be easily determined from documentation maintained by the network administrators and technicians. If a problem arises that is affecting a large number of network users or whole segments of the network, you can check the documentation and see whether anyone has made any major or minor changes to network devices or servers.

Select the Most Probable Cause

Once they've reached this point, most technicians and administrators formulate a few ideas as to the problem that has occurred and what caused it. There is no definitive manual to assist anyone in determining a problem's cause from a given set of issues; this kind of insight is mainly gained from experience. The more issues you resolve, the easier this step will be for you.

Selecting the most probable cause not only draws on your knowledge of networks in general, it also draws on your knowledge of the specific network you are working on at the time. Most employers do not realize that being onsite full time helps technicians or administrators know and understand their specific network better than a technician brought in from a computer repair shop. You can draw on past experiences and be able to determine the causes of problems that might be similar to other problems you've solved in the past. If a technician is around a network long enough, he or she will know the ins and outs of the specific network and be able to notice a problem before it becomes too major and thus noticeable to users.

If a technician or administrator has not formulated any ideas about the problem by this point in the problem-solving process, he or she will at least have an idea where to look or whom to ask. This type of knowledge can be as important as determining the cause of the problem itself. If you have no idea of the cause, you need to have a backup way of determining the cause.

Implement a Solution

As noted in the preceding section, an administrator or technician will have an idea as to a problem's cause and will most likely also have a solution or multiple solutions in mind to solve the problem. Again, this step comes with experience and knowledge.

You not only need to determine the problem's cause, you also need to come up with a solution that might or might not be easily known. You might need to consult other people on how to fix the problem, requiring access to the Internet or technical support telephone numbers for specific manufacturers.

Once you have a solution in mind that seems as though it will fix the problem, you need to implement the solution. Again, you might not be able to implement the solution in a timely manner, since the problem could be of low priority.

Test the Result

Testing the result of your solution is a more important step than the previous ones. Still, some technicians and administrators forget to take this step when troubleshooting problems. There is nothing more frustrating to a network user than contacting a tech support person to fix a problem and have that person arrive to say that the problem has been fixed; but instead of testing the solution, the support person leaves the user's office. The network user then resumes work and finds that the problem still exists.

Once you have implemented a solution, make sure that you return to the user to attempt to perform the task that was exhibiting the problem and make sure that the problem no longer exists.

Recognize the Potential Effects of the Solution

Once you have implemented and tested the solution, you need to make sure that the solution has not adversely affected anything else on the network. In some cases, you should consider this step before implementing the solution.

In some cases, when a service pack or patch is installed, certain .DLL files that are used by other programs could be overwritten; as a result, existing software may not be able to run. Installing software such as service packs often enough leads to compatibility problems with other software on the system, which is why you want to be sure to test the new addition before implementing it in production.

Once you fix a problem via a solution and have tested that solution, make sure you test other network issues that could be affected by the fix. For example, if you make a change to a router's configuration, make sure that you do some testing from all segments of the network that are joined by the router and verify that a change to the routing table has not affected traffic flow from functioning network segments.

Documenting the Solution

The final and most important step in the troubleshooting process is documenting the solution. This step helps avoid wasted time later on as you or someone else tries to resolve the same problem, going through all the steps you have already performed to arrive at the same solution.

Every help desk technician and administrator needs to have some type of database to store all the problems and solutions that are found. In a company in which all hardware and software are standardized, the same problems can keep recurring. If time has passed since the last time you solved a particular problem, you might not remember the solution and would have to perform all the same steps again. Or a problem could be sporadic, appearing only every few months. Keeping up-to-date documentation helps you be sure of the solutions you have tried so that you do not implement that same solution multiple times with no effect.

Documentation is also important for anyone who is hired later to assist or replace you. If you are on vacation and return to find that your assistant has spent a week trying to solve a problem for which you already found a resolution months ago, you will not be too happy (and neither will your assistant). Other work has been put aside in favor of working on a problem that's already been solved.

Sample Troubleshooting Situations

To follow up on the troubleshooting steps, let's look at an example of network issues and the troubleshooting steps you can use to help you diagnose the problem.

In this example, you get a call from a network user who says she cannot print to the laser printer in her department but has no problem accessing the servers or any other PC. She was able to print to the printer yesterday but is unable to print to it today. In fact, no one in the department is able to print to the printer, which is a network printer. The user verifies that the printer is turned on; she has even powered off the printer and turned it back on. No error messages are displayed on the front panel. What do you do?

The first step of troubleshooting is to identify the symptoms, which have just been reported by your caller. The second step is to determine the affected area; in this case, the whole department that uses the laser printer is affected.

The third step is to determine what has changed. You would consult the documentation of what has been performed on the printer or the print server from the time they worked yesterday. While searching, you might find that the network interface card in the printer was changed at the end of yesterday. You check the printer and determine that the NIC was improperly configured.

In Step 4, you would determine that the most probable cause of the problem is that the NIC was not configured correctly, so it cannot be contacted by the print server to receive print jobs. You may also determine that the TCP/IP settings on the network card of the print server are configured incorrectly. You need to be open to all possible causes of the problem.

For a solution in Step 5, you would want to configure the NIC correctly. After consulting the documentation for the printer configuration, you change the settings as they should be to allow proper connectivity. If you had determined that the IP address settings were incorrect in the preceding step, you would configure the addressing information correctly in this step.

For Step 6, you would test the result by waiting to see whether the print jobs that have been sent to the print server will start spooling to the printer. After about a minute, the printer starts printing all the spooled print jobs.

Step 7 would dictate that you determine any adverse effects, but if there were none before the NIC was changed (except the problem for which the NIC configuration was corrected), all should be fine.

The last step is to add to the printer's documentation that the configuration was done improperly and has been redone. You might also document the correct settings once more to make sure that this problem does not occur again.

CERTIFICATION OBJECTIVE 13.03

System or Operator Problems

In some cases, it is very clear whether a system or operator error has occurred. A system error can be classified as an error on the part of a computer or network device or process that was not associated with a user's direct actions. This error can be a result of hardware failure or of something involved in the process of transferring or manipulating data. An operator problem is the result of a user's action, such as not logging on correctly, connecting to the wrong server, or printing to the wrong printer. The sources of most operator-related problems are obvious. However, operator problems can stem from misconfiguration of a device, program, or service by the initial operator—the network administrator. If a device is misconfigured, it might not be apparent until the device is promoted to a production area and fails in the process. For the Network+ exam, you need to understand the various ways a system or network device error occurs, the symptoms of such an error, and how to go about resolving the problem. First, you need to learn the areas that will provide you with a clue as to the problem's nature.

CERTIFICATION OBJECTIVE 13.04

Checking Physical and Logical Indicators

When you begin troubleshooting a network-related problem, several indicators can help you determine the problem. These indicators are a combination of physical and logical elements. From a physical level, you can determine many things about the nature of the problem from the device in question by looking at its various indicator lights, error displays, and monitors. Let's look at these tools now.

Link Lights

Link lights are invaluable in determining whether a network connection is present. A link light is a green or amber light-emitting diode (LED) that shines if the networking device detects a network connection. Many network devices, such as routers, switches, and network cards, are equipped with link lights for this very reason. Most network cards have two lights—a link light, which remains on while there is a physical network connection, and a light that displays the current activity of the network card and pulses as data is transferred to and from the computer or device. This second light can be an obvious indicator that the device is functioning on the network. Link lights on some network connectivity devices (e.g., switches) won't light up if the wrong type of

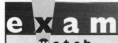

w **a t c h**   *The link light and the activity light are great aids when troubleshooting network issues and will definitely appear on the Network+ exam.*

cable is plugged in (e.g., crossover cables are sometimes required to cascade switches together). If you are troubleshooting a network-related problem, it is best to start by examining the device's link light to determine whether a network connection is detected.

Collision Lights

Troubleshooting network issues can also be determined by collision lights on a hub. Collision lights show whether a specific connection is having problems caused by packets colliding with one another. Collision lights can sometimes be the same as activity lights; the activity light is green when sending or receiving data and turns yellow or orange when a collision occurs.

A collision results in the loss of the packet being received and the packet being sent. Sometimes a faulty cable or hub can cause packets to be generated from other packets or electrical interference. Sometimes called chatter, these disruptive packets can cause major collisions and can even halt an entire network due to collisions of all packets. Administrators and technicians need to watch these lights to verify that network chatter is not occurring.

Power Lights

Even more rudimentary than the link light in the network troubleshooting area is the power light. Simply put, absence of a power light means no power is present in the device or the power light is burned out. If the power light is not present, check that the device is receiving proper power. If it is not, you should check the power supply, the power cable, or the wall connector. If you have verified that all these are working, the device could literally be dead. In this case, you will have to replace it.

Error Displays

An error display is a means of alerting you to a malfunction or failure in a device. This display can be a visual error dialog box on a computer when the error occurs or an LED error display on a network device. Such error messages should describe the problem that is occurring; however, they might not provide the necessary course of action required to solve the problem.

The error display might refer to an error code that you must look up in order to determine the cause of the problem and the ways to resolve it. Referring to documentation for the device is helpful when you're troubleshooting a network device, because each manufacturer has its own special procedure to resolve a physical or logical problem. Sometimes you must check the error codes on the manufacturer's web site because they cannot easily or immediately be deciphered.

Error Logs and Displays

Similar to the error display is the error log, which maintains a listing of errors encountered on a device. This error log should contain the time the problem occurred, the nature of the problem, and quite possibly the procedure for resolving the problem. Unfortunately, error logs usually don't contain enough information to solve a problem, and you must consult documentation to diagnose and resolve it. However, error logging is important because it can help you determine when the problem occurred, what might have caused the problem, and what other processes are affected by this problem. Often, error displays give a visual alert of the problem and log the error into the error log for future reference. Many entries in the error log are not critical-stop errors. Some entries are warnings that do not currently indicate a problem but are worthy of your attention. Other entries, such as those indicating when the computer was restarted or when a service started or stopped, are purely informative.

Windows-based operating systems such as Windows clients and Windows servers each have an error log mechanism called the Event Viewer that is critical to the diagnosis and resolution of problems within those operating systems. It is recommended that you consult the Event Viewer during the troubleshooting process, watching for the critical, red-X error entries that have occurred.

The Event Viewer is an application that reads the binary log files stored in the <windows directory>\system32\config folder. You will not need to go to the config folder to view the logs because the Event Viewer console retrieves the information from the files located in that folder for you. There are three main types of logs within the Windows-based operating systems that you should monitor on a regular basis:

- **The system log**   Records events that are provided by the Windows operating system and contains error messages that typically deal with device drivers failing to load, services failing to start, or general information about something that happens within the OS, such as purging a printer.
- **The security log**   Contains all security-related events when auditing has been enabled. If you have audited events such as the failure to log on, success or failure to access a file or folder, or the success of account management, this is where that information would be recorded.

■ **The application log**   Contains events that have been generated by applications that run on top of the operating system. For example, if you install SQL Server or Exchange Server on the system, those applications typically record their errors in the application log.

Checking Event Logs

If you are having a problem with a Windows 2000/XP/2003 system, you can view one of three logs depending on the type of problem. This exercise will show you how to view the system log for problems with the Windows Server 2003 network operating system.

1. Go to Start | right-click My Computer and choose Manage.
2. Expand out the Event Viewer by clicking the plus sign (+) to the left.
3. To view the system log, click system on the left side. You can see the contents of the system log on the right-hand side (as shown in the following illustration). In the illustration notice that there are errors (red X), warnings (yellow triangle), and information (blue i) events.

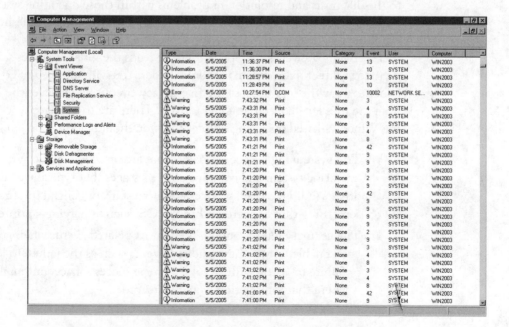

4. To investigate a warning or error, double-click the entry to view the details.

5. A dialog box opens and you will need to try to decipher the information presented. Notice that you can see the date and time the event happened at the top of the dialog box, and you can see an error message at the bottom of the dialog box (as shown in the following illustration).

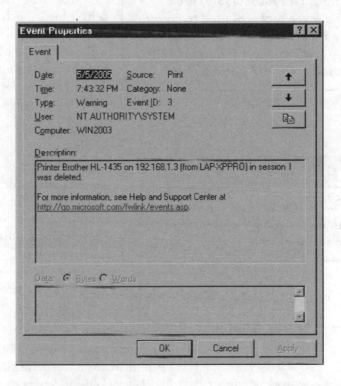

6. Once you see the error message, you can close all the windows and start fixing the problem.

Performance Issues and Optimization

There are a number of terms in the Network+ objectives that you need to be familiar with that deal with network performance, bandwidth, and availability. This section will introduce you to those terms and also give you a tour of two popular network troubleshooting tools.

Part of network optimization is ensuring that only needed traffic travels along the wire and uses up precious network bandwidth. There are a number of applications that are considered high-bandwidth applications, such as Voice over IP (VoIP) and video applications that deliver media such as movies or videos to the desktops. When using such applications, you will need to know how to optimize network bandwidth. The following text describes some popular technologies that deal with network performance issues.

QoS

Quality of Service (QoS) is used to control the network bandwidth that is used by different applications or users. QoS is critical to high-bandwidth applications such as Voice over IP or streaming multimedia where the network engineer will need to ensure that enough bandwidth is available to those applications in order for them to function correctly.

Traffic Shaping

Traffic shaping is when the network administrator controls network traffic in order to reach a desired level of performance on the network. With traffic shaping, the network administrator will delay packets for delivery according to certain criteria, such as the type of traffic, which then leaves the bandwidth available for mission-critical applications.

Caching Engines

A *caching engine* is another method to optimize traffic. When you add a caching engine device to the network, it will download content from the Internet and store it in memory for other clients that request the same content.

You can purchase such a device from Cisco. When you use the caching engine, you need to configure the router to forward the request to the caching engine first so that the engine can decide if a trip to the Internet is required or if it already has the content cached.

Performance Monitoring

There are a number of tools that you can use to monitor network and server performance. Two of the most popular tools in the Windows environment are Network Monitor to monitor network traffic and the Performance Console to monitor the health of a system.

Network Monitor   Network Monitor is an outstanding tool for monitoring network activity and troubleshooting network performance. If you are troubleshooting communication problems and you need to see the details of the packets, Network Monitor is your tool. Network Monitor, which comes with the Windows operating system, only captures and displays the frames that are sent to or from your system. It does not monitor your entire network segment as does the version of Network Monitor that comes with Microsoft's Systems Management Server (SMS). Switched environments usually require configuring traffic from all ports in the switch to be mirrored to a specific port where the administrator is running Network Monitor; otherwise, the administrator is capturing only traffic sent and received through the port the administrator is plugged into.

You have used Network Monitor (shown in Figure 13-1) at different points in the exercises throughout this book to analyze network traffic, so you have seen how powerful a tool it is to help you understand and troubleshoot network problems by displaying the contents of packets running on the network.

FIGURE 13-1

Looking at network traffic with Network Monitor

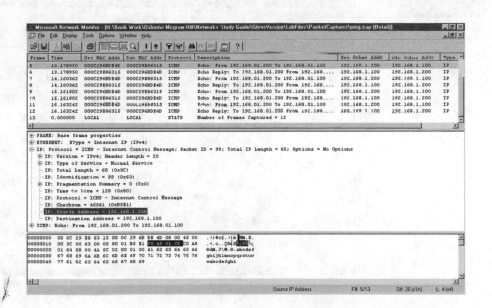

exam
watch

To monitor network traffic when troubleshooting connectivity problems, you can use a tool such as Network Monitor or Wireshark, which is a free download.

System Monitor Another useful tool is the Performance Console in Windows XP, 2003, and Windows 2008. System Monitor (seen in Figure 13-2), a component of the Performance Console, is used to monitor the system's health and to troubleshoot performance-related problems. You can use System Monitor for a variety of tasks, including the following:

- Identifying bottlenecks in CPU, memory, disk I/O, or network I/O
- Identifying performance trends over a period of time
- Monitoring real-time system performance
- Monitoring system performance history
- Determining the system's capacity
- Monitoring system configuration changes

FIGURE 13-2

Using System Monitor on a Windows server

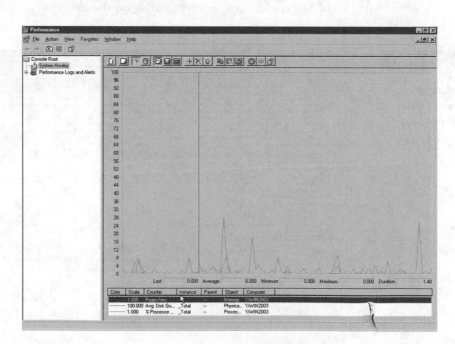

Using System Monitor

When monitoring the system's health, you are trying to determine why the system is running slow. There are four areas of potential bottlenecks on a system:

- **Processor**   The processor may be overworked if you are running too many processes at the same time, or running processor-intensive applications. If you determine that the processor is being overutilized (typically above 85 percent utilization), you may need to upgrade the processor, add another processor, or enable processor hyperthreading (if your processor supports hyperthreading).

- **Memory**   You may notice that the system is getting sluggish because you do not have enough memory. If you don't have enough memory, the system will be doing a lot of paging—that is, swapping information from memory to disk and then disk to memory; this puts a lot of workload on the system. To reduce paging, always add more RAM.

- **Hard disk**   The hard disk is another area of potential bottlenecks. Because the hard disk is servicing all requests for files on the server, you may want to make sure that you have a fast disk or multiple disks to service the request.

- **Network**   The network card is a potential bottleneck as well, especially on a network server, because it is answering all network requests for network resources. You should make certain that you have the fastest network card possible.

When using System Monitor, you will be required to add counters to the monitoring tool. A counter is an element of the computer that you want to monitor. For example, a good counter to measure is percent utilization of the processor to help you determine if the processor is being overworked. The percent utilization counter is a characteristic of the processor object—an object is a component of the system, and a counter is a characteristic of the object. You may add a counter to System Monitor by right-clicking in the detail screen and choosing Add Counters as shown in Figure 13-3.

When you click the + sign to add a counter, a dialog box appears asking you to select the counter to add. When you add a counter, you can choose the object from the drop-down list and then choose the characteristics of that object (as shown in Figure 13-4). You will notice that there are hundreds of objects to measure, and as you add more software to the system the list of objects will increase. For example, if you add SQL Server to the system, there will be objects and counters to keep a close eye on the health of SQL and your databases.

FIGURE 13-3

Using System
Monitor

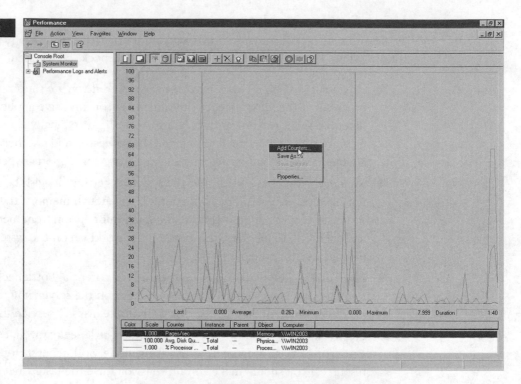

FIGURE 13-3

Using System
Monitor

FIGURE 13-4

Adding a counter
to System
Monitor

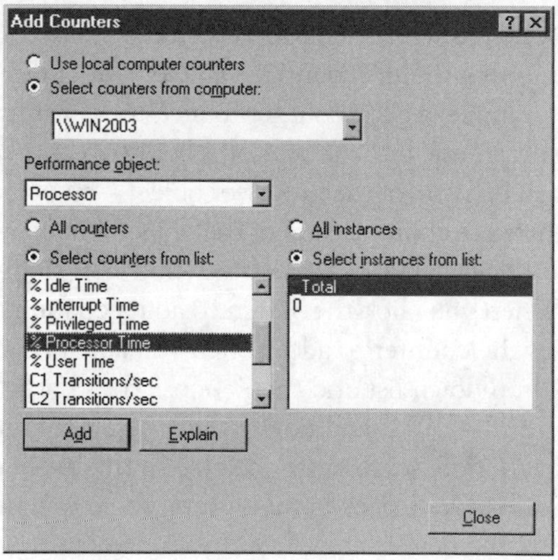

To practice using System Monitor try Exercise 13-3 from LabBook.pdf found on the CD-ROM.

High-Availability Concerns

When dealing with networking applications such as web applications, e-mail servers, database servers, or even something as simple as a file share, you will want to look at ways to ensure high availability. *High availability* means that you are taking steps to ensure that the service is always available. There are a number of technologies that aid in high availability.

High-Availability Clusters *Clustering* is a popular high-availability solution. A typical example of a cluster has two servers in the cluster, each server called a *node*. One of the servers is called the primary node, while the other is the secondary node. The primary node is the server that is available, while the secondary node is in a standby state and is not used unless the primary server becomes unavailable.

An example is your e-mail server. This is a critical service on the network, and users typically have fits of rage if the e-mail server goes down! Your job is to ensure e-mail is always available, so you install two servers in a cluster that is running your e-mail server software. Your e-mail server software is running on both nodes in the cluster with the e-mail data on a drive shared by both nodes.

When the primary server fails, the secondary server automatically becomes the active node and can then service any request from clients wishing to access their e-mails. The clustering technology takes care of automatically detecting when the primary node fails and then making the secondary node the active node.

Load Balancing A very popular method of increasing performance of network resources, such as popular ecommerce web sites, is to load-balance the web site. Load balancing means that you will install the web site on multiple servers and then the requests for the site are distributed among all servers in the load-balancing solution.

The load balance happens as the load-balancing software accepts the request and then uses an algorithm to decide which server to forward the request to. The benefit of a load balance is that if you have a large number of requests coming into the site, you don't have one poor server that is bogged down with requests.

Fault Tolerance We talked about fault tolerance previously in the book, and I just want to stress that high availability and fault tolerance are two totally different things. High availability is about ensuring the service is available, such as the e-mail server, whereas fault tolerance ensures that the data the e-mail server accesses is available through data redundancy.

If you implement fault tolerance without high availability, the e-mail data may be protected through fault tolerance, but if the e-mail service actually fails, then there would be no way to access the fault-tolerant data. High availability will ensure the fault-tolerant data is accessible by having a secondary server with the e-mail service running. This secondary server will come online automatically if the primary e-mail server fails.

Physical and Logical Issues

When it comes to troubleshooting networking issues, you will need to troubleshoot the physical aspects of the network such as devices and cables, but also the logical aspects of the network such as invalid IP address settings or VLAN issues. This section will identity different physical and logical issues you may encounter.

Physical Issues

Most of the physical issues you will encounter deal with cabling problems. To solve cable connection issues, you will use the visual indicators mentioned earlier such as the link light and activity light.

You may encounter a number of other issues that deal with cabling such as

- **Crosstalk**   Crosstalk is interference from adjacent wires. If you experience a lot of signal degradation, it could be due to crosstalk. To fix the problem, look at using another cable type that has more layers of shielding.

- **Attenuation**   Attenuation is the degradation of the signal as it travels great distances. If you find that you cannot communicate with a system that is quite far away, it is possible that you have exceeded the maximum cable length for that type of cable. You can put a repeater in the middle to reamplify the signal or use a different cable type.

- **Collisions**   If you find you have a lot of collisions on the network, it could be because you have too many systems on the network segment and may be using a hub device. Upgrade the hubs to switches because each port on the switch is its own network segment, meaning the data will not collide with any other data because it is the only system on the segment.

- **Shorts**   A short in the network cable could cause network downtime. When experiencing connectivity issues, use a cable analyzer to identify if there is a short in the cable.

- **Open impedance mismatch (echo)**   High impedance can cause signal bounce, which could cause communication issues. This signal bounce could be due to a miswired cable or an incorrect connector. Using a cable tester, or analyzer, will determine if there is connectivity between the two ends of the cable. If there is not, then you will need to recrimp the cable.

- **Interference**   You may receive interference from external components. Be sure to wire the network cable away from power cables and other interference sources.

exam

watch   *Cable disconnections, such as when there is no connectivity between pins at either end of the cable, are called opens. You can use a cable analyzer to determine if there are opens on the cable.*

Logical Issues

I find that most of the problems with networking deal with logical issues such as administrative errors when assigning IP addresses or placing a system in the wrong VLAN. The following is a list of popular logical issues that cause problems on networks:

- **Port speed and duplex settings**   If you have a problem with a system connecting to the network, double-check that the speed and duplex settings of the card are set correctly.

- **Incorrect VLAN**   It is possible that miscommunication is occurring if you place a system on the wrong VLAN. Remember that a system on one VLAN cannot normally talk to a system on another VLAN unless you are routing between VLANs.

- **Incorrect IP address**   One common logical issue is when the IP address of a system is typed incorrectly. When troubleshooting, check the IP addresses of all parties involved.

- **Wrong gateway**   If you have trouble communicating off the network, this is typically a routing issue. Check the default gateway settings on all the systems to verify they are pointing to the IP address of the router.

■ **Wrong DNS** If you can communicate by the IP address but not the DNS name of a system, then you most likely have a name resolution problem. Check the IP address you have configured on the system as the DNS server entry.

■ **Wrong subnet mask** If you have the wrong subnet mask typed into the TCP/IP properties, this could cause miscommunication. When you check the IP address of a system, also verify that you are using the correct subnet mask.

■ **Network loops** Loops on the network will typically bring the network down. This is why Cisco switches use the STP protocol: it is a protocol that prevents loops by placing one of the ports in the loop in a blocking state. If you have intermittent problems with the network where systems seem to just lose connections, then it could be a loop issue. Check how you have everything wired and remove the cable that creates a loop.

■ **Routing issues** If you find all clients on the network cannot communicate with systems on another network, then you most likely have a routing problem. Check the routing table on the router and ensure there is a route to the network you are trying to reach.

■ **Wireless issues** There are a number of potential wireless issues. Your wireless client could have connected to the wrong wireless network automatically. Check to ensure that you are connected to the correct wireless network. If you are losing your wireless connection a lot, then you most likely are getting interference from cordless phones or the microwave.

CERTIFICATION OBJECTIVE 13.05

Network Troubleshooting Resources

Once you have determined the cause of your network problems, the battle is only half over. You still have to figure out how to fix the problem. In many cases, the solution, such as replacing a bad cable, might be obvious. However, in other cases additional solutions could be required. Resources are available to help in your search for the solution to your problems. Let's look at a few of those resources now.

TechNet

TechNet is a Microsoft product that is distributed on a monthly basis to its subscribers. TechNet is a searchable database of all Microsoft's articles and documentation on nearly all its products. Because there is a really good chance that someone else has already had the same problem that you are having, TechNet is likely to contain some documentation about how others have solved the problem that can help you solve yours. Microsoft has a version of TechNet online at www.microsoft.com/technet that you can visit and search for articles and consult a knowledge base for most of the problems you encounter with Microsoft products.

Manufacturer Web Sites

The World Wide Web has simplified network troubleshooting tenfold. The web enables us to find up-to-the-minute information on both hardware and software. If you are having a problem with a NIC that is not properly communicating on the network, a good place to start is the web site of the NIC's manufacturer. Most sites provide troubleshooting information, suggested steps to resolve common problems, phone numbers with which you can contact technical support, and the latest updated drivers. Figure 13-5 illustrates the Microsoft Technical Support web site's interface.

FIGURE 13-5

The Microsoft Support web site

Resource Kits and Knowledgebase

Resource kits provide a wealth of information about your operating system, including technical information that is not available anywhere else. Resource kits contain additional documentation on your operating system that is too comprehensive to cover in the standard documentation. Whenever you are faced with a problem that you cannot solve, check the resource kit's knowledgebase articles—your problem could already have been solved.

Trade Publications and White Papers

Other excellent sources of information are trade publications and white papers. These documents provide valuable information on current techniques and new practices that cannot be acquired anywhere else. In the event of actual network problems, these publications will probably be of little direct use to you, but the information you absorb over time from reading them will become one of your most helpful tools.

Telephone Technical Support

Often, after you have exhausted your resources—vendor web sites, resource kits, and documentation—it is common to open up a technical support incident with the vendor to solve the problem. Who is better qualified to solve your problem than highly skilled technicians who work for the company that makes your equipment and who field similar requests on a daily basis? Chances are, the support personnel have already encountered the specific problem with their own software or hardware and have documented fixes. A problem that boggles you could be a very common tech support call for these professionals.

To improve the speed and accuracy of your technical support incident, make sure you have the following ready to assist the support technician when you call:

- Hardware and software environment information, such as the operating system you are running
- Version numbers of affected hardware or software
- Serial numbers
- A detailed account of the problem

- Troubleshooting steps taken so far and their results
- Contract number for your maintenance contract

Vendor CDs

Vendor-provided CDs that come with hardware and software are important references for installation, configuration, and troubleshooting. Many technicians overlook these CDs and spend countless hours troubleshooting on their own or head straight to the phone for technical support. These CDs should be the first consultation resource, even before the product is installed, because usually the CDs provide preinstallation tips and warnings that are critical for a smooth installation. A vendor-provided CD also can include a technical information base, similar to Microsoft's TechNet, detailing a number of problems and their resolutions. Other CDs have tutorials, documentation, and software patches. Whatever these CDs contain, they should not be overlooked, whether you are planning to implement, support, or troubleshoot the product.

CERTIFICATION OBJECTIVE 13.06

Other Symptoms and Causes of Network Problems

It may sound obvious, but you need to closely examine the symptoms of a network problem in order to determine the cause. Now that you have seen the various causes for network problems, let's look at Table 13-2, which identifies some network-related problems and the appropriate solutions.

You've seen some examples of the most common problems you will encounter in your networking professional journey. You are beginning to see that the same problems will continue to arise, but the causes and solutions could be different.

TABLE 13-2	Problem	Potential Cause
Network Problems and Potential Solutions	I cannot connect to a computer on a remote network.	This sounds like a routing issue. Check to see whether you can connect to a computer on your local network. If you can connect, try to ping the router or another host on the remote network. You need to determine whether the host or the link to the host is down.
	No one can communicate on the entire network.	If this is a coax-based network, make sure that the bus has not been accidentally segmented, meaning that a connection came loose somewhere. If this is a twisted-pair network, make sure that the hub is operational. If this is a Token Ring network, make sure that a computer is not beaconing, indicating a problem.
	It takes way too long to connect to a network resource.	Make sure that the network is not being overloaded. Most network devices, such as hubs and routers, display a percentage of bandwidth being used; check this display to determine whether the network is being saturated. You can also use network monitoring software to do the same thing. Further, you should determine who and what is being affected. Maybe you are experiencing a broadcast storm on one segment and not another.
	A domain controller cannot be found.	Is anyone else receiving this error? This is most commonly a local workstation issue, either an incorrect TCP/IP configuration or a problem with the network adapter or cable. Make certain that the network card has a link light and the cable is firmly plugged in. You should also try replacing the cable to the workstation.
	A device in my system is not functioning and I can't connect to the network.	This sounds like a network card configuration error. Make sure that the NIC is configured correctly. Be sure to use a free IRQ and I/O address when configuring the card. In addition, the driver might not have loaded correctly. What has changed since this adapter worked correctly?
	No one in this department can communicate, but other departments can.	Make sure that the hub/switch is not locked up. Resetting the hub/switch usually fixes this problem. Sometimes an incorrectly configured network adapter causes it. Communication issues can arise from a card with a different speed being set. For example, on an Ethernet network, setting a NIC to 10 Mbps on a 100 Mbps network could cause the system or network to lock up.

	Problem	Potential Cause
TABLE 13-2 Network Problems and Potential Solutions *(continued)*	No one can access the Internet.	This problem can be caused by many things, but make sure that there is no problem with the Internet gateway, if you are using one; this gateway is a computer that acts as an intermediary between the Internet and your local intranet. This problem also could be a routing issue if you are using a dedicated connection to the Internet. Verify that the router or gateway is functional and try pinging key computers on remote networks and the Internet. Use tracert to an Internet host to see if the problem is with your network or your Internet provider's network.
	I can't reach the mainframe using its hostname.	Make sure that you are not having a name resolution problem. Did this problem just start occurring? Test for connectivity by pinging the host. If you can connect to the host using an IP address instead, you definitely have a name resolution problem. If you can't connect with an IP address, try pinging another computer on that network. Maybe you are having routing problems.
	Our Token Ring network suddenly locked up.	Someone on the network is beaconing. Therefore, the nearest active upstream neighbor (NAUN) is having a problem. The network cannot continue until the problem is fixed. Sometimes the problem occurs because a bridge is locking up too.

Recognizing Abnormal Physical Conditions

The key to recognizing abnormal physical conditions on the network is knowing what a normal physical condition is. Such a condition could be different from one network to another. For example, it could take your network only three seconds to spool up a print document, but it could take another network one minute to spool up a document of the same size. This doesn't mean that the second network has a problem; it could be merely a normal physical condition for that network. The following are things to look for when you attempt to determine whether an abnormal condition is occurring on your network:

- Printing takes longer.
- Authentication takes longer.
- You are receiving more errors than usual.
- Connecting to remote resources takes longer, if you can connect at all.

- You are losing connections to resources.
- Network applications are not running.

To determine whether these situations are abnormal occurrences on your network, you need to ask yourself a few questions:

- How many users are affected by this problem?
- Is the problem consistent?
- Is the problem replicable?
- Was there a recent upgrade to the network or computer?
- Has any of the equipment been moved?
- Have we encountered this problem before?
- Has anyone else attempted to fix the problem?
- How many applications is this problem affecting?
- Are there new users or computers on the network?
- Is this a busy or congested time of day?
- Which products are involved?

Your mind should be going at top speed, thinking of what could have contributed to the problem. With knowledge of what constitutes a normal network environment, you can determine rather quickly what is not normal.

Isolating and Correcting Problems in the Physical Media

Experienced network administrators know that cabling is one of the most common causes of network failure. For this reason, you should check cabling first during your network troubleshooting process. Most often the cable that is damaged is the cable from the workstation to the wall jack. This cable receives the most abuse. Sometimes you can fix the problem by simply plugging the cable back in, if it has become loose or fallen out.

If you have determined that a cable could be the culprit of a network-related problem, the next logical step is to test your hypothesis by replacing the cable with a known good cable. The results are simple to assess: if you

exam

watch

The information in this section is important for the exam. Make sure you know the symptoms of cable problems and how to correct them.

can communicate once again, the old cable was bad. If once again you cannot communicate, you need to continue troubleshooting or find another cable to test.

There are devices you can use to determine whether cables have gone bad, but these devices can be expensive. Most of the time you can swap out cables to determine whether they are bad. Table 13-3 lists some common cable-related problems and their solutions.

Checking the Status of Servers

Checking server status is critical because servers can be plagued with ongoing problems that are not so obvious, and if the problems are not corrected, they can become worse. There are many ways to continually monitor the status of your servers, and each is operating system–specific. Some general monitoring tasks are listed here:

- Check error logs
- Check services
- Verify connectivity
- Monitor the performance and the network
- Verify backup logs, including test restores
- Test alerts

TABLE 13-3	Cable Problem	Likely Solution
Common Cable Problems	None of the workstations on the network are able to communicate with each other. They use a thinnet coax Ethernet to connect to each other.	The backbone has been severed. Find the point at which the bus became severed and reconnect it.
	You have a brand-new UTP cable, but the workstation is still not able to communicate on the network. The workstation worked with your test cable.	The brand-new UTP cable might be a crossover cable. Use a cable tester to verify the cable is wired correctly and then obtain a regular UTP cable if it is not.
	A workstation was just moved to a new location and is no longer able to communicate on the network. There is nothing wrong with the workstation's configuration.	Cables were damaged in the move. Replace each cable one at a time to find the problematic cable.

The error logs can give you an indication of a failed device or service and a good idea of how to fix the problem. The errors listed vary from critical to informational. Some errors, such as a service failing to start, warrant immediate action. A service failing to start can be critical, and it often has dependencies that require the running of another service to allow the services themselves to run.

It is important to develop a maintenance plan for your network and to include in that plan daily tasks such as monitoring the event logs for potential problems. Make it part of your early morning or end-of-day routine.

You can test for connectivity with a server using utilities such as Ping to determine whether the server is responding to network requests, and performance and network monitoring can determine whether the server is overloaded or is broadcasting unnecessarily. An overloaded server can increase the length of time needed to fulfill network requests.

If you are backing up a server, which is always recommended, you need to verify that the backups have finished successfully. This is imperative, because in the event of an emergency you will need to recover data from the backup tapes. You must also do test restores to make sure that the data can be restored correctly and that you understand the restore process. A disaster is the worst time to discover that your backup routine hasn't been working correctly.

Finally, you can configure your server to send alerts to specific computers or users in the event of emergencies or when the system encounters thresholds that you have predefined. A threshold is a peak in the rate of activity, about which you would like to be notified so that you can correct the situation. Setting thresholds includes baselining your system so that you know the normal rate of activity.

Checking for Configuration Problems

When you are bringing a new server online or configuring a server with a new service such as DNS or WINS, it is imperative that you begin by verifying that the configuration is correct. Sometimes you will incorrectly configure a server and it will continually deteriorate or it will not work at all. You must make sure that the base operating system, TCP/IP, networking, error logs, and memory allocation are configured correctly. You must also correctly configure the additional services that run on top of the operating system. You will frequently have an application or database server that also runs a backup service, such as ARCserve or Backup Exec.

When you are configuring the backup server, you might have to reboot the machine for changes to take effect. This means downing a critical server for a few minutes, thus breaking connections with all users and services that are currently using that machine. You might have to do this during off hours; be very careful about configuring services for mission-critical machines during business hours.

on the !Job

It is important to have a change log book beside the servers and to train your network administrators to record any of their changes in the log book. This will help you identify potential causes of problems by having a history of the changes and who made them.

It is important that the following services be correctly configured, because they have the capability to affect the entire network, not just the local server—a catastrophe waiting to happen. Most networking environments rely on one of the services discussed in the following subsections.

DNS

DNS is now a requirement of most networking environments such as Microsoft Active Directory and any Internet-based application. Configuring DNS for these environments requires a great deal of planning. You need to gather the following information prior to installing the service:

- Your domain name
- The IP address of each server for which you want to provide name resolution
- The hostname of each server

This information must be correct; otherwise, your network will experience ongoing name resolution problems that will be difficult to diagnose. This is especially the case with hostname–to–IP address mappings. DNS entries can be entered manually, so you must be very careful not to enter a wrong IP address or hostname. You will not be prompted with an error message informing you that you have entered an incorrect IP address.

WINS

WINS is much like DNS in that it provides name resolution; however, DNS resolves hostnames to IP addresses, and WINS resolves NetBIOS names to IP addresses. WINS does not require you to manually enter mappings before you begin—this is because WINS is a dynamic service that can add, modify, and delete name registrations dynamically, saving valuable time for the network administrator. At times you will want to add a static mapping for important clients or servers.

WINS, like DNS, has many configuration possibilities. Although most WINS configuration parameters will not be covered on the Network+ exam, you will be required to know how to configure each client to point to the WINS server in a WINS environment.

The Hosts File

As you have learned, when you use DNS you must manually add hostname–to–IP address mappings in order to resolve hostnames. With the hosts file, you also have to manually configure a database with these exact mappings. Unlike DNS, which uses a centrally located database of hostname mappings, the hosts file resides on every computer. This makes the process of updating the hosts file very difficult. The hosts file is usually located under windows\system32\drivers\etc.

All the DNS rules apply to the hosts file: You must be careful to enter the correct hostname–to–IP address mappings. A helpful tip for configuring the hosts file is to copy to the remaining hosts the newly created file that you have guaranteed to be accurate. This step ensures that you don't make any clerical errors on each of the remaining machines.

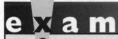

Make sure that you know the definition of WINS, DNS, the hosts file, and the LMHOSTS file. You won't be expected to know any in-depth information about them, just the purpose of each one. For more information, review Chapter 4.

Checking for Viruses

If you have ever been a network administrator in the midst of a virus attack, you know how frustrating the situation can be. Once the virus gets in from the outside, whether from the Internet, a user's home computer, or the local intranet, it poses a huge problem. But how can you eradicate the viruses before they come into the network? A server running a virus-scanning program can make all the difference in applying "preventive maintenance."

Many companies engage in multipronged attacks against viruses, including continually scanning for viruses on the file and messaging servers and installing virus-scanning software on every workstation. Both precautions are critical for stopping the spread of viruses. The server can catch viruses coming in from the messaging servers, such as Microsoft Exchange, and from files stored on the file servers. The workstation virus-scanning programs can catch viruses on users' machines before the viruses get a chance to replicate to the servers and to other users' computers on the network. In any case, the virus-definition files must be updated on a continual basis. Many virus-scanning utilities enable workstations to automatically update the virus definition files from a central server, which means you, the network administrator, do not have to visit every workstation once a month to apply the new definition files.

Checking the Validity of the Account Name and Password

Usually you configure services or applications to log on with a certain account in order to perform their functions. A number of services usually use the built-in system account, but if the service requires logging on to a remote computer, it requires an account name and password that resides in the network account database, such as Active Directory. Some services require administrative privileges or membership in certain groups on the network to accomplish their tasks, so you will need to make sure that the account a service is using is the correct account, has the appropriate level of rights, and is in the correct groups. You must document these special system and service accounts and remember not to delete or tamper with them in any way. If you mistakenly disable, delete, or affect the account details, you could find yourself with a service, or application, that fails to start—a problem that is often very difficult to diagnose.

I have seen network administrators install applications and specify their own administrator account for the service to use. When the network administrator leaves the company, his account is disabled or deleted, and, mysteriously, some of the programs fail. If the other members of the department were not aware of this configuration, they could be scratching their heads for days wondering why this program or service does not work anymore.

Rechecking Operator Logon Procedures

The most obvious problems often involve logging on. If a user mistakenly tries to log on to a network or domain in which he doesn't have an account, he will be denied, and he will call you, the network administrator. Users often forget their passwords or the fact that the password is case sensitive. After three attempts (or however many times you have configured the system to accept guesses), the user is normally locked out and will need to contact you to re-enable the account.

Sometimes users return from vacation to find that their accounts have been disabled or their passwords have expired. You may need to reset a user's password when he or she returns from vacation so that the user can access network resources. Figure 13-6 shows how to change the user's password in Microsoft's Active Directory.

Selecting and Running Appropriate Diagnostics

To build a strong network, you need to run diagnostics to search for bottlenecks or problematic situations. These diagnostics may reveal problems or limitations that you can fix before they get too bad.

You need to choose diagnostic programs that correlate with your specific network needs. For example, you can purchase extensive protocol-analyzing and packet-sniffing products, but they would be overkill for a 20-node network. Often the free diagnostic products, such as Performance Monitor and Network Monitor, are capable of determining computer and network problems.

Whichever tool you choose, you must spend plenty of time with the product to determine the most effective way to deploy it. You must also be trained to analyze the results and determine what needs to be adjusted in order to remedy the situation. It will take more than one trial to establish a reliable baseline of activity for your testing.

FIGURE 13-6

Resetting a user's password

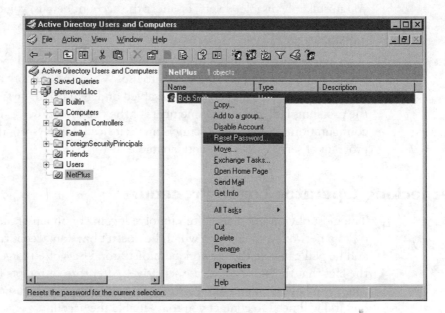

For example, running a diagnostics or performance test at 8:00 A.M., when all the users are logging on, gives entirely different results from running the diagnostics at noon, when they are at lunch. Taking snapshots of activity from various periods of the day, week, and month gives you the most accurate assessment of your network. The longer you spend baselining your network, the more accurate the results. From there, you can begin assigning thresholds to chart and alert for abnormal activity. Furthermore, you are training yourself to read the various diagnostics so that you can quickly determine how, why, and where a problem is occurring. The following section gives more examples of devices that can help you troubleshoot your network.

CERTIFICATION OBJECTIVE 13.07

Network Tools

In most network troubleshooting sessions, there comes a time at which a simple isolation of problems is just not feasible. In that situation, it's time to use some electronic tools to determine your problem and its source. This section discusses the most common network tools and how they are used.

Cable Crimper

A tool that will prove to be useful from time to time is a cable crimper, like the one shown in Figure 13-7. A cable crimper should have the actual crimping tool to "crimp" or close the connector on the end of the cable, along with a wire cutter to cut the ends of the wire, and a wire stripper.

FIGURE 13-7

A network cable crimper

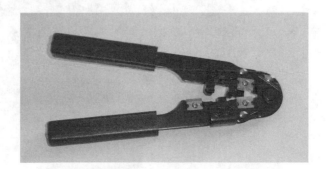

Cable Tester

You should also have some cable testers handy to help you determine whether the cable is crimped properly. A cable tester should have two parts to allow it to plug into each end of the cable, and it should have light indicators that light up as it tests for connectivity from one end of the cable to another on each wire (see Figure 13-8).

The tester should have a light for each wire in the cable. The tester will light up an indicator for each wire, one after the other—you will need to watch the lights light up at both ends and make sure that the order is the same on both parts of the tester. If the order is different, you have an incorrectly positioned wire and you will need to re-crimp an end.

A *certifier* is a type of cable tester that will report the same information as a normal cable tester, but will also report on data such as speed and duplex settings.

Crossover Cables

A *crossover* cable appears to be just another twisted-pair cable, but two wires are crossed, which makes the cable not fit for plugging into a computer and a hub for normal use. The crossover cable is used to directly connect two computers to each other, without the use of a hub. This can be extremely useful when you are troubleshooting a system and want to have it disconnected from the network but also need to be able to connect your own system because it has diagnostic tools on it.

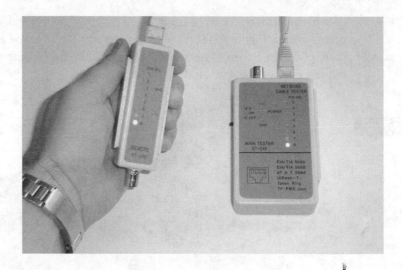

FIGURE 13-8

Testing wiring of a cable with a cable tester

A crossover cable is also used to interconnect some hubs and switches. If you were to substitute a crossover cable for a regular twisted-pair cable to connect two hubs, it would not work correctly (there would be no link light for that port). Therefore, it is important that you mark your crossover cables or use a different color cable to designate a crossover cable. Many companies use yellow or black cables for regular cables and blue for crossover cables. You will not need many crossover cables, and you can make them yourself if you have the correct pinout.

Hardware Loopback

A hardware loopback adapter is a way to test the ports on a system without having to connect to an external device. For example, you can use a serial loopback adapter to verify that a transmitted signal is leaving your serial port and returning through the loopback adapter, thereby ensuring that your serial port is working correctly.

Tone Generators

A tone generator is used to perform tests on phone and network lines in what is referred to as a fox-and-hound process. The device clips to a wire, terminal panel, or standard modular jack and aids in the identification of wires during the wire-tracing process. You begin by attaching the "fox" to the cable, jack, or panel that you want to trace, and you continue with the "hound" on the other end of the cable to find the fox's tone. When you find the tone, you know that you have correctly tracked the cable. This is very helpful for determining which cable in a group of many cables, such as a wiring closet, has gone bad and needs to be replaced.

Time Domain Reflectometers

A time domain reflectometer (TDR) is used to troubleshoot problems with a cable by sending a signal down the cable, where it is reflected at some point. The TDR then calculates the distance down the cable that the signal traveled before being reflected by measuring the amount of time it took for the signal to be returned. If this distance is less than your overall cable length, a cable problem exists at that distance from your location. (Yes, this means that it is in the most inconvenient location possible. It is a law of networking that when something breaks, it will be in the worst possible place to fix it.)

Optical time domain reflectometers are similar to TDRs but are used to test the performance of fiber optic cables.

Oscilloscopes

Oscilloscopes and toner probes can determine when there are shorts, crimps, or attenuation in a cable. An oscilloscope formats its output in a graphical format. Oscilloscopes are commonly used to test cables that have been recently run through walls to ensure that there are no problems with the cables before you use them.

e x a m
ᴡatch

There are other network troubleshooting tools to know about for the exam, such as multimeters or voltage event recorders to monitor voltage. A butt set is used to test telephone lines. System & Network Integrated Polling Software (SNIPS) monitor network activity from a Unix system. And temperature monitors are used to monitor the temperature of computer components.

CERTIFICATION SUMMARY

In this chapter you have learned quite a lot that will not only help you on the Network+ exam, but will give you a troubleshooting methodology that you can use for the rest of your career. You have learned the general model for troubleshooting, which involves establishing the problem symptoms, identifying the affected area of the network, determining what has changed, selecting the most probable cause, implementing a solution, testing the result, recognizing possible side effects of the solution, and documenting the solution.

You have learned to ask yourself questions such as these:

■ Does the problem exist across the network?

■ Is this a workstation, workgroup, LAN, or WAN problem?

■ Is the problem consistent and replicable?

You have learned the physical and logical indicators of network problems, such as link, collision, and power lights as well as error messages and error logs, which give you a good indication of the problem that is occurring.

You have discovered network troubleshooting resources such as TechNet, manufacturers' web sites, and vendor CDs. Each of these resources is invaluable for solving network problems; they are highly recommended.

Finally, you have learned about the various network tools that are available to you to obtain more information about the problem, to solve the problem, or simply to make your networking life a little bit easier.

TWO-MINUTE DRILL

Managing Network Problems

- ❑ Learning how each device coexists and contributes to the network will provide you with a strong foundation for understanding how and why network-related problems occur and how to resolve them.

- ❑ When you first encounter a problem, it is important to determine its symptoms.

- ❑ You need to determine whether the problem relates to a workstation, workgroup, LAN, or WAN.

- ❑ Determine whether the problem is consistent and replicable.

- ❑ It is important to isolate the subsystem involved with the problem process.

Troubleshooting Network Problems

- ❑ When you troubleshoot network problems, it is important to follow a logical troubleshooting methodology.

- ❑ Having others troubleshoot the problem as a team will give you many different perspectives and theories as to the cause of the problem.

- ❑ Sometimes it is possible to recreate the problem, learning exactly why and how it occurred.

- ❑ The most important step of network troubleshooting is isolating the problem.

- ❑ Often there is more than one way to correct a problem, each with its own set of related issues and consequences.

System or Operator Problems

- ❑ In some cases, it is very clear whether a system or operator error has occurred.

Checking Physical and Logical Indicators

- ❑ When you begin troubleshooting a network-related problem, you have several indicators available that will help you determine the problem.

- ❑ Link lights are invaluable in determining whether a network connection is present.

❑ Collision lights can help determine whether a network element has failed and is causing chatter.

❑ Even more rudimentary in the network troubleshooting area than the link light is the power light.

❑ An error display is a means of alerting you to a malfunction or failure in a device.

❑ Similar to the error display is the error log, which maintains a listing of errors encountered.

❑ Network Monitor is an outstanding tool for monitoring the network performance of your system.

❑ Performance Monitor tracks the use of resources by the system components and applications.

Network Troubleshooting Resources

❑ There are some resources available to help in your search for the solution to your problems. For instance, TechNet is a searchable database of all Microsoft articles and documentation on nearly all its products.

❑ The web provides up-to-the-minute information on both hardware and software issues.

❑ Resource kits contain a wealth of information about your operating system and provide technical information that is not available anywhere else.

❑ Other excellent sources of information are trade publications and white papers.

❑ It is common to open up a technical support incident with the vendor to solve a problem.

❑ Vendor-provided CDs that come with hardware and software are important references for installation, configuration, and troubleshooting.

Other Symptoms and Causes of Network Problems

❑ Experienced network administrators know that cabling is one of the most common causes of network failure.

❑ Make sure that you know the symptoms of cable problems and how to correct them.

❑ There are many ways to continually monitor the status of your servers, and each is operating system–specific.

❑ When you are bringing a new server online or configuring a server with a new service such as DNS or WINS, it is imperative that you begin by verifying that the configuration is correct.

❑ Make sure that you know the definition of WINS, DNS, the hosts file, and the LMHOSTS file. You won't be expected to know any in-depth information about each, just the purpose of each. For more information, review Chapter 4.

❑ A server running a virus-scanning program can make all the difference in keeping viruses out of your network.

Network Tools

❑ To build a strong network, you need to run diagnostics to search for bottlenecks or problematic situations.

❑ A hardware loopback adapter is a way to test the ports on a system without having to connect to an external device.

❑ A TDR is a device that sends an electronic pulse down a cable. The pulse then travels until it is reflected back, and the distance traveled is calculated. This process is similar to the way sonar works.

❑ An oscilloscope can determine when there are shorts, crimps, or attenuation in a cable.

❑ Network monitors and protocol analyzers monitor traffic on the network and display the packets that have been transmitted across it.

SELF TEST

The following Self Test questions will help you measure your understanding of the material presented in this chapter. Read all the choices carefully because there might be more than one correct answer. Choose all correct answers for each question.

Managing Network Problems

1. A few computers on the engineering segment are having problems reaching the AutoCAD design segment on the network, but they can access all other segments. What is your initial diagnosis of the problem?

   A. It's a default gateway issue.

   B. It's a routing issue.

   C. The computers are having cable problems.

   D. A hub is locked up.

2. All users on a coaxial bus topology network have suddenly complained that the network is not functioning and they can no longer access resources on the local or remote networks. What is your initial diagnosis of the problem?

   A. It's a routing issue.

   B. It's a default gateway issue.

   C. The network is no longer terminated.

   D. A hub is locked up.

3. You think you are having problems with the UNIX server in another region. Two users have already complained this morning. What would be the next logical step in your troubleshooting methodology?

   A. Check the router.

   B. Check the hub.

   C. Ping the UNIX server by name.

   D. Ping the UNIX server by IP address.

4. You have a workstation that you moved from one cubicle to another. Nothing on the workstation was changed, but the computer refuses to connect to the network. Which of the following is a likely cause?

   A. The network drop has not been activated in the wiring closet.

   B. The cable was damaged in the move.

   C. The TCP/IP configuration is incorrect.

   D. The network adapter was damaged in the move.

Troubleshooting Network Problems

5. You are experiencing problems on a coax bus network. How can you quickly determine where the problem is occurring?

    A. Divide the network in half, terminate it, and find which side is still not functioning. That is the affected area. Continue this process until the break is found.

    B. Use a network packet sniffer to determine where the packets eventually stop responding. This will tell you which computer is the closest to the break.

    C. Use a fox-and-hound process to determine the location of the break in the network backbone.

    D. Use Network Monitor to determine what is causing the broadcast storm. One computer's faulty network card is the likely culprit and must be found.

System or Operator Problems

6. Steve, a user on your network, just got back from a two-week vacation. He calls you the first thing Monday morning. Which of the following is most likely the reason for Steve's call?

    A. He forgot his password.

    B. His account has been disabled.

    C. His password has expired.

    D. A coworker changed Steve's password while he was on vacation.

Checking Physical and Logical Indicators

7. You came to work on Monday morning only to notice that you are having network problems. Your domain controller, which also functions as a database server, appears to be having problems. How can you further investigate the situation?

    A. Check the error log.

    B. Ping the server to see if it responds.

    C. Run diagnostics on the server.

    D. Restart the computer and then begin troubleshooting.

8. You have made system configuration changes to one of your servers. How can you tell if the changes have made a difference?

    A. Watch the server closely for a few hours, especially during peak usage.

    B. Run Network Monitor to perform an assessment of the current system activity and compare that with your previous baseline, taken before the configuration change took place.

    C. Run Performance Monitor to perform an assessment of the current system activity and compare that with your previous baseline, taken before the configuration change took place.

    D. Check the Event Viewer for errors, warnings, or any indicators that system degradation has occurred.

9. Which of the following is the most reliable indicator that a network server could be overloaded?
    A. The activity light on the network card is constantly lit.
    B. Performance Monitor shows network requests are backing up in the queue.
    C. Network Monitor shows too many packets are leaving this server.
    D. The computer is very slow to respond when you log on.

10. Which of the following is not a good recommendation when it comes to performing a baseline of your network?
    A. Monitor traffic at different times of the day.
    B. Configure the snapshots to take place at midnight each night.
    C. Monitor traffic for days, even weeks.
    D. Take as many traffic snapshots as possible.

Network Troubleshooting Resources

11. You feel you are having driver incompatibility problems with your network adapter. What is the best resource for finding another network adapter driver?
    A. TechNet
    B. Resource kit
    C. Vendor web site
    D. Documentation CD

12. You are instructed to migrate the DHCP service from a Windows NT 4.0 server to a Windows 2000 server. What is the best resource to begin preparing for the migration?
    A. A Windows magazine
    B. Telephone tech support
    C. Vendor CDs
    D. Resource kits

13. You are experiencing lockup problems with a new version of the virus-scanning utility that you just implemented. Which of the following is probably not needed when you open a technical support incident?
    A. The version of affected software or hardware
    B. The number of users on the network
    C. Troubleshooting steps taken so far and their results
    D. Current operating system

14. You have a user receiving the error message, "A domain controller cannot be found." Assuming that no one else has called you with this error, which of the following is not likely to be the problem?

    A. The TCP/IP configuration is not correct on the computer.

    B. The domain controller could be down.

    C. The network card is not functioning correctly.

    D. A cable might be faulty or not plugged in.

15. Which of the following is not likely to be an abnormal condition on a network?

    A. It takes a long time to print a large document that contains images.

    B. It takes longer to become authenticated.

    C. Users are having problems connecting to the SQL database.

    D. You continually lose connection to the mainframe.

16. Which of the following will you not need prior to installing DNS?

    A. The DHCP address scope

    B. Your domain name

    C. The hostnames of each server

    D. The IP address of each server for which you want to provide name resolution

17. Which of the following is not true regarding WINS?

    A. It resolves NetBIOS names to IP addresses.

    B. You must replicate with all other WINS servers.

    C. You must manually enter the address mappings.

    D. WINS dynamically updates the WINS database.

Other Symptoms and Causes of Network Problems

18. You can't seem to surf the Internet or connect to the servers in a remote office location, but you can communicate with systems on your local LAN. What would you do to verify what the problem is?

    A. Run ipconfig.

    B. Ping the router.

    C. Ping a local server.

    D. Ping a local workstation.

19. During any network troubleshooting call, which should you check first?
   A. The printer
   B. IP address
   C. Cabling and connections
   D. User

Network Tools

20. How can you eliminate complicated cable problems in your troubleshooting process?
   A. Visually inspect the cables.
   B. Use a "fox and hound" to find cables in a tangled mess.
   C. Examine cables with a TDR to find any problems.
   D. Swap suspect cables with known good cables.

21. What is the best tool to determine where a break has occurred in a cable?
   A. A tone generator
   B. A spectrum division analyzer
   C. A time domain reflectometer
   D. A fox and hound

SELF TEST ANSWERS

Managing Network Problems

1. ☑ **B.** It's a routing issue. If you have a very good understanding of routers and routing, and one segment of your network cannot communicate with another segment, you will immediately know that there is a problem with routing—possibly a router is malfunctioning.

   ☒ **A, C,** and **D** are incorrect. Segments are usually created by routers or bridges, and one of these will be the issue when one segment has problems contacting another. Default gateways are used to connect to the gateway or router that is used to contact other segments. Since some segments in the question can be contacted, the default gateway is fine. Since some PCs can be contacted, the hub is not locked up.

2. ☑ **C.** The network is no longer terminated. One segment of the network is not able to communicate with another segment; therefore, you should quickly determine that you have a routing problem. Another symptom is that everyone on the coaxial-based bus network is not able to communicate. The cause of this problem most likely lies with the network bus backbone, which requires terminators on each end.

   ☒ **A, B,** and **D** are incorrect. The terminator is a problem with bus networks and should be checked whenever the whole network is the issue. If none of the PCs on the local segment can be contacted, the problem is not a router or gateway. Hubs do not simply lock up, so this is not the issue.

3. ☑ **D.** Ping the UNIX server by IP address. You can test the routing problem by trying to communicate with another computer on the corporate headquarters network. For example, you can ping another computer on this network or use a program that connects to a computer on this network. Name resolution is usually not an issue when using terminal-type programs. They usually use the IP address, not the name of the server, when contacting the server.

   ☒ **A, B,** and **C** are incorrect. Ping allows you to determine whether the problem is the hub, a router, or another network device.

4. ☑ **A, C,** and **D.** The network drop was not activated, TCP/IP is not configured correctly, or the network adapter was damaged in the move. When new cable drops have been run, sometimes they are not correctly connected in the wiring closet to a hub and therefore will not allow connection to the network. If TCP/IP is statically configured, the configuration needs to be updated, especially if the PC is on a new segment. Sometimes cards or other PC hardware become damaged if proper care is not taken in handling the PC.

   ☒ **B** is incorrect because cables are not usually moved with a PC.

Troubleshooting Network Problems

5. ☑ **A.** Divide the network in half, terminate it, and find which side is still not functioning. The best example of this is in thinnet coax. Determine the midpoint of the cable and place a terminator on each end. One-half of the cable should now be working, and it is obviously not the source of your problem. Repeat this step until you solve the problem.

☒ **B, C,** and **D** are incorrect because using a sniffer or fox-and-hound tool would require about as much work, but moving the terminator would allow you to find the source of the problem with no extra tool other than the terminator, which is readily available. These tools might not be available to all technicians. Network Monitor might not always determine which computer is causing the problem. If the problem is in a cable rather than a computer, Network Monitor will be of no help.

System or Operator Problems

6. ☑ **A, B,** and **C.** He forgot his password, his account has been disabled, or his password has expired. You need to intervene to correct the situation.

☒ **D** is incorrect because a coworker cannot change Steve's password while he is on vacation.

Checking Physical and Logical Indicators

7. ☑ **A.** Check the error log. Error logs usually don't contain enough information to solve a problem, and documentation must be consulted to diagnose and resolve it. However, checking the error logs is important because you can determine when the problem occurred, what might have caused the problem, and what other processes are affected by this problem.

☒ **B, C,** and **D** are incorrect. Pinging the server verifies that TCP/IP is running and functional on the server, and if there are no calls from users unable to contact the server, this is not an issue. Running diagnostics can help, but you are not sure what diagnostics to run. Diagnostics can be run on all the physical hardware, the database, or the network. Restarting the computer and troubleshooting the system still require you know where to start troubleshooting.

8. ☑ **C.** Run Performance Monitor to perform an assessment of the current system activity and compare that with your previous baseline, taken before the configuration change took place. Performance Monitor can be used for a variety of purposes, including the following: identifying bottlenecks in CPU, memory, disk I/O, or network I/O; identifying trends over a period of time; monitoring real-time system performance; monitoring system performance history; determining the capacity the system can handle; and monitoring system configuration changes.

☒ **A, B,** and **D** are incorrect. Visual inspection of system performance is not a very good measure. It is hard to visually determine CPU and hard disk performance as well as other system resources. Network Monitor does not show system degradation or problems. Event Viewer shows only system-generated errors, not performance issues from configuration changes.

9. ☑ **B.** Performance Monitor shows network requests are backing up in the queue. Performance and network monitoring can determine whether the server is overloaded or broadcasting unnecessarily. An overloaded server can increase the length of time needed to fulfill network requests.

☒ **A, C,** and **D** are incorrect. A constant network light shows that the network or even the server network card is overburdened. Network Monitor is used to check for an overburdened network, not a server. When logging on, if you do not give the system enough time to start, services could still be in the process of being loaded, which can cause slow logon issues but does not mean that the server is overburdened.

10. ☑ **B.** Configure the snapshots to take place at midnight each night. Taking snapshots of activity from various periods of the day, week, and month gives you the most accurate assessment of your network. The longer you spend baselining your network, the more accurate the results. If you are taking network activity snapshots only at midnight, you are not getting an accurate assessment of the normal network activity that occurs throughout the day.

☒ **A, C,** and **D** are incorrect because they are all good recommendations.

Network Troubleshooting Resources

11. ☑ **C.** If you are having a problem with a NIC not properly communicating on the network, a good place to start is the web site of the NIC's manufacturer. Most sites provide troubleshooting information, suggested steps to resolve common problems, phone numbers with which to contact technical support, and the latest updated drivers.

☒ **A, B,** and **D** are incorrect. TechNet offers specific publications dealing with the Microsoft Windows and applications, not hardware drivers. Resource kits provide more information and tools for a software product. The documentation CD does not have the most up-to-date driver, if it contains drivers at all.

12. ☑ **D.** Resource kits contain additional operating system documentation that was too comprehensive to cover in the standard documentation. Whenever you are faced with a problem that you cannot solve, check the resource kit—your problem might already have been solved by someone else.

☒ **A, B,** and **C** are incorrect. Windows magazines have information on various topics, and it could require some searching to find an article on migration, if any exist in a specific magazine. Telephone tech support is for problematic issues, not migration strategies. Vendor CDs contain documentation and drivers for specific products.

13. ☑ **B.** You probably don't need the number of users on the network. To improve the speed and accuracy of your technical support incident, make sure that you have the following ready to assist the support technician: hardware and software environment details, such as the operating system you are running; version numbers of affected hardware or software; serial numbers; a detailed account of the problem; and troubleshooting steps taken so far and their results.

    ☒ **A, C,** and **D** are incorrect because they are needed for your session with tech support.

14. ☑ **B.** The domain controller could be down. If no one else is receiving this error message, it is probably a local workstation issue, either with an incorrect TCP/IP configuration or a problem with the network adapter or cable. Make sure that the network card has a link light and the cable is firmly plugged in. You should also try replacing the cable to the workstation.

    ☒ **A, C,** and **D** are incorrect because they are valid potential causes of the problem.

15. ☑ **A.** It takes a long time to print a large document that contains images. For example, it might take your network only three seconds to spool up a print document, but it could take another network one minute to spool up a document of the same size. This doesn't mean the second network has a problem; it could be a normal physical condition for their network.

    ☒ **B, C,** and **D** are incorrect. Authentication is a process that requires information sent to a server for verification, which could take awhile if the network is busy. This is a common problem in the morning, when many users are attempting to log on at the same time. Sometimes portions of a database can be locked out when one user is updating the information. Mainframes can cause issues; users being kicked off the mainframe can be a common occurrence at those times.

16. ☑ **A.** The DHCP addresses scope. You need to gather information prior to installing the service. This information includes your domain name, the IP address of each server for which you want to provide name resolution, and the hostname of each server. Otherwise, you will not know how to configure the service for proper use on your network.

    ☒ **B, C,** and **D** are incorrect because they are all needed to install a DNS service.

17. ☑ **B** and **C.** WINS does not require replication with all other WINS servers. You must manually enter the address mappings. A few of the WINS configuration settings are the duration of the client renewal and extinction of names and the replication partners with which this WINS server replicates. You can strategically replicate with other WINS servers based on frequency and location.

    ☒ **A** and **D** are incorrect. WINS does resolve NetBIOS names to IP addresses. The WINS database is dynamically managed by WINS.

Other Symptoms and Causes of Network Problems

18. ☑ **B.** When you can communicate with systems on the local network, but not remote networks or the Internet, the problem is typically related to the router. As a result, you should ping the router to see if it is up and running.

    ☒ **A, C,** and **D** are incorrect. You may run ipconfig, but you don't really need to because you are communicating with other systems on the local network. There is no need to ping a local server or workstation because you know that you can already communicate with systems on the local LAN.

19. ☑ **C.** A number of network issues arise because of faulty cables or cables being accidentally disconnected. Always check the simple stuff like connections first!

    ☒ **A, B,** and **D** are incorrect because they are not items that you would check first. You may verify the IP address, but you check that the network cable is plugged in first.

Network Tools

20. ☑ **C.** Eliminate complicated cable problems by examining cables with a TDR to find any problems.

    ☒ **A, B,** and **D** are incorrect. Visually inspecting a cable cannot determine whether the cable is faulty. You need more advanced tools to determine whether a cable is faulty. Using tools saves time and money if you catch a potentially faulty cable before it is put into production.

21. ☑ **C.** Use a TDR or an oscilloscope to find the exact spot where the cable is broken. If you don't have access to such a tool, you might be able to replace the cable without determining the exact area of breakage.

    ☒ **A, B,** and **D** are incorrect. A tone generator is used to determine the two ends of a specific cable within a large bulk of cables. A spectrum division analyzer is used with fiber-optic cables to determine their quality. A fox and hound is the same as a tone generator.

A

About the CD

The CD-ROM included with this book comes complete with MasterExam and the electronic version of the book. The software is easy to install on any Windows 2000/ XP/Vista computer and must be installed to access the MasterExam feature. You may, however, browse the electronic book directly from the CD without installation. To register for a second bonus MasterExam, simply click the Bonus MasterExam link on the Main Page and follow the directions to the free online registration.

System Requirements

Software requires Windows 2000 or higher and Internet Explorer 6.0 or above and 20MB of hard disk space for full installation. The electronic book requires Adobe Acrobat Reader.

Installing and Running MasterExam

If your computer CD-ROM drive is configured to auto run, the CD-ROM will automatically start up upon inserting the disk. From the opening screen you may install MasterExam by pressing the MasterExam button. This will begin the installation process and create a program group named LearnKey. To run MasterExam use Start | All Programs | LearnKey | MasterExam. If the auto run feature did not launch your CD, browse to the CD and click on the LaunchTraining.exe icon.

MasterExam

MasterExam provides you with a simulation of the actual exam. The number of questions, the type of questions, and the time allowed are intended to be an accurate representation of the exam environment. You have the option to take an open book exam, including hints, references, and answers; a closed book exam; or the timed MasterExam simulation.

When you launch MasterExam, a digital clock display will appear in the bottom right-hand corner of your screen. The clock will continue to count down to zero unless you choose to end the exam before the time expires.

Electronic Book

The entire contents of the Study Guide are provided in PDF files. Adobe's Acrobat Reader has been included on the CD.

CertCam

The CertCam clips are provided as .exe files and provide detailed examples of key certification objectives. These clips walk you step-by-step through various networking tasks. You can access the CertCam video clips by clicking the CertCams link off the main splash page, which appears when you place the CD in the CD-ROM tray. Once you click the CertCams link, a folder will appear containing all of the CertCams—simply double-click a CertCam to play it.

The CertCam clips are recorded and produced using TechSmith's Camtasia Studio. We have compiled each .avi file into an .exe that contains TechSmith's special AVI codec, custom player, and the AVI itself. When you double-click on the .exe file, the player is launched automatically and the video is played in the player.

Lab Files

There are a number of lab files that are used throughout the exercises in the book. The lab files are included in the LabFiles folder in the root directory of the CD-ROM. The lab files contain items such as packet capture files used to view precaptured traffic, a test web page, and a Security and Backup Plan checklist you can use as a base to build your own checklist.

Lab Book Exercises

There are a number of step-by-step exercises included on the CD that do not appear in the book. This lab file, LabBook.pdf, is included in the root directory of the CD-ROM.

Help

A help file is provided through the help button on the main page in the lower left-hand corner. An individual help feature is also available through MasterExam.

Removing Installation(s)

MasterExam is installed to your hard drive. For best results removing programs, use the Start | All Programs | LearnKey | Uninstall option to remove MasterExam.

Technical Support

For questions regarding the technical content of the electronic book or MasterExam, please visit www.mhprofessional.com or e-mail customer.service@mcgraw-hill.com. For customers outside the 50 United States, e-mail international_cs@mcgraw-hill.com.

LearnKey Technical Support

For technical problems with the software (installation, operation, removing installations), please visit www.learnkey.com, e-mail techsupport@learnkey.com, or call toll free at 1-800-482-8244.

INDEX